W9-CCD-620

THE
Earth
and Its Peoples

A GLOBAL HISTORY

VOLUME II: SINCE 1500

Richard W. Bulliet
Columbia University

Pamela Kyle Crossley
Dartmouth College

Daniel R. Headrick
Roosevelt University

Steven W. Hirsch
Tufts University

Lyman L. Johnson
University of North Carolina–Charlotte

David Northrup
Boston College

WADSWORTH
CENGAGE Learning

Australia • Brazil • Japan • Korea • Mexico • Singapore • Spain • United Kingdom • United States

WADSWORTH
CENGAGE Learning

The Earth and Its Peoples: A Global History, Volume II: Since 1500
Richard W. Bulliet,Pamela Kyle Crossley, Daniel R. Headrick, Steven W. Hirsch, Lyman L. Johnson, and David Northrup

Publisher for History and Political Science: Suzanne Jeans

Senior Sponsoring Editor: Nancy Blaine

Senior Marketing Manager: Katherine Bates

Senior Discipline Product Manager: Lynn Baldridge

Senior Development Editor: Tonya Lobato

Senior Project Editor: Carol Newman

Senior Media Producer: Lisa Ciccolo

Content Manager: Janet Edmonds

Art and Design Manager: Jill Haber

Cover Design Director: Tony Saizon

Senior Photo Editor: Jennifer Meyer Dare

Senior Composition Buyer: Chuck Dutton

New Title Project Management: James Lonergan

Editorial Assistant: Stacey Walker

Marketing Assistant: Lauren Bussard

Editorial Assistant: Paola Moll

Cover Image: *Awon Obirin* by Moses Zibor (contemporary Nigerian artist), Lithograph. Painting by Moses Zibor, *Awon Obirin* www.grainsofafrica.com.

© 2009 Wadsworth, Cengage Learning

ALL RIGHTS RESERVED. No part of this work covered by the copyright herein may be reproduced, transmitted, stored or used in any form or by any means graphic, electronic, or mechanical, including but not limited to photocopying, recording, scanning, digitizing, taping, Web distribution, information networks, or information storage and retrieval systems, except as permitted under Section 107 or 108 of the 1976 United States Copyright Act, without the prior written permission of the publisher.

For product information and technology assistance, contact us at **Cengage Learning Customer & Sales Support, 1-800-354-9706**

For permission to use material from this text or product, submit all requests online at **www.cengage.com/permissions**
Further permissions questions can be emailed to **permissionrequest@cengage.com**

Library of Congress Control Number: 2008924207

ISBN-13: 978-0-618-99240-9

ISBN-10: 0-618-99240-5

Wadsworth
20 Channel Center Street
Boston, MA 02210
USA

Cengage Learning is a leading provider of customized learning solutions with office locations around the globe, including Singapore, the United Kingdom, Australia, Mexico, Brazil, and Japan. Locate your local office at **international.cengage.com/region**

Cengage Learning products are represented in Canada by Nelson Education, Ltd.

To learn more about Wadsworth, visit **www.cengage.com/wadsworth**

Purchase any of our products at your local college store or at our preferred online store **www.ichapters.com**

Printed in the United States of America
2 3 4 5 6 7 11 10 09

Brief Contents

iii

Contents

Maps

Features

ENVIRONMENT AND TECHNOLOGY

DIVERSITY AND DOMINANCE

MATERIAL CULTURE

ISSUES IN WORLD HISTORY

Preface

When a textbook reaches its fourth edition, the authors feel justified in assessing their work a success. The first edition contained a basic concept. The second used the myriad valuable comments made by teachers and reviewers to make major adjustments in the presentation of that concept. The third edition incorporated a further round of comments and suggestions aimed at filling lacunae and improving the flow of the exposition. At the same time, pedagogical aids were steadily improved to make the text more accessible to both students and teachers.

The principal change from past editions of *The Earth and Its Peoples,* both Brief and Comprehensive, is not be found in the textual narrative, but in the layout of the pages. Moving from a two-column to a one-column format not only makes the text easier to read, but it also makes it possible to gloss key terms in the margins when they first appear and to add cues for referencing computer-based supplementary materials. Preview questions at the start of each chapter, section summaries, and chapter reviews keyed to the preview questions further our intent of making studying more efficient and effective. Pronunciation guides for unfamiliar names and terms have also been integrated into the text.

The Brief Edition is produced in two formats: A complete edition covers the entire chronology from prehistory to the present, and a two-volume edition can be used for the two-semester survey. Volume I covers the period from prehistory to 1550, and Volume II covers 1500 to the present. There is a brief introduction to Volume II that orients students to the general political and social climate of the world before and up to 1500.

Our overall goal in *The Earth and Its Peoples* remains unchanged: to produce a textbook that not only speaks for the past, but speaks to today's student and today's teacher. Students and instructors alike should take away from this text a broad vision of human societies beginning as sparse and disconnected communities reacting creatively to local circumstances; experiencing ever more intensive stages of contact, interpenetration, and cultural expansion and amalgamation; and arriving at a twenty-first-century world situation in which people increasingly visualize a single global community.

Process, not progress, is the keynote of this book: a steady process of change over time, at first differently experienced in various regions, but eventually interconnecting peoples and traditions from all parts of the globe. Students should come away from this book with a sense that the problems and promises of their world are rooted in a past in which people of every sort, in every part of the world, confronted problems of a similar character and coped with them as best they could. We believe our efforts will help students see where their world has come from and learn thereby something useful for their own lives.

CENTRAL THEMES

We have subtitled *The Earth and Its Peoples* "A Global History" because the book explores the common challenges and experiences that unite the human past. Although the dispersal of early humans to every livable environment resulted in many different economic, social, political, and cultural systems, all societies displayed analogous patterns in meeting their needs and exploiting their environments. Our challenge was to select the particular data and episodes that would best illuminate these global patterns of human experience.

To meet this challenge, we adopted two themes to serve as the spinal cord of our history: "technology and environment" and "diversity and dominance." The first theme represents the commonplace material bases of all human societies at all times. It grants no special favor to any cultural group even as it embraces subjects of the broadest topical, chronological, and geographical range. The second theme expresses the reality that every human society has constructed or inherited structures of domination. We examine practices and institutions of many sorts: military, economic, social, political, religious, and cultural, as well as those based on kinship, gender, and literacy. Simultaneously we recognize that alternative ways of life and visions of societal organization continually manifest themselves both within and in dialogue with every structure of domination.

With respect to the first theme, it is vital for students to understand that technology, in the broad sense of experience-based knowledge of the physical world, underlies all human activity. Writing is a technology, but so is oral transmission from generation to generation of lore about medicinal or poisonous plants. The magnetic compass is a navigational technology, but so is a Polynesian mariner's hard-won knowledge of winds, currents, and tides that made possible the settlement of the Pacific islands.

All technological development has come about in interaction with environments, both physical and human, and has, in turn, affected those environments. The story of how humanity has changed the face of the globe is an integral part of this central theme. Yet technology and the environment do not explain or underlie all important episodes of human experience. The theme of "diversity and dominance" informs all our discussions of politics, culture, and society. Thus, when narrating the histories of empires, we describe a range of human experiences within and beyond the imperial frontiers without assuming that the imperial institutions are a more fit topic for discussion than the economic and social organization of pastoral nomads or the lives of peasant women. When religion and culture occupy our narrative, we focus not only on the dominant tradition but also on the diversity of alternative beliefs and practices.

CHANGES IN THE FOURTH EDITION

In addition to transforming the visual layout of *The Earth and Its Peoples,* we have added a new category of historical essays. These new essays expand the scope of one of the improvements in the third edition, the essays on *Issues in World History.* While those essays were designed to alert students to broad and recurring conceptual issues that are of great interest to contemporary historians, the new essays on *Material Culture* call particular attention to the many ways in which objects and processes of everyday life can play a role in understanding human history on a broad scale. Thus essays like "Wine and Beer in the Ancient World" and "Fast Food" are not only interesting in and of themselves but also suggestive of how today's world historians find meaning in the ordinary dimensions of human life.

As for the text itself, material on the Western Hemisphere in Chapters 10 and 14 has been significantly updated and revised. Coverage of Japan and Korea has been expanded in Chapters 9 and 11. The sequence of Chapters 21 and 22 has been reversed to avoid divided coverage of Egypt and to improve the transition from topic to topic. And Chapter 30 has been thoroughly revised and updated to cover the war in Iraq and other contemporary problems.

Suggested reading lists have been revised to include a smaller selection of readily available historical studies. Expanded supplementary reading list selections are available on the textbook website, accessible through www.cengage.com/highered.

ORGANIZATION

The Earth and Its Peoples uses eight broad chronological divisions to define its conceptual scheme of global historical development. In **Part One: The Emergence of Human Communities, to 500 B.C.E.,** we examine important patterns of human communal organization. Small, dispersed human communities living by foraging spread to most parts of the world over tens of thousands of years. They responded to enormously diverse environmental conditions, at different times and in different ways discovering how to cultivate plants and utilize the products of domestic animals. On the basis of these new modes of sustenance, population grows, permanent towns appear, and political and religious authority, based on collection and control of agricultural surpluses, spreads over extensive areas.

Part Two: The Formation of New Cultural Communities, 1000 B.C.E.–600 C.E., introduces the concept of a "cultural community," in the sense of a coherent pattern of activities and symbols pertaining to a specific human community. While all human communities develop distinctive cultures, including those discussed in Part One, historical development in this stage of global history prolonged and magnified the impact of some cultures more than others. In the geographically contiguous African-Eurasian land mass, the cultures that proved to have the most enduring influence traced their roots to the second and first millennia B.C.E.

Part Three: Growth and Interaction of Cultural Communities, 600–1200, deals with early episodes of technological, social, and cultural exchange and interaction on a continental scale both within and beyond the framework of imperial expansion. These are so different from earlier interactions arising from more limited conquests or extensions of political boundaries that they constitute a distinct era in world history, an era that set the world on the path of increasing global interaction and interdependence that it has been following ever since.

In **Part Four: Interregional Patterns of Culture and Contact, 1200–1550,** we take a look at the world during three centuries that saw both intensified cultural and commercial contact and increasingly confident self-definition of cultural communities in Europe, Asia, and Africa. The Mongol conquest of a vast empire extending from the Pacific Ocean to eastern Europe greatly stimulated trade and interaction. In the West, strengthened European kingdoms began maritime expansion in the Atlantic, forging direct ties with sub-Saharan Africa and laying the base for expanded global contacts after 1500.

Part Five: The Globe Encompassed, 1500–1800, treats a period dominated by the global effects of European expansion and continued economic growth. European ships took over, expanded, and extended the maritime trade of the Indian Ocean, coastal Africa, and the Asian rim of the Pacific Ocean. This maritime commercial enterprise had its counterpart in European colonial empires in the Americas and a new Atlantic trading system. The contrasting capacities and fortunes of traditional land empires and new maritime empires, along with the exchange of domestic plants and animals between the hemispheres, underline the technological and environmental dimensions of this first era of complete global interaction.

In **Part Six: Revolutions Reshape the World, 1750–1870,** the word *revolution* is used in several senses: in the political sense of governmental overthrow, as in France and the Americas; in the metaphorical sense of radical transformative change, as in the Industrial Revolution; and in the broadest sense of a perception of a profound change in circumstances and world-view. Technology and environment lie at the core of these developments. With the rapid ascendancy of the Western belief that science and technology could overcome all challenges, technology became not only an instrument of transformation but also an instrument of domination, to the point of threatening the integrity and autonomy of cultural traditions in nonindustrial lands.

Part Seven: Global Diversity and Dominance, 1850–1949, examines the development of a world arena in which people conceived of events on a global scale. Imperialism, world war, international economic connections, and world-encompassing ideological tendencies, like nationalism and socialism, present the picture of a globe becoming increasingly interconnected. European dominance took on a worldwide dimension, seeming at times to threaten the diversity of human cultural experience with permanent subordination to European values and philosophies, while at other times triggering strong political or cultural resistance. The accelerating pace of technological change deepened other sorts of cleavages as well.

For **Part Eight: Perils and Promises of a Global Community, 1945 to the Present,** we decided to divide the last half of the twentieth century into three time periods: 1945 to 1975, 1975 to 1991, and 1991 to the present. Nevertheless, there is a good deal of continuity from chapter to chapter. The challenges of the Cold War, postcolonial nation building, and post-Cold War frictions between different powers and cultures dominate the period and involve global economic, technological, and political forces that become increasingly important factors in all aspects of human life. Technology plays a central role in this part both because of its integral role in the growth of a global community and because its many benefits in improving the quality of life seem clouded by real and potential negative impacts on the environment.

SUPPLEMENTS

In keeping with Cengage Learning's goal of being your primary source for history, we are proud to provide a wealth of supplementary assets for students and instructors.

HistoryFinder is a comprehensive searchable database that offers instructors thousands of online resources including art, photographs, maps, primary source documents, videos, multimedia content, Associated Press interactive modules, and ready-made *PowerPoint* slides. *HistoryFinder* assets can be easily located by keyword, media type, or textbook-specific searches, as well as through a list of drop-down topical menus. Instructors will appreciate the ease of previewing and downloading resources for use in their classroom directly from the website.

Diploma Testing, a computerized bank of test items enables instructors to alter, replace, or add questions to create unique quizzes and tests with minimal effort. *Diploma Testing* also contains a thoroughly updated electronic version of the ***Instructor's Resource Manual.*** The test items and electronic *IRM* have been thoroughly revised by John Reisbord (Ph.D. Northwestern University) and Leslie Kauffman (LEAP Publishing), respectively. Instructors can also access all of these resources, among others, on the textbook's ***Instructor Website***. To reach the site, log on to www.cengage.com/ history and select this book.

The ***Student Website*** is a free online study center that contains a wealth of assets to help students succeed in the classroom. Among the assets are ACE practice quizzes that allow students to test their knowledge of chapter key points, flashcards that quiz students on key terms, downloadable MP3 chapter summaries for the busy student on the go, and interactive maps that depict relevant geographical events. Other assets include learning objectives, suggested reading, an audio pronunciation guide, and numerous weblinks to notable and informative history Internet sites. To access the *Student Website,* please logon to www.cengage.com/history and select this book.

ACKNOWLEDGMENTS

As always we are grateful to the following colleagues who took the time to review and comment upon *The Earth and Its Peoples:* Henry Abramson, Florida Atlantic University; Joseph Adams, Walton High School, Cobb County, Georgia; Paul V. Adams, Shippensburg University/University of San Carlos; Siamak Adhami, Saddleback College; William H. Alexander, Norfolk State University; Maria S. Arbelaez, University of Nebraska at Omaha; Monty Armstrong, Cerritos High School, Cerritos, California; William J. Astore, United States Air Force Academy; David G. Atwill, Pennsylvania State University; Lawrence Backlund, Montgomery County Community College; Fritz Blackwell, Washington State University; Corinne Blake, Rowan University; Olwyn M. Blouet, Virginia State University; Eric Bobo, Hinds Community College; Thomas Borstelmann, Cornell University; James Boyden, Tulane University; Richard M. Brabander, University of New Hampshire; Byron Cannon, University of Utah; Bruce Castleman, San Diego State University; Craige B. Champion, Syracuse University; David A. Chappell, University of Hawaii; Nancy Clark, California Polytechnic State University at San Luis Obispo; Aaron Cohen, California State University, Sacramento; Eleanor A. Congdon, Youngstown State University; Lee Congdon, James Madison University; James Coolsen, Shippensburg University; Ransom P. Cross, University of Texas at El Paso; Bruce Cruikshank, Hastings College; Philip Daileader, The College of William and Mary; Linda T. Darling, University of Arizona; Jennifer Deane, University of Minnesota, Morris; Susan Deans-Smith, University of Texas at Austin; Krista Feinberg, Lakeland College; Gregory C. Ference, Salisbury State University; Alan Fisher, Michigan State University; Donald M. Fisher, Niagara County Community College; Nancy Fitch, California State University, Fullerton; Peter Fraunholtz, Northeastern University; Cathy A. Frierson, University of New Hampshire; Jeffrey S. Gaab, SUNY at Farmingdale; Rosanna Gatens, Belmont University; Lorne E. Glaim, Pacific Union College; Moshe Gershovich, University of Omaha; Matthew S. Gordon, Miami University; Steve Gosch, University of Wisconsin at Eau Claire; Kolleen M. Guy, University of Texas at San Antonio; James R. Hansen, Auburn University; Jay Harmon, Catholic High School, Baton Rouge, Louisiana; Randolph C. Head, University of California at Riverside; Kenneth E. Hendrickson, Sam Houston State University; David Hertzel, Southwestern Oklahoma State University; Catherine Higgs, University of Tennessee; Richard J. Hoffman, San Francisco State University; Diana Honey, Kennesaw State University; Roy W. Hopper, The University of Memphis; Amy J. Johnson, Berry College; Catherine M. Jones, North Georgia College and State University; Joy Kammerling, Eastern Illinois University; Carol A. Keller, San Antonio College; James Krippner, Haverford College; Patricia Kollander, Florida Atlantic University; Hal Langfur, University of North Carolina, Wilmington; Jinhee Lee, Eastern Illinois University; Jonathan Lee, San Antonio College; Miriam R. Levin, Case Western Reserve University; Richard Lewis, St. Cloud State University; James E. Lindsay, Colorado State University; Susan Maneck, Jackson State University; Laurie S. Mannino, Magruder High School, North Potomac, Maryland; Margaret Malamud, New Mexico State University; Harold Marcus, University of California, Santa Barbara; Dorothea A. L. Martin, Appalachian State University; Charles W. McClellan, Radford University; Patrick F. McDevitt, SUNY at Buffalo; Andrea McElderry, University of Louisville; Stephen L. McFarland, Auburn University; Randall McGowen, University of Oregon; Margaret McKee, Castilleja School, Palo Alto, California; Megan McLean, Central Washington University; Mark McLeod, University of Delaware; Gregory McMahon, University of New Hampshire; Stephen S. Michot, Mississippi County Community College;

Shawn W. Miller, Brigham Young University; Stephen Morillo, Wabash College; Andrew Muldoon, Metropolitan State College of Denver; Kalala Joseph Ngalamulume, Central Washington University; Peter A. Ngwafu, Albany State University; Patricia O'Neill, Central Oregon Community College; Chandrika Paul, Shippensburg University; John R. Pavia, Ithaca College; Thomas Earl Porter, North Carolina A&T State University; Diethelm Prowe, Carleton College; Jean H. Quataert, SUNY at Binghamton; Stephen Rapp, Georgia State University; William Reddy, Duke University; Stephen A. Reed, Santiago Canyon College; Thomas Reeves, Roxbury Community College; Dennis Reinhartz, University of Texas at Arlington; Richard Rice, University of Tennessee at Chattanooga; Michael D. Richards, Sweet Briar College; Jane Scimeca, Brookdale Community College; William Schell, Murray State University; Alyssa Goldstein Sepinwall, California State University at San Marcos; Deborah Shackleton, United States Air Force Academy; Anita Shelton, Eastern Illinois University; Jeffrey M. Shumway, Brigham Young University; Jonathan Skaff, Shippensburg University of Pennsylvania; David R. Smith, California State Polytechnic University at Pomona; Linda Smith, Samford University; Mary Frances Smith, Ohio University; George E. Snow, Shippensburg University; Charlotte D. Staelin, Washington College; Tracy L. Steele, Sam Houston State University; Paul D. Steeves, Stetson University; Robert Shannon Sumner, State University of West Georgia; Yi Sun, University of San Diego; Willard Sunderland, University of Cincinnati; Karen Sundwick, Southern Oregon University; Thaddeus Sunseri, Colorado State University; Joel E. Tishken, Columbus State University; Robert Topmiller, Eastern Kentucky University; Sara W. Tucker, Washburn University; David J. Ulbrich, Ball State University; John M. VanderLippe, SUNY at New Paltz; Mary A. Watrous-Schlesinger, Washington State University; James A. Wood, North Carolina A&T State University; Eric Van Young, University of California at San Diego; Peter von Sivers, University of Utah; and Alex Zukas, National University, San Diego.

We also want to extend our thanks to Lynda Schaffer for her early conceptual contributions and to the history departments of Shippensburg University, the United States Air Force Academy, and the State University of New York at New Paltz for arranging reviewer conferences that provided crucial feedback for our revisions.

Our debt to the staff of Cengage Learning remains undiminished in the fourth edition. Nancy Blaine, Senior Sponsoring Editor, has offered us firm but sympathetic guidance throughout the revision process. Tonya Lobato, Senior Development Editor, provided editorial support and facilitated the implementation of new ideas for this edition. Carol Newman, Senior Project Editor, moved the work through the production stages. Carole Frohlich did an outstanding job of photo research, and Jessyca Broekman did an excellent job revising the maps and timelines.

Finally, we thank the many students whose questions and concerns, expressed directly or through their instructors, shaped much of this revision. We continue to welcome all our readers' suggestions, queries, and criticisms. Please contact us at our respective institutions or at this e-mail address: higheredcs@cengage.com.

About the Authors

Richard W. Bulliet Professor of Middle Eastern History at Columbia University, Richard W. Bulliet received his Ph.D. from Harvard University. He has written scholarly works on a number of topics: the social history of medieval Iran *(The Patricians of Nishapur),* the historical competition between pack camels and wheeled transport *(The Camel and the Wheel),* the process of conversion to Islam *(Conversion to Islam in the Medieval Period),* and the overall course of Islamic social history *(Islam: The View from the Edge).* His most recent books include a global history of human-animal relations *(Hunters, Herders, and Hamburgers),* and an affirmation of the historical kinship of Islam and Christianity *(The Case for Islamo-Christian Civilization).* He is the editor of the *Columbia History of the Twentieth Century.* He has published four novels, co-edited *The Encyclopedia of the Modern Middle East,* and hosted an educational television series on the Middle East. He was awarded a fellowship by the John Simon Guggenheim Memorial Foundation.

Pamela Kyle Crossley Pamela Kyle Crossley received her Ph.D. in Modern Chinese History from Yale University. She is Professor of History and Rosenwald Research Professor in the Arts and Sciences at Dartmouth College. Her books include *A Translucent Mirror: History and Identity in Qing Imperial Ideology; The Manchus; Orphan Warriors: Three Manchu Generations and the End of the Qing World;* and (with Lynn Hollen Lees and John W. Servos) *Global Society: The World Since 1900.* Her research, which concentrates on the cultural history of China, Inner Asia, and Central Asia, has been supported by the John Simon Guggenheim Memorial Foundation and the National Endowment for the Humanities.

Daniel R. Headrick Daniel R. Headrick received his Ph.D. in History from Princeton University. Professor of History and Social Science at Roosevelt University in Chicago, he is the author of several books on the history of technology, imperialism, and international relations, including *The Tools of Empire: Technology and European Imperialism in the Nineteenth Century; The Tentacles of Progress: Technology Transfer in the Age of Imperialism; The Invisible Weapon: Telecommunications and International Politics;* and *When Information Came of Age: Technologies of Knowledge in the Age of Reason and Revolution, 1700–1850.* His articles have appeared in the *Journal of World History* and the *Journal of Modern History,* and he has been awarded fellowships by the National Endowment for the Humanities, the John Simon Guggenheim Memorial Foundation, and the Alfred P. Sloan Foundation.

Steven W. Hirsch Steven W. Hirsch holds a Ph.D. in Classics from Stanford University and is currently Associate Professor Classics and History at Tufts University. He has received grants from the National Endowment for the Humanities and the Massachusetts Foundation for Humanities and Public Policy. His research and publications include *The Friendship of the Barbarians: Xenophon and the Persian Empire,* as well as articles and reviews in the *Classical Journal,* the *American Journal of Philology,* and the *Journal of Interdisciplinary History.* He is currently working on a comparative study of ancient Mediterranean and Chinese civilizations.

Lyman L. Johnson Professor of History at the University of North Carolina at Charlotte, Lyman L. Johnson earned his Ph.D. in Latin American History from the University of Connecticut. A two-time Senior Fulbright-Hays Lecturer, he also has received fellowships from the Tinker Foundation, the Social Science Research Council, the National Endowment for the Humanities, and the American Philosophical Society. His recent books include *Death, Dismemberment, and Memory; The Faces of Honor* (with Sonya Lipsett-Rivera); *The Problem of Order in Changing Societies; Essays on the Price History of Eighteenth-Century Latin America* (with Enrique Tandeter); and *Colonial Latin America* (with Mark A. Burkholder). He also has published in journals, including the *Hispanic American Historical Review,* the *Journal of Latin American Studies,* the *International Review of Social History, Social History,* and *Desarrollo Económico.* He recently served as president of the Conference on Latin American History.

David Northrup Professor of History at Boston College, David Northrup earned his Ph.D. in African and European History from the University of California at Los Angeles. He earlier taught in Nigeria with the Peace Corps and at Tuskegee Institute. Research supported by the Fulbright-Hays Commission, the National Endowment for the Humanities, and the Social Science Research Council led to publications concerning precolonial Nigeria, the Congo (1870–1940), the Atlantic slave trade, and Asian, African, and Pacific Islander indentured labor in the nineteenth century. A contributor to the *Oxford History of the British Empire* and *Blacks in the British Empire,* his latest book is *Africa's Discovery of Europe, 1450–1850.* For 2004 and 2005 he served as president of the World History Association.

Note on Spelling and Usage

Where necessary for clarity, dates are followed by the letters C.E. or B.C.E. The abbreviation C.E. stands for "Common Era" and is equivalent to A.D. (*anno Domini,* Latin for "in the year of the Lord"). The abbreviation B.C.E. stands for "before the Common Era" and means the same as B.C. ("before Christ"). In keeping with our goal of approaching world history without special concentration on one culture or another, we chose these neutral abbreviations as appropriate to our enterprise. Because many readers will be more familiar with English than with metric measurements, however, units of measure are generally given in the English system, with metric equivalents following in parentheses.

In general, Chinese has been romanized according to the *pinyin* method. Exceptions include proper names well established in English (e.g., Canton, Chiang Kaishek) and a few English words borrowed from Chinese (e.g., kowtow). Spellings of Arabic, Ottoman Turkish, Persian, Mongolian, Manchu, Japanese, and Korean names and terms avoid special diacritical marks for letters that are pronounced only slightly differently in English. An apostrophe is used to indicate when two Chinese syllables are pronounced separately (e.g., Chang'an).

For words transliterated from languages that use the Arabic script—Arabic, Ottoman Turkish, Persian, Urdu—the apostrophe indicating separately pronounced syllables may represent either of two special consonants, the *hamza* or the *ain.* Because most English-speakers do not hear the distinction between these two, they have not been distinguished in transliteration and are not indicated when they occur at the beginning or end of a word. As with Chinese, some words and commonly used place-names from these languages are given familiar English spellings (e.g., Quran instead of Qur'an, Cairo instead of al-Qahira). Arabic romanization has normally been used for terms relating to Islam, even where the context justifies slightly different Turkish or Persian forms, again for ease of comprehension.

Before 1492 the inhabitants of the Western Hemisphere had no single name for themselves. They had neither a racial consciousness nor a racial identity. Identity was derived from kin groups, language, cultural practices, and political structures. There was no sense that physical similarities created a shared identity. America's original inhabitants had racial consciousness and racial identity imposed on them by conquest and the occupation of their lands by Europeans after 1492. All of the collective terms for these first American peoples are tainted by this history. *Indians, Native Americans, Amerindians, First Peoples, and Indigenous Peoples* are among the terms in common usage. In this book the names of individual cultures and states are used wherever possible. *Amerindian* and other terms that suggest transcultural identity and experience are used most commonly for the period after 1492.

There is an ongoing debate about how best to render Amerindian words in English. It has been common for authors writing in English to follow Mexican usage for Nahuatl and Yucatec Maya words and place-names. In this style, for example, the capital of the Aztec state is spelled Tenochtitlán, and the important late Maya city-state is spelled Chichén Itzá. Although these forms are still common even in the specialist literature, we have chosen to follow the scholarship that sees these accents as unnecessary. The exceptions are modern place-names, such as Mérida and Yucatán, which are accented. A similar problem exists for the spelling of Quechua and Aymara words from the Andean region of South America. Although there is significant disagreement among scholars, we follow the emerging consensus and use the spellings khipu (not quipu), Tiwanaku (not Tiahuanaco), and Wari (not Huari). However, we keep Inca (not Inka) and Cuzco (not Cusco), since these spellings are expected by most of our potential readers and we hope to avoid confusion.

The World Before 1500

- Antiquity: Humans, Cultures, and Conquests, to 400 C.E.

- Growth and Interaction, 400–1200

- Interregional Conquests and Exchanges, 1200–1500

This icon will direct you to the website where you can Prepare for Class, Improve Your Grade, and Ace the Test: college.cengage.com/pic/bullietbrief4e

istory occurs in a continuous stream. Because new events are the products of their past, each historical period is intimately linked to what preceded it. As a Roman historian put it, "History doesn't make leaps." Nevertheless, modern historians find it useful to divide the past into eras or ages to make sense of the sweep of history. The longest historical eras are antiquity, the Middle Ages, and modern times. Volume II of *The Earth and Its Peoples* is devoted to the third of these—modern world history, the five centuries since about 1500.

World historians largely agree that the intensity of interaction around the world during the modern period distinguishes it from all earlier times. European maritime exploration opened up or intensified these contacts. The modern era is also characterized by the steady expansion of European political, economic, and cultural leadership in every part of the world.

How and when different parts of the world felt the impact of the West varied. By 1500 parts of the Americas were already reeling under the impact of their first contacts with Europeans, but in most other parts of the world the West did not make a big difference until the century after 1750 or even later. Thus, while in hindsight Western ascendancy seems to be a defining theme of modern history, for the people of Asia, Africa, and elsewhere the modern era was a time in which the internal patterns of historical change only gradually became altered by the growing influence of Westerners and by their own reactions to these influences.

In order to explain how the modern era came into being, the first chapter of Volume II of *The Earth and Its Peoples* (Chapter 16) begins in about 1450. To help the reader understand the broader sweep of history, this Introduction provides an overview of earlier eras. The Introduction reviews three periods of decreasing temporal length. The first is the very long period from human origins until the end of ancient history in about 400 C.E. Next comes the early medieval period down to about 1200; and, finally, the three hundred years immediately preceding 1500. Because the centuries after 1200 were most important for shaping the transition to the modern era, they receive the most detailed treatment.

▌ ANTIQUITY: HUMANS, CULTURES, AND CONQUESTS, TO 400 C.E.

▌ All historical periods were shaped by natural environment and human technology (whether simple tools, techniques, or complex machines). The paramount role played by environmental forces is apparent when historians seek to explain how human beings—and thus history—began. Like all other living creatures, early humans were products of biological adjustments to changing environments. Over millions of years, our ancestors in eastern and southern Africa evolved biologically to enhance their chances for survival. The evolution of an upright posture enabled early people to walk and run on two legs, thereby freeing their hands for tool making. The evolution of larger brains gave them the capacity to learn and understand all sorts of new things and devise techniques for putting them to use. Finally, evolutionary changes in the throat gave humans the capacity for speech, which, as language developed, had the dual effect of making complex social relations easier and fostering the development of intellectual culture.

With these physical traits in place, humans were able to develop in a direction taken by no other creature. Instead of relying on the glacially slow process of biological evolution to adapt their bodies to new environments, our ancestors used their minds to devise technologies for transforming nature to suit their needs. By the standards of today, these early technologies may seem crude—stone tools for cutting and chopping, clothing made from plants and animal skins, shelters in caves and huts—but they were sufficient to enable humans to survive environmental changes in their homelands. They also enabled bands of humans to migrate to new environments in every part of the world. Through trial and error Stone Age people learned what could safely be eaten in new environments. Other primates acted primarily by instinct; humans acted according to the dictates of culture. The capacity to create and change material and intellectual culture marked the beginning of human history.

Agricultural Civilizations

Beginning about 10,000 years ago, the transition from food gathering to food production marked a major turning point in history. Human communities in many different parts of the world learned to alter the natural food supply. Some people promoted the growth of foods they liked by scattering seeds on good soils and restricting the growth of competing plants. In time some people became full-time farmers. Other communities tamed wild animals whose meat, milk, fur, and hides they desired, and they controlled their breeding to produce animals with the most desired characteristics. Promoted by a warmer world climate, these agricultural revolutions slowly spread from the Middle East around the Mediterranean. People in South and East Asia, Africa, and the Americas domesticated other wild plants and animals for their use. Just as humans had ceased to rely on evolution to enable them to adjust to new surroundings, so too they had bypassed evolution in bringing new species of plants and animals into existence (see Map I.1).

The agricultural revolutions greatly enhanced people's chances for survival in two ways. One was a rapid increase in population fostered by the ability to grow and store more food (see Issues in World History: Climate and Population, to 1500). A second change was taking place in the composition of human communities. The earliest communities consisted of small bands of biologically related people and their spouses from other bands. However, more complex societies made their first appearances as more and more unrelated people concentrated in lush river valleys, where the soils, temperatures, and potential to irrigate with river water produced conditions suitable for farming.

In the Fertile Crescent of the Middle East, Egypt, India, and China the existence of a regular food surplus enabled a few people to develop highly specialized talents and tools that were not tied to food production. Some talented military leaders became rulers of large areas and headed government with specialized administrators. Specialists constructed elaborate irrigation systems, monumental palaces, and temples. Others made special metal tools and weapons, first of bronze, then of iron. Because of the value of their talents these specialists acquired privileges. It was grandest to be a king, queen, or head priest. For the average person, life was harder in complex societies than in parts of the world where such specialization had not yet occurred.

Culture and Civilization

Complex and populous agricultural societies developed specialists who dealt with abstract and unseen forces. This development was not entirely new. For tens of thousands of years before the first settled societies, humans had used their minds to think about the meaning of life. The remains of elaborate burials and sites of worship suggest that some early societies had clear beliefs in an afterlife and in spiritual forces that controlled their lives. Many cultures believed the sun, moon, and nature had supernatural powers.

Another form of intellectual activity was the collection of technical knowledge about the environment. Cultural communities learned what plants were best for food, clothing, or building materials and passed this knowledge along to later generations. Most specialized was the knowledge of how to make medicines and poisons. Assigning names for all these facilitated the transmission of this knowledge. In

Scene from the Egyptian Book of the Dead, ca. 1300 B.C.E.
The mummy of a royal scribe named Hunefar is approached by members of his household before being placed in the tomb. Behind Hunefar is jackel-headed Anubis, the god who will conduct the spirit of the deceased to the afterlife. The Book of the Dead provided Egyptians with the instructions they needed to complete this arduous journey and gain a blessed existence in the afterlife.
(Courtesy of the Trustees of the British Museum)

the absence of written records, very little specific information about these early treasuries of knowledge exists, but the elaborate and beautiful paintings in caves dating to tens of thousands of years before the emergence of early agricultural societies provide the clearest evidence of the cultural sophistication of early humans.

Cultural change surged as settled agricultural communities became more specialized. Temple priests devised elaborate rituals and prayers for the gods who protected the community, and they studied the movements of stars, planets, and the moon for signs of the progress of the seasons or the will of the gods. In Mesopotamia, Egypt, and elsewhere a new class of scribes used written symbols to preserve administrative and commercial records, laws, and bodies of specialized knowledge. Thoughtful people recorded the myths and legends passed down orally from earlier days, systematizing them and often adapting them to new social conditions, as well as creating new literary forms. Communications could now be sent unchanged over long distances. Some of these works were lost for millennia only to be rediscovered in recent times, allowing us to know much more about the lives, thoughts, and values of ancient peoples.

Empires and Regional Cultures

In time governments weakened or fell victim to conquest. Egypt, for example, fell to Nubians from up the Nile then to the Assyrians from Mesopotamia. Some conquerors created vast new empires. Late in the fourth century B.C.E., Alexander the Great brought everything from the eastern Mediterranean to India and Egypt under his sway, spreading Greek culture and language. After the collapse of Alexander's empire, the first of a series of Indian empires arose. In the second and first centuries B.C.E., Latin-speakers spread their rule, language, and culture throughout the Roman Empire, which encompassed the Mediterranean and reached across the Alps into Gaul (France) and Britain. At much the same time, the Han consolidated control over the densely populated lands of China, and successive rulers extended the sway of imperial China over much of East Asia. In the isolated continents of the Americas, advanced agricultural societies were also building larger states in late antiquity.

Essential to empire formation was the significant enhancement of old technologies and the development of new ones. In many parts of the world iron replaced bronze as the preferred metal for tools and weapons. In the Middle East and China

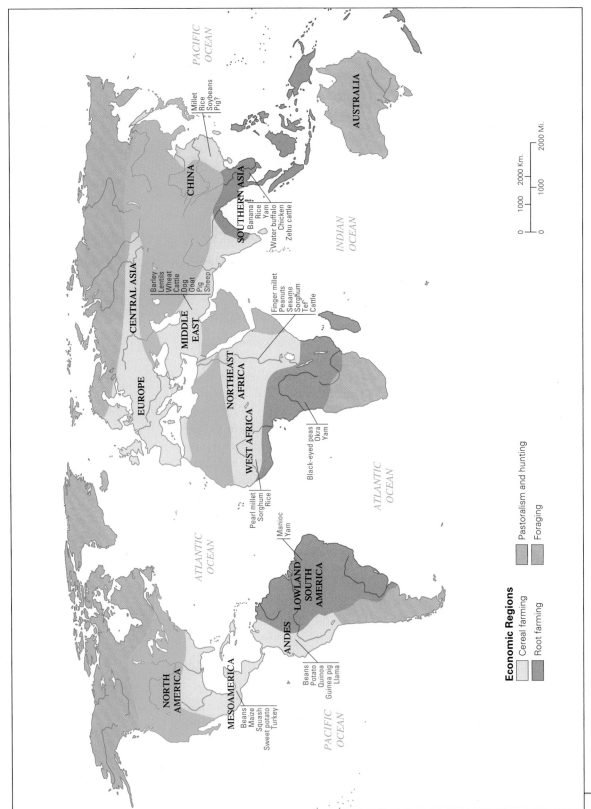

Map I.1 Early Centers of Plant and Animal Domestication

Many different parts of the world made original contributions to domestication during the Agricultural Revolutions that began about 10,000 years ago. Later interactions helped spread these domesticated animals and plants to new locations. In lands less suitable for crop cultivation, pastoralism and hunting remained more important for supplying food.

Economic Regions

- Cereal farming
- Root farming
- Pastoralism and hunting
- Foraging

Labels on map:

- PACIFIC OCEAN
- AUSTRALIA
- CHINA — Millet, Rice, Soybeans, Pig?
- SOUTHERN ASIA — Banana, Rice, Yam, Water buffalo, Chicken, Zebu cattle
- CENTRAL ASIA
- MIDDLE EAST — Barley, Lentils, Wheat, Cattle, Dog, Goat, Pig, Sheep
- EUROPE
- NORTHEAST AFRICA — Finger millet, Peanuts, Sesame, Sorghum, Tef, Cattle
- WEST AFRICA — Black-eyed peas, Okra, Yam
- INDIAN OCEAN
- ATLANTIC OCEAN
- Pearl millet, Sorghum, Rice
- Manioc, Yam
- LOWLAND SOUTH AMERICA
- ANDES — Beans, Potato, Quinoa, Guinea pig, Llama
- NORTH AMERICA
- MESOAMERICA — Beans, Maize, Squash, Sweet potato, Turkey
- PACIFIC OCEAN

Scale: 0 1000 2000 Km. / 0 1000 2000 Mi.

soldiers on horseback played important military roles. In most places there were advances in the fighting techniques and in defensive strategies and fortifications.

Empires encouraged the growth of cities to serve as administrative, economic, and cultural centers. Temples, palaces, monuments, markets, and public amenities advertised the glory of these imperial centers. Large states regularly mobilized large pools of labor for massive construction projects. By late antiquity, a few cities had populations in the hundreds of thousands—Alexandria in Egypt, Rome in Italy, Chang'an in China, Pataliputra in India—though such large numbers strained cities' capacities to supply food and water and dispose of waste. Such architectural monuments established "classical" styles that were frequently imitated and affected wide areas even after the empires were gone.

Other imperial building projects were more practical. The Roman and Chinese governments built thousands of miles of paved roads for moving troops and communication; long barrier walls and strings of forts defended frontier areas from invasion. Trade often flourished on these political frontiers, and good roads further encouraged trade. Improvements in shipping also encouraged the movement of goods over long distances and allowed transport of bulkier goods. Much long-distance trade in antiquity was in luxury goods for the privileged classes in urban civilizations. The search for exotic items tied remote parts of the world together and gave rise to new specialists both within the urban civilizations and in less stratified parts of the world. Gold, ivory, animal pelts, and exotic feathers from inner Africa reached Egypt. Phoenician mariners marketed lumber, papyrus (for paper), wine, and fish around the Mediterranean Sea. Other merchants carried silk from China across arid Central Asia to the Middle East and lands to the west. The advent of coinage in the first millennium B.C.E. stimulated local and regional economies.

The routes that carried goods also helped spread religions, inventions, and ideas. The Zoroastrian religion of the Persians became one of the great ethical creeds of antiquity. The diaspora of Jews from Palestine after their southern kingdom was destroyed by the Neo-Babylonian Empire in the seventh century B.C.E. also helped spread monotheistic beliefs. The beliefs and culture of the Greeks and Romans spread throughout their empires, largely because many of their subjects saw the advantages in adopting the ways of the ruling elite. Similarly, Indian traders introduced Hinduism and Buddhism to Southeast Asia.

▌ GROWTH AND INTERACTION, 400–1200

During the Early Middle Ages expanding political and commercial links drew regions closer together. In addition, the growth of interregional trade and the spread of new world religions helped unite and redefine the boundaries of cultural regions, though divisions within religions undercut some of this cultural unity. All of these factors were interrelated, but let's begin with the one that left the most enduring impression on the course of history: the spread of world religions.

World Religions The first religious tradition to experience widespread growth in this period was Buddhism, which spread from the Indian homeland where it had arisen around 500

B.C.E. One direction of growth was eastward into Southeast Asia. After 500 C.E. there were particular strongholds of the faith on the large islands of Ceylon, Sumatra, and Java, whose kings supported the growth of schools and monasteries and constructed temple complexes. Traders also carried Buddhism to China and from there to Korea, Japan, and Tibet. In some places Buddhism's growing strength led to political reactions. In China the Tang emperors reduced the influence of the monasteries in 840 by taking away their tax exemption and by promoting traditional Confucian values. A similar effort by the Tibetan royal family to curtail Buddhism failed, and Buddhist monks established their political dominance in mountainous Tibet. In India, however, Buddhism gradually lost support during this period and by 1200 had practically disappeared from the land of its origin.

Meanwhile, people in western Eurasia were embracing two newer religious systems. In the fourth century, Christianity became the official religion of the Roman Empire, adding new followers all around the Mediterranean to this once persecuted faith. But when the western half of the empire collapsed under the onslaught of "barbarian" invasions in the late fifth century, the Latin Church had to shoulder alone the tasks of converting these peoples to Christianity and preserving the intellectual, political, and cultural heritage of Roman antiquity. In its religious mission the Latin Church was quite successful. One by one Frankish, German, English, Irish, Hungarian, and other leaders were converted, and their subjects gradually followed suit. Preserving other Roman achievements was more difficult. The church continued to use the Latin language and Roman law, and Christian monasteries preserved manuscripts of many ancient works. But the trading economy and urban life that had been the heart blood of ancient Rome became only a memory in most of the Latin West.

In the eastern Mediterranean, Byzantine Roman emperors continued to rule, and the Greek-speaking Christian church continued to enjoy political protection. Greek monks were also active Christian missionaries among the Slavic peoples of eastern Europe. The conversion of the Russian rulers in the tenth century was a notable achievement. However, by the middle of the next century, cultural, linguistic, and theological differences led to a deep rift between Greek and Russian Christians in the east and Latin Christians in the west.

Meanwhile, prophetic religion founded by Muhammad in the seventh century was spreading like a whirlwind out of its Arabian homeland. With great fervor Arab armies introduced Islam and an accompanying state system into the Middle East, across North Africa, and into the Iberian Peninsula. Over time most Middle Eastern and African Christians and members of other religions chose to adopt the new faith. Muslim merchants helped spread the faith along trade routes into sub-Saharan Africa and across southern Asia. Like Christianity, Islam eventually split along cultural, theological, and political lines as it expanded. Beginning in 1095, Latin Christians launched military Crusades against Muslim dominance of Christian holy places in Palestine. In later

Armored Knights in Battle

This painting from around 1135 shows the armament of knights at the time of the Crusades. Chain mail, a helmet, and a shield carried on the left side protect the rider. The lance carried underarm and the sword are the primary weapons. Notice that riders about to make contact with lances have their legs straight and braced in the stirrups, while riders with swords and in flight have bent legs.   (Pierpont Morgan Library/ Art Resource, NY)

Crusades, political and commercial ends became more important than religious goals, and the boundaries between Christianity and Islam changed little.

Commercial and Political Contacts

In many other parts of the world empires played a fundamental role in defining and unifying cultural areas. Under the Tang and Song dynasties (618–1279) China continued to have stability and exhibited periods of remarkable economic growth and technological creativity. Ghana, the first notable empire in sub-Saharan Africa, emerged to control one end of the trans-Saharan trade. In the isolated continents of the Americas a series of cultural complexes formed in the Andes, among the Maya of the Yucatán, along the Mississippi, and in the arid North American southwest. But despite efforts by Christian northern Europeans to create a loosely centralized "Holy Roman Empire," a very decentralized political system prevailed in most of western Europe. In Japan development was moving in a similar direction.

Political and religious expansion helped stimulate regional and long-distance trade. The challenge of moving growing quantities of goods over long distances produced some important innovations in land and sea travel. Two of the most important land-based, long-distance routes in this period depended on pack animals, especially the camel. One was the Silk Road, a caravan route across Central Asia. On the other trade route, between sub-Saharan Africa and North Africa, camels carried goods across the Sahara, the world's largest desert.

The Silk Road took its name from the silk textiles that were carried from eastern China to the Mediterranean Sea. In return, the Chinese received horses and other goods from the West. In existence since about 250 B.C.E., this series of roads nearly 6,000-miles (9,000-kilometers) in length passed through arid lands whose pastoral populations provided guides, food, and fresh camels (specially bred for caravan work).

After 900 C.E. the Silk Road declined for a time. By coincidence, the trans-Saharan caravan routes were growing more important during the period from 700 to 1200. Here, too, horses were an important trade purchased by African rulers to the south in return for gold, slaves, and other goods. The pastoralists who controlled the Saharan oases became essential guides for the camel caravans.

Since ancient times sea travel had been important in moving goods over relatively short distances, usually within sight of land, as around the Mediterranean Sea, the Red Sea, the Persian Gulf, and among the islands of the East Indies. During this period the water links around and through the Indian Ocean were increasing enough to make it an alternative to moving goods from China to the Middle East. Shipments went from port to port and were exchanged many times. Special ships known as dhows made use of the seasonal shifts in the winds across the Indian Ocean to plan their voyages in each direction. These centuries also saw remarkable maritime voyages in the Pacific (see Chapter 16).

■ INTERREGIONAL CONQUESTS AND EXCHANGES, 1200–1500

■ Between 1200 and 1500, cultural and commercial contacts grew rapidly across wide expanses of Eurasia, Africa, the Americas, and the Indian Ocean. In part, the increased contacts were the product of an unprecedented era of empire building around the world. The Mongols conquered a vast empire spanning Eurasia from the Pacific to eastern Europe. Muslim peoples created new empires in India, the Middle East, and sub-Saharan Africa. Amerindian empires united extensive regions of the Americas. Most of Europe continued to lack political unity, but unusually powerful European kingdoms were expanding their frontiers.

Empires stimulated commercial exchanges. The Mongol conquests revived the Silk Road across Central Asia, while a complex maritime network centered on the Indian Ocean stretched around southern Eurasia from the South China Sea to the North Atlantic, with overland connections in all directions (see Map I.2). Trade in the Americas and Africa also expanded. In the fifteenth century, Portuguese and Spanish explorers began an expansion southward along the Atlantic coast of Africa that by 1500 had opened a new all-water route to the riches of the Indian Ocean and set the stage for transoceanic routes that for the first time were to span the globe.

Mongol, Muslim, and European expansion promoted the spread of technologies. Printing, compasses, crossbows, gunpowder, and firearms—all East Asian inventions found broader applications and new uses in western Eurasia. Both the Ottomans and the kingdoms of western Europe made extensive use of gunpowder technologies. However, the highly competitive and increasingly literate peoples of the Latin West surpassed all others of this period in their use of technologies that they borrowed from elsewhere or devised themselves. Europeans mined and refined

Map I.2   Arteries of Trade and Travel in the Islamic World, to 1500

Ibn Battuta's journeys across Africa and Asia made use of land and sea routes along which Muslim traders and the Islamic faith had long traveled.

Silk Painting Depicting Khitan Hunters Resting Their Horses
The artist shows the Khitans' soft riding boots, leggings, and robes (much like those used by the Mongols) and the Khitans' patterned hairstyle, with part of the skull shaved and some of the hair worn long. Men in Central and North Asia (including Japan) used patterned hairstyles to indicate their political allegiance. The custom was documented in the 400s (but is certainly much older) and continued up to the twentieth century.   (National Palace Museum, Taipai, Taiwan, Republic of China)

more metals, produced more books, built more kinds of ships, and made more weapons than did people in any other comparable place on earth.

Why was so much change taking place all at once? Historians attribute many of the changes in South and Central Asia directly or indirectly to the empire building of the Mongols. But other changes took place far from that area. The role of simple coincidence, of course, should never be overlooked in history. And some historians believe that larger environmental factors were also at work—changes in climate that promoted population growth, trade, and empire building.

Mongols and Turks

The earliest and largest of the new empires was the work of the Mongols of northeastern Asia. Using their extraordinary command of horses and refinements in traditional forms of military and social organization, Mongols and allied groups united under Genghis Khan overran northern China in the early thirteenth century and spread their control westward across Central Asia to eastern Europe. By the later part of the century, the Mongol Empire stretched from Korea to Poland. It was ruled initially in four separate khanates: one in Russia, one in Iran, one in Central Asia, and one in China.

By ensuring traders protection from robbers and excessive tolls, the Mongol Empire revitalized the Silk Road. Never before had there been such a volume of commercial exchanges between eastern and western Eurasia. Easier travel also helped Islam and Buddhism spread to new parts of Central Asia.

The strains of holding such vast territories together caused the Mongol Empire to disintegrate over the course of the fourteenth and early fifteenth centuries. The Ming rulers of China overthrew Mongol rule in 1368 and began an expansionist foreign policy to reestablish China's predominance and prestige. Their armies repeatedly invaded Mongolia, reestablished dominion over Korea, and occupied northern Vietnam (Annam). One by one the other khanates collapsed.

The Mongols left a formidable legacy, but it was not Mongolian. Instead, Mongol rulers tended to adopt and promote the political systems, agricultural practices, and local customs of the peoples they ruled. Their encouragement of local languages helped later literary movements to flower. The political influence of the administrations the Mongols established in China, Iran, and Russia lingered even after locals had overthrown their rule, creating the basis for new national regimes.

At about the same time as the early Mongol expansion, Turkic war leaders from what is now Afghanistan were surging through the Khyber Pass and established a Muslim empire centered at Delhi. In short order, they overwhelmed the several Hindu states of north and central India and established a large empire ruled from the city of Delhi. The subsequent migration of large numbers of Muslims into India and the prestige and power of the Muslim ruling class brought India into the Islamic world. After their conquests in the Middle East, Mongols had recruited other Turkic-speaking Muslims from Central Asia to serve as their agents. In the decades after 1250, a large Turkic community in Anatolia (now Turkey) known as Ottomans took advantage of the weakness of the Byzantine Empire to extend their base in Anatolia. They then crossed into the Balkan Peninsula of southeastern Europe.

In the late 1300s, the Central Asian conqueror Timur (Tamerlane) shattered the Delhi Sultanate and stopped the expansion of the Ottoman Empire. The conquest and pillage of Timur's armies left the Delhi Sultanate a shadow of its former self, but the Ottoman Turks were able to reconstitute their empire in the fifteenth century. Ottoman conquerors swept deep into southeastern Europe (taking Constantinople, the last surviving remnant of the Byzantine Empire, in 1453) and southward into the Middle East, establishing a stable presence that was to endure into the twentieth century.

Indian Ocean Exchanges

In the wake of the Mongol Empire's collapse, the Indian Ocean assumed greater importance in the movement of goods across Eurasia. Alliances among Muslim merchants of many nationalities made these routes the world's richest trading area. Merchant dhows sailed among the trading ports, carrying cotton textiles, leather goods, grains, pepper, jewelry, carpets, horses, ivory, and many other goods. Chinese silk and porcelain and Indonesian spices entered from the east, meeting Middle Eastern and European goods from the west. It is important to note that Muslim merchant networks were almost completely independent of the giant Muslim land empires.

As a consequence of the Islamic world's political and commercial expansion, the number of adherents to the Muslim faith also grew. By 1500 Islam had replaced Buddhism as the second most important faith in India and was on its way to displacing Hinduism and Buddhism in Southeast Asia. The faith was also spreading in the Balkans. Meanwhile, raids by Arab pastoralists undermined ancient Christian states along Africa's upper Nile, leaving Ethiopia as the only Christian-ruled state in Africa. In the trading cities below the Sahara and along the Indian Ocean coast where Islam had established itself well before 1200, the strength and sophistication of Islamic religious practice was growing.

Mediterranean Exchanges

The Mediterranean Sea, which since antiquity had been a focus of commerce and cultural exchange for the peoples of Europe, the Middle East, and Africa, saw increased activity in the later Middle Ages. Part of the Mediterranean's importance derived from its trading links to the Indian Ocean by land and water routes. Another area that contributed to expanded trade was northern Africa. Camel caravans brought great quantities of gold and large numbers of slaves to the Mediterranean from the lands below the Sahara. This trade facilitated the growth of the powerful empire of Mali, which controlled some of the main gold-producing regions of West Africa. The rulers of Mali became rich and Muslim. Their wars and those of other states produced the captives that were sold north. In the fourteenth century the disruption of supplies of slaves from the eastern Mediterranean led to more slaves being purchased in southern Europe.

Another part of the expansion of Mediterranean trade was tied to the revival of western Europe. In 1204 the Italian city-state of Venice had shown its determination to be a dominant player in the eastern Mediterranean by attacking the Greek city of Constantinople and ensuring access to the Black Sea. Trade routes from the Mediterranean spread northward to the Netherlands and connected by sea to the British Isles, the Baltic Sea, and the Atlantic. The growth of trade in Europe accompanied a revival of urban life and culture. Both the cities and the countryside saw increased use of energy, minerals, and technologies from printing to gunpowder. Despite a high level of warfare among European states and devastating population losses in the fourteenth century, much of Europe was exhibiting cultural and economic vitality that was to have great consequences for the entire world in the centuries that followed.

The Aztecs and Inca

In the continents of the Western Hemisphere, American peoples were also creating important empires in the period from 1200 to 1500, although they had more limited resources with which to do so. For thousands of years their cultures had developed in isolation from the rest of humanity and thus had been unable to borrow any plants, animals, or technologies. Amerindian conquests were made without the aid of riding animals like the Mongols' horses, without the iron weapons all Old World empire builders had been using for many centuries, and without the new gunpowder weaponry that some Eurasians were employing in their conquests in this period.

In the wake of the collapse of the Toltec Empire, a martial people known as the Aztecs pushed southward into the rich agricultural lands of central Mexico. At first the Aztecs placed themselves at the service of strong indigenous residents, but after 1300 they began to build their own empire. Relying on their military skills, members of the Aztec warrior elite were able to conquer territories and reduce peasants to their service. The growth of a servile class at the bottom of society was paralleled by the growth of a powerful ruling class housed in well-constructed two-story dwellings in the Aztec capital cities. The servile laborers supplied the food needs of the growing cities and were impressed into building elaborate canals and land reclamation projects. Underpinning the power of the Aztec rulers were religious rituals that emphasized human sacrifice, mostly captives of the armies. By 1500 the Aztecs ruled a densely populated empire of subject and allied peoples.

The Mesoamerican Ball Game

From Guatemala to Arizona, archaeologists have found evidence of an ancient ball game played with a solid rubber ball on slope-sided courts shaped like a capital T. Among the Maya the game was associated with a creation myth and thus had deep religious meaning. There is evidence that some players were sacrificed. In this scene from a ceramic jar, players wearing elaborate ritual clothing—which includes heavy, protective pads around the chest and waist—play with a ball much larger than the ball actually used in such games. Some representations show balls drawn to suggest a human head.   (Chrysler Museum of Art/Justin Kerr)

Meanwhile, in the Andean highlands of western South America another powerful Amerindian empire was forming. Like central Mexico this region already had a rich agricultural base and a dense population when, in the fifteenth century, the Inca began using military skills to expand from a chiefdom into an empire. The Inca rulers, like the Aztecs, built impressive cities, promoted irrigation projects, and relied on religious rituals to bolster their authority. Tribute in goods and labor from their subject peoples supported their projects, and a network of mountain roads tied together the pieces of an empire that stretched for more than 3,000 miles (nearly 5,000 kilometers) north to south.

Both empires were cultural and commercial centers as well as political ones. In the Aztec Empire, well-armed private merchants controlled a long-distance trade in luxuries for the elites, including gold, jewels, feathered garments, and animal skins. There was also a network of local markets, large and small, that supplied the needs of more ordinary folks. State direction featured more prominently in Inca-ruled areas and promoted a vast exchange of specialized goods and a huge variety of foodstuffs grown at different altitudes.

SUGGESTED READING

Bulliet, Richard, "Themes, Conquerors, and Commerce," in Heidi Roupp, ed., *World History: A Resource Book* (1997). A brief overview of world history both before and after 1500.

American Historical Association, "Essays on Global and Comparative History." A series of sixty-page pamphlets on major topics featuring the latest scholarship. See in particular:

Abu-Lughod, Janet Lippman, *The World System in the Thirteenth Century: Dead-End or Precursor* (1993)

Burstein, Stanley M., *The Hellenistic Period in World History* (1996)

Eaton, Richard M., *Islamic History as World History* (1990)

Ehret, Christopher, *Sudanic Civilization* (2003)

Golden, Peter B., *Nomads and Sedentary Societies in Medieval Eurasia* (1998)

Hughes, Sarah Shaver and Brady Hughes, *Women in Ancient Civilizations* (1998)

Kicza, John E., *The Peoples and Civilizations of the Americas Before Contact* (1998)

Liu, Xinru, *The Silk Road: Overland Trade and Cultural Interactions in Eurasia* (1998)

Mears, John A., *Agricultural Origins in Global Perspective* (2003)

Walters, Jonathan S., *Finding Buddhists in Global History* (1998)

The Maritime Revolution

to 1550

In 1511, the young Ferdinand Magellan sailed from Europe around the southern tip of Africa and eastward across the Indian Ocean as a member of the first Portuguese expedition to explore the East Indies (maritime Southeast Asia). Eight years later, in the service of Spain, he headed an expedition that sought to reach the East Indies by sailing westward from Europe. By the middle of 1521, Magellan's expedition had sailed across the Atlantic, rounded the southern tip of South America, and crossed the Pacific Ocean—but at a high price.

One of the five ships wrecked on a reef; the captain of another deserted and sailed back to Spain. The passage across the Pacific took much longer than anticipated. Dozens of sailors died of starvation and disease. In the Philippines, Magellan himself was killed

This icon will direct you to the website where you can Prepare for Class, Improve Your Grade, and Ace the Test: college.cengage.com/pic/bullietbrief4e

385

on April 27, 1521, while aiding a local king who had promised to become a Christian. Magellan's successor met the same fate a few days later.

The expedition's survivors consolidated their resources by burning the least seaworthy of their remaining three ships and transferring the men and supplies to the smaller *Victoria*, which continued westward across the Indian Ocean, around Africa, and back to Europe. Magellan's flagship, the *Trinidad*, tried unsuccessfully to recross the Pacific to Central America. However, the *Victoria*'s return to Spain on September 8, 1522, confirmed Europe's ability and determination to master the oceans. The Portuguese crown had backed a century of daring and dangerous voyages to open routes to Africa, Brazil, and the Indian Ocean. Since 1492, Spain had opened contacts with the American continents. Now the broad Pacific Ocean had been crossed.

Before 1500, powerful states and the rich trading networks of Asia had led the way in overland and maritime expansion. The Iberians set out on their voyages of exploration to reach Eastern markets, and their success began a new era in which the West gradually became the world's center of power, wealth, and innovation.

GLOBAL MARITIME EXPANSION BEFORE 1450

What were the objectives and major accomplishments of the voyages of exploration undertaken by Chinese, Polynesians, and other non-Western peoples?

By 1450, mariners had discovered and settled most of the islands of the Pacific, the Atlantic, and the Indian Oceans, and a great trading system united the peoples around the Indian Ocean. But we know of no individual crossing the Pacific in either direction. Even the narrower Atlantic formed a barrier that kept the peoples of the Americas, Europe, and Africa in ignorance of each other's existence. The inhabitants of Australia were also completely cut off from contact with the rest of humanity. All this was about to change.

The Pacific Ocean

The vast distances that Polynesian peoples voyaged out of sight of land across the Pacific Ocean are one of the most impressive feats in maritime history before 1450 (see Map 14.1). Though they left no written records, over several thousand years mariners from the Malay (may-LAY) Peninsula of Southeast Asia explored and settled the island chains of the East Indies and continued on to New Guinea and the smaller islands of Melanesia (mel-uh-NEE-zhuh). Beginning sometime before the Common Era (C.E.), a wave of expansion from the area of Fiji brought the first humans to the islands of the central Pacific known as Polynesia. Their sailing canoes reached the easternmost Marquesas (mar-KAY-suhs) Islands about 400 C.E.; Easter Island, 2,200 miles (3,540 kilometers) off the coast of South America, a century later; and the Hawaiian Islands by 500 C.E. Settlement in New Zealand began about 1200. Between 1100 and 1300, new voyages northward from Tahiti brought more Polynesian settlers to Hawaii.

Historians have puzzled over how the Polynesians reached the eastern Pacific islands without compasses to plot their way, particularly in view of the difficulties Magellan's flagship encountered sailing eastward across the Pacific. In 1947, explorer

Chronology

	Pacific Ocean	Atlantic Ocean	Indian Ocean
Pre-1400	**400–1300** Polynesian settlement of Pacific islands	**700–1200** Viking voyages **1300s** Settlement of Madeira, Azores, Canaries **Early 1300s** Mali voyages	
1400 to 1500		**1418–1460** Voyages of Henry the Navigator **1440s** Slaves from West Africa **1482** Portuguese at Gold Coast and Kongo **1486** Portuguese at Benin **1492** Columbus reaches Caribbean **1493** Columbus returns to Caribbean (second voyage) **1493–1502** Spanish conquer Hispaniola **1498** Columbus reaches mainland of South America (third voyage) **1500** Cabral reaches Brazil	**1405–1433** Voyages of Zheng He **1498** Vasco da Gama reaches India
1500 to 1550	**1519–1522** Magellan expedition	**1513** Ponce de Léon explores Florida **1519–1520** Cortés conquers Aztec Empire **1532–1533** Pizarro conquers Inca Empire	**1505** Portuguese bombard Swahili Coast cities **1510** Portuguese take Goa **1511** Portuguese take Malacca **1515** Portuguese take Hormuz **1535** Portuguese take Diu **1538** Portuguese defeat Ottoman fleet **1539** Portuguese aid Ethiopia

Map 14.1   Exploration and Settlement in the Indian and Pacific Oceans Before 1500
Over many centuries, mariners originating in Southeast Asia gradually colonized the islands of the Pacific and Indian Oceans. The Chinese voyages led by Zheng He in the fifteenth century were lavish official expeditions.

Interactive Map

Thor Heyerdahl (HIGH-uhr-dahl) argued that Easter Island and Hawaii were settled from the Americas and sought to prove his theory by sailing his balsawood raft *Kon Tiki* westward from Peru.

Although some Amerindian voyagers did use ocean currents to travel northward from Peru to Mexico between 300 and 900 C.E., there is now considerable evidence that planned expansion by Polynesian mariners accomplished the settlement of the islands of the eastern Pacific. The languages of the islanders relate closely to the languages of the western Pacific and ultimately to those of Malaysia and Indonesia. In addition, accidental voyages could not have brought sufficient numbers of men and women for founding a new colony along with all the plants and domesticated animals common to other Polynesian islands.

In 1976, a Polynesian crew led by anthropologist Ben Finney used traditional navigational methods to sail the *Hokulea,* a 62-foot-long (19-meter-long) double canoe, from Hawaii south to Tahiti. Patterned after old oceangoing canoes, some of which measured 120 feet (35 meters) long, it used inverted triangular sails and was steered by paddles (not by a rudder). The *Hokulea*'s crew navigated using only their observation of the currents, stars, and evidence of land.

The Indian Ocean

While Polynesian mariners settled the Pacific islands, other Malayo-Indonesians sailed westward across the Indian Ocean and colonized the large island of Madagascar off the southeastern coast of Africa. These voyages continued through the fifteenth century. To this day, the inhabitants of Madagascar speak Malayo-Polynesian languages. However, part of the island's population is descended from Africans who crossed the 600 miles (1,000 kilometers) from the mainland to Madagascar, most likely in the centuries just before 1500.

The rise of Islam gave Indian Ocean trade an important boost. The great Muslim cities of the Middle East provided a demand for valuable commodities, and networks of Muslim traders tied the region together. The Indian Ocean traders operated largely independent of the empires and states that they served, but in East Asia, China's early Ming emperors took an active interest in these wealthy ports of trade, sending Admiral **Zheng He** (jung huh) on a series of expeditions.

The first Ming fleet in 1405 consisted of sixty-two specially built "treasure ships," large Chinese junks each about 300 feet long by 150 feet wide (90 by 45 meters). Most of the one hundred smaller accompanying vessels exceeded in size the flagship in which Columbus later sailed across the Atlantic. Each treasure ship had nine masts, twelve sails, many decks, and a carrying capacity of 3,000 tons (six times the capacity of Columbus's entire fleet). One expedition carried over 27,000 individuals, including infantry and cavalry troops. Although the ships carried small cannon, highly accurate crossbows dominated most Chinese sea battles.

One Chinese-Arabic interpreter kept a journal recording the customs, dress, and beliefs of the people visited, along with the trade, towns, and animals of their countries. Among his observations were these: exotic animals such as the black panther

Zheng He (1371–1433) An imperial eunuch and Muslim, entrusted by the Ming emperor Yongle with a series of state voyages that took his gigantic ships through the Indian Ocean, from Southeast Asia to Africa.

Polynesian Canoes

Pacific Ocean mariners sailing canoes such as these, shown in an eighteenth-century painting, made epic voyages of exploration and settlement. A large platform connects two canoes at the left, providing more room for the members of the expedition, and a sail supplements the paddlers.   ("Tereoboo, King of Owyhee, bringing presents to Captain Cook," D. L. Ref. p. xx 2f. 35. Courtesy, The Dixson Library, State Library of New South Wales) of Malaya and the tapir of Sumatra; beliefs in legendary "corpse-headed barbarians" whose heads left their bodies at night and caused infants to die; the division of coastal Indians into five classes, which correspond to the four Hindu varnas and a separate Muslim class; and the fact that traders in the Indian port of Calicut (KAL-ih-kut) could perform error-free calculations by counting on their fingers and toes rather than using the Chinese abacus. After his return, the interpreter went on tour in China, telling of these exotic places and "how far the majestic virtue of [China's] imperial dynasty extended."[1]

Interest in new contacts was not confined to the Chinese side. In 1415–1416, at least three trading cities on the Swahili (swah-HEE-lee) Coast of East Africa sent delegations to China. Although no record of African and Chinese reactions to one another survives, China's lavish gifts to local rulers stimulated the Swahili market for silk and porcelain.

The Atlantic Ocean

The Vikings, northern European raiders and pirates, used their small, open ships to attack coastal European settlements for several centuries. They also discovered and settled one island after another in the North Atlantic. Like the Polynesians, the Vikings had neither maps nor navigational devices. They found their way using their knowledge of the heavens and the seas.

The Vikings first settled Iceland in 770. From there, some moved on to Greenland in 982, and one group sighted North America in 986. Fifteen years later, Leif Ericsson established a short-lived Viking settlement on the island of Newfoundland, which he called Vinland. When the climate turned colder after 1200, the northern settlements in Greenland went into decline. Vinland became a mysterious place mentioned in Norse sagas.

Some southern Europeans also explored the Atlantic. In 1291, two Vivaldo brothers from Genoa set out to sail around Africa to India. They were never heard of again. Other Genoese and Portuguese expeditions into the Atlantic in the fourteenth century discovered (and settled) the islands of Madeira (muh-DEER-uh), the Azores (A-zorz), and the Canaries.

Mention also occurs of African voyages of exploration in the Atlantic. The Syrian geographer al-Umari (1301–1349) relates that when Mansa Kankan Musa (MAHN-suh KAHN-kahn MOO-suh), the ruler of the West African empire of Mali, passed through Egypt on his lavish pilgrimage to Mecca in 1324, he told of voyages to cross the Atlantic undertaken by his predecessor, Mansa Muhammad. Muhammad had sent out four hundred vessels with men and supplies, telling them, "Do not return until you have reached the other side of the ocean or if you have exhausted your food or water." After a long time, one canoe returned, reporting the others had been swept away by a "violent current in the middle of the sea." Muhammad himself then set out at the head of a second, even larger, expedition, from which no one returned.

On the other side of the Atlantic, Amerindian voyagers from South America colonized the West Indies. By the year 1000, Amerindians known as the **Arawak** (AR-uh-wahk) had moved from the small islands of the Lesser Antilles (Barbados, Martinique, Guadaloupe) into the Greater Antilles (Cuba, Hispaniola, Jamaica, and

SECTION REVIEW

- Before 1450, the Atlantic and Pacific Oceans were barriers that kept the peoples of Europe, Africa, and the Americas ignorant of each other.

- In the Pacific, Malayan seafarers settled the East Indies and Melanesia, and mariners from around Fiji colonized the Polynesian islands.

- In the Indian Ocean, Southeast Asians and Africans colonized Madagascar.

- Ming China sent expeditions to Indian Ocean ports, and the Swahili city-states dispatched delegations to China.

- Vikings colonized the islands of the North Atlantic, eventually reaching North America.

- Southern Europeans and Africans attempted to explore the Atlantic, and South American Amerindians colonized the West Indies.

Arawak Amerindian peoples who inhabited the Greater Antilles of the Caribbean at the time of Columbus.

Puerto Rico), as well as into the Bahamas. Another people, the Carib, followed their route. By the late fifteenth century, they had overrun most Arawak settlements in the Lesser Antilles and were raiding parts of the Greater Antilles. From the West Indies, Arawak and Carib also undertook voyages to the North American mainland.

IBERIAN EXPANSION, 1400–1550

In this era of long-distance exploration, did Europeans have any special advantages over other cultural regions?

The preceding survey shows that maritime exploration occurred in many parts of the world before 1450. The sea voyages sponsored by the Iberian kingdoms of Portugal and Spain attract special interest because they began a maritime revolution that profoundly altered the course of world history. The Portuguese and Spanish expeditions ended the isolation of the Americas and increased global interaction. The influence in world affairs of the Iberians and other Europeans who followed them overseas rose steadily after 1500.

Iberian overseas expansion arose from two related phenomena. First, Iberian rulers had strong economic, religious, and political motives to expand their contacts and increase their dominance. Second, improvements in maritime and military technologies gave them the means to master treacherous and unfamiliar ocean environments, seize control of existing maritime trade routes, and conquer new lands.

Background to Iberian Expansion

In many ways, these voyages continued four trends evident in the Latin West from about the year 1000: (1) the revival of urban life and trade, (2) a struggle with Islamic powers for dominance of the Mediterranean that mixed religious motives with the desire for trade with distant lands, (3) growing intellectual curiosity about the outside world, and (4) a peculiarly European alliance between merchants and rulers.

The city-states of northern Italy took the lead in all of these developments. By 1450, they had well-established trade links to northern Europe, the Indian Ocean, and the Black Sea, and their merchant princes had sponsored an intellectual and artistic Renaissance. But the Italian states did not take the lead in exploring the Atlantic, even after the expansion of the Ottoman Empire in the fourteenth and fifteenth centuries disrupted their trade to the East, because Venice and Genoa preferred to continue the lucrative alliances with Muslims that had given their merchants privileged positions and because Mediterranean ships were ill suited to the more violent weather of the Atlantic. However, many individual Italians played leading roles in Atlantic exploration.

By contrast, the Iberian kingdoms had engaged in anti-Muslim warfare since the eighth century, when Muslim forces overran most of the peninsula. By about 1250, the Iberian kingdoms of Portugal, Castile, and Aragon had conquered all the Muslim lands in Iberia except the southern kingdom of Granada, which finally fell to the united kingdom of Castile and Aragon in 1492. These territories gradually amalgamated to form Spain, sixteenth-century Europe's most powerful state.

Christian militancy continued to drive Portugal and Spain in their overseas ventures. But the Iberian rulers and their adventurous subjects also sought material returns. Their small share of the Mediterranean trade made them more willing than the Italians to take risks to find new routes to Africa and Asia through the Atlantic. Moreover, both kingdoms participated in the shipbuilding changes and the gunpowder revolution under way in Atlantic Europe. Though not centers of Renaissance learning, both states had exceptional rulers who appreciated new geographical knowledge.

Portuguese Voyages

When the Muslim government of Morocco in northwestern Africa weakened in the fifteenth century, the Portuguese went on the attack, beginning with the city of Ceuta (say-OO-tuh) in 1415. This assault combined aspects of a religious crusade, a plundering expedition, and a military tournament in which young Portuguese knights displayed their bravery. Despite the capture of several more ports along Morocco's Atlantic coast, the Portuguese could not push inland and gain access to the gold trade they learned about, so they sought more direct contact with the gold producers by sailing down the African coast.

Young Prince Henry (1394–1460), third son of the king of Portugal, led the attack on Ceuta. Because he devoted the rest of his life to promoting exploration, he is known as **Henry the Navigator.** His official biographer emphasized his desire to convert Africans to Christianity, make contact with Christian rulers believed to exist in Africa, and launch joint crusades with them against the Ottomans. Profit also figured in his dreams. His initial explorations focused on Africa. His ships established

Henry the Navigator (1394–1460) Portuguese prince who promoted the study of navigation and directed voyages of exploration down the western coast of Africa.

Portuguese Map of Western Africa, 1502

This map shows in great detail a section of African coastline that Portuguese explorers charted and named in the fifteenth century. The cartographer illustrated the African interior, which was almost completely unknown to Europeans, with drawings of birds and views of coastal sights: Sierra Leone (Serra lioa), named for a mountain shaped like a lion, and the Portuguese Castle of the Mine (Castello damina) on the Gold Coast. (akg-images) permanent contact with the islands of Madeira in 1418 and the Azores in 1439. Only later did reaching India become a goal.

"The Navigator" himself never ventured farther from home than North Africa. Instead, he founded a sort of research institute at Sagres (SAH-gresh) for studying navigation and collecting information about new lands. His staff drew on the pioneering efforts of Italian merchants, especially the Genoese, who had learned some of the secrets of the trans-Saharan trade, and of fourteenth-century Jewish cartographers who used information from Arab and European sources to produce remarkably accurate sea charts and maps of distant places. They also studied and improved navigational instruments that had come into Europe from China and the Islamic world: the magnetic compass, first developed in China, and the astrolabe, an instrument of Arab or Greek invention that enabled mariners to determine their latitude by measuring the position of the sun or the stars.

The Portuguese developed a new type of long-distance sailing vessel, the **caravel** (KAR-uh-vel). The many-oared galleys of the Mediterranean could not carry enough food and water for long ocean voyages. The three-masted ships of the North Atlantic, powered by square sails, could not sail at much of an angle against the wind. The caravel, which was only one-fifth the size of the largest European ships and the large Chinese junks, could enter shallow coastal waters and explore upriver, yet it had the strength to weather ocean storms. When equipped with lateen sails, caravels had great maneuverability and could sail deeply into the wind; when sporting square Atlantic sails, they had great speed. The addition of small cannon made them good fighting ships as well. The caravels' economy, speed, agility, and power justified a contemporary's claim that they were "the best ships that sailed the seas."[2]

caravel A small, highly maneuverable three-masted ship used by the Portuguese and Spanish in the exploration of the Atlantic.

Pioneering captains had to overcome crews' fears that the South Atlantic waters were boiling hot and contained ocean currents that would prevent their ever returning home. It took Prince Henry from 1420 to 1434 to coax an expedition to venture beyond southern Morocco in northwest Africa (see Map 14.2). The next stretch of coast, 800 miles (1,300 kilometers) of desert, offered little of interest to the explorers. Finally in 1444, the mariners reached the Senegal River and the populous, well-watered lands below the Sahara beginning at what they named Cape Verde (Green Cape) because of its vegetation.

In the years that followed, Henry's explorers learned how to return speedily to Portugal. Instead of battling the prevailing northeast trade winds and currents back up the coast, they discovered that by sailing northwest into the Atlantic to the latitude of the Azores, ships could pick up prevailing westerly winds that would blow them back to Portugal. The knowledge that ocean winds tend to form large circular patterns helped explorers discover many other ocean routes.

To pay for the research, ships, and expeditions, Prince Henry drew partly on the income of the Order of Christ, a military religious order of which he was the governor. The Order of Christ had been founded to inherit the Portuguese properties and the crusading tradition of the Order of Knights Templar, which had disbanded in 1314. The Order of Christ received the exclusive right to promote Christianity in all the lands that were discovered, and the Portuguese emblazoned their ships' sails with the crusaders' red cross.

The first financial returns came from selling into slavery Africans captured in raids on the northwest coast of Africa and the Canary Islands during the 1440s. The

Map 14.2   European Exploration, 1420–1542

Portuguese and Spanish explorers showed the possibility and practicality of intercontinental maritime trade. Before 1540 European trade with Africa and Asia was much more important than that with the Americas, but after the Spanish conquest of the Aztec and Inca Empires transatlantic trade began to increase. Notice the Tordesillas line, which in theory separated the Spanish and Portuguese spheres of activity.

Interactive Map

Portuguese had captured or purchased eighty thousand Africans by the end of the century. However, gold quickly became more important than slavery. By 1457, enough African gold was coming back to Portugal for the kingdom to issue a new gold coin called the *cruzado* (crusade), another reminder of how deeply the Portuguese entwined religious and secular motives.

By the time Prince Henry died in 1460, his explorers had established a base of operations in the uninhabited Cape Verde Islands and explored 600 miles (950 kilometers) of coast beyond Cape Verde, as far as what they named Sierra Leone (see-ER-uh lee-OWN) (Lion Mountain). From there, they knew the coast of Africa curved sharply toward the east. After spending four decades covering the 1,500 miles (2,400 kilometers) from Lisbon to Sierra Leone, Portuguese explorers traveled the remaining 4,000 miles (6,400 kilometers) to the continent's southern tip in only three decades.

Royal sponsorship continued, but private commercial participation sped the progress. In 1469, a Lisbon merchant named Fernão Gomes purchased from the Crown the privilege of exploring 350 miles (550 kilometers) of new coast a year for five years and a monopoly on any resulting trade. Gomes discovered the uninhabited island of São Tomé (sow toh-MAY) on the equator; in the next century, it became a major source of sugar produced with African slave labor. He also explored what later Europeans called the **Gold Coast,** which became the headquarters of Portugal's West African trade.

The expectation of finding a passage around Africa to the Indian Ocean spurred the final thrust down the African coast. **Bartolomeu Dias** rounded the southern tip of Africa (in 1488) and entered the Indian Ocean. In 1497–1498, **Vasco da Gama** led a Portuguese expedition around Africa to India (see Environment and Technology: Vasco da Gama's Fleet). In 1500, ships in an expedition under Pedro Alvares Cabral (kah-BRAHL), while swinging wide to the west in the South Atlantic to catch the winds that would sweep them around southern Africa and on to India, came on the eastern coast of South America, laying the basis for Portugal's later claim to Brazil.

Spanish Voyages

Spain's early discoveries owed more to haste and blind luck than to careful planning. Only in the last decade of the fifteenth century did the Spanish monarchs turn their attention from reconquest and organization of previously Muslim territories to overseas exploration. By this time, the Portuguese had already found their route to the Indian Ocean.

The leader of their overseas mission would be **Christopher Columbus** (1451–1506), a Genoese mariner. His three voyages between 1492 and 1498 would reveal the existence of vast and unexpected lands across the Atlantic. But this momentous discovery fell disappointingly short of Columbus's intention of finding a new route to the Indian Ocean even shorter than that of the Portuguese.

As a younger man, Columbus had gained considerable experience while participating in Portuguese explorations along the African coast, but he dreamed of a shorter way to the riches of the East. By his reckoning (based on a serious misreading of a ninth-century Arab authority), a mere 2,400 nautical miles (4,450 kilometers) separated the Canary Islands from Japan. The actual distance was five times greater.

Portuguese authorities twice rejected his plan to reach the East by sailing west, first in 1485 following a careful study and again in 1488 after Dias had established

Gold Coast (Africa) Region of the Atlantic coast of West Africa occupied by modern Ghana; named for its gold exports to Europe from the 1470s onward.

Bartolomeu Dias (1450?–1500) Portuguese explorer who in 1488 led the first expedition to sail around the southern tip of Africa from the Atlantic and sight the Indian Ocean.

Vasco da Gama (1460?–1524) Portuguese explorer. In 1497–1498 he led the first naval expedition from Europe to sail to India, opening an important commercial sea route.

Christopher Columbus (1451–1506) Genoese mariner who in the service of Spain led expeditions across the Atlantic, reestablishing contact between the peoples of the Americas and the Old World and opening the way to Spanish conquest and colonization.

Vasco da Gama's Fleet

The four small ships that sailed for India from Lisbon in June 1497 may seem a puny fleet compared to the sixty-two Chinese vessels that Zheng He had led into the Indian Ocean ninety-five years earlier. But given the fact that China had a hundred times as many people as Portugal, Vasco da Gama's fleet represented at least as great a commitment of resources. In any event, the Portuguese expedition had a far greater impact on the course of history. Having achieved its aim of inspiring awe at China's greatness, the Chinese throne sent out no more expeditions after 1432. Although da Gama's ships seemed more odd than awesome to Indian Ocean observers, that modest fleet began a revolution in global relations.

Portugal spared no expense in ensuring that the fleet would make it to India and back. Craftsmen built extra strength into the hulls to withstand the powerful storms that Dias had encountered in 1488 at the tip of Africa. Small enough to be able to navigate any shallow harbors and rivers they might encounter, the ships were crammed with specially strengthened casks and barrels of water, wine, oil, flour, meat, and vegetables far in excess of what was required even on a voyage that would take the better part of a year. Arms and ammunition were also in abundance.

Three of da Gama's ships were rigged with square sails on two masts for speed and a lateen sail on the third mast. The fourth vessel was a caravel with lateen sails. Each ship carried three sets of sails and plenty of extra rigging so as to be able to repair any damages due to storms. The crusaders' red crosses on the sails signaled one of the expedition's motives.

The captains and crew—Portugal's most talented and experienced—received extra pay and other rewards for their

VASCO DA GAMA'S FLAGSHIP This vessel carried the Portuguese captain on his second expedition to India in 1505.
(The Pierpont Morgan Library/Art Resource, NY)

service. Yet there was no expectation that the unprecedented sums spent on this expedition would bring any immediate return. According to a contemporary chronicle, the only immediate return the Portuguese monarch received was "the knowledge that some part of Ethiopia and the beginning of Lower India had been discovered." However, the scale and care of the preparations suggest that the Portuguese expected the expedition to open up profitable trade to the Indian Ocean. And so it did.

the feasibility of the African route. Columbus received more sympathy, but initially no support, from Queen Isabella of Castile. A Castilian commission appointed by Isabella studied the proposal for four years and concluded that a westward sea route to the Indies rested on questionable geographical assumptions. Nevertheless, Columbus's persistence finally won over the queen and her husband, King Ferdinand of Aragon. In 1492, elated perhaps by finally expelling the Muslims from Granada, they agreed to fund a modest expedition.

Columbus recorded in his log that the *Santa María,* the *Santa Clara* (nicknamed the *Niña*), and a vessel now known only by its nickname, the *Pinta,* with a mostly Spanish crew of ninety men "departed Friday the third day of August of the year 1492," toward "the regions of India." Their mission, the royal contract stated, was "to discover and acquire certain islands and mainland in the Ocean Sea." Columbus carried letters of introduction from the Spanish sovereigns to Eastern rulers, including one to the "Grand Khan" (meaning the Chinese emperor). An Arabic-speaking Jewish convert to Christianity had the job of communicating with the peoples of eastern Asia.

Unfavorable headwinds had discouraged other attempts to explore the Atlantic west of the Azores. But on earlier voyages along the African coast, Columbus had learned about winds blowing westward at the latitude of the Canaries. After reaching the Canaries, he replaced the *Niña*'s lateen sails with square sails, for he knew that from then on, speed would be more important than maneuverability since his supplies would last for only a fixed number of days.

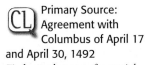

Primary Source: Agreement with Columbus of April 17 and April 30, 1492

Find out what sort of material wealth Christopher Columbus stood to gain when he undertook his famous voyage of 1492.

Columbus Prepares to Cross the Atlantic, 1492

This later representation shows Columbus with the ships, soldiers, priests, and seaman that were part of Spain's enterprise. (G. Dagli Orti/The Art Archive)

History in Focus Notice the figures in the foreground aboard the ships and small boat. How do they reflect attitudes and goals that drove Spanish overseas expansion? Now, look at the figures in the background. Who do you think they are? What might they suggest about the attitude of the general Spanish populace to early overseas expansion? *Find the answer online.*

SECTION REVIEW

- The Portuguese and Spanish expeditions prompted a maritime revolution of global significance.

- The voyages extended from cultural trends in the Latin West since 1000, but Christian militancy and material gain were especially strong motives.

- Urged by Henry the Navigator, Portuguese explorers ventured farther into the Atlantic and colonized Madeira, the Azores, and the Canaries.

- Portuguese explorer-traders and missionaries established bases along the coast of Africa, pushed into the Indian Ocean, and crossed to South America.

- Spanish overseas expansion began with Columbus's voyages to find a western route to the Indian Ocean.

- The Treaty of Torsedillas divided the world between Spain and Portugal, a division clarified by Magellan's circumnavigation of the world.

Ferdinand Magellan (1480?–1521) Portuguese navigator who led the Spanish expedition of 1519–1522 that was the first to sail around the world.

In October, the expedition encountered the islands of the Caribbean. Columbus called the inhabitants "Indians" because he believed he had reached the East Indies. A second voyage in 1493 did nothing to change his mind. On a third voyage in 1498, two months after Vasco da Gama reached India, Columbus sighted the mainland of South America, which he insisted was part of Asia. But by then, other Europeans had become convinced that his discoveries were of lands previously unknown to the Old World (Europe, Asia, and Africa). Amerigo Vespucci's explorations, first on behalf of Spain and then for Portugal, led mapmakers to name the new continents "America," after him.

To prevent disputes about exploiting these new lands and spreading Christianity among their peoples, Spain and Portugal agreed to split the world between them. Modifying an earlier papal proposal, the Treaty of Tordesillas (tor-duh-SEE-yuhs), negotiated by the pope in 1494, drew an imaginary north-south line down the middle of the Atlantic Ocean. Lands east of the line in Africa and southern Asia could be claimed by Portugal; lands to the west in the Americas belonged to Spain. Cabral's discovery of Brazil, however, gave Portugal a valid claim to the part of South America that bulged east of the line.

But if the Tordesillas line were extended around the earth, where would Spain's and Portugal's spheres of influence divide in the East? Given European ignorance of the earth's true size in 1494, no one knew whether the Moluccas (muh-LOO-kuhz), the source of the valuable spices of the East Indies, belonged to Portugal or Spain. The missing information concerned the size of the Pacific Ocean, which a Spanish adventurer named Vasco Núñez de Balboa (bal-BOH-uh) had spotted in 1513 when he crossed the isthmus (a narrow neck of land) of Panama from the east. The 1519 expedition of **Ferdinand Magellan** (ca. 1480–1521) sought to complete Columbus's interrupted westward voyage by sailing around the Americas and across the Pacific. The Moluccas turned out to lie well within Portugal's sphere, as Spain formally acknowledged in 1529.

Magellan's voyage laid the basis for Spanish colonization of the Philippine Islands after 1564. It also gave Magellan credit, despite his death, for being the first person to encircle the globe, for a decade earlier he had sailed from Europe to the East Indies on an expedition sponsored by his native Portugal.

Columbus and those who followed in his path laid the basis for the colonial empires of Spain and other European nations. In turn, these empires promoted, among the four Atlantic continents, a new trading network whose importance rivaled and eventually surpassed that of the Indian Ocean. Of more immediate importance, Portugal's entry into the Indian Ocean led quickly to a major European presence and profit. Both the eastward and the westward voyages of exploration marked a tremendous expansion of Europe's role in world history.

ENCOUNTERS WITH EUROPE, 1450–1550

What were the different outcomes of European interactions with Africa, India, and the Americas?

The ways in which Africans, Asians, and Amerindians perceived their European visitors and interacted with them influenced their future relations. Some welcomed the Europeans as potential allies; others viewed them as rivals or enemies. In general, Africans and Asians readily recognized the benefits and dangers of European contact. However, the long isolation of the Amerindians added to the strangeness of their encounter with the Spanish and made them more vulnerable to the unfamiliar diseases the Spanish inadvertently introduced.

Western Africa

Many Africans welcomed trade with the Portuguese, which gave them new markets for their exports and access to imports cheaper than those coming by caravan across the Sahara. Miners in the hinterland of the Gold Coast, which the Portuguese first visited in 1471, had long sold their gold to merchants from trading cities along the southern edge of the Sahara for transshipment to North Africa. Recognizing the possibility of more favorable trading terms, coastal Africans negotiated with the royal representative of Portugal, who arrived in 1482 seeking permission to erect a trading fort.

The Portuguese noble in charge and his officers (likely including the young Christopher Columbus, who had entered Portuguese service in 1476) strove to make a proper impression. They dressed in their best clothes, erected a fancy reception platform, celebrated a Catholic Mass, and signaled the start of negotiations with trumpets, tambourines, and drums. The African king, Caramansa, staged his entrance with equal ceremony, arriving with a large retinue of attendants and musicians. Through an African interpreter, the two leaders exchanged flowery speeches pledging goodwill and mutual benefit. Caramansa then gave permission for a small trading fort, assured, he said, by the appearance of these royal delegates that they were honorable persons, unlike the "few, foul, and vile" Portuguese visitors of the previous decade.

Neither side made a show of force, but Caramansa warned that if the Portuguese failed to be peaceful and honest traders, he and his people would move away and deprive their post of food and trade. Trade at the post of Saint George of the Mine (later called Elmina) enriched both sides. The Portuguese crown was soon purchasing gold amounting to one-tenth of the world's production at the time. In return, Africans received shiploads of goods brought by the Portuguese from Asia, Europe, and other parts of Africa.

Early contacts involved a mixture of commercial, military, and religious interests. Some African rulers quickly saw the value of European firearms. Coastal rulers also proved willing to test the value of Christian practices, which the Portuguese eagerly promoted. The rulers of Benin and Kongo, the largest coastal kingdoms, invited Portuguese missionaries and soldiers to accompany them into battle to test the Christians' religion along with their muskets.

The kingdom of Benin in the Niger Delta, near the peak of its power after a century of aggressive expansion, had a large capital city, also known as Benin. Its *oba* (king) responded to a Portuguese visit in 1486 by sending an ambassador to Portugal to learn more about their homeland. Then he established a royal monopoly on Portuguese trade, selling pepper and ivory tusks (to be taken back to Portugal) as well as stone beads, textiles, and prisoners of war (to be resold at Elmina). In return, Portuguese merchants provided Benin with copper and brass, fine textiles, glass beads, and a horse for the king's royal procession. In the early sixteenth century, as the demand for slaves for the Portuguese sugar plantations on the nearby island of São Tomé grew, the oba first raised the price of slaves and then imposed restrictions on their sale.

Efforts to spread Catholicism ultimately failed. Early kings showed some interest, but after 1538, the rulers declined to receive further missionaries. They also closed the market in male slaves for the rest of the sixteenth century. Both steps illustrate their power to control how much interaction they wanted.

Farther south, on the lower Congo River, the *manikongo* (mah-NEE-KONG-goh) (king) of Kongo also sent delegates to Portugal, established a royal monopoly on trade, and expressed interest in missionary teachings. But here the royal family made Catholicism the kingdom's official faith. Lacking ivory and pepper, Kongo sold more and more slaves to acquire the goods brought by the Portuguese and to pay missionary expenses.

Soon the royal trade monopoly broke down. In 1526, the Christian manikongo, Afonso I (r. 1506–ca. 1540), wrote to his royal "brother," the king of Portugal, begging for his help in stopping the slave trade because unauthorized Kongolese were kidnapping and selling people, even members of good families. Afonso's appeal that contacts be limited to "some priests and a few people to teach in the schools, and no other goods except wine and flour for the holy sacrament" received no reply. After 1540, the major part of the slave trade from this part of Africa moved farther south.

Eastern Africa

As Vasco da Gama sailed up the eastern coast of Africa in 1498, most rulers of the coastal trading states received him coolly. Visitors who painted crusader crosses on their sails raised their suspicions. The ruler of Malindi, however, saw in the Portuguese an ally who could help him expand Malindi's trade, and he provided da Gama with a pilot to guide

Bronze Figure of Benin Ruler

Both this prince and his horse are protected by chainmail introduced in the fifteenth century to Benin by Portuguese merchants.   (Antenna Gallery Dakar Senegal / G.Dagli Orti / The Art Archive)

him to India. The suspicions of most rulers came to fruition seven years later when a Portuguese war fleet bombarded and looted most of the coastal cities in the name of Christ and commerce. It spared Malindi.

Christian Ethiopia also saw benefits in allying with the Portuguese. In the four-teenth and fifteenth centuries, Ethiopian conflicts with Muslim states along the Red Sea increased. After the Ottoman Turks conquered Egypt and launched a fleet in the Indian Ocean to counter the Portuguese in 1517, the warlord of the Muslim state of Adal attacked Ethiopia. A decisive victory in 1529 put the Christian kingdom in jeopardy, making Portuguese support a crucial matter.

For decades, delegations from Portugal and Ethiopia had talked of a Christian alliance. Queen Helena of Ethiopia, who acted as regent for her young sons after her husband's death in 1478, sent a letter in 1509 to "our very dear and well-beloved brother," the king of Portugal, along with a gift of two tiny crucifixes said to be made of wood from the cross on which Christ was crucified. She proposed to combine her land army and Portugal's fleet against the Turks. At her death in 1522, no alliance had come into being, but the worsening situation brought renewed Ethiopian appeals.

Finally, a small Portuguese force commanded by Vasco da Gama's son Christopher reached Ethiopia in 1539. With Portuguese help, another queen rallied the desperate Ethiopians. Muslim foes captured Christopher da Gama and tortured him to death but lost heart when their leader fell in battle. Portuguese aid helped save the Ethiopian kingdom from extinction, but Ethiopia's refusal to transfer its Christian affiliation from the patriarch of Alexandria to the pope prevented a permanent alliance.

As these examples illustrate, African encounters with the Portuguese before 1550 varied considerably. Africans and Portuguese might become royal brothers, bitter opponents, or partners in a mutually profitable trade, but Europeans were still a minor presence in most of Africa in 1550. The Indian Ocean trade by then was occupying most of their attention.

Indian Ocean States

Vasco da Gama's arrival on the Malabar Coast of India in May 1498 did not impress the citizens of Calicut. The Chinese fleets of gigantic junks that had called at Calicut sixty-five years earlier dwarfed his four small ships, which were no larger than many of the dhows (dow) already filling the harbor. The *samorin* (ruler) of Calicut and his Muslim officials showed mild interest, but the gifts da Gama brought evoked derisive laughter: twelve pieces of striped cloth, four scarlet hoods, six hats, and six wash basins. When da Gama defended his gifts as those of an explorer, not a merchant, the samorin cut him short, asking whether he had come to discover men or stones: "If he had come to discover men, as he said, why had he brought nothing?"

Coastal rulers soon discovered that the Portuguese had no intention of remaining poor competitors in the Indian Ocean trade. Upon da Gama's return to Portugal in 1499, the jubilant King Manuel styled himself "Lord of the Conquest, Navigation, and Commerce of Ethiopia, Arabia, Persia, and India." Previously, the Indian Ocean had been an open sea, used by merchants (and pirates) of all the surrounding coasts. Now the Portuguese crown intended to make it Portugal's sea, which others might use only on Portuguese terms.

Portugal's hope of controlling the Indian Ocean stemmed from the superiority of its ships and weapons over the smaller and lightly armed merchant dhows. In 1505, the Portuguese fleet of 81 ships and some 7,000 men bombarded Swahili Coast cities. Goa, on the west coast of India, fell to a well-armed fleet in 1510, becoming the base from which the Portuguese menaced the trading cities of Gujarat (goo-juh-RAHT) to the north and Calicut and other Malabar Coast cities to the south. The port of Hormuz, controlling the entry to the Persian Gulf, fell in 1515. Aden, at the entrance to the Red Sea, preserved its independence, but the capture of the Gujarati port of Diu in 1535 consolidated Portuguese dominance of the western Indian Ocean.

Farther east, the independent city of Malacca (muh-LAH-kuh) on the strait separating the Malay Peninsula and Sumatra became the focus of their attention. During the fifteenth century, Malacca had become the main entrepôt (ON-truh-poh) (a place where goods are stored or deposited and from which they are distributed) for the trade from China, Japan, India, the Southeast Asian mainland, and the Moluccas. The city's 100,000 residents spoke eighty-four different languages, according to a Portuguese source, and included merchants from Cairo, Ethiopia, and the Swahili Coast. Many non-Muslim residents supported letting the Portuguese join this cosmopolitan trading community, perhaps to offset the growing solidarity of Muslim traders. In 1511, however, the Portuguese seized Malacca with a force of a thousand fighting men, including three hundred recruited in southern India.

On the China coast, local officials and merchants persuaded the imperial government to allow the Portuguese to establish a trading post at Macao (muh-COW) in 1557. Subsequently, Portuguese ships nearly monopolized trade between China and Japan.

Control of the major port cities enabled the Portuguese to enforce their demands that all spices be carried in Portuguese ships, as well as all goods on the major ocean routes such as between Goa and Macao. The Portuguese also tried to control and tax other Indian Ocean trade. Merchant ships entering and leaving their ports had to carry a Portuguese passport and pay customs duties. Portuguese patrols seized vessels that did not comply, confiscated their cargoes, and either killed the captain and crew or sentenced them to forced labor.

Reactions to this power grab varied. Like the emperors of China, the Mughal (MOO-gahl) emperors of India largely ignored Portugal's maritime intrusions. The Ottomans confronted the Christian intruders more aggressively. They supported Egypt's defensive efforts from 1501 to 1509 and then sent their own fleet into the Indian Ocean in 1538. However, Ottoman galleys proved no match for the faster, better-armed Portuguese vessels in the open ocean. They retained their advantage only in the Red Sea and Persian Gulf, where they controlled many ports.

Smaller trading states could not challenge the Portuguese. Mutual rivalry kept them from forming a common front. Some cooperated with the Portuguese to safeguard their prosperity and security. Others engaged in evasion and resistance.

When the merchants of Calicut put up sustained resistance, the Portuguese embargoed all trade with Aden, Calicut's principal trading partner, and centered their trade on the port of Cochin, which had once been a dependency of Calicut. Some Calicut merchants evaded their patrols, but Calicut's importance shrank as Cochin gradually became the major pepper-exporting port on the Malabar Coast.

Farther north, Gujarat initially resisted Portuguese attempts at monopoly and in 1509 joined Egypt's futile effort to sweep the Portuguese from the Arabian Sea.

But in 1535, with his state weakened by Mughal attacks, the ruler allowed the Portuguese to build a fort at Diu in return for their support. Once established, the Portuguese gradually extended their control. By midcentury, they were licensing and taxing all Gujarati ships. Even after the Mughals took control of Gujarat in 1572, the Mughal emperor, Akbar, permitted the Portuguese to continue their maritime monopoly in return for allowing one pilgrim ship a year to sail to Mecca without paying a fee.

The Portuguese never gained complete control of the Indian Ocean trade, but their domination of key ports and trade routes brought them considerable profit in the form of spices and other luxury goods. The Portuguese broke the trading monopoly of Venice and Genoa by selling pepper for less than what they charged for shipments obtained through Egyptian middlemen.

The Americas

In the Americas, the Spanish established a vast territorial empire, in contrast to the trading empire of the Portuguese. The Spanish kingdoms drew on somewhat greater resources, but the Spanish and Portuguese monarchies had similar motives for expansion and used identical ships and weapons. The isolation of the Amerindian peoples provided a key difference. The first European settlers in the Caribbean resorted to conquest and plunder rather than trade. They later extended this practice to the more powerful Amerindian kingdoms on the American mainland. After 1518, deadly epidemics weakened the Amerindians' ability to resist.

The Arawak whom Columbus first encountered on Hispaniola (modern Haiti and the Dominican Republic) in the Greater Antilles and the Bahamas to the north cultivated maize (corn), cassava (a tuber), sweet potatoes, and hot peppers, as well as cotton and tobacco. They mined and worked gold, but they did not trade gold, nor did they have iron. They extended a cautious welcome to Columbus but told him exaggerated stories about gold in other places to persuade him to move on.

Columbus brought with him several hundred settlers from southern Iberia, as well as missionaries, on his second trip to Hispaniola in 1493. The settlers stole gold ornaments, confiscated food, and raped women, provoking the Hispaniola Arawak to war in 1495. With the advantage of horses and body armor, the Spaniards slaughtered tens of thousands of Arawak and forced the survivors to pay a heavy tax in gold, spun cotton, and food. Whoever failed to meet the quotas faced forced labor. Meanwhile, the cattle, pigs, and goats introduced by the settlers devoured the Arawak's food crops, causing deaths from famine and disease. A governor appointed by the Spanish crown in 1502 forced the Arawak on Hispaniola to become laborers under the control of Spanish settlers.

The actions of the Spanish in the Antilles reflected Spanish behavior during the wars against the Muslims in the previous centuries. They sought to serve God by defeating, controlling, and converting nonbelievers and to become rich in the process. Individual **conquistadors** (kon-KEY-stuh-dor) (conquerors) extended that pattern around the Caribbean. Some raided the Bahamas for gold and labor as both grew scarce on Hispaniola. Arawak from the Bahamas served as slaves on Hispaniola. Juan Ponce de León (1460–1521), a veteran of the conquest of Muslim Spain and the seizure of Hispaniola, conquered the island of Borinquen (Puerto Rico) in 1508 and in 1513 explored southeastern Florida.

conquistadors Early-sixteenth-century Spanish adventurers who conquered Mexico, Central America, and Peru.

Hernán Cortés (1485–1547)
Spanish explorer and conquistador who led the conquest of Aztec Mexico in 1519–1521 for Spain.

Primary Source: General History of the Things of New Spain
Learn the details of the horrible disaster that befell the Aztecs when the Spaniards and the plague descended upon them simultaneously.

Moctezuma II (1466?–1520)
Last Aztec emperor, overthrown by the Spanish conquistador Hernán Cortés.

An ambitious and ruthless nobleman, **Hernán Cortés** (kor-TEZ) (1485–1547), led the most audacious expedition to the mainland. Cortés left Cuba in 1519 with six hundred fighting men and most of the island's weapons to assault the Mexican mainland in search of slaves and trade. Learning of the rich Aztec Empire in central Mexico, Cortés expanded on the American mainland the exploitation and conquest carried out in the Greater Antilles.

Many of the Amerindians whom the Aztecs had subjugated during the previous century resented the tribute, forced labor, and the large-scale human sacrifices to Aztec gods their rulers imposed on them. Consequently, some gave the Spanish their support as allies against the Aztecs. Like the Caribbean people, the mainland Amerindians had no precedent by which to judge these strangers. Later accounts suggest that some believed Cortés to be the legendary ruler Quetzalcoatl (ket-zahl-COH-ah-tal), whose return to earth had been prophesied, and treated him with great deference.

Another consequence of millennia of isolation proved even more fatal: the lack of acquired immunity to Old World diseases. Smallpox, the most deadly of the early epidemics, appeared for the first time on the island of Hispaniola late in 1518. An infected member of the Cortés expedition then transmitted smallpox to Mexico in 1519, where it spread with deadly efficiency.

The Aztec emperor **Moctezuma** (mock-teh-ZOO-ma) II (r. 1502–1520) sent messengers to greet Cortés and determine whether he was god or man, friend or foe. Cortés advanced steadily toward the capital, Tenochtitlan (teh-noch-TIT-lan), overcoming Aztec opposition with cavalry charges and steel swords and gaining the support of discontented tributary peoples. When the Spaniards drew near, the emperor went out in a great procession, dressed in all his finery, to welcome Cortés with gifts and flower garlands.

Despite Cortés's initial promise of friendship, Moctezuma quickly found himself a prisoner in his own palace. The Spaniards looted his treasury, melting down its gold. Soon full-scale battle broke out. The Aztecs and their supporters briefly gained the upper hand. They destroyed half the Spanish force and four thousand of their Amerindian allies, sacrificing fifty-three Spanish prisoners and four horses to their gods and displaying their severed heads in rows on pikes. Reinforcements from Cuba enabled Cortés to regain the advantage. Smallpox, which weakened and killed more of the city's defenders than died in the fighting, also assisted his capture of Tenochtitlan in 1520. One source remembered that the disease "spread over the people as a great destruction."

After the capital fell, the conquistadors took over other parts of Mexico. Then some Spaniards began eyeing the Inca Empire, stretching nearly 3,000 miles (5,000 kilometers) south from the equator and containing half of the population in South America. The Inca had conquered the inhabitants of the Andes Mountains and the Pacific coast of South America during the previous century, and their rule was not fully accepted by the subjugated peoples.

The Inca rulers administered a well-organized empire with highly productive agriculture, exquisite stone cities (such as the capital, Cuzco), and rich gold and silver mines. The power of the Inca emperor rested on the belief that he was descended from the sun-god and on an efficient system of roads and messengers that kept him informed about major events. Yet at the end of the 1520s, before the Spanish had even been heard of, smallpox claimed countless lives, perhaps including the Inca emperor in 1530.

Coronation of Emperor Moctezuma

This painting by an unnamed Aztec artist depicts the Aztec ruler's coronation. Moctezuma, his nose pierced by a bone, receives the crown from a prince in the palace at Tenochtitlan.
(Oronoz)

An even more devastating threat loomed: **Francisco Pizarro** (pih-ZAHR-oh) (ca. 1478–1541) and his motley band of 180 men, 37 horses, and 2 cannon. With limited education and some military experience, Pizarro had come to the Americas in 1502 at the age of twenty-five to seek his fortune. He had participated in the conquest of Hispaniola and in Balboa's expedition across the isthmus of Panama. By 1520 a wealthy landowner and official in Panama, he nevertheless gambled his fortune on exploring the Pacific coast to a point south of the equator, where he learned of the riches of the Inca. With a license from the king of Spain, he set out from Panama in 1531 to conquer them.

In November 1532, Pizarro arranged to meet the new Inca emperor, **Atahualpa** (ah-tuh-WAHL-puh) (r. 1531–1533), near the Andean city of Cajamarca (kah-hah-MAHR-kah). With supreme boldness and brutality, Pizarro's small band grabbed Atahualpa from a rich litter borne by eighty nobles as it passed through an enclosed courtyard. Though surrounded by an Inca army of at least 40,000, the Spaniards used their cannon to create confusion while their swords sliced the emperor's lightly armed retainers and servants to pieces.

Noting the glee with which the Spaniards seized gold, silver, and emeralds, the captive Atahualpa offered them what he thought would satisfy even the greediest among them in exchange for his freedom: a roomful of gold and silver. But after receiving 13,400 pounds (6,000 kilograms) of gold and 26,000 pounds (12,000 kilograms) of silver, the Spaniards gave Atahualpa a choice: being burned at the stake as a heathen or being strangled after a Christian baptism. He chose the latter. His death and the Spanish occupation broke the unity of the Inca Empire.

Francisco Pizarro (1478?–1541)
Spanish explorer who led the conquest of the Inca Empire of Peru in 1531–1533.

Atahualpa (1502?–1533) Last ruling Inca emperor of Peru. He was executed by the Spanish.

In 1533, the Spaniards took Cuzco and from there set out to conquer and loot the rest of the empire. The defeat of a final rebellion in 1536 spelled the end of Inca rule. Five years later, Pizarro himself met a violent death at the hands of Spanish rivals, but the conquest of the mainland continued. Incited by the fabulous wealth of the Aztecs and Inca, conquistadors extended Spanish conquest and exploration in South and North America, dreaming of new treasuries to loot.

Patterns of Dominance Within fifty years of Columbus's first landing, the Spanish had located and occupied the major population centers of the Americas and penetrated many of the more thinly populated areas. Why did the peoples of the Americas suffer a fate so different from that of peoples in Africa and Asia? Why were the Spanish able to erect a vast land empire in the Americas so quickly?

First, unfamiliar illnesses devastated the Caribbean islands and then the mainland. Contemporaries estimated that between 25 and 50 percent of those infected with smallpox died. Repeated epidemics inhibited the Amerindians' ability to regain control. Estimates of the size of the population before Columbus's arrival, based on sparse evidence, vary widely. Yet historians agree that the Amerindian population fell sharply during the sixteenth century. The Americas became a "widowed land," open to resettlement from across the Atlantic.

A second factor was Spain's superior military technology. Steel swords, protective armor, and horses gave the Spaniards an advantage over their Amerindian opponents. Though few in number, muskets and cannon provided a psychological edge. However, the Spanish conquests depended heavily on large numbers of Amerindian allies armed with indigenous weapons. The most decisive military advantage may have been the no-holds-barred fighting techniques the Spaniards had developed during their wars at home.

The third factor in Spain's conquest was the precedent established by the reconquest of Granada in 1492: forced labor, forced conversion, and the incorporation of conquered lands into a new empire.

The same three factors help explain the different outcomes elsewhere. Centuries of contacts before 1500 meant that Europeans, Africans, and Asians shared the same Old World diseases. Only very isolated peoples in Africa and Asia suffered a demographic calamity. The Iberians enjoyed a military advantage at sea, but on land they had no decisive advantage against more numerous indigenous armies. Everywhere, Iberian religious zeal went hand in hand with a desire for riches. In Iberia and America, conquest itself brought wealth. But in Africa and Asia, existing trading networks made wealth dependent on commercial domination rather than conquest.

COMPARATIVE PERSPECTIVES

The rapid expansion of European empires and the projection of European military power around the world is one of the most important topics in world history, but it would have seemed unlikely in 1492. No European power matched the mili-

SECTION REVIEW

- Portugal and western African kingdoms forged commercial, military, and religious contacts, but missionary work and slave trading became points of tension.

- Portuguese contacts with East African states were mixed from the start, often marred by religious differences and the Portuguese focus on Indian Ocean trade.

- Naval superiority helped Portugal win control of Indian Ocean ports, and diplomacy gained it Macao in China.

- Benefiting from the Amerindians' isolation, Spain conquered a vast territorial empire in the Americas.

- Small conquistador armies subjugated island peoples and toppled the mainland Aztec and Inca Empires.

- Spain's conquest of the Americas happened as it did because of new diseases, military superiority, and precedents established by the reconquest of Spain.

tary and economic strength of China, and few could rival the Ottomans. Spain lacked strong national institutions and Portugal had a small population, and both had limited economic resources. Because of these limitations the monarchs of Spain and Portugal allowed their subjects greater initiative. While royal sponsorship was often crucial in, for example, the Portuguese contacts with Africa and the first voyages to Asia, many of the commercial and military expeditions were effectively organized and financed as private companies. Very often the kings of Spain and Portugal struggled to catch up with their restless and ambitious subjects, sometimes taking decades to establish royal control in new colonies.

The pace and character of European expansion were different in Africa and Asia than in the Americas. In Africa local rulers were generally able to limit European military power to coastal outposts and to control European trade. Only in the Kongo were the Portuguese able to project their power inland. When Europeans arrived in the Indian Ocean, mature markets and specialized production for distant consumers already existed. Although Portuguese (and later Dutch and British) naval power allowed Europeans to harvest large profits and influence local commercial patterns, most native populations continued to enjoy autonomy for centuries.

In the Americas the terrible effects of epidemic disease and the destructiveness of the conquest led to the rapid creation of European settlements and the subordination of the surviving indigenous population. The Spanish and Portuguese found few long-distance markets and little large-scale production of goods that could be exported profitably to Europe. The gold, silver, and sugar that eventually produced great wealth resulted from the introduction of new technologies, the imposition of oppressive new forms of labor, such as slavery, and the development of new roads and ports.

Chapter Review

DOWNLOAD THE MP3 AUDIO FILE OF THE CHAPTER REVIEW TO LISTEN TO ON THE GO.

What were the objectives and major accomplishments of the voyages of exploration undertaken by Chinese, Polynesians, and other non-Western peoples? (page 386)

The voyages of exploration undertaken by the Chinese and Polynesians pursued diverse objectives. In the Chinese case, the great voyages of the early fifteenth century were made out of interest in trade, curiosity, and the projection of imperial power. For the Polynesians, exploration opened the opportunity to both project power and demonstrate expertise while at the same settling satellite populations that would relieve population pressures on limited resources. In both cases new connections were made and societies were invigorated. The Vikings had similarly explored new lands in the North Atlantic, using their knowledge

KEY TERMS

Zheng He *(p. 389)*

Arawak *(p. 390)*

Henry the Navigator *(p. 392)*

caravel *(p. 393)*

Gold Coast (Africa) *(p. 395)*

Bartolomeu Dias *(p. 395)*

Vasco da Gama *(p. 395)*

Christopher Columbus *(p. 395)*

Ferdinand Magellan *(p. 398)*

conquistadors *(p. 403)*

Hernán Cortés *(p. 404)*

(Continued)

of the heavens and seas to establish settlements. There is also written evidence of African voyages in the Atlantic during this same period, although their purpose is less clear.

In this era of long-distance exploration, did Europeans have any special advantages over other cultural regions? (page 391)

The projection of European influence between 1450 and 1550 was in some ways similar to that of other cultural regions in that it expanded commercial linkages, increased cross-cultural contacts, and served the ambitions of political leaders. But the result was a major turning point in world history. During those years European explorers opened new long-distance trade routes across the world's three major oceans, for the first time establishing regular contact among all the continents. As a result, a new balance of power arose in parts of Atlantic Africa, the Indian Ocean, and the Americas.

What were the different outcomes of European interactions with Africa, India, and the Americas? (page 399)

Europeans created colonial empires in the Americas quite rapidly, while their progress in Africa and Asia was much slower. Many Amerindians welcomed the Spanish settlers at first, only to have them tax their labors, steal their food, introduce disease and warfare, and eventually subjugate them. In contrast, Portuguese visitors to Africa remained a minor presence in 1550. In some regions, the Portuguese were welcomed as trading partners; in others they were regarded as potential political and military allies. The real focus of the Portuguese was to capture the rich trade of the Indian Ocean. While they never gained complete control, they used their superior military strength to dominate key ports and major trade routes.

As dramatic and momentous as these events were, they were not completely unprecedented. The riches of the Indian Ocean trade that brought a gleam to the eye of many Europeans had been developed over many centuries by the trading peoples who inhabited the surrounding lands. While rapid, the European conquest of the Americas was no more rapid or brutal than the earlier Mongol conquests of Eurasia. Even the crossing of the Pacific had been done before, though in stages, by Polynesians.

What gave this maritime revolution unprecedented importance had more to do with what happened after 1550 than with what happened earlier. The overseas empires of the Europeans would endure longer than the Mongols' and would continue to expand for three and a half centuries after 1550. Unlike the Chinese, the Europeans did not turn their backs on the world after an initial burst of exploration. Not content with dominance in the Indian Ocean trade, Europeans opened an Atlantic maritime network that grew to rival the Indian Ocean network in the wealth of its trade; they also pioneered trade across the Pacific. The maritime expansion begun in the period from 1450 to 1550 marked the beginning of a new age of growing global interaction.

Moctezuma II *(p. 404)*
Francisco Pizarro *(p. 405)*
Atahualpa *(p. 405)*

WEB RESOURCES

Pronunciation Guide
Interactive Maps
MAP 14.1 Exploration and Settlement in the Indian and Pacific Oceans Before 1500
MAP 14.2 European Exploration, 1420–1542
Primary Sources
Agreement with Columbus of April 17 and April 30, 1492
General History of the Things of New Spain
Answer to the History in Focus Question
See the photo on page 397, "Columbus Prepares to Cross the Atlantic, 1492."
Plus
Chapter Objectives
ACE multiple-choice quiz
Flashcards

SUGGESTED READING

Abu-Lughod, Janet. *Before European Hegemony: The World System, A.D. 1250–1350*. 1989. A speculative reassessment of the Mongols and the Indian Ocean trade in the creation of an economic world system.

Cipolla, Carlo M. *Guns, Sails, and Empires: Technological Innovation and the Early Phases of European Expansion, 1400–1700*. 1965. A simple introduction to the technologies of European expansion.

Cuyvers, Luc. *Into the Rising Sun: The Journey of Vasco da Gama and the Discovery of the Modern World*. 1998. Examines the impact of finding a sea route to India.

Fernandez-Armesto, Felipe. *Before Columbus: Exploration and Colonization from the Mediterranean to the Atlantic, 1229–1492*. 1987. Examines the medieval background to European intercontinental voyages.

Jennings, Jesse D., ed. *The Prehistory of Polynesia*. 1979. A reliable guide to Polynesian expansion.

Kamen, Henry. *Spain, 1469–1714: A Society of Conflict*. 2d ed. 1991. Spain in the age of maritime empire.

Northrup, David. *Africa's Discovery of Europe, 1450–1850*. 2002. Looks at the perceptions of the peoples European explorers encountered.

Parry, J. H. *The Age of Reconnaissance: Discovery, Exploration, and Settlement, 1450–1650*. 1963. A general history with an emphasis on maritime techniques.

Phillips, William D., and Carla Rhan Phillips. *The Worlds of Christopher Columbus*. 1992. Examines the mariner and his times in terms of modern concerns.

Reid, Anthony. *Southeast Asia in the Age of Commerce, 1450–1680*. 2 vols. 1988, 1993. Deals with what were known as the East Indies.

Restall, Matthew. *Seven Myths of the Spanish Conquest*. 2003. Concentrates on continuities of Amerindian life in the face of European onslaught.

Russell-Wood, A. J. R. *The Portuguese Empire: A World on the Move*. 1998. The earliest European maritime empire.

Severin, Tim. *The Brendan Voyage*. 2000. Vividly recounts a modern retracing of pre-Columbian Irish voyages.

Thornton, John. *Africa and Africans in the Making of the Atlantic World, 1400–1800*. 2d ed. 1998. Examines Africans' encounters with Europeans and their involvement in the Atlantic economy.

Todorov, Tzvetan. *The Conquest of America*. 1985. Focuses on the shortcomings of Columbus and his Spanish peers.

NOTES

1. Ma Huan, *Ying-yai Sheng-lan: "The Overall Survey of the Ocean's Shores,"* ed. Feng Ch'eng-Chün, trans. J. V. G. Mills (Cambridge, England: Cambridge University Press, 1970), 180.

2. Alvise da Cadamosto in *The Voyages of Cadamosto and Other Documents,* ed. and trans. G. R. Crone (London: Hakluyt Society, 1937), 2.

Climate and Population, to 1500

DURING THE MILLENNIA before 1500 human populations expanded in three momentous surges. The first occurred after 50,000 B.C.E. when humans emigrated from their African homeland to all of the inhabitable continents. After that, the global population remained steady for several millennia. During the second expansion, between about 5000 and 500 B.C.E., population rose from about 5 million to 100 million as agricultural societies spread around the world (see Figure 1). Again population growth then slowed for several centuries before a third surge took world population to over 350 million by 1200 C.E. (see Figure 2).

For a long time historians tended to attribute these population surges to cultural and technological advances. Indeed, a great many changes in culture and technology are associated with adaptation to different climates and food supplies in the first surge and with the domestication of plants and animals in the second. However, historians have not found a cultural or technological change to explain the third surge, nor can they explain why creativity would have stagnated for long periods between the surges. Something else must have been at work.

Recently historians have begun to pay more attention to the impact of long-term variations in global climate. By examining ice cores drilled out of glaciers, scientists have been able to compile records of thousands of years of climate change. The comparative width of tree rings from ancient forests has provided additional data on periods of favorable and unfavorable growth. Such evidence shows that cycles of population growth and stagnation followed changes in global climate.

Historians now believe that global temperatures were above normal for extended periods from the late 1100s to the late 1200s C.E. In the temperate lands where most of the world's people lived, above-normal temperatures meant a longer growing season, more bountiful harvests, and thus a more adequate and reliable food supply. The ways in which societies responded to the medieval warm period are as important as the climate change, but it is unlikely that human agency alone would have produced the medieval surge. One notable response was that of the Vikings, who increased the size and range of their settlements in the North Atlantic, although their raids also caused death and destruction.

Some of the complexities involved in the interaction of human agency, climate, and other natural factors are also evident in the demographic changes that followed the medieval warm period. During the 1200s the Mongol invasions caused death and disruption of agriculture across Eurasia. China's population, which had been over 100 million in 1200, declined by a third or more by 1300. The Mongol invasions did not cause harm west of Russia, but climate changes in the 1300s resulted in population losses in Europe. Unusually heavy rains caused crop failures and a prolonged famine in northern Europe from 1315 to 1319.

The freer movement of merchants within the Mongol empire also facilitated the spread of disease across Eurasia, culminating in the great pandemic known as the Black Death in Europe. The demographic recovery under way in China was reversed. The even larger population losses in Europe may have been affected by the decrease in global temperatures to their lowest point in many millennia between 1350 and 1375. Improving economic conditions enabled population to recover more rapidly in Europe after 1400 than in China, where the conditions of rural life remained harsh.

Because many other historical circumstances interact with changing weather patterns, historians have a long way to go in deciphering the role of climate in history. Nevertheless, it is a factor that can no longer be ignored.

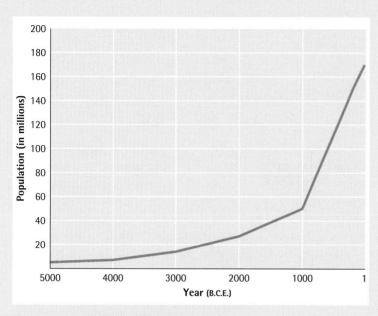

Figure 1   World Population, 5000–1 B.C.E.

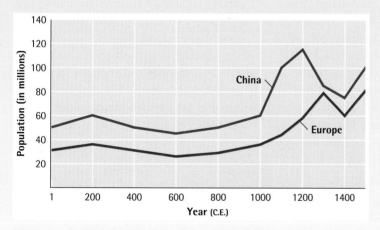

Figure 2   Population in China and Europe, 1–1500 C.E.

The Globe Encompassed, 1500–1800

The decades between 1500 and 1800 witnessed a tremendous expansion of commercial, cultural, and biological exchanges around the world. New long-distance sea routes linked Europe with sub-Saharan Africa and the existing maritime networks of the Indian Ocean and East Asia. Spanish and Portuguese voyages ended the isolation of the Americas and created new webs of exchange in the Atlantic and Pacific. Overland expansion of Muslim, Russian, and Chinese empires also increased global interaction.

These expanding contacts had major demographic and cultural consequences. Domesticated animals and crops from the Old World transformed agriculture in the Americas, while Amerindian foods such as the potato became staples of the diet of the Old World. European diseases, meanwhile, devastated the Amerindian population, facilitating the establishment of large Spanish, Portuguese, French, and British empires. Europeans introduced enslaved Africans to relieve the labor shortage. Immigrant Africans and Europeans brought new languages, religious practices, music, and forms of personal adornment.

In Asia and Africa, by contrast, the most important changes owed more to internal forces than to European actions. The Portuguese seized control of some important trading ports and networks in the Indian Ocean and pioneered new contacts with China and Japan. In time, the Dutch, French, and English expanded these profitable connections, but in 1750 Europeans were still primarily a maritime force. Asians and Africans generally retained control of their lands and participated freely in overseas trade.

The Islamic world saw the dramatic expansion of the Ottoman Empire in the Middle East and the establishment of the Safavid Empire in Iran and the Mughal Empire in South Asia. In northern Eurasia, Russia and China acquired vast new territories and populations, while a new national government in Japan promoted economic development and stemmed foreign influence.

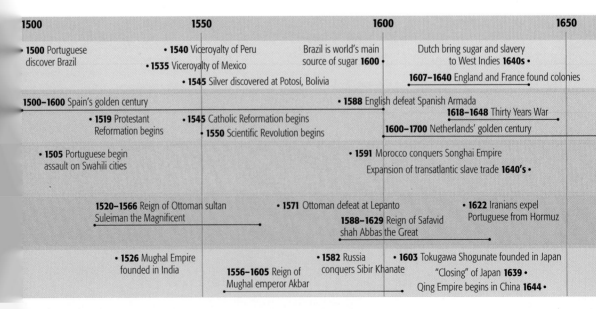

1500	1550	1600	1650
• **1500** Portuguese discover Brazil	• **1540** Viceroyalty of Peru • **1535** Viceroyalty of Mexico	Brazil is world's main source of sugar **1600** •	Dutch bring sugar and slavery to West Indies **1640s** • **1607–1640** England and France found colonies
1500–1600 Spain's golden century	• **1545** Silver discovered at Potosí, Bolivia	• **1588** English defeat Spanish Armada	
• **1519** Protestant Reformation begins	• **1545** Catholic Reformation begins • **1550** Scientific Revolution begins		**1618–1648** Thirty Years War **1600–1700** Netherlands' golden century
• **1505** Portuguese begin assault on Swahili cities		• **1591** Morocco conquers Songhai Empire Expansion of transatlantic slave trade **1640's** •	
	1520–1566 Reign of Ottoman sultan Suleiman the Magnificent	• **1571** Ottoman defeat at Lepanto **1588–1629** Reign of Safavid shah Abbas the Great	• **1622** Iranians expel Portuguese from Hormuz
• **1526** Mughal Empire founded in India	**1556–1605** Reign of Mughal emperor Akbar	• **1582** Russia conquers Sibir Khanate	• **1603** Tokugawa Shogunate founded in Japan "Closing" of Japan **1639** • Qing Empire begins in China **1644** •

ARCTIC OCEAN

NORTH AMERICA
Quebec
New York
NORTH ATLANTIC OCEAN
New Orleans
Mexico
West Indies
PACIFIC OCEAN
SOUTH AMERICA
Peru
Potosí
Brazil
SOUTH ATLANTIC OCEAN

England
Netherlands
St. Petersburg
Russian Empire
EUROPE
ASIA
Spain
Ottoman Empire
Safavid Empire
China
Korea
Japan
MIDDLE EAST
Mughal Empire
Calcutta
AFRICA
West Africa
Asante Dahomey
Swahili Coast
INDIAN OCEAN
East Indies
PACIFIC OCEAN
AUSTRALIA

0 1000 2000 3000 Km.
0 1000 2000 3000 Mi.

	1700	1750	1800
• **1660** English take Jamaica	• **1700** West Indies are world's main source of sugar	**1754–1763** French and Indian War; British take Canada	
	• **1718** French found New Orleans		**1780–1782** Revolt of Tupac Armaru in Peru
1667–1697 Wars of Louis XIV	• **1712** Peter the Great founds St. Petersburg	**1772–1795** Poland partitioned	
England's Glorious Revolution **1688** •	**1700–1800** The Enlightenment		
	1701–1714 War of the Spanish Succession		
• **1680s** Rise of Asante kingdom	• **1720s** Rise of kingdom of Dahomey	**1750–1800** Growing slave trade reduces population	
• **1683** Last Ottoman siege of Vienna	**1718–1730** Tulip Period of Ottoman Empire; Ottoman military decline		
Fall of Safavid Empire **1722** •	**1736–1747** Nadir Shah reunites Iran		
• **1689** Treaty of Nerchinsk			
• **1691** British found trading post at Calcutta	**1736–1799** Reign of Qing emperor Qianlong		

Transformations in Europe

CHAPTER 15

1500–1750

CHAPTER PREVIEW

Culture and Ideas

How was the cultural history of early modern Europe determined by the interplay of traditional beliefs and revolutionary ideas?

Social and Economic Life

What factors contributed to the wealth of some Europeans and the great poverty of others?

Political Innovations

How did differing policies on religion, foreign relations, and economics influence the history of early modern European states?

Comparative Perspectives

DIVERSITY AND DOMINANCE: Political Craft and Craftiness

s he neared the end of his life in 1575, the French scholar and humanist Loys Le Roy (lwa-EES le RWAH) reflected on the times in which he lived. It was, he believed, a golden age for Europe, and he ticked off the names of more than 130 scholars and translators, writers and poets, artists and sculptors, and explorers and philosophers whose work over the preceding two centuries had restored the standards of ancient learning. Later ages would call this scholarly and artistic revival the European **Renaissance**.

In addition, Le Roy enumerated a series of technological innovations that he believed had also transformed his age: printing, the marine compass, and cannonry. He put printing first because its rapid spread across Europe had done so much to communicate the literary and scholarly revival. The marine compass had

 This icon will direct you to the website where you can Prepare for Class, Improve Your Grade, and Ace the Test: college.cengage.com/pic/bullietbrief4e

made possible the sea voyages that now connected Europe directly to Africa and Asia and had led to the discovery and conquest of the Americas.

Le Roy gave third place to firearms because they had transformed warfare. Cannon and more recently devised hand-held weapons had swept before them all older military instruments. His enthusiasm for this transformation was dampened by the demonstrated capacity of firearms to cause devastation and ruin. Among the other evils of his age Le Roy enumerated syphilis and the spread of religious heresies and sects.

Reading Loys Le Roy's analysis more than four centuries later, one is struck not only by the acuity of his judgment and the beauty and clarity of his prose, but also by the astonishing geographical and historical range of his understanding. He credits both ancient and modern Greeks and Italians for their cultural contributions, the Germans for their role in perfecting printing and cannonry, and the Spanish for their overseas voyages. But his frame of reference is not confined to Europe. He cites the mathematical skills of ancient Egyptians; the military conquests of Mongols, Turks, and Persians (Iranians); Arabs' contributions to science and medicine; and China's contributions to the development of printing.

The global framework of Le Roy's analysis led him to conclude that he was living at a turning point in world history. For long centuries, he argued, the military might of the Mongols and Turks had threatened the peoples of Europe, and Safavid Iran and Mamluk Egypt had surpassed any European land in riches. Now the West was in the ascendancy. Europeans' military might equaled that of their Middle Eastern neighbors. They were amassing new wealth from Asian trade and American silver. Most of all, the explosion of learning and knowledge had given Europe intellectual equality and perhaps superiority. Le Roy noted perceptively that while printing presses were in use all across Europe, the Islamic world had closed itself off from the benefits of this new technology, refusing to allow presses to be set up and even forbidding the printing of Arabic works about their lands in Europe.

> **Renaissance (European)** A period of intense artistic and intellectual activity, said to be a "rebirth" of Greco-Roman culture. Usually divided into an Italian Renaissance, from roughly the mid-fourteenth to mid-fifteenth century, and a Northern (trans-Alpine) Renaissance, from roughly the early fifteenth to early seventeenth century.

CULTURE AND IDEAS

How was the cultural history of early modern Europe determined by the interplay of traditional beliefs and revolutionary ideas?

The period from 1500 to 1750 saw both conflict and continuity in the world of ideas. Theological controversies broke the religious unity of the Latin Church and contributed to violent wars. A huge witch scare showed the power of Christian and folk beliefs about the Devil. Although classical ideas from Greco-Roman antiquity impressed many better-educated people, some thinkers challenged the authority of the ancients. Their new models of planetary motion encouraged others to challenge traditional social and political systems, with important implications for the period after 1750. The technology of the printing press enhanced the impact of all of these developments.

Religious Reformation

In 1500 the **papacy**, the central government of Latin Christianity, was simultaneously gaining stature and suffering from corruption and dissent. Larger donations and tax

> **papacy** The central administration of the Roman Catholic Church, of which the pope is the head.

St. Peter's Basilica in Rome

Extravagant spending on church buildings and ornamentation helped spark Martin Luther's break with the papacy. The luxurious St. Peter's Basilica, with room for 60,000 worshipers, provided the most outstanding example. Work on the basilica began in 1506 and continued for more than a century. Shown here is the spectacular *baldacchino*, a sculptured bronze canopy above the main altar. It is 98 feet (30 meters) high and was executed by Gian Lorenzo Bernini between 1623 and 1633. (Scala/Art Resource, NY)

receipts let popes fund ambitious construction projects in Rome, their capital city. During the sixteenth century Rome gained fifty-four new churches and other buildings, which showcased the artistic Renaissance then under way. However, such wealth and power also attracted ambitious men, including some who led scandalous personal lives.

The jewel of the building projects was the new Saint Peter's Basilica in Rome. The unprecedented size and splendor of this church were intended to glorify God and enhance the standing of the papacy. Such a project required refined tastes and vast sums of money. Pope Leo X (r. 1513–1521), a member of the wealthy Medici (MED-ih-chee) family of Florence, oversaw the design and financing of the new basilica. Pope Leo's artistic taste was superb and his personal life free from scandal, but he was more a man of action than a spiritual leader. One way he raised building funds was by authorizing **indulgences**—absolutions for past sins granted to reward a pious act such as making a pilgrimage, saying a particular prayer, or making a financial donation.

A young professor of sacred scripture, Martin Luther (1483–1546), objected to the way the new indulgences were preached. Having forsaken money and marriage for a monastic life of prayer, self-denial, and study, Luther found personal consolation in a passage in Saint Paul's Epistle to the Romans stating that salvation came not from "doing certain things" but from religious faith. That passage led Luther to object to the indulgence preachers' emphasis on giving money more than on the faith behind the donation. He complained about this abuse to Pope Leo and challenged the preachers to debate the theology of indulgences.

Largely ignoring Luther's theological objections, Pope Leo regarded his letter as a challenge to papal power and moved to silence him. During a debate in 1519, a papal representative led Luther into open disagreement with church doctrines, for which the papacy condemned him. Unable to reform the church from within, Luther burned the papal bull (document) of condemnation, rejecting the pope's authority and beginning the movement known as the **Protestant Reformation**.

Accusing those whom he called "Romanists" (Roman Catholics) of relying on "good works," Luther insisted that the only way to salvation was through faith in Jesus Christ. He further declared that Christian belief must be based on the word of God in the Bible and on Christian tradition, not on the authority of the pope. Eventually his conclusions led him to abandon his monastic prayers and penances and to marry a former nun.

indulgence The forgiveness of the punishment due for past sins, granted by the Catholic Church authorities as a reward for a pious act. Martin Luther's protest against the sale of indulgences is often seen as touching off the Protestant Reformation.

CL **Primary Source: Table Talk** *Find out what word "creates more alarm at Rome than thunderbolts from heaven or the day of judgment."*

Protestant Reformation Religious reform movement within the Latin Christian Church beginning in 1519. It resulted in the "protesters" forming several new Christian denominations, including the Lutheran and Reformed Churches and the Church of England.

Chronology

	Politics and Culture	Environment and Technology	Warfare
1500	**1500s** Spain's golden century	**Mid-1500s** Increasing land drainage in Holland	
	1519 Protestant Reformation begins		
			1526 1571 Ottoman wars
	1540s Scientific Revolution begins		
	1545 Catholic Reformation begins		
			1546–1555 German Wars of Religion
			1562–1598 French Wars of Religion
			1566–1648 Netherlands Revolt
		1590s Dutch develop flyboats; Little Ice Age begins	
	Late 1500s Witch-hunts increase		
1600	**1600s** Holland's golden century	**1600s** Depletion of forests growing	
		1609 Galileo's astronomical telescope	
			1618–1648 Thirty Years War
			1642–1648 English Civil War
			1652–1678 Anglo-Dutch Wars
			1667–1697 Wars of Louis XIV
		1682 Canal du Midi completed	
			1683–1697 Ottoman wars
1700	**1700s** The Enlightenment begins		**1700–1721** Great Northern War
			1701–1714 War of the Spanish Succession
		1750 English mine nearly 5 million tons of coal a year	
		1755 Lisbon earthquake	

Today Roman Catholics and Lutherans have resolved many of their theological differences, but in the sixteenth century stubbornness on both sides made reconciliation impossible. Moreover, Luther's use of the printing press to promote his ideas won him the support of powerful Germans, who responded to his portrayal of the dispute as an effort by an Italian pope to beautify his city with German funds.

Inspired by Luther's denunciation of corruption, leaders elsewhere called for a return to authentic Christian practices and beliefs. John Calvin (1509–1564), a Frenchman who turned from the study of law to theology after experiencing a religious conversion, became a highly influential Protestant leader. Calvin's *The Institutes of the*

Christian Religion (1535) set forth his synthesis of Christian teachings, which differed from that of Roman Catholics and Lutherans in two respects. First, while exalting faith over works, Calvin nevertheless denied that faith alone could ensure salvation. Heaven, said Calvin, was a gift God gave to those he "predestined" for salvation. Second, Calvin went beyond Luther in curtailing the power of the clergy and simplifying religious rituals. Calvinist congregations elected their governing committees and in time created regional and national synods (councils) to regulate doctrinal issues. Calvinists also emphasized simplicity in dress, life, and worship. In an age of ornate garments, they wore simple black clothes, avoided ostentatious living, and worshiped in churches devoid of statues, most musical instruments, stained-glass windows, incense, and vestments.

The Reformers appealed to genuine religious sentiments, but their successes and failures were also due to political circumstances (discussed below) and the social agendas of their followers. Lutheranism appealed strongly to German speakers and linguistically related Scandinavians. Peasants and urban laborers sometimes defied their masters by adopting a different faith. Protestants were no more inclined than Roman Catholics to question male dominance in the church and the family, but most Protestants rejected the tradition of celibate priests and nuns and advocated Christian marriage for all adults.

Shaken by the Protestant Reformers' popularity, the Catholic Church undertook its own reforms. A council that met at the city of Trent, in northern Italy, in three sessions between 1545 and 1563 painstakingly distinguished proper Catholic doctrines from Protestant "errors." It also reaffirmed the supremacy of the pope and called for a number of reforms, including requiring each bishop to reside in his diocese and each diocese to have a theological seminary to train priests. Also important to this **Catholic Reformation** were the activities of a new religious order—the Society of Jesus, or "Jesuits," that Ignatius of Loyola (1491–1556), a Spanish nobleman, founded in 1540. Well-educated Jesuits helped win back some adherents by their teaching and preaching (see Map 15.1). Other Jesuits became missionaries overseas (see Chapters 16 and 18).

Given the intensity of the emotions that the Protestant Reformation stirred, it is not surprising that violence often flared up. Both sides persecuted and even executed those of differing views. Bitter "wars of religion," fought over a mixture of religious and secular issues, continued in parts of Europe until 1648.

Catholic Reformation Religious reform movement within the Latin Christian Church, begun in response to the Protestant Reformation. It clarified Catholic theology and reformed clerical training and discipline.

Traditional Thinking and Witch-Hunts

Religious differences continued to generate animosity long after the first generation of reformers, but from a global perspective European Christians still had much in common both in their theology and in the local folk customs and pre-Christian beliefs that remained powerful everywhere in Europe. The widespread **witch-hunts** pursued by both Protestants and Catholics arose from those common beliefs.

Two distinct traditions marked European ideas about the natural world: folklore about magic and forest spirits passed down orally from pre-Christian times, and biblical teachings heard in church and read by growing numbers in vernacular translations. Christian teachings about miracles, saints, and devils mingled with folklore in the minds of many.

witch-hunt The pursuit of people suspected of witchcraft, especially in northern Europe in the late sixteenth and seventeenth centuries.

Interactive Map

Predominant Religion in 1555

- Lutheran
- Calvinist (Reformed)
- Church of England
- Roman Catholic
- ◄ Huguenot centers
- → Spread of Calvinism

0   150   300 Km.
0   150   300 Mi.

Map 15.1 Religious Reformation in Europe

The Reformation brought greater religious freedom but also led to religious conflict and persecution. In many places the Reformation accelerated the trend toward state control of religion and added religious differences to the motives for wars among Europeans.

Like people elsewhere, most Europeans believed that natural events could have supernatural causes. When crops failed or domestic animals died unexpectedly, many people blamed unseen spirits. People also attributed human triumphs and tragedies to supernatural causes. When an earthquake destroyed much of Lisbon, Portugal's capital city, in November 1755, for example, both educated and uneducated people saw the event as a divine punishment. A Jesuit charged it "scandalous to pretend that the earthquake was just a natural event." An English Protestant leader agreed, comparing Lisbon's fate with that of Sodom, the sinful biblical city that God destroyed.

The fear of witches that swept across northern Europe in the late sixteenth and seventeenth centuries grew out of these beliefs. Secular and church authorities tried over a hundred thousand people—some three-fourths of them women—for practicing witchcraft. Some were acquitted; some recanted; but more than half were executed—mostly in Protestant lands. Torture and harsh interrogation persuaded many accused witches to confess to casting spells and to describe in vivid detail their encounters with the Devil and their attendance at nighttime assemblies of witches.

Trial records make it clear that both the accusers and the accused believed that it was possible for angry and jealous individuals to use evil magic and the power of the Devil to attack people and domestic animals or to cause crops to wither in the fields. Though researchers think that at least some of those accused may really have tried using witchcraft to harm their enemies, it was the Reformation's focus on the Devil that made such malevolence a serious crime and helped revive pre-Christian fears of witchcraft.

Modern historians also argue that accusations against widows and independent-minded women arose from a widespread distrust of women not directly controlled by fathers or husbands. Such women played important roles in tending animals and the sick and in childbirth, which also made them suspects if death occurred.

No single reason can explain the witchcraft hysteria in early modern Europe, but, for both the accusers and the accused, there are plausible connections between the witch-hunts and rising social tensions, rural poverty, and environmental strains. Far from being a bizarre aberration, witch-hunts reflected the larger social climate.

The Scientific Revolution

Educated people ignored folklore and looked to the Bible and the writings of antiquity, many of them newly discovered by Renaissance scholars, for guides to the natural world. Their authority on physics was Aristotle, who taught that everything on earth was re-

Death to Witches

This woodcut from 1574 depicts three women convicted of witchcraft being burned alive in Baden, Switzerland. The well-dressed townsmen look on stolidly.   (Zentralbibliothek Zurich, Ms.F. 54) ducible to four elements: earth and water on the surface and air and fire floating above the ground. Higher still were the sun, moon, planets, and stars, light, pure bodies embedded in crystalline spheres. This theory accorded perfectly with the common-sense perception that all heavenly bodies revolved around the earth.

The ideas of the ancient Greek mathematician Pythagoras supported this view. Pythagoreans attached special significance to the simplest (to them perfect) geometrical shapes: the circle (a point rotated around another point) and the sphere (a circle rotated on its axis). They believed that celestial objects were perfect spheres orbiting the earth in perfectly circular orbits.

In the sixteenth century, however, careful observations and mathematical calculations, many of them made by Muslim and translated into Latin, led some imaginative European investigators to challenge these views. These pioneers of the **Scientific Revolution** rejected the accumulation of ingenious theories used to explain some seemingly irregular celestial movements. A Polish monk and mathematician named Nicholas Copernicus (1473–1543), possibly building on the theories of Muslim astronomers, came up with a mathematically simpler solution: switching the center of the different orbits from the earth to the sun.

Scientific Revolution The intellectual movement in Europe, initially associated with planetary motion and other aspects of physics, that by the seventeenth century had laid the groundwork for modern science.

Copernicus did not challenge the idea that the sun, moon, and planets were light, perfect spheres or that they moved in circular orbits. But his placement of the sun, not the earth, at the center of things began a revolution in understanding the structure of the heavens and the place of humans in the universe. To escape the anticipated controversies, Copernicus delayed the publication of his heliocentric (sun-centered) theory until the end of his life.

Other astronomers, including the Dane Tycho Brahe (1546–1601) and his German assistant Johannes Kepler (1571–1630), improved on the Copernican model by showing that planets actually move in elliptical, not circular orbits. The most brilliant of the Copernicans was the Italian Galileo Galilei (gal-uh-LAY-oh gal-uh-LAY-ee) (1564–1642). In 1609 Galileo built a telescope through which he took a closer look at the heavens. Viewing distant objects at a magnification thirty times that of the naked eye, Galileo perceived that heavenly bodies were not the perfectly smooth spheres of the Aristotelians.

Tycho Brahe at Work
Between 1576 and 1597, on the island of Ven between Denmark and Sweden, Tycho built the best observatory in Europe and set a new standard for accurate celestial observations before the invention of the telescope. The contemporary hand-colored engraving shows the Danish astronomer at work. (Maritime Museum Kronberg Castle Denmark/ G. Dagli Orti/The Art Archive)

The moon, he reported in *The Starry Messenger* (1610), had mountains and valleys; the sun had spots; other planets had their own moons. In other words, the earth was not alone in being heavy and changeable.

At first, the Copernicans endured much criticism because their views so directly challenged not just popular ideas but also classical and biblical authority. How, demanded Aristotle's defenders, could the heavy earth rotate around the sun without shaking to pieces? Does the Bible lie, asked the theologians, when the Book of Joshua says that, by God's command, "the sun [not the earth] stood still . . . for about a whole day" to give the ancient Israelites victory in their conquest of Palestine? If Aristotle's physics was wrong, worried other traditionalists, would not the theological synthesis built on other parts of his philosophy be open to question?

Most Protestant leaders, following the lead of Martin Luther, condemned the heliocentric universe as contrary to the Bible. Catholic authorities waited longer to act. After all, both Copernicus and Galileo were Roman Catholics. Copernicus had dedicated his book to the pope, and in 1582 another pope, Gregory XIII, had used the latest astronomical findings to issue a new and more accurate calendar (still used today). Galileo ingeniously argued that the conflict between scripture and science was only apparent: the word of God revealed in the Bible was expressed in the imperfect language of ordinary people, but in nature God's truth was revealed in a language that could be learned by careful observation and scientific reasoning.

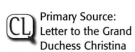

Primary Source: Letter to the Grand Duchess Christina
Hear what the quick-witted Galileo Galilei has to say to his detractors.

Unfortunately, Galileo ridiculed those who were slow to accept his findings, charging that Copernican ideas were "mocked and hooted at by an infinite multitude . . . of fools." Stung by such sarcasm, some Jesuits and other critics got his ideas condemned by the Roman Inquisition in 1616. *The Starry Messenger* went onto the Index of Forbidden Books, and Galileo was barred from publishing further on the subject. (In 1992 the Catholic Church officially retracted its condemnation of Galileo.)

Index or no Index, printed books spread the new scientific ideas among scholars across Europe. In England, Robert Boyle (1627–1691) used experimental methods and a trial-and-error approach to examine the inner workings of chemistry. Through the Royal Society, chartered in London in 1662 to promote knowledge of the natural world, Boyle and others became enthusiastic missionaries of mechanical science and fierce opponents of the Aristotelians.

Meanwhile, English mathematician Isaac Newton (1642–1727) was carrying Galileo's demonstration that the heavens and earth share a common physics to its logical conclusion. Newton formulated a set of mathematical laws that all physical objects obeyed. It was the force of gravity—not angels—that governed the elliptical orbits of heavenly bodies. It was gravitation that caused cannonballs to fall back to earth. From 1703 until his death Newton served as president of the Royal Society and as an icon of the new science.

Galileo's condemnation demonstrates that in 1700 most religious and intellectual leaders viewed the new science with suspicion or outright hostility. Yet the principal pioneers of the Scientific Revolution were convinced that scientific discoveries and revealed religion were not in conflict. At the peak of his fame Newton promoted a series of lectures devoted to proving the validity of Christianity. However, by showing that Aristotelian and biblical ideas about the natural world were naive and not based on facts, these pioneers opened the door for others who used reason to challenge a broader range of traditions and superstitions.

The Early Enlightenment

The advances in scientific thought inspired a few brave souls to question the reasonableness of everything from agricultural methods to laws, religion, and social hierarchies. The belief that human reason could discover scientific laws governing social behavior, parallel to those governing physical properties, energized a movement known as the **Enlightenment**. Like the Scientific Revolution, this movement was the work of a few "enlightened" individuals, who often faced bitter opposition. Leading Enlightenment thinkers became accustomed to having their books banned and spending long periods in exile to escape imprisonment.

The partisan bickering and bloodshed of the Reformation had led some people to doubt the superiority of any theological position and to recommend toleration of all religions. The killing of suspected witches also shocked many thoughtful people. The leading French thinker Voltaire (1694–1778) declared: "No opinion is worth burning your neighbor for."

Explorers' accounts of cultures in other parts of the world raised questions about Europe's superiority. Romantic reports of Amerindian life, for example, led some to conclude that so-called "savages" were in many ways nobler than European Christians. Matteo Ricci, a Jesuit missionary to China whose journals were widely read, contrasted the lack of territorial ambition of the Chinese with the constant warfare in the West and attributed the difference to China's being ruled by educated men whom he called "Philosophers."

Although many circumstances shaped "enlightened" thinking, the new scientific methods and discoveries provided the clearest model for changing European society. Voltaire posed the issues in these terms: "it would be very peculiar that all nature, all the planets, should obey eternal laws" but a human being, "in contempt of these laws, could act as he pleased solely according to his caprice." The English poet Alexander Pope (1688–1774) made a similar point in verse: "Nature and Nature's laws lay hidden in night; / God said, 'Let Newton be' and all was light."

The Enlightenment was more a frame of mind than a coherent movement. By 1750 its proponents were clearer about what they disliked than about what new institutions should be created. Nearly all were optimistic that—at least in the long run—human beliefs and institutions could be improved. This belief in progress would help foster political and social revolutions after 1750, as Chapter 19 recounts.

Despite the enthusiasm the Enlightenment aroused in some circles, it was decidedly unpopular with many absolutist rulers and with most clergymen. Europe in 1750 was neither enlightened nor scientific.

SECTION REVIEW

- Conflicts among ideas, enhanced by print technology, profoundly affected the culture of early modern Europe.

- Outraged by corrupt church practices, reformers like Luther and Calvin challenged papal authority and traditional Catholic theology.

- In response to the Protestant reformers, the Church launched a Catholic Reformation.

- At the same time, both Protestants and Catholics, driven by traditional ideas, undertook widespread witch-hunts.

- The thinkers of the Scientific Revolution challenged traditional biblical and Greco-Roman conceptions of the cosmos.

- The advances in science prompted Enlightenment thinkers to question many conventional ideas and practices.

Enlightenment A philosophical movement in eighteenth-century Europe that fostered the belief that one could reform society by discovering rational laws that governed social behavior and were just as scientific as the laws of physics.

Primary Source: Treatise on Tolerance *Discover Voltaire's eloquent argument for tolerance and learn why he calls human beings "atoms of the moment."*

SOCIAL AND ECONOMIC LIFE

What factors contributed to the wealth of some Europeans and the great poverty of others?

From a distance European society seemed quite rigid. At the top of the social pyramid a small number of noble families monopolized church, government, and military offices and enjoyed many privileges, including exemption from taxation. Merchants and professionals, who had acquired wealth but no legal privileges, ranked well below them. At the base of the pyramid were the masses, mostly rural peasants and land-less laborers. The subordination of women to men seemed equally rigid.

Nevertheless, some social mobility did occur, particularly in the middle. The principal engine of social change was the economy, and the places where social change occurred most readily were the cities. A secondary means of change was education—for those who could get it.

The Bourgeoisie

Europe's growing cities were the products of a changing economy. In 1500 Paris was the only northern European city with over 100,000 inhabitants. By 1700 both Paris and London had populations over 500,000, and twenty other European cities contained over 60,000 people.

The wealth of the cities came from manufacturing, finance, and especially trade, both within Europe and overseas. The French called the economically dynamic urban class the **bourgeoisie** (boor-zwah-ZEE) (burghers, town dwellers). Members of the bourgeoisie poured much of their profit back into their businesses or into new ventures. Even so, they had enough money to live comfortably in large houses with many servants. In the seventeenth and eighteenth centuries they could buy exotic luxuries imported from the far corners of the earth—Caribbean and Brazilian sugar and rum, Mexican chocolate, Virginia tobacco, North American furs, East Indian cottons and spices, and Chinese tea.

bourgeoisie In early modern Europe, the class of well-off town dwellers whose wealth came from manufacturing, finance, commerce, and allied professions.

The Netherlands flourished in the seventeenth century with a wide variety of goods flowing from factories and workshops. The highly successful textile industry concentrated on weaving and printing cloth, leaving the spinning of thread to low-paid workers elsewhere. Along with fine woolens and linens the Dutch made cheaper textiles for mass markets. Other factories in Holland refined West Indian sugar, brewed beer from Baltic grain, processed Virginia tobacco, and made imitations of Chinese ceramics. Free from the censorship imposed in neighboring countries, Holland's printers published books in many languages, including manuals with the latest advances in machinery, metallurgy, and agriculture. For a small province barely above sea level, lacking timber and other natural resources, this was a remarkable achievement.

Burgeoning from a fishing village to a metropolis of some 200,000 by 1700, Amsterdam was Holland's largest city and Europe's major port. The bourgeoisie there and in other cities developed huge commercial fleets that dominated sea trade in Europe and overseas. Eighty percent of the trade between Spain and northern Europe sailed on Dutch ships, even while Spain and the Netherlands were at war. Amsterdam also served as Europe's financial center. Seventeenth-century Dutch banks had such a reputation for security that wealthy individuals and governments from all over western Europe entrusted them with their money. The banks in turn invested these funds in real estate, loaned money to factory owners and governments, and provided capital for business operations overseas.

Maritime expansion led to new ship designs. In this, too, the Dutch played a dominant role, using timber imported from northern Europe to build their own fleets as well as ships for export. Especially successful was the fluit, or "flyboat," a large-capacity cargo ship developed in the 1590s. It was inexpensive to build and required only a

Port of Amsterdam
Ships, barges, and boats of all types are visible in this busy seventeenth-century scene. The large building in the center is the Admiralty House, the headquarters of the Dutch East India Company.   (Mansell/TimeLife Pictures/Getty Images)

small crew. Another successful type was the heavily armed "East Indiaman," which helped the Dutch establish their supremacy in the Indian Ocean. The Dutch also excelled at mapmaking.

Like merchants elsewhere, Europeans relied on family and ethnic networks. Many northern cities contained merchant colonies from Venice, Florence, Genoa, and other Italian cities. Amsterdam and Hamburg sheltered Jewish merchants who had fled religious persecution in Iberia. Other Jewish communities expanded out of eastern Europe into the German states, especially after the Thirty Years War. Armenian merchants from Iran were moving into the Mediterranean and became important in Russia in the seventeenth century.

Leading merchants sought alliances with European monarchs who believed that economic growth would increase state revenues. The Dutch government pioneered chartering **joint-stock companies**. The Dutch East India Company received a monopoly over trade to the East Indies, as did the Dutch West India Company for the New World. France and England chartered companies of their own. The companies sold shares to individuals, thus spreading the risks (and profits) among many investors (see Chapter 16). Investors bought and sold shares in specialized markets called **stock exchanges**, an Italian innovation transferred to the cities of northwestern Europe in the sixteenth century. The greatest stock market in the seventeenth and eighteenth centuries was the Amsterdam Exchange, founded in 1530. Large insurance companies also emerged in this period, and insuring long voyages against loss became a standard practice after 1700.

joint-stock company A business, often backed by a government charter, that sold shares to individuals to raise money for its trading enterprises and to spread the risks (and profits) among many investors.

stock exchange A place where shares in a company or business enterprise are bought and sold.

Governments undertook large projects to improve water transport. The Dutch built canals for transport and to drain the lowlands for agriculture. Other governments also financed canals. One of the most important was the 150-mile (240-kilometer) Canal du Midi in France, built by the French government between 1661 and 1682 to link the Atlantic and the Mediterranean. By the seventeenth century rulers sought the talents of successful businessmen as administrators. Jean Baptiste Colbert (kohl-BEAR) (1619–1683), Louis XIV's able minister of finance, was a notable example.

Successful bourgeoisie in England and France traded wealth for social status. By retiring from their businesses and buying country estates, they could become members of the **gentry** and follow the lifestyle of the old aristocracy. The gentry loaned money to impoverished peasants and to members of the nobility and in time increased their ownership of land. Some families sought aristocratic husbands for their daughters. The old nobility found such alliances attractive because of the large dowries that the bourgeoisie provided. In France a family could gain the exemption from taxation by living in gentility for three generations or, more quickly, by purchasing a title from the king.

gentry The term *gentry* denotes the class of landholding families in England and France below the aristocracy. In China, the class of prosperous families, next in wealth below the rural aristocrats, from which the emperors drew their administrative personnel. Respected for their education and expertise, these officials became a privileged group and made the government more efficient and responsive than in the past.

Peasants and Laborers

At the other end of society things were bad, but they had been worse. Though serfdom expanded in eastern Europe, in the west it faded away after the Black Death of the mid-fourteenth century. Slavery, which had briefly expanded in southern Europe around 1500 as the result of the Atlantic slave trade from sub-Saharan Africa, declined. After 1600, Europeans shipped nearly all African slaves to the Americas. Thus western Europe continued to depend on unfree labor, though at a distance rather than at home.

Hunters in the Snow, 1565

This January scene by the Flemish artist Pieter Bruegel, the Elder, shows many everyday activities.   (Kunsthistorisches Museum, Vienna/The Bridgeman Art Library)

Legal freedom did not make a peasant's life more secure. Agricultural efficiency had improved little since 1300. As a result, bad years brought famine; good ones provided only small surpluses. Indeed, prolonged warfare, environmental problems, and varying economic conditions may have lowered the conditions of life for the average person between 1500 and 1750. In addition, Europeans felt the effects of a century of relatively cool weather that began in the 1590s. During this **Little Ice Age** an average temperature decline of only a few degrees had startling results (see Issues in World History: The Little Ice Age, page 521).

By 1700 high-yielding new crops from the Americas were helping the rural poor avoid starvation. Potatoes sustained life in northeastern and central Europe and in Ireland, and poor peasants in Italy subsisted on maize. Ironically, all of these lands were major exporters of wheat, which the agricultural laborers could not afford to eat. Instead, the grain was shipped to the cities of western Europe. Other fleets brought wine from southern to northern Europe. Parisians downed 100,000 barrels of wine a year at the end of the seventeenth century. Some of the grain was made into beer, which the poor drank because it was cheaper than wine. In 1750 Parisian breweries brewed 23 million quarts (22 million liters) of beer for local consumption.

The expanding iron industry in England provided work for woodcutters and charcoal makers, but the high consumption of wood fuel for this and other purposes caused serious **deforestation**. One early-seventeenth-century observer lamented: "within man's memory, it was held impossible to have any want of wood in England. But . . . at present, through the great consuming of wood . . . and the neglect of planting of woods, there is a great scarcity of wood throughout the whole kingdom."[1] Ironworks managers in England met the shortages by importing timber and charcoal from heavily forested Scandinavian countries and Russia. Eventually, the high price of wood and charcoal encouraged smelters to use coal as an alternative fuel. England's coal mining increased twelvefold, from 210,000 tons in 1550 to 2,500,000 tons in 1700. Starting in 1709, coke—coal refined to remove impurities—gradually replaced charcoal in the smelting of iron. These new demands drove English coal production to nearly 5 million tons a year by 1750.

France was more forested than England, but deforestation there prompted Colbert to predict that "France will perish for lack of wood." By the late eighteenth century, local iron production made deforestation an issue even in Sweden and Russia. Fear of running out of the high-quality timbers of exceptional size and curvature needed for naval vessels spurred new laws to protect forests in France and England. Although wood consumption remained high, rising prices encouraged some individuals to plant trees for future harvest. Everywhere in Europe the rural poor felt the depletion of the forests most strongly, since for centuries they had depended on woodlands for wild nuts and berries, free firewood and building materials, and wild game.

Improvements in food production were sometimes overwhelmed by population growth. Rural women had long supplemented household incomes by spinning yarn. From the mid-1600s rising wages in towns led textile manufacturers to farm more and more weaving out to rural areas with high underemployment. This provided men and women with enough to survive on, but the piecework paid very little for long hours of tedious labor.

Many rural poor migrated to the towns and cities in hopes of better jobs, but few met success. Even in the prosperous Dutch towns, half the population lived in

Little Ice Age A century-long period of cool climate that began in the 1590s. Its ill effects on agriculture in northern Europe were notable.

deforestation The removal of trees faster than forests can replace themselves.

acute poverty. Authorities estimated that those permanent city residents who were too poor to tax, the "deserving poor," made up 10 to 20 percent of the population. This left out the large numbers of "unworthy poor"—recent migrants, peddlers traveling from place to place, and beggars (many with horrible deformities and sores) who tried to survive on charity. Desperation forced many young women into prostitution and many men into crime. Organized gangs practiced everything from picking pockets to highway robbery.

The pervasive poverty shocked those who were not hardened to it. Around 1580 the mayor of the French city of Bordeaux (bor-DOH) asked a group of visiting Amerindian chiefs what impressed them most about European cities. The chiefs are said to have expressed astonishment at the disparity between the fat, well-fed people and the poor, half-starved men and women in rags. Why, the visitors wondered, did the poor not grab the rich by the throat or set fire to their homes?[2]

In fact, misery provoked many rebellions. For example, in 1525 peasant rebels in the Alps attacked both nobles and clergy as representatives of the privileged and landowning classes. They had no love for merchants either, whom they denounced for lending at interest and charging high prices. In southwestern France alone some 450 uprisings occurred between 1590 and 1715, many of them set off by food shortages and tax increases. The exemption of the wealthy from taxation was a frequent source of complaint. A rebellion in southern France in 1670 began when a mob of townswomen attacked the tax collector. It quickly spread to the country, where peasant leaders cried, "Death to the people's oppressors!" Authorities dealt severely with such revolts and executed or maimed their leaders.

Women and the Family

Women's status and work were closely tied to those of their husbands and families. In rare instances, a woman in a royal family might inherit a throne (see Table 15.1 for examples) in the absence of a male heir, but such exceptions do not negate the rule that women everywhere ranked below men. Nevertheless, class and wealth defined a woman's position in life more than gender. A wife or daughter in a rich family, for example, had a much better life than any poor man. Occasionally, a single woman might be secure and respected, as in the case of women from good families heading convents of nuns in Catholic countries. But unmarried women and widows fared poorly compared to their married sisters.

Men and women most often chose their own spouses. Privileged families controlled marriage plans more often than poor ones. Royal and noble families carefully plotted their children's marriages to further the family's status. Bourgeois parents were less likely to force their children into arranged marriages. Nevertheless, nearly all found spouses within their social class, sometimes to buttress business connections.

Europeans also married late. The children of craftspeople and the poor had to delay marriage until they could afford to live on their own. Young men served long apprenticeships to learn trades. Young women worked helping their parents, or as domestic servants, or in some other capacity to save money for their dowry: the money and household goods—the amount varied by social class—that enabled a young couple to begin marriage independent of their parents. The typical groom in western and central Europe could not hope to marry before his late twenties. His bride would be a few years younger. Marriage also came late in bourgeois families, in part to allow young men to complete their education.

The late age of marriage held down the birthrate and thus limited family size. Even so, about one in ten urban babies was born to an unmarried woman, often a servant. Such newborns were generally left on the doorsteps of churches, convents, or rich homes. Many perished. Public brothels also went with delayed marriage. They provided a place for young men to satisfy their desires at the expense of unfortunate young women, often newly arrived from impoverished villages. Nevertheless, rape was a common occurrence, especially assaults by gangs of young men. Some historians believe these crimes reflect the envy poor young men had of older men's easier access to women.

Bourgeois parents focused on giving their children the education and training necessary for success. They promoted the establishment of municipal schools where they could learn Latin and perhaps Greek. Then they sent their sons abroad to learn modern languages or to a university to earn a law degree. Legal training helped them conduct business and was necessary for obtaining a judgeship or treasury position. Daughters were less likely to be groomed for business careers, but wives often helped their husbands as bookkeepers and sometimes inherited businesses.

The fact that most schools, like most guilds and professions, barred females explains why women were not prominent in the cultural movements of the period. Yet from a global perspective, women in early modern Europe were more prominent in the creation of high culture than were women in most other parts of the world. Recent research has identified successful women who were painters, musicians, and writers. Indeed, the spread of learning, the stress on religious reading, and the growth of business may have made Europe the leading area of the world in female literacy. Nevertheless, illiteracy was widespread for both sexes, and only women in wealthier families might have a good education. From the late 1600s some wealthy French women ran intellectual gatherings in their homes. Others were prominent letter writers. Galileo's daughter, Maria Celeste Galilei, carried on a detailed correspondence with her father from behind the walls of her convent, which she had vowed never to leave.

SECTION REVIEW

- Early modern European society was less rigid than it appeared, with the economy and education the primary means of social change.

- The urban bourgeoisie, especially in the Netherlands, created much of Europe's wealth through trade, manufacture, finance, and technological innovation.

- Governments sought lucrative alliances with the bourgeoisie, whose wealth afforded them political and social advancement.

- Oppressed by economic and environmental trends, peasants and laborers generally lived in poverty, and their misery often provoked rebellion.

- Although women remained subordinate to men, class and wealth were the main determinants of their positions in life.

POLITICAL INNOVATIONS

How did differing policies on religion, foreign relations, and economics influence the history of early modern European states?

The monarchs of early modern Europe occupied the apex of the social order, arbitrated intellectual and religious conflicts, and influenced economic life. In addition, royal political agendas introduced new elements of conflict and change.

Though no unified European empire emerged, political centralization increased in separate kingdoms. The frequent civil and international conflicts of this era sometimes promoted cooperation and often encouraged innovation. Leadership and success passed from Spain to the Netherlands and then to England and France.

Holy Roman Empire Loose federation of mostly German states and principalities, headed by an emperor elected by the princes. It lasted from 962 to 1806.

Habsburg A powerful European family that provided many Holy Roman Emperors, founded the Austrian (later Austro-Hungarian) Empire, and ruled sixteenth- and seventeenth-century Spain.

State Development

Political diversity characterized Europe. City-states and principalities abounded, either independently or bound into loose federations, of which the **Holy Roman Empire** of the German heartland was the foremost example. In western Europe the strong monarchies that had emerged earlier were acquiring national identities, but some rulers dreamed of a European empire comparable to that of Rome.

In 1519 electors of the Holy Roman Empire chose Charles V (r. 1519–1556) as emperor. Like his predecessors for three generations, Charles belonged to the powerful **Habsburg** (HABZ-berg) family of Austria, but he had recently inherited the Spanish thrones of Castile and Aragon. With the vast resources of these lands behind him, Charles hoped to centralize his imperial power and lead a Christian coalition to halt the advance into southeastern Europe of the Ottoman Empire, which had recently conquered Egypt and Syria.

Stout defense and bad weather prevented the Ottomans from taking Vienna in 1529, but Ottoman attacks continued on and off until 1697. King Francis I of France, who had lost to Charles in the imperial election, openly supported the Ottomans, whom the Europeans usually called Turks, to weaken his rival. In addition, some imperial states used Luther's religious Reformation to frustrate Charles's efforts to control them. Luther's appeals to German national sentiment encouraged many German princes to oppose Charles's defense of Catholic doctrine in the imperial Diet (assembly).

After decades of bitter squabbles turned to open warfare in 1546 (the German Wars of Religion), Charles V finally gave up on unification, handed his various possessions over to different heirs, and retired to a monastery. By the Peace of Augsburg (1555), he recognized the princes' right to choose either Catholicism or Lutheranism as their state religion, and he allowed them to keep any church lands they had seized before 1552. The triumph of religious diversity postponed German political unification for three centuries.

Meanwhile, the rulers of Spain, France, and England met greater success in political centralization and religious unity. Getting control of the church in the sixteenth century was a stormy process, but the outcome was clear. Bringing the nobles and other powerful interests into a centralized political system took longer and led to more diverse outcomes (see Diversity and Dominance: Political Craft and Craftiness).

Religious Policies

The rulers of Spain and France successfully defended the Catholic tradition against Protestant challenges. Learning from his predecessors how to suppress Jews and Muslims, King Philip II of Spain used an ecclesiastical court, the Spanish Inquisition, to bring into line those who resisted his authority. Suspected Protestants, as well as critics of the king, were accused of heresy, an offense punishable by death. Those who were acquitted learned not to oppose the king again.

In France the Calvinist opponents of the Valois rulers gained the military advantage in the French Wars of Religion (1562–1598), but in the interest of forging lasting unity, their leader Prince Henry of Navarre then embraced the Catholic faith of the majority of his subjects. The Bourbon king who followed him, Henry IV, his son King Louis XIII, and his grandson King Louis XIV supported the Catholic

Political Craft and Craftiness

Political power was becoming more highly concentrated in early modern Europe, but absolute dominance was more a goal than a reality. Whether subject to constitutional checks or not, rulers were very concerned with creating and maintaining good relations with their more powerful subjects. Their efforts to manipulate public opinion and perceptions have much in common with the efforts of modern politicians to manage their "image."

A diplomat and civil servant in the rich and powerful Italian city-state of Florence, Niccolò Machiavelli, is best known for his book The Prince *(1532). This influential essay on the proper exercise of political power has been interpreted as cynical by some and as supremely practical and realistic by others. Because Machiavelli did not have a high opinion of the intelligence and character of most people, he urged rulers to achieve obedience by fear and deception. But he also suggested that genuine mercy, honesty, and piety may be superior to feigned virtue.*

Of Cruelty and Clemency, and Whether It Is Better to Be Loved Than Feared

It will naturally be answered that it would be desirable to be both the one and the other; but, as it is difficult to be both at the same time, it is much safer to be feared than to be loved, when you have to choose between the two. For it may be said of men in general that they are ungrateful and fickle, dissemblers, avoiders of danger, and greedy of gain. So long as you shower benefits on them, they are all yours; they offer you their blood, their substance, their lives, and their children, provided the necessity for it is far off; but when it is near at hand, then they revolt. And the prince who relies on their words, without having otherwise provided for his security, is ruined; for friendships that are won by rewards, not by greatness and nobility of soul, although deserved, yet are not real, and cannot be depended upon in time of adversity.

Besides, men have less hesitation in offending one who makes himself beloved than one who makes himself feared; for love holds by a bond of obligation which, as mankind is bad, is broken on every occasion whenever it is for the interest of the obligated party to break it. But fear holds by the apprehension of punishment, which never leaves men. A prince, however, should make himself feared in such a manner that, if he has not won the affection of his people, he shall at least not incur their hatred.

In What Manner Princes Should Keep Their Faith

It must be evident to every one that it is more praiseworthy for a prince always to maintain good faith, and practice integrity rather than craft and deceit. And yet the experience of our own times has shown those princes have achieved great things who made small account of good faith, and who understood by cunning to circumvent the intelligence of others; and that in the end they got the better of those whose actions were dictated by loyalty and good faith. You must know, therefore, that there are two ways of carrying on a struggle; one by law and the other by force. The first is practiced by men, and the other by animals; and as the first is often insufficient, it becomes necessary to resort to the second.

. . . If men were altogether good, this advice would be wrong; but since they are bad and will not keep faith with you, you need not keep faith with them. Nor will a prince ever be short of legitimate excuses to give color to his breaches of faith. Innumerable modern examples could be given of this; and it could easily be shown how many treaties of peace, and how many engagements, have been made null and void by the faithlessness of princes; and he who has best known how to play the fox has ever been the most successful.

But it is necessary that the prince should know how to color this nature well, and how to be a great hypocrite and dissembler. For men are so simple, and yield so much to immediate necessity, that the deceiver will never lack dupes. I will mention one of the most recent examples. [Pope] Alexander VI never did nor ever thought of anything but to deceive, and always found a reason for doing so . . . and yet he was always successful in his deceits, because he knew the weakness of men in that particular.

It is not necessary, however, for a prince to possess all the above-mentioned qualities; but it is essential that he should at least seem to have them. I will even venture to say, that to have and practice them constantly is pernicious, but to seem to have them is useful. For instance, a prince should seem to be merciful, faithful, humane, religious, and upright, and should even be so in reality; but he should have his mind so trained that, when occasion requires it, he may know how to change to the opposite.

431

And it must be understood that a prince, and especially one who has but recently acquired his state, cannot perform all those things which cause men to be esteemed as good; he being obligated, for the sake of maintaining his state, to act contrary to humanity, charity, and religion. And therefore, it is necessary that he should have a versatile mind, capable of changing readily, according as the winds and changes of fortune bid him; and, as has been said above, not to swerve from the good if possible, but to know how to resort to evil if necessity demands it.

A prince then should be very careful never to allow anything to escape his lips that does not abound in the abovementioned five qualities, so that to see and to hear him he may seem all charity, integrity, and humanity, all uprightness and all piety. And more than all else is it necessary for a prince to seem to possess the last quality; for mankind in general judge more by what they see than by what they feel, every one being capable of the former, and few of the latter. Everybody sees what you seem to be, but few really feel what you are; and those few dare not oppose the opinion of the many, who are protected by the majority of the state; for the actions of all men, and especially those of princes, are judged by the result, where there is no other judge to whom to appeal.

A prince should look mainly to the successful maintenance of his state. For the means which he employs for this will always be counted honorable, and will be praised by everybody; for the common people are always taken in by appearances and by results, and it is the vulgar mass that constitutes the world.

*B*ecause, as Machiavelli argued, appearances count for as much in the public arena as realities, it is difficult to judge whether rulers' statements expressed their real feelings and beliefs or what may have been the most expedient to say at the moment. An example is this speech Queen Elizabeth of England made at the end of November 1601 to Parliament after a particularly difficult year. One senior noble had led a rebellion and was subsequently executed. Parliament was pressing for extended privileges. Having gained the throne in 1558 after many difficulties (including a time in prison), the sixty-eight-year-old queen had much experience in the language and wiles of politics and was well aware of the importance of public opinion. Reprinted many times, the speech became famous as "The Golden Speech of Queen Elizabeth."

I do assure you, there is no prince that loveth his subjects better, or whose love can countervail our love. There is no jewel, be it of never so rich a price, which I set before this jewel: I mean your love. For I do esteem it more than any treasure or riches; for that we know how to prize, but love and thanks I count invaluable.

And, though God has raised me high, yet this I count the glory of my crown, that I have reigned with your loves. This makes me that I do not so much rejoice that God hath made me to be a Queen, as to be Queen over so thankful a people.

Therefore, I have cause to wish nothing more than to content the subjects; and that is the duty I owe. Neither do I desire to live longer days than I may see your prosperity; and that is my only desire.

And as I am that person that still (yet under God) has delivered you, so I trust, by the almighty power of God, that I shall be His instrument to preserve you from every peril, dishonour, shame, tyranny, and oppression. . . .

Of myself I must say this: I was never any greedy scraping grasper, nor a straight, fast-holding prince, nor yet a waster. My heart was never set on worldly goods, but only for my subjects' good. What you bestow on me, I will not hoard it up, but receive it to bestow on you again. Yea, mine own properties I count yours, and to be expended for your good. . . .

To be a king and wear a crown is a thing more glorious to them that see it, than it is pleasing to them that bear it. For myself, I was never so much enticed with the glorious name of king, or royal authority of a queen, as delighted that God made me his instrument to maintain his truth and glory, and to defend this Kingdom (as I said) from peril, dishonour, tyranny and oppression.

There will never Queen sit in my seat with more zeal to my country, care for my subjects, and that sooner with willingness will venture her life for your good and safety than myself. For it is not my desire to live nor reign longer than my life and reign shall be for your good. And though you have had and may have many more princes more mighty and wise sitting in this state, yet you never had or shall have any that will be more careful and loving. Shall I ascribe anything to myself and my sexly weakness? I were not worthy to live then; and of all, most unworthy of the great mercies I have had from God, who has even yet given me a heart, which never feared foreign or home enemy. I speak to give God the praise. . . . That I should speak for any glory, God forbid.

QUESTIONS FOR ANALYSIS

1. **Do you find Machiavelli's advice to be cynical or realistic?**

2. **Describe how a member of Parliament might have responded to Queen Elizabeth's declarations of her concern for the welfare of her people above all else.**

3. **Can a ruler be sincere and manipulative at the same time?**

Source: From *The Historical, Political, and Diplomatic Writings of Niccolo Machiavelli*, trans. Christian E. Detmold (Boston: Houghton Mifflin and Company, 1891), II: 54–59; and Heywood Townshend, *Historical Collections, or an Exact Account of the Proceedings of the Last Four Parliaments of Q. Elizabeth* (London: Basset, Crooke, and Cademan, 1680), 263–266.

Church as ardently as the Spanish kings did. In 1685 Louis XIV even revoked the Edict of Nantes (nahnt), by which his grandfather had granted the Protestants religious freedom in 1598.

In England King Henry VIII initially defended the papacy against Lutheran criticism. But when the pope refused to annul his marriage to Catherine of Aragon, who had not produced a male heir, Henry ordered the English archbishop of Canterbury to annul the marriage in 1533. The breach with Rome was sealed the next year when Parliament made the English monarch head of the Church of England.

Like many Protestant rulers, Henry disbanded monasteries and convents and seized their lands. He gave some lands to his powerful allies and sold others to pay for his new navy. Yet the ritual and theology of the new Anglican Church resembled their Catholic counterparts too closely to satisfy English Puritans (Calvinists who wanted to "purify" the Anglican Church of Catholic practices and beliefs). In 1603 the first Stuart king, James I, dismissed a Puritan petition to eliminate bishops with the statement "No bishops, no king"—a reminder of the essential role of the church in supporting royal power.

Monarchies in England and France

Over the course of the seventeenth century, the rulers of England and France contested with their leading subjects over the limits of royal authority. Religion was never absent in these struggles, but the different constitutional outcomes were more significant in the long run.

To evade any check on his power, King Charles I of England (see Table 15.1) ruled for eleven years without summoning Parliament, his kingdom's representative body. Lacking Parliament's consent to new taxes, he raised funds by coercing "loans" from wealthy subjects and applying existing tax laws more broadly. Then in 1640 a rebellion in Scotland forced him to summon a Parliament to approve new taxes to pay for an army. Noblemen and churchmen sat in the House of Lords. Representatives from the towns and counties sat in the House of Commons. Before it would authorize new taxes, Parliament insisted on strict guarantees that the king would never again ignore the body's traditional rights. Charles refused. When he ordered the arrest of his leading critics in the House of Commons in 1642, he plunged the kingdom into the **English Civil War**.

Even after defeat on the battlefield, Charles refused to compromise. In 1649 a "Rump" Parliament (one purged of his supporters) ordered him executed and replaced the monarchy with a republic under Oliver Cromwell, a Puritan general. Cromwell expanded England's presence overseas and imposed firm control over Ireland and Scotland, but he was as unwilling as the Stuart kings to share power with Parliament. After his death Parliament restored the Stuart line, making it unclear, for a time, which side had won the war.

King James II clarified matters when he refused to respect Parliament's rights and had his heir baptized a Roman Catholic. Parliament responded by forcing James into exile in the bloodless coup known as "the Glorious Revolution of 1688." The Bill of Rights of 1689 specified that Parliament had to be called frequently and had to consent to changes in laws and to the raising of an army in peacetime. Another law reaffirmed the official status of the Church of England but extended religious toleration to the Puritans.

English Civil War (1642–1648)
A conflict over royal versus parliamentary rights, caused by King Charles I's arrest of his parliamentary critics and ending with his execution. Its outcome checked the growth of royal absolutism and, with the Glorious Revolution of 1688 and the English Bill of Rights of 1689, ensured that England would be a constitutional monarchy.

TABLE 15.1 | RULERS IN EARLY MODERN WESTERN EUROPE

SPAIN	FRANCE	ENGLAND/GREAT BRITAIN
HABSBURG DYNASTY	VALOIS DYNASTY	TUDOR DYNASTY
Charles I (1516–1556) (Holy Roman Emperor Charles V) Philip II (1556–1598)	Francis I (1515–1547) Henry II (1547–1559) Francis II (1559–1560) Charles IX (1560–1574) Henry III (1574–1589)	Henry VIII (1509–1547) Edward VI (1547–1553) Mary I (1553–1558) Elizabeth I (1558–1603)
	BOURBON DYNASTY	STUART DYNASTY
Philip III (1598–1621) Philip IV (1621–1665) Charles II (1665–1700)	Henry IV (1589–1610)[a] Louis XIII (1610–1643) Louis XIV (1643–1715)	James I (1603–1625) Charles I (1625–1649) [a,b] (Puritan Republic, 1649–1660) Charles II (1660–1685) James II (1685–1688)[b] William III (1689–1702) and Mary II (1689–1694) Anne (1702–1714)
BOURBON DYNASTY		HANOVERIAN DYNASTY
Philip V (1700–1746)		
	Louis XV (1715–1774)	George I (1714–1727)
Ferdinand VI (1746–1759)		George II (1727–1760)

[a] Died a violent death.   [b] Was overthrown.

Versailles The huge palace built for French King Louis XIV south of Paris in the town of the same name. The palace symbolized the preeminence of French power and architecture in Europe and the triumph of royal authority over the French nobility.

A similar struggle in France produced a different outcome. There the Estates General represented the traditional rights of the clergy, the nobility, and the towns (that is, the bourgeoisie). The Estates General had asserted its rights during the sixteenth-century French Wars of Religion, when the monarchy was weak. But thereafter the Bourbon monarchs generally ruled without calling it into session. They avoided financial crises by more efficient tax collection and by selling appointments to high government offices. In justification they claimed that the monarch had absolute authority to rule in God's name.

Louis XIV's gigantic new palace at **Versailles** (vuhr-SIGH) symbolized the monarch's triumph over the nobility, clergy, and towns. Capable of housing ten thousand people and surrounded by elaborately landscaped grounds and parks, the palace was a sort of theme park of royal absolutism. Elaborate ceremonies and banquets centered on the king deterred the nobles who lived at Versailles from plotting rebellion. According to one of them, the duke of Saint-Simon (san-see-MOHN), "no one was so clever in devising petty distractions" as the king.

Most European rulers admired and imitated the centralized powers and absolutist claims of the French until well after 1750. Some built imitations of Versailles. The English model of balanced powers gained influence more slowly. In his *Second Treatise of Civil Government* (1690), the English political philosopher John Locke

Versailles, 1722

This painting by P.-D. Martin shows the east expanse of buildings and courtyards that make up the palace complex built by King Louis XIV.

(Giraudon/Art Resource, NY)

CL HISTORY IN FOCUS
Look closely at how this scene is laid out—that is, the relationship between the individual buildings and the open spaces. Try also to pick out a few of the architectural features: windows, doorways/gates, sculptures, and so forth. What does the layout of the palace and its features suggest about the artistic values that prevailed under Louis XIV's absolutist monarchy? *Find the answer online.*

(1632–1704) disputed monarchial claims to absolute authority by divine right. Rather, he argued, rulers derived their authority from the consent of the governed and, like everyone else, were subject to the law. If monarchs overstepped the law, citizens had not only the right but also the duty to rebel.

Warfare and Diplomacy

In addition to their bitter civil wars, European monarchies engaged in numerous international conflicts. Warfare was almost constant (see the Chronology at the beginning of the chapter). The worst of the international conflicts, the Thirty Years War (1618–1648), caused long-lasting depopulation and economic decline in much of the Holy Roman Empire.

Not surprisingly, weaponry and war-making skills improved dramatically, making European armed forces the most powerful in the world. The numbers of men in arms increased steadily. French forces, for example, grew from about 150,000 in 1630 to 400,000 by the early eighteenth century. Sweden, with under a million people, had one of the best-armed military forces in seventeenth-century Europe. Prussia, a country with fewer than 2 million inhabitants in 1700, had an army that made it a major power.

Larger armies required better command structures. As a modern historian remarked, European armies "evolved . . . the equivalent of a central nervous system, capable of activating technologically differentiated claws and teeth."[3] New signaling techniques improved battlefield maneuvers. Frequent marching drills trained troops to obey orders instantly and gave them a close sense of comradeship. Since battles between evenly matched armies often ended in prolonged stalemates, victory increasingly depended on naval superiority.

England alone did without a peacetime standing army, but England's rise as a sea power had begun under King Henry VIII, who spent heavily on ships and promoted a domestic iron-smelting industry to supply cannon. The Royal Navy also copied innovative ship designs from the Dutch. By the early eighteenth century the Royal Navy surpassed the rival French fleet in numbers. By then, England had merged with Scotland to become Great Britain, annexed Ireland, and built a North American empire.

Although France was Europe's most powerful state, Louis XIV's efforts to expand were increasingly frustrated by coalitions of other powers. In a series of eighteenth-century wars beginning with the War of the Spanish Succession (1701–1714), the combination of Britain's naval strength and the land armies of its Austrian and Prussian allies blocked French ambitions and prevented the Bourbons from uniting the thrones of France and Spain.

balance of power The policy in international relations by which, beginning in the eighteenth century, the major European states acted together to prevent any one of them from becoming too powerful.

France's defeat illustrates the principle of **balance of power** in international relations: the major European states formed temporary alliances to prevent any one state from becoming too powerful. Russia emerged as a major power after its modernized armies defeated Sweden in the Great Northern War (1700–1721). During the next two centuries, though adhering to four different branches of Christianity, the great powers of Europe—Catholic France, Anglican Britain, Catholic Austria, Lutheran Prussia, and Orthodox Russia (see Map 15.2)—maintained an effective balance of power by shifting their alliances for geopolitical rather than religious reasons. These pragmatic alliances were the first successful efforts at international peacekeeping.

Paying the Piper

European rulers needed revenue to pay for their wars. The most successful of them after 1600 allied with the rising commercial elite. Both sides understood that trade thrived where government taxation and regulation were not excessive, where courts enforced contracts and collected debts, and where military power protected overseas expansion.

Spain, sixteenth-century Europe's mightiest state, illustrates how the financial drains of an aggressive military policy and the failure to promote economic development could lead to decline. Expensive wars against the Ottomans, northern European Protestants, and rebellious Dutch subjects caused the treasury to default on its debts four times during the reign of King Philip II. Insistence on religious uniformity and aristocratic privilege further undermined the economy. In the name of religious uniformity the rulers expelled Jewish merchants, persecuted Protestant dissenters, and forced tens of thousands of farmers and artisans into exile because of their Muslim ancestry. In the name of aristocratic privilege the 3 percent of the population that controlled 97 percent of the land in 1600 was exempt from taxation. Yet high sales taxes discouraged manufacturing.

Vast imports of silver and gold bullion from Spain's American colonies filled the government treasury, but they also triggered severe inflation (rising prices) in Spain

Map 15.2 Europe in 1740

By the middle of the eighteenth century the great powers of Europe were France, the Austrian Empire, Great Britain, Prussia, and Russia. Spain, the Holy Roman Empire, and the Ottoman Empire were far weaker in 1740 than they had been two centuries earlier.

Ruled by Bourbons
Ruled by Habsburgs
Boundary of Holy Roman Empire

and throughout the rest of Europe. As a Spanish saying put it: American silver was like rain on the roof—it poured down and washed away. Huge debts for foreign wars drained bullion from Spain to its creditors. More wealth flowed out to purchase manufactured goods and even food in the seventeenth century.

Opposite policies supported the rise of the Netherlands as an economic power. The Spanish crown had acquired the Netherlands as part of Charles V's inheritance. But King Philip II's decision to impose Spain's ruinously heavy sales tax and enforce Catholic orthodoxy drove the Dutch to revolt in 1566 and again in 1572. If successful, those measures would have discouraged business and driven away the Calvinists, Jews, and other key contributors to Dutch prosperity. The Dutch raised and trained an army and a navy that were among the most effective in Europe. In 1609 Spain agreed to a truce that recognized the autonomy of the northern part of the Netherlands. In 1648, after eight decades of warfare, the independence of these seven United Provinces of the Free Netherlands (their full name) became final.

Rather than being ruined by the long war, the United Netherlands emerged as the dominant commercial power in Europe and the world's greatest trading nation. This economic success owed much to a decentralized government. During the struggle against Spain, the provinces united around the prince of Orange, their sovereign and commander-in-chief. But in economic matters each province pursued its own interests. The maritime province of Holland grew rich by favoring commercial interests.

After 1650 the Dutch faced growing competition from England, where business was also allied with government. In a series of wars (1652–1678) England's naval might broke Dutch dominance in overseas trade. With government support, the English merchant fleet doubled between 1660 and 1700, and foreign trade rose by 50 percent. State revenue from customs duties tripled. During the eighteenth century Britain's trading position strengthened still more.

The debts run up by the Anglo-Dutch Wars persuaded the English monarchy to enlarge the government's role in managing the economy. The outcome has been called a "financial revolution." The government increased revenues by taxing the formerly exempt landed estates of the aristocrats and by collecting taxes directly. Previously, private individuals known as tax farmers had advanced the government a fixed sum of money; in return they could keep whatever money they were able to collect from taxpayers. England also followed the Dutch lead in creating a central bank, from which the government was able to obtain long-term loans at low rates.

Under the leadership of Colbert, the French too experienced economic development. He streamlined tax collection, promoted French manufacturing and shipping by imposing taxes on foreign goods, and improved inland transportation. Yet the power of the wealthy aristocrats kept the French government from following England's lead in taxing wealthy landowners, collecting taxes directly, and securing low-cost loans. Nor did France succeed in managing its debt as efficiently as England.

SECTION REVIEW

- Greater political centralization enabled early modern monarchs to exert considerable influence on economic, religious, and social life.

- While the Holy Roman Empire fragmented along religious and political lines, Spain, France, and England achieved greater centralization and religious unity.

- Spain enforced Catholic unity through the Inquisition and France through Bourbon policy, while in England the church became an arm of royal power.

- In both England and France, monarchs struggled with other powers over the limits of royal authority.

- Armies grew larger and more sophisticated, and through diplomacy and nearly constant warfare, the European powers strove to maintain the balance of power.

- High military costs drove the European powers to attempt a variety of tax and financial policies, the most successful being those of England and the Netherlands.

COMPARATIVE PERSPECTIVES

European historians have used the word *revolution* to describe many different changes taking place in Europe between 1500 and 1750. The expansion of trade has been called a commercial revolution, the reform of state spending a financial revolution, and the changes in weapons and warfare a military revolution. We have also encountered a scientific revolution and the religious revolution of the Reformation.

Yet the years from 1500 to 1750 were not simply—perhaps not even primarily—an age of progress for Europe. For many, the ferocious competition of European armies, merchants, and ideas was a wrenching experience. The growth of powerful states exacted a terrible price in death, destruction, and misery. The Reformation brought greater individual choice in religion but widespread persecution as well. The expanding economy benefited the emerging merchant elite and their political allies, but most Europeans became worse off as prices rose faster than wages. New scientific and enlightened ideas ignited controversies long before they yielded any tangible benefits.

The historical significance of this period of European history is clearer when viewed in a global context. What stands out are the powerful and efficient European armies, economies, and governments. From a global perspective, the balance of political and economic power was shifting slowly, but inexorably, in the Europeans' favor. In 1500 the Ottomans threatened Europe. By 1750, Europeans had brought the world's seas and a growing portion of its lands and peoples under their control. No single group of Europeans accomplished this. The Dutch eclipsed the pioneering Portuguese and Spanish; then the English and French bested the Dutch. Competition, too, was a factor in European success.

Chapter Review

 DOWNLOAD THE MP3 AUDIO FILE OF THE CHAPTER REVIEW TO LISTEN TO ON THE GO.

How was the cultural history of early modern Europe determined by the interplay of traditional beliefs and revolutionary ideas? (page 415)

Early modern Europe underwent the Scientific Revolution as well as the fragmentation of the Catholic Church. Traditional antifeminist beliefs and pagan folklore about witchcraft fed a witch-hunting craze that took thousands of lives. Supporting the belief in witchcraft was a more fundamental idea that human misfortune could be blamed on supernatural forces, but this idea was powerfully challenged by pioneers of the Scientific Revolution such as Copernicus and Newton, who showed that the workings of the physical universe could be explained in natural terms. These scientists did not see any conflict between science and religion, and they paved the way for influential figures of the Enlightenment, who believed that human reason was capable of discovering the laws that govern social behavior.

KEY TERMS

Renaissance (European) *(p. 414)*
papacy *(p. 415)*
indulgence *(p. 416)*
Protestant Reformation *(p. 416)*
Catholic Reformation *(p. 418)*
witch-hunt *(p. 418)*
Scientific Revolution *(p. 421)*
Enlightenment *(p. 423)*
bourgeoisie *(p. 424)*
joint-stock company *(p. 425)*
stock exchange *(p. 425)*

(Continued)

What factors contributed to the wealth of some Europeans and the great poverty of others? (page 423)

Thanks to foreign and domestic trade, European cities experienced rapid growth and the rise of a wealthy commercial class. The Netherlands in particular prospered from expanded manufacturing and trade. For peasants and laborers, however, life did not improve much: serfdom ended in western Europe but rose in eastern Europe. Agricultural techniques had not improved since medieval times, and deforestation brought great difficulties to the poor. Rural poverty, coupled with aristocratic exemption from taxation, sparked numerous armed rebellions.

How did differing policies on religion, foreign relations, and economics influence the history of early modern European states? (page 429)

Monarchs like Charles V of the Holy Roman Empire and Louis XIV of France impressed contemporaries with their military might and aggressive ambitions. In the long run, however, tolerance of religious diversity and cooperation between rulers and the rising class of merchants brought a country greater success. The Netherlands, a group of provinces marked by their religious tolerance, won independence from their intolerant Spanish overlord and went on to become Europe's most prosperous trading nation. England endured a civil war based on religious disagreement and conflict between kings and Parliament but eventually rose to contest the maritime supremacy of the Dutch. Here too religious tolerance and collaboration between merchants and the Crown proved a winning combination.

SUGGESTED READING

Bergin, Joseph. *The Short Oxford History of Europe: The Seventeenth Century*. 2001. A general overview.

Braudel, Fernand. *Civilization and Capitalism, 15th–18th Century*. Trans. Siân Reynolds. 3 vols. 1992. A sweeping interpretation by an eminent historian.

Casey, James. *Early Modern Spain: A Social History*. 1999. A general look at an important country.

Cipolla, Carlo M. *Before the Industrial Revolution: European Society and Economy, 1000–1700*. 3d ed. 1993. An excellent introduction to social and economic life.

Fagan, Brian. *The Little Ice Age: How Climate Made History, 1300–1850*. 2000. An important episode in climate history.

Israel, Jonathan. *The Dutch Republic: Its Rise, Greatness and Fall, 1477–1806*. 1995. Study of a key country.

Jütte, Robert. *Poverty and Deviance in Early Modern Europe*. 1994. Looks at nonelite perspectives.

Le Roy Ladurie, Emmanuel. *The Royal French State, 1460–1610*. Trans. Juliet Vale. 1994. *The Ancien Régime: A History of France, 1610–1774*. Trans. Mark Greengrass. 1996. A two-volume look at a key country by an eminent historian.

Levack, Brian P. *The Witch-Hunt in Early Modern Europe*. 2d ed. 1995. A good starting point for studying Europe's obsession with witchcraft.

Outram, Dorinda. *The Enlightenment*. 2d ed. 2005. Provides a recent summary of research.

Parker, Geoffrey. *Military Revolution: Military Innovation and the Rise of the West, 1500–1800*. 2d ed. 1996. Technological development in a violent era.

Shapin, Steven. *The Scientific Revolution*. 1996. An accessible introduction.

---

gentry *(p. 426)*

Little Ice Age *(p. 427)*

deforestation *(p. 427)*

Holy Roman Empire *(p. 430)*

Habsburg *(p. 430)*

English Civil War *(p. 433)*

Versailles *(p. 434)*

balance of power *(p. 436)*

WEB RESOURCES

Pronunciation Guide

Interactive Maps

  MAP 15.1 Religion Reformation in Europe

Primary Sources

  Table Talk

  Letter to the Grand Duchess Christina

  Treatise on Tolerance

Answer to the History in Focus Question

  See photo on page 435, "Versailles, 1722."

Plus

  Chapter Objectives

  ACE multiple-choice quiz

  Flashcards

Sharpe, J. A. *Early Modern England: A Social History, 1550–1760*. 2d ed. 1997. A good single-country survey.

Wallerstein, Immanuel. *The Modern World-System*. vol. 2. *Mercantilism and the Consolidation of the European World-Economy, 1600–1750*. 1980. Presents an influential economic theory of Europe's relation to the world.

Wiesner, Merry E. *Women and Gender in Early Modern Europe*. 2d ed. 2000. Examines topics in women's history.

NOTES

1. Quoted by Carlo M. Cipolla, "Introduction," *The Fontana Economic History of Europe*, vol. 2, *The Sixteenth and Seventeenth Centuries* (Glasgow: Collins/Fontana Books, 1974), 11–12.
2. Michel de Montaigne, *Essais* (1588), ch. 31, "Des Cannibales."
3. William H. McNeill, *The Pursuit of Power: Technology, Armed Force, and Society Since A.D. 1000* (Chicago: University of Chicago Press, 1982), 124.

CHAPTER 16

The Americas, the Atlantic, and Africa

1530–1770

CHAPTER PREVIEW

Because of their long isolation from other continents, the peoples of the New World lacked immunity to diseases introduced from the Old World by explorers and settlers. Smallpox arrived in the Caribbean in 1518, killing most of the native peoples there. Smallpox was then spread to the mainland by the conquest of the Aztecs and Incas. Fifty percent or more of the mainland Amerindian population died after repeated epidemics. Other diseases added to the toll: measles in the 1530s, followed by diphtheria, typhus, influenza, and perhaps pulmonary plague. By the mid-seventeenth century, malaria and yellow fever were also present in tropical regions. When between 1520 and 1521 influenza and other ailments attacked the Cakchiquel of Guatemala, their chronicler recalled:

 This icon will direct you to the website where you can Prepare for Class, Improve Your Grade, and Ace the Test: college.cengage.com/pic/bullietbrief4e

Great was the stench of the dead. After our fathers and grandfathers succumbed, half the people fled to the fields. The dogs and vultures devoured the bodies. . . . So it was that we became orphans, oh my sons! . . . We were born to die![1]

The development of English and French colonies in North America in the seventeenth century led to similar patterns of contagion and mortality. In 1616 and 1617, epidemics nearly exterminated many of New England's indigenous groups. French fur traders transmitted measles, smallpox, and other diseases as far as Hudson Bay and the Great Lakes.

Although there is very little evidence that Europeans consciously used disease as a tool of empire, the deadly results of contact clearly undermined the ability of native peoples to resist European settlement. Europeans and their African slaves occupied these depopulated lands. Transformed biologically and culturally, the Americas were subjected to Europeans' political and economic demands.

The colonies of the Americas were crucial pieces of a new **Atlantic system**. This network of trading links moved people and cultures as well as goods and wealth around the Atlantic. The Atlantic system also affected Africa, but less severely than the Americas. Despite the loss of millions of people to the slave trade, Africa did not suffer such severe population loss due to epidemics as the Americas. Most important, Africans remained in control of their lands.

Atlantic system The network of trading links after 1500 that moved goods, wealth, people, and cultures around the Atlantic Ocean Basin.

Amerindians, Europeans, and Africans all contributed to the creation of new cultures in the Americas. The societies that arose reflected each colony's mix of native peoples, its connections to the slave trade, and the policies of its European rulers.

SPANISH AMERICA AND BRAZIL

What role did forced labor play in the main industries in Spanish America and Brazil?

Within one hundred years of Columbus's first voyage to the Western Hemisphere, the Spanish Empire in America included most of the islands of the Caribbean, Mexico, the American Southwest, Central America, the Caribbean and Pacific coasts of South America, the Andean highlands, and the vast plains of the Río de la Plata region (a region that includes the modern nations of Argentina, Uruguay, and Paraguay). Portuguese settlement in the New World developed more slowly. But before the end of the sixteenth century, Portugal occupied most of the Brazilian coast.

Early settlers from Spain and Portugal sought to create colonial societies based on the institutions and customs of their homelands. They viewed society as a vertical arrangement of estates (classes of society), as uniformly Catholic, and as an arrangement of patriarchal extended-family networks. Despite the imposition of foreign institutions and the massive loss of life caused by epidemics, indigenous peoples still exercised a powerful influence on the development of colonial societies. Aztec and Inca elite families sought to protect their traditional privileges and rights through marriage or less formal alliances with the Spanish settlers. They also often used colonial courts to defend their claims to land. Nearly everywhere, Amerindian religious beliefs and practices survived beneath the surface of an imposed Christianity. Amerindian languages, cuisine, medical practices, and agricultural techniques also survived the conquest and influenced the development of Latin American culture.

The African slave trade added a third cultural stream to colonial Latin American society. By the end of the colonial era, Africans and their descendants were living throughout Latin America, enriching colonial societies with their traditional agricultural practices, music, religious beliefs, cuisine, and social customs.

State and Church

The Spanish crown moved quickly to curb the independent power of the conquistadors and establish royal authority over both the defeated native populations and the rising tide of European settlers. Created in 1524, the **Council of the Indies** in Spain supervised all government, ecclesiastical, and commercial activity in the Spanish colonies. Political and economic power was concentrated in Mexico City, capital of the Viceroyalty of New Spain (created in 1535), and in Lima, capital of the Viceroyalty of Peru (created in the 1540s). Each viceroyalty was divided into a number of judicial and administrative districts. Until the seventeenth century, almost all of the officials appointed to high positions in Spain's colonial bureaucracy were born in Spain. Later, local-born members of the colonial elite gained many offices.

In the sixteenth century, Portugal concentrated its resources and energies on Asia and Africa, because early settlers found neither mineral wealth nor rich native empires in Brazil. Finally, the king appointed a governor-general in 1549 and designated Salvador, in the northern province of Bahia, Brazil's capital. In 1720, the first viceroy of Brazil was named (see Map 16.1).

Just as these colonial bureaucracies imposed Iberian economic and political institutions, the Catholic Church became the primary agent for the introduction and transmission of Christian belief and European culture in South America. Spain and Portugal justified their American conquests by assuming an obligation to convert native populations to Christianity. In Mexico alone, hundreds of thousands of conversions and baptisms were achieved within a few years of the conquest.

The Catholic clergy sought to win over the Amerindians by converting native elites. But these efforts were abandoned when church authorities discovered that many converts were secretly observing old beliefs and rituals. As Amerindian populations declined from the effects of epidemics, priests in both Spanish America and Brazil forced native populations to relocate, often worsening the disease mortality. At times priests used forced conversions, such as in the 1560s among the Maya. Repelled by these excesses, the Church ended both the violent repression of native religious practice and ambitious efforts to recruit Amerindians for the clergy.

Despite its failures, the Catholic clergy did provide native peoples with some protections against the abuse and exploitation of settlers. For example, the priest **Bartolomé de Las Casas** (1474–1566) was an important advocate for native peoples. His most important achievement was the enactment of the New Laws of 1542, which outlawed the enslavement of Amerindians and limited other forms of forced labor in the Spanish colonies.

Despite European disapproval, Amerindians blended Catholic Christian beliefs with important elements of traditional native cosmology and ritual. Most commonly, indigenous beliefs and rituals came to be embedded in the celebration of saints' days or Catholic rituals associated with the Virgin Mary. This cultural borrowing and innovation contributed to a distinct and original Latin American culture.

Council of the Indies The institution responsible for supervising Spain's colonies in the Americas from 1524 to the early eighteenth century, when it lost all but judicial responsibilities.

CL Primary Source: A Dominican Voice in the Wilderness: Preaching Against Tyranny in Hispaniola *Listen to the story of one friar who bravely speaks out against the brutality of the Spanish toward the native people of Hispaniola.*

Bartolomé de Las Casas (1474–1566) First bishop of Chiapas, in southern Mexico. He devoted most of his life to protecting Amerindian peoples from exploitation. His major achievement was the New Laws of 1542, which limited the ability of Spanish settlers to compel Amerindians to labor for them.

Chronology

	Latin America	North America	West Indies	Atlantic
1500			**ca. 1500** Spanish settlers introduce sugar-cane cultivation	
	1518 Smallpox arrives in Caribbean	**1524–1554** French explore Newfoundland and Gulf of St. Lawrence		
				1530 Amsterdam Exchange opens
	1535 Creation of Viceroyalty of New Spain			
	1540s Creation of Viceroyalty of Peru			
	1542 New Laws outlaw Amerindian enslavement			
	1545 Silver discovered at Potosí, Bolivia			
1600		**1607** Jamestown founded		
		1608 Quebec founded		
	By 1620 African slaves the majority of Brazilian plantation workers	**1620** Plymouth founded	**1620s and 1630s** English and French colonies in Caribbean	
				1621 Dutch West India Company chartered
			1640s Dutch bring sugar plantation system from Brazil	
			1655 English take Jamaica	
		1660 Slavery in Virginia begins to grow rapidly		**1660s** English Navigation Acts
		1664 English take New York from Dutch		
			1670s French occupy western half of Hispaniola	
				1672 Royal African Company chartered
				1698 French *Exclusif*
		1699 Louisiana founded		
1700	**1713** Beginning of Bourbon dynasty in Spain		**1700** West Indies surpass Brazil in sugar production	**1700–1830** Slave trade at its peak
	1750–1790 Reforms in Brazil and Spanish America	**1756–1763** French and Indian War		

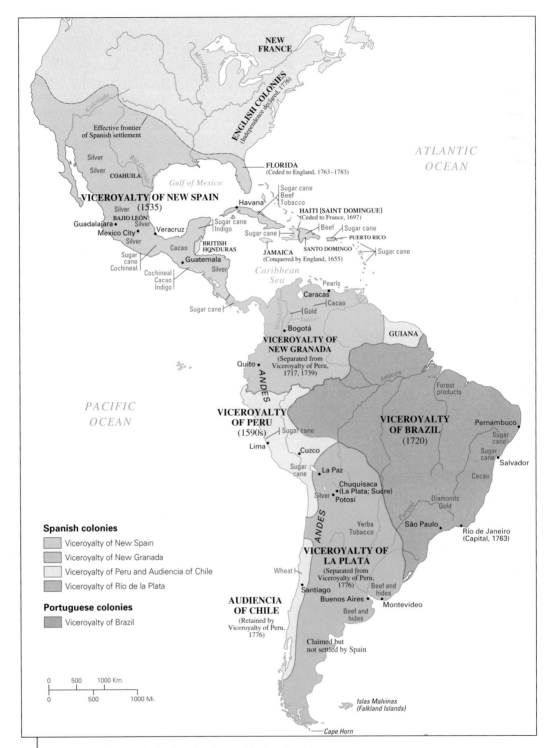

Map 16.1   Colonial Latin America in the Eighteenth Century

Spain and Portugal controlled most of the Western Hemisphere in the eighteenth century. In the sixteenth century they had created new administrative jurisdictions—viceroyalties—to defend their respective colonies against European rivals. Taxes assessed on colonial products helped pay for this extension of governmental authority.

Interactive Map

After 1600, the Catholic Church redirected most of its resources from the countryside to growing colonial cities and towns with large European populations. This altered mission included the founding of universities and secondary schools, which stimulated urban intellectual life.

Colonial Economies

The silver mines of Peru and Mexico and the sugar plantations of Brazil dominated the colonial economy and fueled the early development of European capitalism. Profits produced in these economic centers also promoted the growth of colonial cities, concentrated scarce investment capital and labor resources, and stimulated the development of livestock raising and agriculture in neighboring rural areas. Dependence on mineral and agricultural exports was an enduring theme in Latin America. Although millions of pesos of gold were mined in Latin America, silver mines generated more wealth and exercised greater economic influence. In 1545, the single richest silver deposit in the Americas was discovered at **Potosí** (poh-toh-SEE), in what is now Bolivia, and until 1680 the silver production of Bolivia and Peru dominated the Spanish colonial economy.

Silver mining also greatly altered the environment. Within a short time, wasteful use of forest resources for fuel destroyed forests near the mining centers. Faced with rising fuel costs, miners developed an efficient method of chemical extraction that relied on mixing mercury with the silver ore. But mercury is a poison, and its use contaminated the environment and sickened the Amerindian work force.

From the time of Columbus, indigenous populations had been compelled to provide labor for European settlers in the Americas. Until the 1540s in Spanish

Potosí Located in Bolivia, one of the richest silver mining centers and most populous cities in colonial Spanish America.

Silver Mines at Potosi
This town in Bolivia was founded in 1546 below a mountain with such rich deposits of silver ore that over 45,000 tons of the precious metal were refined and exported over the following two centuries. This drawing shows a water wheel operating the trip-hammers that crushed the ore and the rectangular ponds where the crushed ore was mixed with mercury, which bonded with the silver. Drying the amalgam, as the mixture was called, gave off poisonous mercury fumes that contributed to a high death rate among the workers. (Courtesy, the Hispanic Society of America)

colonies, Amerindian peoples were divided among the settlers and were forced to provide them with labor or with textiles, food, or other goods. This form of forced labor was called the **encomienda** (in-co-mee-EN-dah). The discovery of silver in Peru led to a new form of compulsory labor called the mita (MEE-tah). Under this system, one-seventh of the adult male Amerindians were compelled to work for six months each year in mines or on farms or in textile factories. The most dangerous working conditions existed in the silver mines.

encomienda A grant of authority over a population of Amerindians in the Spanish colonies. It provided the grant holder with a supply of cheap labor and periodic payments of goods by the Amerindians. It obliged the grant holder to Christianize the Amerindians.

In the Spanish mita, few Amerindian workers could survive on their wages. Wives and children were commonly forced to join the work force to help meet expenses. Even those who remained behind in the village were forced to send food and cash to support mita workers.

The Portuguese, who had developed sugar plantations that depended on slave labor on the Atlantic islands of Madeira, the Azores, the Cape Verdes, and São Tomé, transferred this profitable form of agriculture to Brazil. By the seventeenth century, sugar dominated the Brazilian economy. At first, the Portuguese enslaved Amerindians as field hands, but sugar planters eventually came to rely more on African slaves as Amerindian populations fell due to epidemics. Imports of African slaves rose from an average of 2,000 per year in the late sixteenth century to approximately 7,000 per year a century later, far outstripping the immigration of free Portuguese settlers.

The mining centers of Latin America exercised global economic influence. American silver increased the European money supply, promoting commercial expansion. Large amounts of silver also flowed across the Pacific, where it was exchanged for Asian spices, silks, and porcelain.

The sugar plantations of Brazil played a similar role in integrating the economy of the South Atlantic region. At the end of the seventeenth century, the discovery of gold in Brazil helped overcome this large region's currency shortage and promoted further economic integration.

Both Spain and Portugal attempted to control the trade of their American colonies, but the combination of monopoly commerce and convoy shipping slowed the flow of European goods to the colonies and kept prices high. Frustrated by these restraints, colonial populations established illegal commercial relations with the English, French, and Dutch. By the middle of the seventeenth century, a majority of European imports were arriving in Latin America illegally.

Society in Colonial Latin America

With the exception of a few early viceroys, few members of Spain's great noble families came to the New World. *Hidalgos* (ee-DAHL-goes)—lesser nobles—were well represented, as were Spanish merchants, artisans, miners, priests, and lawyers. Small numbers of criminals, beggars, and prostitutes also found their way to the colonies. Spanish settlers, however, were always a tiny minority in a colonial society numerically dominated by Amerindians and rapidly growing populations of Africans, **creoles** (whites born in America to European parents), and people of mixed ancestry (see Diversity and Dominance: Race and Ethnicity in the Spanish Colonies: Negotiating Hierarchy).

creole In colonial Spanish America, term used to describe someone of European descent born in the New World. Elsewhere in the Americas, the term is used to describe all nonnative peoples.

Conquistadors and early settlers who received from the Crown grants of labor and tribute goods (encomienda) from Amerindian communities as rewards for service to Spain sought to create a hereditary social and political class comparable to the nobles

Race and Ethnicity in the Spanish Colonies: Negotiating Hierarchy

*M*any European visitors to colonial Latin America were interested in the mixing of Europeans, Amerindians, and Africans in the colonies. Many also commented on the treatment of slaves. The passages that follow allow us to examine two colonial societies.

The first selection was written by two young Spanish naval officers and scientists, Jorge Juan and Antonio de Ulloa, who arrived in the colonies in 1735 as members of a scientific expedition. They visited the major cities of the Pacific coast of South America and traveled across some of the most difficult terrain in the hemisphere. In addition to performing their scientific chores, they described architecture, local customs, and the social order.

The second selection was published in Lima under the pseudonym Concolorcorvo around 1776. We now know that the author was Alonso Carrío de la Vandera. Born in Spain, he traveled to the colonies as a young man. He served in many minor bureaucratic positions, one of which was the inspection of the postal route between Buenos Aires and Lima. Carrío turned his long and often uncomfortable trip into an insightful, and sometimes highly critical, examination of colonial society.

Juan and Ulloa and Carrío seem perplexed by colonial efforts to create and enforce a racial taxonomy that stipulated and named every possible mixture of European, Amerindian, and African, noting the vanity and social presumptions of the dominant white population. We are fortunate to have these contemporary descriptions of the diversity of colonial society, but it is important to remember that these authors were clearly rooted in their time and confident in the superiority of Europe. Although they noted many of the abuses of Amerindian, mixed, and African populations while puncturing the pretensions of the colonial elites, they were also quick to assume the inferiority of the nonwhite population.

Quito [currently the capital of Ecuador]

This city is very populous, and has, among its inhabitants, some families of high rank and distinction; though their number is but small considering its extent, the poorer class bearing here too great a proportion. The former are the descendants either of the original conquerors, or of presidents, auditors, or other persons of character [high rank], who at different times came over from Spain invested with some lucrative post, and have still preserved their luster, both of wealth and descent, by intermarriages, without intermixing with meaner families though famous for their riches. The commonalty may be divided into four classes: Spaniards or Whites, Mestizos, Indians or Natives, and Negroes, with their progeny. These last are not proportionally so numerous as in the other parts of the Indies; occasioned by it being something inconvenient to bring Negroes to Quito, and the different kinds of agriculture being generally performed by Indians.

The name of Spaniard here has a different meaning from that of Chapitone [sic] or European, as properly signifying a person descended from a Spaniard without a mixture of blood. Many Mestizos, from the advantage of a fresh complexion, appear to be Spaniards more than those who are so in reality; and from only this fortuitous advantage are accounted as such. The Whites, according to this construction of the word, may be considered as one sixth part of the inhabitants.

The Mestizos are the descendants of Spaniards and Indians, and are to be considered here in the same different degrees between the Negroes and Whites, as before at Carthagena [sic]; but with this difference, that at Quito the degrees of Mestizos are not carried so far back; for, even in the second or third generations, when they acquire the European color, they are considered as Spaniards. The complexion of the Mestizos is swarthy and reddish, but not of that red common in the fair Mulattos. This is the first degree, or the immediate issue of a Spaniard and Indian. Some are, however, equally tawny with the Indians themselves, though they are distinguished from them by their beards: while others, on the contrary, have so fine a complexion that they might pass for Whites, were it not for some signs which betray them, when viewed attentively. Among these, the most remarkable is the lowness of the forehead, which often leaves but a small space between their hair and eye-brows; at the same time the hair grows remarkably forward on the temples, extending to the lower part of the ear. Besides, the hair itself is harsh, lank, coarse, and very black; their nose very small, thin, and has a little rising on the middle, from whence it forms a small curve, terminating in a point, bending towards the upper lip. These marks, besides some dark spots on the body, are so constant and invariable, as to make it very difficult to conceal the fallacy of their complexion. The Mestizos may be reckoned a third part of the inhabitants.

The next class is the Indians, who form about another third; and the others, who are about one sixth, are the Castes [mixed]. These four classes, according to the most authentic accounts taken from the parish register, amount to between 50 and 60,000 persons, of all ages, sexes, and ranks. If among these classes the Spaniards, as is natural to think, are the most eminent for riches, rank, and power, it must at the same time be owned, however melancholy the truth may appear, they are in proportion the most poor, miserable and distressed; for they refuse to apply themselves to any mechanic business, considering it as a disgrace to that quality they so highly value themselves upon, which consists in not being black, brown, or of a copper color. The Mestizos, whose pride is regulated by prudence, readily apply themselves to arts and trades, but choose those of the greatest repute, as painting, sculpture, and the like, leaving the meaner sort to the Indians.

Córdoba, Argentina

There was not a person who would give me even an estimate of the number of residents comprising this city, because neither the secular nor the ecclesiastical council has a register, and I know not how these colonists prove the ancient and distinguished nobility of which they boast; it may be that each family has its genealogical history in reserve. In my computation, there must be within the city and its limited common lands around 500 to 600 residents, but in the principal houses there are a very large number of slaves, most of them Creoles [native born] of all conceivable classes, because in this city and in all of Tucumán there is no leniency about granting freedom to any of them. They are easily supported since the principal aliment, meat, is of such moderate price, and there is a custom of dressing them only in ordinary cloth which is made at home by the slaves themselves, shoes being very rare. They aid their masters in many profitable ways and under this system do not think of freedom, thus exposing themselves to a sorrowful end, as is happening in Lima.

As I was passing through Córdoba, they were selling 2,000 Negroes, all Creoles from Temporalidades [property confiscated from the Jesuit order in 1767], from just the two farms of the [Jesuit] colleges of this city. I have seen the lists, for each one has its own, and they proceed by families numbering from two to eleven, all pure Negroes and Creoles back to the fourth generation, because the priests used to sell all of those born with a mixture of Spanish, mulatto, or Indian blood. Among this multitude of Negroes were many musicians and many other crafts; they proceeded with the sale by families. I was assured that the nuns of Santa Teresa alone had a group of 300 slaves of both sexes, to whom they give their just ration of meat and dress in the coarse cloth which they make, while these good nuns content themselves with what is left from other ministrations. The number attached to other religious establishments is much smaller, but there is a private home which has 30 or 40, the majority of whom are engaged in various gainful activities. The result is a large number of excellent washerwomen whose accomplishments are valued so highly that they never mend their outer skirts in order that the whiteness of their undergarments may be seen. They do the laundry in the river, in water up to the waist, saying vaingloriously that she who is not soaked cannot wash well. They make ponchos [hand-woven capes], rugs, sashes, and sundries, and especially decorated leather cases which the men sell for 8 reales each, because the hides have no outlet due to the great distance to the port; the same thing happens on the banks of the Tercero and Cuarto rivers, where they are sold at 2 reales and frequently for less.

The principal men of the city wear very expensive clothes, but this is not true of the women, who are an exception in both Americas and even in the entire world, because they dress decorously in clothing of little cost. They are very tenacious in preserving the customs of their ancestors. They do not permit slaves, or even freedmen who have a mixture of Negro blood, to wear any cloth other than that made in this country, which is quite coarse. I was told recently that a certain bedecked mulatto [woman] who appeared in Córdoba was sent word by the ladies of the city that she should dress according to her station, but since she paid no attention to this reproach, they endured her negligence until one of the ladies, summoning her to her home under some other pretext, had the servants undress her, whip her, burn her finery before her eyes, and dress her in the clothes befitting her class; despite the fact that the [victim] was not lacking in persons to defend her, she disappeared lest the tragedy be repeated.

QUESTIONS FOR ANALYSIS

1. **What do the authors of these selections seem to think about the white elites of the colonies? Are there similarities in the ways that Juan and Ulloa and Carrío describe the mixed population of Quito and the slave population of Córdoba?**

2. **Are there differences in the way that the authors characterize the relationship between color and class?**

3. **What does the humiliation of the mixed-race woman in Córdoba tell us about ideas of race and class in the Spanish colony?**

Sources: Jorge Juan and Antonio de Ulloa, *A Voyage to South America*, The John Adams translation (abridged), Introduction by Irving A. Leonard (New York: Alfred A. Knopf, 1964), 135–137, copyright © 1964 by Alfred A. Knopf, Inc. Used by permission of Alfred A. Knopf, a division of Random House, Inc.; Concolorcorvo, *El Lazarillo, A Guide for Inexperienced Travelers between Buenos Aires and Lima*, 1773, translated by Walter D. Kline (Bloomington: Indiana University Press, 1965), 78–80. Copyright © 1965. Reprinted by permission of the publisher, Indiana University Press.

of Europe. But the position of these *encomenderos* was undermined by their abuse of Amerindian communities, the catastrophic epidemics of the sixteenth century, and the growing power of colonial viceroys, judges, and bishops appointed by the king.

By the end of the sixteenth century, the elite of Spanish America included both European immigrants and creoles. Europeans dominated the highest levels of the church and government, as well as commerce. Creoles commonly controlled colonial agriculture and mining. Although tensions between Spaniards and creoles were inevitable, most elite families had members from both groups.

Before the Europeans arrived in the Americas, the native peoples were members of a large number of distinct cultural and linguistic groups. Cultural diversity and class distinctions were present even in the highly centralized Aztec and Inca Empires. The loss of life provoked by the European conquest undermined this rich social and cultural complexity, and the imposition of Catholic Christianity further eroded ethnic boundaries among native peoples. Colonial administrators and settlers broadly applied the racial label *Indian,* which facilitated the imposition of special taxes and labor obligations while erasing long-standing class and ethnic differences.

Indigenous Amerindian elites survived only briefly. Some of the conquistadors and early settlers married or established less formal relations with elite Amerindian women, but these alliances diminished after European women began to arrive. Some descendants of the powerful Amerindian families prospered as ranchers, muleteers, and merchants; many others lived in the same materially deprived conditions as Amerindian commoners.

Thousands of blacks participated in the conquest and settlement of Spanish America, and the opening of a direct slave trade with Africa added millions more. Settlers' views of African slaves' cultural differences as signs of inferiority ultimately served as a justification for slavery. By 1600, anyone with black ancestry was barred from positions in church, government, and many skilled crafts. Even so, African languages, religious beliefs, and marriage customs mixed with European (and in some cases Amerindian) languages and beliefs to forge distinct local cultures. The rapid growth of an American-born slave population accelerated cultural change.

The colonial development of Brazil took place in the absence of rich and powerful indigenous civilizations such as those of the Aztecs and Inca. Fewer Europeans immigrated to Brazil than to the Spanish colonies, but those who did exercised the same sort of domination. The growth of cities and the creation of imperial institutions eventually duplicated in outline the social structures found in Spanish America, but with an important difference. By the early seventeenth century, Africans and their American-born descendants were by far the largest racial group in Brazil. As a result, Brazilian colonial society (unlike Spanish Mexico and Peru) was influenced more by African culture than by Amerindian culture.

African slaves became skilled artisans, musicians, servants, artists, cowboys, and even soldiers in Brazil and Spanish America. However, the vast majority worked in agriculture. To escape harsh discipline, brutal punishments, and backbreaking labor, many slaves rebelled or ran away. Communities of runaways (called *quilombos* [key-LOM-bos] in Brazil and *palenques* [pah-LEN-kays] in Spanish colonies) were common. The largest quilombo was Palmares, where thousands of slaves defended themselves against Brazilian authorities for sixty years until they were finally overrun in 1694.

SECTION REVIEW

- European, Amerindian, and African elements combined to form the hybrid culture of colonial Latin America.

- Spain and Portugal imposed Iberian political and economic institutions on their colonies and tried to promote Catholic uniformity, with mixed success.

- Silver and sugar dominated the economy of colonial Latin America and integrated it with the global economy.

- A social order developed that was stratified along lines of ethnicity and birthplace, but Amerindian and African languages and cultural practices survived and blended with European ways.

ENGLISH AND FRENCH COLONIES IN NORTH AMERICA

How did the English and French colonies of North America evolve?

The North American colonial empires of England and France and the colonies of Spain and Portugal had many characteristics in common. The governments of England and France hoped to find precious metals or great indigenous empires like those of the Aztecs or Inca. Like the Spanish and Portuguese, English and French settlers responded to native peoples with a mixture of diplomacy and violence. African slaves proved crucial to the development of all four colonial economies.

There were also important differences. The English and French colonies were founded nearly a century after Cortés's conquest of Mexico and initial Portuguese settlement in Brazil. Distracted by ventures elsewhere, neither England nor France imitated the large and expensive colonial bureaucracies that Spain and Portugal established. Instead, private companies and individual proprietors pioneered development. This practice led to greater regional variety in economic activity, political institutions and culture, and social structure than was evident in Latin American colonies.

The South

London investors, organized as the privately funded Virginia Company, got off to a rocky start. Nearly 80 percent of the settlers at Jamestown in 1607 and 1608 soon died of disease or Amerindian attacks. After the English crown dissolved the Virginia Company in 1624 because of its mismanagement, colonists pushed deeper into the interior, developing a sustainable economy based on furs, timber, and, increasingly, tobacco. The profits from tobacco soon attracted new immigrants and new capital. Along the shoreline of Chesapeake Bay and the rivers that fed it, settlers spread out, developing plantations and farms.

Choctaw Village in Louisiana at Time of French Colonial Rule

In this scene of village life we see strong indications of integration in the colonial economy. While natives are shown pursuing traditional tasks, a black slave and European trade goods obtained in exchange for deerskins are arrayed along the riverbank.   (© 2006 Harvard University Peabody Museum Photo 41-72 10/20 T2377)

Indentured servants eventually accounted for approximately 80 percent of all English immigrants to the Chesapeake Bay region. Young men and women unable to pay for their transportation to the New World accepted indentures (contracts) that bound them to a term ranging from four to seven years of labor in return for passage, a small parcel of land, and some tools and clothes. During the seventeenth century, approximately fifteen hundred indentured servants, mostly male, arrived each year. As life expectancy improved, planters began to purchase more slaves. They calculated that greater profits could be secured by paying the higher initial cost of slaves owned for life than by purchasing the contracts of indentured servants bound for short periods of time. As a result, Virginia's slave population grew rapidly, from 950 in 1660 to 120,000 by 1756.

Ironically, this increase in the colony's slave population occurred along with the expansion in colonial liberties and political rights. At first, colonial government had been administered by a Crown-appointed governor and his council, as well as by representatives of towns meeting together as the **House of Burgesses**. When these representatives began to meet alone as a deliberative body, they initiated a form of democratic representation that distinguished the English colonies of North America from the colonies of other European powers. The intertwined evolution of freedom and slavery gave England's southern colonies a unique and conflicted political character.

Colonial South Carolina was the most hierarchical society in British North America. Planters controlled the economy and political life. The richest maintained households in both the countryside and Charleston, the largest city in the southern colonies. Small farmers, cattlemen, artisans, merchants, and fur traders held an intermediate but clearly subordinate social position. South Carolina depended on slavery. African slaves were present from the founding of Charleston and were instrumental in introducing irrigated rice agriculture and in developing indigo (a plant that produced a blue dye) plantations. Native peoples remained influential participants in colonial society through commercial contacts and alliances, but they were increasingly marginalized.

New England

New England was colonized by two separate groups of Protestant dissenters. The **Pilgrims** established the coastal colony of Plymouth in present-day Massachusetts in 1620. Although nearly half of the settlers died during the first winter, the colony survived. In 1691, Plymouth was absorbed into the larger Massachusetts Bay Colony of the **Puritans**. By 1643, more than 20,000 Puritans had settled in the Bay Colony.

Unlike in the southern colonies, most newcomers to Massachusetts arrived with their families. A normal gender balance and a healthy climate resulted in a rapid increase in population. Massachusetts also was more homogeneous and less hierarchical than the southern colonies.

Political institutions evolved out of the terms of the Puritans' royal charter. A governor was elected, along with a council of magistrates drawn from the board of directors of the Massachusetts Bay Company. Disagreements between this council and elected representatives of the towns led, by 1650, to the creation of a lower legislative house that selected its own speaker and began to develop procedures and rules similar to those of the House of Commons in England.

indentured servant A migrant to British colonies in the Americas who paid for passage by agreeing to work for a set term ranging from four to seven years.

House of Burgesses Elected assembly in colonial Virginia, created in 1618.

Pilgrims Group of English Protestant dissenters who established Plymouth Colony in Massachusetts in 1620 to seek religious freedom after having lived briefly in the Netherlands.

Puritans English Protestant dissenters who believed that God predestined souls to heaven or hell before birth. They founded Massachusetts Bay Colony in 1629.

Economically, agriculture met basic needs, but the poor soils and harsh climate did not favor cash crops like tobacco or rice. To pay for imported tools, textiles, and other essentials, the colonists provided commercial and shipping services to the southern colonies, the smaller Caribbean islands, Africa, and Europe.

In contrast to Latin America's heavily capitalized monopolies, New England merchants depended on market intelligence, flexibility, and streamlined organization. With 16,000 inhabitants in 1740, Boston was the largest city in British North America.

Middle Atlantic Region

The rapid economic development and cultural diversity of the Middle Atlantic colonies added to the success of English-speaking North America. The **Iroquois Confederacy**, an alliance of several native peoples, established treaties and trading relationships with the Dutch. When confronted by an English military expedition in 1664, the Dutch surrendered their colony of New Netherland without a fight. Renamed New York, the colony's success depended on the development of New York City as a commercial and shipping center. Located at the mouth of the Hudson River, the city connected the region's grain farmers to the booming markets of the Caribbean and southern Europe. By the early eighteenth century, New York Colony had a diverse population that included (in addition to English colonists) Dutch, German, and Swedish settlers, as well as a large slave community.

Pennsylvania began as a proprietary colony in 1682 and as a refuge for Quakers, a persecuted religious minority. The founder, William Penn, quickly lost control of the colony's political life, but the colony enjoyed remarkable success. By 1700, Pennsylvania had a population of more than 21,000, and Philadelphia, its capital, soon passed Boston to become the largest city in the British colonies. Healthy climate, excellent land, and relatively peaceful relations with native peoples attracted free workers, including many German families. As a result, Pennsylvania's economic expansion in the late seventeenth century occurred without reproducing South Carolina's hierarchical and repressive social order based on slavery. By the early eighteenth century, however, the prosperous city of Philadelphia included a large population of black slaves, servants, and skilled tradesmen.

French North America

French settlement patterns more closely resembled those of Spain and Portugal than of England. The French were committed to missionary activity among Amerindian peoples and emphasized extracting resources—in this case, furs.

Coming to Canada after spending years in the West Indies, Samuel de Champlain founded the colony of **New France** at Quebec (kwuh-BEC), on the banks of the St. Lawrence River, in 1608. The European market for fur, especially beaver, fueled French settlement. Young Frenchmen were sent to live among native peoples to master their languages and customs. These men and their children by native women organized the fur trade and led French expansion to the west and south. Amerindians actively participated

Iroquois Confederacy An alliance of five northeastern Amerindian peoples (six after 1722) that made decisions on military and diplomatic issues through a council of representatives. Allied first with the Dutch and later with the English, the Confederacy dominated the area from western New England to the Great Lakes.

New France French colony in North America, with a capital in Quebec, founded in 1608. New France fell to the British in 1763.

SECTION REVIEW

- In contrast to Spanish colonies, the development of English and French colonies was shaped by private companies and individuals.
- In England's southern colonies, settlers spread inland and planted cash crops, enjoying unique rights and liberties even as slavery expanded.
- New England developed a more homogeneous, less hierarchical society than the South and an economy based on more varied commercial activities.
- The Middle Atlantic colonies benefited from diverse populations, hospitable climates, and rapid economic expansion without the South's social hierarchy.
- The development of French America was shaped by missionary activity and the fur trade, which was dependent on Amerindian participation.

in this trade because they came to depend on the goods they received in exchange for furs: firearms, metal tools and utensils, textiles, and alcohol.

The Iroquois Confederacy responded to the increased military strength of France's Algonquin allies by forging commercial and military links with Dutch and later English settlements in the Hudson River Valley. Well armed by the Dutch and English, the Iroquois Confederacy nearly eradicated the Huron in 1649 and inflicted a series of humiliating defeats on the French. At the high point of their power in the early 1680s, Iroquois hunters and military forces gained control of much of the Great Lakes region and the Ohio River Valley. A large French military expedition and a relentless attack focused on Iroquois villages and agriculture finally checked Iroquois power in 1701.

Use of firearms in hunting and warfare moved west and south, reaching indigenous plains cultures that previously had adopted the horse introduced by the Spanish. This intersection of horse and gun frontiers in the early eighteenth century multiplied the military power and hunting efficiency of the Sioux, Comanche, Cheyenne, and other indigenous peoples and slowed the pace of European settlement.

In French Canada, the Jesuits led the effort to convert native peoples to Christianity. Building on earlier evangelical efforts in Brazil and Paraguay, French Catholic missionaries mastered native languages, created boarding schools for young boys and girls, and set up model agricultural communities for converts. Their greatest successes coincided with a wave of epidemics and renewed warfare among native peoples in the 1630s. Nevertheless, local cultures persisted.

Although the fur trade flourished, settlers were few. Founded at about the same time, Virginia had twenty times as many European residents as Canada by 1627. Canada's small settler population and the fur trade's dependence on Amerindians allowed indigenous peoples to retain greater independence and more control over their encounters with new religious, technological, and market realities.

The French aggressively expanded. Louisiana, founded in 1699, depended on the fur trade with Amerindians. France's North American colonies were threatened by a series of wars with England and the neighboring English colonies. The "French and Indian War" (also known as the Seven Years War, 1756–1763) proved to be the final contest for the North American empire. England committed a larger military force to the struggle and, despite early defeats, took the French capital of Quebec in 1759. The peace agreement forced France to yield Canada to the English and cede Louisiana to Spain.

Canadian Fur Traders
The fur trade provided the economic foundation of early Canadian settlement. Fur traders were cultural intermediaries. They brought European technologies and products like firearms and machine-made textiles to native peoples and native technologies and products like canoes and furs to European settlers. This canoe with sixteen paddlers was adapted from the native craft by fur traders to transport large cargoes. (Frances Anne Hopkins, "Shooting the Rapids," Library and Archives Canada, Ref. # C-2774)

PLANTATIONS IN THE WEST INDIES

What factors contributed to the development of plantations in the West Indies?

The West Indies was the first place in the Americas that Columbus reached and the first part of the Americas where native populations collapsed. It took a long time to repopulate these islands from abroad and forge new economic links between them and other parts of the Atlantic. But after 1650, sugar plantations, African slaves, and European capital made these islands a major center of the Atlantic economy.

Spanish settlers had introduced sugar-cane cultivation into the West Indies shortly after 1500, but these colonies soon fell into neglect as attention shifted to colonizing the American mainland. In the 1620s and 1630s, the West Indies revived as a focus of colonization, this time by English and French settlers interested in growing tobacco and other crops. The islands' value mushroomed after the Dutch reintroduced sugar cultivation from Brazil in the 1640s and supplied the African slaves and European capital necessary to create a new economy.

Sugar and Slaves

The English colony of Barbados illustrates the dramatic transformation that sugar brought to the seventeenth-century Caribbean. In 1640, Barbados's economy depended largely on tobacco, mostly grown by European settlers, both free and indentured. By the 1680s, sugar had become the colony's principal crop, and enslaved Africans were three times as numerous as Europeans. Exporting up to 15,000 tons of sugar a year, Barbados had become the wealthiest and most populous of England's American

Caribbean Sugar Mill

The windmill crushes sugar cane, whose juice is boiled down in the smoking building next door.   (From William Clark, Ten Views in the Islands of Antigua, 1823. British Library)

Market in Rio de Janeiro

In many of the cities of colonial Latin America female slaves and black free women dominated retail markets. In this scene from late colonial Brazil, Afro-Brazilian women sell a variety of foods and crafts.   (Sir Henry Chamberlain, *Views and Costumes of the City and Neighborhoods of Rio de Janeiro*, London, 1822)

HISTORY IN FOCUS Examine this image, paying special attention to what the figures are wearing and appear to be doing. What does the image suggest about the nature of the economy that black women dominated? Who were their most likely customers, and what kind of a living was it possible for them to make? *Find the answer online.*

colonies. By 1700, the West Indies had surpassed Brazil as the world's principal source of sugar.

The expansion of sugar plantations in the West Indies required a sharp increase in the volume of the slave trade from Africa. During the first half of the seventeenth century, about 10,000 slaves a year had arrived from Africa, most destined for Brazil and the mainland Spanish colonies. In the second half of the century, the trade averaged 20,000 slaves a year. More than half were intended for the English, French, and Dutch West Indies and most of the rest for Brazil. A century later, the volume of the Atlantic slave trade was three times larger.

What produced this shift in favor of African slaves? Recent scholarship has cast doubt on the once-common assertion that Africans were more suited than Europeans to field labor; in fact, both died in large numbers in the American tropics. The West Indian historian Eric Williams has also refuted the idea that the rise of African slave labor was primarily motivated by prejudice. Citing the West Indian colonies' prior use of enslaved Amerindians and indentured Europeans, along with European convicts and prisoners of war, he argued, "Slavery was not born of racism: rather, racism was the consequence of slavery."[2] Williams suggested that the shift was due to the lower cost of African labor.

Yet slaves were far from cheap. Cash-short tobacco planters in the seventeenth century preferred indentured Europeans because they cost half as much as African slaves. Poor European men and women were willing to work for little to get to the Americas, where they could acquire their own land cheaply at the end of their term of service. However, as the cultivation of sugar spread after 1750, rich speculators drove the price of land in the West Indies up so high that end-of-term indentured servants could not afford to buy it. As a result, poor Europeans chose to indenture themselves in the mainland North American colonies, where cheap land was still available. Rather than raise wages to attract European laborers, Caribbean sugar planters switched to slaves.

Rising sugar prices helped the West Indian sugar planters afford the higher cost of African slaves. The planters could rely on the Dutch and other traders to supply them with enough new slaves to meet the demands of the expanding plantations. Rising demand drove slave prices up steadily during the eighteenth century. These high labor costs were one more factor favoring large plantations over smaller operations.

To find more land for sugar plantations, France and England founded new Caribbean colonies. In 1655, the English had wrested the island of Jamaica from the Spanish (see Map 16.1). The French seized the western half of the large Spanish island of Hispaniola in the 1670s. During the eighteenth century, this new French colony of Saint Domingue (san doh-MANGH) (present-day Haiti) became the greatest producer of sugar in the Atlantic world, while Jamaica surpassed Barbados as England's most important sugar colony.

Technology and Environment

What made the sugar plantation a complex investment was that it had to be a factory as well as a farm. Freshly cut canes needed to be crushed within a few hours to extract the sugary sap. Thus, for maximum efficiency, each plantation needed its own expensive crushing and processing equipment.

At the heart of the sugar works was the mill where canes were crushed between sets of heavy rollers. From the mill, lead-lined wooden troughs carried the cane juice to a series of large copper kettles in the boiling shed, where the excess water boiled off, leaving a thick syrup. Workers poured the syrup into conical molds in the drying shed. The sugar crystals that formed in the molds were packed in wooden barrels for shipment to Europe.

To make their operation more efficient and profitable, investors gradually increased the size of the typical West Indian plantation from around 100 acres (40 hectares) in the seventeenth century to at least twice that size in the eighteenth century. A plantation became a huge investment. One source estimated that a planter had to invest nearly £20,000 ($100,000) to acquire a Jamaican plantation of 600 acres (240 hectares) in 1774: a third for land, a quarter for equipment, and £8,000 for 200 slaves. Jamaica specialized so heavily in sugar production that the island had to import most of its food. Saint Domingue was more diverse in its economy.

In some ways, the mature sugar plantation was environmentally responsible. The crushing mill was powered by water, wind, or animal power, not fossil fuels. The boilers were largely fueled by burning the crushed canes, and the fields were fertilized by cattle manure. In two respects, however, the plantation was very damaging to the environment: soil exhaustion and deforestation.

Instead of rotating sugar with other crops to restore the nutrients naturally, planters found it more profitable to clear new lands when yields declined too much in the old fields. When land close to the sea was exhausted, planters moved on to new islands. Many of the English who first settled Jamaica were from Barbados, and the pioneer planters on Saint Domingue came from older French sugar colonies. In the second half of the eighteenth century, Jamaican sugar production began to fall behind that of Saint Domingue, which still had access to virgin land. Thus, the plantations of this period were not a stable form of agriculture but one that gradually laid waste to the landscape.

Deforestation, the second form of environmental damage, continued a trend begun in the sixteenth century. By the end of the eighteenth century, only land in the interior of the islands retained dense forests.

The most tragic and dramatic transformation in the West Indies occurred in the human population. During the eighteenth century, West Indian plantation colonies were the world's most polarized societies. On most islands, 90 percent or more of the inhabitants became slaves. A small number of very rich men owned most of the slaves and most of the land as well. Between the slaves and the masters might be found only a few others: a few estate managers and government officials and, in the French islands, some small farmers, both white and black. The profitability of a Caribbean plantation depended on extracting as much work as possible from the slaves through the use and threat of force.

On a typical Jamaican plantation, about 80 percent of the slaves actively engaged in productive tasks; the only exceptions were infants, the seriously ill, and the very old. Slave labor was organized by age, sex, and ability. About 70 percent of the able-bodied slaves worked in the fields, generally in one of three labor gangs. Women formed the majority of the field laborers, even in the great gang. A little over half of the adult males were employed in nongang work, tending the livestock or serving as blacksmiths and carpenters. The most important artisan slave was the head boiler, who oversaw the delicate process of reducing the cane sap to crystallized sugar and molasses.

Skilled slaves received rewards of food and clothing or time off for good work, but the most common reason for working hard was to escape punishment. A slave gang was headed by a privileged male slave, appropriately called the **driver**, whose job was to ensure that the gang completed its work. Production quotas were high, and slaves toiled in the fields from sunup to sunset, except for meal breaks. Those who fell behind because of fatigue or illness soon felt the sting of the whip. Openly rebellious slaves who refused to work, disobeyed orders, or tried to escape were punished with flogging, confinement in irons, or mutilation.

driver A privileged male slave whose job was to ensure that a slave gang did its work on a plantation.

The harsh conditions of plantation life played a major role in shortening slaves' lives, but the greatest killer was disease. The very young were carried off by dysentery caused by contaminated food and water. Slaves newly arrived from Africa went through a period of adjustment to the new environment known as **seasoning**, during which one-third on average died of unfamiliar diseases. Slaves also suffered from diseases they brought with them, including malaria. On one plantation, for example, more than half of the slaves incapacitated by illness had yaws, a painful and debilitating skin disease common in Africa.

seasoning An often difficult period of adjustment to new climates, disease environments, and work routines, such as that experienced by slaves newly arrived in the Americas.

SECTION REVIEW

- During the seventeenth and eighteenth centuries, sugar planting and African slavery expanded rapidly in the West Indies.
- The preference for African slaves grew from the effects of rising sugar prices and land speculation.
- As demand for land grew, England and France established more island colonies.
- The need for efficiency made plantations into large, self-sufficient, and expensive units.
- The plantation system caused environmental damage and exacted huge human costs.
- Harsh conditions provoked rebellions and flight, and fugitives created maroon communities.

maroon A slave who ran away from his or her master. Often a member of a community of runaway slaves in the West Indies and South America.

Such high mortality greatly added to the volume of the Atlantic slave trade, since plantations had to purchase new slaves every year or two to replace those who had died. The additional imports of slaves to permit the expansion of the sugar plantations meant that the majority of slaves on most West Indian plantations were African-born. As a result, African religious beliefs, patterns of speech, styles of dress and adornment, and music were prominent parts of West Indian life.

Given the harsh conditions of their lives, it is not surprising that slaves in the West Indies often sought to regain the freedom into which most had been born. Individual slaves often ran away, hoping to elude the men and dogs that would track them. Sometimes large groups of plantation slaves rose in rebellion against their bondage and abuse. For example, a large rebellion in Jamaica in 1760 was led by a slave named Tacky, who had been a chief on the Gold Coast of Africa. One night, his followers broke into a fort and armed themselves. Joined by slaves from nearby plantations, they stormed several plantations, setting them on fire and killing the planter families. Tacky died in the fighting that followed, and three other rebel leaders stoically endured cruel deaths by torture that were meant to deter others from rebellion.

Because they believed rebellions were usually led by slaves with the strongest African heritage, European planters tried to curtail African cultural traditions. They required slaves to learn the colonial language and discouraged the use of African languages by deliberately mixing slaves from different parts of Africa. In French and Portuguese colonies, slaves were encouraged to adopt Catholic religious practices, though African deities and beliefs also survived. In the British West Indies, where only Quaker slave owners encouraged Christianity among their slaves before 1800, African herbal medicine remained strong, as did African beliefs concerning nature spirits and witchcraft.

As in Latin America, slavery also provoked flight. In the Caribbean, runaways were known as **maroons**. Maroon communities were especially numerous in the mountainous interiors of Jamaica and Hispaniola, as well as in the island parts of the Guianas (guy-AHN-uhs). The Jamaican maroons, after withstanding several attacks by the colony's militia, signed a treaty in 1739 that recognized their independence in return for their cooperation in stopping new runaways and suppressing slave revolts. Similar treaties with the large maroon population in the Dutch colony of Surinam (Dutch Guiana) recognized their possession of large inland regions.

CREATING THE ATLANTIC ECONOMY

What conditions created the Atlantic economy?

The West Indian plantation colonies were at once archaic in their cruel system of slavery and oddly modern in their specialization in a single product. Yet they played a crucial role in the emerging Atlantic economy. The plantation system profitably dominated a broad region from the Chesapeake to the Caribbean and then to northern South America and Brazil. The African slave made the plantation economies possible, and profits from the exports of plantation products helped finance commercial and manufacturing expansion. Three other elements went into the creation of the new Atlantic economy: new economic institutions, new partnerships between private investors and governments in Europe, and new working relationships between European and African merchants. The new trading system is a prime example of how European capitalist relationships were reshaping the world.

Capitalism and Mercantilism

The Spanish and Portuguese voyages of exploration in the fifteenth and sixteenth centuries were government ventures, and both countries tried to keep their overseas trade and colonies royal monopolies. Monopoly control, however, proved both expensive and inefficient. The success of the Atlantic economy in the seventeenth and eighteenth centuries owed much to private enterprise, which made trading venues more efficient and profitable.

Two European innovations, capitalism and mercantilism, enabled private investors to fund the rapid growth of the Atlantic economy. **Capitalism** was a system of large financial institutions—banks, stock exchanges, and chartered trading companies—that enabled wealthy investors to reduce risks and increase profits. Early capitalism was buttressed by **mercantilism**, policies adopted by European states to promote their citizens' overseas trade and defend it, by armed force when necessary.

Chartered companies were one of the first examples of mercantilist capitalism. A charter issued by the government of the Netherlands in 1602 gave the Dutch East India Company a legal monopoly over all Dutch trade in the Indian Ocean. This privilege encouraged private investors to buy shares in the company. They were amply rewarded when the Dutch East India Company captured control of the long-distance trade routes in the Indian Ocean from the Portuguese (see Chapter 17). A sister firm, the **Dutch West India Company**, was chartered in 1621 to engage in the Atlantic trade and to seize sugar-producing areas in Brazil and African slaving ports from the Portuguese.

Such successes inspired other governments to set up their own chartered companies. In 1672, a royal charter placed all English trade with West Africa in the hands of the new **Royal African Company**, which established its headquarters at Cape Coast Castle, just east of Elmina on the Gold Coast. The French government chartered East India and West India companies to reduce French colonies' dependence on Dutch and English traders. The Spanish and Portuguese governments imitated this model.

French and English governments also used military force in pursuit of commercial dominance, especially to break the trading advantage of the Dutch in the Americas. Restrictions on Dutch access to French and English colonies provoked a series of wars with the Netherlands between 1652 and 1678, during which the larger English and French navies defeated the Dutch and drove the Dutch West India Company into bankruptcy.

With Dutch competition in the Atlantic reduced, the French and English governments moved to revoke the monopoly privileges of their chartered companies. England opened trade in Africa to any English subject in 1698 on the grounds that ending monopolies would be "highly beneficial and advantageous to this kingdom." It was hoped that such competition would also cut the cost of slaves to West Indian planters, though the demand for slaves soon drove the prices up again.

capitalism The economic system of large financial institutions—banks, stock exchanges, investment companies—that first developed in early modern Europe. *Commercial capitalism,* the trading system of the early modern economy, is often distinguished from *industrial capitalism,* the system based on machine production.

mercantilism European government policies of the sixteenth, seventeenth, and eighteenth centuries designed to promote overseas trade between a country and its colonies and accumulate precious metals by requiring colonies to trade only with their motherland country. The British system was defined by the Navigation Acts, the French system by laws known as the *Exclusif.*

chartered companies Groups of private investors who paid an annual fee to France and England in exchange for a monopoly over trade to the West Indies colonies.

Dutch West India Company (1621–1794) Trading company chartered by the Dutch government to conduct its merchants' trade in the Americas and Africa.

Royal African Company Trading company chartered by the Dutch English government to conduct its merchants' trade in the Americas and Africa.

SECTION REVIEW

- Capitalism and mercantilism encouraged private funding of the Atlantic economy.

- These systems often worked through chartered companies and military force.

- Mercantilism promoted competition among a country's citizens while blocking foreign competition.

Such new mercantilist policies fostered competition among a nation's own citizens, while using high tariffs and restrictions to exclude foreigners. In the 1660s, England had passed a series of Navigation Acts that confined trade with its colonies to English ships and cargoes. The French called their mercantilist legislation, first codified in 1698, the *Exclusif* (ek-skloo-SEEF), highlighting its exclusionary intentions. Other mercantilist laws defended manufacturing and processing interests in Europe against competition from colonies, imposing prohibitively high taxes on any manufactured goods and refined sugar imported from the colonies.

As a result of such mercantilist measures, the Atlantic became Britain, France, and Portugal's most important overseas trading area in the eighteenth century. Britain's imports from its West Indian colonies in this period accounted for over one-fifth of the value of total British imports. The French West Indian colonies played an even larger role in France's overseas trade. Only the Dutch, closed out of much of the American trade, found Asian trade of greater value. Profits from the Atlantic economy, in turn, promoted further economic expansion and inreased the revenues of European governments.

COLONIAL EXPANSION AND CONFLICT

What were the effects of the colonial reforms and wars among imperial powers that dominated the Americas during the eighteenth century?

In the last decades of the seventeenth century, all of the European colonies in the Americas began to experience a long period of economic and demographic expansion. In the next century, the imperial powers responded by strengthening their administrative and economic controls in the colonies. They also sought to force colonial populations to pay a larger share of the costs of administration and defense. These efforts at reform and restructuring coincided with a series of imperial wars fought along Atlantic trade routes and in the Americas. France's loss of its North American colonies in 1763 was one of the most important results of these struggles. Equally significant, colonial populations throughout the Americas became more aware of separate national identities and more aggressive in asserting local interests against the will of distant monarchs.

Imperial Reform in Spanish America and Brazil

Spain's Habsburg dynasty ended when the Spanish king Charles II died without an heir in 1700. After thirteen years of conflict involving the major European powers and factions within Spain, Philip of Bourbon, grandson of Louis XIV of France, gained the Spanish throne. Under Philip V and his Bourbon heirs, Spain's colonial administration and tax collection were reorganized. For most of the Spanish Empire, the eighteenth century was a period of remarkable economic expansion associated with population growth and enhanced commerce. Mining, the heart of the Spanish colonial economy, increased as silver production in Mexico and Peru rose steadily into the 1780s. Agricultural exports also expanded: tobacco, dyes, hides, chocolate, cotton, and sugar joined the flow of goods to Europe.

Brazil experienced a similar period of expansion and reform after 1700, as Portugal created new administrative positions and gave monopoly companies exclusive rights to little-developed regions. As in Spanish America, this led to rebellions and plots. The discovery of gold in the 1690s and diamonds after 1720 in Brazil financed an aggressive period of reform. This economic expansion led to an increase in the slave trade: nearly 2 million African slaves were imported in the eighteenth century.

The Spanish and Portuguese kings also sought to reduce the power of the Catholic Church in their colonies while at the same time transferring some church wealth to their treasuries. These efforts led to a succession of confrontations between colonial officials and the church hierarchy. In both the Spanish and Portuguese empires, these disputes began to undermine the clergy's previously reliable support for the colonial state. Many colonists saw the reforms as an abuse of power. In Spanish America tax rebellions, urban riots, and Amerindian uprisings tied to these reforms began in the 1770s. In Brazil, as in Spanish America, a more intrusive colonial government that imposed new taxes led to rebellions and plots, including open warfare in 1707 between "sons of the soil" and "outsiders" in São Paulo.

SECTION REVIEW

- Under the leadership of Philip V and his heirs, Spain's colonial interests expanded rapidly.

- In Brazil, economic expansion depended on a dramatic increase in the slave trade.

- Efforts by Spain and Portugal to reduce the power of the Catholic Church in their colonies led to disputes with the clergy and increasing dissatisfaction among the colonists.

- In British America Charles II worked to establish greater control over the colonies by restricting colonial trading and appointing colonial governors.

Reform and Reorganization in British America

After the period of Cromwell's Puritan Republic (see Chapter 15), the restored Stuart king, Charles II, undertook an ambitious campaign to establish greater Crown control over the colonies. Between 1651 and 1673 a series of Navigation Acts sought to severely limit colonial trade and production that competed directly with English manufacturers. Because the New England colonies were viewed as centers of smuggling, the king temporarily suspended their elected assemblies. At the same time, he appointed colonial governors and granted them new fiscal and legislative powers.

During the eighteenth century the English colonies experienced renewed economic growth and attracted a new wave of European immigration, but social divisions were increasingly evident. The colonial population in 1770 was more urban, more clearly divided by class and race, and more vulnerable to economic downturns. Crises were provoked when imperial wars with France and Spain disrupted trade in the Atlantic, increased tax burdens, forced military mobilizations, and provoked frontier conflicts with the Amerindians.

AFRICA AND THE ATLANTIC

How did the Atlantic system affect Africa?

The Atlantic system took a terrible toll in African lives both during the Middle Passage (the journey from Africa to America) and under the harsh conditions of plantation slavery. Many other Africans died while being marched to African coastal ports for sale overseas. The overall effects on Africa of these losses and of other aspects of the slave trade have been the subject of considerable historical debate. It is clear that the trade's impact depended on the intensity and terms of different African regions' involvement.

Any assessment of the Atlantic system's effects in Africa must also take into consideration the fact that some Africans profited from the trade by capturing and selling slaves. They chained the slaves together or bound them to forked sticks for the march to the coast, then bartered them to the European slavers for trade goods. The effects on the enslaver were different from the effects on the enslaved.

The Gold Coast and the Slave Coast

The transition to slave trading was not sudden. Even as slaves were becoming Atlantic Africa's most valuable export, nonslave goods remained a significant part of the total trade. For example, during its eight decades of operation from 1672 to 1752, the English Royal African Company made 40 percent of its profits from dealings in gold, ivory, and forest products. In some parts of West Africa, such nonslave exports remained predominant even at the peak of the trade.

African merchants were very discriminating about what merchandise they received in return for slaves or other goods. A European ship that arrived with goods of low quality or unsuited to local tastes found it hard to purchase a cargo at a profitable price. Africans' greatest demands were for textiles, hardware, and guns. Of the goods the Royal African Company traded in West Africa in the 1680s, over 60 percent were Indian and European textiles and 30 percent hardware and weaponry. Beads and other jewelry formed 3 percent. The rest consisted of cowrie shells, which were used as money. In the eighteenth century, tobacco and rum from the Americas became welcome imports.

Both Europeans and Africans naturally attempted to drive the best bargain for themselves and sometimes engaged in deceitful practices. The strength of the African bargaining position, however, may be inferred from the fact that as the demand for slaves rose, so too did their price in Africa. In the course of the eighteenth century, the goods needed to purchase a slave on the Gold Coast doubled and in some places tripled or quadrupled.

Primary Source: A Voyage to New Calabar River in the Year 1699 *Learn the details of a transaction in which men and women are traded for bars of iron.*

African governments on the Gold Coast and the Slave Coast just east of it made Europeans observe African trading customs and prevented them from taking control of African territory. Rivalry among European nations, each of which established its own trading "castles" along the Gold Coast, also reduced Europeans' bargaining strength.

How did African kings and merchants obtain slaves for sale? Most accounts agree that prisoners taken in war were the greatest source of slaves for the Atlantic trade, but it is difficult to say how often capturing slaves for export was the main cause of warfare. An early-nineteenth-century king of Asante stated, "I cannot make war to catch slaves in the bush, like a thief. My ancestors never did so. But if I fight a king, and kill him when he is insolent, then certainly I must have his gold, and his slaves, and his people are mine too. Do not the white kings act like this?"[3] English rulers had indeed sentenced seventeenth-century Scottish and Irish prisoners to forced labor in the West Indies.

The Bight of Biafra and Angola

In the eighteenth century, the slave trade expanded eastward to the Bight (bay) of Biafra. In contrast to the Gold and Slave Coasts, where strong kingdoms predominated, the densely populated interior of the Bight of Biafra contained no large states. Even so, the powerful merchant princes of the coastal ports made European traders give them rich presents. Because of the absence of sizeable states, there were no large-scale wars and consequently few prisoners of war. Instead, kidnapping was the major means of getting slaves.

As the volume of the Atlantic trade along the Bight of Biafra expanded in the late eighteenth century, some inland markets evolved into giant fairs, with different sections specializing in slaves and imported goods. An English ship's doctor reported that in the 1780s slaves were "bought by the black traders at fairs, which are held for that purpose, at a distance of upwards of two hundred miles from the sea coast." He reported seeing from twelve hundred to fifteen hundred enslaved men and women arriving at the coast from a single fair.[4]

Angola, south of the Congo estuary, was the greatest source of slaves for the Atlantic trade. This was also the one place along the Atlantic coast where a single European nation, Portugal, controlled a significant amount of territory. Portuguese residents of the main coastal ports served as middlemen between caravans that arrived from the far interior and ships from Brazil.

Many of the slaves sold at Angolan markets were prisoners of war captured by expanding African states. As elsewhere in Africa, such prisoners seem to have been a byproduct of African wars rather than the purpose for which the wars were fought.

Recent research has linked other enslavement with environmental crises in the hinterland of Angola. During the eighteenth century, these southern grasslands periodically suffered severe droughts, which drove famished refugees to areas with more plentiful water. In return for food and water, powerful African leaders gained control of many refugees and sold into the Atlantic trade the men, who were more likely than the women and children to escape or challenge the ruler's authority. The most successful of these inland Angolan leaders became heads of powerful new states that stabilized areas devastated by war and drought and repopulated them with the refugees and prisoners they retained. The slave frontier then moved farther inland. This cruel system worked to the benefit of a few African rulers and merchants at the expense of the many thousands of Africans who were sent to death or perpetual bondage in the Americas.

It is impossible to assess with precision the complex effects of the goods received in sub-Saharan Africa from these trades. Africans were very particular about what they received, so it is unlikely that they could have been consistently cheated. Some researchers have suggested that imports of textiles and metals undermined African weavers and metalworkers, but most economic historians calculate that, on a per capita basis, the volume of these imports was too small to have idled many African artisans. Imports supplemented rather than replaced local production. The goods received in sub-Saharan Africa were intended for consumption and thus did not develop the economy. Likewise, the sugar, tea, and chocolate Europeans consumed did little to promote economic development in Europe. However, both African and European merchants profited from trading these consumer goods. Because they directed the whole Atlantic system, Europeans gained far more wealth than Africans did.

Historians disagree in their assessment of how deeply European capitalism dominated Africa before 1800, but Europeans clearly had much less

SECTION REVIEW

- The impact of the slave trade, in which many Africans participated, varied from region to region.

- Slaves—mostly war captives—were only one of the many goods traded on the West African coasts.

- Demand for slaves and European rivalries strengthened the bargaining positions of Slave and Gold Coast kings.

- The slave trade expanded to the Bight of Biafra, but Portuguese-held Angola became the greatest source of slaves.

- The combination of warfare, environmental crises, and state formation helped to feed the Angolan slave markets.

- Both Africans and Europeans profited from trade in consumer goods, but before 1800 Europe had less impact on Africa than on the West Indies and the Americas.

political and economic impact in Africa than in the West Indies or in other parts of the Americas. Still, it is significant that Western capitalism was expanding rapidly in the seventeenth century, while the Ottoman Empire, the dominant state of the Middle East, was entering a period of economic and political decline (see Chapter 17). The tide of influence in Africa was thus running in the Europeans' direction.

THE COLUMBIAN EXCHANGE

How did the Columbian Exchange alter the natural environment of the Americas?

Columbian Exchange The exchange of plants, animals, diseases, and technologies between the Americas and the rest of the world following Columbus's voyages.

The term **Columbian Exchange** refers to the transfer of peoples, animals, plants, diseases, and technology between the New and Old Worlds that European trade in the Atlantic opened up. We have already seen how Old World diseases devastated Amerindian peoples and led to the resettlement of the Americas by Europeans and Africans. In addition, the domesticated livestock and major agricultural crops of the Old World spread over much of the Americas, and Amerindians' staple crops enriched the agricultures of Europe and Africa. This vast exchange of plants and animals radically altered diets and lifestyles around the Atlantic.

Transfers to the Americas

Within a century of Columbus's first voyage, new settlers in the Americas were growing all the staples of southern European agriculture—wheat, olives, grapes, and garden vegetables—along with African and Asian crops such as rice, bananas, coconuts, breadfruit, and sugar cane. Native peoples remained loyal to their traditional staples but added many Old World plants to their diet. Citrus fruits, melons, figs, and sugar, as well as onions, radishes, and salad greens, all found a place in Amerindian cuisine.

By the eighteenth century, nearly all of the domesticated animals and cultivated plants in the Caribbean were ones that Europeans had introduced. The Spanish had brought cattle, pigs, and horses, all of which multiplied rapidly. They had also introduced new plants. Of these, bananas and plantain from the Canary Islands were a valuable addition to the food supply, and sugar and rice formed the basis of plantation agriculture, along with native tobacco. Other food crops arrived with the slaves from Africa, including okra, black-eyed peas, yams, grains such as millet and sorghum, and mangoes. Many of these new animals and plants were useful additions to the islands, but they crowded out indigenous species. The central importance of sugar cane in transforming Brazil and the Caribbean has already been noted.

The introduction of European livestock to the mainland had a dramatic impact. Faced with few natural predators, cattle, pigs, horses, and sheep, as well as pests like rats and rabbits, multiplied rapidly in the open spaces of the Americas. On the vast plains of present-day southern Brazil, Uruguay, and Argentina, herds of wild cattle and horses exceeded 50 million by 1700. Large herds of both animals also appeared in northern Mexico and what became the Southwest of the United States.

Where Old World livestock spread most rapidly, environmental changes were most dramatic. Marauding livestock often had a destructive impact on Amerindian agriculturists. But on the plains of South America, northern Mexico, and Texas, cattle provided indigenous peoples with abundant supplies of meat and hides. In the present-day southwestern United States, the Navajo became sheepherders and expert weavers of woolen cloth. Individual Amerindians became muleteers, cowboys, and sheepherders.

No animal had a more striking effect on the cultures of native peoples than the horse, which increased the efficiency of hunters and the military capacity of warriors on the plains. The horse permitted the Apache, Sioux, Blackfoot, Comanche, Assiniboine, and others to hunt the vast herds of buffalo in North America more efficiently.

Transfers from the Americas

In return, the Americas offered the Old World an abundance of useful plants. The New World staples of maize and potatoes revolutionized agriculture and diet in parts of Europe, because they provided more calories per acre than any of the Old World staples except rice. Beans, squash, tomatoes, sweet potatoes, peanuts, chilis, and chocolate also gained widespread acceptance in Europe and other parts of the Old World. The New World also provided the Old with plants that provided dyes, medicines, and tobacco.

Maize and cassava (a Brazilian plant cultivated for its edible roots) moved across the Atlantic to Africa. Cassava became the most important New World food in Africa. Truly a marvel, cassava had the highest yield of calories per acre of any staple food and thrived even in poor soils and during droughts. Both the leaves and the root could be eaten. Ground into meal, the root could be made into a bread that would keep for up to six months, or it could be fermented into a beverage.

Cassava and maize were probably introduced accidentally into Africa by Portuguese ships from Brazil that discarded leftover supplies after reaching Angola. It did not take long for local Africans to recognize the food value of these new crops, especially in drought-prone areas. By the eighteenth century, Central African rulers hundreds of miles from the Angolan coast were actively promoting the cultivation of maize and cassava on their royal estates in order to provide a more secure food supply. Some historians believe that in the inland areas these Amerindian food crops provided the nutritional base for a population increase that partially offset losses due to the Atlantic slave trade.

SECTION REVIEW

- The Columbian Exchange brought to the Americas southern European, African, and Asian crops.
- Old World plants and livestock altered New World environments and cultures.
- New World crops revolutionized agriculture and diet in Europe and Africa.

COMPARATIVE PERSPECTIVES

The New World colonial empires of Spain, Portugal, France, and England had many characteristics in common. All subjugated Amerindian peoples, introduced large numbers of enslaved Africans, and transformed the American environment by introducing Old World animals, plants, and technologies. Each of the New World empires also reflected the distinctive cultural and institutional heritages of its colonizing power.

Spain's discovery of mineral wealth allowed it to develop the largest and most centralized colonial government. Portugal and France pursued similar objectives, but neither Brazil's agricultural economy, based on sugar, nor France's Canadian fur trade permitted the level of political control achieved by Spain. There was greater cultural and religious diversity in British North America. British colonial government was less centralized and in some cases more responsive to local interests.

From the seventeenth century European powers expanded and created new colonies in the Caribbean. Spain's early control of the region was lost as settlers moved to the mainland once gold and silver were discovered. The British, French, and Dutch established colonies. While tobacco dominated these economies early, sugar made these once-isolated islands part of a dynamic trading system controlled from Europe and dependent on slave labor. Spain's most important Caribbean colony, Cuba, joined the sugar revolution late and became the major producer of sugar by 1820.

Historians have seen the Atlantic system that tied European colonies in the Americas to Africa and Europe as a model of the kind of highly interactive economy that became global in later centuries. For that reason the Atlantic system was a milestone in a much larger historical process. Its transformations were destructive as well as creative, producing victims, Amerindians and African slaves, as well as victors, European commercial and manufacturing interests. Africa played an essential role in the Atlantic system, importing trade goods and exporting slaves to the Americas. However, it was less dominated by the Atlantic system than were Europe's American colonies. Africans remained in control of their continent and interacted culturally and politically with the Islamic world more than with the Atlantic.

Chapter Review

DOWNLOAD THE MP3 AUDIO FILE OF THE CHAPTER REVIEW TO LISTEN TO ON THE GO.

What role did forced labor play in the main industries in Spanish America and Brazil? (page 443)

The development of Spanish colonies was promoted by the discovery of rich gold and silver mines and by the encomienda and mita, which forced tens of thousands of indigenous laborers to work in mines, farms, and factories. The sugar industry was crucial to Brazil. At first the enslavement of Amerindians provided labor for the sugar plantations, but eventually Brazil depended on the African slave trade, importing nearly 2 million slaves in the eighteenth century.

How did the English and French colonies of North America evolve? (page 452)

While French Canada was founded with the hope that mineral wealth would be discovered, it survived because of the modest profits of the fur trade. Population grew slowly, and France relied on alliances with native peoples to exploit the fur trade and protect its North American colony. The English colonies of

KEY TERMS

Atlantic system *(p. 443)*
Council of the Indies *(p. 444)*
Bartolomé de Las Casas *(p. 444)*
Potosí *(p. 447)*
encomienda (p. 448)
creole *(p. 448)*
indentured servant *(p. 453)*
House of Burgesses *(p. 453)*
Pilgrims *(p. 453)*
Puritans *(p. 453)*
Iroquois Confederacy *(p. 454)*
New France *(p. 454)*
driver *(p. 459)*
seasoning *(p. 459)*
maroon *(p. 460)*

North America followed a different path. Settlements were first created by groups of private investors or by religious minorities, and England never established centralized political institutions to control all its colonies as did the Spanish and later Portuguese. As a result, settlers exercised greater political power. The economies of Britain's North American colonies were more diverse and much less profitable than were the colonies of Spain and Portugal. The northern English-speaking colonies relied on diverse economic activities such as commercial services and shipbuilding and attracted large numbers of free immigrants. England's southern colonies depended on agricultural exports like rice and tobacco and on slave labor.

What factors contributed to the development of plantations in the West Indies? (page 456)

The islands of the West Indies were divided among a number of European powers. After devastating epidemics eliminated the indigenous populations, settlers relied heavily on slavery to produce a range of export crops. When settlers and European investors realized sugar's profitability, they were willing to finance the forced transfer of hundreds of thousands of Africans to work the Caribbean plantations. Since Africans and their American-born descendants outnumbered Europeans across the area, African culture took root and served as an important basis for these new American societies.

What conditions created the Atlantic economy? (page 460)

European merchants and investors played a central role in the creation of the Atlantic system. In the century before Columbus they traded over longer distances and introduced new credit mechanisms. By the seventeenth century a more confident and adventurous European investor class was ready to promote colonial production and long-distance trade in a much more aggressive way. The development of banks, stock exchanges, and chartered companies supported new ambitions.

What were the effects of the colonial reforms and wars among imperial powers that dominated the Americas during the eighteenth century? (page 462)

In the eighteenth century the European colonies in the Americas experienced economic and population growth. The century also witnessed a series of destructive and costly wars among the European colonial powers. In an effort to force the colonies to pay a greater share of the costs of imperial defense, Spain, Portugal, England, and France all introduced new taxes and created more intrusive colonial governments. With these reforms came increased resentment among colonial populations as well as tax rebellions and riots.

How did the Atlantic system affect Africa? (page 463)

Sub-Saharan Africa had long-established trade connections with the Islamic world before the arrival of Europeans on the African coast. Among the goods transported along these trade routes were slaves. The slave trade to the Islamic north persisted long after the Atlantic trade began to decline. Islamic trade

capitalism *(p. 461)*

mercantilism *(p. 461)*

chartered companies *(p. 461)*

Dutch West India Company *(p. 461)*

Royal African Company *(p. 461)*

Columbian Exchange *(p. 466)*

WEB RESOURCES

Pronunciation Guide

Interactive Map

MAP 16.1 Colonial Latin America in the Eighteenth Century

Primary Sources

A Dominican Voice in the Wilderness: Preaching Against Tyranny in Hispaniola

A Voyage to New Calabar River in the Year 1699

Answer to the History in Focus Question

See photo on page 457, "Market in Rio de Janeiro."

Plus

Chapter Objectives

ACE multiple-choice quiz

Flashcards

was accompanied by the spread of the religion south of the Sahara and the creation of Islamic states like Mali and Songhai (see Chapter 16). But the volume of the Atlantic slave trade was much larger than the Islamic trade, especially to the Caribbean islands after the introduction of sugar. The production of sugar in the Americas and the volume of the African slave trade crested together in the eighteenth century.

How did the Columbian Exchange alter the natural environment of the Americas? (page 466)

The creation of colonies in the Western Hemisphere led to the introduction of new plants and animals that affected the environment and forced indigenous peoples to adapt. Europeans also brought over Old World diseases, such as smallpox, that had a devastating effect on the native populations. The exchange of plants and animals altered diets and lifestyles in dramatic ways. In their relentless effort to discover a viable basis for their settlements, European colonists introduced sugar, rice, and coffee. They also took Western Hemisphere domesticates, like indigo, cacao, and tobacco, and spread them to new regions.

SUGGESTED READING

Burkholder, Mark A., and Lyman L. Johnson. *Colonial Latin America.* 2d ed. 1994. Provides a good introduction to the field.

Crosby, Alfred W., Jr. *The Columbian Exchange: Biological and Cultural Consequences of 1492.* 1972; and *Ecological Imperialism.* 1986. Pioneering works in the study of cross-Atlantic history.

Curtin, Philip D. *The Rise and Fall of the Plantation Complex.* 1990. Excellent introduction to the Atlantic system.

Davis, David Brion. *The Problem of Slavery in Western Culture.* 1966. A classic study from a broad perspective.

Eccles, William J. *France in America.* Rev. ed. 1990. An excellent overview of French colonialism in North America.

Ellis, David. *The Rise of African Slavery in the Americas.* 2000.

Fischer, David Hackett. *Albion's Seed: Four British Folkways in America.* 1989. A general study of the British colonies.

Klein, Herbert S. *African Slavery in Latin America and the Caribbean.* 1986. An exceptionally fine synthesis of research on New World slavery, including North American slave systems.

Klein, Herbert S. *The Atlantic Slave Trade.* 1999.

Lovejoy, Paul. *Transformations in Slavery: A History of Slavery in Africa.* 2d ed. 2000. Contains recent research on slavery and the African, Atlantic, and Muslim slave trades.

McAlister, Lyle N. *Spain and Portugal in the New World, 1492–1700.* 1984. A useful introduction to the era of Iberian rule.

Melville, Elinor G. K. *A Plague of Sheep: Environmental Consequences of the Spanish Conquest of Mexico.* 1994. Looks at what happens when a new domestic species is introduced.

Nash, Gary B. *Red, White, and Black: The Peoples of Early America.* 5th ed. 2005. Studies the complexity of colonial society in North America.

Thornton, John. *Africa and Africans in the Making of the Atlantic World, 1400–1800.* 2d ed. 1998. Examines cultural connections among African communities on both sides of the Atlantic.

NOTES

1. Quoted in Alfred W. Crosby, Jr., *The Columbian Exchange: Biological and Cultural Consequences of 1492* (Westport, CT: Greenwood, 1972), 58.
2. Eric Williams, *Capitalism and Slavery* (Charlotte: University of North Carolina Press, 1944), 7.
3. King Osei Bonsu, quoted in David Northrup, ed., *The Atlantic Slave Trade,* 2d ed. (Boston: Houghton Mifflin, 2001), 176.
4. Alexander Falconbridge, *Account of the Slave Trade on the Coast of Africa* (London: J. Phillips, 1788), 12.

Southwest Asia and the Indian Ocean

1500–1750

CHAPTER PREVIEW

I n 1541 a woman named Sabah appeared before an Ottoman judge in the town of Aintab in southern Turkey to answer several charges: that she had brought men and women together illegally and that she had fostered heresy. In her court testimony, she stated the following:

> I gather girls and brides and women in my home. I negotiated with Ibrahim b. Nazih and the two youths who are his apprentices, and in exchange for paying them a month's fee, I had them come every day to the girls and brides in my house and I had them preach and give instruction. There are no males at those sessions besides the said Ibrahim and his apprentices; there are only women and girls and young brides. This kind of thing is what I have always done for a living.[1]

This icon will direct you to the website where you can Prepare for Class, Improve Your Grade, and Ace the Test: college.cengage.com/pic/bullietbrief4e

471

Two male neighbors testified differently:

> She holds gatherings of girls and brides and women in her home. . . . While she says that she has [Ibrahim] preach, she actually has him speak evil things. She has him conduct spiritual conversations with these girls and brides. . . . [I]n the ceremonies, the girls and brides and women spin around waving their hands, and they bring themselves into a trancelike state by swaying and dancing. They perform the ceremonies according to Kizilbash teachings. We too have wives and families, and we are opposed to illegal activities like this.[2]

The judge made no finding on the charge of heresy, but he ordered Sabah to be publicly humiliated and banished from town for unlawfully mixing the sexes. Ibrahim was also banished.

This uncommon story taken from Ottoman religious court records sheds light on several aspects of daily life in a provincial town. It provides an example of a woman making her living by arranging religious instruction for other women. It also demonstrates the willingness of neighbors, in this case males, to complain in court about activities they considered immoral. And its suggestion that Sabah was promoting the qizilbash heresy, which at that time was considered a state threat because it was the ideology of the enemy Safavid Empire next door, shows that townspeople thought it plausible that women could act to promote religious doctrines.

Studies of everyday life through court records and other state and nonstate documents are a recent development in Ottoman and Safavid history. They produce an image of these societies that differs greatly from the pomp and formality conveyed by European travelers and official histories. As a consequence, accounts of capricious and despotic actions taken by shahs and sultans are increasingly being balanced by stories of common people, who were much more concerned with the maintenance of a sound legal and moral order than were some of the denizens of the imperial palaces. The doings of rulers remain an important historical focus, of course, but stories about ordinary folk perhaps give a better picture of the habits and mores of the majority of the population.

THE OTTOMAN EMPIRE

How did the Ottoman Empire rise to power, and what factors contributed to its transformation?

Ottoman Empire Islamic state founded by Osman in northwestern Anatolia ca. 1300. After the fall of the Byzantine Empire, the Ottoman Empire was based at Istanbul (formerly Constantinople) from 1453 to 1922. It encompassed lands in the Middle East, North Africa, the Caucasus, and eastern Europe.

The most long-lived of the post-Mongol Muslim empires was the **Ottoman Empire**, founded around 1300 (see Map 17.1). By extending Islamic conquests into eastern Europe, starting in the late fourteenth century, and by taking Syria and Egypt from the Mamluk rulers in the early sixteenth, the Ottomans seemed to recreate the might of the original Islamic caliphate, the empire established by the Muslim Arab conquests in the seventh century. However, the empire was actually more like the new centralized monarchies of France and Spain (see Chapter 15) than any medieval model.

Enduring more than five centuries, until 1922, the Ottoman Empire survived several periods of wrenching change, some caused by internal problems, others by the growing power of European adversaries. These periods of change reveal the problems faced by huge land-based empires around the world.

Chronology

	Ottoman Empire	Safavid Empire	Mughal Empire
1500			
		1502–1524 Shah Ismail establishes Safavid rule in Iran	
	1516–1517 Selim I conquers Egypt and Syria		
	1520–1566 Reign of Suleiman the Magnificent; peak of Ottoman Empire		
			1526 Babur defeats last sultan of Delhi
	1529 First Ottoman siege of Vienna		
			1556–1605 Akbar rules in Agra; peak of Mughal Empire
	1571 Ottoman naval defeat at Lepanto		
		1587–1629 Reign of Shah Abbas the Great; peak of Safavid Empire	
1600			
	1610 End of Anatolian revolts		
			1658–1707 Aurangzeb imposes conservative Islamic regime
1700			
		1722 Afghan invaders topple last Safavid shah	
	1730 Janissary revolt begins period of Ottoman conservatism		
		1736–1747 Nadir Shah temporarily reunites Iran; invades India (1739)	
			1739 Iranians under Nadir Shah sack Delhi

Expansion and Frontiers

Established around 1300, the Ottoman Empire grew from a tiny state in northwestern Anatolia because of three factors: (1) the shrewdness of its founder, Osman (from which the name *Ottoman* comes), and his descendants, (2) control of a strategic link between Europe and Asia on the Dardanelles strait, and (3) the creation of an army that took advantage of the traditional skills of the Turkish cavalryman and the new military possibilities presented by gunpowder.

Interactive Map

Map 17.1 Muslim Empires in the Sixteenth and Seventeenth Centuries

Iran, a Shi'ite state flanked by Sunni Ottomans on the west and Sunni Mughals on the east, had the least exposure to European influences. Ottoman expansion across the southern Mediterranean Sea intensified European fears of Islam. The areas of strongest Mughal control dictated that Islam's spread into Southeast Asia would be heavily influenced by merchants and religious figures from Gujarat instead of from eastern India.

At first, Ottoman armies concentrated on Christian enemies in Greece and the Balkans, in 1389 conquering a strong Serbian kingdom at the Battle of Kosovo (KO-so-vo). Much of southeastern Europe and Anatolia was under the control of the sultans by 1402. In 1453, Sultan Mehmed II, "the Conqueror," laid siege to Constantinople. His forces used enormous cannon to bash in the city's walls, dragged warships over a high hill from the Bosporus strait to the city's inner harbor to get around its sea defenses, and finally penetrated the city's land walls through a series of direct infantry assaults. The fall of Constantinople—henceforth commonly known as Istanbul—brought to an end over eleven hundred years of Byzantine rule and made the Ottomans seem invincible.

Selim (seh-LEEM) I, "the Grim," conquered Egypt and Syria in 1516 and 1517, making the Red Sea the Ottomans' southern frontier. His son, **Suleiman** (SOO-lay-man) **the Magnificent** (r. 1520–1566), presided over the greatest Ottoman assault on Christian Europe. Suleiman seemed unstoppable: he conquered Belgrade in 1521, expelled the Knights of the Hospital of St. John from the island of Rhodes the following year, and laid siege to Vienna in 1529. Vienna was saved by the need to retreat before the onset of winter more than by military action. In later centuries, Ottoman historians looked back on the reign of Suleiman as the period when the imperial system worked to perfection, and they spoke of it as the golden age of Ottoman greatness.

Suleiman the Magnificent (1494–1566) The most illustrious sultan of the Ottoman Empire (r. 1520–1566); also known as Suleiman Kanuni, "The Lawgiver." He significantly expanded the empire in the Balkans and eastern Mediterranean.

While Ottoman armies pressed deeper and deeper into eastern Europe, the sultans also sought to control the Mediterranean. Between 1453 and 1502, the Ottomans fought the opening rounds of a two-century war with Venice, the most powerful of Italy's commercial city-states. The initial fighting left Venice in control of its lucrative islands for another century. But it also left Venice a reduced military power compelled to pay tribute to the Ottomans.

In the early sixteenth century, merchants from southern India and Sumatra sent emissaries to Istanbul requesting naval support against the Portuguese. The Ottomans responded vigorously to Portuguese threats close to their territories, such as at Aden at the southern entrance to the Red Sea, but their efforts farther afield were insufficient to stifle growing Portuguese domination.

Eastern luxury products still flowed to Ottoman markets. Portuguese power was territorially limited to fortified coastal points, such as Hormuz at the entrance to the Persian Gulf, Goa in western India, and Malacca in Malaya. It never occurred to the Ottomans that a sea empire held together by flimsy ships could truly rival a great land empire fielding an army of a hundred thousand men. Why commit major resources to subduing an enemy whose main threat was a demand that merchant vessels, mostly belonging to non-Ottoman Muslims, buy protection from Portuguese attack? The Ottomans did send a small naval force to Indonesia, but they never formulated a consistent or aggressive policy with regard to political and economic developments in the Indian Ocean.

Central Institutions

By the 1520s, the Ottoman Empire was the most powerful and best-organized state in either Europe or the Islamic world. Its military was balanced between cavalry archers, primarily Turks, and **Janissaries** (JAN-nih-say-rees), Christian prisoners of war induced to serve as military slaves.

Janissaries Infantry, originally of slave origin, armed with firearms and constituting the elite of the Ottoman army from the fifteenth century until the corps was abolished in 1826.

An Ottoman Janissary Soldier
The Venetian artist Gentile Bellini (d. 1507) was sent by his government to Constantinople in 1478, only 24 years after its capture by the Ottomans. Among the images he produced was this one of a soldier wearing the distinctive headgear of the Janissary corps. Though the Janissaries were noted for their training in gunpowder weapons, this soldier is equipped with the more traditional bow and sword.   (Courtesty of the Trustees of the British Museum)

Slave soldiery had a long history in Islamic lands, but the conquest of Christian territories in the Balkans in the late fourteenth century gave the Ottomans access to a new military resource. Converted to Islam, these "new troops," called *yeni cheri* in Turkish and *Janissaries* in English, gave the Ottomans unusual military flexibility. Since horseback riding and bowmanship were not part of their cultural backgrounds, they readily accepted the idea of fighting on foot and learning to use guns, which at that time were still too heavy and awkward for a horseman to load and fire. The Janissaries lived in barracks and trained all year round.

The process of selection for Janissary training changed early in the fifteenth century. The new system imposed a regular levy of male children on Christian villages in the Balkans and occasionally elsewhere. Recruited children were placed with Turkish families to learn their language and then were sent to the sultan's palace in Istanbul for an education that included instruction in Islam, military training, and, for the most talented, what we might call liberal arts. This regime, sophisticated for its time, produced not only the Janissary soldiers but also, from among the chosen few who received special training, senior military commanders and heads of government departments up to the rank of grand vizier.

The cavalrymen were supported by land grants and administered most rural areas in Anatolia and the Balkans. They maintained order, collected taxes, and reported for each summer's campaign with their horses, retainers, and supplies, all paid for from the taxes they collected. When not campaigning, they stayed at home.

A galley-equipped navy was manned by Greek, Turkish, Algerian, and Tunisian sailors, usually under the command of an admiral from one of the North African ports. The balance of the Ottoman land forces brought success to Ottoman arms in recurrent wars with the Safavids, who were much slower to adopt firearms, and in the inexorable conquest of the Balkans. Expansion by sea was less dramatic. A major expedition against Malta in the western Mediterranean failed in 1565. Combined Christian forces also achieved a massive naval victory at the Battle of Lepanto, off Greece, in 1571. But the Ottomans' resources were so extensive that in a year's time they had replaced all of the galleys sunk in that battle.

The Ottoman Empire became cosmopolitan in character. The sophisticated court language, Osmanli (os-MAHN-lee) (the Turkish form of *Ottoman*), shared basic grammar and vocabulary with Turkish, but Arabic and Persian elements made it distinct from the language spoken by Anatolia's nomads and villagers. Everyone

Ottoman Glassmakers on Parade
Celebrations of the circumcisions of the sultan's sons featured parades organized by the craft guilds of Istanbul. This float features glassmaking, a common craft in Islamic realms. The most elaborate glasswork included oil lamps for mosques and colored glass for the small stained-glass windows below mosque domes.   (Topkapi Saray Museum)

CL HISTORY IN FOCUS   Examine the dress of the figures in this image and consider the public nature of their display. What do you think the social status of the craftsmen in the Ottoman Empire was? Why? *Find the answer online.*

who served in the military or the bureaucracy and conversed in Osmanli was considered to belong to the *askeri* (AS-keh-ree), or "military," class. Members of this class were exempt from taxes and owed their well-being to the sultan.

The Ottomans saw the sultan as providing justice for his "flock of sheep" (*raya* [RAH-yah]) and the military protecting them. In return, the raya paid the taxes that supported both the sultan and the military. In reality, the sultan's government remained comparatively isolated from the lives of most subjects. As Islam gradually became the majority religion in Balkan regions, Islamic law (the Shari'a [sha-REE-ah]) conditioned urban institutions and social life. Local customs prevailed among non-Muslims and in many rural areas; and non-Muslims looked to their own religious leaders for guidance in family and spiritual matters.

Crisis of the Military State, 1585–1650

As military technology evolved, cannon and lighter-weight firearms played an ever-larger role on the battlefield. Accordingly, the size of the Janissary corps—and its cost to the government—grew steadily, and the role of the Turkish cavalry diminished. To pay the Janissaries, the sultan started reducing the number of landholding cavalrymen. Revenues previously spent on their living expenses and military equipment went directly into the imperial treasury. Inflation caused by a flood of cheap silver from the New World bankrupted many of the remaining landholders, who were restricted by law to collecting a fixed amount of taxes. Their land was returned to the state. Displaced cavalrymen, armed and unhappy, became a restive element in rural Anatolia.

This complicated situation resulted in revolts that devastated Anatolia between 1590 and 1610. Former landholding cavalrymen, short-term soldiers released at the end of the campaign season, peasants overburdened by emergency taxes, and even impoverished students of religion formed bands of marauders. Anatolia experienced the worst of the rebellions and suffered greatly from emigration and the loss of agricultural production. But an increase in banditry, made worse by the government's inability to stem the spread of muskets among the general public, beset other parts of the empire as well.

In the meantime, the Janissaries took advantage of their growing influence to gain relief from prohibitions on their marrying and engaging in business. Janissaries who involved themselves in commerce lessened the burden on the state budget, and married Janissaries who enrolled sons or relatives in the corps made it possible in the seventeenth century for the government to save state funds by abolishing forced recruitment. These savings, however, were more than offset by the increase in the total number of Janissaries and in their steady deterioration as a military force, which necessitated the hiring of more and more supplemental troops.

Economic Change and Growing Weakness   A very different Ottoman Empire emerged from this crisis. The sultan once had led armies. Now he mostly resided in his palace and had little experience of the real world, and the affairs of government were overseen more and more by the chief administrators—the grand viziers.

The Janissaries took advantage of their increased power to make membership in their corps hereditary. Their involvement in crafts and trading took a toll on their military skills, but they continued to be a powerful faction in urban politics. Land grants in return for military service also disappeared, and tax farming arose in their place. Tax farmers paid specific taxes, such as customs duties, in advance in return for the privilege of collecting a greater amount from the actual taxpayers.

Rural administration, already disrupted by the rebellions, suffered from the transition to tax farms. The former military landholders had kept order on their lands in order to maintain their incomes. Tax farmers were less likely to live on the land. The imperial government therefore faced greater administrative burdens and came to rely heavily on powerful provincial governors or on wealthy men who purchased life-long tax collection rights and behaved more or less like private landowners.

Rural disorder and decline in administrative control sometimes opened the way for new economic opportunities. The port of Izmir (IZ-meer), known to Europeans by the ancient name "Smyrna," had a population in 1580 of around two thousand, many of them Greek-speaking Christians. By 1650 the population had increased to between thirty thousand and forty thousand. Along with refugees from the Anatolian uprisings and from European pirate attacks along the coast came European merchants and large colonies of Armenians and Jews. A French traveler in 1621 wrote: "At present, Izmir has a great traffic in wool, beeswax, cotton, and silk, which the Armenians bring there instead of going to Aleppo . . . because they do not pay as many dues."[3]

Izmir transformed itself between 1580 and 1650 from a small town into a multiethnic, multireligious, multilinguistic entrepôt because of the Ottoman government's inability to control trade and the slowly growing dominance of European traders in the Indian Ocean. Spices from the East, though still traded in Aleppo and other long-established Ottoman centers, were not to be found in Izmir. Aside from Iranian silk brought in by caravan, European traders at Izmir purchased local agricultural products—dried fruits, sesame seeds, nuts, and olive oil. As a consequence, local farmers who previously had grown grain for subsistence shifted their plantings more and more to cotton and other cash crops, including, after its introduction in the 1590s, tobacco, which quickly became popular in the Ottoman Empire despite government prohibitions (see Environment and Technology: Tobacco and Water-pipes). In this way, the agricultural economy of western Anatolia, the Balkans, and the Mediterranean coast—the Ottoman lands most accessible to Europe (see Map 17.1)—became enmeshed in a growing European commercial network.

At the same time, military power slowly ebbed. The ill-trained Janissaries some-times resorted to hiring substitutes to go on campaign, and the sultans relied on partially trained seasonal recruits and on armies raised by the governors of frontier provinces. A second mighty siege on Vienna failed in 1683, and by the middle of the eighteenth century it was obvious to the Austrians and Russians that the Ottoman Empire was weakening. On the eastern front, however, Ottoman exhaustion after many wars was matched by the demise in 1722 of their perennial adversary, the Safavid state of Iran.

The Ottoman Empire lacked both the wealth and the inclination to match Eu-ropean economic advances. Overland trade from the East dwindled as political dis-order in Safavid Iran cut deeply into Iranian silk production. Coffee, an Arabian product that rose from obscurity in the fifteenth century to become the rage first in the Ottoman Empire and then in Europe, was grown in the highlands of Yemen and exported by way of Egypt. By 1770, however, Muslim merchants trading in the Yemeni port of Mocha (MOH-kuh) (literally "the coffee place") were charged 15 per-cent in duties and fees. But European traders, benefiting from long-standing trade agreements with the Ottoman Empire, paid little more than 3 percent.

Such trade agreements, called capitulations, were first granted as favors by pow-erful sultans, but they eventually led to European domination of Ottoman seaborne trade. Nevertheless, the Europeans did not control strategic ports in the Mediter-ranean comparable to Malacca in the Indian Ocean and Hormuz on the Persian Gulf, so their economic power stopped short of colonial settlement or direct control in Ottoman territories.

A few astute Ottoman statesmen observed the growing disarray of the empire and advised the sultans to reestablish the land-grant and devshirme systems of Suleiman's reign. Most people, however, could not perceive the downward course of imperial power, much less the reasons behind it. Ottoman historians named the pe-riod between 1718 and 1730 the **"Tulip Period"** because of the craze for high-priced tulip bulbs that swept Ottoman ruling circles. The craze echoed a Dutch tulip ma-nia that had begun in the mid-sixteenth century, when the flower was introduced into Holland from Istanbul, and had peaked in 1636 with particularly rare bulbs go-ing for 2,500 florins apiece—the value of twenty-two oxen. Far from seeing Europe as the enemy that would eventually dismantle the empire, the Istanbul elite experi-mented with European clothing and furniture styles and purchased printed books from the empire's first (and short-lived) press.

In 1730, however, gala soirees at which guests watched turtles with candles on their backs wander in the dark through massive tulip beds gave way to a conserva-tive Janissary revolt with strong religious overtones. Sultan Ahmed III abdicated, and the leader of the revolt, Patrona Halil (pa-TROH-nuh ha-LEEL), an Albanian for-mer seaman and stoker of the public baths, swaggered around the capital for several months dictating government policies before he was seized and executed.

Tulip Period (1718–1730) Last years of the reign of Ottoman sultan Ahmed III, during which European styles and attitudes became briefly popular in Istanbul.

Tobacco and Waterpipes

Tobacco, a plant native to the Western Hemisphere, may have been introduced into Ottoman Syria as early as 1570 and was certainly known in Istanbul by 1600. In Iran, one historian noted that when an Uzbek ruler entered the northeast province of Khurasan in 1612 and called for tobacco, it was quickly provided for him, while a Spanish diplomat remarked just a few years later that Shah Abbas, who had banned smoking as a sinful practice, nevertheless permitted an envoy from the Mughal sultan to indulge. European traders initially brought tobacco by sea, but it quickly became a cultivated crop in Mughal India, whence it was exported to Iran. By the middle of the seventeenth century, however, it had also become a significant crop in Ottoman and Safavid territories.

The waterpipe became a distinctive means of smoking in the Islamic world, but when the device came into use is disputed. Iranian historians assert that it was invented in Iran, where one reference in poetry goes back to before 1550. This early date suggests that waterpipes may have been used for smoking some other substance before tobacco became known. Straight pipes of clay or wood were also used, especially in Turkish areas and among poorer people.

The Persian word for a waterpipe, *qalyan*, comes from an Arabic verb meaning "to boil, or bubble." Arabic has two common words: *nargila*, which derives ultimately from the Sanskrit word for "coconut," and *shisha*, which means "glass" in Persian. In India, where coconuts were often used to contain the water, the usual term was *hookah*, meaning "jar." The absence of a clear linguistic indication of the country of origin enhances the possibility that waterpipes evolved and spread before the introduction of tobacco.

All levels of society took to smoking, with women enjoying it as much as men. The leisurely ceremony of preparing and lighting the waterpipe made it an ideal pastime in coffeehouses, which became popular in both the Ottoman and Safavid Empires. In other settings, the size

IRANIAN WATERPIPE Moistened tobacco is placed in cup A, and a glowing coal is put on top of it to make it smolder. When the smoker draws on the stem sticking out to the side, the smoke bubbles up from beneath the water, which cools and filters it. The sophisticated manufacture shown in this drawing, which was rendered in 1622, supports the theory that the waterpipe went through a lengthy period of development before the seventeenth century.   (From J. Neander, *tabacolga medico-chemurgical pharmaceutica* [Leiden, 1622])

and fragility of the waterpipe could cause inconvenience. When traveling, wealthy Iranian men sometimes had a pipe carrier in their entourage who carried the *qalyan* in his hand and had a small pot containing hot coals dangling from his saddle in case his master should wish to light up on the road.

The Patrona Halil rebellion confirmed the perceptions of a few that the Ottoman Empire was facing severe difficulties. Yet decay at the center spelled benefit elsewhere. In the provinces, ambitious and competent governors, wealthy landholders, urban notables, and nomad chieftains took advantage of the central government's weakness. By the middle of the eighteenth century groups of Mamluks had regained a dominant position in Egypt. Though Selim I had defeated the Mamluk sultanate in the early sixteenth century, the practice of buying slaves in the Caucasus and training them as soldiers reappeared by the end of the century in several Arab cities. In Baghdad, Janissary commanders and Georgian mamluks competed for power, with the latter emerging triumphant by the mid-eighteenth century. In Aleppo and Damascus, however, the Janissaries came out on top. Meanwhile, in central Arabia, a puritanical Sunni movement inspired by Muhammad ibn Abd al-Wahhab began a remarkable rise beyond the reach of Ottoman power. Although no region declared full independence, the sultan's power was slipping away to the advantage of a broad array of lower officials and upstart chieftains in all parts of the empire while the Ottoman economy was reorienting itself toward Europe.

SECTION REVIEW

• The Ottoman Empire grew through the skill of its founding rulers, control of strategic territory, and military power.

• The empire expanded into southern and eastern Europe, the Middle East, and Africa, reaching its height under Suleiman the Magnificent.

• Unwilling to build a strong navy, the Ottomans never adapted to developments in the Indian Ocean.

• The empire rested on the military led by the sultan, and changes in military structure ultimately weakened the state.

• As the imperial economy reoriented toward Europe, the central government weakened, permitting the rise of local powers.

THE SAFAVID EMPIRE, 1502–1722

How did the Safavid Empire both resemble and differ from its neighbors?

The **Safavid Empire** of Iran (see Map 17.1) resembled its long-time Ottoman foe in many ways: it initially relied militarily on cavalry paid through land grants; its population spoke several different languages; and it was oriented inward away from the sea. It also had distinct qualities that to this day set Iran off from its neighbors: it derived part of its legitimacy from the pre-Islamic dynasties of ancient Iran, and it adopted the Shi'ite form of Islam.

Safavid Empire Iranian kingdom (1502–1722) established by Ismail Safavi, who declared Iran a Shi'ite state.

Safavid Society and Religion

The ultimate victor in a complicated struggle for power among Turkish chieftains west of the Ottoman Empire was Ismail (IS-ma-eel), a boy of Kurdish, Iranian, and Greek ancestry. In 1502, at the age of sixteen, Ismail proclaimed himself shah of Iran and declared that from that time forward his realm would be devoted to **Shi'ite** Islam, which revered the family of Muhammad's son-in-law Ali. Although Ismail's reasons for compelling Iran's conversion to Shi'ism are unknown, the effect of this radical act was to create a deep chasm between Iran and its neighbors, all of which were Sunni. Iran became a truly separate country for the first time since its incorporation into the Islamic caliphate in the seventh century.

The imposition of Shi'ite belief made the split permanent, but differences between Iran and its neighbors had long been in the making. Persian, written in the Arabic script from the tenth century onward, had emerged as the second language of Islam. Iranian scholars and writers normally read Arabic as well as Persian and sprinkled their writings with Arabic phrases, but their Arab counterparts were much less

Shi'ites Muslims belonging to the branch of Islam believing that God vests leadership of the community in a descendant of Muhammad's son-in-law Ali. Shi'ism is the state religion of Iran.

inclined to learn Persian. After the Mongols destroyed Baghdad, the capital of the Islamic caliphate, in 1258, Iran developed largely on its own, having more extensive contacts with India—where Muslim rulers favored the Persian language—than with the Arabs.

In the post-Mongol period, artistic styles in Iran, Afghanistan, and Central Asia also went their own way. Painted and molded tiles and tile mosaics, often in vivid turquoise blue, became the standard exterior decoration of mosques in Iran but never were used in Syria and Egypt. Persian poets raised verse to peaks of perfection that had no reflection in Arabic poetry, generally considered to be in a state of decline.

To be sure, Islam itself provided a tradition of belief, learning, and law that crossed ethnic and linguistic borders, but Shah Ismail's imposition of Shi'ism set Iran significantly apart. Shi'ite doctrine says that all temporal rulers, regardless of title, are temporary stand-ins for the **"Hidden Imam"**: the twelfth descendant of Ali, the prophet Muhammad's cousin and son-in-law who disappeared as a child in the ninth century. Some Shi'ite scholars concluded that the faithful should calmly accept the world as it was and wait quietly for the Hidden Imam's return. Others maintained that they themselves should play a stronger role in political affairs because they were best qualified to know the Hidden Imam's wishes. These two positions, which still play a role in Iranian Shi'ism, tended to enhance the self-image of religious scholars as independent of imperial authority and stood in the way of their becoming subordinate government functionaries, as happened in the Ottoman Empire.

Shi'ism also affected the psychological life of the people. Annual commemoration of the martyrdom of Imam Husayn (d. 680), Ali's son and the third Imam, regularized an emotional outpouring with no parallel in Sunni lands. Day after day for two weeks, preachers recited the woeful tale to crowds of weeping believers, and elaborate street processions, often organized by craft guilds, paraded chanting and self-flagellating men past crowds of reverent onlookers. Of course, Shi'ites elsewhere observed rites of mourning for Imam Husayn, but the impact of these rites was especially great in Iran, where 90 percent of the population was Shi'ite. Over time, the subjects of the Safavid shahs came to feel more than ever a people apart.

A Tale of Two Cities: Isfahan and Istanbul

Outwardly, the Ottoman capital of Istanbul looked quite different from Isfahan (is-fah-HAHN), which became Iran's capital in 1598 by decree of **Shah Abbas I** (r. 1587–1629). Built on seven hills on the south side of the narrow Golden Horn inlet, Istanbul boasted a skyline punctuated by the gray stone domes and thin, pointed minarets of the great imperial mosques. The mosques surrounding the royal plaza in Isfahan, in contrast, had unobtrusive minarets and brightly tiled domes that rose to gentle peaks. High walls surrounded the sultan's palace in Istanbul. Shah Abbas in Isfahan focused his capital on the giant royal plaza, which was large enough for his army to play polo, and he used an airy palace overlooking the plaza to receive dignitaries and review his troops.

The harbor of Istanbul, the primary Ottoman seaport, teemed with sailing ships and smaller craft, many of them belonging to a colony of European merchants perched on a hilltop on the north side of the Golden Horn. Isfahan, far from the sea, was only occasionally visited by Europeans. Most of its trade was in the hands of Jews, Hindus, and especially a colony of Armenian Christians brought in by Shah Abbas.

CL Primary Source: **Letter to Shah Ismail of Persia** *Discover why Sultan Selim I, animated by the spirit of a fatwa, launches an attack on Shah Ismail of Persia.*

Hidden Imam Last in a series of twelve descendants of Muhammad's son-in-law Ali, whom Shi'ites consider divinely appointed leaders of the Muslim community. In occlusion since ca. 873, he is expected to return as a messiah at the end of time.

Shah Abbas I (r. 1587–1629) The fifth and most renowned ruler of the Safavid dynasty in Iran. Abbas moved the royal capital to Isfahan in 1598.

Istanbul Family on the Way to a Bath House

Public baths, an important feature of Islamic cities, set different hours for men and women. Young boys, such as the lad in the turban shown here, went with their mothers and sisters. Notice that the children wear the same styles as the adults.   (Austrian National Library, Vienna, picture archives)

Beneath these superficial differences, the two capitals had much in common. Wheeled vehicles were scarce in hilly Istanbul and nonexistent in Isfahan. Both cities were built for walking and, aside from the royal plaza in Isfahan, lacked the open spaces common in contemporary European cities. Streets were narrow and irregular. Houses crowded against each other in dead-end lanes. Residents enjoyed their privacy in interior courtyards. Artisans and merchants organized themselves into guilds that had strong social and religious as well as economic bonds. The shops of each guild adjoined each other in the markets.

Women were seldom seen in public, even in Istanbul's mazelike covered market or in Isfahan's long, serpentine bazaar. At home, the women's quarters—called *anderun* (an-deh-ROON), or "interior," in Iran and *harem,* or "forbidden area," in Istanbul—were separate from the public rooms where the men of the family received visitors. In both areas, low cushions, charcoal braziers for warmth, carpets, and small tables constituted most of the furnishings.

The private side of family life has left few traces, but it is apparent that women's society—consisting of wives, children, female servants, and sometimes one or more eunuchs—was not entirely cut off from the outside world. Ottoman court records reveal that women, using male agents, were very active in the urban real estate market. Often they were selling inherited shares of their father's estate, but some both bought and sold real estate on a regular basis and even established religious endowments for pious purposes. The fact that Islamic law, unlike some European codes, permitted a wife to retain her property after marriage gave some women a stake in the general economy and a degree of independence from their spouses. Women also appeared in other types of court cases, where they often testified for themselves, for Islamic courts did not recognize the role of attorney. Although comparable Safavid court records do not survive, historians assume that a parallel situation prevailed in Iran.

European travelers commented on the veiling of women outside the home, but the norm for both sexes was complete coverage of arms, legs, and hair. Miniature paintings indicate that ordinary female garb consisted of a long, ample dress with a scarf or long shawl pulled tight over the forehead to conceal the hair. Lightweight trousers, either close-fitting or baggy, were often worn under the dress. This mode of dress was not far different from that of men. Poor men wore light trousers, a long shirt, a jacket, and a hat or turban. Wealthier men wore over their trousers ankle-length caftans, often closely fitted around the chest. Public life was almost entirely the domain of men. Poetry and art, both somewhat more elegantly developed in Isfahan than in Istanbul, were as likely to extol the charms of beardless boys as pretty

Aya Sofya Mosque in Istanbul   Originally a Byzantine cathedral, Aya Sofya (in Greek, Hagia Sophia) was transformed into a mosque after 1453, and four minarets were added. It then became a model for subsequent Ottoman mosques. To the right behind it is the Bosporus strait dividing Europe and Asia, to the left the Golden Horn inlet separating the old city of Istanbul from the newer parts. The gate to the Ottoman sultan's palace is to the right of the mosque. The pointed tower to the left of the dome is part of the palace.
(Robert Frerck/Odyssey/Chicago)

women. Despite religious disapproval of homosexuality, attachments to adolescent boys were neither unusual nor hidden. Women who appeared in public—aside from non-Muslims, the aged, and the very poor—were likely to be slaves. Miniature paintings frequently depict female dancers, musicians, and even acrobats in attitudes and costumes that range from decorous to decidedly erotic.

Despite social similarities, the overall flavors of Isfahan and Istanbul were not the same. Isfahan had its prosperous Armenian quarter across the river from the city's center, but it was not a truly cosmopolitan capital, just as the peoples of the Safavid realm were not remarkably diverse. Like other rulers of extensive land empires, Shah Abbas located his capital toward the center of his domain within comparatively easy reach of any threatened frontier. Istanbul, in contrast, was a great seaport and a crossroads located on the straits separating the sultan's European and Asian possessions. People of all sorts lived or spent time in Istanbul: Venetians, Genoese, Arabs, Turks, Greeks, Armenians, Albanians, Serbs, Jews, Bulgarians, and more. In this respect, Istanbul conveyed the cosmopolitan character of major seaports from London to Canton (Guangzhou) and belied the fact that its prosperity rested on the vast reach of the sultan's territories rather than on the voyages of its merchants.

Economic Crisis and Political Collapse

The silk fabrics of northern Iran were the mainstay of the Safavid Empire's foreign trade. However, the manufacture that eventually became most powerfully associated with Iran was the deep-pile carpet made by knotting colored yarns around stretched warp threads. Different cities produced distinctive carpet designs. Women and girls did much of the actual knotting work.

Overall, Iran's manufacturing sector was neither large nor notably productive. Most of the shah's subjects, whether Iranians, Turks, Kurds, or Arabs, lived by subsistence farming or herding. Neither area of activity recorded significant technological advances during the Safavid period.

The Safavids, like the Ottomans, had difficulty finding the money to pay troops armed with firearms. This crisis occurred somewhat later in Iran because of its greater distance from Europe. By the end of the sixteenth century, it was evident that a more systematic adoption of cannon and firearms in the Safavid Empire would be needed to hold off the Ottomans and the Uzbeks (UHZ-bex) (Turkish rulers who had succeeded the Timurids on Iran's Central Asian frontier; see Map 17.1). Like the Ottoman cavalry a century earlier, the warriors furnished by the nomad leaders were not inclined to trade in their bows for firearms. Shah Abbas responded by establishing a slave corps of year-round soldiers and arming them with guns. The Christian converts to Islam who initially provided the manpower for the new corps were mostly captives taken in raids on Georgia in the Caucasus (CAW-kuh-suhs).

In the late sixteenth century, the inflation caused by cheap silver spread into Iran; then overland trade through Safavid territory declined because of mismanagement of the silk monopoly after Shah Abbas's death in 1629. As a result, the country faced the unsolvable problem of finding money to pay the army and bureaucracy. Trying to unseat the nomads from their lands to regain control of taxes was more difficult and more disruptive militarily than the piecemeal dismantlement of the land-grant system in the Ottoman Empire. The nomads were still a cohesive military force, and pressure from the center simply caused them to withdraw to their mountain pastures until the pressure subsided. By 1722, the government had become so weak and commanded so little support from the nomadic groups that an army of marauding Afghans was able to capture Isfahan and effectively end Safavid rule.

SECTION REVIEW

- The rise of the Shi'ite Safavid Empire completed the long-growing split between Iran and its neighbors.

- Despite significant differences, Istanbul and Isfahan showed some cultural similarities between the Ottoman and Safavid Empires.

- Silks and carpets were important manufactures, but most Safavid subjects made a living by farming or herding.

- High military costs, inflation, and decline of overland trade weakened the state, which fell to Afghan invaders in 1722.

THE MUGHAL EMPIRE

How did the Mughal Empire combine Muslim and Hindu elements into an effective state?

What distinguished the Indian empire of the Mughal (MOH-guhl) sultans from the empires of the Ottomans and Safavids was the fact that India was a land of Hindus ruled by a Muslim minority. Muslim dominion in India was the result of repeated military campaigns from the early eleventh century onward, and the Mughals had to contend with the Hindus' long-standing resentment of the destruction of their culture by Muslims. Thus, the challenge facing the Mughals was not just conquering and organizing a large territorial state but also finding a formula for Hindu-Muslim coexistence.

Mughal Empire Muslim state (1526–1857) exercising dominion over most of India in the sixteenth and seventeenth centuries.

Akbar (1542–1605) Most illustrious sultan of the Mughal Empire in India (r. 1556–1605). He expanded the empire and pursued a policy of conciliation with Hindus.

mansabs In India, grants of land given in return for service by rulers of the Mughal Empire.

Primary Source: Akbarnama
Learn about life in the court of Akbar where arts and customs from conquered lands were routinely presented for the sultan's review.

Rajputs Members of a mainly Hindu warrior caste from northwest India. The Mughal emperors drew most of their Hindu officials from this caste, and Akbar married a Rajput princess.

Political Foundations

Babur (BAH-bur) (1483–1530), the founder of the **Mughal Empire**, was a Muslim descendant of both Timur and Genghis Khan (*Mughal* is Persian for "Mongol"). Invading from Central Asia, Babur defeated the last Muslim sultan of Delhi (DEL-ee) in 1526. Babur's grandson **Akbar** (r. 1556–1605), a brilliant but mercurial man, established the central administration of the expanding state. Under him and his three successors—the last of whom died in 1707—all but the southern tip of India fell under Mughal rule, administered first from Agra and then from Delhi.

Akbar granted land revenues to military officers and government officials in return for their service. Ranks, called ***mansabs*** (MAN-sabz), some high and some low, entitled their holders to revenue assignments. As in the other Islamic empires, revenue grants were not considered hereditary, and the central government kept careful track of their issuance.

With a population of 100 million, a thriving trading economy based on cotton cloth, and a generally efficient administration, India under Akbar was probably the most prosperous empire of the sixteenth century. He and his successors faced few external threats and experienced generally peaceful conditions in their northern Indian heartland.

Foreign trade boomed at the port of Surat in the northwest, which also served as an embarkation point for pilgrims on their way to Mecca. Like the Safavids, the Mughals had no navy or merchant ships. The government saw the Europeans—after Akbar's time, primarily Dutch and English, the Portuguese having lost most of their Indian ports—less as enemies than as shipmasters whose naval support could be procured as needed in return for trading privileges.

Hindus and Muslims

The Mughal state inherited traditions of unified imperial rule from both the Islamic caliphate and the more recent examples of Genghis Khan and Timur. Those traditions did not necessarily mean religious intolerance. Seventy percent of the *mansabdars* (man-sab-DAHRZ) (officials holding land revenues) appointed under Akbar were Muslim soldiers born outside India, but 15 percent were Hindus. Most of the Hindu appointees were warriors from the north called **Rajputs** (RAHJ-putz), one of whom rose to be a powerful revenue minister.

Akbar, the most illustrious ruler of his dynasty, differed from his Ottoman and Safavid counterparts—Suleiman the Magnificent and Shah Abbas the Great—in his striving for social harmony and not just for more territory and revenue. His marriage to a Rajput princess signaled his desire for reconciliation and even intermarriage between Muslims and Hindus. The birth of a son in 1569 ensured that future rulers would have both Muslim and Hindu ancestry.

Akbar ruled that in legal disputes between two Hindus, decisions would be made according to village custom or Hindu law as interpreted by local Hindu scholars. Shari'a law was in force for Muslims. Akbar made himself the legal court of last resort, creating an appeals process not usually present in Islamic jurisprudence.

Akbar also made himself the center of a new "Divine Faith" incorporating Muslim, Hindu, Zoroastrian, Sikh (seek), and Christian beliefs. He was strongly attracted by Sufi ideas, which permeated the religious rituals he instituted at his court. To promote serious consideration of his religious principles, he oversaw, from a catwalk high above the audience, debates among scholars of all religions assembled in his octagonal private audience chamber. When courtiers uttered the Muslim exclamation "Allahu Akbar"—"God is great"—they also understood it in its second grammatical meaning: "God is Akbar."

Akbar's religious views did not survive him, but the court culture he fostered, reflecting a mixture of Muslim and Hindu traditions, flourished until his zealous great-grandson Aurangzeb (ow-rang-ZEB) (r. 1658–1707) reinstituted many restrictions on Hindus. Mughal and Rajput miniature paintings reveled in precise portraits of political figures and depictions of scantily clad women, even though they brought frowns to the faces of pious Muslims, who deplored the representation of human beings. Most of the leading painters were Hindus. In addition to the florid style of Persian verse favored at court, a new taste developed for poetry and prose in the popular language of the Delhi region. The modern descendant of this language is called *Urdu* in Pakistan and *Hindi* in India.

Central Decay and Regional Challenges

Mughal power did not long survive Aurangzeb's death in 1707. Some historians consider the land-grant system a central element in the rapid decline of imperial authority, but other factors were at play as well. Aurangzeb's additions to Mughal territory in southern India were not all well integrated into the imperial structure, and strong regional powers arose to challenge Mughal military supremacy. A climax came in 1739 when Nadir Shah, a warlord who had seized power in Iran after the fall of the Safavids, invaded the Mughal capital and carried off to Iran the "peacock throne," the priceless jewel-encrusted symbol of Mughal grandeur. Another throne was found for the later Mughals to sit on; but their empire, which survived in name to 1857, was finished.

In 1723, Nizam al-Mulk (nee-ZAHM al-MULK), the powerful vizier of the Mughal sultan, gave up on the central government and established his own nearly independent state at Hyderabad in the eastern Deccan. Other officials bearing the title *nawab* (NAH-wab) became similarly independent in Bengal and Oudh (OW-ad) in the northeast, as did the Marathas in the center. In the northwest, simultaneous Iranian and Mughal weakness allowed the Afghans to establish an independent kingdom.

Some of these regional powers, and the smaller princely states that arose on former Mughal territory, were prosperous and benefited from the removal of the sultan's heavy hand. Linguistic and religious communities, freed from the religious intolerance instituted during the reign of Aurangzeb, similarly enjoyed greater opportunity for political expression. However, this disintegration of central power favored the intrusion of European adventurers.

Joseph François Dupleix (doo-PLAY) took over the presidency of the French stronghold of Pondicherry (pon-dih-CHER-ree) in 1741 and began a new phase of European involvement in India. He captured the English trading center of Madras and used his small contingent of European and European-trained Indian troops to become a power broker in southern India. Though offered the title *nawab*, Dupleix preferred to operate behind the scenes, using

SECTION REVIEW

- Founded by Babur, the Mughal Empire grew under Akbar and his successors to encompass most of India.

- The empire prospered through trade and granted trade privileges to Europeans in exchange for naval support.

- Akbar included both Muslims and Hindus in his government, respected Hindu customs, and strove for religious harmony.

- A hybrid culture flourished, but Aurangzeb practiced Muslim intolerance.

- After Aurangzeb's death, the empire declined through foreign invasion, the rise of regional powers, and European encroachment.

Indian princes as puppets. His career ended in 1754 when he was called home. Deeply involved in wars in Europe, the French government was unwilling to pursue further adventures in India. Dupleix's departure opened the way for the British, whose ventures in India are described in Chapter 22.

THE MARITIME WORLDS OF ISLAM, 1500–1750

What role does maritime history play in the political and economic life of this period?

As land powers, the Mughal, Safavid, and Ottoman Empires faced similar problems in the seventeenth and eighteenth centuries. Complex changes in military technology and in the world economy, along with the increasing difficulty of basing an extensive land empire on military forces paid through land grants, affected them all adversely. These difficulties contributed to the often dynamic development of power centers away from the imperial capital.

The new pressures faced by land powers were less important to seafaring countries intent on turning trade networks into maritime empires. Improvements in ship design, navigation accuracy, and the use of cannon gave an ever-increasing edge to European powers competing with local seafaring peoples. Moreover, the development of joint-stock companies, in which many merchants pooled their capital, provided a flexible and efficient financial instrument for exploiting new possibilities. The English East India Company was founded in 1600; the Dutch East India Company in 1602.

Although the Ottomans, Safavids, and Mughals did not effectively contest the growth of Portuguese and then Dutch, English, and French maritime power, the majority of non-European shipbuilders, captains, sailors, and traders were Muslim. Groups of Armenian, Jewish, and Hindu traders were also active, but they remained almost as aloof from the Europeans as the Muslims did. The presence in every port of Muslims following the same legal traditions and practicing their faith in similar ways cemented the Muslims' trading network. Islam, from its very outset in the life and preaching of Muhammad (570–632), had favored trade and traders. Unlike Hinduism, it was a proselytizing religion, a factor that encouraged the growth of coastal Muslim communities as local non-Muslims associated with Muslim commercial activities converted and intermarried with Muslims from abroad.

Although European missionaries, particularly the Jesuits, tried to extend Christianity into Asia and Africa (see Chapters 14 and 18), most Europeans, the Portuguese excepted, did not treat local converts or the offspring of mixed marriages as full members of their communities. Islam was generally more welcoming. As a consequence, Islam spread extensively into East Africa and Southeast Asia during precisely the same time as rapid European commercial expansion. Even without the support of the Muslim land empires, Islam became a source of resistance to growing European domination.

Muslims in Southeast Asia

Historians disagree about the chronology and manner of Islam's spread in Southeast Asia. Arab traders appeared in southern China as early as the eighth century, so Muslims probably reached the East Indies (the island portions of Southeast Asia) at a similarly early date. Nevertheless, the dominance of Indian cultural influences in the area for several centuries thereafter indicates that early Muslim visitors had little impact on local beliefs. Clearer indications of conversion and the formation of Muslim communities date from roughly the fourteenth century, with the strongest overseas linkage being to the port of Cambay in India (see Map 17.2) rather than to the Arab world. Islam first took root in port cities and in some royal courts and spread inland only slowly, possibly transmitted by itinerant Sufis.

Although appeals to the Ottoman sultan for support against the Europeans ultimately proved futile, Islam strengthened resistance to Portuguese, Spanish, and Dutch intruders. When the Spaniards conquered the Philippines during the decades following the establishment of their first fort in 1565, they encountered Muslims on the southern island of Mindanao (min-duh-NOW) and the nearby Sulu archipelago. They called them "Moros," the Spanish term for their old enemies, the Muslims of North Africa. In the ensuing Moro wars, the Spaniards portrayed the Moros as greedy pirates who raided non-Muslim territories for slaves. In fact, they were political, religious, and commercial competitors whose perseverance enabled them to establish the Sulu Empire based in the southern Philippines, one of the strongest states in Southeast Asia from 1768 to 1848.

Other local kingdoms that looked on Islam as a force to counter the aggressive Christianity of the Europeans included the actively proselytizing Brunei (BROO-nie) Sultanate in northern Borneo and the **Acheh** (AH-cheh) **Sultanate** in northern Sumatra. At its peak in the early seventeenth century, Acheh succeeded Malacca as the main center of Islamic expansion in Southeast Asia. It prospered by trading pepper for cotton cloth from Gujarat in India. Acheh declined after the Dutch seized Malacca from Portugal in 1641.

Acheh Sultanate Muslim kingdom in northern Sumatra. Main center of Islamic expansion in Southeast Asia in the early seventeenth century, it declined after the Dutch seized Malacca from Portugal in 1641.

How well Islam was understood in these Muslim kingdoms is open to question. In Acheh, for example, a series of women ruled between 1641 and 1699. This practice ended when local Muslim scholars obtained a ruling from scholars in Mecca and Medina that Islam did not approve of female rulers. After this ruling, scholarly understandings of Islam gained greater prominence in the East Indies.

Historians have looked at merchants, Sufi preachers, or both as the first propagators of Islam in Southeast Asia. The scholarly vision of Islam, however, took root in the sixteenth century by way of pilgrims returning from years of study in Mecca and Medina. Islam promoted the dissemination of writing in the region. Some of the returning pilgrims wrote in Arabic, others in Malay or Javanese. As Islam continued to spread, adat ("custom"), a form of Islam rooted in pre-Muslim religious and social practices, retained its preeminence in rural areas over practices centered on the Shari'a, the religious law. But the royal courts in the port cities began to heed the views of the pilgrim teachers. Though different in many ways, both varieties of Islam provided believers with a firm basis of identification in the face of the growing European presence. Christian missionaries gained most of their converts in regions that had not yet converted to Islam, such as the northern Philippines.

Muslims in Coastal Africa

Muslim rulers also governed the East African ports that the Portuguese began to visit in the fifteenth century, though they were not allied politically (see Map 17.2). People living

Interactive Map

Map 17.2   European Colonization in the Indian Ocean, to 1750

Since Portuguese explorers were the first Europeans to reach India by rounding Africa, Portugal gained a strong foothold in both areas. Rival Spain was barred from colonizing the region by the Treaty of Tordesillas in 1494, which limited Spanish efforts to lands west of a line drawn through the mid-Atlantic Ocean. The line carried around the globe provided justification of Spanish colonization in the Philippines. French, British, and Dutch colonies date from after 1600, when joint-stock companies provided a new stimulus for overseas commerce.

in the millet and rice lands of the Swahili Coast—from the Arabic sawahil (suh-WAH-hil) meaning "coasts"—had little contact with those in the dry hinterlands. Throughout this period, the East African lakes region and the highlands of Kenya witnessed unprecedented migration and relocation of peoples because of drought conditions that persisted from the late sixteenth through most of the seventeenth century.

Cooperation among the trading ports of Kilwa, Mombasa, and Malindi was hindered by the thick bush country that separated the cultivated tracts of coastal land and by the fact that the ports competed with one another in the export of ivory; ambergris (AM-ber-grees) (a whale byproduct used in perfumes); and forest products such as beeswax, copal tree resin, and wood. Kilwa also exported gold. In the eighteenth century slave trading, primarily to Arabian ports but also to India, increased in importance. Because Europeans—the only peoples who kept consistent records of slave-trading activities—played a minor role in this slave trade, few records have survived to indicate its extent. Perhaps the best estimate is that 2.1 million slaves were exported between 1500 and 1890, a little over 12.5 percent of the total traffic in African slaves during that period (see Chapter 16).

The Portuguese conquered all the coastal ports from Mozambique northward except Malindi, with whose ruler Portugal cooperated. A Portuguese description of the ruler names some of the cloth and metal goods that Malindi imported, as well as some local manufactures:

> The King wore a robe of damask trimmed with green satin and a rich [cap]. He was seated on two cushioned chairs of bronze, beneath a rough sunshade of crimson satin attached to a pole. An old man, who attended him as a page, carried a short sword in a silver sheath. There were many players on [horns], and two trumpets of ivory richly carved and of the size of a man, which were blown through a hole in the side, and made sweet harmony with the [horns].[4]

Initially, the Portuguese favored the port of Malindi, which caused the decline of Kilwa and Mombasa. Repeatedly plagued by local rebellion, Portuguese power suffered severe blows when the Arabs of **Oman** in southeastern Arabia captured their south Arabian stronghold at Musqat (1650) and then went on to seize Mombasa (1698), which had become the Portuguese capital in East Africa. The Portuguese briefly retook Mombasa but lost control permanently in 1729. From then on, the Portuguese had to content themselves with Mozambique in East Africa and a few remaining ports in India (Goa) and farther east (Macao and Timor).

Oman Arab state based in Musqat, the main port in the southeastern region of the Arabian peninsula. Oman succeeded Portugal as a power in the western Indian Ocean in the eighteenth century.

The Omanis created a maritime empire of their own, one that worked in greater cooperation with the African populations. The Bantu language of the coast, broadened by the absorption of Arabic, Persian, and Portuguese loanwords, developed into **Swahili** (swah-HEE-lee), which was spoken throughout the region. Arabs and other Muslims who settled in the region intermarried with local families, giving rise to a mixed population that played an important role in developing a distinctive Swahili culture.

Swahili Bantu language with Arabic loanwords spoken in coastal regions of East Africa.

Islam also spread in the southern Sudan in this period, particularly in the dry areas away from the Nile River. This growth coincided with a waning of Ethiopian power as a result of Portugal's stifling of trade in the Red Sea. Yet no significant contact developed between the emerging Muslim Swahili culture and that of the Muslims in the Sudan to the north.

In northwest Africa the seizure by Portugal and Spain of coastal strongholds in Morocco provoked a militant response. The Sa'adi family, which claimed descent from

Portuguese Fort Guarding Musqat Harbor

Musqat in Oman and Aden in Yemen, the best harbors in southern Arabia, were targets for imperial navies trying to establish dominance in the Indian Ocean. Musqat's harbor is small and circular, with one narrow entrance overlooked by this fortress. The palace of the sultan of Oman is still located at the opposite end of the harbor. (Robert Harding World Imagery)

SECTION REVIEW

- From its inception in the time of Muhammad, Islam flowered in places of trade, and beginning around 1500, the majority of non-European shipbuilders, captains, sailors, and traders were Muslim.

- A number of local kingdoms in Southeast Asia took on Islam as a force to resist the aggressive Christianity of the Europeans.

- Many Muslims in coastal Africa intermarried with locals, creating a mixed population that played a key part in the development of a distinctive Swahili culture.

- Over time the successes of European trading companies changed the balance of power in the southern seas, but local merchants never completely disappeared from the commercial scene.

the Prophet Muhammad, led a resistance to Portuguese aggression that climaxed in victory at the battle of al-Qasr al-Kabir (Ksar el Kebir) in 1578. The triumphant Moroccan sultan, Ahmad al-Mansur, restored his country's strength and independence. By the early seventeenth century naval expeditions from the port of Salé, referred to in British records as "the Sally Rovers," raided European shipping as far as Britain itself.

Corsairs, or sea raiders, working out of Algerian, Tunisian, and Libyan ports brought the same sort of warfare to the Mediterranean. European governments called these Muslim raiders pirates and slave-takers, and they leveled the same charges against other Muslim mariners in the Persian Gulf and the Sulu Sea. But there was little distinction between the actions of the Muslims and of their European adversaries.

European Powers in Southern Seas

The Dutch played a major role in driving the Portuguese from their possessions in the East Indies. They were better organized than the Portuguese through the Dutch East India Company. Just as the Portuguese had tried to dominate the trade in spices, so the Dutch concentrated at first on the spice-producing islands of Southeast Asia. The Portuguese had seized Malacca, a strategic town on the narrow strait at the end of the Malay Peninsula, from a local Malay ruler in 1511 (see Chapter 14). The Dutch took it away from them in 1641, leaving Portugal little foothold in the East Indies except the islands of Ambon (am-BOHN) and Timor (see Map 17.2).

Although the United Netherlands was one of the least autocratic countries of Europe, the governors-general appointed by the Dutch East India Company deployed almost unlimited powers in their efforts to maintain their trade monopoly. They could even order the execution of their own employees for "smuggling"—that is, trading on their own. Under strong governors-general, the Dutch fought a series of wars against Acheh and other local kingdoms on Sumatra and Java. In 1628 and 1629 their new capital at **Batavia**, now the city of Jakarta on Java, was besieged by a fleet of fifty ships belonging to the sultan of Mataram (MAH-tah-ram), a Javanese kingdom. The Dutch held out with difficulty and eventually prevailed when the sultan was unable to get effective help from the English.

Suppressing local rulers, however, was not enough to control the spice trade once other European countries adopted Dutch methods, learned more about where goods might be acquired, and started to send more ships to Southeast Asia. In the course of the eighteenth century, therefore, the Dutch gradually turned from being middlemen between Southeast Asian producers and European buyers to producing crops in areas they controlled, notably in Java. Javanese teak forests yielded high-quality lumber, and coffee, transplanted from Yemen, grew well in the western hilly regions. In this new phase of colonial export production, Batavia developed from being the headquarters town of a far-flung enterprise to being the administrative capital of a conquered land.

Beyond the East Indies, the Dutch utilized their discovery of a band of powerful eastward-blowing winds (called the "Roaring Forties" because they blow throughout the year between 40 and 50 degrees south latitude) to reach Australia in 1606. In 1642 and 1643 Abel Tasman became the first European to set foot on Tasmania and New Zealand and to sail around Australia, signaling European involvement in that region (see Chapter 22).

Batavia Fort established ca. 1619 as headquarters of Dutch East India Company operations in Indonesia; today the city of Jakarta.

Chapter Review

 DOWNLOAD THE MP3 AUDIO FILE OF THE CHAPTER REVIEW TO LISTEN TO ON THE GO.

How did the Ottoman Empire rise to power, and what factors contributed to its transformation? (page 472)

Strategic location and a centralized army well balanced between mounted bowmen and an infantry armed with gunpowder weapons were keys to Ottoman success during the empire's first two centuries. With territorial growth, however, the borders became too distant from the capital for the efficient deployment of a centralized army, and economic pressures, notably those associated with a flood of cheap silver from the New World, forced modifications in the ruling system. Military, and increasingly political, power devolved to commanders and governors in provincial capitals and border districts, while new fiscal arrangements captured more tax revenue for the central government and the Istanbul elite.

How did the Safavid Empire both resemble and differ from its neighbors? (page 481)

The Safavid Empire embodied some of the same Turkish tribal traditions and Islamic governing institutions that were found among the Ottomans, but the formal adoption of Shi'ism as the state religion at the beginning of the sixteenth century created such a gulf between them that these similarities were seldom recognized. In some respects, such as their practice of using Christian prisoners of war as infantry, the Safavids followed the Ottoman lead. By contrast, the Mughals drew military forces from Central Asia and Afghanistan and adopted Persian as the language of government but never enjoyed the religious and cultural homogeneity that was a hallmark of Safavid Iran.

How did the Mughal Empire combine Muslim and Hindu elements into an effective state? (page 485)

Dealing with the Hindu majority in their domain was a continuing problem for the Mughal rulers. Akbar took the path of accommodation by appointing Hindu officials and trying to harmonize religious differences. Aurangzeb, his great-grandson, took the opposite path of persecuting Hindus and exalting Islam. Both rulers enjoyed military success against various Indian adversaries,

KEY TERMS

Ottoman Empire *(p. 472)*
Suleiman the Magnificent *(p. 475)*
Janissaries *(p. 475)*
Tulip Period *(p. 479)*
Safavid Empire *(p. 481)*
Shi'ites *(p. 481)*
Hidden Imam *(p. 482)*
Shah Abbas I *(p. 482)*
Mughal Empire *(p. 486)*
Akbar *(p. 486)*
mansabs (p. 486)
Rajputs *(p. 486)*
Acheh Sultanate *(p. 489)*
Oman *(p. 491)*
Swahili *(p. 491)*
Batavia *(p.492)*

WEB RESOURCES

Pronunciation Guide
Interactive Maps
MAP 17.1 Muslim Empires in the Sixteenth and Seventeenth Centuries
MAP 17.2 European Colonization in the Indian Ocean, to 1750
Primary Sources
Letter to Shah Ismail of Persia
Akbarnama
(Continued)

but neither hit on a formula that would permanently bridge the gap between the Muslim ruling minority and the non-Muslim majority. Nevertheless, by comparison with most earlier Indian states, and measured by the problems and successes of the contemporary Ottoman and Safavid realms, Mughal rule must be deemed effective.

What role does maritime history play in the political and economic life of this period? (page 488)

Muslim rulers who saw greater opportunities and dangers along imperial land frontiers than at sea saw nothing threatening in the vigorous commercial activity of the non-Muslim merchants in their realms—Jews, Christians, and Hindus—or even the European trading companies. To be sure, the Ottoman navy was a formidable military force in the Mediterranean, and Muslim rulers in Morocco, Oman, and Southeast Asia sometimes reacted effectively to European maritime pressure. But the greatest battles were fought on land, and acquisition or loss of territory was taken by Muslims and non-Muslims alike as a more important sign of an empire's strength than its command of maritime trade routes. Over time, the economic gains made by the European trading companies changed the balance of power in the region, but local merchants never disappeared from the commercial scene, either as maritime traders or as manufacturers producing goods like Indian cotton cloth for export.

> ### Answer to the History in Focus Question
> See photo on page 477, "Ottoman Glassmakers on Parade."
> ### Plus
> Chapter Objectives
> ACE multiple-choice quiz
> Flashcards

SUGGESTED READING

Arjomand, Said Amir. *The Shadow of God and the Hidden Imam: Religion, Political Order, and Societal Change in Shiite Iran from the Beginning to 1890.* 1984. Contains the best analysis of the complicated relationship between Shi'ism and monarchy.

Braude, Benjamin, and Bernard Lewis, eds. *Christians and Jews in the Ottoman Empire: The Functioning of a Plural Society.* 1982. Diverse studies dealing with religious minorities.

Goffman, Daniel. *The Ottoman Empire and Early Modern Europe.* 2002. Compares the Ottomans with contemporary European kingdoms.

Hattox, Ralph S. *Coffee and Coffeehouses: The Origins of a Social Beverage in the Medieval Near East.* 1988. An excellent contribution to Ottoman social history.

Ikram, S. M. *History of Muslim Civilization in India and Pakistan.* 1989. A broad treatment of the entire development of Islamic society in India with emphasis on the Mughal period.

Imber, Colin. *The Ottoman Empire, 1300–1650: The Structure of Power.* 2002. On the Ottoman Empire in its prime.

Inalcik, Halil, and Donald Quataert, eds. *An Economic and Social History of the Ottoman Empire, 1300–1914.* 1994. A valuable collection of articles on nonpolitical matters.

Lapidus, Ira. *A History of Islamic Societies.* 2d ed. 2002. Offers the best comprehensive and comparative account of the post-Mongol Islamic land empires

Marcus, Abraham. *The Middle East on the Eve of Modernity: Aleppo in the Eighteenth Century.* 1989. An outstanding study of an Arab city under Ottoman rule.

Martin, Esmond Bradley, and Chryssee Perry Martin. *Cargoes of the East: The Ports, Trade and Culture of the Arabian Seas and Western Indian Ocean.* 1978. A popular and well-illustrated work on the western Indian Ocean.

Matthee, Rudi. *The Pursuit of Pleasure: Drugs and Stimulants in Iranian History, 1500–1900.* 2005. Studies court life and popular culture through wine, tobacco, opium, coffee, and tea.

Newman, Andrew. *Safavid Iran: Rebirth of a Persian Empire.* 2006. A provocative reinterpretation of Safavid rule.

Ogot, B. A., ed. *UNESCO General History of Africa.* Vol. 5. *Africa from the Sixteenth to the Eighteenth Century.* 1992. A useful collection of articles on an understudied field.

Peirce, Leslie. *The Imperial Harem: Women and Sovereignty in the Ottoman Empire.* 1993. Skillfully treats the role of women in the governance of the empire.

Richards, John F. *The Mughal Empire.* 1993. A comprehensive history.

NOTES

1. Leslie Peirce, *Morality Tales: Law and Gender in the Ottoman Court of Aintab* (Berkeley: University of California Press, 2003), 258.

2. Ibid., 262.

3. Daniel Goffman, *Izmir and the Levantine World, 1550–1650* (Seattle: University of Washington Press, 1990), 52.

4. Edmund Bradley Martin and Chryssee Perry Martin, *Cargoes of the East: The Ports, Trade and Culture of the Arabian Seas and Western Indian Ocean* (1978), 17.

CHAPTER 18

Northern Eurasia

1500–1800

CHAPTER PREVIEW

Japanese Reunification
How did Japan respond to domestic social changes and the challenges posed by contact with foreign cultures?

The Later Ming and Early Qing Empires
How did China deal with military and political challenges both inside and outside its borders?

The Russian Empire
To what extent was Russia's expanding empire influenced by relations with western Europe in this period?

Comparative Perspectives

DIVERSITY AND DOMINANCE: Gendered Violence: The Yangzhou Massacre

In the seventeenth century, the Ming dynasty in China was threatened by Manchu armies from Manchuria in the northeast. To pay the army defending Beijing (bay-JING), the emperor slashed the government payroll. Among those thrown out of his job as an apprentice ironworker was one Li Zicheng (lee ZUH-cheng). By 1630 Li Zicheng had found work as a soldier, but he and his fellow soldiers mutinied when the government failed to provide needed supplies. A natural leader, Li soon headed several thousand Chinese rebels. In 1635 he and other rebel leaders gained control over much of north central China.

Wedged between the Manchu armies to the north and the rebels to the southwest, the Ming government tottered. Li Zicheng's forces began to move toward Beijing, along the way conscripting young men

CL This icon will direct you to the website where you can Prepare for Class, Improve Your Grade, and Ace the Test: college.cengage.com/pic/bullietbrief4e

495

from captured towns into their army. The rebels promised to end the abuses of the Ming and restore peace and prosperity. In April 1644 Li's forces took over Beijing without a fight. The last Ming emperor hanged himself in the palace garden, bringing to an end the dynasty that had ruled China since 1368.

Victory was short-lived, however. Fearful of uneducated, violent men like Li ruling the land, the Ming general Wu Sangui joined forces with the **Manchus**. Li had incidentally captured one of the general's favorite concubines and taken her for himself. Together Wu and the Manchus retook Beijing in June. Li's forces scattered, and a year later he was dead, either a suicide or beaten to death by peasants whose food he tried to steal.[1]

Meanwhile, the Manchus made it clear that they were the new masters of China. They installed their young sovereign as emperor and over the next two decades hunted down the last of the Ming loyalists and heirs to the throne.

China was not the only state in northern Eurasia facing foreign threats and uprisings from within. In the period from 1500 to 1800 Japan and Russia experienced similar turbulence as they underwent massive political and economic change and economic growth. Besides challenges from nearby neighbors, the three also faced new contacts and challenges from the commercially and militarily powerful European states.

Manchu Federation of Northeast Asian peoples who founded the Qing Empire.

JAPANESE REUNIFICATION

How did Japan respond to domestic social changes and the challenges posed by contact with foreign cultures?

Like China and Russia in the centuries between 1500 and 1800, Japan experienced three major changes: internal and external military conflicts, political growth and strengthening, and expanded commercial and cultural contacts. Along with its culturally homogenous population and natural boundaries, Japan's smaller size made the process of political unification shorter than in the great empires of China and Russia. Japan also differed in its responses to new contacts with western Europeans.

Civil War and the Invasion of Korea, 1500–1603

In the twelfth century different parts of Japan had fallen under the rule of warlords known as *daimyo* (DIE-mee-oh) (see Chapter 11). Each daimyo had a castle town, a small bureaucracy, and a band of warriors, the *samurai* (SAH-moo-rye). Daimyo pledged a loose allegiance to the Japanese emperor residing in the capital city of Kyoto (KYOH-toh) and to the shogun, the hereditary chief of the emperor's government and armies. But neither figure held significant political power.

Warfare among the different daimyo was common, and in the late 1500s it culminated in a prolonged civil war. The warlord to emerge from the war was Hideyoshi (HEE-duh-YOH-shee). In 1592, buoyed with his success in Japan, the supremely confident Hideyoshi invaded the Asian mainland with 160,000 men. His apparent intention was not just to conquer the Korean peninsula but also to make himself emperor of China.

daimyo Literally, great name(s). Japanese warlords and great landowners, whose armed samurai gave them control of the Japanese islands from the eighth to the later nineteenth century. Under the Tokugawa Shogunate they were subordinated to the imperial government.

samurai Literally "those who serve," the hereditary military elite of the Tokugawa Shogunate.

Chronology

	Korea and Japan	China and Central Asia	Russia
1500			
		1517 Portuguese embassy to China	
	1543 First Portuguese contacts		
			1547 Ivan IV adopts title of tsar
			1582 Russians conquer Khanate of Sibir
	1592 Japanese invasion of Korea		
1600			
		1601 Matteo Ricci allowed to reside in Beijing	
	1603 Tokugawa Shogunate formed		
			1613–1645 Rule of Mikhail, the first Romanov tsar
	1633–1639 Edicts close down trade with Europe		
		1644 Qing conquest of Beijing	
			1649 Subordination of serfs complete
		1662–1722 Rule of Emperor Kangxi	
		1689 Treaty of Nerchinsk with Russia	1689–1725 Rule of Peter the Great
		1691 Qing control of Inner Mongolia	
1700			
	1702 Trial of the Forty-Seven Ronin		
			1712 St. Petersburg becomes Russia's capital
		1736–1796 Rule of Emperor Qianlong	
			1762–1796 Rule of Catherine the Great
	1792 Russian ships first spotted off the coast of Japan		
			1799 Alaska becomes a Russian colony

The Korean and Japanese languages are closely related, but the dominant influence on Korean culture had long been China, to which Korean rulers generally paid tribute. In many ways the Yi dynasty that ruled Korea from 1392 to 1910 was a model Confucian state. Although Korea had developed its own system of writing in 1443 and made extensive use of printing with movable type from the fifteenth century on, most printing continued to use Chinese characters.

Against Hideyoshi's invaders the Koreans employed all the technological and military skill for which the Yi period was renowned. Ingenious covered warships, or "turtle boats," intercepted a portion of the Japanese fleet. The mentally unstable Hideyoshi countered with brutal punitive measures as his armies advanced through the Korean peninsula and into the Chinese province of Manchuria. However, after Hideyoshi's death in 1598, the other Japanese military leaders withdrew their forces, and the Japanese government made peace in 1606.

The invasion devastated Korea. In the turmoil after the Japanese withdrawal, the Korean *yangban* (nobility) were able to lay claim to so much taxpaying land that royal revenues may have fallen by two-thirds. China, however, suffered even more dire consequences. The battles in Manchuria weakened Chinese garrisons there, permitting Manchu opposition to consolidate. Manchu forces invaded Korea in the 1620s and eventually compelled the Yi to become a tributary state. As already related, the Manchus would be in possession of Beijing, China's capital, by 1644.

The Tokugawa Shogunate, to 1800

After Hideyoshi's demise, Tokugawa Ieyasu (TOH-koo-GAH-wah ee-ay-YAH-soo) (1543–1616) asserted his domination over other daimyo and in 1603 established a new military government known as the **Tokugawa Shogunate**. The shoguns created a new administrative capital at Edo (ED-oh) (now Tokyo). Trade along the well-maintained road between Edo and the imperial capital of Kyoto promoted the development of the Japanese economy and the formation of other trading centers (see Map 18.1).

Tokugawa Shogunate (1603–1868) The last of the three shogunates of Japan.

Although the Tokugawa Shogunate gave Japan more political unity than the islands had seen in centuries, the regionally based daimyo still had a great deal of power and autonomy. Ieyasu and his successors worked hard to keep the political system from disintegrating; nevertheless, economic integration was more a feature of Tokugawa Japan than political centralization. Because shoguns required the daimyo to visit Edo frequently, good roads and maritime transport linked the city to the castle towns on three of Japan's four main islands. Commercial traffic developed along these routes. The shogun paid the lords in rice, and the lords paid their followers in rice. Recipients converted much of this rice into cash, a practice that led to the development of rice exchanges at Edo and at Osaka (OH-sah-kah), where merchants speculated in rice prices. By the late seventeenth century Edo was one of the largest cities in the world, with nearly a million inhabitants.

The domestic peace of the Tokugawa era forced the warrior class to adapt itself to the growing bureaucratic needs of the state. As the samurai became better educated and more attuned to the tastes of the civil elite, they became important customers for merchants dealing in silks, *sake* (SAH-kay) (rice wine), fans, porcelain, lacquer ware, books, and moneylending. The state attempted—unsuccessfully—to curb the independence of the merchants when the economic well-being of the samurai was threatened by low rice prices or high interest rates.

The 1600s and 1700s were centuries of high achievement in artisanship, and Japanese skills in steel making, pottery, and lacquer ware were joined by excellence in the production and decoration of porcelain, thanks in no small part to Korean experts brought back to Japan after the invasion of 1592. In the early 1600s manufacturers and merchants amassed enormous family fortunes. Several of the most important industrial and financial enterprises—for instance, the Mitsui (MIT-soo-ee) companies—had their origins in sake breweries of the early Tokugawa period and then branched out into manufacturing, finance, and transport.

Wealthy merchants weakened the Tokugawa policy of controlling commerce by cultivating close alliances with their regional daimyo and, if possible, with the shogun himself. By the end of the 1700s the merchant families of Tokugawa Japan held the key to future modernization and the development of heavy industry.

Primary Source: Some Observations on Merchants
Discover what happens to merchants who try to trick samurai.

Japan and the Europeans

Direct contacts with Europeans presented Japan with new opportunities and problems. Within thirty years of the arrival of the first Portuguese in 1543, the daimyo were fighting with Western-style firearms, copied and improved upon by Japanese armorers.

The Japanese welcomed but closely regulated traders from Portugal, Spain, the Netherlands, and England. Aside from the brief boom in porcelain exports in the seventeenth century, few Japanese goods went to Europe, and not much from Europe found a market in Japan. The Japanese sold the Dutch copper and silver, which the Dutch exchanged in China for silks that they then resold in Japan. The Japanese, of course, had their own trade with China.

Portuguese and Spanish merchant ships also brought Catholic missionaries. One of the first, Francis Xavier, went to India in the mid-sixteenth century looking for converts and later traveled throughout Southeast and East Asia. He spent two years in Japan and died in 1552, hoping to gain entry to China.

Japanese responses to Xavier and other Jesuits (members of the Catholic religious order the Society of Jesus) were decidedly mixed. Many ordinary Japanese found the new faith deeply meaningful, but the Japanese elite more often opposed it as disruptive and foreign. By 1580 more than 100,000 Japanese had become Christians, and one daimyo gave Jesuit missionaries the port city of Nagasaki (NAH-guh-SAHK-kee). In 1613 Date Masamune (DAH-tay mah-suh-MOO-nay), the fierce and independent daimyo of northern Honshu (HOHN-shoo), sent his own embassy to the Vatican, by way of the Philippines (where there were significant communities of Japanese merchants and pirates) and Mexico City. Some daimyo converts ordered their subjects to become Christians as well.

By the early seventeenth century there were some 300,000 Japanese Christians and even some Japanese priests. However, suspicions about the intentions of the Europeans and their well-armed ships turned the new shogunate in Edo into a center of hostility toward Christianity. A decree issued in 1614 banned Christianity and charged its adherents with seeking to overthrow true doctrine, change the government, and seize the country. Some missionaries left Japan; others worked underground. The government began persecutions in earnest in 1617, and the beheadings, crucifixions, and forced recantations over the next several decades destroyed almost the entire Christian community.

To keep Christianity from resurfacing, a series of decrees issued between 1633 and 1639 sharply curtailed trade with Europe. Europeans who entered illegally faced the death penalty. Japanese subjects were required to produce certificates from Buddhist temples attesting to their religious orthodoxy and loyalty to the regime.

The exclusion of Europe was not total. A few Dutch were permitted to reside on a small artificial island in Nagasaki's harbor, and a few Japanese were licensed to supply their needs. What these intermediaries learned about European weapons technology, shipbuilding, mathematics and astronomy, anatomy and medicine, and geography was termed "Dutch studies."

Tokugawa restrictions on the number of Chinese ships that could trade in Japan were harder to enforce. Regional lords in northern and southern Japan not only pursued overseas trade and piracy but also claimed dominion over islands between Japan and Korea and southward toward Taiwan, including present-day Okinawa. Despite such evasions, the new shogunate unquestionably achieved substantial success in exercising its authority.

Elite Decline and Social Crisis

During the 1700s population growth put a great strain on the well-developed lands of central Japan. In more remote provinces, where the lords promoted new settlements and agricultural expansion, the rate of economic growth was significantly greater.

Also troubling the Tokugawa government in the 1700s was the shogunate's inability to stabilize rice prices and halt the economic decline of the samurai. The Tokugawa government realized that the rice brokers could manipulate rice prices and interest rates to enrich themselves at the expense of the samurai, who had to convert their rice allotments into cash. Early Tokugawa laws designed to regulate interest and prices were later supplemented by laws requiring moneylenders to forgive samurai debts. But these laws were not always enforced. By the early 1700s many lords and samurai were dependent on the willingness of merchants to provide credit.

The legitimacy of the Tokugawa shoguns rested on their ability to reward and protect the interests of the lords and samurai who had supported their rise to power. Moreover, the Tokugawa government, like the governments of China, Korea, and Vietnam, accepted the Confucian idea that agriculture should be the basis of state wealth and that merchants, who were considered morally weak, should occupy lowly positions in society. Tokugawa decentralization, however, not only failed to hinder but actually stimulated the growth of commercial activities. From the founding of the Tokugawa Shogunate in 1603 until 1800, the economy grew faster than the population. Household amenities and cultural resources that in China appeared only in the cities were common in the Japanese countryside. Despite official disapproval, merchants enjoyed relative freedom and influence in eighteenth-century Japan. They produced a vivid culture of their own, fostering the development of *kabuki* theater, colorful woodblock prints and silk-screened fabrics, and restaurants.

The "Forty-Seven Ronin" (ROH-neen) incident of 1701–1703 exemplified the ideological and social crisis of Japan's transformation from a military to a civil society. A senior minister provoked a young daimyo into drawing his sword at the shogun's court. For this offense the young lord was sentenced to commit *seppuku* (SEP-poo-koo), the ritual suicide of the samurai. His

SECTION REVIEW

- From the civil war among the daimyo emerged Hideyoshi, who, as supreme warlord, invaded Korea and China.

- After Hideyoshi's death, Tokugawa Ieyasu established the Tokugawa Shogunate, with its capital at Edo.

- The Tokugawa shoguns provided political unity and fostered economic expansion but failed to control commerce.

- The Japanese engaged in regulated trade with Europeans, but rising suspicions caused the Tokugawa shoguns to restrict foreign contacts.

- Economic growth nourished a new merchant-class culture, but the position of the samurai deteriorated under economic and social pressures.

Woodblock Print of the "Forty-Seven Ronin" Story
The saga of the forty-seven ronin and the avenging of their fallen leader has fascinated the Japanese public since the event occurred in 1702. This watercolor from the Tokugawa period shows the leaders of the group pausing on the snowy banks of the Sumida River in Edo (Tokyo) before storming their enemy's residence.   (Archives Charmet/The Bridgeman Art Library)

own followers then became *ronin*, "masterless samurai," obliged by the traditional code of the warrior to avenge their deceased master. They broke into the house of the senior minister and killed him and others in his household. Then they withdrew to a temple in Edo and notified the shogun of what they had done out of loyalty to their lord and to avenge his death.

A legal debate ensued. To deny the righteousness of the ronin would be to deny samurai values. But to approve their actions would create social chaos, undermine laws against murder, and deny the shogunal government the right to try cases of samurai violence. The shogun ruled that the ronin had to die but would be permitted to die honorably by committing seppuku. Traditional samurai values had to surrender to the supremacy of law. The purity of purpose of the ronin is still celebrated in Japan, but since then Japanese writers, historians, and teachers have recognized that the self-sacrifice of the ronin for the sake of upholding civil law was necessary.

THE LATER MING AND EARLY QING EMPIRES

How did China deal with military and political challenges both inside and outside its borders?

Like Japan, China after 1500 experienced civil and foreign wars, an important change in government, and new trading and cultural relations with Europe and its neighbors. The internal and external forces at work in China were different and operated on a much larger scale, but they led in similar directions. By 1800 China had a greatly enhanced empire, an expanding economy, and growing doubts about the importance of European trade and Christianity.

Ming Empire (1368–1644)
Empire based in China that Zhu Yuanzhang established after the overthrow of the Yuan Empire. The Ming emperor Yongle sponsored additions to the Forbidden City and the voyages of Zheng He. The later years of the Ming saw a slow-down in technological development and economic decline.

The Ming Empire, 1500–1644

The economic and cultural achievements of the early **Ming Empire** (see Chapter 11) continued during the 1500s. But this productive period was followed by many decades of political weakness, warfare, and rural woes until a new dynasty, the Qing (ching) from Manchuria, guided China back to peace and prosperity.

The Europeans whose ships began to seek out new contacts with China in the early sixteenth century left many accounts of their impressions. They were astonished at Ming China's imperial power, exquisite manufactures, and vast population. European merchants bought such large quantities of the high-grade blue-on-white porcelain commonly used by China's upper classes that in English all fine dishes became known simply as "china."

The growing integration of China into the world economy stimulated rapid growth in the silk, cotton, and porcelain industries. Agricultural regions that supplied raw materials to these industries and food for the expanding urban populations also prospered. In exchange for Chinese exports, tens of thousands of tons of silver from Japan and Latin America flooded into China in the century before 1640. The influx of silver led many Chinese to substitute payments in silver for land taxes, labor obligations, and other kinds of dues.

Ming cities had long been culturally and commercially vibrant. Many large landowners and absentee landlords lived in town, as did officials, artists, and rich merchants who had purchased ranks or prepared their sons for the examinations. The elite classes had created a brilliant culture in which novels, operas, poetry, porcelain, and painting were all closely interwoven. Small businesses catering to the urban elites prospered through printing, tailoring, running restaurants, or selling paper, ink, ink-stones, and writing brushes. The imperial government operated factories for the production of ceramics and silks. Enormous government complexes at Jingdezhen and elsewhere invented assembly-line techniques and produced large quantities of high-quality ceramics for sale in China and abroad.

Despite these achievements, serious problems developed that left the Ming Empire economically and politically exhausted. There is evidence that the climate changes known as the Little Ice Age in seventeenth-century Europe affected the climate in China as well (see Issues in World History: The Little Ice Age). Annual temperatures dropped, reached a low point about 1645, and remained low until the early 1700s. The resulting agricultural distress and famine fueled large uprisings that speeded the end of the Ming Empire. The devastation caused by these uprisings and the spread of epidemic disease resulted in steep declines in local populations.

The rapid urban growth and business speculation that were part of the burgeoning of the trading economy also produced problems. Some provinces suffered from price inflation caused by the flood of silver. In contrast to the growing involvement of European governments in promoting economic growth, the Ming government pursued some policies that hindered growth. Despite the fact that earlier experiments with paper currency had failed, Ming governments persisted in issuing new paper money and copper coinage, even after abundant supplies of silver had won the approval of the markets. Corruption was also a serious government problem. By the end of the Ming period disorder and inefficiency plagued the imperial factories, touching off strikes in the late sixteenth and seventeenth centuries. During a labor protest at Jingdezhen in 1601, workers threw themselves into the kilns to protest working conditions.

Yet the urban and industrial sectors of later Ming society fared much better than the agricultural sector, which failed to maintain the strong growth of early Ming times. Despite knowledge of new African and American crops gained from European traders, farmers were slow to change their ways. Neither the rice-growing regions in southern China nor the wheat-growing regions in northern China experienced a meaningful increase in productivity under the later Ming. After 1500 economic depression in the countryside, combined with recurring epidemics in central and southern China, kept rural population growth in check.

Ming Collapse and the Rise of the Qing

Although these environmental, economic, and administrative problems existed, the primary reasons for the fall of the Ming Empire were internal rebellion and rising Manchu power. Insecure boundaries had been a recurrent peril. The Ming had long been under pressure from the powerful Mongol federations of the north and west. In the late 1500s large numbers of Mongols were unified by their devotion to the Dalai Lama (DAH-lie LAH-mah), or universal teacher of Tibetan Buddhism. Building on this spiritual unity, a brilliant leader named Galdan restored Mongolia as a regional military power around 1600. The Manchus, an agricultural people who controlled the region north of Korea, grew stronger in the northeast.

In the southwest, native peoples repeatedly resisted the immigration of Chinese farmers. Pirates based in Okinawa and Taiwan, many of them Japanese, frequently looted the southeast coast. Ming military resources, concentrated against the Mongols and the Manchus in the north, could not be deployed to defend the coasts. As a result, many southern Chinese migrated to Southeast Asia to profit from the sea-trading networks of the Indian Ocean.

The Japanese invasion of 1592 to 1598 (see section on Japan) prompted the Ming to seek the assistance of Manchu troops that they were then unable to restrain. With the rebel leader Li Zicheng in possession of Beijing (see the beginning of this chapter) and the emperor dead by his own hand, a Ming general joined forces with the Manchu leaders in the summer of 1644. Instead of restoring the Ming, however, the Manchus claimed China for their own and began a forty-year conquest of the rest of the Ming territories, as well as Taiwan and parts of Mongolia and Central Asia (see Map 18.1 on page 506 and Diversity and Dominance: Gendered Violence: The Yangzhou Massacre).

A Manchu family headed the new **Qing Empire**, and Manchu generals commanded the military forces. But Manchus made up a very small portion of the population. The overwhelming majority of Qing officials, soldiers, merchants, and farmers were ethnic Chinese. Like other successful invaders of China, the Qing soon adopted Chinese institutions and policies.

Qing Empire Empire established in China by Manchus who overthrew the Ming Empire in 1644. At various times the Qing also controlled Manchuria, Mongolia, Turkestan, and Tibet. The last Qing emperor was overthrown in 1911.

Trading Companies and Missionaries

For European merchants, the China trade was second in importance only to the spice trade of southern Asia. China's vast population and manufacturing skills drew a steady stream of ships from western Europe, but enthusiasm for the trade developed only slowly at the imperial court.

A Portuguese ship reached China at the end of 1513 but was not permitted to trade. A formal Portuguese embassy in 1517 got bogged down in Chinese protocol

Gendered Violence: The Yangzhou Massacre

The Qing were not eager for reminders of their brutal takeover to circulate. This rare eyewitness account smuggled out of China reveals not just the violence of the conquest but also the diversity of its impact on men and women.

The account begins in 1645 as rumors of approaching Manchu soldiers spread through Yangzhou, an important city near the juncture of the Yangzi River and the Grand Canal, and the soldiers charged with its defense begin to flee.

Crowds of barefoot and disheveled refugees were flocking into the city. When questioned, they were too distraught to reply. At that point dozens of mounted soldiers in confused waves came surging south looking as though they had given up all hope. Among them appeared a man who turned out to be the commandant himself. It seems he had intended to leave by the east gate but could not because the enemy soldiers outside the wall were drawing too near; he was therefore forced to cut across this part of town to reach the south gate. This is how we first learned for sure that the enemy troops would enter the city. . . .

My house backed against the city wall, and peeping through the chinks in my window, I saw the soldiers on the wall marching south then west, solemn and in step. Although the rain was beating down, it did not seem to disturb them. This reassured me because I gathered that they were well-disciplined units.

. . . For a long time no one came. I retreated again to the back window and found that the regiment on the wall had broken ranks; some soldiers were walking about, others standing still.

All of a sudden I saw some soldiers escorting a group of women dressed in Yangzhou fashion. This was my first real shock. Back in the house, I said to my wife, "Should things go badly when the soldiers enter the city, you may need to end your life."

"Yes," she replied, "Whatever silver we have you should keep. I think we women can stop thinking about life in this world." She gave me all the silver, unable to control her crying. . . .

Soon my younger brother arrived, then my two older brothers. We discussed the situation and I said, "The people who live in our neighborhood are all rich merchants. It will be disastrous if they think we are rich too." I then urged my brothers to brave the rain and quickly take the women by the back route to my older brother's house. His home was situated behind Mr. He's graveyard and was surrounded by the huts of poor families. . . .

The cunning soldiers, suspecting that many people were still hidden, tried to entice them out by posting a placard promising clemency. About fifty to sixty people, half of them women, emerged. My elder brother said, "We four by ourselves will never survive if we run into these vicious soldiers, so we had better join the crowd. Since there are so many of them, escape will be easier. . . ."

The leaders were three Manchu soldiers. They searched my brothers and found all the silver they were carrying, but left me untouched. At that point some women appeared, two of whom called out to me. I recognized them as the concubines of my friend Mr. Zhu Shu and stopped them anxiously. They were disheveled and partly naked, their feet bare and covered with mud up to the ankles. One was holding a girl whom the soldiers hit with a whip and threw into the mud. Then we were immediately driven on. One soldier, sword in hand, took the lead; another drove us from behind with a long spear; and a third walked along on our right and left flanks alternately, making sure no one escaped. In groups of twenty or thirty we were herded along like sheep and cattle. If we faltered we were struck, and some people were even killed on the spot. The women were tied together with long chains around their necks, like a clumsy string of pearls. Stumbling at every step, they were soon covered with mud. Here and there on the ground lay babies, trampled by people or horses.

. . . We then entered the house of [a] merchant, . . . which had been taken over by the three soldiers. Another soldier was already there. He had seized several attractive women and was rifling their trunks for fancy silks, which he piled in a heap. Seeing the three soldiers arrive, he laughed and pushed several dozen of us into the back hall. The women he led into a side chamber. . . .

The three soldiers stripped the women of their wet clothing all the way to their underwear, then ordered the seamstress to measure them and give them new garments. The women, thus coerced, had to expose themselves and stand naked. What shame they endured! Once they had changed, the soldiers grabbed them and forced them to join them in eating and drinking, then did whatever they pleased with them, without any regard for decency.

[The narrator escapes and hides atop a wooden canopy over a bed.] Later on a soldier brought a woman in and wanted her to sleep with him in the bed below me. Despite her refusal he forced her to yield. "This is too near the street. It is not a good place to stay," the woman said. I was almost discovered, but after a time the soldier departed with the woman. . . . [The narrator flees again and is reunited with his wife and relatives.]

At length, however, there came a soldier of the "Wolf Men" tribe, a vicious-looking man with a head like a mouse and eyes like a hawk. He attempted to abduct my wife. She was obliged to creep forward on all fours, pleading as she had with the others, but to no avail. When he insisted that she stand up, she rolled on the ground and refused. He then beat her so savagely with the flat of his sword that the blood flowed out in streams, totally soaking her clothes. Because my wife had once admonished me, "If I am unlucky I will die no matter what; do not plead for me as a husband or you will get caught too," I acted as if I did not know she was being beaten and hid far away in the grass, convinced she was about to die. Yet the depraved soldier did not stop there; he grabbed her by the hair, cursed her, struck her cruelly, and then dragged her away by the leg. . . . Just then they ran into a body of mounted soldiers. One of them said a few words to the soldier in Manchu. At this he dropped my wife and departed with them. Barely able to crawl back, she let out a loud sob, every part of her body injured. . . .

Unexpectedly there appeared a handsome looking man of less than thirty, a double-edged sword hung by his side, dressed in Manchu-style hat, red coat, and a pair of black boots. His follower, in a yellow jacket, was also very gallant in appearance. Immediately behind them were several residents of Yangzhou. The young man in red, inspecting me closely, said, "I would judge from your appearance that you are not one of these people. Tell me honestly, what class of person are you?"

I remembered that some people had obtained pardons and others had lost their lives the moment they said that they were poor scholars. So I did not dare come out at once with the truth and instead concocted a story. He pointed to my wife and son and asked who they were, and I told him the truth. "Tomorrow the prince will order that all swords be sheathed and all of you will be spared," he said and then commanded his followers to give us some clothes and an ingot of silver. He also asked me, "How many days have you been without food?"

"Five days," I replied.

"Then come with me," he commanded. Although we only half trusted him, we were afraid to disobey. He led us to a well-stocked house, full of rice, fish, and other provisions. "Treat these four people well," he said to a woman in the house and then left. . . .

The next day was [April 30]. Killing and pillaging continued, although not on the previous scale. Still the mansions of the rich were thoroughly looted, and almost all the teenage girls were abducted. . . . every grain of rice, every inch of silk now entered these tigers' mouths. The resulting devastation is beyond description.

[May 2]. Civil administration was established in all the prefectures and counties; proclamations were issued aimed at calming the people, and monks from each temple were ordered to burn corpses. The temples themselves were clogged with women who had taken refuge, many of whom had died of fright or starvation. The "List of Corpses Burned" records more than eight hundred thousand, and this list does not include those who jumped into wells, threw themselves into the river, hanged themselves, were burned to death inside houses, or were carried away by the soldiers. . . .

When this calamity began there had been eight of us: my two elder brothers, my younger brother, my elder brother's wife, their son, my wife, my son, and myself. Now only three of us survived for sure, though the fate of my wife's brother and sister-in-law was not yet known. . . .

From the 25th of the fourth month to the 5th of the fifth month was a period of ten days. I have described here only what I actually experienced or saw with my own eyes; I have not recorded anything I picked up from rumor or hearsay.

QUESTIONS FOR ANALYSIS

1. **What accounts for the soldiers' brutal treatment of the women?**

2. **What did different women do to protect themselves?**

3. **Having conquered, what did the Manchu do to restore order?**

Source: Reprinted with permission of the Free Press, a division of Simon and Schuster Adult Publishing Group from *Chinese Civilization: A Sourcebook*, Second Edition, edited by Patricia Buckley Ebrey, pp. 272–279. Copyright © 1993 by Patricia Buckley Ebrey.

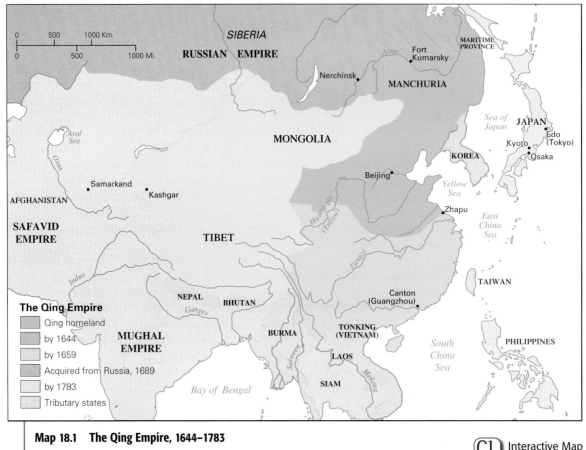

Map 18.1   The Qing Empire, 1644–1783

The Qing Empire began in Manchuria and captured north China in 1644. Between 1644 and 1783 the Qing conquered all the former Ming territories and added Taiwan, the lower Amur River Basin, Inner Mongolia, eastern Turkestan, and Tibet. The resulting state was more than twice the size of the Ming Empire.

CL   Interactive Map

and procrastination, and China expelled the Portuguese in 1522. Finally, in 1557 the Portuguese gained the right to trade from a base in Macao (muh-KOW) on the southern coast. Spain's Asian trade was conducted from Manila in the Philippines, which also linked with South America across the Pacific. For a time, the Spanish and the Dutch both maintained trading outposts on the island of Taiwan, but in 1662 they were forced to concede control to the Qing, who for the first time incorporated Taiwan into China.

By then, the Dutch East India Company (VOC) had displaced the Portuguese as the major European trader in the Indian Ocean and was establishing itself as the main European trader in East Asia. VOC representatives courted official favor in China by acknowledging the moral superiority of the emperor. They performed the ritual kowtow (in which the visitor knocked his head on the floor while crawling toward the throne) to the Ming emperor.

Catholic missionaries accompanied the Portuguese and Spanish merchants to China, just as they did to Japan. While the Franciscans and Dominicans pursued the conversion efforts at the bottom of society that had worked so well in Japan, the Jesuits focused on China's intellectual and political elite. In this they were far more successful than they had been in Japan—at least until the eighteenth century.

The outstanding Jesuit of late Ming China, Matteo Ricci (mah-TAY-oh REE-chee) (1552–1610), became expert in the Chinese language and an accomplished scholar of the Confucian classics. Under Ricci's leadership, the Jesuits adapted Catholicism to Chinese cultural traditions while introducing the Chinese to the latest science and technology from Europe. From 1601 Ricci resided in Beijing on an imperial stipend as a Western scholar. Later Jesuits headed the office of astronomy that issued the official calendar.

Emperor Kangxi

The seventeenth and eighteenth centuries—particularly the reigns of the **Kangxi** (KAHNG-shee) (r. 1662–1722) and Qianlong (chee-YEN-loong) (r. 1736–1796) emperors—were a period of economic, military, and cultural achievement in China. The early Qing emperors repaired the roads and waterworks, lowered transit taxes, cut rents and interest rates, and established incentives for resettling areas devastated by peasant rebellions. Foreign trade was encouraged. Vietnam, Burma, and Nepal sent embassies to the Qing tribute court and carried the latest Chinese fashions back home. Overland routes from Korea to Central Asia revived.

The Manchu aristocrats who led the conquest of Beijing and north China dominated the first Qing emperor and served as regents for his young son, who was declared emperor in 1662. This child-emperor, Kangxi, sparred politically with the regents until 1669, when at age sixteen he executed the chief regent and thereby gained real control of the government. An intellectual prodigy who had mastered classical Chinese, Manchu, and Mongolian and memorized the Chinese classics, Kangxi guided imperial expansion and maintained stability until his death in 1722.

In the north, the Qing rulers feared an alliance between Galdan's Mongol state and the expanding Russian presence along the **Amur** (AH-moor) **River**. In the 1680s Qing forces attacked the wooden forts built by hardy Russian scouts on the river's northern bank. Neither empire sent large forces into the Amur territories, so the contest was partly a struggle for the goodwill of the local peoples. The Qing emperor emphasized the importance of treading lightly in the struggle:

> Upon reaching the lands of the Evenks and the Dagurs you will send to announce that you have come to hunt deer. Meanwhile, keep a careful record of the distance and go, while hunting, along the northern bank of the Amur until you come by the shortest route to the town of Russian settlement at Albazin. Thoroughly reconnoiter its location and situation. I don't think the Russians will take a chance on attacking you. If they offer you food, accept it and show your gratitude. If they do attack you, don't fight back. In that case, lead your people and withdraw into our own territories.[2]

Qing forces twice attacked Albazin. The Qing were worried about Russian alliances with other frontier peoples, while Russia wished to protect its access to the furs, timber, and metals concentrated in Siberia, Manchuria, and Yakutsk. The Qing and Russians were also rivals for control of northern Asia's Pacific coast. Seeing little benefit in continued conflict, in 1689 the two empires negotiated the Treaty of Nerchinsk, using Jesuit missionaries as interpreters. The treaty fixed the border along the Amur River and regulated trade across it. Although this was a thinly settled area, the treaty proved important, and the frontier it demarcated has long endured.

CL **Primary Source: Journals** *Find out what happens when a contingent of Chinese locals accuse certain Jesuit priests of treason against the throne and call for them to be either sentenced to death or "banished from the realm, to some deserted island in the sea."*

Kangxi (1654–1722) Qing emperor (r. 1662–1722) who oversaw the greatest expansion of the Qing Empire.

Amur River This river valley was a contested frontier between northern China and eastern Russia until the settlement arranged in the Treaty of Nerchinsk (1689).

Emperor Kangxi

In a portrait from about 1690, the young Manchu ruler is portrayed as a refined scholar in the Confucian tradition. He was a scholar and had great intellectual curiosity, but this portrait would not suggest that he was also a capable battlefield leader. (The Palace Museum, Beijing)

CL HISTORY IN FOCUS The caption for this image calls your attention to the emperor's representation as a refined Confucian scholar. Look carefully at his dress, the furnishings of the space he occupies, and the paper on the desk. What do you notice about those features, and what more do they suggest about how Kangxi wished to be seen? *Find the answer online.*

The next step was to settle the Mongolian frontier. Kangxi personally led troops in the great campaigns that defeated Galdan and brought Inner Mongolia under Qing control by 1691.

Unlike the rulers of Japan, who drove Christian missionaries out, Kangxi welcomed Jesuit advisers, discussed scientific and philosophical issues with them, and put them in important offices. Jesuits helped create maps in the European style as practical guides to newly conquered regions and as symbols of Qing dominance. Kangxi considered introducing the European calendar, but protests from the Confucian elite caused him to drop the plan. When he fell ill with malaria in the 1690s, Jesuit medical treatment (in this case, South American quinine) aided his recovery. Kangxi also ordered the creation of illustrated books in Manchu detailing European anatomical and pharmaceutical knowledge.

To gain converts, the Jesuits made important compromises in their religious teaching. Most importantly, they tolerated Confucian ancestor worship. This aroused controversy between the Jesuits and their Catholic rivals in China, the Franciscans and Dominicans, and also between the Jesuits and the pope. In 1690 the disagreement reached a high pitch. Kangxi wrote to Rome supporting the Jesuit position and after further dispute ordered the expulsion of all missionaries who refused to sign a certificate accepting his position. The Jesuit presence in China declined in the eighteenth century, and later Qing emperors persecuted Christians rather than naming them to high offices.

From the Jesuit Library at Beijing

Jesuits such as Matteo Ricci were willing to share books on technology and science with Chinese scholars. But without firsthand experience it was impossible for Chinese translators to convey how the devices actually worked. Here, a man walking in a wheel drives a shaft that changes the pressure inside two pumps. In the Chinese translation of the drawing, the mechanisms were all lost. (Left: From Zonca, *Trombe da Rota per Cavar Aqua* [1607]. Right: "Diagram Number Eight" from *Qi tushuo* [*Illustrations on Energy*] [1627].

Chinese Influences on Europe

The exchange of information that Kangxi had fostered was never one-way. While the Jesuits brought forward new knowledge of anatomy, for example, the Qing demonstrated an early form of inoculation, called "variolation," that had helped curtail smallpox after the conquest of Beijing. The technique inspired Europeans to develop other vaccines.

Similarly, Jesuit writings about China excited admiration in Europe. The wealthy and the aspiring middle classes demanded Chinese things—or things that looked to Europeans as if they could be Chinese. Silk, porcelain, and tea were avidly sought, along with cloisonné jewelry, jade, lacquered and jeweled room dividers, painted fans, and carved ivory (which originated in Africa and was finished in China). Wallpaper began as an adaptation of the Chinese practice of covering walls with enormous loose-hanging watercolors or calligraphy scrolls. By the mid-1700s special workshops throughout China were producing wallpaper and other consumer items according to the specifications of European merchants. The items were exported to Europe via Canton.

Qing political philosophy impressed Europeans, too. In the late 1770s poems supposedly written by Emperor Qianlong were translated into French and disseminated in intellectual circles. In them the Qing emperors rule as benevolent despots campaigning against superstition and ignorance, curbing aristocratic excesses, and patronizing science and the arts. This image of a practical, secular, compassionate ruler impressed the French thinker Voltaire, who proclaimed that Qing emperors were model philosopher-kings and advocated such rulership as a protection against the growth of aristocratic privilege.

Tea and Diplomacy

To maintain control over trade, facilitate tax collection, and suppress piracy, the Qing permitted only one market point for each foreign sector. Thus Europeans could trade only at Canton.

Chinese Export Ware
Though Europe developed its own porcelain industry, dishes from China continued to command a large market. Some, like the one depicted here, featured Chinese interpretations of European landscapes and patterns.   (©Christie's Images Ltd.)

Macartney mission (1792–1793) The unsuccessful attempt by the British Empire to establish diplomatic relations with the Qing Empire.

Primary Source: Edit on Trade with Great Britain
Find out why Emperor Qianlong accuses England of making impossible requests and setting a bad example for barbarian tribes the world over.

This system worked well enough until the late 1700s, when Britain became worried about its massive trade deficit with China. From bases in India and Singapore, British traders moved eastward and by the early 1700s dominated European trading in Canton, displacing the Dutch. The directors of the East India Company (EIC) anticipated limitless profits from China's gigantic markets and advanced technologies.

Tea from China had spread overland to Russia, Central Asia, and the Middle East in medieval and early modern times to become a prized import. Consumers knew it by its northern Chinese name, *cha*—as did the Portuguese. Other western Europeans acquired tea from the sea routes and with it the name used in the Fujian province of coastal China and Taiwan: *te*. In much of Europe, tea competed with chocolate and coffee as a fashionable drink by the mid-1600s.

British tea importers accumulated great fortunes. However, the Qing Empire took payment in silver and rarely bought anything from Britain. With domestic revenues declining in the later 1700s, the Qing government needed the silver and was disinclined to loosen import restrictions. To make matters worse, the East India Company had managed its worldwide holdings badly. As it teetered on bankruptcy, its attempts to manipulate Parliament became increasingly intrusive. In 1792 the British government dispatched Lord George Macartney, a well-connected peer with practical experience in Russia and India, to China. Staffed by scientists, artists, and translators as well as guards and diplomats, the **Macartney mission** showed Britain's great interest in the Qing Empire as well as the EIC's desire to revise the trade system.

To fit Chinese traditions, Macartney portrayed himself as a "tribute emissary" come to salute the Qianlong emperor's eightieth birthday. However, he steadfastly refused to perform the kowtow, though he did agree to bow on one knee as he would to King George III. The Qianlong emperor received Macartney courteously in September 1793 but refused to alter the Canton trading system, open new ports of trade, or allow the British to establish a permanent mission in Beijing. The emperor sent a letter to King George explaining that China had no need to increase its foreign trade, had no use for Britain's ingenious devices and manufacturers, and set no value on closer diplomatic ties.

Dutch, French, and Russian missions to achieve what Macartney could not do also failed. European frustration mounted while admiration for China faded. The

Qing court would not communicate with foreign envoys or observe the simplest rules of the European diplomatic system. In Macartney's view, China was like a venerable old warship, well maintained and splendid to look at, but obsolete and no longer up to the task.

Population and Social Stress

The Chinese who escorted Macartney and his entourage in 1792–1793 took them through China's prosperous cities and productive farmland. They did not see, however, the economic and environmental decline that had set in during the last decades of the 1700s.

Population growth—a tripling in size since 1500—had intensified demand for food and for more intensive agriculture. With an estimated 350 million people in the late 1700s, China had twice the population of all of Europe. Despite efficient farming and the gradual adoption of New World crops like corn and sweet potatoes, population pressure touched off social and environmental problems. Increased demand for building materials and firewood reduced woodlands. Deforestation, in turn, accelerated wind and water erosion and increased flooding. Dams and dikes were not maintained, and silted-up river channels were not dredged. By the end of the eighteenth century parts of the thousand-year-old Grand Canal linking the rivers of north and south China were nearly unusable, and the towns that bordered it were starved for commerce.

Some interior districts responded to this misery by increasing their output of export goods like tea, cotton, and silk. Some peasants sought seasonal jobs in better-off agricultural areas or worked in low-status jobs as barge pullers, charcoal burners, or night soil (human waste) carriers. Begging, prostitution, and theft increased in the cities. Rebellions broke out in flood-ravaged central and southwestern China. Indigenous peoples concentrated in the less fertile lands in the south and in the northern and western borderlands of the empire often joined in revolts.

The Qing government was not up to controlling its vast empire. It was twice the size of the Ming geographically, but it employed about the same number of officials. The government's dependence on working alliances with local elites had led to widespread corruption and shrinking government revenues. The Qing's spectacular rise had ended, and decline had set in.

SECTION REVIEW

- Ming economic and cultural achievement continued, but after the year 1500, financial, environmental, and administrative problems weakened the empire, and it fell to the Manchus.

- European merchants pursued trade contacts with China despite official resistance, and missionaries worked successfully until the eighteenth century.

- Kangxi expanded the Qing Empire's borders, subdued or contained rival powers, and presided over a flourishing economy and culture.

- The Qing and Europeans engaged in productive exchanges of ideas, and Chinese producers supplied growing European consumer markets.

- The one-sided Qing trade system prompted the Macartney mission and other European embassies to the Qing court, but the Qing refused all requests for more equitable trading conditions.

- By the late eighteenth century, population growth had created social and environmental problems that the Qing could not control.

THE RUSSIAN EMPIRE

To what extent was Russia's expanding empire influenced by relations with western Europe in this period?

From modest beginnings in 1500, Russia expanded rapidly during the next three centuries to create an empire that stretched from eastern Europe across northern Asia and into North America. Russia also became one of the major powers of Europe by 1750.

The Drive Across Northern Asia

During the centuries just before 1500, the history of the Russians had been dominated by steppe nomads (see Chapter 11). The Mongol Khanate of the Golden Horde ruled the Russians and their neighbors from the 1240s until 1480.

Under the Golden Horde Moscow became the most important Russian city and the center of political power. Moscow lay in the forest zone that stretched across Eurasia north of the treeless steppe (grasslands) favored by Mongol horsemen. The princes of **Muscovy** (MUSS-koe-vee), the territory surrounding the city of Moscow, led the movement against the Golden Horde and ruthlessly annexed the territories of the neighboring Russian state of Novgorod in 1478.

Once free from Mongol domination, the princes of Moscovy set out on conquests that in time made them masters of all the Golden Horde territories and then of a far greater empire. Prince Ivan IV (r. 1533–1584) pushed the conquests south and east at the expense of the Khanates of Kazan and Astrakhan (see Map 18.2).

At the end of the sixteenth century, Russians ruled the largest state in Europe and large territories on the Asian side of the **Ural Mountains** as well. Since 1547 the Russian ruler used the title **tsar** (zahr) (from the Roman imperial title *caesar*), the term Russians had used for the rulers of the Mongol Empire. The Russian church promoted the idea of Moscow as the "third Rome," successor to the Roman Empire's second capital, Constantinople, which had fallen to the Ottoman Turks in 1453.

Yet Russian claims to greatness were also exaggerated: in 1600 the empire was poor, backward, and landlocked. Only one seaport—often frozen Arkhangelsk in the north—connected to the world's oceans. The Crimean Turks to the south were powerful enough to sack Moscow in 1571. Beyond them, the Ottoman Empire controlled access to the Black Sea, while the Safavid rulers of Iran dominated the trade of southern Central Asia. The powerful kingdoms of Sweden and Poland-Lithuania to the west similarly blocked Russian access to the Baltic Sea.

The one route open to expansion, **Siberia**, had much to recommend it. Many Russians preferred the forested north to the open steppes; and the thinly inhabited region abounded in valuable resources, most notably the soft, dense fur that forest animals grew to survive the long winters. Like their counterparts in Canada (see Chapter 16), Russian pioneers in Siberia made a living from animal pelts. The

Muscovy The Russian principality that emerged gradually during the era of Mongol domination. The Muscovite dynasty ruled without interruption from 1276 to 1598.

Ural Mountains This north-south range separates Siberia from the rest of Russia. It is commonly considered the boundary between the continents of Europe and Asia.

tsar (czar) From Latin *caesar*, this Russian title for a monarch was first used in reference to a Russian ruler by Ivan III (r. 1462–1505).

Siberia The extreme northeastern sector of Asia, including the Kamchatka Peninsula and the present Russian coast of the Arctic Ocean, the Bering Strait, and the Sea of Okhotsk.

Russian Ambassadors to Holland Display Their Furs, 1576

Representatives from Muscovy impressed the court of King Maximilian II of Bohemia with their sable coats and caps.   (Ria-Novositi)

Map 18.2   The Expansion of Russia, 1500–1800

Sweden and Poland initially blocked Russian expansion in Europe, while the Ottoman Empire blocked the southwest. In the sixteenth century, Russia began to expand east, toward Siberia and the Pacific Ocean. By the end of the rule of Catherine the Great in 1796, Russia encompassed all of northern and northeastern Eurasia.

foreign merchants who came to buy these furs in Moscow provided the tsars with revenue and European contacts.

The Strogonovs, a wealthy Russian trading family, led the early Russian exploration of Siberia. The small indigenous bands of foragers had no way of resisting the armed adventurers the Strogonovs hired. Using rifles, their troops attacked and destroyed the only political power in the region, the Khanate of Sibir, in 1582. Moving through the dense forests by river, Russian fur trappers were able to reach the Pacific during the seventeenth century and soon crossed over into Alaska. Russian political control followed more slowly into what was more a frontier zone with widely scattered forts than a province under full control. Beginning in the early seventeenth century the tsar also used Siberia as a penal colony for criminals and political prisoners.

In the 1640s Russian settlers began to grow grain in the Amur River Valley east of Mongolia. As seen already, by the time the Qing reacted to the Russian presence, the worrisome threat of Galdan's Mongol military power had arisen. Equally concerned about the Mongols, the Russians were pleased to work out a frontier agreement. The 1689 Treaty of Nerchinsk recognized Russian claims west of Mongolia but required the Russians to withdraw their settlements farther east.

Russian Society and Politics, to 1725

Russian expansion involved demographic changes as well as new relations between the tsar and the elite classes. A third transformation affected the freedom and mobility of the Russian peasantry.

As the empire expanded, it incorporated people with different languages, religious beliefs, and ethnic identities. Orthodox missionaries made great efforts to Christianize the peoples of Siberia in much the same way that Catholic missionaries did in Canada. But among the relatively more populous steppe peoples, Islam prevailed over Christianity as the dominant religion. Differences in how people made their living were equally fundamental. Russians tended to live as farmers, hunters, builders, scribes, or merchants, while those newly incorporated into the empire were mostly herders, caravan workers, and soldiers.

As people mixed, individual and group identities became complex. There was diversity even among Russian speakers who were Russian Orthodox in faith. The name *Cossack*, which applied to bands of people living on the steppes between Moscovy and the Caspian and Black Seas, probably comes from a Turkic word for a warrior or mercenary soldier. Actually, Cossacks had diverse origins and beliefs, but they all belonged to close-knit bands, fought superbly from the saddle, and terrified both villagers and legal authorities. Cossack allegiances with rulers were temporary; loyalty to the chiefs of their bands was paramount.

Cossacks provided most of the soldiers and settlers employed by the Strogonovs, and they founded every major town in Russian Siberia. They also manned the Russian camps on the Amur River. West of the Urals the Cossacks defended Russia against Swedish and Ottoman incursions, but they also preserved their political autonomy. Those in the rich and populous lands of the Ukraine, for example, rebelled when the tsar agreed to a division of their lands with Poland-Lithuania in 1667.

In the early seventeenth century Swedish and Polish forces briefly occupied Moscow on separate occasions. This "Time of Troubles" marked the end of the old line of Muscovite rulers. The Russian aristocracy—the boyars (BOY-ar)—allowed one of their

Cossacks Peoples of the Russian Empire who lived outside the farming villages, often as herders, mercenaries, or outlaws. Cossacks led the conquest of Siberia in the sixteenth and seventeenth centuries.

own, Mikhail Romanov (ROH-man-off or roh-MAN-off) (r. 1613–1645), to inaugurate a dynasty that would soon consolidate its own authority while successfully competing with neighboring powers. The Romanovs often represented conflicts between Slavic Russians and Turkic steppe peoples as being between Christians and "infidels" or between the civilized and the "barbaric." Despite this rhetoric, it is important to understand that these cultural groups were defined less by blood ties than by the ways in which they lived.

As centralized tsarist power rose, the freedom of the peasants who tilled the land in European Russia fell. The Moscovy rulers and early tsars rewarded their loyal nobles with grants of land that obliged the local peasants to work for the lords. Law and custom permitted peasants to change masters during a two-week period each year, which encouraged lords to treat their peasants well; but the rising commercialization of agriculture also raised the value of these labor obligations.

Long periods of warfare in the late sixteenth and early seventeenth centuries disrupted peasant life and caused many to flee to the Cossacks or across the Urals. Some who couldn't flee sold themselves into slavery to keep from starving. When peace returned, landlords sought to recover the runaways and bind them more tightly to their land. A law change in 1649 finally transformed the peasants into **serfs** by eliminating the period when they could change masters and ordering runaways to return to their masters.

Like slavery, serfdom was hereditary. In theory the serf was tied to a piece of land, not owned by a master. In practice, strict laws narrowed the difference between serf and slave. In the Russian census of 1795, serfs made up over half the population. Landowners made up only 2 percent, or roughly the same as they did in the Caribbean.

serf In medieval Europe, an agricultural laborer legally bound to a lord's property and obligated to perform set services for the lord. In Russia some serfs worked as artisans and in factories; serfdom was not abolished there until 1861.

Peter the Great

The greatest of the Romanovs, Tsar **Peter the Great** (r. 1689–1725), reduced Russia's isolation and increased the empire's size and power. He turned Russia away from its Asian cultural connections and toward what he deemed the advanced civilization of the West. In fact, he accelerated trends under way for some time. When he ascended the throne, there were already hundreds of foreign merchants in Moscow. Military officers from western Europe had already trained a major part of the army in new weapons and techniques, and Italian builders were already influencing church and palace architecture. Peter accelerated these tendencies.

Peter matured quickly both physically and mentally. In his youth the government was in the hands of his half-sister Sophia, who was regent for him and her sickly brother Ivan. Living on an estate near the foreigners' quarter outside Moscow, Peter learned what he could of life outside Russia and busied himself gaining practical skills in blacksmithing, carpentry, shipbuilding, and the arts of war. He organized his own military drill unit among other young men. When Princess Sophia tried to take complete control of the government in 1689, Peter rallied enough support to send her to a monastery, secure the abdication of Ivan, and take charge of Russia. He was still in his teens.

Peter concerned himself with Russia's expansion and modernization. To secure a port on the Black Sea, he constructed a small but formidable navy. Describing his wars with the Ottoman Empire as a new crusade to liberate Constantinople from the Muslim sultans, Peter also fancied himself the legal protector of Orthodox

Peter the Great (1672–1725) Russian tsar (r. 1689–1725). He enthusiastically introduced Western languages and technologies to the Russian elite and moved the capital from Moscow to the new city of St. Petersburg.

CL Primary Source: Edicts and Decrees
Learn about Peter the Great's feelings on such things as freedom of religion, proper dress, shaving, and military advancement.

Christians living under Ottoman rule. Peter's forces seized the port of Azov in 1696 but lost it again in 1713, thus calling a halt to southward expansion.

In the winter of 1697–1698, after his Black Sea campaign, Peter traveled in disguise across Europe to discover how western European societies were becoming so powerful and wealthy. He paid special attention to ships and weapons, even working for a time as a ship's carpenter in the Netherlands. With great insight, he perceived that western European success owed as much to trade and toleration as to technology. Trade generated the money to spend on weapons, while toleration attracted talented persons fleeing persecution. Upon his return to Russia, Peter resolved to expand and reform his vast and backward empire.

In the long and costly Great Northern War (1700–1721), his modernized armies broke Swedish control of the Baltic Sea, making possible more direct contacts between Russia and Europe. Peter's victory forced the European powers to recognize Russia as a major power for the first time.

On land captured from Sweden at the eastern end of the Baltic, Peter built St. Petersburg, his window on the West. In 1712 the city became Russia's capital. To demonstrate Russia's new sophistication, Peter ordered architects to build St. Petersburg's houses and public buildings in the baroque style then fashionable in France.

Peter also pushed the Russian elite to imitate European fashions. He personally shaved off his noblemen's long beards to conform to Western styles. To end the traditional seclusion of upper-class Russian women, Peter required officials, military officers, and merchants to bring their wives to the social gatherings he organized in the capital. He also directed the nobles to educate their children.

Another strategy was to reorganize Russian government along the lines of the powerful German state of Prussia. He sharply reduced the traditional roles of the boyars in government and the army. A group of appointed advisers in St. Petersburg replaced the old boyar council. Members of the traditional nobility continued to serve as generals and admirals, but officers in Peter's modern, professional army and navy were promoted according to merit, not birth.

The Fontanka Canal in St. Petersburg in 1753

The Russian capital continued to grow as a commercial and administrative center. As in Amsterdam, canals were the city's major arteries. On the right is a new summer palace built by Peter's successor. (British Library, Maps Department, Engraving, after M. I. Makhaiev, from the official series of 1753, Maps K Top, 112.76.5)

A decree of 1716 proclaimed that the tsar "is not obliged to answer to anyone in the world for his doings, but possesses power and authority over his kingdom and land, to rule them at his will and pleasure as a Christian ruler." Under this expansive definition of his role, Peter brought the Russian Orthodox Church more firmly under state control, built factories and iron and copper foundries to provide munitions and supplies for the military, and increased the burdens of taxes and forced labor on the serfs. Peter was an absolutist ruler of the sort then common in western Europe, and he had no more intention of improving the conditions of the serfs than did the European slave owners of the Americas.

Consolidation of the Empire

Russia's eastward expansion continued under Peter the Great and his successors. The frontier settlement with China and Qianlong's quashing of Inner Mongolia in 1689 freed Russians to concentrate on the northern Pacific. The Pacific northeast was colonized, and in 1741 an expedition led by Captain Vitus Bering crossed the strait (later named for him) into North America. In 1799 a Russian company of merchants received a monopoly over the Alaskan fur trade, and its agents were soon active along the entire northwestern coast of North America.

Far more important than these immense territories in the cold and thinly populated north were the populous agricultural lands to the west acquired during the reign of Catherine the Great (r. 1762–1796). A successful war with the Ottoman Empire gave Russia control of the north shore of the Black Sea by 1783, though not of the straits leading to the Mediterranean. Three successive partitions of the once powerful kingdom of Poland between 1772 and 1795 advanced Russia's frontiers 600 miles (nearly 1,000 kilometers) to the west (see Map 18.2). When Catherine died, the Russian Empire extended from Poland in the west to Alaska in the east, from the Barents Sea in the north to the Black Sea in the south.

Catherine also made important additions to Peter's policies of promoting industry and building a canal system to improve trade. Besides furs, the Russians had also become major exporters of gold, iron, and timber. Catherine implemented administrative reforms and showed a special talent for diplomacy. Through her promotion of the ideas of the Enlightenment, she expanded Peter's policies of westernizing the Russian elite.

SECTION REVIEW

- Muscovy became the center of Russian political power and led the movement against Mongol domination.

- Ivan IV expanded Muscovy, and the Strogonovs sponsored exploration of fur-rich Siberia.

- Russian society blended diverse ethnicities, religions, and cultural practices, a mixture embodied in the Cossacks.

- Emerging from the Time of Troubles, the Romanov tsars worked to centralize royal authority and to institutionalize serfdom.

- Peter the Great accelerated Russia's westernization, fought wars of expansion, and enlarged the power of the tsar.

- Expansion continued eastward and westward, and Catherine the Great continued Peter's westernizing policies.

COMPARATIVE PERSPECTIVES

China and Russia are examples of the phenomenal flourishing of empires in Eurasia between 1500 and 1800. Already a vast empire under the Ming, China doubled in size under the Qing, mostly through westward expansion into less densely populated areas. In expanding from a modestly sized principality into the world's largest land empire, Russia added rich and well-populated lands to the west and south and far larger but less populous lands to the east. Russia and China were land based, just like the Ottoman and Mughal Empires, with the strengths and problems of administrative control and tax collection that size entailed.

Japan was different. Though nominally headed by an emperor, Japan's size and ethnic homogeneity do not support calling it an empire in the same breath with China and Russia. Tokugawa Japan was similar in size and population to France, the most powerful state of western Europe, but its political system was much more decentralized. Japan's efforts to add colonies on the East Asian mainland had failed.

China had once led the world in military innovation (including the first uses of gunpowder), but the modern "gunpowder revolution" of the fifteenth and sixteenth centuries was centered in the Ottoman Empire and western European states. Although the centuries after 1500 were full of successful military operations, Chinese armies continued to depend on superior numbers and tactics for their success, rather than on new technology. As in the past, infantrymen armed with guns served alongside others armed with bows and arrows, swords, and spears.

The military forces of Japan and Russia underwent more innovative changes than those of China, in part through Western contacts. In the course of its sixteenth-century wars of unification, Japan produced its own gunpowder revolution but thereafter lacked the motivation and the means to stay abreast of the world's most advanced military technology. By the eighteenth century Russia had made greater progress in catching up with its European neighbors, but its armies still relied more on their size than on the sophistication of their weapons.

Naval power provides the greatest military contrast among China, Russia, and Japan. Eighteenth-century Russia constructed modern fleets of warships in the Baltic and Black Seas, but neither China nor Japan developed navies commensurate with their size and coastlines. China's defenses against pirates and other sea invaders were left to its maritime provinces, whose small war junks were armed with only a half-dozen cannon. Japan's naval capacity was similarly decentralized. In 1792, when Russian ships exploring the North Pacific turned toward the Japanese coast, the local daimyo used his own forces to chase them away. All Japanese daimyo understood that they would be on their own if foreign incursions increased.

The expansion of China and Russia incorporated not just new lands but also diverse new peoples. Chinese society had long been diverse, and its geographical, occupational, linguistic, and religious differences grew as the Qing expanded (see Map 18.1). China had also long used Confucian models, imperial customs, and a common system of writing to transcend such differences and to assimilate elites. Russia likewise approached its new peoples with a mixture of pragmatic tolerance and a propensity for seeing Russian ways and beliefs as superior. The Russian language was strongly promoted. Religion was a particular sore point, as Russian Orthodox missionaries, with the support of the tsars, encouraged conversion of Siberian peoples. Russia absorbed new ideas and styles from western Europe, although even among the elite these influences often overlay Russian traditions in a very superficial way. In contrast, Japan remained more culturally homogeneous, and the government reacted with great intolerance to the growing influence of converts to western Christianity.

Forced labor remained common in the Russian and Chinese Empires. Serfdom grew more brutal and widespread in Russia in the seventeenth and eighteenth centuries, although the expansion of the frontier eastward across Siberia also opened an escape route for many peasants and serfs. Some Chinese peasants also improved their lot by moving to new territories, but population growth increased overall misery in the eighteenth century. China was also notable for the size of its popular insurrections, especially the one that toppled the Ming.

Chapter Review

DOWNLOAD THE MP3 AUDIO FILE OF THE CHAPTER REVIEW TO LISTEN TO ON THE GO.

How did Japan respond to domestic social changes and the challenges posed by contact with foreign cultures? (page 496)

The formation of the Tokugawa Shogunate in Japan is a clear example of a society changing from within. The decisions of the government to suppress Christianity and sharply curtail commercial and intellectual contacts with distant Europe illustrate how easily even the most decentralized state could control its dealings with outsiders.

How did China deal with military and political challenges both inside and outside its borders? (page 501)

China's history illustrates a complex interplay of internal and external forces. During the final days of the Ming dynasty, China suffered from internal rebellions caused by deteriorating economic conditions, to which the Ming responded ineffectively. When Japan invaded, the Ming sought help from the Manchus, who then turned on them and established the Qing Empire. The Qing's settlement of the Amur frontier with Russia illustrates how diplomacy and compromise could serve mutual interests. Finally, the Chinese added new European customers to already extensive internal and external markets and developed both positive and problematic cultural relations with the Jesuits and some other Europeans. From a Chinese perspective, European contacts could be useful but were neither essential nor of great importance.

To what extent was Russia's expanding empire influenced by relations with western Europe in this period? (page 511)

During this period Russia increased its trade with the West and through its conquests and territorial expansion emerged as a Great Power. Moreover, both Peter the Great and Catherine the Great labored to westernize their people. Clearly, Western influences were very important, but their importance can easily be exaggerated. The impetus for Muscovy's expansion came out of its own history and domination by the Mongols, and trade with western Europe was not the center of the Russian economy. Tsar Peter was more interested in Western technology than in the full range of Western culture. The Russian church was quite hostile to the Catholics and Protestants to the west, whom it regarded as heretics. Finally, Peter the Great banned the Jesuits from Russia, considering them a subversive and backward influence.

KEY TERMS

Manchu *(p. 496)*
daimyo *(p. 496)*
samurai *(p. 496)*
Tokugawa Shogunate *(p. 498)*
Ming Empire *(p. 502)*
Qing Empire *(p. 503)*
Kangxi *(p. 507)*
Amur River *(p. 507)*
Macartney mission *(p. 510)*
Muscovy *(p. 512)*
Ural Mountains *(p. 512)*
tsar (czar) *(p. 512)*
Siberia *(p. 512)*
Cossacks *(p. 514)*
serf *(p. 515)*
Peter the Great *(p. 515)*

WEB RESOURCES

Pronunciation Guide
Interactive Maps
  The Qing Empire, 1644–1783
Primary Sources
  Some Observations on Merchants
  Journals
  Edict on Trade with Great Britain
  Edicts and Decrees
Answer to the History in Focus Question
  See photo on page 508, "Emperor Kangxi."
Plus
  Chapter Objectives
  ACE multiple-choice quiz
  Flashcards

SUGGESTED READING

Berry, Mary Elizabeth. *Hideyoshi.* 1982. An account of the reunification of Japan at the end of the sixteenth century.

Cooper, Michael, and Jonathan D. Spence. *The Memory Palace of Matteo Ricci.* 1984. An engrossing account of Jesuits in East Asia in the sixteenth and seventeenth centuries.

Crossley, Pamela Kyle. *The Manchus.* 2002. A history of the people who ruled China during the Qing dynasty.

Crummey, Robert O. *Aristocrats and Servitors: The Boyar Elite in Russia, 1613–1689.* 1983. Russia before Peter the Great.

Kappeler, Andreas. *The Russian Empire: A Multiethnic History.* 2001. Deals with all of the empire's peoples, not just the Russians.

Keay, John. *The Honourable Company: A History of the English East India Company.* 1994. A study of Indian Ocean trade and colonization.

Massie, Robert K. *Peter the Great: His Life and World.* 1980. A highly readable biography for a general audience.

Morris-Suzuki, Tessa. *The Technological Transformation of Japan from the Seventeenth to the Twenty-first Century.* 1994. Analyzes the roots of modern Japanese technological development.

Nakane, Chie and Shinzaburo Oishi. *Tokugawa Japan: The Social and Economic Antecedents of Modern Japan.* Trans. Conrad Totman. 1990. Early modern Japan from a contemporary perspective.

Rawski, Evelyn Sakakida. *The Last Emperors: A Social History of Qing Imperial Institutions.* 1998. A reinterpretation of the success of the Manchus' Qing Empire.

Spence, Jonathan D. *The Search for Modern China.* 1990. China during the transition from the Ming to Qing periods.

Wills, John E. *Pepper, Guns, and Parleys: The Dutch East India Company and China, 1662–1681.* 2005. Describes China's relations with European traders.

Wills, John E., Jr. *1688: A Global History.* 2001. Part III, "Three Worlds Apart: Russia, China, and Japan," provides stimulating comparisons.

NOTES

1. Adapted from Jonathan D. Spence, *The Search for Modern China* (New York: W. W. Norton, 1990), 21–25.

2. Adapted from G. V. Melikhov, "Manzhou Penetration into the Basin of the Upper Amur in the 1680s," in S. L. Tikhvinshii, ed., *Manzhou Rule in China* (Moscow: Progress Publishers, 1983).

The Little Ice Age

A GIANT VOLCANIC ERUPTION in the Peruvian Andes in 1600 affected the weather in many parts of the world for several years. When volcanic ash from the eruption of Mount Huanyaputina (hoo-AHN-yah-poo-TEE-nuh) shot into the upper atmosphere and spread around the world, it screened out sunlight. As a result, the summer of 1601 was the coldest in two hundred years in the Northern Hemisphere.

Archaeologist Brian Fagan has pointed out that Mount Huanyaputina's chilling effects were a spectacular event in a much longer pattern of climate change that has been called the Little Ice Age.[1] Although global climate had been cooling since the late 1200s, in the northern temperate regions the 1590s had been exceptionally cold. Temperatures remained cooler than normal throughout the seventeenth century.

The most detailed information on the Little Ice Age comes from Europe. Glaciers in the Alps grew much larger. Trade became difficult when rivers and canals that had once been navigable in winter froze solid from bank to bank. In the coldest years, the growing season in some places was as much as two months shorter than normal. Unexpectedly late frosts withered the tender shoots of newly planted crops in spring. Wheat and barley ripened more slowly during cooler summers and were often damaged by early fall frosts.

People could survive a smaller-than-average harvest in one year by drawing on food reserves, but when cold weather damaged crops in two or more successive years, the consequences were devastating. Deaths due to malnutrition and cold increased sharply when summer temperatures in northern Europe registered 2.7F (1.5C) lower than average in 1674 and 1675 and again in 1694 and 1695. The cold spell of 1694 and 1695 caused a famine in Finland that carried off a quarter to a third of the population.

At the time people had no idea what was causing the unusual cold of the Little Ice Age. Advances in climate history make it clear that the cause was not a single terrestrial event such as the eruption of Mount Huanyaputina. Nor was the Little Ice Age the product of human actions, unlike some climate changes such as today's global warming.

Ultimately, the earth's weather is governed by the sun. In the seventeenth century astronomers in Europe reported seeing fewer sunspots, dark spots on the sun's surface that are indicative of solar activity and thus the sun's warming power. Diminished activity in the sun was primarily responsible for the Little Ice Age.

If the sun was the root cause, the effects of global cooling should not have been confined to northern Europe. Although contemporary accounts are much scarcer in other parts of the world, there is evidence of climate changes around the world in this period. Observations of sunspots in China, Korea, and Japan drop to zero between 1639 and 1700. China experienced unusually cool weather in the seventeenth century, but the warfare and disruption accompanying the fall of the Ming and the rise of the Qing probably were much more to blame for the famines and rural distress of that period.

By itself, a relatively slight decrease in average annual temperature would not have a significant effect on human life outside the northern temperate areas. However, evidence suggests that there was also a significant rise in humidity in this period in other parts of the world. Ice cores drilled into ancient glaciers in the Arctic and Antarctic show increased snowfall. Information compiled by historian James L. A. Webb, Jr., shows that lands south of the Sahara received more rainfall between 1550 and 1750 than they had during the previous era.[2] Increased rainfall would have been favorable for pastoral people, whose herds found new pasture in what had once been desert, and for the farmers farther south whose crops got more rain.

In the eighteenth century the sun's activity began to return to normal. Rising temperatures led to milder winters and better harvests in northern Eurasia. Falling rainfall allowed the Sahara to advance southward, forcing the agricultural frontier to retreat.

NOTES

1. Brian Fagan, *The Littlest Ice Age: How Climate Made History, 1300–1850* (New York: Basic Books, 2000).
2. James L. A. Webb, Jr., *Desert Frontier: Ecological Change Along the Western Sahel, 1600–1850* (Madison: University of Wisconsin Press, 1995).

Revolutions Reshape the World, 1750–1870

*B*etween 1750 and 1870, nearly every part of the world experienced dramatic political, economic, and social change. The beginnings of industrialization, the American and French Revolutions, and the revolutions for independence in Latin America transformed political and economic life. European nations expanded into Africa, Asia, and the Middle East while Russia and the United States acquired vast new territories.

The Industrial Revolution introduced new technologies and patterns of work that made these societies wealthier and militarily more powerful. Western intellectual life became more secular. The Atlantic slave trade and later slavery itself were abolished, and the first efforts to improve the status of women were initiated.

The Industrial Revolution led to a new wave of imperialism. France conquered Algeria, and Great Britain expanded its colonial rule in India and established colonies in Australia and New Zealand. European political and economic influence also expanded in Africa and Asia. The Ottoman Empire and the Qing Empire met this challenge by implementing reform programs that preserved traditional structures while adopting elements of Western technology and organization. Though lagging behind western Europe in transforming its economy and political institutions, Russia attempted modernization efforts, including the abolition of serfdom.

The economic, political, and social revolutions that began in the mid-eighteenth century shook the foundations of European culture and led to the expansion of Western power around the globe. Some of the nations of Asia, Africa, and Latin America reformed and strengthened their own institutions and economies, while others pushed for more radical change. After 1870 Western imperialism became more aggressive, and few parts of the world were able to resist it.

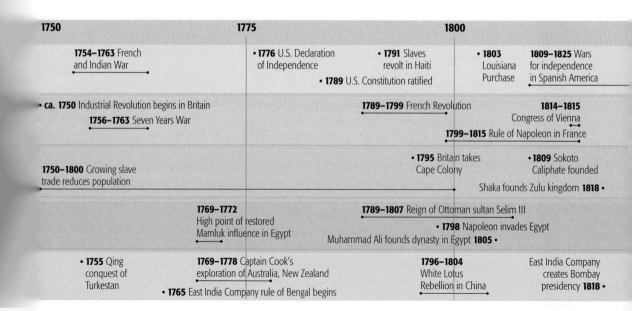

1750	1775	1800
1754–1763 French and Indian War	• **1776** U.S. Declaration of Independence	• **1791** Slaves revolt in Haiti • **1803** Louisiana Purchase **1809–1825** Wars for independence in Spanish America
	• **1789** U.S. Constitution ratified	
• **ca. 1750** Industrial Revolution begins in Britain	**1789–1799** French Revolution	**1814–1815** Congress of Vienna
1756–1763 Seven Years War		**1799–1815** Rule of Napoleon in France
1750–1800 Growing slave trade reduces population	• **1795** Britain takes Cape Colony	• **1809** Sokoto Caliphate founded
		Shaka founds Zulu kingdom **1818** •
	1769–1772 High point of restored Mamluk influence in Egypt	**1789–1807** Reign of Ottoman sultan Selim III
		• **1798** Napoleon invades Egypt
		Muhammad Ali founds dynasty in Egypt **1805** •
• **1755** Qing conquest of Turkestan	**1769–1778** Captain Cook's exploration of Australia, New Zealand	**1796–1804** White Lotus Rebellion in China
	• **1765** East India Company rule of Bengal begins	East India Company creates Bombay presidency **1818** •

523

1825	1850	1875
• **1822** Independence of Brazil	• **1848** Women's Rights Convention in Seneca Falls, New York	**1862–1867** French invasion of Mexico **1861–1865** U.S. Civil War • **1867** Creation of Dominion of Canada
• **1830** Revolutions of 1830 • **1834** Abolition of slavery in British Empire	**1852–1870** Rule of Napoleon III in France • **1848** Revolutions of 1848 • **1861** Russia abolishes serfdom **1853–1856** Crimean War	
• **1821** Republic of Liberia founded	**1836–1839** Afrikaners' Great Trek	• **1869** Jaja founds Opobo
• **1826** Ottoman ruler Mahmud II dissolves Janissary corps • **1839** Ottoman ruler Abdul Mejid launches Tanzimat reforms		• **1860s** Beginning of Young Turk movement • **1869** Suez Canal opens
• **1826** East India Company annexes Assam, northern Burma **1839–1842** Opium War **1829–1864** Russia completes conquest of Central Asia	**1850–1864** Taiping Rebellion in China **1857–1858** Sepoy Rebellion in India	

Revolutionary Changes in the Atlantic World

CHAPTER 19

1750–1850

CHAPTER PREVIEW

On the evening of August 14, 1791, more than two hundred slaves and black freedmen met in secret in the plantation district of northern Saint Domingue (san doe-MANG) (present-day Haiti) to set the date for an armed uprising against local slave owners. Although the delegates agreed to delay the attack for a week, violence began almost immediately. During the following decade, the Haitian rebels abolished slavery, defeated military forces from Britain and France, and gained independence.

News and rumors about revolutionary events in France that had spread through the island incited the slave community and divided the island's white population between royalists (supporters of France's King Louis XVI) and republicans (supporters of democracy). The free mixed-race population initially gained some

 This icon will direct you to the website where you can Prepare for Class, Improve Your Grade, and Ace the Test: college.cengage.com/pic/bulletbrief4e

political rights from the French Assembly but was then forced to rebel when the slave-owning elite reacted violently.

Among those planning the insurrection was Toussaint L'Ouverture (too-SAN loo-ver-CHORE), a black freedman. This remarkable revolutionary organized the rebels into a potent military force, negotiated with the island's royalist and republican factions, and, with representatives of Great Britain and France, wrote his nation's first constitution. Throughout the Western Hemisphere, Toussaint became a towering symbol of resistance to oppression for slaves and a fiend in the eyes of slave owners.

The Haitian slave rebellion was an important episode in the long and painful political and cultural transformation of the modern Western world. Economic expansion and the growth of trade were creating unprecedented wealth. Intellectuals were questioning the traditional place of monarchy and slavery in society. An emerging class of merchants, professionals, and manufacturers began to press for a larger political role, and economies were increasingly opened to competition.

Imperial powers resisted the loss of colonies, and monarchs and nobles struggled to retain their ancient privileges. Revolutionary steps forward were often matched by reactionary steps backward. The liberal and nationalist ideals of the eighteenth-century revolutionary movements were only imperfectly realized in Europe and the Americas in the nineteenth century.

PRELUDE TO REVOLUTION: WAR AND THE ENLIGHTENMENT

How did the costs of imperial wars and the Enlightenment challenge the established authority of monarchs and religion in Europe and the American colonies?

In large measure, the cost of wars fought among Europe's major powers over colonies and trade precipitated the revolutionary era that began in 1775 with the American Revolution. The struggle of Britain, France, and Spain for political preeminence in western Europe and overseas produced many violent conflicts during the eighteenth century. In the Seven Years War (1756–1763), known as the French and Indian War in America, Britain gained dominance in North America and in India. All parties suffered from the enormous costs of these conflicts.

However, new Western ideas and political environments now made people much more critical of any effort to extend the power of a monarch or impose new taxes, and they also raised questions about the rights of individuals. As Chapter 15 recounted, the **Enlightenment** applied the methods and questions of the Scientific Revolution to the study of human society. Some thinkers challenged long-established religious and political institutions. They argued that if scientists could understand the laws of nature, then surely similar forms of disciplined investigation might reveal laws of human nature. Others wondered whether society and government might be better regulated and more productive if guided by reason rather than by hereditary rulers and the church.

These new perspectives and the intellectual optimism that fed them were to help guide the English political philosopher John Locke (1632–1704). Locke argued

Enlightenment A philosophical movement in eighteenth-century Europe that fostered the belief that one could reform society by discovering rational laws that governed social behavior and were just as scientific as the laws of physics.

Beer Street (1751)

This engraving by William Hogarth shows an idealized London street scene where beer drinking is associated with manly strength, good humor, and prosperity. The self-satisfied corpulent figure in the left foreground has been reading a copy of the king's speech to Parliament. We can imagine him offering a running commentary to his drinking companions as he reads.
(Courtesy, Dover Publications)

in 1690 that governments were created to protect life, liberty, and property and that the people had a right to rebel when a monarch violated these natural rights. In *The Social Contract,* published in 1762, the French-Swiss intellectual Jean-Jacques Rousseau (zhahn-zhock roo-SOE) (1712–1778) asserted that the will of the people was sacred and that the legitimacy of the monarch depended on the consent of the people. Although both men believed that government rested on the will of the people rather than divine will, Locke emphasized the importance of individual rights, and Rousseau envisioned the people acting collectively because of their shared historical experience.

The Enlightenment is commonly associated with hostility toward monarchy, but Voltaire, one of the Enlightenment's most critical intellects, believed that Europe's monarchs were likely agents of political and economic reform, and he wrote favorably of China's Qing (ching) emperors. Indeed, some sympathetic members of the nobility and reforming monarchs in Spain, Russia, Austria, and Prussia actively sponsored and promoted the dissemination of new ideas, providing patronage for many intellectuals. They recognized that elements of the Enlightenment critique of the *ancien régime* (ahn-see-EN ray-ZHEEM) buttressed their own efforts to expand royal authority at the expense of religious institutions, the nobility, and regional autonomy. Monarchs also understood that the era's passion for science and technology held the potential of fattening national treasuries and improving economic performance.

The Western Hemisphere shared in the debates of Europe. In colonial societies where political rights were even more limited than in Europe, the idea that government authority ultimately rested on the consent of the governed was potentially explosive. The efforts of ordinary men and women to resist the growth of government power and the imposition of new cultural forms provide an important political undercurrent to much of the revolutionary agitation and conflict from 1750 to 1850. But spontaneous popular uprisings gained revolutionary potential only when they coincided with ideological divisions and conflicts within the governing class itself.

CL **Primary Source: Rousseau Espouses Popular Sovereignty and the General Will**
What is "the government"? Find out what Jean-Jacques Rousseau believes, and consider how his ideas helped shape the revolutionary movements of his time.

SECTION REVIEW

- The costs of the imperial wars among England, France, and Spain helped to spark the era of revolutions.

- Also important were the ideas and critical spirit of the Enlightenment, particularly the political ideas of Locke and Rousseau.

- These new ideas received support of reformist nobility and monarchs.

- Progressive intellectual debate spread to the colonial societies of the Western Hemisphere.

Chronology

The Americas	Europe
1750	
1756–1763 French and Indian War	**1756–1763** Seven Years War
1770 Boston Massacre	
1776 American Declaration of Independence	
1783 Treaty of Paris ends American Revolution	
	1789 Storming of Bastille begins French Revolution
1791 Slaves revolt in Saint Domingue (Haiti)	
	1793–1794 Reign of Terror in France
	1795–1799 The Directory rules France
1798 Toussaint L'Ouverture defeats British in Haiti	
	1799 Napoleon overthrows the Directory
1800	
1804 Haitians defeat French invasion and declare independence	**1804** Napoleon crowns himself emperor
1808 Portuguese royal family arrives in Brazil	
1808–1809 Revolutions for independence begin in Spanish South America	
	1814 Napoleon abdicates; Congress of Vienna opens
1822 Brazil gains independence	
1825	
	1830 Greece gains independence; revolution in France
1848 Women's Rights Convention in Seneca Falls, New York	**1848** Revolutions in France, Austria, Germany, Hungary, and Italy
1850	
1861–1865 American Civil War	
1865 End of slavery in United States	
1875	
1886 End of slavery in Cuba	
1888 End of slavery in Brazil	

THE AMERICAN REVOLUTION

What were the direct causes of the American Revolution?

After defeating the French in the French and Indian War, the British government faced two related problems in its North American colonies. One was the likelihood of armed conflict with Amerindian peoples as settlers quickly pushed west of the Appalachian Mountains and across the Ohio River. Already burdened with war debts, Britain desperately wanted to avoid additional expenditures for frontier defense. The other problem was how to get the colonists to shoulder more of the costs of imperial defense and colonial administration. Every effort to impose new taxes or prevent the settlement of the trans-Appalachian frontier provoked angry protests in the colonies. The confrontational and impolitic way in which a succession of weak British governments responded made the situation politically explosive.

Frontiers and Taxes

The British Proclamation of 1763, which sought to establish an effective western limit for settlement, threw into question the claims of thousands of already established farmers without effectively protecting Amerindian land. The Quebec Act of 1774 annexed disputed lands to the province of Quebec, thus denying eastern colonies the authority to distribute lands claimed as a result of original charters. Colonists saw the Quebec Act as punitive and tyrannical, and Amerindian peoples received no relief from the continuous assault on their land.

New commercial regulations that increased the cost of foreign molasses and endangered New England's profitable trade with Spanish and French Caribbean sugar colonies provoked widespread boycotts of British goods. The Stamp Act of 1765, which imposed a tax on all legal documents, newspapers, pamphlets, and other types of printed material, led to violent protest and more effective boycotts. Parliament imposed new taxes and duties soon after repealing the Stamp Act in 1766, even sending British

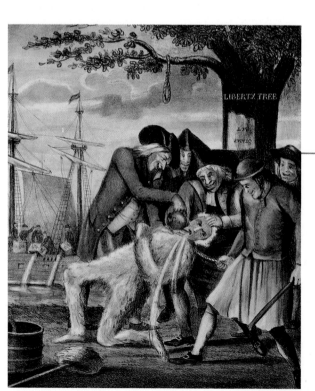

LIBERTY TREE

The Tarring and Feathering of a British Official, 1774

This illustration from a British periodical shows the unfortunate John Malcomb, commissioner of customs at Boston. By the mid-1770s British periodicals were focusing public opinion on mob violence and the breakdown of public order in the colonies. British critics of colonial political protests viewed the demand for liberty as little more than an excuse for mob violence.   (The Granger Collection, New York)

(CL) HISTORY IN FOCUS In addition to what the caption tells, what do the figures and their surroundings, particularly the Liberty Tree, tell you about how some in Britain viewed the American colonists and their cause? If this picture had appeared in an American magazine, how might it have been different? *Find the answer online.*

troops to quell urban riots. Unable to control the streets of Boston, British authorities reacted by threatening traditional liberties, dissolving the colonial legislature of Massachusetts, and dispatching a warship and two regiments of soldiers to reestablish control. Support for a complete break with Britain grew when a British force fired on an angry Boston crowd on March 5, 1770, killing five civilians. This "Boston Massacre," which seemed to expose the naked force on which colonial rule rested, radicalized public opinion throughout the colonies.

Parliament attempted to calm public opinion by repealing some of the taxes and duties, then stumbled into another crisis by granting the British East India Company a monopoly for importing tea to the colonies, which raised anew the constitutional issue of Parliament's right to tax the colonies. It also offended wealthy colonial merchants, who were excluded from this profitable commerce. The crisis came to a head in the already politically overheated port of Boston when tea worth £10,000 was dumped into the harbor by protesters disguised as Amerindians.

The Course of the Revolution

As the crisis mounted, patriots created new governing bodies, effectively deposed many British governors and other officials, passed laws, appointed judges, and even took control of colonial militias. Simultaneously, radical leaders organized crowds to intimidate loyalists—people who were pro-British—and to enforce the boycott of British goods.

Events were propelling the colonies toward revolution. Elected representatives, meeting in Philadelphia as the Continental Congress in 1775, assumed the powers of government, creating a currency and organizing an army. **George Washington** (1732–1799), a Virginia planter who had served in the French and Indian War, was named commander. On July 4, 1776, Congress approved the Declaration of Independence, the document that proved to be the most enduring statement of the revolutionary era's ideology:

> We hold these truths to be self evident: That all men are created equal; that they are endowed by their creator with certain unalienable rights; that among these are life, liberty and the pursuit of happiness; that, to secure these rights, governments are instituted among men, deriving their just powers from the consent of the governed.

This affirmation of popular sovereignty and individual rights influenced the language of revolution and popular protest around the world.

To shore up British authority, Great Britain sent more than 400 ships, 50,000 soldiers, and 30,000 German mercenaries. But this military commitment proved futile. Although British forces won most of the battles, Washington slowly built a competent Continental army and civilian support networks that provided supplies and financial resources. In the final decisive battle, fought at Yorktown, Virginia, an American army, supported by French soldiers, besieged a British army led by General Charles Cornwallis. With escape cut off by a French fleet, Cornwallis surrendered to Washington as the British military band played "The World Turned Upside-Down."

George Washington (1732–1799) Military commander of the American Revolution. He was the first elected president of the United States (1789–1799).

Primary Source: The United States Declaration of Independence *Consider Thomas Jefferson's famous words, and find out how he and his cohorts justified their separation from Great Britain.*

New Republican Institutions

Ignoring the British example of an unwritten constitution, representatives in each of the newly independent states drafted formal charters and submitted the results

SECTION REVIEW

- The American Revolution grew from British settlement and tax policies after the French and Indian War.

- New taxes and duties and the British East India Company tea monopoly sparked popular outrage and riots in the colonies.

- Meeting as the Continental Congress, patriots assumed government powers, formed an army under Washington, and declared independence.

- The independent states developed republican institutions and procedures on the state and national levels.

- Although the new government was quite democratic, only a minority of adults gained full rights.

Constitutional Convention
Meeting in 1787 of the elected representatives of the thirteen original states to write the Constitution of the United States.

to voters for ratification. Europeans were fascinated by these written constitutions and by their formal ratification by the people. Here was the social contract of Locke and Rousseau made manifest. The state constitutions also placed severe limits on executive authority but granted legislatures greater powers than in colonial times. Many states also inserted in their constitutions a bill of rights to provide further protection against government tyranny.

An effective constitution for the new national government was developed more slowly and hesitantly. The Articles of Confederation—the first constitution of the United States—were not accepted by all the states until 1781. With the coming of peace in 1783, there was an effort to fashion a new constitution.

Debate at the **Constitutional Convention**, which began meeting in May 1787, focused on several issues: representation, electoral procedures, executive powers, and the relationship between the federal government and the states. The final compromise provided for a two-house legislature: the lower house (the House of Representatives) to be elected directly by voters and the upper house (the Senate) to be elected by state legislatures. The chief executive—the president—was to be elected indirectly by "electors" selected by ballot in the states (each state had a number of electors equal to the number of its representatives and senators).

Although the U.S. Constitution created the most democratic government of the era, only a minority of the adult population was given full rights. Southern leaders were able to protect the institution of slavery by counting three-fifths of the slave population in the calculations that determined their states' congressional representatives. Although women had led prewar boycotts and had organized relief and charitable organizations during the war, they were denied political rights in the new republic.

THE FRENCH REVOLUTION

What were the origins and accomplishments of the French Revolution?

The French Revolution confronted the entrenched privileges of an established church, monarchy, and aristocracy more directly than the American Revolution did. It also expanded mass participation in political life and radicalized the democratic tradition. But in the end, the passions unleashed in France by revolutionary events could not be sustained.

French Society and Fiscal Crisis

French society was divided into three groups. The clergy, the First Estate, numbered about 130,000 in a nation of 28 million. The Catholic Church owned about 10 percent of the nation's land and extracted substantial amounts of wealth from the economy in the form of tithes and ecclesiastical fees. Despite its substantial wealth, the church was exempted from nearly all taxes.

The 300,000 members of the nobility, the Second Estate, controlled about 30 percent of the land and retained ancient rights on much of the rest. Nobles held the vast majority of high administrative, judicial, military, and church positions. Though traditionally barred from some types of commercial activity, nobles were important participants in wholesale trade, banking, manufacturing, and mining.

The Third Estate included everyone else. There were three times as many members of the bourgeoisie (boor-zhwah-ZEE) in 1774, when Louis XVI took the throne, as there had been in 1715, at the end of Louis XIV's reign. Peasants accounted for 80 percent of the French population. They owned some property and lived decently when crops were good and prices stable. By 1780, poor harvests had decreased their incomes.

The nation's poor were a large, growing, and troublesome sector. Urban streets swarmed with beggars and prostitutes. Unable to afford decent housing, obtain steady employment, or protect their children, the poor periodically erupted in violent protest and rage. In the countryside, violence was often the reaction to increased dues and fees. In towns and cities, an increase in the price of bread often provided the spark.

These explosive episodes, however, were not revolutionary in character. The remedies sought were conventional and immediate rather than structural and long term. That was to change when the Crown tried to solve its fiscal crisis by imposing new taxes on the nobility and on other groups that in the past had enjoyed exemptions. But this effort failed in the face of widespread protest and the refusal of the Parlement of Paris, a court of appeal that heard appeals from local courts throughout France, to register the new tax. In 1768, frustrated authorities exiled the members of that Parlement and pushed through a series of unpopular fiscal measures. Despite the worsening fiscal crisis, the French took on the heavy burden of supporting the American Revolution, delaying collapse by borrowing enormous sums. By the end of the war with Britain, more than half of France's national budget was required to service the debt alone. In 1787, the desperate king called an Assembly of Notables to approve a radical and comprehensive reform of the economy and fiscal policy. Although the members of this assembly were selected by the king's advisers from the high nobility, the judiciary, and the clergy, they proved unwilling to act as a rubber stamp for the proposed reforms or new taxes. Instead, these representatives of France's most privileged classes sought to protect their interests by questioning the competence of the king and his ministers to supervise the nation's affairs, thus creating the conditions for political revolution.

Protest Turns to Revolution

Unable to extract needed tax concessions from the notables, King Louis XVI was forced to call the **Estates General**, the French national legislature, which had not met since 1614. Traditionally, the three estates met separately, and a positive vote by two of the three was required for action. Tradition, however, was quickly overturned when the Third Estate refused to conduct business until the king ordered the other two estates to sit with it in a single body. During a six-week period of stalemate, many parish priests deserted the First Estate to meet with them.

When this expanded Third Estate declared itself the **National Assembly**, the king and his advisers recognized that the reformers intended to force them to accept a constitutional monarchy. Louis's agenda for fiscal reform was being displaced by the central ideas of the era: the people were sovereign, and the legitimacy of political institutions and individual rulers ultimately depended on their carrying out the

Estates General France's traditional national assembly with representatives of the three estates, or classes, in French society: the clergy, nobility, and commoners. The calling of the Estates General in 1789 led to the French Revolution.

National Assembly French Revolutionary assembly (1789–1791). Called first as the Estates General, the three estates came together and demanded radical change. It passed the Declaration of the Rights of Man in 1789.

people's will. Louis prepared for a confrontation with the National Assembly by moving military forces to Versailles. But before he could act, the people of Paris intervened.

A succession of bad harvests beginning in 1785 had propelled bread prices upward throughout France and provoked an economic depression. By the time the Estates General met, nearly a third of the Parisian work force was unemployed. Hunger and anger marched hand in hand through working-class neighborhoods.

When the people of Paris heard that the king was massing troops to arrest their representatives, crowds of common people began to seize arms and mobilize. On July 14, 1789, a crowd searching for military supplies attacked the Bastille (bass-TEEL), a medieval fortress used as a prison. The futile defense of the Bastille cost ninety-eight lives before its garrison surrendered. Enraged, the attackers hacked the commander to death and then paraded through the city with his head and that of Paris's chief magistrate stuck on pikes.

These events coincided with uprisings in the country. Peasants sacked manor houses and destroyed documents that recorded their traditional obligations. They refused to pay taxes and dues to landowners and seized common lands. Forced to recognize the fury raging through rural areas, the National Assembly voted to end traditional obligations and to reform the tax system. Having forced acceptance of their narrow agenda, the peasants ceased their revolt.

Declaration of the Rights of Man (1789) Statement of fundamental political rights adopted by the French National Assembly at the beginning of the French Revolution.

These popular uprisings strengthened the hand of the National Assembly in its dealings with the king. One manifestation of this altered relationship was passage of the **Declaration of the Rights of Man**. The French declaration, however, was more sweeping in its language than the American Declaration of Independence. Among the enumerated natural rights were "liberty, property, security, and resistance to oppression." The Declaration of the Rights of Man also guaranteed free expression of ideas, equality before the law, and representative government.

While delegates debated political issues in Versailles, the economic crisis worsened in Paris. Because the working women of Paris faced high food prices every day as they struggled to feed their families, their anger had a hard edge. On October 5, market women organized a crowd of thousands to march the 12 miles (19 kilometers) to Versailles (vuhr-SIGH). Once there, they forced their way into the National Assembly to demand action from the frightened representatives: "The point is that

Playing Cards from the French Revolution

Even playing cards could be used to attack the aristocracy and Catholic Church. In this pack of cards, "Equality" and "Liberty" replaced kings and queens.   (Archives Charmet/ The Bridgeman Art Library)

we want bread." The crowd then entered the royal apartments, killed some of the king's guards, and searched for Queen Marie Antoinette (ann-twah-NET), whom they loathed as a symbol of extravagance. Eventually, the crowd demanded that the royal family return to Paris. Preceded by the heads of two aristocrats carried on pikes and hauling away the palace's supply of flour, the triumphant crowd escorted the royal family to Paris.

The National Assembly achieved a radically restructured French society in the next two years. It passed a new constitution that dramatically limited monarchical power and abolished the nobility as a hereditary class. Economic reforms swept away monopolies and trade barriers within France. The Legislative Assembly created by the new constitution seized church lands to use as collateral for a new paper currency, and priests, who were to be elected, were put on the state payroll. When the government tried to force priests to take a loyalty oath, however, many Catholics joined a growing counterrevolutionary movement.

At first, many European monarchs had welcomed the weakening of the French king, but by 1791 Austria and Prussia threatened to intervene in support of the monarchy. The Legislative Assembly responded by declaring war. Although the war went badly at first for French forces, people across France responded patriotically to foreign invasions, forming huge new volunteer armies and mobilizing national resources to meet the challenge. By the end of 1792, French armies had gained the upper hand everywhere.

In this period of national crisis and foreign threat, the French Revolution entered its most radical phase. A failed effort by the king and queen to escape from Paris and find foreign allies cost the king any remaining popular support. As foreign armies crossed into France, his behavior was increasingly viewed as treasonous. In August 1792, the Legislative Assembly suspended the king, ordered his imprisonment, and called for the formation of a new National Convention to be elected by the vote of all men. Swept along by popular passion, the newly elected National Convention convicted Louis XVI of treason, sentencing him to death and proclaiming France a republic.

The guillotine ended the king's life in January 1793. Invented in the spirit of the era as a more humane way to execute the condemned, this machine was to become the bloody symbol of the Revolution (see Environment and Technology: The Guillotine). During the period of repression called the Reign of Terror (1793–1794), approximately 40,000 people were executed or died in prison. This radical phase ended in July 1794 when the Terror's leaders were executed by guillotine.

CL   Primary Source: The Declaration of the Rights of Man and of the Citizen   *Learn about the assertions of the French National Assembly and see how its views compare to those expressed in the American Declaration of Independence.*

Reaction and Dictatorship

Purged of the radicals, the National Convention—the new legislative assembly of the French republic—began to undo the radical reforms. It removed many of the emergency economic controls that had been holding down prices and protecting the working class. When the Paris working class rose in protest in 1795, the Convention approved the use of overwhelming military force. The Convention also permitted the Catholic Church to regain much of its former influence, but it would not return the church's confiscated wealth. Finally, it ratified a more conservative constitution, which protected property, established a voting process that reduced the power of the

The Guillotine

No machine more powerfully symbolizes the revolutionary era than the guillotine. The machine immortalizes Joseph Ignace Guillotin (1738–1814), a physician and member of the French Constituent Assembly. In 1789 Guillotin recommended that executions be made more modern and more humane by the use of a beheading device. He sought to replace hangings, used for commoners, and beheadings by axe, used for the nobility. Both forms of execution were often administered with little skill, leading to gruesome and painful deaths. Guillotin believed that a properly designed machine would produce predictable, nearly painless deaths. The universal application of this penalty would also remove the social distinction between commoners and nobles, now embarrassing in a more egalitarian age. As Guillotin said, the "privilege of decapitation will no longer be confined to nobles."

After 1791 execution by beheading became the common sentence for all capital crimes. The actual machine was invented by another physician, Antoine Louis, secretary of the College of Surgeons. Once directed to produce a suitable device, Louis, in many ways a typical technician of his time, systematically examined devices used elsewhere and experimented until satisfied with his results. At first called Louisette after its inventor, the guillotine was first used on a highwayman in 1792. Praised by contemporaries because it seemed to remove human agency, and therefore revenge, from the execution of the death penalty, the guillotine became the physical symbol of the Terror.

THE GUILLOTINE The guillotine, introduced as a more humane and democratic alternative to traditional executions, came to symbolize the arbitrary violence of the French Revolution. In this contemporary cartoon Robespierre, the architect of the Terror, is shown as an executioner surrounded by these terrifying machines. (The Art Archive)

Napoleon Bonaparte (Napoleon I) (1769–1832)
Overthrew French Directory in 1799 and became emperor of the French in 1804. Failed to defeat Great Britain and abdicated in 1814. Returned to power briefly in 1815 but was defeated and died in exile.

masses, and created a new executive authority, the Directory. Once installed in power, however, the Directory proved unable to end the foreign wars or solve domestic economic problems.

After losing the election of 1797, the Directory suspended the results. The republican phase of the Revolution was clearly dead. Legitimacy was now based on coercive power rather than on elections. Two years later, **Napoleon Bonaparte** (1769–1821), a brilliant young general in the French army, seized power. Just as the American and French Revolutions had been the start of the modern democratic tradition, the military intervention that brought Napoleon to power in 1799 marked the advent of another modern form of government: popular authoritarianism.

In contrast to the National Convention, Napoleon proved capable of realizing France's dream of dominating Europe and providing effective protection for persons and property at home. Negotiations with the Catholic Church led to the Concordat of 1801, which gave French Catholics the right to practice their religion freely. Napoleon's Civil Code of 1804 asserted two basic principles inherited from the moderate first stage of the French Revolution: equality in law and protection of property. Even some members of the nobility became supporters after Napoleon declared himself emperor and France an empire in 1804.

While providing personal security, the Napoleonic system denied or restricted many individual rights. Women were denied basic political rights. Free speech and free expression were limited. Criticism of the government, viewed as subversive, was proscribed, and most opposition newspapers disappeared.

Ultimately, the Napoleonic system depended on the success of French arms and French diplomacy (see Map 19.1). From Napoleon's assumption of power until his fall, no single European state could defeat the French military. Austria and Prussia were forced to become allies of France. Only Britain, protected by its powerful navy, remained able to thwart Napoleon's plans to dominate Europe. In June 1812, Napoleon made the fateful decision to invade Russia with the largest army ever assembled in Europe, approximately 600,000 men. Five weeks after occupying Moscow, he was forced to retreat. The brutal Russian winter and attacks by Russian forces destroyed his army. A broken and battered fragment of 30,000 men returned home to France.

After the debacle in Russia, Austria and Prussia deserted Napoleon and entered an alliance with Britain and Russia. Unable to defend Paris, Napoleon was forced to abdicate the French throne in April 1814. The allies exiled Napoleon to the island of Elba off the coast of Italy and restored the French monarchy.

Retrenchment, Reform, and Revolution

The French Revolution and Napoleon's imperial ambitions had threatened the survival of the European old order. Ancient monarchies had been overturned and long-established political institutions tossed aside. The very existence of the nobility and church had been put at risk. Under the leadership of the Austrian foreign minister, Prince Klemens von Metternich (MET-uhr-nik) (1773–1859), Britain, Russia, Austria, and Prussia, along with representatives of other nations, worked together in Vienna to create a comprehensive peace settlement that they hoped would safeguard the conservative order. Because the participants in the **Congress of Vienna** believed that a strong and stable France was the best guarantee of future peace, the French monarchy was reestablished. Metternich sought to offset French strength with a balance of power.

Congress of Vienna (1814–1815) Meeting of representatives of European monarchs called to reestablish the old order after the defeat of Napoleon I.

Despite the power of the conservative monarchs, popular support for national self-determination and democratic reform grew throughout Europe. In 1821, Greek patriots launched a movement for independence from Ottoman control. In 1830, Russia, France, and Great Britain forced the Ottoman Empire to recognize Greek independence. That same year, the people of Paris rose up and forced King Charles X to abdicate. His successor, Louis Philippe (loo-EE fee-LEEP) (r. 1830–1848), reestablished the constitution and extended voting privileges.

Despite limited political reform, conservatives continued to hold the upper hand in Europe. Finally, in 1848, the desire for democratic reform and national

Map 19.1 Napoleon's Europe, 1810

By 1810 Great Britain was the only remaining European power at war with Napoleon. Because of the loss of the French fleet at the Battle of Trafalgar in 1805, Napoleon was unable to threaten Britain with invasion, and Britain was able to actively assist the resistance movements in Spain and Portugal, thereby helping weaken French power.

self-determination and the frustrations of urban workers led to upheavals across Europe. The **Revolutions of 1848** began in Paris, where members of the middle class and workers united to overthrow the regime of Louis Philippe and create the Second French Republic. Adult men were given voting rights, slavery was abolished in French colonies, the death penalty was ended, and a ten-hour workday was legislated for Paris. But Parisian workers' demand for programs to reduce unemployment and lower prices provoked conflicts with the middle class, which wanted to protect property rights. Desiring the reestablishment of order, the French elected Louis Napoleon, nephew of the former emperor, president in December 1848. Three years later, he overturned the constitution as a result of popular plebiscite and, after ruling briefly as dictator, became Emperor Napoleon III. He remained in power until 1871.

Despite their heroism on the barricades of Vienna, Rome, and Berlin, the revolutionaries of 1848 also failed to gain either their nationalist or their republican objectives. Metternich, the symbol of reaction, fled Vienna in disguise, but little lasting change occurred. Monarchs retained the support not only of aristocrats but also of professional militaries, largely recruited from among peasants who had little sympathy for urban workers.

REVOLUTION IN HAITI AND LATIN AMERICA

How did revolution in one country help incite revolution elsewhere?

In the Americas, the revolutionary ideology of the American and French Revolutions was spreading and taking hold. On the island of Hispaniola, a revolution ended slavery and French rule in Saint Domingue. The same economic and political forces that had undermined British rule in the colonies that became the United States were present in Spanish America and Brazil.

The Haitian Revolution The French colony of Saint Domingue produced two-thirds of France's tropical imports and generated nearly one-third of all French foreign trade. This impressive wealth depended on a brutal slave regime. Saint Domingue's harsh punishments and high mortality were notorious throughout the Caribbean.

In 1789, when news of the calling of France's Estates General arrived on the island, wealthy white planters sent a delegation to Paris charged with seeking more home rule and greater economic freedom. The *gens de couleur* (zhahn deh koo-LUHR) also sent representatives. Mostly small planters or urban merchants, these free mixed-race delegates focused on ending race discrimination and political inequality. They did not seek freedom for slaves, because the most prosperous gens de couleur were slave owners themselves.

The political turmoil in France weakened colonial authority, permitting rich planters, poor whites, gens de couleur, and slaves to pursue their narrow interests, in an increasingly bitter and confrontational struggle. By 1791, whites and the gens de

SECTION REVIEW

- The French Revolution grew from mounting social and financial crises after 1765.

- The crisis within the Estates General sparked the Revolution when the Third Estate declared itself the National Assembly.

- Popular uprisings thwarted military intervention and enabled the National Assembly to press its reforms on the monarchy.

- Economic crisis and foreign intervention radicalized the Revolution, resulting in the execution of Louis XVI and the Reign of Terror.

- Reaction against the Terror resulted in the conservative Directory and the dictatorship of Napoleon.

- Despite conservative retrenchment after Napoleon's fall, liberal reform and revolution continued through the failed 1848 revolutions.

Revolutions of 1848 Democratic and nationalist revolutions that swept across Europe. The monarchy in France was overthrown. In Germany, Austria, Italy, and Hungary the revolutions failed.

gens de couleur Free men and women of color in Haiti. They sought greater political rights and later supported the Haitian Revolution.

Toussaint L'Ouverture
(1743–1803) Leader of the
Haitian Revolution. He freed
the slaves and gained effective
independence for Haiti despite
military interventions by the
British and French.

couleur were engaged in open warfare. This breach between the two groups of slave owners gave the slaves an opening. Their rebellion began on the plantations of the north and spread throughout the colony. Plantations were destroyed, masters and overseers killed, and crops burned.

The rebellious slaves eventually gained the upper hand under the military leadership of **Toussaint L'Ouverture**, a former domestic slave. Politically strengthened in 1794 when the radical National Convention in Paris abolished slavery in all French possessions, Toussaint overcame his rivals in Saint Domingue, defeated a British expeditionary force in 1798, and then led an invasion of neighboring Santo Domingo, freeing the slaves there. Toussaint continued to assert his loyalty to France but gave the French government no effective role in local affairs.

In 1802, Napoleon sent a large military force to Saint Domingue to reestablish both French authority and slavery. At first, the French forces were successful. Toussaint was captured and sent to France, where he died in prison. Eventually, however, French losses to yellow fever and the resistance of the revolutionaries turned the tide. Whereas few slave women had taken up arms during the early stages of the Haitian Revolution, now they joined the armed resistance. In 1804, the free republic

Burning of Cap Français, Saint Domingue, in 1793
In 1791, the slaves of Saint Domingue, France's richest colony, began a rebellion that, after years of struggle, ended slavery and created the Western Hemisphere's second independent nation, Haiti.   (Archives Charmet/The Bridgeman Art Library)

of Haiti joined the United States as the second independent nation in the Western Hemisphere. But independence and emancipation were achieved at a terrible price. Tens of thousands had died, and the economy was destroyed.

Latin American Revolutions

The great works of the Enlightenment as well as revolutionary documents like the Declaration of Independence and the Declaration of the Rights of Man circulated widely in Latin America. But it was Napoleon's decision to invade Portugal (1807) and Spain (1808), not revolutionary ideas, that ignited Latin America's struggle for independence.

In 1808, the royal family of Portugal fled to Brazil and maintained court there for over a decade. In Spain, in contrast, Napoleon forced King Ferdinand VII to abdicate and placed his own brother, Joseph Bonaparte, on the throne. When Spanish patriots fighting against the French created a new political body, the Junta (HUN-tah) Central, and claimed the right to exercise the king's powers over Spain's colonies, a vocal minority of powerful colonists objected. In late 1808 and 1809, popular movements overthrew Spanish colonial officials in Venezuela, Mexico, and Bolivia and created local juntas. In each case, Spanish officials' harsh repression gave rise to a greater sense of a separate American nationality. By 1810, Spanish colonial authorities were facing a new round of revolutions more clearly focused on the achievement of independence.

In Caracas (the capital city of modern Venezuela), a revolutionary junta led by creoles (colonial-born whites) declared independence in 1811. Its leaders were large landowners who espoused popular sovereignty and representative democracy, defended slavery, and opposed full citizenship for the black and mixed-race majority. The junta's narrow agenda spurred loyalists in the colonial administration and church hierarchy to rally thousands of free blacks and slaves to defend the Spanish Empire. **Simón Bolívar** (see-MOAN bow-LEE-varh) (1783–1830) became the preeminent leader of the independence movement in Spanish South America.

Between 1813 and 1817, military advantage shifted back and forth between the patriots and loyalists, but by 1820, momentum swung irreversibly to the patriots. After liberating present-day Venezuela, Colombia, Ecuador, Peru, and Bolivia, Bolívar's army defeated the last Spanish armies in 1824. But Bolívar's attempt to draw the former Spanish colonies into a formal confederation failed (see Map 19.2).

Buenos Aires (the capital city of modern Argentina) was the second important center of revolutionary activity in Spanish South America. In the south, a coalition of militia commanders, merchants, and ranchers declared independence as the United Provinces of the Río de la Plata in 1816. Patriot leaders in Buenos Aires at first sought to retain control over the old Viceroyalty of Río de la Plata, but a separatist movement defeated these ambitions. A mixed force of Chileans and Argentines, led by José de San Martín (hoe-SAY deh san mar-TEEN) (1778–1850), liberated Chile in 1820. Simón Bolívar overcame final Spanish resistance in Peru in 1824.

The arrival of the Portuguese royal family in Brazil in 1808 had helped to maintain the loyalty of the colonial elite and to stimulate the local economy. But when King John VI returned to Portugal in 1821, Brazilians began to reevaluate Brazil's relationship with Portugal and to talk openly of independence.

Unwilling to return to Portugal and committed to maintaining his family's hold on Brazil, King John's son Pedro aligned himself with the rising tide of indepen-

Simón Bolívar (1783–1830)
The most important military leader in the struggle for independence in South America. Born in Venezuela, he led military forces there and in Colombia, Ecuador, Peru, and Bolivia.

 Primary Source: The Jamaica Letter *Read from this famous political manifesto and see what grand hopes Simón Bolívar was able to sustain for South America even at the lowest of times.*

Map 19.2   Latin America by 1830

By 1830 patriot forces had overturned the Spanish and Portuguese Empires of the Western Hemisphere. Regional conflicts, local wars, and foreign interventions challenged the survival of many of these new nations following independence.

dence sentiment. In 1822, he declared Brazilian independence. Unlike its neighbors, which became constitutional republics, Brazil gained independence as a constitutional monarchy with Pedro I, heir to the throne of Portugal, as emperor. The monarchy lasted until 1889, when it was overthrown by republicans.

Mexico

In 1810, Mexico was Spain's richest and most populous colony. But the sharp distinctions among its creole, native, and Spanish populations made it ripe for revolution. The first stage of the revolution against Spain occurred in central Mexico, where wealthy ranchers and farmers had aggressively forced many Amerindian communities from their traditional agricultural lands. By the time news of Napoleon's invasion of Spain reached the region, crop failures and epidemics had further afflicted the poor.

On September 16, 1810, **Miguel Hidalgo y Costilla** (mee-GEHL ee-DAHL-go ee cos-TEA-ah), parish priest of the small town of Dolores, rang the church bells, attracting thousands. In a fiery speech, he urged the crowd to rise up against the oppression of Spanish officials. Tens of thousands of the rural and urban poor joined his movement. They lacked military discipline and adequate weapons but knew who

Miguel Costilla

Miguel Hidalgo y Costilla (1753–1811) Mexican priest who led the first stage of the Mexican independence war in 1810. He was captured and executed in 1811.

The Revolutionary Tradition in Mexico

This 1948 mural by José Clemente Orozco commemorates the Mexican struggle to restore its republican tradition after France intervened—using collection of overdue debts as a pretext—and enthroned the Austrian archduke Maximilian as emperor of Mexico. Maximilian reigned from 1864 to 1867, when he was overthrown and executed by a popular movement led by Benito Juarez, shown in the center of the painting. Orozco depicts Maximilian's bandage-swathed body being borne by the Catholic clergy, military commanders, and foreign interlopers who constituted the conservative opposition to Juarez's republicanism.

(Courtesy, Muséo Nacional de Antropologia e Historia, Mexico City/photo: CENIDIAP-INBA)

SECTION REVIEW

- Revolutionary events in France prompted Saint Domingue's whites and *gens de couleur* to demand reforms.

- As the revolution radicalized, these groups fought in open warfare, enabling slaves under Toussaint L'Ouverture to defeat both and establish the republic of Haiti.

- Napoleon invaded Portugal and Spain, Portugal's royal family fled to Brazil, and popular uprisings broke out in Venezuela, Mexico, and Bolivia.

- Throughout Latin America, loyalists battled separatists, while Spanish-born colonists, creoles, Amerindians, and mixed-race people struggled for control.

- Bolívar and San Martín won the independence of the Spanish South American nations, while Brazil broke from Portugal as a constitutional monarchy.

- Mexico's revolution unfolded as both an independence and class struggle with conservative elements retaining considerable power.

their oppressors were. At first sympathetic to Hidalgo's objectives, wealthy Mexicans eventually turned against Hidalgo, who was captured, tried, and executed in 1811.

Although insurgents continued to wage war against Spanish forces, colonial rule seemed secure in 1820. However, news of the military revolt in Spain unsettled the conservative groups and church officials who had defended Spanish rule against Hidalgo and José Morelos, who continued the revolution after Hidalgo's execution. In 1821, Colonel Agustín de Iturbide (ah-goos-TEEN deh ee-tur-BEE-deh) and other loyalist commanders forged an alliance with remaining insurgents and declared Mexico's independence. The conservative origins of Mexico's transition to independence were highlighted by the decision to create a monarchial form of government and crown Iturbide as emperor. In early 1823, however, the army overthrew Iturbide and Mexico became a republic.

ECONOMIC AND SOCIAL LIBERATION MOVEMENTS

What economic and social liberation movements rose during the nineteenth century?

During the nineteenth century, the newly independent nations of the Western Hemisphere struggled to realize the Enlightenment ideals of freedom and individual liberty. The persistence of slavery and women's inequality raised troubling questions about these ideals. By century's end, reform movements in many of the hemisphere's nations had made significant progress, but much remained to be done.

The Abolition of Slavery

In both the United States and Latin America, strong antislavery sentiments were expressed during the struggles for independence. In nearly all the new nations of the Western Hemisphere, revolutionary leaders asserted universal ideals of freedom and citizenship that contrasted sharply with the reality of slavery. Men and women who wanted to outlaw slavery were called **abolitionists**. Despite their efforts, slavery survived in much of the hemisphere until the 1850s. In regions where the export of plantation products was most important—such as the United States, Brazil, and Cuba—the abolition of slavery was achieved with great difficulty.

In the United States, some northern states had abolished slavery after the Revolution, and Congress banned the importation of new slaves in 1808. But this progress was stalled by the profitable expansion of cotton agriculture after the War of 1812. In Spanish America, tens of thousands of slaves gained freedom by joining revolutionary armies during the wars for independence. After independence, most Spanish American republics prohibited the slave trade. Counteracting that trend was the growing international demand for sugar and coffee, products traditionally produced on plantations by slaves. As prices rose for plantation products in the first

abolitionists Men and women who agitated for a complete end to slavery. Abolitionist pressure ended the British transatlantic slave trade in 1808 and slavery in British colonies in 1834. In the United States the activities of abolitionists were one factor leading to the Civil War (1861–1865).

half of the nineteenth century, Brazil and Cuba (a Spanish colony until 1899) increased their imports of slaves.

During the long struggle to end slavery in the United States, American abolitionists argued that slavery offended both morality and the universal rights asserted in the Declaration of Independence. Two groups denied full rights of citizenship under the Constitution, women and free African Americans, played important roles in the abolition of slavery. Women served on the executive committee of the American Anti-Slavery Society and produced some of the most effective propaganda against slavery. Many women abolitionists advocated female suffrage as well. Frederick Douglass, a former slave, became one of the most effective abolitionist speakers and writers. More radical black leaders saw civil war or slave insurrection as necessary for ending slavery.

During the Civil War, pressure for emancipation rose as tens of thousands of black freemen and escaped slaves joined the Union army. Hundreds of thousands of other slaves fled their masters' plantations and farms for the protection of advancing northern armies. In 1863, in the midst of the Civil War, President Lincoln began the abolition of slavery by issuing the Emancipation Proclamation, which ended slavery in rebel states not occupied by the Union army. Final abolition was accomplished in 1865, by the Thirteenth Amendment to the Constitution.

After Britain ended its participation in the slave trade in 1807, it negotiated treaties with Spain, Brazil, and other importers of slaves to eliminate the slave trade to the Americas. But enforcement proved difficult. For example, Brazil, despite its treaty of 1830, illegally imported over a half-million more African slaves before the British navy finally forced compliance in the 1850s. The Brazilian parliament passed legislation abolishing slavery in 1888.

Slavery lasted longest in Cuba. Despite strong British pressure, the Spanish colony continued to import large numbers of African slaves until the 1860s. More important, however, was the growth of support for abolition in these colonies. Both Cuba and Puerto Rico had larger white and free colored populations than did the Caribbean colonies of Britain and France. As a result, there was less fear in Cuba and Puerto Rico that abolition would lead to the political ascendancy of former slaves (as had occurred in Haiti). In Puerto Rico, where slaves numbered approximately thirty thousand, local reformers sought and gained the abolition of slavery in 1873. Eventually, during a decade-long war to defeat forces seeking the independence of Cuba, the Spanish government moved toward gradual abolition. Finally, in 1886, slavery was abolished.

Equal Rights for Women and Blacks

The abolition of slavery in the Western Hemisphere did not end racial discrimination or provide full political rights for every citizen. Not only blacks but also women suffered political and economic discrimination during the nineteenth century.

In 1848, a group of women angered by their exclusion from an international antislavery meeting issued a call for a meeting to discuss women's rights. The **Women's Rights Convention** at Seneca Falls, New York, issued a statement that said in part, "We hold these truths to be self-evident: that all men and women are equal." While moderates focused on the issues of greater economic independence and full legal rights,

Women's Rights Convention An 1848 gathering of women angered by their exclusion from an international antislavery meeting. They met at Seneca Falls, New York, to discuss women's rights.

Elizabeth Cady Stanton and Children

This pioneer leader of the women's suffrage movement was thirty-two with three children under the age of six when the first women's rights convention met in 1848 in Seneca Falls, where she lived. An early interest in her father's law practice stimulated her interest in social reforms, including abolitionism and temperance. But women's rights of all sorts, not just suffrage, became her primary cause, and she wrote many of the stirring speeches given by Susan B. Anthony, an unmarried colleague who had enjoyed greater freedom to travel and organize. (Coline Jenkins/Elizabeth Cady Stanton Trust)

increasing numbers of women demanded the right to vote. Others lobbied to provide better conditions for women working outside the home, especially in textile factories.

Progress toward equality between men and women was equally slow in Canada and Latin America. Canada's first women doctors received their training in the United States because no woman was able to receive a medical degree in Canada until 1895. Argentina and Uruguay were among the first Latin American nations to provide public education for women. Both nations introduced coeducation in the 1870s. Chilean women gained access to some careers in medicine and law in the 1870s. In Brazil, where many women were active in the abolitionist movement, four women graduated in medicine by 1882. Throughout the hemisphere, more rapid progress was achieved in lower-status careers that threatened male economic power less directly, and by the end of the century, women dominated elementary school teaching throughout the Western Hemisphere.

From Canada to Argentina and Chile, the majority of working-class women had no direct involvement in these reform movements, but in their daily lives, they succeeded in transforming gender relations. By the end of the nineteenth century, large numbers of poor women worked outside the home on farms, in markets, and, increasingly, in factories.

Throughout the hemisphere, there was little progress toward eliminating racial discrimination. Blacks were denied the vote throughout the southern United States and subjected to the indignity of segregation. Racial discrimination against men and women of African descent was also common in Latin America, though seldom spelled out in legal codes. Latin Americans tended to view racial identity across a continuum of physical characteristics rather than in the narrow terms of black and white that defined race relations in the United States.

SECTION REVIEW

- Despite professions of Enlightenment ideals, economic trends during the early nineteenth century strengthened slavery in the southern United States and parts of Latin America.

- American abolitionists produced effective antislavery propaganda, but final abolition did not happen until after the Civil War in 1865.

- Britain worked to end the Atlantic slave trade, but slavery persisted in Brazil, Cuba, and Puerto Rico until the late nineteenth century.

- Racial discrimination persisted after abolition, and women continued to live without equal rights.

- The Women's Rights Convention sparked the women's rights movement in the United States, but progress was slow throughout the Western Hemisphere.

▍COMPARATIVE PERSPECTIVES

▍The last decades of the eighteenth century began a long period of revolutionary upheaval in the Atlantic world. Costly wars in Europe and along Europe's colonial frontiers in the Americas and Asia helped to provoke change, forcing European monarchs to impose new and unpopular taxes. The American Revolution initiated these transformations. Having defeated Britain, the citizens of this new American republic created the most democratic government of the time. While full rights were limited and slavery persisted, many Europeans saw this experiment as demonstrating the efficacy of the Enlightenment's most revolutionary political ideas. In the end, however, the compromises over slavery that had made the Constitution possible in 1787 failed, and the new nation nearly disintegrated after 1860.

The French Revolution led temporarily to a more radical formulation of representative democracy, but it also led to the Terror, which cost thousands of lives, and the militarization of western Europe and a destructive cycle of wars. Yet, despite these terrible costs, the French Revolution propelled the idea of democracy and the ideal of equality far beyond the boundaries established earlier by the American Revolution. The Haitian Revolution, set in motion by events in France, not only created the second independent nation of the Western Hemisphere but also delivered a powerful blow to the institution of slavery. In Europe the excesses of the French Revolution and the wars that followed in its wake promoted the political ascent of Napoleon Bonaparte and democracy's modern nemesis, popular authoritarianism.

Each revolution had its own character. The revolutions in France and Haiti proved to be more violent and destructive than the American Revolution. First, there was no slave rebellion in North America. Although slavery was crucial to the most profitable exports, such as tobacco, cotton, and rice, slaves in British North America remained a minority except along the South Carolina coast. In addition, revolutionaries in France and Haiti faced more strongly entrenched and more powerful oppositions as well as greater social inequalities than did the revolutionaries in North America. The resistance of entrenched and privileged elites led inexorably to greater violence. Both French and Haitian revolutionaries also faced powerful foreign interventions that intensified the bloodshed and destructiveness of these revolutions.

The conservative retrenchment that followed the defeat of Napoleon succeeded in the short term. Monarchy, multinational empires, and the established church retained their hold on the loyalty of millions of Europeans and could count on the support of many of Europe's wealthiest and most powerful individuals. But liberalism and nationalism continued to stir revolutionary sentiment. The contest between adherents of the old order and partisans of change was to continue well into the nineteenth century. In the end, the nation-state, the Enlightenment legacy of rational inquiry, broadened political participation, and secular intellectual culture prevailed. This outcome was determined in large measure by the old order's inability to satisfy the new social classes that appeared with the emerging industrial economy. The material transformation produced by industrial capitalism could not be contained in the narrow confines of a hereditary social system, nor could the rapid expansion of scientific learning be contained within the doctrines of traditional religion.

The revolutions of the late eighteenth century began the transformation of Western society, but they did not complete it. Only a minority gained full political rights. Women did not achieve full political rights until the twentieth century. Democratic institutions, as in revolutionary France, often failed. Moreover, slavery endured in the Americas past the mid-1800s, despite the revolutionary era's enthusiasm for individual liberty.

Chapter Review

 DOWNLOAD THE MP3 AUDIO FILE OF THE CHAPTER REVIEW TO LISTEN TO ON THE GO.

KEY TERMS

Enlightenment (p. 525)
George Washington (p. 529)
Constitutional Convention (p. 530)
Estates General (p. 531)
National Assembly (p. 531)
Declaration of the Rights of Man (p. 532)
Napoleon Bonaparte (p. 534)
Congress of Vienna (p. 535)
Revolutions of 1848 (p. 537)
gens de couleur (p. 537)
Toussaint L'Ouverture (p. 538)
Simón Bolívar (p. 539)
Miguel Hidalgo y Costilla (p. 541)
abolitionists (p. 542)
Women's Rights Convention (p. 543)

How did the costs of imperial wars and the Enlightenment challenge the established authority of monarchs and religion in Europe and the American colonies? (page 525)

This era of revolution was, in large measure, the product of a long period of costly warfare among the imperial nations of Europe. Britain and France in particular faced fiscal crises as a result of colonial wars. Using taxes and institutions inherited from the past, they found it increasingly difficult to fund distant wars in the Americas or in Asia. In the British case, the costs of the French and Indian War led the government to attempt to impose unpopular taxes on its colonies. France faced an even more dire fiscal emergency as a result of this war and later aid to the American revolutionaries. The refusal of powerful French interests to accept new taxes would force the king to call the Estates General and lead ultimately to the French Revolution. Meanwhile, the spread of literacy and the greater availability of books helped create an Enlightenment culture more open to reform and to the revolutionary change of existing institutions in Europe and in the Americas. But there were many distinct, even contradictory, currents in the Enlightenment. If the ideas of Locke and Rousseau guided critics of monarchy toward a new political culture of elections and representative institutions, these ideas were difficult to reconcile. Nevertheless, the intellectual ferment of the era gave educated men and women tools to criticize existing political institutions and the confidence to design new ones. The language of liberty and equality, even if poorly realized in the actions of revolutionary governments, proved a powerful solvent when applied to hierarchy and privilege.

What were the direct causes of the American Revolution? (page 528)

The American Revolution grew from British colonial policy after the French and Indian War. To avoid new military costs, Britain tried unsuccessfully through the Quebec Act to restrict western settlement and thus reduce conflict with the Amerindians. To pay its war debt, Britain imposed new taxes, duties, and commercial regulations on the colonies, including the Stamp Act. These acts led to violent unrest that culminated with the "Boston Massacre." Parliament repealed some of these acts but then gave the British East India Company a tea monopoly, thus provoking more violence. Colonial patriots met in the Continental Congress, assumed government powers, raised an army, and issued the Declaration of Independence.

What were the origins and accomplishments of the French Revolution? (page 530)

The French Revolution erupted from the crises provoked by France's archaic social and tax system, financial collapse, urban unrest, and division between the monarchy and aristocracy. The immediate cause was the crisis within the Estates General, during which the Third Estate broke away and declared itself the National Assembly. Uprisings in Paris and the countryside strengthened the Assembly's position, enabling it to press reforms embodied in the Declaration of the Rights of Man. Further reforms restructured France's society and economy. However, foreign intervention pushed the Legislative Assembly to radical extremes that culminated with the execution of Louis XVI and the Reign of Terror. Reaction against the Terror resulted in the conservative Directory and the even more repressive dictatorship of Napoleon Bonaparte. Napoleon's military adventures ultimately led to his fall, and the Congress of Vienna sought to establish a conservative balance of power. Despite this retrenchment, revolutionary struggles continued, especially in France, where the 1830 uprising replaced Charles X with Louis-Philippe. In 1848 nationalist and republican revolutions flared throughout Europe. These won few lasting gains, however, and in France they resulted in the imperial rule of Napoleon III.

How did revolution in one country help incite revolution elsewhere? (page 537)

Each new revolutionary development served as example and provocation for dissatisfied women and men elsewhere. French officers who took part in the American Revolution helped ignite the French Revolution. The constitutions of new American states and the new national constitution were published across Europe and read by thousands. Free black militiamen from Saint Domingue served along French units in support of the American Revolution. With the first stage of the French Revolution black freemen from Haiti traveled to France to seek their rights and returned to spread revolutionary passions. With the success of the Haitian Revolution, slaves throughout the Western Hemisphere took heart, and some rose in rebellion.

What economic and social liberation movements rose during the nineteenth century? (page 542)

In the newly independent nations of the Americas, the persistence of slavery and gender inequality clashed with the Enlightenment ideals that had fostered their revolutions. Rising demand for export crops after 1800 strengthened slavery in the southern United States and parts of Latin America. U.S. abolitionists, many of whom were women and free blacks, produced powerful antislavery propaganda. Although Lincoln issued the Emancipation Proclamation during the Civil War, final abolition did not come until the Thirteenth Amendment

WEB RESOURCES

Pronunciation Guide

Primary Sources

Rousseau Espouses Popular Sovereignty and the General Will

The United States Declaration of Independence

The Declaration of the Rights of Man and of the Citizen

The Jamaica Letter

Answer to the History in Focus Question

See photo on page 528, "The Tarring and Feathering of a British Official, 1774."

Plus

Chapter Objectives

ACE multiple-choice quiz

Flashcards

Handwritten notes:
Toussaint L'ouverture
Simon Bolivar
Miguel Hidalgo y Costilla
abolitionists
Women's rights Gral

passed in 1865. Britain ceased to participate in the slave trade in 1807 and worked to end the Atlantic trade through treaties with slave importers. Britain's navy forced compliance on Latin American importers, but slavery continued in Brazil, Cuba, and Puerto Rico until late in the nineteenth century. The movement for women's rights in the United States began with the Seneca Falls Women's Rights Convention, but progress on gender equality was slow throughout the Western Hemisphere. Equally slow was the elimination of racial discrimination. Legalized in the southern United States, it also persisted in Latin America without formal codification.

SUGGESTED READING

Bonwick, Colin. *The American Revolution.* 1991. A good general introduction.

Craveri, Benedetta. *The Age of Conversation.* 2005. Illuminates the culture of the French aristocracy prior to the French Revolution.

Fick, Carolyn E. *The Making of Haiti: The Saint Domingue Revolution from Below.* 1990. The best recent synthesis of the Haitian Revolution.

Furet, François. *Interpreting the French Revolution.* 1981. A reinterpretation that challenges works emphasizing class and ideology.

Goodman, Dena. *The Republic of Letters: A Cultural History of the Enlightenment.* 1994. Studies male and female intellectuals in the era of revolutions.

Hobsbawm, Eric. *The Age of Revolution.* 1962. Provides a clear analysis of the class issues that appeared during this era.

Holtman, Robert B. *The Napoleonic Revolution.* 1967. Provides a reliable summary of the period.

Hunt, Lynn. *The Family Romance of the French Revolution.* 1992. Examines the gender content of revolutionary politics.

James, C. L. R. *The Black Jacobins.* 2d ed. 1963. Classic study of the Haitian Revolution.

Lefebvre, Georges. *The Coming of the French Revolution.* Trans. R. R. Palmer. 1947. A classic class-based analysis.

Lindemann, Albert. *History of European Socialism.* 1983. Surveys the development of European social reform movements.

Norton, Mary Beth. *Liberty's Daughters: The Revolutionary Experience of American Women, 1750–1800.* 1980. Studies the role of women in the revolutionary era.

Rudé, George. *The Crowd in History: Popular Disturbances in France and England.* 1981. The best introduction to the role of mass protest in the revolutionary period.

Taylor, Barbara. *Eve and the New Jerusalem: Socialism and Feminism in the Nineteenth Century.* 1983. Analyzes connections between workers' and women's rights issues in England.

Wood, Gordon S. *The Radicalism of the American Revolution.* 1992. Brilliantly examines the ideological and cultural meanings of the Revolution.

CHAPTER 20

The Early Industrial Revolution

1760–1851

CHAPTER PREVIEW

Causes of the Industrial Revolution   *What caused the Industrial Revolution?*

The Technological Revolution   *What were the key innovations that increased productivity and drove industrialization?*

The Impact of the Industrial Revolution   *What was the impact of these changes on the society and environment of the industrializing countries?*

New Economic and Political Ideas   *How did the Industrial Revolution influence the rise of new economic and political ideas?*

The Limits of Industrialization Outside the West   *How did the Industrial Revolution affect the relations between the industrialized and the nonindustrialized parts of the world?*

ENVIRONMENT AND TECHNOLOGY: Gas Lighting

Manchester was a small town in northern England in the early eighteenth century. A hundred years later, it had become the fastest-growing city in history. To contemporary visitors, it was both a marvel and a horror. In the inner city, cotton mills and other factories were interspersed with workers' housing, built as cheaply as possible. Here is how the economist Nassau Senior described these workers' quarters:

> But when I went through their habitations . . . my only wonder was that tolerable health could be maintained by the inmates of such houses. These towns . . . have been erected by small speculators with an utter disregard to everything except immediate profit. . . . Not a house in this street escaped cholera. And, generally speaking, . . . the streets are unpaved, with a

This icon will direct you to the website where you can Prepare for Class, Improve Your Grade, and Ace the Test: college.cengage.com/pic/bullietbrief4e

dunghill or a pond in the middle; the houses built back to back, without venti-
lation or drainage, and whole families occupy each a corner of a cellar or of a
garret.[1]

Not everyone deplored the living conditions in the new industrial city. Friedrich Engels, one of the foremost critics of industrial capitalism, recounts a meeting with a
well-to-do citizen:

> One day I walked with one of these middle-class gentlemen into Manchester. I
> spoke to him about the disgraceful unhealthy slums and drew his attention to
> the disgusting condition of that part of the town in which the factory workers
> lived. I declared that I had never seen so badly built a town in my life. He listened
> patiently and at the corner of the street at which we parted company, he remarked:
> "And yet there is a great deal of money made here. Good morning, Sir!"[2]

Industrial Revolution The
transformation of the economy,
the environment, and living
conditions, occurring first in
England in the eighteenth century, that resulted from the
use of steam engines, the mechanization of manufacturing
in factories, and innovations
in transportation and communication.

Manchester's rise was a result of what historians call the **Industrial Revolution**, the
most profound and wrenching transformation in human life since the development
of agriculture 10,000 years earlier. The Industrial Revolution made it possible for increasing numbers of people (including those in Manchester) to lead longer, healthier, richer, and more productive lives than could have been possible before.

This revolution involved dramatic innovations in manufacturing, mining, transportation, and communications and equally rapid changes in society and commerce.
New relationships between social groups created an environment that was con-
ducive to technical innovation and economic growth. New technologies and new social and economic arrangements allowed the industrializing countries—first Britain,
then western Europe and the United States—to unleash massive increases in production and productivity, exploit the world's natural resources as never before, and
transform the environment and human life in unprecedented ways.

The distribution of power and wealth generated by the Industrial Revolution
was very uneven, for industrialization widened the gap between rich and poor. The
people who owned and controlled the innovations amassed wealth and power over
nature and over other people. While some of them lived lives of spectacular luxury,
workers, including children, worked long hours in dangerous factories and lived
crowded together in unsanitary tenements.

The effect of the Industrial Revolution around the world was also very uneven.
The first countries to industrialize grew rich and powerful. In Egypt and India, the
economic and military power of the European countries stifled the tentative beginnings of industrialization. Regions that had little or no industry were easily taken
advantage of. The disparity between the industrial and the developing countries
that exists today has its origins in the early nineteenth century

CAUSES OF THE INDUSTRIAL REVOLUTION

What caused the Industrial Revolution?

What caused the Industrial Revolution, and why did it begin in England in the
late eighteenth century? The basic preconditions of this momentous event seem to
have been population growth, an agricultural revolution, the expansion of trade,
and an openness to innovation.

Chronology

	Technology	Economy, Society, and Politics
1750		
	1759 Josiah Wedgwood opens pottery factory	
	1764 Spinning jenny	
	1769 Richard Arkwright's water frame; James Watt patents steam engine	
		1776 Adam Smith's *Wealth of Nations*
		1776–1783 American Revolution
	1779 First iron bridge	
	1785 Boulton and Watt sell steam engines; Samuel Crompton's mule	
		1789–1799 French Revolution
	1793 Eli Whitney's cotton gin	
1800		
	1800 Alessandro Volta's battery	
		1804–1815 Napoleonic Wars
	1807 Robert Fulton's *North River*	
	1820s Construction of Erie Canal	**1820s** U.S. cotton industry begins
		1833 Factory Act in Britain
		1834 Robert Owen's Grand National Consolidated Trade Union
	1837 Wheatstone and Cooke's telegraph	
	1838 First ships steam across the Atlantic	
	1840 *Nemesis* sails to China	
	1843 Samuel Morse's Baltimore-to-Washington telegraph	
		1847–1848 Irish famine
		1848 Collapse of Chartist movement; revolutions in Europe
1850		
	1851 Crystal Palace opens in London	

Preconditions for Industrialization

The population of Europe rose in the eighteenth century—slowly at first, faster after 1780, then even faster in the early nineteenth century. The population of England and Wales rose unusually fast—from 5.5 million in 1688 to 18 million by 1851. Industrialization and the population boom reinforced each other. A high birthrate meant a large percentage of children, which explains both the vitality of the British people in that period and the widespread use of child labor.

This population explosion and urbanization depended upon an **agricultural revolution** that provided food for city dwellers and forced poorer peasants off the land. Long before the eighteenth century, the acceptance of the potato and maize from the Americas had increased food supplies in Europe. In the cool and humid regions of Europe, from Ireland to Russia, potatoes yielded two or three times more food per acre than grain. Maize (American corn) was grown across Europe from southwestern France to the Balkans.

agricultural revolution (eighteenth century) The transformation of farming that resulted in the eighteenth century from the spread of new crops, improvements in cultivation techniques and livestock breeding, and the consolidation of small holdings into large farms from which tenants and sharecroppers were forcibly expelled.

During the seventeenth century, rich English landowners began draining marshes, improving the soil, and introducing crop rotation using turnips, legumes, and clover that did not deplete the soil and could be fed to cattle. Additional manure from improved breeds of livestock fertilized the soil for other crops. Some also "enclosed" land—that is, consolidated their holdings, including commons that in the past had been open to all. This "enclosure movement" also turned tenants and sharecroppers into landless farm laborers. Many moved to the cities to seek work; others became homeless migrants and vagrants; still others emigrated.

Trade expansion accompanied the growth in population and food supply. Most of it was local, but a growing share involved imports, like tea and sugar, and simple goods that even middle-class people could afford, such as cotton textiles, iron hardware, and pottery.

Trade stimulated a growing interest in technology and innovation among educated people throughout Europe and eastern North America. They read descriptions of new techniques and inventions in many publications, and some experimented on their own.

Britain's Advantages

These changes were widespread, but Britain in the eighteenth century had the fastest-growing population, food supply, and overseas trade. The British also put inventions into practice more quickly than other people, thus making Britain the world's leading exporter of tools, guns, hardware, and other craft goods. Its mining and metal industries employed engineers willing to experiment with new ideas. It also had the largest merchant marine and produced more ships, naval supplies, and navigation instruments than other countries.

Moreover, Britain had a fluid society. Political power was not as centralized as on the European continent, and the government employed fewer bureaucrats and officials. Class lines eased as members of the gentry, and even some aristocrats, married into merchant families. Intermarriage among the families of petty merchants, yeoman farmers, and town craftsmen was common.

With land transportation as costly as ever, Great Britain had good water transportation, thanks to its indented coastline, navigable rivers, and growing network of canals (see Map 20.1). Its unified internal market, with none of the duties and tolls that goods had to pay every few miles in France, encouraged specialization and trade. More people there were involved in production for export and in trade and finance than in any other major country. Finally, Britain's financial and insurance institutions sup-

SECTION REVIEW

- The Industrial Revolution began in Britain because of rapid population growth, agricultural revolution, expansion of trade, and technological innovation.

- Britain's advantages included a large merchant marine, its position as an exporter, and the ability of its people to put inventions to practical use.

- Britain also had a relatively fluid society, good water transportation, and a unified internal market.

- By 1830, conditions elsewhere in Europe had caught up with those in Britain.

Map 20.1   The Industrial Revolution in Britain, ca. 1850

The first industries arose in northern and western England. These regions had abundant coal and iron-ore deposits for the iron industry and moist climate and fast-flowing rivers for the cotton textile industry.

ported growing business enterprises, and its patent system protected inventors' profits.

By 1830, western Europe had as favorable a climate for business as Britain had had a half-century earlier. Industrialization first took hold in Belgium and northern France, as their businessmen visited Britain to observe the changes and to spy out industrial secrets. In spite of British laws forbidding the emigration of skilled workers and the export of textile machinery, many slipped through, setting up machines, training workers in the new methods, and even starting their own businesses. European governments created technical schools; eliminated internal tariff barriers, tolls, and other hindrances to trade; and encouraged the formation of joint-stock companies and banks to channel private savings into industrial investments. On the European continent, as in Britain, cotton was the first industry to industrialize.

THE TECHNOLOGICAL REVOLUTION

What were the key innovations that increased productivity and drove industrialization?

Five revolutionary innovations spurred industrialization: (1) mass production through the division of labor, (2) new machines and mechanization, (3) a great increase in the supply of iron, (4) the steam engine and the changes it made possible in industry and transportation, and (5) the electric telegraph.

Mass Production and Mechanization

The pottery industry offers a good example of **mass production**, the making of many identical items by breaking the process into simple repetitive tasks. **Josiah Wedgwood** opened a pottery business in 1759 that was able to produce porcelain cheaply, by means of the **division of labor**. He subdivided the work into highly specialized and repetitive tasks, such as unloading the clay, mixing it, pressing flat pieces, dipping the pieces in glaze, putting handles on cups, packing kilns, and carrying things from one part of his plant to another. He used molds instead of the potter's wheel wherever possible, a change that both saved labor and created identical plates and bowls that could be stacked. These innovations allowed Wedgwood to lower the cost of his products while improving their quality. Accordingly, his factory grew far larger

mass production The manufacture of many identical products by the division of labor into many small repetitive tasks. This method was introduced into the manufacture of pottery by Josiah Wedgwood and into the spinning of cotton thread by Richard Arkwright.

Josiah Wedgwood (1730–1795) English industrialist whose pottery works were the first to produce fine-quality pottery by industrial methods.

division of labor A manufacturing technique that breaks down a craft into many simple and repetitive tasks that can be performed by unskilled workers. Pioneered in the pottery works of Josiah Wedgwood and in other eighteenth-century factories, it greatly increased the productivity of labor and lowered the cost of manufactured goods.

Wedgwood's Potteries
In Staffordshire, England, Josiah Wedgwood established a factory to mass-produce beautiful and inexpensive china. The bottle-shaped buildings are kilns in which thousands of pieces of china could be fired at one time. Kilns, factories, and housing were all mixed together in pottery towns, and smoke from burning coal filled the air. (Mary Evans Picture Library)

than his competitors' factories, and his salesmen traveled throughout England touting his goods.

New technologies intrigued Wedgwood. He invested in toll roads and canals so that clay could be shipped economically from southwestern England to his factories in the Midlands. In 1782, to mix clay and grind flint, he purchased one of the first steam engines to be used in industry. Wedgwood's interest in applying technology to manufacturing was reflected in his membership in the Birmingham Lunar Society, a group of manufacturers, scientists, and inventors who met to exchange ideas and discoveries. Similar societies throughout Britain were creating a vogue for science and giving the word *progress* a new meaning: "change for the better."

mechanization The application of machinery to manufacturing and other activities. Among the first processes to be mechanized were the spinning of cotton thread and the weaving of cloth in late-eighteenth- and early-nineteenth-century England.

The cotton industry, the largest of the period, illustrates the role of **mechanization**, the use of machines to do work previously done by hand. The cotton plant did not grow in Europe, but the cloth was so much cooler, softer, and cleaner than wool that wealthy Europeans developed a liking for this costly import. When the powerful English woolen industry persuaded Parliament to forbid the import of cotton cloth into England, it stimulated attempts to import cotton fiber and make the cloth locally. Here was an opportunity for enterprising inventors to reduce costs with laborsaving machinery.

Beginning in the 1760s, a series of inventions—the spinning jenny, the water frame, and the mule—revolutionized the spinning of cotton thread and allowed British industry to undersell high-quality handmade cotton cloth from India. British cotton output increased tenfold between 1770 and 1790.

When the boom in thread production and the soaring demand for cloth created bottlenecks in weaving, inventors rose to the challenge with power looms, carding machines, chlorine bleach, and cylindrical printing presses. By the 1830s, large English textile mills powered by steam engines were turning raw cotton into printed cloth. This was a far cry from the cottage industries of the previous century.

Mechanization offered two advantages: (1) productivity for the manufacturer and (2) economy for the consumer. In India it took 500 hours to spin a pound of cotton; the improved mule of 1830 required only 80 minutes. Cotton mills needed few skilled workers, and managers often hired children to tend the spinning machines. Mechanization and cheap labor allowed the price of cloth to fall by 90 percent from 1782 to 1812, and it kept on dropping.

Manchester, the First Industrial City
The first cotton mills, built on the banks of the River Irwell in northern England, transformed Manchester from a country town into a booming industrial city. The use of chemicals to bleach and dye the cloth and the introduction of steam engines in the early nineteenth century to power the spinning and weaving machines made Manchester, for a time, the most polluted city on earth.   (The Royal Collection ©2006 Her Majesty Queen Elizabeth II)

Britain's industrialization made cotton America's most valuable crop. In 1793, the American Eli Whitney patented his cotton gin, a simple device that separated the seeds from the fiber and made the growing of short-staple cotton economical. This permitted the spread of cotton farming into Georgia, then into Alabama, Mississippi, and Louisiana, and finally as far west as Texas. By the late 1850s, the southern states were producing a million tons of cotton a year, five-sixths of the world's total.

With the help of British craftsmen who introduced jennies, mules, and power looms, Americans developed a cotton industry in the 1820s. By 1840, the United States had 1,200 cotton mills, two-thirds of them in New England, powered by water rather than steam.

The Iron Industry

For over two thousand years iron had been used for tools, weapons, and household items such as knives, pots, hinges, and locks. Wherever it was produced, however, deforestation eventually drove up the cost of charcoal (used for smelting) and restricted output. Furthermore, iron had to be repeatedly heated and hammered to drive out impurities, a difficult and costly process. Then in 1709, Abraham Darby discovered that coke (coal from which the impurities have been cooked out) could be used in place of charcoal. The resulting metal was of lower quality than charcoal iron but much cheaper to produce, for coal was plentiful. Just as importantly, in 1784 Henry Cort found a way to remove some of the impurities in coke-iron by puddling—stirring the molten iron with long rods. Cort's process made it possible to turn high-sulfur English coal into coke to produce wrought iron (a soft and malleable form of iron) very cheaply. By 1790 four-fifths of Britain's iron was made with coke, while other countries were still using charcoal. Coke-iron allowed a great expansion in the size of individual blast furnaces, substantially reducing its cost. There seemed almost no limit to the quantity of iron that could be produced with coke. Britain's iron production began rising fast, from 17,000 tons in 1740 to 3 million tons in 1844, as much as in the rest of the world put together.

In turn, there seemed no limit to the amount of iron that an industrializing society would purchase or to the novel applications for this cheap and useful material. In 1779 the iron manufacturer Abraham Darby III (grandson of the first Abraham Darby) built a bridge of iron across the Severn River. In 1851 Londoners marveled at the **Crystal Palace**, a huge greenhouse made entirely of iron and glass and large enough to enclose the tallest trees.

The availability of cheap iron made the mass production of objects such as guns, hardware, and tools appealing. However, fitting together the parts of these products required a great deal of labor. To reduce labor costs, manufacturers turned to the idea of interchangeable parts. This idea originated in the eighteenth century when French army officers attempted, without success, to persuade gun makers to produce precisely identical parts. Craftsmen continued to use traditional methods to make parts that had to be filed to fit together with other parts. By the mid-nineteenth century, however, interchangeable-parts procedures had been adopted in the manufacture of firearms, farm equipment, and sewing machines. At the Crystal Palace exhibition of 1851, Europeans called it the "American system of manufactures." In the next hundred years the use of machinery to mass-produce consumer items was to become the hallmark of American industry.

The Steam Engine

The first machine to transform fossil fuel into mechanical energy was the **steam engine**. Although the mechanization of manufacturing was very important, the steam engine was what set the Industrial Revolution apart from all previous periods of growth and innovation.

Before the eighteenth century, lack of energy had limited many activities. For example, deep mines filled with water faster than horses could pump it out. Scientists understood the concept of atmospheric pressure and had created experimental devices to turn heat into motion, but they had not found a way to put those devices to practical use. Then, between 1702 and 1712 Thomas Newcomen developed the first practical steam engine, a crude but effective device. One engine could pump water out of a mine as fast as four horses and could run day and night without getting tired.

The Newcomen engine's voracious appetite for fuel mattered little in coal mines, where fuel was cheap, but it made the engine too costly for other uses. In 1764 **James Watt**, an instrument maker at Glasgow University in Scotland, was asked to repair the university's model Newcomen engine. Watt realized that the engine wasted fuel because the cylinder had to be alternately heated and cooled. He developed a separate condenser—a vessel into which the steam was allowed to escape after it had done work, leaving the cylinder always hot and the condenser always cold. Watt patented his idea in 1769 and enlisted the help of the iron manufacturer Matthew Boulton to turn his invention into a commercial product. Their first engines were sold to pump water out of copper and tin mines, where fuel was too costly for Newcomen engines. In 1781 Watt invented the sun-and-planet gear, which turned the back-and-forth action of the piston into rotary motion. This allowed steam engines to power machinery in flour and cotton mills, pottery factories, and other industries.

Crystal Palace Building erected in Hyde Park, London, for the Great Exhibition of 1851. Made of iron and glass, like a gigantic greenhouse, it was a symbol of the industrial age.

steam engine A machine that turns the energy released by burning fuel into motion. Thomas Newcomen built the first crude but workable steam engine in 1712. James Watt vastly improved his device in the 1760s and 1770s. Steam power was later applied to moving machinery in factories and to powering ships and locomotives.

James Watt (1736–1819) Scot who invented the condenser and other improvements that made the steam engine a practical source of power for industry and transportation. The watt, an electrical measurement, is named after him.

Watt's steam engine was the most celebrated invention of the eighteenth century. Because coal supplies seemed unlimited, steam-generated energy seemed an inexhaustible source of power that could be used where animal, wind, and water power were lacking.

Inspired by Watt's engine, inventors in France in 1783, in the United States in 1787, and in England in 1788 put steam engines on boats. The first commercially successful steamboat was Robert Fulton's *North River,* which steamed between New York City and Albany in 1807. Soon steamboats were launched on other American rivers. In the 1820s the Erie Canal linked the Atlantic seaboard with the Great Lakes and opened Ohio, Indiana, and Illinois to European settlement. Steamboats proliferated west of the Appalachian Mountains; by 1830 some three hundred plied the Mississippi and its tributaries. To counter the competition from New York State, Pennsylvania built a thousand miles of canals by 1840. The United States was fast becoming a nation that moved by water.

Oceangoing steam-powered ships were much more difficult to build than riverboats, for the first steam engines used so much coal that no ship could carry more than a few days' supply. The *Savannah,* which crossed the Atlantic in 1819, was a sailing ship with an auxiliary steam engine that was used for only ninety hours of its twenty-nine-day trip. However, engineers soon developed more efficient engines,

Pit Head of a Coal Mine

This is a small coal mine. In the center of this picture stands a Newcomen engine used to pump water. The work of hauling coal out of the mine was still done by horses and mules. The smoke coming out of the smokestack is a trademark of the early industrial era.   (National Museums and Galleries on Merseyside, Walker Art Gallery [WAG 659])

 HISTORY IN FOCUS   What do you think the artist's attitude toward the new industrial technology is? Why? *Find the answer online.*

and in 1838 two steamers, the *Great Western* and the *Sirius,* crossed the Atlantic on steam power alone.

SECTION REVIEW

- The technological revolution involved the development of cost-saving machines and processes, such as mass production through the division of labor.

- Beginning in the 1760s a series of inventions mechanized the British cotton industry and encouraged cotton farming and industry in the United States.

- Innovations in processing transformed the British iron industry, making cheap iron widely available for various applications.

- With the perfection of the steam engine, steamboats and railroads proliferated, the latter spurring the industrialization of Europe.

- Practical electric telegraphs appeared in England and America and quickly spread.

Railroads

Steam engines were initially too heavy and weak to pull any weight. After Watt's patent expired in 1800, however, inventors experimented with lighter, more powerful high-pressure engines and in the early 1800s built several steam-powered vehicles able to travel on roads or rails. Between 1830 and 1850, a railroad-building mania swept Britain. The first lines linked towns and mines with the nearest harbor or waterway. As passenger traffic soared, entrepreneurs built lines between the major cities and then to small towns as well. Railroads were far cheaper, faster, and more comfortable than stagecoaches.

In the United States, entrepreneurs built railroads as fast and cheaply as possible. By the 1840s, 6,000 miles (10,000 kilometers) of track radiated westward from Boston, New York, Philadelphia, and Baltimore. The boom of the 1840s was dwarfed by the mania of the 1850s, when 21,000 miles (34,000 kilometers) of new track were laid, much of it westward across the Appalachians to Memphis, St. Louis, and Chicago. The trip from New York to Chicago, which once took three weeks by boat and on horseback, could be made in forty-eight hours. The railroads opened up the Midwest, turning the vast prairie into wheat fields and pasture for cattle to feed the industrial cities of the eastern United States.

Railways triggered the industrialization of Europe. Belgium, independent since 1830, quickly copied the British. State-planned and -supervised railroad construction in the mid-1840s in France and Prussia not only satisfied the long-standing need for transportation but also stimulated the iron, machinery, and construction industries. In the 1850s and 1860s, the states of Germany also experienced an industrial boom.

electric telegraph A device for rapid, long-distance transmission of information over an electric wire. It was introduced in England and North America in the 1830s and 1840s and replaced telegraph systems that utilized visual signals such as semaphores.

Communication over Wires

The advent of railroads coincided with the development of the **electric telegraph**. After the Italian scientist Alessandro Volta invented the battery in 1800, making it possible to produce an electric current, many inventors tried to apply electricity to communication. The first practical telegraphy systems were developed almost simultaneously in England and America. In England, Wheatstone and Cooke introduced a five-needle telegraph in 1837; it remained in use until the early twentieth century. That same year, the American Samuel Morse introduced a code of dots and dashes that could be transmitted with a single wire; in 1843, he erected a line between Washington and Baltimore.

By the late 1840s, telegraph wires were being strung throughout the eastern United States and western Europe. In 1851, the first submarine telegraph cable was laid across the English Channel from England to France. Thus began a network that eventually enclosed the entire globe. The world was rapidly shrinking, to the applause of Europeans and Americans, for whom speed was a clear measure of progress. No longer were communications limited to the speed by which a ship could sail or a horse could gallop.

THE IMPACT OF THE INDUSTRIAL REVOLUTION

What was the impact of these changes on the society and environment of the industrializing countries?

The Industrial Revolution brought many changes in society, politics, and the economy. Early changes—smoky cities, slum neighborhoods, polluted water, child labor in mines and textile mills—were being alleviated by the mid-nineteenth century. But by then national or even international problems were replacing these local ones: business cycles, labor conflicts, and the transformation of entire regions into industrial landscapes.

New Industrial Cities

The most dramatic environmental changes occurred in the towns. Never before had towns grown so fast. London, one of the largest cities in Europe in 1700 with 500,000 inhabitants, grew to 959,000 by 1800 and to 2,363,000 by 1850, by then the largest city in the world. Smaller towns grew even faster. Manchester's population increased eightfold in a century. Liverpool grew sixfold in the first sixty years of the nineteenth century. New York City, already 100,000 strong in 1815, reached 600,000 (including Brooklyn) in 1850. In some areas, towns merged and formed megalopolises, such as Greater London, the English Midlands, central Belgium, and the Ruhr district of Germany.

Industrialization generated wealth that manifested itself in fine new homes, churches, museums, and theaters. Yet by all accounts, the industrial cities grew much too fast. As poor migrants streamed in from the countryside, developers built cheap, shoddy row houses for them to rent. These tenements were dangerously overcrowded. Often, several families had to live in one small room. Town dwellers recently arrived from the country brought country ways with them. People threw their sewage and trash out the windows to be washed down

Paris Apartment at Night

This cutaway drawing in a French magazine shows the vertical segregation by social class that prevailed in the 1840s. The lower level is occupied by the concierge and her family. The first floor belongs to a wealthy family throwing a party for high-society friends. Middle-class people living on the next floor seem annoyed by the noise coming from below. Above them, a thief has entered an artist's studio. A poor seamstress and her child live in the garret under the roof. When elevators were introduced in the late nineteenth century, people of different income levels became segregated by neighborhoods instead of by floors. (Bibliothèque nationale de France) the gutters in the streets. The poor kept pigs and chickens, the rich kept horses, and pedestrians stepped into the street at their own risk. Air pollution from burning coal got steadily worse. People drank water drawn from wells and rivers contaminated by sewage and industrial runoff. The River Irwell, which ran through Manchester, was, in the words of one visitor, "considerably less a river than a flood of liquid manure."[3] To the long list of preindustrial urban diseases such as smallpox, dysentery, and tuberculosis, industrialization added new ailments. Rickets, a bone disease caused by lack of sunshine, became endemic in dark and smoky industrial cities. Steamships brought cholera from India, causing great epidemics that struck the poor neighborhoods especially hard. In the 1850s, when the average life expectancy in England was forty years, it was only twenty-four years in Manchester, and around seventeen years in Manchester's poorest neighborhoods, because of the high infant mortality. Shocking reports of slum life led to municipal reforms, such as garbage removal, water and sewage systems, and parks and schools. These measures began to alleviate the ills of urban life after midcentury.

Rural Environments

Wilderness areas had largely disappeared in Britain and much of western Europe long before the Industrial Revolution. Human activity had turned almost every exploitable piece of land into fields, pastures, or towns. The most serious problem was deforestation. People cut timber to build ships and houses, to heat homes, and to manufacture bricks, iron, glass, beer, bread, and many other items.

Americans transformed their environment even faster than Europeans did. Settlers viewed forests not as a valuable resource but as a hindrance to development. In their haste to "open up the West," pioneers felled trees and burned them, built houses and abandoned them when they moved on. The cultivation of cotton was especially harmful. Planters cut down forests, grew cotton for a few years until it depleted the soil, and then moved west, abandoning the land to scrub pines. The American idea of nature as an obstacle to be overcome and dominated persisted long after the entire continent was occupied.

To contemporaries, the new transportation systems brought the most obvious changes in rural life. Governments and private trusts built numerous roads. Canal building boomed in Britain, France, and the Low Countries in the late eighteenth century. Canals were marvels of construction, with deep cuts, tunnels, and even aqueducts that carried barges over rivers. They also were a sort of school where engineers learned skills they were able to apply to the next great transportation system: the railroads. They laid track across rolling country by cutting deeply into hillsides and erecting daringly long bridges of stone and iron across valleys. Soon, clanking trains pulled by puffing, smoke-belching locomotives were invading long-isolated districts.

Thus, in the century after industrialization began, the landscape of industrializing countries was transformed more rapidly than ever before. But the ecological changes, like the technological and economic changes that caused them, were only beginning.

Working Conditions

Most industrial jobs were unskilled, repetitive, and boring. Factory work did not vary with the seasons or the time of day but began and ended by the clock. Factories used the invention of gas lighting to expand the working day past sunset (see Environment and Technology: Gas Lighting). Workdays were long, there were few breaks, and foremen watched constantly. Workers who performed one simple task over and over had little sense of achievement or connection to the final product. Industrial accidents were common and could ruin a family. Unlike even the poorest preindustrial farmer or artisan, factory workers had no control over their tools, jobs, or working hours.

Women workers were concentrated in textile mills, partly because of ancient traditions, partly because textile work required less strength than metalworking, construction, or hauling. On average, women earned one-third to one-half as much as men. Young unmarried women worked to support themselves or to save for marriage. Married women took factory jobs when their husbands were unable to support the family. Mothers of infants faced a hard choice: whether to leave their babies with wet nurses at great expense and danger or to bring them to the factory and keep them quiet with opiates. Rather than working together as family units, husbands and wives increasingly worked in different places.

Factory work was never the main occupation of working women. Most young women who sought paid employment in the early years of industrialization became domestic servants in spite of the low pay, drudgery, and risk of sexual abuse. Other women with small children tried hard to find work they could do at home, such as laundry, sewing, embroidery, millinery, or taking in lodgers.

Even with both parents working, poor families found it hard to make ends meet. As in preindustrial societies, parents thought children should contribute to their upkeep as soon as they were able to. The first generation of workers brought their children with them to the factories and mines as early as age five or six; they had little choice, since there were no public schools or day-care centers. Employers encouraged the practice and even hired orphans. They preferred children because they were cheaper and more docile than adults and were better able to tie broken threads or crawl under machines to sweep the dust. Mine operators used children to pull coal carts along the low passageways from the coal face to the mine shaft. In the mid-nineteenth century, when the British government began restricting child labor, mill owners increasingly recruited Irish immigrants.

American industry began on a somewhat different note than the British. When Francis Cabot Lowell built a cotton mill in Massachusetts, he deliberately hired the unmarried daughters of New England farmers, promising decent wages and housing in dormitories under careful moral supervision. Other manufacturers eager to combine profits with morality followed his example. But soon the profit motive won out, and manufacturers imposed longer hours, harsher working conditions, and lower wages. When the young women went on strike, the factory owners replaced them with Irish immigrant women willing to accept lower pay and worse conditions.

The rising demand for cotton and the abolition of the African slave trade in the United States in 1808 caused an increase in the price of slaves. As the "Cotton Kingdom" expanded, the number of slaves rose through natural increase, from 700,000 in the 1790s to 3,200,000 slaves by 1850. Similarly, Europe and North America's surging demand for tea and coffee prolonged slavery on sugar plantations in the West Indies and caused it to spread to the coffee-growing regions of southern Brazil. Slavery was part and parcel of the Industrial Revolution, just as much as child labor in Britain, the clothes that people wore, and the beverages they drank.

Gas Lighting

Before the nineteenth century, the night was a danger- ous time to be out. Oil lanterns and candles made of tallow or beeswax were too expensive for everyday use. Some hardy souls—like the engine designer James Watt, the pottery manufacturer Josiah Wedgwood, the chem- ist Joseph Priestley, the iron manufacturer Matthew Boulton, and the naturalist Erasmus Darwin—called themselves the Lunar Society because they only met on nights when there was a full moon so they could find their way home in the dark. Almost everyone else went to bed at sundown and got up at dawn.

There was a big demand for better lighting. For the managers of cotton mills and other industrial estab- lishments, daylight hours were too short, especially in the winter months; they knew that they could keep running after sunset if they had light, but lanterns and candles were costly and dangerous. Wealthy people wanted to light up their homes. Businesses and gov- ernment offices also needed light. The demand in- spired inventors to look for new ways to produce light.

In France, the engineer Philippe Lebon knew that heating wood to make charcoal let off a flammable gas. In the 1790s he was able to channel this gas through pipes to illuminate a home and garden. In Britain, William Murdock, an engineer who worked for the steam engine manufacturers Boulton and Watt, extracted gas released in the process of heating coal to make coke and used it to light up a house. Moving from these ex- periments to commercial applications was a long and complicated process, however. Coal gas was smelly and explosive and full of impurities that gave off toxic fumes and smoke when it burned. Engineers had to learn ways to extract the gas efficiently, make strong pipes that did not leak, and market the product. In 1806 a German immigrant to England, Frederick Albert Winsor, founded the National Light and Heat Company to produce and distribute gas in London. By 1816, London had 26 miles of gas mains bringing gas to several neighborhoods. That same year, Baltimore became the first American city to install gas mains and streetlamps. In the follow- ing decades, engineers developed ways of removing the impurities from the gas to make it safer and cleaner. They also invented meters to measure the amount of gas consumed and burners that produced a brighter

GAS LIGHTING   For city dwellers, one of the most dramatic improvements brought by industrializa- tion was the introduction of gas lighting. The gas used was a byproduct of heating coal to make coke for the iron industry, and the gas was distributed in iron pipes throughout the wealthier neighborhoods of big cities. Every evening at dusk, lamplighters went around lighting the street lamps.   (Mary Evans Picture Library/The Image Works)

light. As a result of these improvements, the cost of gas dropped to less than a third of that of oil lamps of equivalent lighting power. From the 1840s until the early twentieth century, gaslights were installed in homes, businesses, and factories and even along streets in the major cities of Europe and America.

The results were astonishing and delighted city dwell- ers. Mills and factories could operate on two eight- to ten-hour shifts instead of one long dawn-to-dusk shift. Businesses stayed open late. Theaters gave evening performances. And people could now walk the streets safely. Evening illumination also contributed to the tre- mendous increase in adult education, as working peo- ple attended classes after work. Sales of books soared, in part because the increasing number of people with gaslights in their homes could stay up late reading. The brightly lit cities attracted migrants from the still-dark countryside. Long before electricity, gas lighting had banished the terrors of the night.

Changes in Society

Industrialization accentuated the polarization of society and disparities of income. In Britain, the worst-off were those who clung to an obsolete skill or craft, such as handloom weavers in a time of power looms. Even by working more hours, they could not escape destitution.

The wages and standard of living of factory workers did not decline steadily like those of handloom weavers; they fluctuated wildly with the cycles of economic growth and contraction. During the war years 1792 to 1815, the poor suffered hardship when the price of food rose faster than wages. Then, in the 1820s, real wages and public health began to improve, as industrial production grew at over 3 percent a year, pulling the rest of the economy along. Prices fell so that even the poor could afford comfortable, washable cotton clothes.

Overall, the benefits of industrialization—cheaper food, clothing, and utensils—did not improve workers' standard of living until the 1850s. The real beneficiaries of the early Industrial Revolution were the entrepreneurs whose money came from manufacturing. Most were the sons of middling shopkeepers, craftsmen, or farmers who had a little capital to start a cotton-spinning or machine-building business. Many tried and some succeeded, largely by plowing their profits back into the business. A generation later, in the nineteenth century, some newly rich industrialists bought their way into high society. With industrialization also came a "cult of domesticity" that removed middle-class women from contact with the business world and left them responsible for the home, the servants, the education of children, and the family's social life.

SECTION REVIEW

- The Industrial Revolution spurred rapid urbanization, causing severe pollution, overcrowding, and myriad health and hygiene problems.

- Industrialization hastened deforestation and brought pollution to rural environments.

- Industrial working conditions were harsh and dangerous, especially for children, until Britain passed child-labor laws.

- Women often faced difficult choices between factory work and family obligations, and slavery persisted because of industrialization.

- Industrialization benefited owners more quickly than workers, the former often being able to rise in society, while the cult of domesticity shaped women's lives.

NEW ECONOMIC AND POLITICAL IDEAS

How did the Industrial Revolution influence the rise of new economic and political ideas?

Changes as profound as the Industrial Revolution could not occur without political ferment and ideological conflict. So many other momentous events took place during those years—the American Revolution (1776–1783), the French Revolution (1789–1799), the Napoleonic Wars (1804–1815), the reactions and revolts that periodically swept over Europe after 1815—that we cannot neatly separate out the consequences of industrialization from the rest. But it is clear that the Industrial Revolution strengthened the ideas of laissez faire and socialism and sparked workers' protests.

Laissez Faire

The most celebrated exponent of **laissez faire** (lay-say fair) ("let them do") was Adam Smith (1723–1790), a Scottish economist. In *The Wealth of Nations* (1776), Smith argued that if individuals were allowed to seek their personal gain, the effect, as though guided by an "invisible hand," would be to increase the general welfare. Except to protect

laissez faire The idea that government should refrain from interfering in economic affairs. The classic exposition of laissez-faire principles is Adam Smith's *Wealth of Nations* (1776).

private property, the government should refrain from interfering in business; it should even allow duty-free trade with foreign countries.

Although it was true that governments at the time were incompetent at regulating their national economies, it was becoming obvious that industrialization was not improving the general welfare but was for some causing great misery. Other thinkers blamed the workers' plight on the population boom, which outstripped the food supply and led to falling wages. The workers' poverty, they claimed, was as much a result of "natural law" as the wealth of successful businessmen, and the only way the working class could avoid mass famine was to delay marriage and practice self-restraint and sexual abstinence.

Laissez faire provided an ideological justification for a special kind of capitalism: banks, stock markets, and chartered companies allowed investors to obtain profits with reasonable risks but with much less government control and interference than in the past. But not everyone accepted the grim conclusions of the "dismal science," as economics was then known. Jeremy Bentham (1748–1832) believed that it was possible to maximize "the greatest happiness of the greatest number," if only a Parliament of enlightened reformers would study the social problems of the day and pass appropriate legislation; his philosophy became known as utilitarianism.

Positivism and Utopian Socialism

positivism A philosophy developed by the French count of Saint-Simon. Positivists believed that social and economic problems could be solved by the application of the scientific method, leading to continuous progress. Their ideas became popular in France and Latin America in the nineteenth century.

utopian socialism A philosophy introduced by the Frenchman Charles Fourier in the early nineteenth century. Utopian socialists hoped to create humane alternatives to industrial capitalism by building self-sustaining communities whose inhabitants would work cooperatively.

Some French social thinkers, moved by sincere concern for the poor, offered a more radically new vision of a just civilization. Espousing a philosophy called **positivism**, the count of Saint-Simon (1760–1825) argued that the scientific method could solve social as well as technical problems. He recommended that the poor, guided by scientists and artists, form workers' communities under the protection of benevolent business leaders. These ideas found no following among workers, but they attracted the enthusiastic support of bankers and entrepreneurs, who were inspired by visions of railroads, canals, and other symbols of progress and invested their money accordingly.

Meanwhile, the **utopian** (you-TOE-pee-uhn) **socialism** of Charles Fourier (1768–1837), who loathed capitalists, imagined an ideal society in which groups of sixteen hundred workers would live in dormitories and work together on the land and in workshops where music, wine, and pastries would soften the hardships of labor. For this idea, critics called him a "utopian"—a dreamer.

The person who came closest to creating a utopian community was the Englishman Robert Owen (1771–1858), a successful cotton manufacturer who believed that industry could provide prosperity for all. Conscience-stricken by the appalling plight of the workers, Owen took over the management of New Lanark, a mill town south of Glasgow. He improved the housing and added schools, a church, and other amenities. He also testified before Parliament against child labor and for government inspection of working conditions, thereby angering his fellow industrialists.

Protests and Reforms

Workers benefited little from the ideas of these middle-class philosophers. Instead, they resisted the harsh working conditions in their own ways. They changed jobs frequently and were often absent, especially on Mondays. Periodically, workers rioted or went on strike. Such acts of resistance did nothing, however, to change the nature of industrial work. Not until workers learned to act together could they hope to have much influence.

Gradually, they formed benevolent societies and organizations to demand universal male suffrage and shorter workdays. In 1834, Robert Owen organized the Grand National Consolidated Trade Union to lobby for an eight-hour workday; it gained half a million members but failed a few months later in the face of government prosecution of trade union activities. The Chartist movement had more success, gathering petitions by the thousands to present to Parliament. Although Chartism collapsed in 1848, it left a legacy of labor organizing. Eventually, mass movements persuaded political leaders to look into the abuses of industrial life, despite the prevailing laissez-faire philosophy.

In the 1820s and 1830s, the British Parliament began investigating conditions in the factories and mines. The Factory Act of 1833 prohibited the employment of children under age nine in textile mills and limited the working hours of children between the ages of nine and eighteen. The Mines Act of 1842 prohibited the employment of all women and of boys under age ten underground. Several decades passed before the government appointed enough inspectors to enforce the new laws.

The British learned to seek reform through accommodation. On the European continent, in contrast, the revolutions of 1848 (see Chapter 19) revealed widespread discontent with repressive governments but failed to soften the hardships of industrialization.

Emigration

Another response to growing population, rural crises, and business cycles was emigration. Many poor Irish emigrated to England in search of work in construction and factories. After the potato crop failed in Ireland in 1847–1848, one-quarter of the Irish population died in the resulting famine, and another quarter emigrated to England and America. On the European continent, the negative effects of economic downturns were tempered by the existence of small family farms to which urban workers could return when they were laid off, but vast numbers still left Europe in search of better opportunities in the Western Hemisphere.

The United States received approximately 600,000 European immigrants in the 1830s, 1.5 million in the 1840s, and then 2.5 million per decade until 1880. In the 1890s, an astonishing total of 5.2 million immigrants arrived. European immigration to Latin America also increased dramatically after 1880. Immigrants from Europe faced prejudice and discrimination from those who believed they

Irish Mill Workers

Immigrant women provided cheap, docile, and minimally skilled labor for American mills. Faced with a constant shortage of skilled craftsmen, American factory owners pioneered assembly line methods that made it possible to employ new arrivals from various parts of the world.

(New York Public Library/Art Resource, NY)

SECTION REVIEW

- Industrialization reinforced Adam Smith's theories even in the face of conditions that prompted competing ideas such as utilitarianism.

- French social thinkers responded to industrialization with positivism and utopian socialism, but Robert Owen came closest to realizing such visions.

- Britain led the way in both labor organization and government reform, while on the continent the 1848 revolutions did little to ease workers' conditions.

- The broad economic effects of industrialization prompted emigration from Europe and Asia to the Western Hemisphere.

threatened the well-being of native-born workers by accepting low wages, and they threatened national culture by resisting assimilation.

Asian immigration to the Western Hemisphere also increased after 1850. Between 1849 and 1875, approximately 570,000 Chinese immigrants arrived in the Americas, half in the United States. India also contributed more than a half-million immigrants to the Caribbean region. Asians faced more obstacles to immigration than did Europeans and were often victims of violence and more extreme forms of discrimination in the New World.

Despite discrimination, most immigrants were also motivated to assimilate. Many intellectuals and political leaders wondered if the evolving mix of culturally diverse populations could sustain a common citizenship. As a result, efforts were directed toward compelling immigrants to assimilate. They learned the language spoken in their adopted countries as fast as possible in order to improve their earning capacity.

Union movements and electoral politics in the hemisphere also felt the influence of new arrivals who aggressively sought to influence government and improve working conditions. Immigrants also introduced new languages, foods, and customs. Mutual benevolent societies and less formal ethnic associations pooled resources to help immigrants open businesses, aid the immigration of their relatives, or bury their family members, sometimes worsening the fears of the native-born that immigration posed a threat to national culture. They also established links with political movements, sometimes exchanging votes for favors.

THE LIMITS OF INDUSTRIALIZATION OUTSIDE THE WEST

How did the Industrial Revolution affect the relations between the industrialized and the nonindustrialized parts of the world?

The spread of the Industrial Revolution in the early nineteenth century transformed the relations of western Europe and North America with the rest of the world. In Egypt and India cheap industrial imports, backed by the power of Great Britain, delayed industrialization for a century or more. China was defeated and humiliated by the products of industrial manufacture. In these three cases, we can discern the outlines of the Western domination that has characterized the history of the world since the late nineteenth century.

Egypt, strongly influenced by European ideas since the French invasion of 1798, began to industrialize in the early nineteenth century. The driving force was its ruler, Muhammad Ali (1769–1849), a man who was to play a major role not only in the history of Egypt but also in the Middle East and East Africa (see Chapters 21 and 22). He wanted to build up the Egyptian economy and military in order to become less dependent on the Ottoman sultan, his nominal overlord. To do so, he imported advisers and technicians from Europe and built cotton mills, foundries, shipyards, weapons factories, and other industrial enterprises. To pay for all this, he made the peasants grow wheat and cotton, which the government bought at a low price and exported at a profit. He also imposed high tariffs on imported goods to force the pace of industrialization.

Muhammad Ali's efforts fell afoul of the British, who did not want a powerful country threatening to interrupt the flow of travelers and mail across Egypt, the shortest route between Europe and India. When Egypt went to war against the Ottoman Empire in 1839, Britain intervened and forced Muhammad Ali to eliminate all import duties in the name of free trade. Unprotected, Egypt's fledgling industries could not compete with the flood of cheap British products. Thereafter, Egypt exported raw cotton, imported manufactured goods, and became, in effect, an economic dependency of Britain.

Until the late eighteenth century, India had been the world's largest producer and exporter of cotton textiles, handmade by skilled spinners and weavers. The British East India Company took over large parts of India just as the Industrial Revolution was beginning in Britain (see Chapter 22 and Map 22.2). It allowed cheap British factory-made yarn and cloth to flood the Indian market duty-free, putting spinners and later handloom weavers out of work. Unlike Britain, India had no factories to which displaced handicraft workers could turn for work. Most of them became landless peasants, eking out a precarious living.

Like other tropical regions, India became an exporter of raw materials and an importer of British industrial goods. To hasten the process, British entrepreneurs and colonial officials introduced railroads into the subcontinent. The construction of India's railroad network began in the mid-1850s, along with coal mining to fuel the locomotives and the installation of telegraph lines to connect the major cities.

Some Indian entrepreneurs saw opportunities in the atmosphere of change that the British created. In 1854 the Bombay merchant Cowasjee Nanabhoy Davar imported an engineer, four skilled workers, and several textile machines from Britain and started India's first textile mill. This was the beginning of India's mechanized cotton industry. Despite many gifted entrepreneurs, India's industrialization proceeded at a snail's pace, for the government was in British hands and the British did nothing to encourage Indian industry.

China's stagnation in the late eighteenth and early nineteenth centuries, at the very time when first Britain and then western Europe and North America were becoming industrialized, has long puzzled historians. China had the resources, both human and natural, to advance technologically and economically, but a conservative elite and a growing population of poor peasants stood in the way of change (see Chapter 18). As a result, when faced with Western industrial technology, China became weaker rather than stronger.

In January 1840 a shipyard in Britain launched a radically new ship. The *Nemesis* had an iron hull, a flat bottom that allowed it to navigate in shallow waters, and a steam engine to power it upriver and against the wind. In November it arrived off the coast of China, heavily armed. Though ships from Europe had been sailing to China for three hundred years, the *Nemesis* was the first steam-powered iron gunboat seen in Asian waters. A Chinese observer noted: "Iron is employed to make it strong. The hull is painted black, weaver's shuttle fashion. On each side is a wheel, which by the use of coal fire is made to revolve as fast as a running horse. . . . At the vessel's head is a Marine God, and at the head, stern, and sides are cannon, which give it a terrific appearance. Steam vessels are a wonderful invention of foreigners, and are calculated to offer delight to many."[4]

SECTION REVIEW

- Industrialization contributed to Europe's and North America's domination of large parts of the world.

- Egypt's modernization drive collapsed because of British military and economic intervention.

- Despite strong efforts, India's handicraft cotton industry was slow to develop because the government was in British hands and the British did nothing to encourage the fledgling industry.

- Steam-powered iron warships enabled Britain to defeat China.

Instead of offering delight, the *Nemesis* and other steam-powered warships that soon joined it steamed up the Chinese rivers, bombarded forts and cities, and transported troops and supplies from place to place along the coast and up rivers far more quickly than Chinese soldiers could move on foot. With this new weapon, Britain, a small island nation half a world away, was able to defeat the largest and most populated country in the world (see Chapter 21).

Chapter Review

 DOWNLOAD THE MP3 AUDIO FILE OF THE CHAPTER REVIEW TO LISTEN TO ON THE GO.

What caused the Industrial Revolution? (page 550)

The Industrial Revolution arose from a combination of factors in European society in the eighteenth and early nineteenth centuries. The population grew, but so did the food supply, thanks to improvements in agriculture. Among upper- and middle-class Europeans, practical subjects like business, science, and technology became fashionable. Great Britain had a particularly fluid society open to talents and enterprise. On the European continent, the revolutions of 1789–1815 swept away the restrictions of the old aristocratic regimes.

What were the key innovations that increased productivity and drove industrialization? (page 553)

A series of technological and organizational innovations transformed the manufacture of many products, reducing their costs and increasing their productivity. New machines, assembled in mills, mass-produced cotton yarn and cloth. Work formerly done by skilled craftsmen was divided into many simple tasks assigned to workers in factories. New techniques made iron cheap and abundant. Steam engines provided power to factories, ships, and railroads. And electricity found its first practical application in telegraphy.

What was the impact of these changes on the society and environment of the industrializing countries? (page 559)

The Industrial Revolution changed people's lives and the environments in which they lived. Cities grew huge and, for most of their inhabitants, unsightly and unhealthy. While middle-class women were consigned to caring for the home and children, working-class women and children as well as men were obliged to earn their living in mines and factories. In the industrial cities, social problems such as unemployment, alcoholism, and the abandonment of children became acute. Rural environments were also transformed as roads, canals, and railroads crisscrossed open land.

KEY TERMS

Industrial Revolution *(p. 550)*

agricultural revolution (eighteenth century) *(p. 552)*

mass production *(p. 553)*

Josiah Wedgwood *(p. 553)*

division of labor *(p. 553)*

mechanization *(p. 554)*

Crystal Palace *(p. 556)*

steam engine *(p. 556)*

James Watt *(p. 556)*

electric telegraph *(p. 558)*

laissez faire *(p. 563)*

positivism *(p. 564)*

utopian socialism *(p. 564)*

WEB RESOURCES

Pronunciation Guide

Answer to the History in Focus Question

See photo on page 557, "Pit Head of a Coal Mine."

Plus

Chapter Objectives

ACE multiple-choice quiz

Flashcards

How did the Industrial Revolution influence the rise of new economic and political ideas? (page 563)

Some thinkers defended the growing disparities between rich and poor in the name of laissez faire. Governments and businesspeople eagerly adopted many of the free-market capitalist views of Adam Smith. Others, such as positivists and utopian socialists, criticized the injustices caused by industrialization and offered a new vision of just communities. Workers created labor unions, leading political leaders to reexamine the working conditions of factories and mines, especially as they concerned women and children. However, not until the mid-nineteenth century did industrialization begin to raise living standards in the industrialized countries.

How did the Industrial Revolution affect the relations between the industrialized and the nonindustrialized parts of the world? (page 566)

The Industrial Revolution changed life not only in the industrializing nations but also around the world because it gave the newly industrial nations of the West new powers to coerce non-Western societies. In particular, Britain snuffed out the incipient industrialization of Egypt and India and turned those countries into producers of raw materials, and British steam-powered gunboats forced China to open its doors to unequal trade.

SUGGESTED READING

Ashton, T. S. *The Industrial Revolution, 1760–1830.* 1948. A classic account of the British industrial revolution.

Goodman, J., and K. Honeyman. *Gainful Pursuits: The Making of Industrial Europe: 1600–1914.* 1988. Industrialization outside of Britain.

Harris, John. *Industrial Espionage and Technology Transfer: Britain and France in the Eighteenth Century.* 1998. Looks at the underside of industrial development.

Jeremy, David. *Artisans, Entrepreneurs and Machines: Essays on the Early Anglo-American Textile Industry, 1770–1840.* 1998. Discusses the beginnings of American industrialization.

Landes, David. *The Unbound Prometheus: Technological Change and Industrial Development in Western Europe from 1750 to the Present.* 2d ed. 2003. A broad synthesis of modern industrial development.

McClellan, James, III, and Harold Dorn. *Science and Technology in World History.* 1999. Emphasizes the intersection of technology and science.

Mokyr, Joel. *The Gifts of Athena: Historical Origins of the Knowledge Economy.* 2002. Examines the role and institutional bases of knowledge in the growth of the modern industrial world.

Mokyr, Joel. *The Lever of Riches: Technological Creativity and Economic Progress.* 1990. An optimistic overview of technological change.

Pomeranz, Kenneth. *The Great Divergence: Europe, China, and the Making of the Modern World Economy.* 2000. An important work comparing China and Europe in the eighteenth century.

Stearns, Peter. *The Industrial Revolution in World History.* 1993. The first book to treat industrialization as a global phenomenon.

Thompson, E. P. *The Making of the English Working Class.* 1963. A classic work on the impact of industrialization on workers.

Tucker, Richard, and John Richards. *Global Deforestation in the Nineteenth-Century World Economy.* 1983. Looks at the negative consequences of industrialization.

Uglow, Jenny. *The Lunar Men: Five Friends Whose Curiosity Changed the World.* 2002. Explores interactions between scientists, technologists, and businessmen.

Weiner, Lynn Y. *From Working Girl to Working Mother: The Female Labor Force in the United States, 1820–1980.* 1985. The role of women in an industrializing society.

Wilkinson, Richard. *Poverty and Progress: An Ecological Perspective on Economic Development.* 1973. Explores the environmental impact of industrialization.

NOTES

1. Nassau W. Senior, *Letters on the Factory Act, as it affects the cotton manufacture, addressed to the Right Honourable, the President of the Board of Trade,* 2d ed. (London: Fellows, 1844), 20.

2. Friedrich Engels, *Condition of the Working Class in England,* trans. and ed. by W. O. Henderson and W. H. Chaloner (Oxford: Blackwell, 1958), 312.

3. Quoted in Lewis Mumford, *The City in History* (New York: Harcourt Brace, 1961), 460.

4. *Nautical Magazine* 12 (1843): 346.

CHAPTER 21

Land Empires in the Age of Imperialism

1800–1870

Wﾠhen the emperor of the Qing (ching) (the last empire to rule China) died in 1799, the imperial court received a shock. For decades officials had known that the emperor was indulging his handsome young favorite, Heshen (huh-shun), allowing him extraordinary privileges and power. Senior bureaucrats hated Heshen, suspecting him of overseeing a widespread network of corruption. They believed he had been scheming to prolong the inconclusive wars against the native Miao (mee-ow) peoples of southwest China in the late 1700s. Glowing reports of successes against the rebels had poured into the capital, and enormous sums of government money had flowed to the battlefields. But there was no adequate accounting for the funds, and the war persisted.

After the emperor's death, Heshen's enemies ordered his arrest. When they searched his mansion,

 This icon will direct you to the website where you can Prepare for Class, Improve Your Grade, and Ace the Test: college.cengage.com/pic/bullietbrief4e

they discovered a magnificent hoard of silk, furs, porcelain, furniture, and gold and silver. His personal cash alone exceeded what remained in the imperial treasury. The new emperor ordered Heshen to commit suicide with a rope of gold silk. The government seized Heshen's fortune, but the financial damage could not be undone. The declining agricultural base could not replenish the state coffers, and much of the income that did flow in was squandered by an increasingly corrupt bureaucracy. In the 1800s the Qing Empire faced increasing challenges from Europe and the United States with an empty treasury, a stagnant economy, and a troubled society.

The Qing Empire's problems were not unique. They were common to all the land-based empires of Eurasia, where old and inefficient ways of governing put states at risk. The international climate was increasingly dominated by industrializing European economies drawing on the wealth of their overseas colonies. During the early 1800s rapid population growth and slow agricultural growth affected much of Eurasia. Earlier military expansion had stretched the resources of imperial treasuries (see Chapter 18), leaving the land-based empires vulnerable to European military pressure. Responses to this pressure varied, with reform and adaptation gaining headway in some lands and tradition being reasserted in others. In the long run, attempts to meet western Europe's economic and political demands produced financial indebtedness to France, Britain, and other Western powers.

This chapter contrasts the experiences of the Qing Empire with those of the Russian and Ottoman Empires. Whereas the Qing opted for resistance, the others made varying attempts to adapt and reform. Russia eventually became part of Europe and shared in many aspects of European culture, while the Ottomans and the Qing became subject to ever-greater imperialist pressure. These different responses raise the question of the role of culture in shaping western Europe's relations with the rest of the world in the nineteenth century.

THE OTTOMAN EMPIRE

What were the benefits and the drawbacks to the Ottoman Empire of the reforms adopted during the Tanzimat period?

During the eighteenth century the central government of the Ottoman Empire lost much of its power to provincial governors, military commanders, ethnic leaders, and bandit chiefs. In several parts of the empire local officials and large landholders tried to increase their independence and divert imperial funds into their own coffers.

A kingdom in Arabia led by the Saud family, following the puritanical and fundamentalist religious views of an eighteenth-century leader named Muhammad ibn Abd al-Wahhab (moo-HAH-muhd ib-uhn ab-dahl-wa-HAHB), took control of the holy cities of Mecca and Medina and deprived the sultan of the honor of organizing the annual pilgrimage. In Egypt factions of mamluk slave-soldiers purchased as boys in Georgia and nearby parts of the Caucasus and educated for war reasserted their influence. Such soldiers had ruled Egypt between 1260 and 1517, when they were defeated by the Ottomans. Now Ottoman weakness allowed mamluk factions based on a revival of the slave-soldier tradition to reemerge as local military forces.

CL Primary Source: The History and Doctrine of the Wahhabis *Find out what happens when the Wahhabis enter the holy city of Mecca.*

For the sultans, the outlook was bleak. At the end of the eighteenth century, the inefficient Janissary corps used the political power it enjoyed in Istanbul to force Sultan Selim III to abandon efforts to train a modern, European-style army. This situation unexpectedly changed when France invaded Egypt.

Egypt and the Napoleonic Example

Napoleon Bonaparte and an invasion force of 36,000 men and four hundred ships invaded Egypt in May 1798. The French quickly defeated the mamluk forces that for several decades had dominated the country under the loose jurisdiction of the Ottoman sultan in Istanbul. Fifteen months later, after being stopped by Ottoman land and British naval forces in an attempted invasion of Syria, Napoleon secretly left Cairo and returned to France. Three months later he seized power and made himself emperor.

Back in Egypt, his generals tried to administer a country that they only poorly understood. Cut off from France by British ships in the Mediterranean, they had little hope of remaining in power and agreed to withdraw in 1801. For the second time in three years, a collapse of military power produced a power vacuum in Egypt. The winner of the ensuing contest was **Muhammad Ali** (moo-HAM-mad AH-lee), the commander of a contingent of Albanian soldiers sent by the sultan to restore imperial control. By 1805 he had taken the place of the official Ottoman governor, and by 1811 he had dispossessed the mamluks of their lands and privileges.

Muhammad Ali's rise to power coincided with the meteoric career of Emperor Napoleon I. It is not surprising, therefore, that he adopted many French practices in rebuilding the Egyptian state. Militarily, he established special schools for training artillery and cavalry officers, army surgeons, military bandmasters, and others. The curricula of these schools featured European skills and sciences, and Muhammad Ali began to send promising officer trainees to France for education. In 1824 he started a gazette devoted to official affairs, the first newspaper in the Islamic world.

As discussed in Chapter 20, Muhammad Ali built all sorts of factories to outfit his new army. These did not prove efficient enough to survive, but they showed a determination to achieve independence and parity with the European powers.

In the 1830s Muhammad Ali's son Ibrahim invaded Syria and instituted some of the changes already under way in Egypt. The improved quality of the new Egyptian army had been proven during the Greek war of independence (see below), when Ibrahim had commanded an expeditionary force to help the sultan. In response, the sultan embarked on building his own new army in 1826. The two armies met when Ibrahim attacked northward into Anatolia in 1839 and defeated the army of his suzerain, the Ottoman sultan. The road to Istanbul seemed open until the European powers intervened and forced a withdrawal to the present-day border between Egypt and Israel.

Muhammad Ali remained Egypt's ruler, under the suzerainty of the sultan, until his death in 1849; and his family continued to rule the country until 1952. But his dream of making Egypt a mighty country capable of standing up to Europe faded. What survived was the example he had set for the sultans in Istanbul.

Muhammad Ali (1769–1849) Leader of Egyptian modernization in the early nineteenth century. He ruled Egypt as an Ottoman governor, but had imperial ambitions. His descendants ruled Egypt until overthrown in 1952.

Chronology

	Ottoman Empire	Russian Empire	Qing Empire
			1794–1804 White Lotus Rebellion
1800		**1801–1825** Reign of Alexander I	
	1805–1849 Muhammad Ali governs Egypt		
	1808–1839 Rule of Mahmud II		
		1812 Napoleon's retreat from Moscow	
		1825 Decembrist revolt	
		1825–1855 Reign of Nicholas I	
	1826 Janissary corps dissolved		
	1829 Greek independence		
	1839 Abdul Mejid begins Tanzimat reforms		**1839–1842** Opium War
1850			**1850–1864** Taiping Rebellion
	1853–1856 Crimean War	**1853–1856** Crimean War	
		1855–1881 Reign of Alexander II	
			1856–1860 Arrow War
		1861 Emancipation of the serfs	
	1876 First constitution by an Islamic government		

Ottoman Reform and the European Model, 1807–1853

At the end of the eighteenth century Sultan Selim (seh-LEEM) III (r. 1789–1807), a forward-looking ruler who stayed abreast of events in Europe, introduced reforms to create European-style military units, bring provincial governors under central government control, and standardize taxation. The rise in government expenditures to implement the reforms was supposed to be offset by taxes on selected items, primarily tobacco and coffee.

The reforms failed for political more than economic reasons. The most violent and persistent opposition came from the **Janissary** (JAN-nih-say-ree) military corps (see Chapter 17). Originally Christian boys taken from their homes in the Balkans, converted to Islam, and required to serve for life in the Ottoman army, in the eighteenth century the Janissaries became a significant political force in Istanbul and in provincial capitals like Damascus and Aleppo. Their interest in preserving special economic privileges made them resist the creation of new military units.

At times, Janissary power produced military uprisings. In the Ottoman territory of **Serbia**, local residents intensely resented the control exercised by Janissary governors. The Orthodox Christians claimed that the Janissaries abused them. In response,

Janissaries Infantry, originally of slave origin, armed with firearms and constituting the elite of the Ottoman army from the fifteenth century until the corps was abolished in 1826.

Serbia The Ottoman province in the Balkans that rose up against Janissary control in the early 1800s. After World War II the central province of Yugoslavia. Serb leaders struggled to maintain dominance as the Yugoslav federation dissolved in the 1990s.

Selim threatened to reassign the Janissaries to Istanbul. Suspecting that the sultan wanted to curb their political power, in 1805 the Janissaries revolted and massacred Christians in Serbia. Unable to reestablish central Ottoman rule over Serbia, the sultan had to rely on the ruler of Bosnia, another Balkan province, who joined his troops with the peasants of Serbia to suppress the Janissary uprising. The threat of Russian intervention prevented the Ottomans from disarming the victorious Serbians, so Serbia became effectively independent.

Other opponents of reform included ulama, or Muslim religious scholars, who distrusted the secularization of law and taxation that Selim proposed. In the face of widespread rejection of his reforms, Selim suspended his program in 1806. Nevertheless, a massive military uprising occurred at Istanbul, and the sultan was deposed and imprisoned. Reform forces recaptured the capital, but not before Selim had been executed. Selim's cousin, Sultan Mahmud (MAH-mood) II (r. 1808–1839), cautiously revived Selim's program, but he realized that reforms needed to be more systematic and imposed more forcefully. The effectiveness of radical reform in Muhammad Ali's Egypt drove this lesson home, as did the insurrection in Greece, during which the Egyptian military performed much better than the main Ottoman army.

Greek independence in 1829 had dramatic international significance. A combination of Greek nationalist organizations and interlopers from Albania formed the independence movement. Europe's interest in the classical age of Greece and Rome led many Europeans to consider the Greeks' struggle for independence a campaign to recapture their classical glory from Muslim oppression. Some—including the "mad, bad and dangerous to know" English poet Lord Byron, who lost his life in the war—went to Greece to fight as volunteers. When the combined squadrons of the British, French, and Russian fleets, under orders to observe but not intervene in the war, made an unauthorized attack that sank the Ottoman fleet at the Battle of Navarino, Greek victory was assured (see Map 21.1).

Mahmud II concurred with the pro-Greek Europeans in viewing Ottoman military reversals in Greece as a sign of profound weakness. With popular outrage over the military setbacks strong, the sultan made his move in 1826. First he announced the creation of a new artillery unit, which he had secretly been training. When the Janissaries rose in revolt, he ordered the new unit to bombard the Janissary barracks. The Janissary corps was officially dissolved.

Like Muhammad Ali, Mahmud felt he could not implement major changes without reducing the political power of the religious elite. He visualized restructuring the bureaucracy and the educational and legal systems, where ulama power was strongest. Before such strong measures could be undertaken, however, Ibrahim attacked from Syria in 1839. Battlefield defeat, the decision of the rebuilt Ottoman navy to switch sides and support Egypt, and the death of Mahmud, all in the same year, left the empire completely dependent on the European powers for survival.

Mahmud's reforming ideas received their widest expression in the **Tanzimat** (TAHNZ-ee-MAT) ("reorganization"), a series of reforms announced by his sixteen-year-old son and successor, Abdul Mejid (ab-dul meh-JEED), in 1839 and strongly endorsed by the European ambassadors. One proclamation called for public trials and equal protection under the law for all, whether Muslim, Christian, or Jew. It also guaranteed some rights of privacy, equalized the eligibility of men for conscription into the army (a practice copied from Egypt), and provided for a new, formalized

Tanzimat "Restructuring" reforms by the nineteenth-century Ottoman rulers, intended to move civil law away from the control of religious elites and make the military and the bureaucracy more efficient.

Map 21.1 The Ottoman and Russian Empires, 1829–1914

At its height the Ottoman Empire controlled most of the perimeter of the Mediterranean Sea. But in the 1800s Ottoman territory shrank as many countries gained their independence. The Black Sea, where the Turkish coast was vulnerable to assault, became a weak spot as Russian naval power grew. Russian challenges to the Ottomans at the eastern end of the Black Sea and to the Persians east and west of the Caspian aroused fears in Europe that Russia was trying to reach the Indian Ocean.

 Interactive Map

method of tax collection that legally ended tax farming in the Ottoman Empire. It took many years and strenuous efforts by reforming bureaucrats, known as the "men of the Tanzimat," to give substance to these reforms.

European observers praised the reforms for their noble principles and rejection of religious influence. Ottoman citizens were more divided; the Christians and Jews, for whom the Europeans showed the greatest concern, were generally more enthusiastic than the Muslims. Many historians see the Tanzimat as the dawn of modern thought and enlightened government in the Middle East. Others point out that removing the religious elite from influence in government also removed the one remaining check on authoritarian rule.

Over time, one legal code after another—commercial, criminal, civil procedure—was introduced to take the place of the corresponding areas of religious legal juris-

CL Primary Source: Imperial Rescript

Learn about the rights and freedoms granted to the Ottoman citizens during the first half of the nineteenth century.

diction. All the codes were modeled closely on those of Europe. The Shari'a, or Islamic law, gradually became restricted to matters of family law such as marriage and inheritance. As the Shari'a was displaced, job opportunities for the ulama shrank.

Like Muhammad Ali, Sultan Mahmud sent military cadets to France and the German states for training. In the 1830s an Ottoman imperial school of military sciences, later to become Istanbul University, was established. Instructors from western Europe taught chemistry, engineering, mathematics, and physics in addition to military history. Military education became the model for more general educational reforms. In 1838 the first medical school was established to train army doctors and surgeons. Later, a national system of preparatory schools was created to feed graduates into the military schools. The subjects that were taught and many of the teachers were foreign, raising the issue of whether Turkish should be a language of instruction. Because it was easier to import and use foreign textbooks than to write new ones in Turkish, French became the preferred language in all advanced professional and scientific training. In numerical terms, however, the great majority of students still learned to read and write in Quran schools down to the twentieth century.

Modernized Ottoman Troops

This photograph of a contingent of Imperial Guards in the late nineteenth century shows them equipped and uniformed much like any other European army of the time. The only distinctive feature is the fez, a brimless hat adopted earlier in the century as a symbol of reform.   (From one of the original photographic albums of Sultan Abdul Hamid II, 1842–1918/Library of Congress)

In the capital city of Istanbul, the reforms stimulated the growth of a small but cosmopolitan milieu embracing European language and culture. The first Turkish newspaper, a government gazette modeled on that of Muhammad Ali, appeared in 1831. Other newspapers followed, many written in French. Travel to Europe—particularly to England and France—became popular among wealthy Turks. Interest in importing European military, industrial, and communications technology remained strong through the 1800s.

Changes in military practice had unforeseen cultural and social effects. Accepting the European notion that modern weapons and drill required modern military dress, beards were deemed unhygienic and, in artillery units, a fire hazard. Military headgear also became controversial. European military caps, which had leather bills on the front to protect against the glare of the sun, were not acceptable because they interfered with Muslim soldiers' touching their foreheads to the ground in prayer. The compromise was the brimless cap now called the *fez*, which was adopted by the military and then by Ottoman civil officials in the early years of Mahmud II's reign.

The empire's new orientation spread beyond the military. Government ministries that normally recruited from traditional bureaucratic families and relied on on-the-job training were gradually transformed into formal civil services hiring men educated in the new schools. Among self-consciously progressive men, particularly those in government service, European dress became the fashion in the Ottoman cities of the later 1800s. Traditional dress became a symbol of the religious, the rural, and the parochial.

Secularization of the legal code particularly affected non-Muslim Ottoman subjects. Islamic law had required non-Muslims to pay a special head tax that was sometimes explained as a substitute for military service. Under the Tanzimat, the tax was abolished and non-Muslims became liable for military service—unless they bought their way out by paying a new military exemption tax. The new law codes gave all male subjects equal access to the civil courts, while the operations of the Islamic law courts shrank. What enhanced the status of non-Muslims most, however, was the strong concern for their welfare consistently expressed by the European powers. The Ottoman Empire became a rich field of operation for Christian missionaries and European supporters of Jewish community life in the Muslim world.

The public rights and political participation granted during the Tanzimat applied specifically to men. Private life, including everything connected to marriage and divorce, remained within the sphere of religious law, and at no time was there a question of political participation or reformed education for women. Indeed, the reforms may have decreased the influence of women. The political changes ran parallel to economic changes that also narrowed women's opportunities.

After silver from the Americas began to flood the empire in the 1600s, workers were increasingly paid in cash rather than in goods, and businesses associated with banking and finance developed. But women were barred from the early industrial labor and the professions, and traditional "woman's work" such as weaving was increasingly mechanized and done by men.

Nevertheless, in the early 1800s women retained considerable power in the management and disposal of their own property, gained mostly through fixed shares of inheritance. After marriage a woman was often pressured to convert her landholdings to cash in order to transfer her personal wealth to her husband's family, with

Primary Source: An Ottoman Government Decree Defines the Official Notion of the "Modern" Citizen, June 19, 1870 *Find out how progress and modernization among the Ottomans affected the area's nomadic tribespeople.*

Interior of the Ottoman Financial Bureau
This engraving from the eighteenth century depicts the governing style of the Ottoman Empire before the era of westernizing reforms. By the end of the Tanzimat period in 1876, government offices and the costumes of officials looked much more like those in contemporary European capitals.   (From Ignatius Mouradgea d'Ohsson, *Tableau General de l'Empire Ottoman,* large folio edition, Paris, 1787–1820, pl. 178, following p. 340)

whom she and her husband would reside. However, this was not a requirement, since men were legally obligated to support their families single-handedly. Until the 1820s many wealthy women retained their say in the distribution of property through the creation of charitable trusts for their sons. Because these trusts were set up in the religious courts, they could be designed to conform to the wishes of family members. Then, in the 1820s and 1830s the secularizing reforms of Mahmud II, which did not always produce happy results, transferred jurisdiction over the charitable trusts from religious courts to the state and ended women's control over this form of property.

The Crimean War and Its Aftermath

Since the reign of Peter the Great (r. 1689–1725) the Russian Empire had been attempting to expand southward at the Ottomans' expense (see "Russia and Asia," below). By 1815 Russia had pried the Georgian region of the Caucasus away from the Ottomans, and the threat of Russian intervention had prevented the Ottomans from crushing Serbian independence. When Muhammad Ali's Egyptian army invaded Syria in 1833, Russia signed a treaty in support of the Ottomans. In return, the sultan recognized Russia's claim to being the protector of all of the empire's Orthodox subjects. This set the stage for an obscure dispute that resulted in war.

Bowing to British and French pressure, the sultan named France Protector of the Holy Sepulchre in Jerusalem in 1852. Russia protested, but the sultan held firm. So Russia invaded Ottoman territories in what is today Romania, and Britain and France went to war as allies of the sultan. The real causes of the war went beyond church quarrels in Jerusalem and involved diplomatic maneuvering among European powers over whether the Ottoman Empire should continue to exist and, if not, who should take over its territory. The Eastern Question was the simple name given to this complex issue. Though the powers, including Russia, had agreed to save the empire in 1839, Britain subsequently became suspicious of Russian ambitions.

Prominent anti-Russian politicians in Britain feared that Russia would threaten the British hold on India.

Between 1853 and 1856 the **Crimean** (cry-ME-uhn) **War** raged in Romania, on the Black Sea, and on the Crimean peninsula. Britain, France, and the Italian kingdom of Sardinia-Piedmont sided with the Ottomans. Austria mediated the outcome. Britain and France trapped the Russian fleet in the Black Sea, where its commanders decided to sink the ships to protect the approaches to Sevastopol, their main base in Crimea. An army largely made up of British and French troops landed and laid siege to the city. Official corruption and lack of railways hampered the Russians' attempts to supply their forces. On the Romanian front, the Ottomans resisted effectively. At Sevastopol, the Russians were outmatched militarily and suffered badly from disease. Tsar Nicholas died as defeat loomed, leaving his successor, Alexander II (r. 1855–1881), to sue for peace when Sevastopol finally fell three months later.

The Crimean War brought significant changes to all the combatants. The tsar and his government, already beset by demands for the reform of serfdom, education, and the military (discussed later), were further discredited. In Britain and France, the conflict was accompanied by massive propaganda campaigns. For the first time newspapers effectively mobilized public support for a war. British press accounts so glamorized British participation that the false impression has lingered that Ottoman troops played a negligible role in the conflict. At the time, however, British and French commanders noted the massive losses among Turkish troops in particular. The French press, dominant in Istanbul, promoted a sense of unity between Turkish and French society that continued to influence many aspects of Turkish urban culture.

The larger significance of the Crimean War was that it marked the transition from traditional to modern warfare. All the combatants had previously prided themselves on the use of highly trained cavalry to smash through the front lines of infantry. Cavalry coexisted with firearms until the early 1800s, primarily because early rifles were awkward to load and not very accurate. Cavalry could attack during the intervals between volleys. Then in the 1830s and 1840s percussion caps that did away with pouring gunpowder into the barrel of a musket came into use. In Crimean War battles many cavalry units were destroyed by the rapid fire of rifles that loaded at the breech rather than down the barrel. That was the fate of the famed British Light Brigade, which was sent to relieve an Ottoman unit surrounded by Russian troops.

After the Crimean War, the Ottoman Empire increased its involvement with European commerce. The Ottoman imperial bank was founded in 1840, and a few years later currency reform pegged the value of Ottoman gold coins to the British pound. Sweeping changes in the 1850s expedited the creation of banks, insurance companies, and legal firms throughout the empire. Bustling trade also encouraged a migration from country to city between about 1850 and 1880. Many of the major cities of the empire—Istanbul, Damascus, Beirut, Alexandria, Cairo—expanded. A small but influential urban professional class emerged, as did a considerable class of wage laborers. Other demographic shifts involved refugees from Poland and Hungary, where rivalry between the European powers and the Russian Empire caused political tension and sporadic warfare, and from Georgia and other parts of the Caucasus, where Russian expansion forced many Muslims to emigrate (discussed later).

Crimean War (1853–1856)
Conflict between the Russian and Ottoman Empires fought primarily in the Crimean peninsula. To prevent Russian expansion, Britain and France sent troops to support the Ottomans.

SECTION REVIEW

- After French withdrawal from Egypt, Muhammad Ali seized control and began a French-influenced modernization program.

- His successors continued the program and attacked the Ottoman Empire, but they were thwarted by the European powers.

- The Greek insurrection, European intervention, and Egyptian attack drove the westernizing reform efforts of Mahmud II and his successors.

- The most comprehensive reform initiative was Abdul Mejid's Tanzimat program.

- The Crimean War marked the transition from traditional to modern warfare and drew the Ottoman Empire into greater involvement with European commerce.

- Declining power and prosperity led to the rise of the Young Ottomans.

extraterritoriality The right of foreign residents in a country to live under the laws of their native country and disregard the laws of the host country. In the nineteenth and early twentieth centuries, European and American nationals living in certain areas of Chinese and Ottoman cities were granted this right.

Young Ottomans Movement of young intellectuals to institute liberal reforms and build a feeling of national identity in the Ottoman Empire in the second half of the nineteenth century.

However, commercial vigor and urbanization could not make up for declining revenues and the chronic insolvency and corruption of the imperial government. From the conclusion of the Crimean War in 1856 on, the Ottoman government became heavily dependent on foreign loans. In return it lowered tariffs to favor European imports and allowed European banks to open in Ottoman cities. Europeans living in Istanbul and other commercial centers enjoyed **extraterritoriality**, the right to be subject to their own laws and exempt from Ottoman jurisdiction.

As the result of these measures, imported goods multiplied, but—apart from tobacco and the Turkish opium that American traders took to China to compete against British opium from India—Anatolia produced few exports. As foreign debt grew, so did inflationary trends that left urban populations in a precarious position. By contrast, Egyptian cotton exports soared during the American Civil War, when American cotton exports plummeted; but the profits benefited Muhammad Ali's descendants, who had become the hereditary governors of Egypt, rather than the Ottoman government. The Suez Canal, which was partly financed by cotton profits, opened in 1869, and Cairo was redesigned and beautified. Eventually overexpenditure on such projects plunged Egypt into the same debt crisis that plagued the empire as a whole.

The decline of Ottoman power and prosperity had a strong impact on a group of well-educated young urban men who aspired to wealth and influence. They doubted that the empire's rulers and the Tanzimat officials who worked for them would ever stand up to European domination. Though lacking a sophisticated organization, these **Young Ottomans** (sometimes called Young Turks, though that term properly applies to a later movement) promoted a mixture of liberal ideas derived from Europe, national pride in Ottoman independence, and modernist views of Islam. Prominent Young Ottomans helped draft a constitution that was promulgated in 1876 by a new and as yet untried sultan, Abdul Hamid II. This apparent triumph of liberal reform was short-lived. With war against Russia again threatening in the Balkans in 1877, Abdul Hamid suspended the constitution and the parliament that had been elected that year. Though he ruthlessly opposed further political reforms, the Tanzimat programs of extending modern schooling, utilizing European military practices and advisers, and making the government bureaucracy more orderly continued during his reign.

THE RUSSIAN EMPIRE

How did the Russian Empire maintain its status as both a European power and a great Asian land empire?

In 1812, when Napoleon's march on Moscow ended in a disastrous retreat brought on more by what a later tsar called "Generals January and February" than by Russian military action, the European image of Russia changed. Just as Napoleon's withdrawal from Egypt led to Muhammad Ali briefly becoming a political power, so his withdrawal from Russia conferred status on Tsar Alexander I (r. 1801–1825). Conservative Europeans still saw Russia as alien, backward, and oppressive, but they acknowledged its immensity and potential and included the tsar in efforts to suppress revolutionary tendencies throughout Europe.

In several important respects Russia resembled the Ottoman Empire more than the conservative kingdoms of Europe whose autocratic practices it so staunchly supported. Socially dominated by nobles whose country estates were worked by unfree serfs, Russia had almost no middle class. Industry was still at the threshold of development by the standards of the rapidly industrializing European powers, though it was somewhat more dynamic than Ottoman industry. Like Egypt and the Ottoman Empire, Russia engaged in reforms from the top down under Alexander I, but when his conservative brother Nicholas I (r. 1825–1855) succeeded to the throne, iron discipline and suspicion of modern ideas took priority over reform.

Russia and Europe

In 1700 only three Russians out of a hundred lived in cities, two-thirds of them in Moscow alone. By the mid-1800s the town population had grown tenfold, though it still accounted for only 6 percent of the total because the territories of the tsars had grown greatly through wars and colonization (see Chapter 18). These figures demonstrate that, like the Ottoman Empire, Russia was an overwhelmingly agricultural land. However, it had poorer transportation than the Ottoman Empire, since many Ottoman cities were seaports. Both empires encompassed peoples speaking many different languages.

Well-engineered roads did not begin to appear until 1817, and steam navigation commenced on the Volga in 1843. Tsar Nicholas I built the first railroad from St. Petersburg, the Russian capital, to his summer palace in 1837. A few years later his commitment to strict discipline led him to insist that the trunk line from St. Petersburg to Moscow run in a perfectly straight line. American engineers, among them the father of the painter James McNeill Whistler, who learned to paint in St. Petersburg, oversaw the laying of track and built locomotive workshops. Industrialization projects depended heavily on foreign expertise. British engineers set up the textile mills that gave woolens and cottons a prominent place among Russia's industries.

Until the late nineteenth century the Russian government's interest in industry was limited. An industrial revolution required educated and independent-minded artisans and entrepreneurs, but Nicholas feared the spread of literacy and modern education—especially anything smacking of liberalism, socialism, or revolution—beyond the minimum needed to train the officer corps and the bureaucracy. He preferred serfs to factory workers, and he paid for imported industrial goods with exports of grain and timber.

Like Egypt and the Ottoman Empire, Russia aspired to Western-style economic development. But when France and Britain entered the Crimean War, they faced a Russian army equipped with obsolete weapons and bogged down by lack of transportation. At a time when European engineers were making major breakthroughs in loading cannon through an opening at the breech end, muzzle-loading artillery remained the Russian standard.

Yet in some ways Russia bore a closer resemblance to other European countries than the Ottoman Empire did. From the point of view of the French and the British, the Cyrillic alphabet and the Russian Orthodox form of Christianity seemed foreign, but they were not nearly as foreign as the Arabic alphabet and the Muslim faith. Britain and France feared Russia as a rival for power in the east, but they increasingly accepted Tsar Nicholas's view of the Ottoman Empire as "the sick man of Europe," capable of surviving only so long as the European powers permitted.

From the Russian point of view, kinship with western Europe was of questionable value. Westernizers, like the men of the Tanzimat in the Ottoman Empire, put their trust in technical advances and governmental reform. Opposing them were intellectuals known as **Slavophiles**, who considered the Orthodox faith, the solidity of peasant life, and the tsar's absolute rule to be the proper bases of Russian civilization. After Russia's humiliation in the Crimea, the Slavophile tendency gave rise to **Pan-Slavism**, a militant political doctrine advocating unity of all the Slavic peoples, including those living under Austrian and Ottoman rule.

On the diplomatic front, the tsar's inclusion as a major European ruler contrasted sharply with the sultan's exclusion. However, this did not prevent a powerful sense of Russophobia from developing in the West. Britain in particular saw Russia as a threat to India and despised the subjection of the serfs, who gained their freedom from Tsar Alexander II only in 1861, twenty-seven years after the British had abolished slavery. The passions generated by the Crimean War and its outcome affected the relations of Russia, Europe, and the Ottoman Empire for the remainder of the nineteenth century.

Slavophiles Russian intellectuals in the early nineteenth century who favored resisting western European influences and taking pride in the traditional peasant values and institutions of the Slavic people.

Pan-Slavism Movement among Russian intellectuals in the second half of the nineteenth century to identify culturally and politically with the Slavic peoples of eastern Europe.

Russia and Asia

The Russian drive to the east in the eighteenth century brought the tsar's empire to the Pacific Ocean and the frontiers of China (see Map 18.2) by century's end. In the nineteenth century Russian expansionism focused on the south. There the backwardness of the Russian military did not matter since the peoples they faced were even less industrialized and technologically advanced. In 1860 Russia established a military outpost on the Pacific coast that would eventually grow into the great naval port of Vladivostok, today Russia's most southerly city. In Central Asia the steppe lands of the Kazakh nomads came under Russian control early in the century, setting the stage for a confrontation with three Uzbek states farther south. They succumbed one by one, beginning in 1865, giving rise to the new province of Turkestan, with its capital at Tashkent in present-day Uzbekistan. In the region of the Caucasus Mountains, the third area of southward expansion, Russia first took over Christian Georgia (1786), Muslim Azerbaijan (ah-zer-by-JAHN) (1801), and Christian Armenia (1813) before gobbling up the many small principalities in the heart of the mountains. Between 1829 and 1864 Dagestan, Chechnya (CHECH-nee-yah), Abkhazia (ab-KAH-zee-yah), and other regions that would one day gain political prominence after the breakup of the Soviet Union became parts of the Russian Empire.

The drive to the south intensified political friction with Russia's new neighbors: Qing China and Japan in the east, Iran on the Central Asian and Caucasus frontiers, and the Ottoman Empire at the eastern end of the Black Sea. In the latter two instances, Muslim refugees from the territories newly absorbed by Russia spread anti-Russian feelings, though some of them brought with them modern skills and ideas gained from exposure to Russian administration and education.

CL Primary Source: The Treaty of Peace and Commerce (Treaty of Turkmanchai) Between Iran and Russia, February 10–22, 1828 *Learn details of the agreement through which Russia and Iran resolve to live in peace.*

The Russian drive to the south added a new element to the Eastern Question. Many British statesmen and strategists reckoned that a warlike Russia would press on until it had conquered all the lands separating it from British India, a prospect that made them shudder, given India's enormous contribution to Britain's prosperity. The competition that ensued over which power would control southern Central Asia resulted in a standoff in Afghanistan, which became a buffer zone under the control of neither. In Iran, the standoff between the powers helped preserve the weak Qajar dynasty of shahs.

Cultural Trends

Unlike Egypt and the Ottoman Empire, which began to send students to Europe for training only in the nineteenth century, Russia had been in cultural contact with western Europe since the time of Peter the Great (r. 1689–1725). Members of the Russian court knew Western languages, and the tsars employed officials and advisers from Western countries. Peter had also enlisted the well-educated Ukrainian clerics who headed the Russian Orthodox Church to help spread a Western spirit of education. As a result, Alexander I's reforms met a more positive reception than those of Muhammad Ali and Mahmud II. However, his reforms promised more on paper than they brought about in practice. It took many years to develop a sufficient pool of trained bureaucrats to make the reforms effective.

Ironically, much of the opposition to Alexander's reforms came from well-established families that were not at all unfriendly to Western ideas. Their fear was

Raising of the Alexander Monument in St. Petersburg
The death of Alexander I in 1825 brought to power his conservative brother Nicholas I. Yet Alexander remained a heroic figure for his resistance to Napoleon. This monument in Winter Palace Square was erected in 1829.
(Visual Connection Library)

that the new government bureaucrats, who often came from humbler social origins, would act as agents of imperial tyranny. This fear was realized during the conservative reign of Nicholas I in the same way that the Tanzimat-inspired bureaucracy of the Ottoman Empire served the despotic purposes of Sultan Abdul Hamid II after 1877. Individuals favoring more liberal reforms, including military officers who had served in western Europe, intellectuals who read Western political tracts, and members of Masonic lodges who exchanged views with Freemasons in the West, formed secret societies of opposition. Some placed their highest priority on freeing the serfs; others advocated a constitution and a republican form of government. When Alexander I died in December 1825, confusion over who was to succeed him encouraged a group of reform-minded army officers to try to take over the government and provoke an uprising. The so-called **Decembrist revolt** failed, and many of the participants were severely punished. These events ensured that the new tsar, Nicholas I, would pay little heed to calls for reform over the next thirty years.

The great powers meeting in Paris to settle the Crimean War in 1856 forced Russia to return land to the Ottomans in both Europe and Asia. This humiliation spurred Nicholas's son and successor, Alexander II (r. 1855–1881), to institute major new reforms to reinvigorate the country. The greatest of his reforms was the emancipation of the serfs in 1861. He also authorized new joint-stock companies, projected a railroad network to tie the country together, and modernized the legal and administrative arms of government.

Earlier intellectual and cultural trends flourished under Alexander II. More and more people became involved in intellectual, artistic, and professional life. Most prominent intellectuals received some amount of instruction at Moscow University or some German university. Universities also appeared in provincial cities like Kharkov in Ukraine and Kazan on the Volga River. Student clubs, along with Masonic lodges, became places for discussing new ideas. As Russian scholars and scientists began to achieve recognition for their contributions to European thought, scholarly careers attracted young men from clerical families, who in turn helped stimulate reforms in religious education.

Just as the Tanzimat reforms of the Ottoman Empire preceded the emergence of the Young Ottomans as a new and assertive political and intellectual force in the second half of the nineteenth century, so the initially ineffective reforms of Alexander I set in motion cultural currents that would make Russia a dynamic center of intellectual, artistic, and political life under his nephew Alexander II. Thus Russia belonged to two different spheres of development. It entered the nineteenth century a recognized force in European politics, but in other ways it resembled the Ottoman Empire. Rulers in both empires instituted reforms, overcame opposition, and increased the power of their governments. These activities stimulated intellectual and political trends that would ultimately work against the absolute rule of tsar and sultan. Yet Russia would eventually develop much closer relations with western Europe and become an arena for every sort of European intellectual, artistic, and political tendency, while the Ottoman Empire would ultimately succumb to European imperialism.

Decembrist revolt Abortive attempt by army officers to take control of the Russian government upon the death of Tsar Alexander I in 1825.

SECTION REVIEW

- Russian society resembled Ottoman society, but Alexander I undertook top-down westernizing reforms.

- Nicholas I's suspicion of Western ideas stalled reform and slowed industrial development.

- Slavophiles opposed westernizers and, after the Crimean War, embraced Pan-Slavism, contributing to Russophobia in the West.

- Russian expansion southward and eastward added vast territories to the empire and caused friction with China, Japan, Iran, and the Ottoman Empire.

- Resistance to Alexander I's bureaucratic reforms sparked the Decembrist revolt, which stiffened Nicholas I's hostility to Western ideas.

- The humiliation of the Crimean War drove Alexander II's reforms, including emancipation of the serfs.

THE QING EMPIRE

How did the impact of European imperialism on China differ from its impact on Russia and the Ottoman Empire?

In 1800 the Qing Empire faced many problems, but no reform movement of the kind initiated by Sultan Selim III emerged in China. The reasons are not difficult to understand. The Qing emperors had skillfully countered Russian strategic and diplomatic moves in the 1600s. Instead of having a Napoleon threatening them with invasion, they enjoyed the admiration of Jesuit priests, who likened them to enlightened philosopher-kings. In 1793, however, a British attempt to establish diplomatic and trade relations—the Macartney mission—turned European opinion against China (see Chapter 18).

China's most serious crises were domestic, not foreign: rebellions by displaced indigenous peoples and the poor, and protests against the injustice of the local magistrates. The Qing dealt with these problems in the usual way, by suppressing rebels and dismissing incompetent or untrustworthy officials. They paid little attention to the far-off Europeans and brushed aside the complaints from European merchants who chafed against the restrictions of the "Canton system" by which the Qing limited and controlled foreign trade.

Economic and Social Disorder

Early Qing successes and territorial expansion sowed the seeds of the domestic and political chaos of the later period. The early emperors encouraged the recovery of farmland, the opening of previously uncultivated areas, and the restoration and expansion of the road and canal systems. These measures expanded the agricultural base and supported a doubling of the population between about 1650 and 1800. Enormous numbers of farmers, merchants, and day laborers migrated in search of less crowded conditions, and a permanent floating population of the unemployed and homeless emerged. By 1800 population strain had caused serious environmental damage in some parts of central and western China.

While farmers tried to cope with agricultural deterioration, other groups vented grievances against the government: minority peoples in central and southwestern China complained about being driven off their lands during the boom of the 1700s; Mongols resented appropriation of their grazing lands and the displacement of their traditional elites. In some regions, village vigilante organizations took over policing and governing functions from Qing officials who had lost control. Growing numbers of people mistrusted the government, suspecting that all officials were corrupt. The increasing presence of foreign merchants and missionaries in Canton and in the Portuguese colony of Macao aggravated discontent in neighboring districts.

In some parts of China the Qing were hated as foreign conquerors and were suspected of sympathy with the Europeans. In 1794 the White Lotus Rebellion—partly inspired by a messianic ideology that predicted the restoration of the Chinese Ming dynasty and the coming of the Buddha—raged across central China and was not suppressed until 1804. It initiated a series of internal conflicts that continued through the 1800s. Ignited by deepening social instabilities, these movements were sometimes intensified by local ethnic conflicts and by unapproved religions. The ability of some village militias to defend themselves and attack others intensified the conflicts, though the same techniques proved useful to southern coastal populations attempting to fend off British invasion.

The Opium War and Its Aftermath, 1839–1850

Unlike the Ottomans, the Qing knew little about the enormous fortunes being made in the early 1800s by European and American merchants smuggling opium into China. They did not know that silver gained in this illegal trade was helping finance the industrial transformation of England and the United States. Only slowly did Qing officials become aware of British colonies in India that grew and exported opium, and of the major naval base at Singapore through which British opium reached East Asia.

In 1729 the first Qing law banning opium imports was promulgated. By 1800, however, opium smuggling had swelled the annual import level to as many as four thousand chests. Though British merchants had pioneered this profitable trade, Chinese merchants likewise profited from distributing the drugs. A price war in the

Military Modernization in China
The Opium War revealed a serious technology gap between the Manchu Bannermen and the British troops. Many Bannermen still fought with swords and spears as they had in the eighteenth century. After the war China adopted a variety of Western weapons. This later photograph from the Nanjing arsenal shows a Gatling gun. Invented during the American Civil War (1860–1865) by Dr. Richard J. Gatling, each barrel discharged a single shot as the operator turned a crank to make the firing continuous.   (© British Library Board)

early 1820s stemming from competition between British and American importers raised demand so sharply that as many as thirty thousand chests were being imported by the 1830s. Addiction spread to people at all levels of Qing society, including high-ranking officials. The Qing emperor and his officials debated whether to legalize and tax opium or to enforce the existing ban more strictly. Having decided to root out the use and importation of opium, in 1839 they sent a high official to Canton to deal with the matter.

Britain considered the ban on opium importation an intolerable limitation on trade, a direct threat to Britain's economic health, and a cause for war. British naval and marine forces arrived on the south China coast in late 1839. The **Opium War** (1839–1842) broke out when negotiations between the Qing official and British representatives reached a stalemate. The war exposed the fact that the traditional, hereditary soldiers of the Qing Empire—the **Bannermen**—were, like the Janissaries of the Ottoman Empire, hopelessly obsolete. As in the Crimean War, the British excelled at sea, where they deployed superior technology. British ships landed marines who pillaged coastal cities and then sailed to new destinations (see Map 21.2). The Qing had no imperial navy. Thus until they were able to engage the British in prolonged fighting on land, they were unable to defend themselves against British attacks. Even in the land engagements, Qing resources proved woefully inadequate. The British could quickly transport their forces by sea along the coast; Qing troops moved primarily on foot. Moving Qing reinforcements from central to eastern China took more than three months; and when the defense forces arrived, they were exhausted and basically without weapons.

The Bannermen used the few muskets the Qing had imported during the 1700s. The weapons were matchlocks, which required the soldiers to ignite the load of gunpowder in them by hand. Firing the weapons was dangerous, and the canisters of gunpowder that each musketeer carried on his belt were likely to explode if a fire broke out nearby—a frequent occurrence in encounters with British artillery. Most of the Bannermen, however, had no guns at all and fought with swords, knives, spears, and clubs. Soldiers under British command—many of them Indians—carried percussion-cap rifles, which were far quicker, safer, and more accurate than the matchlocks. In addition, the long-range British artillery could be moved from place to place and proved deadly in the cities and villages of eastern China.

Qing commanders thought that British gunboats rode so low in the water that they could not sail up the Chinese rivers. So they evacuated the coastal areas to counter the British threat. But the British deployed new gunboats for shallow waters and moved without difficulty up the Yangzi River (see Chapter 20).

When the invaders approached Nanjing, the former Ming capital, the Qing decided to negotiate. In 1842 the terms of the **Treaty of Nanking** (the British name for Nanjing) dismantled the old Canton system. The number of **treaty ports**—cities opened to foreign residents—increased from one (Canton) to five (Canton, Xiamen, Fuzhou, Ningbo, and Shanghai [shahng-hie]). The island of Hong Kong became a British colony, and British residents in China gained extraterritorial rights. The Qing government agreed to set a low tariff of 5 percent on imports and to pay Britain an indemnity of 21 million ounces of silver as a penalty for having started the war. A supplementary treaty the following year guaranteed **most-favored-nation status** to Britain: any privileges that China granted to another country would be

Primary Source: Letter to Queen Victoria, 1839
Read Lin Zexu's stern warning to England about the consequences of continuing to bring opium into China.

Opium War (1839–1842) War between Britain and the Qing Empire that was, in the British view, occasioned by the Qing government's refusal to permit the importation of opium into its territories. The victorious British imposed the one-sided Treaty of Nanking on China.

Bannermen Hereditary military servants of the Qing Empire, in large part descendants of peoples of various origins who had fought for the founders of the empire.

Treaty of Nanking (1842) The treaty that concluded the Opium War. It awarded Britain a large indemnity from the Qing Empire, denied the Qing government tariff control over some of its own borders, opened additional ports of residence to Britons, and ceded the island of Hong Kong to Britain.

treaty ports Cities opened to foreign residents as a result of the forced treaties between the Qing Empire and foreign signatories. In the treaty ports, foreigners enjoyed extraterritoriality.

most-favored-nation status A clause in a commercial treaty that awards to any later signatories all the privileges previously granted to the original signatories.

Areas of Taiping rebellion
- 1853–1857
- 1857–1863
- Areas of Nian rebellion, 1853–1868
- Areas of Muslim revolts, 1855–1873

← British attacks during the Opium War, 1839–1842
← British and French attacks during the Arrow War, 1858–1860
✦ Conflicts with Romanovs, 1850s
■ Treaty ports

Map 21.2   Conflicts in the Qing Empire, 1839–1870

In both the Opium War of 1839–1842 and the Arrow War of 1856–1860, the seacoasts saw most of the action. Since the Qing had no imperial navy, the well-armed British ships encountered little resistance as they shelled the southern coasts. In inland conflicts, such as the Taiping Rebellion, the opposing armies were massive and slow moving. Battles on land were often prolonged attempts by one side to starve out the other side before making a major assault.

 Interactive Map

automatically extended to Britain as well. This provision effectively prevented the colonization of China, because giving land to one country would have necessitated giving it to all.

With each round of treaties came a new round of privileges for foreigners. In 1860 a new treaty legalized their right to import opium. Later, French treaties established the rights of foreign missionaries to travel in the Chinese countryside and preach their religion. The number of treaty ports grew, too; by 1900 they numbered more than ninety.

The treaty system and the principle of extraterritoriality resulted in the colonization of small pockets of Qing territory, where foreign merchants lived at ease.

Greater territorial losses resulted when outlying regions gained independence or were ceded to neighboring countries. Districts north and south of the Amur River in the northeast fell to Russia by treaty in 1858 and 1860; parts of modern Kazakhstan and Kirgizstan in the northwest met the same fate in 1864. From 1865 onward the British gradually gained control of territories on China's Indian frontier. In the late 1800s France forced the court of Vietnam to end its tribute relationship to the Qing, while Britain encouraged Tibetan independence.

In Canton, Shanghai, and other coastal cities, Europeans and Americans maintained offices and factories that employed local Chinese as menial laborers. The foreigners built comfortable housing in zones where Chinese were not permitted to live, and they entertained themselves in exclusive restaurants and bars. Around the foreign establishments, gambling and prostitution offered employment to part of the local urban population.

Whether in town or in the countryside, Christian missionaries whose congregations sponsored hospitals, shelters, and soup kitchens or gave stipends to Chinese who attended church enjoyed a good reputation. But just as often the missionaries themselves were regarded as another evil. They seemed to subvert Confucian beliefs by condemning ancestor worship, pressuring poor families to put their children into orphanages, or fulminating against footbinding. The growing numbers of foreigners, and their growing privileges, became targets of resentment for a deeply dissatisfied, daily more impoverished, and increasingly militarized society.

The Taiping Rebellion, 1850–1864

The inflammatory mixture of social unhappiness and foreign intrusion exploded in the great civil war usually called the **Taiping** (tie-PING) **Rebellion**. In Guangxi, where the Taiping movement originated, entrenched social problems had been generating disorders for half a century. Agriculture in the region was unstable, and many people made their living from arduous and despised trades such as disposing of human waste, making charcoal, and mining. Ethnic divisions complicated economic distress. The lowliest trades frequently involved a minority group, the Hakkas, and tensions between them and the majority were rising. Problems may have been intensified by sharp fluctuations in the opium trade and reactions to the cultural and economic impact of the Europeans and Americans in Canton.

Hong Xiuquan (hoong shee-OH-chew-an), the founder of the Taiping movement, experienced all of these influences. Hong came from a humble Hakka background. After years of study, he competed in the provincial Confucian examinations, hoping for a post in government. He failed the examinations repeatedly, and it appears that he suffered a nervous breakdown in his late thirties. Afterward he spent some time in Canton, where he met both Chinese and American Protestant missionaries, who inspired him with their teachings. Hong had his own interpretation of the Christian message. He saw himself as the younger brother of Jesus, commissioned by God to found a new kingdom on earth and drive the Manchu conquerors, the Qing, out of China. The result would be universal peace. Hong called his new religious movement the "Heavenly Kingdom of Great Peace."

Hong quickly attracted a community of believers, primarily Hakkas like himself. They believed in the prophecy of dreams and claimed they could walk on air. Hong and his rivals for leadership in the movement went in and out of ecstatic

Taiping Rebellion (1850–1864) The most destructive civil war before the twentieth century. A Christian-inspired rural rebellion threatened to topple the Qing Empire.

Nanjing Encircled

For a decade the Taipings held the city of Nanjing as their capital. For years Qing and international troops attempted to break the Taiping hold. By the summer of 1864, Qing forces had built tunnels leading to the foundations of Nanjing's city walls and had planted explosives. The detonation of the explosives signaled the final Qing assault on the rebel capital. As shown here, the common people of the city, along with their starving livestock, were caught in the crossfire. Many of the Taiping leaders escaped the debacle at Nanjing, but nearly all were hunted down and executed.   (Roger-Viollet/Getty Images)

CL HISTORY IN FOCUS   Examine the image "Nanjing Encircled," paying particular attention to how it depicts warfare in nineteenth-century China. What does it tell you about the disadvantages of the Qing Empire in the face of Western imperialism? *Find the answer online.*

trances. They denounced the Manchus as creatures of Satan. News of the sect reached the government, and Qing troops arrived to arrest the Taiping leaders. But the Taipings soundly repelled the imperial troops. Local loyalty to the Taipings spread quickly, their numbers multiplied, and they began to enlarge their domain.

The Taipings relied at first on Hakka sympathy and the charismatic appeal of their religious doctrine to attract followers. But as their numbers and power grew, they altered their methods of preaching and governing. They replaced the anti-Chinese appeals used to enlist Hakkas with anti-Manchu rhetoric designed to enlist Chinese. They forced captured villages to join their movement. Once people were absorbed, the Taipings strictly monitored their activities. They segregated men and women and organized them into work and military teams. Women were forbidden to bind their feet (the Hakkas had never practiced footbinding) and participated fully in farming and labor. Brigades of women soldiers took to the field against Qing forces.

As the movement grew, it began to move toward eastern and northern China (see Map 21.2). Panic preceded the Taipings. Villagers feared being forced into Taiping units, and Confucian elites recoiled in horror from the bizarre ideology of foreign gods, totalitarian rule, and walking, working, warring women. But the huge numbers the Taipings were able to muster overwhelmed attempts at local defense. The tremendous growth in the number of Taiping followers required the movement to establish a permanent base. When the rebel army conquered Nanjing in 1853, the Taiping leaders decided to settle there and make it the capital of the new "Heavenly Kingdom of Great Peace."

Qing forces attempting to defend north China became more successful as problems of organization and growing numbers slowed Taiping momentum. Increasing Qing military success resulted mainly from the flexibility of the imperial military commanders in the face of an unprecedented challenge. In addition, the military commanders received strong backing from a group of civilian provincial governors who had studied the techniques developed by local militia forces for self-defense. Certain provincial governors combined their knowledge of civilian self-defense and local terrain with more efficient organization and the use of modern weaponry. The result was the formation of new military units, in which many of the Bannermen voluntarily served under civilian governors. The Qing court agreed to special taxes to fund the new armies and acknowledged the new combined leadership.

When the Taipings settled into Nanjing, the new Qing armies surrounded the city, hoping to starve out the rebels. The Taipings, however, had provisioned and fortified themselves well. They also had the services of several brilliant young military commanders, who mobilized enormous campaigns in nearby parts of eastern China, scavenging supplies and attempting to break the encirclement of Nanjing. For more than a decade the Taiping leadership remained ensconced at Nanjing, and the "Heavenly Kingdom" endured.

In 1856 Britain and France, freed from their preoccupation with the Crimean War, turned their attention to China. European and American missionaries had visited Nanjing, curious to see what their fellow Christians were up to. Their reports were discouraging. Hong Xiuquan and the other leaders appeared to lead lives of indulgence and abandon, and more than one missionary accused them of homosexual practices. Relieved of the possible accusation of quashing a pious Christian movement, the British and French surveyed the situation. Though the Taipings were not going to topple the Qing, rebellious Nian ("Bands") in northern China added a new threat in the 1850s. A series of simultaneous large insurrections might indeed destroy the empire. Moreover, since the Qing had not observed all the provisions of the treaties signed after the Opium War, Britain and France were now considering renewing war on the Qing themselves.

In 1856 the British and French launched a series of swift, brutal coastal attacks— a second opium war, called the Arrow War (1856–1860)—which culminated in a British and French invasion of Beijing and the sacking of the Summer Palace in 1860. A new round of treaties punished the Qing for not enacting all the provisions of the Treaty of Nanking. Having secured their principal objective, the British and French forces then joined the Qing campaign against the Taipings. Attempts to co-ordinate the international forces were sometimes riotous and sometimes tragic, but the injection of European weaponry and money helped quell both the Taiping and the Nian rebellions during the 1860s.

The Taiping Rebellion ranks as the world's bloodiest civil war and the greatest armed conflict before the twentieth century. Estimates of deaths range from 20 million to 30 million. The loss of life came primarily from starvation and disease, for most engagements consisted of surrounding fortified cities and waiting until the enemy forces died, surrendered, or were so weakened that they could be easily defeated. Many sieges continued for months. Reports of people eating grass, leather, hemp, and human flesh were widespread. The dead were rarely buried properly, and epidemic disease was common.

The area of early Taiping fighting was close to the regions of southwest China in which bubonic plague had been lingering for centuries. When the rebellion was suppressed, many Taiping followers sought safety in the highlands of Laos and Vietnam, which soon showed infestation by plague. Within a few years the disease reached Hong Kong. From there it spread to Singapore, San Francisco, Calcutta, and London. In the late 1800s there was intense apprehension over the possibility of a world-wide outbreak, and Chinese immigrants were regarded as likely carriers. This fear became a contributing factor in the passage of discriminatory immigration bans on Chinese in the United States in 1882.

The Taiping Rebellion devastated the agricultural centers of China. Many of the most intensely cultivated regions of central and eastern China were depopulated. Some were still uninhabited decades later, and major portions of the country did not recover until the twentieth century.

Cities, too, were hard hit. Shanghai, a treaty port of modest size before the rebellion, saw its population multiplied many times by the arrival of refugees from war-blasted neighboring provinces. The city then endured months of siege by the Taipings. Major cultural centers in eastern China lost masterpieces of art and architecture; imperial libraries were burned or their collections exposed to the weather; and the printing blocks used to make books were destroyed. While the empire faced the mountainous challenge of dealing with the material and cultural destruction of the war, it also was burdened by a major ecological disaster in the north. The Yellow River changed course in 1855, destroying the southern part of impoverished Shandong province with flood and initiating decades of drought along the former riverbed in northern Shandong.

Decentralization at the End of the Qing Empire, 1864–1875

The Qing government emerged from the 1850s with no hope of achieving solvency. The corruption of the 1700s, attempts in the very early 1800s to restore waterworks and roads, and declining yields from land taxes had bank-rupted the treasury. By 1850, before the Taiping Rebellion, Qing government expenditures were ten times revenues. The indemnities demanded by Europeans after the Opium and Arrow Wars compounded the problem. Vast stretches of formerly productive rice land were devastated, and the population was dispersed. Refugees pleaded

Trade Warehouse in Guangzhou
A European merchant enters in background while Chinese workers pack tea and porcelain. (Peabody Essex Museum, Salem, Massachusetts/The Bridgeman Art Library)

for relief, and the imperial, volunteer, foreign, and mercenary troops that had suppressed the Taipings demanded unpaid wages.

Britain and France became active participants in the period of recovery that followed the rebellion (see Diversity and Dominance: Chinese Responses to Imperialism). To ensure repayment of the debt to Britain, Robert Hart was installed as inspector-general of a newly created Imperial Maritime Customs Service. Britain and the Qing split the revenues he collected. Britons and Americans worked for the Qing government as advisers and ambassadors, attempting to smooth communications between the Qing, Europe, and the United States.

The real work of the recovery, however, was managed by provincial governors who had come to the forefront in the struggle against the Taipings. To prosecute the war, they had won the right to levy their own taxes, raise their own troops, and run their own bureaucracies. These special powers were not entirely canceled when the war ended. Chief

SECTION REVIEW

- Social unrest grew in Qing China through a combination of discontent among the poor and displaced indigenous peoples and resentment of growing European influence.

- Qing attempts to ban opium imports provoked the Opium War with Britain, which exposed Qing military inferiority.

- The Treaty of Nanking gave extraterritoriality and other privileges to Britain and led to further losses to other Western powers.

- Social resentment and foreign intrusion ignited the Taiping Rebellion, which, after the Arrow War, the Qing quelled with British and French aid.

- The rebellion encouraged epidemics, devastated agriculture, produced overcrowded cities filled with refugees, and coincided with environmental disasters.

- The rebellion and China's recovery afterward resulted in a process of decentralization led by reformist aristocrats.

Chinese Responses to Imperialism

The Opium War, followed by the Taiping Rebellion, revealed China's weakness for all to see, but there was no agreement on what should be done to restore its strength. A few provincial officials were able to take effective action, but the competing ideas that were heard at the imperial court tended to cancel each other out.

Feng Guifen, an official and a scholar, came into contact with Westerners defending Shanghai when he took refuge there from the Taipings. The following is from a book of essays he published in 1861.

According to a general geography compiled by an Englishman, the territory of China is eight times that of Russia, ten times that of the United States, one hundred times that of France, and two hundred times that of Great Britain. . . . Yet we are shamefully humiliated by the four nations, not because our climate, soil, or resources are inferior to theirs, but because our people are inferior. . . . Now, our inferiority is not due to our allotment from Heaven [i.e., our inherent nature], but is rather due to ourselves. . . .

Why are the Western nations small and yet strong? Why are we large and yet weak? We must search for the means to become their equal, and that depends solely upon human effort. . . .

We have only one thing to learn from the barbarians, and that is strong ships and effective guns. . . . Funds should be allotted to establish a shipyard and arsenal in each trading port. A few barbarians should be employed, and Chinese who are good in using their minds should be selected to receive instruction so that in turn they may teach many craftsmen. When a piece of work is finished and is as good as that made by the barbarians, the makers should be rewarded with an official *juren* degree and be permitted to participate in the metropolitan examinations on the same basis as other scholars. Those whose products are of superior quality should be rewarded with the *jinshi* degree [ordinarily conferred in the metropolitan examinations] and be permitted to participate in the palace examinations like others. The workers should be paid double so that they will not quit their jobs.

Our nation's emphasis on civil service examinations has sunk deep into people's minds for a long time. Intelligent and brilliant scholars have exhausted their time and energy in such useless things as the stereotyped examination essays, examination papers, and formal calligraphy. . . . We should now order one-half of them to apply themselves to the manufacturing of instruments and weapons and to the promotion of physical studies. . . . The intelligence and ingenuity of the Chinese are certainly superior to those of the various barbarians; it is only that hitherto we have not made use of them. When the government above takes delight in something, the people below will pursue it further: their response will be like an echo carried by the wind. There ought to be some people of extraordinary intelligence who can have new ideas and improve on Western methods. At first they may take the foreigners as their teachers and models; then they may come to the same level and be their equals; finally they may move ahead and surpass them. Herein lies the way to self-strengthening.

In 1867 the debate over how to resist foreign military pressure surged through the imperial court. Woren, a Mongol who held the rank of grand secretary, spoke for the conservatives.

Mathematics, one of the six arts, should indeed be learned by scholars as indicated in the imperial decree, and it should not be considered an unworthy subject. But according to the viewpoint of your servant, astronomy and mathematics are of very little use. If these subjects are going to be taught by Westerners as regular studies, the damage will be great. . . . Your servant has learned that the way to establish a nation is to lay emphasis on rites and rightness, not on power and plotting. The fundamental effort lies in the minds of people, not in techniques. Now, if we seek trifling arts and respect barbarians as teachers . . . all that can be accomplished is the training of mathematicians. From ancient down to modern times, your servant has never heard of anyone who could use mathematics to raise the nation from a state of decline or to strengthen it in time of weakness. . . .

Since the conclusion of the peace, Christianity has been prevalent, and half of our ignorant people have been fooled by it. The only thing we can rely on is that our scholars should clearly explain to the people the Confucian tenets, which may be able to sustain the minds of the ignorant populace. Now if these brilliant and talented scholars, who have been trained by the nation and reserved for great future usefulness, have to change from their regular course of study to follow the barbarians, then the correct spirit will not be developed, and accordingly the evil spirit will become stronger. After several years it will end in nothing less than driving the multitudes of the Chinese people into allegiance to the barbarians.

The opposing group of ministers who backed the idea of "self-strengthening" responded.

Your ministers have examined the memorial of Woren: the principles he presents are very lofty and the opinion he maintains is very orthodox. Your ministers' point of view was also like that before they began to manage foreign affairs; and yet today they do not presume to insist on such ideas, because of actual difficulties that they cannot help. . . .

From the beginning of foreign relations to the present there have been twenty or thirty years. At first the officials inside and outside the capital did not grasp the crux of the matter, and whether they negotiated peace or discussed war, generally these were empty words without effect. . . . Therefore your ministers have pondered a long-term policy and discussed the situation thoroughly with all the provincial officials. Proposals to learn the written and spoken languages of foreign countries, the various methods of making machines, the training of troops with foreign guns, the dispatching of officials to travel in all countries, the investigation of their local customs and social conditions . . . all these painstaking and special decisions represent nothing other than a struggle for self-strengthening. . . .

We too are afraid that the people who are learning these things will have no power of discrimination and are likely to be led astray by foreigners, as Woren fears. Therefore we have deliberated and decided that those who participate in these examinations must be persons from regular scholastic channels. It is indeed those students who have read widely and who understand right principles and have their minds set upon upright and grand purposes—and the present situation is just what causes the scholars and officials to feel pain in heart and head—who would certainly be able to lie on faggots and taste gall [i.e., nurse vengeance] in order to encourage each other vigorously to seek the actual achievement of self-strengthening. They are different from those who have vague, easygoing, or indifferent ideas.

QUESTIONS FOR ANALYSIS

1. **How do the views of the writers reflect their own backgrounds as officials who achieved their offices through the traditional examination system?**
2. **In what ways do these passages indicate a deep or a shallow understanding of the West?**
3. **How do the ideas expressed here compare with the attitudes toward reform in the Ottoman and Russian Empires as discussed elsewhere in this chapter?**

Source: Excerpts from Wm. Theodore de Bary and Richard Lafrano, *Sources of Chinese Tradition*, vol. 2, 2d ed. (New York: Columbia University Press, 2000), 235–236, 238–239 © 2001 Columbia University Press. Reprinted with permission of publisher.

among these governors was Zeng Guofan (zung gwoh-FAN), who oversaw programs to restore agriculture, communications, education, and publishing, as well as efforts to reform the military and industrialize armaments manufacture.

Like many provincial governors, Zeng preferred to look to the United States rather than to Britain for models and aid. He hired American advisers to run his weapons factories, shipyards, and military academies. He sponsored a daring program in which promising Chinese boys were sent to Hartford, Connecticut, a center of missionary activity, to learn English, science, mathematics, engineering, and history. They returned to China to assume some of the positions previously held by foreign advisers. Though Zeng was never an advocate of participation in public life by women, his Confucian convictions taught him that educated mothers were more than ever a necessity. He not only encouraged but also partly oversaw the advanced classical education of his own daughters. Zeng's death in 1872 deprived the empire of a major force for reform.

The period of recovery marked a fundamental structural change in the Qing Empire. Although the emperors after 1850 were ineffective rulers, a coalition of aristocrats supported the reform and recovery programs. Without their legitimization of the new powers of provincial governors like Zeng Guofan, the empire might have evaporated within a generation. A crucial member of this alliance was Cixi (TSUH-shee), who was known as the "Empress Dowager" after the 1880s. Later observers, both Chinese and foreign, reviled her as a monster of corruption and arrogance. But in the 1860s and 1870s Cixi supported the provincial governors, some of whom became so powerful that they were managing Qing foreign policy as well as domestic affairs.

No longer a conquest regime dominated by a Manchu military caste and its Chinese civilian appointees, the empire came under the control of a group of reformist aristocrats and military men, independently powerful civilian governors, and a small number of foreign advisers. The Qing lacked strong, central, unified leadership and could not recover their powers of taxation, legislation, and military command once these had been granted to the provincial governors. From the 1860s forward, the Qing Empire disintegrated into a number of large power zones in which provincial governors handed over leadership to their protégés in a pattern that the Qing court eventually could only ritually legitimate.

COMPARATIVE PERSPECTIVES

Most of the subjects of the Ottoman, Russian, and Qing rulers did not think of European pressure or competition as determining factors in their lives during the first half of the nineteenth century. They continued to live according to the social and economic institutions they inherited from previous generations. By the 1870s, however, the challenge of Europe had become widely realized. The Crimean War, where European allies achieved a hollow victory for the Ottomans and then pressured the sultan for more reforms, confirmed both Ottoman and Russian military weakness. The Opium War did the same for China. But China, unlike the other empires, was also stricken by rampaging civil war and regional uprisings.

Though all three empires faced similar problems of reform, military rebuilding, and financial disarray, China was geographically remote from Europe and thus removed from the geostrategic tug-of-war between Britain and Russia. Despite British fears about Russian threats to India, the tsars enjoyed the advantage of being included in high-level deliberations among European powers. The Ottoman Empire, which had once dominated eastern Europe, was largely excluded from these deliberations. To many European diplomats and overseas investors, its final demise seemed only a matter of time, leaving up in the air the question of who would reap the benefits.

In analyzing the crises of the three empires, historians today stress European economic pressures and observe that all three empires ultimately became insolvent and saw the overthrow of their ruling dynasties. However, at the time what most impressed the Ottomans, Russians, and Chinese was European military superiority, as demonstrated in the Greek war of independence, the Crimean War, and the Opium War. Thus for all three empires, dealing with military emergency took priority over deeper reforms throughout most of the time period of this chapter.

Chapter Review

DOWNLOAD THE MP3 AUDIO FILE OF THE CHAPTER REVIEW TO LISTEN TO ON THE GO.

What were the benefits and the drawbacks to the Ottoman Empire of the reforms adopted during the Tanzimat period? (page 571)

Although the Tanzimat period began with the sultan declaring in 1839 a measure of equality for all Ottoman citizens, improving military performance was at the center of the reforming effort. This reform enhanced the role of the military while other administrative changes reduced the social role and governmental influence of the religious elite. The result was an unbalanced reform effort that eventually led to a military takeover of the country.

How did the Russian Empire maintain its status as both a European power and a great Asian land empire? (page 580)

For Russians, defeat in the Crimean War and the revelation that Russian arms were no match for modern European weaponry were counterbalanced by the comparative weakness of the peoples to the east and south into whose territories they aggressively expanded. Thus, while lagging far behind in industrialization and having an inefficient government, Russia, like the other European states, engaged in imperialist expansion.

How did the impact of European imperialism on China differ from its impact on Russia and the Ottoman Empire? (page 585)

The course of Russian expansion into Asia made it a neighbor of Qing China, but other European powers were seen as greater threats. Britain, France, and the United States used every means available to gain the freedom to exploit China economically. With respect to the empires nearer to home, however, European imperialists—the United States had minimal involvement—considered financial investment to be somewhat less important than limiting Russian expansion or weakening the Ottoman state and improving the lives of its Christian and Jewish populations.

KEY TERMS

Muhammad Ali *(p. 572)*
Janissaries *(p. 573)*
Serbia *(p. 573)*
Tanzimat *(p. 574)*
Crimean War *(p. 579)*
extraterritoriality *(p. 580)*
Young Ottomans *(p. 580)*
Slavophiles *(p. 582)*
Pan-Slavism *(p. 582)*
Decembrist revolt *(p. 584)*
Opium War *(p. 587)*
Bannermen *(p. 587)*
Treaty of Nanking *(p. 587)*
treaty ports *(p. 587)*
most-favored-nation status *(p. 587)*
Taiping Rebellion *(p. 589)*

SUGGESTED READING

Bassin, Mark. *Imperial Visions: Nationalist Imagination and Geographical Expansion in the Russian Far East, 1840–1865*. 1999. Addresses Russia's little-studied eastward expansion.

Blackwell, W. L. *The Beginnings of Russian Industrialization, 1800–1860*. 1968. A standard introduction.

Crossley, Pamela Kyle. *Orphan Warriors: Three Manchu Generations and the End of the Qing World*. 1990. Presents a Manchu perspective on the late Qing.

Deringil, Selim. *The Well-Protected Domains: Ideology and the Legitimation of Power in the Ottoman Empire, 1876–1909*. 1998. A revisionist view of the reign of Abdul Hamid II.

Field, Daniel. *The End of Serfdom: Nobility and Bureaucracy in Russia, 1855–1861*. 1976. Studies the primary problem besetting Russian society during this period.

Kappeler, Andreas. *The Russian Multi-Ethnic Empire*. 2001. Puts an emphasis on ethnic diversity.

Lewis, Bernard. *The Emergence of Modern Turkey*. 3d ed. 2001. A treatment of late Ottoman history based on Europeanization as a sign of progress.

Mardin, Serif. *The Genesis of Young Ottoman Thought: A Study in the Modernization of Turkish Political Ideas*. Reprint, 2000. Classic study of intellectual developments.

Pamuk, Sevket. *The Ottoman Empire and European Capitalism, 1820–1913: Trade, Investment, and Production*. 1987. An economic analysis of the Ottoman Empire.

Polachek, James M. *The Inner Opium War*. 1992. Details a major event in Chinese-Western confrontation.

Quataert, Donald. *The Ottoman Empire, 1700–1922*. 2d ed. 2005. A survey of late Ottoman history.

Raeff, Marc. *Understanding Imperial Russia*. 1984. Sets nineteenth-century Russian developments in a broad context and challenges many standard ideas.

Spence, Jonathan D. *God's Chinese Son: The Taiping Heavenly Kingdom of Hong Xiuquan*. 1996. A highly readable account of the Taiping movement that focuses on religious leadership.

Walicki, Andrzej. *The Slavophile Controversy*. 1975. A study in intellectual history.

Zelin, Madeleine. *The Merchants of Zigong: Industrial Entrepreneurship in Early Modern China*. 2005. A revealing study of indigenous economic development.

WEB RESOURCES

Pronunciation Guide

Interactive Maps

MAP 21.1 The Ottoman and Russian Empires, 1829–1914

MAP 21.2 Conflicts in the Qing Empire, 1839–1870

Primary Sources

The History and Doctrine of the Wahhabis

Imperial Rescript

An Ottoman Government Decree Defines the Official Notion of the "Modern" Citizen, June 19, 1870

The Treaty of Peace and Commerce (Treaty of Turkmanchai)

Between Iran and Russia, February 10–22, 1828

Letter to Queen Victoria, 1839

Answer to the History in Focus Question

See photo on page 590, "Nanjing Encircled."

Plus

Chapter Objectives

ACE multiple-choice quiz

Flashcards

CHAPTER 22

Africa, India, and the New British Empire

CHAPTER PREVIEW

In 1782, Tipu Sultan inherited the throne of Mysore (MY-sore), which his father had made the most powerful state in south India. The talented new ruler also inherited a healthy distrust of the British East India Company's territorial ambitions. Before the company could invade Mysore, Tipu Sultan launched his own attack in 1785. He then sent an embassy to France in 1788 seeking an alliance against Britain.

Neither of these ventures was immediately successful, but a decade later the French did agree to a loose alliance to challenge Britain's supremacy in the Indian Ocean. When General Napoleon Bonaparte invaded Egypt in 1798, he hoped to use the alliance with Tipu Sultan to threaten the British in India. When the French withdrew three years later, another military adventurer, Muhammad Ali, retook control of Egypt on behalf of the Ottoman sultan.

 This icon will direct you to the website where you can Prepare for Class, Improve Your Grade, and Ace the Test: college.cengage.com/pic/bullietbrief4e

Meanwhile, Tipu's alliance with France did not protect him from the East India Company, whose military victory in 1792 deprived him of most of his seacoast. Tipu lost his life in 1799 while defending his capital against another British assault. Mysore was divided between the British and their Indian allies.

As these events illustrate, talented local leaders and European powers were both vying to expand their influence in South Asia and Africa between 1750 and 1870. Midway through that period, it was by no means clear who would gain the upper hand. By 1870, Britain had gained a decisive advantage over France and had established commercial dominance in Africa, the Indian Ocean, and East Asia. Moreover, Britain had created a new colonial empire in the East.

CHANGES AND EXCHANGES IN AFRICA

How did different African leaders react to modern times, and how did European nations' relationship to African peoples change during this period?

During the century before 1870, Africa underwent dynamic political changes and a great expansion of foreign trade. Indigenous African leaders as well as Middle Eastern and European imperialists built powerful new states or expanded old ones. As the continent's external slave trades to the Americas and to Islamic lands died slowly under British pressure, trade in goods such as palm oil, ivory, timber, and gold grew sharply. In return, Africans imported large quantities of machine-made textiles and firearms.

New African States

Internal forces produced clusters of new states in two parts of sub-Saharan Africa (see Map 22.1). In the fertile coastlands of southeastern Africa (in modern South Africa), a serious drought at the beginning of the nineteenth century led to conflict for grazing and farming lands among the small, independent chiefdoms of the region. An upstart named Shaka emerged in 1818 as head of a new **Zulu** kingdom, and the Zulus' military discipline and courage soon made them the most feared fighters in southern Africa. Shaka's regiments raided his African neighbors, seized their cattle, and captured their women and children. To protect themselves from the Zulu, some neighboring Africans created their own states.

Although Shaka ruled for little more than a decade, he successfully instilled a new national identity into his newly conquered subjects. He grouped all the young people into regiments that lived together and were taught Zulu customs and fighting methods. At public festivals, regiments of young men and women paraded, danced, and pledged their loyalty to Shaka.

Meanwhile, Islamic reform movements were creating another powerful state in the savannas of West Africa. The reformers followed a classic Muslim pattern: a *jihad* (holy war) added new lands, spreading Islamic beliefs and laws among conquered people. The largest reform movement was led by Usuman dan Fodio (OO-soo-mahn dahn FOH-dee-oh) (1745–1817), whose armed supporters conquered and combined

Zulu A people of modern South Africa whom King Shaka united in 1818.

Chronology

	Africa	India	Empire
1750			
		1756 Black Hole of Calcutta	
			1763 End of Seven Years War
		1765 East India Company (EIC) rule of Bengal begins	
			1769–1778 Captain James Cook explores New Zealand and eastern Australia
	1795 Britain seizes Cape Colony from Dutch	**1795** Britain seizes Ceylon from the Dutch	**1795** End of Dutch East India Company
	1798 Napoleon invades Egypt		
		1799 EIC defeats Mysore	
1800			
	1805 Muhammad Ali seizes Egypt		
	1807–1808 Britain outlaws slave trade and takes over Sierra Leone		
			1808 Britain outlaws slave trade
	1809 Sokoto Caliphate founded		
	1818 Shaka founds Zulu kingdom	**1818** EIC creates Bombay Presidency	
	1821 Foundation of Republic of Liberia; Egypt takes control of Sudan		
		1826 EIC annexes Assam and northern Burma	
		1828 Brahmo Samaj founded	
	1830–1847 Algerians resist French takeover		
	1834 Britain abolishes slavery		**1834** Britain abolishes slavery
	1840 Omani sultan moves capital to Zanzibar		
1850			
		1857–1858 Sepoy Rebellion leads to end of EIC rule and Mughal rule	
	1867 End of Atlantic slave trade		**1867** End of Atlantic slave trade
		1877 Queen Victoria becomes empress of India	**1877** Queen Victoria becomes empress of India
		1885 First Indian National Congress	
	1889 Menelik unites modern Ethiopia		

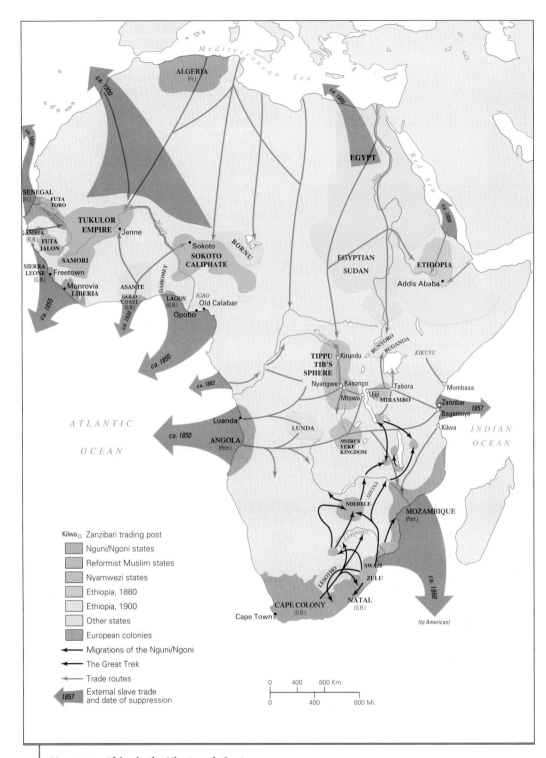

Map 22.1   Africa in the Nineteenth Century

Expanding internal and overseas trade drew much of Africa into global networks, but foreign colonies in 1870 were largely confined to Algeria and southern Africa. Growing trade, Islamic reform movements, and other internal forces created important new states throughout the continent.

the older Hausa states into a new empire ruled by a caliph in the city of Sokoto. The **Sokoto Caliphate** (1809–1906) was the largest state in West Africa since the fall of Songhai in the sixteenth century (see Chapter 12).

In addition to being a center of Islamic learning and reform, the Sokoto Caliphate became a center of slavery. Many captured in the wars were enslaved and put to work in the empire or sold away across the Sahara or the Atlantic.

▎**Sokoto Caliphate** A large Muslim state founded in 1809 in what is now northern Nigeria.

Modernization in Egypt and Ethiopia

In northeastern Africa, the African states of Egypt and Ethiopia were undergoing a period of growth and **modernization**. Napoleon's invasion of Egypt ended in 1801, but the shock of this display of European strength and Egyptian weakness prompted **Muhammad Ali**, who eliminated his rivals and ruled Egypt from 1805 to 1848, to begin military and economic reforms.

As we saw in the last chapter, Muhammad Ali's central aim was to strengthen Egypt militarily by making use of European experts and technology. Despite the shattering of his imperial dreams by the British after 1839, by the end of Muhammad Ali's reign in 1848, modernization was well rooted in Egypt. Trade with Europe had expanded by almost 600 percent.

▎**modernization** The process of reforming political, military, economic, social, and cultural traditions in imitation of the early success of Western societies, often with regard for accommodating local traditions in non-Western societies.

▎**Muhammad Ali** Leader of Egyptian modernization in the early nineteenth century. He ruled Egypt as an Ottoman governor, but had imperial ambitions. His descendants ruled Egypt until overthrown in 1952.

Téwodros's Mighty Cannon
In 1861 Emperor Téwodros of Ethiopia forced resident European missionaries and craftsmen to build guns and cannon, including this 7-ton behemoth nicknamed "Sebastapol" after the Black Sea port that had been the center of the Crimean War. It took five hundred men to haul the cannon across Ethiopia's hilly terrain. (From Hormuzd Rassam, *Narrative of the British Mission to Theodore, King of Abyssinia, II*, London 1869, John Murray)

Muhammad Ali's grandson Ismail (is-MAH-eel) (r. 1863–1879) placed even more emphasis on westernizing Egypt. "My country is no longer in Africa," Ismail declared. "It is in Europe."[1] Massive cotton exports during the American Civil War helped finance a network of new irrigation canals, 800 miles (1,300 kilometers) of railroads, a modern postal service, and dazzling changes in the capital city of Cairo.

State building and reform also were under way in the ancient Christian kingdom of Ethiopia. Beginning in the 1840s, Ethiopian rulers purchased modern weapons from European sources and created strong armies loyal to the ruler. Emperor Téwodros (tay-WOH-druhs) II (r. 1833–1868) and his successor, Yohannes (yoh-HAHN-nehs) IV (r. 1872–1889), brought back under imperial rule large areas of ancient Ethiopia. When King Menelik of Shoa succeeded Yohannes as emperor in 1889, the merger of their separate realms created the modern boundaries of Ethiopia.

European Penetration   France's long and difficult war to conquer the North African country of Algeria from 1830 to 1847 was a rare example of European use of force in Africa before 1870. More typical was the peaceful penetration of European explorers, missionaries, and traders. Small expeditions of adventurous explorers, using their own funds or financed by private geographical societies, sought knowledge of inner Africa and of the course of Africa's great rivers: the Niger, the Nile, and the Congo.

In contrast to these heavily financed expeditions with hundreds of African porters, the Scottish missionary David Livingstone (1813–1873) organized modest treks through southern and Central Africa to scout out locations for Christian missions. His several expeditions in southern and equatorial Africa made him a celebrity. In 1871, he was met by the Welsh-American journalist Henry Morton Stanley (1841–1904) on a publicity-motivated search for the "lost" missionary doctor. On an expedition from 1874 to 1877, Stanley descended the Congo River to its mouth.

Commerce governed most European enterprises. No sooner was the mouth of the Niger River discovered in 1830 than eager adventurers moved up the river to discover its potential for trade. Trade between Africa and the other Atlantic continents more than doubled between the 1730s and the 1780s, then doubled again by 1870.[2] Before about 1825, the slave trade accounted for most of that increase, but thereafter African exports of vegetable oils, gold, ivory, and other goods drove overseas trade to new heights.

As Chapter 19 recounted, Western criticism of slavery was rising. Once the world's greatest slave traders, the British became the most aggressive abolitionists. During the half-century after 1815, Britain spent some $60 million (£12 million) in its efforts to end the slave trade through naval patrols. This equaled the profits British slave traders had made in the fifty years before the trade was banned in 1807. Although British patrols captured 1,635 slave ships and liberated over 160,000 enslaved Africans, continued demand for slaves in Cuba and Brazil kept the trade going until 1867.

To satisfy their desires for cloth, metals, and other imported goods after slavery was outlawed, Africans expanded their **"legitimate" trade** (exports other than slaves). The most successful new export from West Africa was palm oil, a substance used by British manufacturers for soap, candles, and lubricants. From the mid-1830s, the trading states of the Niger Delta emerged as the premier exporters of palm oil. Coastal Africans grew rich and purchased large numbers of male slaves to paddle the giant

CL Primary Source: The Interesting Narrative of Olaudah Equiano as Written by Himself   *Read a boy's personal account of being kidnapped and forced into slavery.*

"legitimate" trade Exports from Africa in the nineteenth century that did not include the newly outlawed slave trade.

dugout canoes that transported palm oil from inland markets along the narrow delta creeks to the trading ports.

Suppressing the slave trade helped spread Western cultural influences in West Africa. In 1808 the British had taken over the small colony of Sierra Leone (see-ER-uh lee-OWN) as a base for their anti–slave trade naval squadron. In the following years, 130,000 men, women, and children taken from "captured" vessels were liberated in Sierra Leone. Christian missionaries helped settle these impoverished and dispirited **recaptives** in and around Freetown, the capital. In time, the mission churches and schools made many willing converts among such unfortunates.

Sierra Leone's schools produced a number of distinguished graduates. For example, Samuel Adjai Crowther (1808–1891), freed as a youth from a slave ship in 1821, became the first Anglican bishop in West Africa in 1864, administering a pioneering diocese along the lower Niger River. James Africanus Horton (1835–1882), the son of a slave liberated in Sierra Leone, became a doctor and the author of many studies of West Africa.

Other Western cultural influences came from people of African birth or descent returning to their ancestral homeland. In 1821, to the south of Sierra Leone, free black Americans began a settlement that grew into the Republic of Liberia, a place of liberty at a time when slavery was legal and flourishing in the United States. Free blacks from Brazil and Cuba chartered ships to return to their West African homelands, bringing with them Roman Catholicism, architectural motifs, and clothing fashions from the New World. Although the number of Africans exposed to Western culture in 1870 was still small, this influence grew rapidly.

recaptives Africans rescued by Britain's Royal Navy from the illegal slave trade of the nineteenth century and restored to free status.

Secondary Empires in Eastern Africa

With the British patrolling West Africa, slavers moved southward and then around the tip of the continent to eastern Africa, where an existing trade in slaves to the Muslim world was still expanding. Two-thirds of the 1.2 million slaves exported from eastern Africa in the nineteenth century went to markets in North Africa and the Middle East; the other third went to European plantations in the Americas and the Indian Ocean.

Between 1800 and 1873 local Arab and Swahili owners purchased some 700,000 slaves from inland eastern Africa to do the labor-intensive work of harvesting cloves on plantations on Zanzibar Island and the neighboring coast. These territories belonged to the sultan of Oman, a realm in southeastern Arabia. The sultan moved his court to Zanzibar in 1840. Zanzibar also exported ivory, mostly to India, where much of it was carved into decorative objects for middle-class Europeans.

Caravans led by African and Arab merchants brought ivory from hundreds of miles inland. Some of these merchants created large personal empires by using capital they had borrowed from Indian bankers and modern firearms they had bought from Europeans and Americans. These modern rifles felled countless elephants for their ivory tusks and inflicted widespread devastation and misery on the inland people.

Since Europeans supplied the weapons used by the invaders and were major consumers of ivory and cloves, historians refer to the states carved out of eastern Africa as "secondary empires," in contrast to the empire that

SECTION REVIEW

- Vital new states rose in Africa: the Zulu kingdom in southeastern Africa and the Sokoto Caliphate in West Africa.

- Egypt under Muhammad Ali and Ismail and Ethiopia under Téwodros and his successors undertook European-influenced modernization programs.

- Before 1870, European penetration of Africa was largely peaceful, small in scale, and concerned mainly with trade, missionary work, and exploration.

- The most important European influence was the suppression of the Atlantic slave trade and its resulting commercial and cultural shifts.

- Secondary slave- and ivory-trading empires grew along the coast of East Africa.

Britain was establishing directly. At the same time, Britain was working to bring the slave trade to an end in eastern Africa. British officials pressured the sultan of Oman into halting the Indian Ocean slave trade from Zanzibar in 1857 and ending the import of slaves into Zanzibar in 1873.

INDIA UNDER BRITISH RULE

How did Britain secure its hold on India, and what colonial policies led to the beginnings of Indian nationalism?

The people of South Asia felt the impact of European commercial, cultural, and colonial expansion more immediately and profoundly than did the Africans. Europeans laid claim to only small parts of Africa between 1750 and 1870, but nearly all of India (with three times the population of Africa) came under Britain's direct or indirect rule. After the founding of the East India Company in 1600, it took British interests 250 years to commandeer the colonies and trade of the Dutch, fight off French and Indian challenges, and pick up the pieces of the decaying Mughal (MOO-guhl) Empire. By 1763 the French were stymied, in 1795 the Dutch company was dissolved, and in 1858 the last Mughal emperor was dethroned, leaving the vast subcontinent in British hands.

Company Men

As Mughal power weakened in the eighteenth century, British, Dutch, and French companies expanded into India (see Map 22.2). The success of these far-flung European enterprises depended on hard-drinking and ambitious young "Company Men," who used hard bargaining, and hard fighting when necessary, to persuade Indian rulers to allow them to establish trading posts at strategic points along the coast. To protect their fortified warehouses from attack by other Europeans or by native states, the companies hired and trained Indian troops known as **sepoys** (SEE-poy). In fragmented India, these private armies came to hold the balance of power.

In 1691, the East India Company (EIC) had convinced the **nawab** (NAH-wab) (the term used for Mughal governors) of Bengal in northeast India to let the company establish a fortified outpost at the fishing port of Calcutta. A new nawab seeking additional tribute from the prospering port overran the fort in 1756 and imprisoned a group of EIC men in a cell so small that many died of suffocation. To avenge their deaths in this "Black Hole of Calcutta," a large EIC force from Madras overthrew the nawab. The weak Mughal emperor was persuaded to acknowledge the EIC's right to rule Bengal in 1765. Calcutta grew into a city of 250,000 by 1788.

In southern India, EIC forces secured victory for the British Indian candidate for nawab of Arcot during the Seven Years War, thereby gaining an advantage over French traders who had supported the loser. The defeat of Tipu Sultan of Mysore at the end of the century (described at the start of this chapter) secured south India for the company and prevented a French resurgence.

Along with Calcutta and Madras, the third major center of British power in India was Bombay, on the western coast. There, after a long conflict with Indian rulers, the EIC gained a decisive advantage in 1818, annexing large territories to form the

sepoy A soldier in South Asia, especially in the service of the British.

nawab A Muslim prince allied to British India; technically, a semi-autonomous deputy of the Mughal emperor.

Map 22.2   India, 1707–1805
As Mughal power weakened during the eighteenth century, other Indian states and the British East India Company expanded their territories.

core of what was called the "Bombay Presidency." Some states were taken over completely, as Bengal had been, but many others remained in the hands of local princes who accepted the political control of the company.

Raj and Rebellion, 1818–1857

In 1818, the EIC controlled an empire with fifty times the population of the colonies the British had lost in North America. One thrust of the **British raj** (regime) was to

British raj The rule over much of South Asia between 1765 and 1947 by the East India Company and then by a British government.

remake India through administrative measures, economic development, and modern technology. But the Company Men—like the Mughals before them—had to temper their interference with Indian social and religious customs lest they provoke rebellion or lose the support of their Indian princely allies. This immense and complex task led to many inconsistencies in Britain's policies toward India.

The main policy was to create a powerful and efficient system of government. British rule before 1850 relied heavily on military power—170 sepoy regiments and 16 European regiments. Another policy was to disarm approximately 2 million warriors who had served India's many states and turn them to civilian tasks, mostly cultivation. A third policy gave freer rein to Christian missionaries eager to convert and uplift India's masses. Few converts were made, but the missionaries kept up steady pressure for social reforms.

Another key British policy was to turn India's complex and overlapping patterns of landholding into private property. In Bengal, this reform worked to the advantage of large landowners, but in Mysore, the peasantry gained. Private ownership made it easier for the state to collect the taxes that were needed to pay for the costs of administration, the army, and economic reform.

Such policies of "westernization, Anglicization, and modernization," as they have been called, were only one side of British rule. The other side was the bolstering of "traditions"—both real and newly invented. In the name of tradition, the Indian princes who ruled nearly half of British India were permitted to expand their power and splendor. The British rulers themselves invented many "traditions"—including elaborate parades and displays—half borrowed from European royal pomp, half freely improvised from Mughal ceremonies (see Diversity and Dominance: Ceremonials of Imperial Domination).

The British and Indian elites danced sometimes in close partnership, sometimes in apparent opposition. But the ordinary people of India—women of every status, members of subordinate Hindu castes, the "untouchables" and "tribals" outside the caste system, and the poor generally—found less benefit in the British reforms and much new oppression in the new taxes and "traditions."

The transformation of British India's economy was doubled-edged. On the one hand, the growth in internal and external trade created many new jobs, as did the expansion of farming: opium in Bengal (largely for export to China), coffee in Ceylon (an island off the tip of India), and tea in Assam (in northeastern India). On the other hand, competition from cheap cotton goods produced in Britain's industrial mills ruined the handicraft textile industry. In the eighteenth century, India had been the world's greatest exporter of cotton textiles; in the nineteenth century, India increasingly shipped raw cotton fiber to Britain.

Economic changes, including beneficial ones, caused disruption. Thus, local rebellions by displaced ruling elites, disgruntled religious traditionalists, and the economically dispossessed were almost constant during the first half of the nineteenth century. The greatest concern was over the loyalty of Indian sepoys in the EIC's army.

In the early decades of EIC rule, most sepoys came from Bengal, one of the first states the company had annexed. The Bengali sepoys resented the recruitment of other ethnic groups into the army after 1848, such as Sikhs (seek) from Punjab and Gurkhas from Nepal. Many high-caste Hindus objected to a new law in 1856 permitting service assignment overseas in the growing Indian Ocean empire, for their

Ceremonials of Imperial Domination

*T*his letter to Queen Victoria from Edward Robert Bulwer-Lytton, the Earl of Lytton and the viceroy of India, describes the elaborate durbar that the government of India staged in 1876 in anticipation of her being named "Empress of India." It highlights the effects these ceremonies had on the Indian princes who governed many parts of India as agents ("feudatories") of the British or as independent rulers. British India's power rested on the threat of military force, but the letter points up how much it also depended on cultivating the allegiance of powerful Indian rulers.

The day before yesterday (December 23), I arrived, with Lady Lytton and all my staff at Delhi. . . . I was received at the [railroad] station by all the native chiefs and princes, and, . . . after shaking hands . . . , I immediately mounted my elephant, accompanied by Lady Lytton, our two little girls following us on another elephant. The procession through Delhi to the camp . . . lasted upwards of three hours. . . . The streets were lined for many miles with troops; those of the native princes being brigaded with those of your Majesty. The crowd along the way, behind the troops, was dense, and apparently enthusiastic; the windows, walls, and housetops being thronged with natives, who salaamed, and Europeans, who cheered as we passed along. . . .

My reception by the native princes at the station was most cordial. The Maharaja of Jeypore informed Sir John Strachey that India had never seen such a gathering as this, in which not only all the great native princes (many of whom have never met before), but also chiefs and envoys from Khelat, Burmah, Siam, and the remotest parts of the East, are assembled to do homage to your Majesty. . . .

On Tuesday (December 26) from 10 A.M. till past 7 P.M., I was, without a moment's intermission, occupied in receiving visits from native chiefs, and bestowing on those entitled to them the banners, medals, and other honours given by your Majesty. The durbar, which lasted all day and long after dark, was most successful. . . . Your Majesty's portrait, which was placed over the Viceregal throne in the great durbar tent, was thought by all to be an excellent likeness of your Majesty. The native chiefs examined it with special interest.

On Wednesday, the 27th, I received visits from native chiefs, as before, from 10 A.M. til 1 P.M., and from 1:30 P.M. to 7:30 P.M., was passed in returning visits. I forgot to mention that on Tuesday and Wednesday evenings I gave great State dinners to the Governors of Bombay and Madras. Every subsequent evening of my stay at Delhi was similarly occupied by state banquets and receptions [for officials, foreign dignitaries, and] many distinguished natives.

The satisfactory and cordial assurances received from [the ruler of] Kashmir are, perhaps, less important, because his loyalty was previously assumed. But your Majesty will, perhaps, allow me to mention, in connection with the name of this prince, one little circumstance which appears to me very illustrative of the effect which the assemblage has had on him and others. In the first interviews which took place months ago . . . I noticed that, though perfectly courteous, he was extremely mistrustful of the British Government and myself. He seemed to think that every word I had said to him must have a hidden meaning against which he was bound to be on his guard. During our negotiations he carefully kept all his councillors round him, and he referred to them before answering any question I put to him. . . . On the day following the Imperial assemblage, I had another private interview with Kashmir for the settlement of some further details. His whole manner and language on this last occasion were strikingly different. [He said:] "I am now convinced that you mean nothing that is not for the good of me and mine. Our interests are identical with those of the empire. Give me your orders and they shall be obeyed."

. . . If the vast number of persons collected together at Delhi, and all almost entirely under canvas, be fairly taken into consideration . . . , no candid person will, I think, deny that to bring together, lodge, and feed so vast a crowd without a single case of sickness, or a single accident due to defective arrangements, without a moment's confusion or an hour's failure in the provision of supplies, and then to have sent them all away satisfied and loud in their expressions of gratitude for the munificent hospitality with which they had been entertained (at an expenditure of public money scrupulously moderate), was an achievement highly creditable to all concerned in carrying it out. Sir Dinkur Rao (Sindiah's great Minister) said to one of my colleagues: "If any man would understand why it is that the English are, and must necessarily remain, the masters of India, he need only go up to the Flagstaff Tower, and look down upon this marvellous camp. Let him notice the method, the order, the cleanliness, the discipline, the perfection of its whole organisation, and he will recognise in it at once the epitome of every title to command and govern which one race can possess over others." This anecdote reminds me of another which may perhaps please your Majesty. [The ruler of] Holkar said to me when I took leave of him: "India has been till now a vast heap of stones, some of them big, some of them small. Now the house is built, and from roof to basement each stone of it is in the right place."

The Khan of Khelat and his wild Sirdars were, I think, the chief objects of curiosity and interest to our Europeans. . . . On the Khan himself and all his Sirdars, the assemblage seems to have made an impression more profound even than I had anticipated. Less than a year ago they were all at war with each other, but they have left Delhi with mutual embraces, and a very salutary conviction that the Power they witnessed there is resolved that they shall henceforth keep the peace and not disturb its frontiers with their squabbles. The Khan asked to have a banner given to him. It was explained to His Highness that banners were only given to your Majesty's feudatories, and that he, being an independent prince, could not receive one without compromising his independence. He replied: "But I am a feudatory of the Empress, a feudatory quite as loyal and obedient as any other. I don't want to be an independent prince, and I do want to have my banner like all the rest. Pray let me have it."

I anticipate an excellent effect by and by from the impressions which the yet wilder envoys and Sirdars of Chitral and Yassin will carry with them from Delhi, and propagate throughout that important part of our frontier where the very existence of the British Government has hitherto been almost unrealised, except as that of a very weak power, popularly supposed in Kafristan to be exceedingly afraid of Russia. Two Burmese noblemen, from the remotest part of Burmah, said to me: "The King of Burmah fancies he is the greatest prince upon earth. When we go back, we shall tell all his people that he is nobody. Never since the world began has there been in it such a power as we have witnessed here."

QUESTIONS FOR ANALYSIS

1. **What is significant about the fact that Lord Lytton and his family arrived in Delhi by train and then chose to move through the city on elephants?**

2. **What impression did the viceroy intend to create in the minds of the Indian dignitaries by assembling so many of them together and bestowing banners, medals, and honors on them?**

3. **What might account for some Indians' remarkable changes of attitude toward the viceroy and the empire? How differently might a member of the Indian middle class or an unemployed weaver have reacted?**

Source: Lady Betty Balfour, *The History of Lord Lytton's Indian Administration, 1876 to 1880* (London: Longmans, Green, and Co., 1899), 116–125.

religion prohibited ocean travel. In 1857 the replacement of the standard musket by the more accurate Enfield rifle sparked outrage because the soldiers were ordered to use their teeth to tear open the ammunition cartridges, which were greased with animal fat. Fat from cattle offended Hindus; fat from pigs offended Muslims.

A quick change of the cartridge-opening procedure could not forestall a rebellion by Hindu sepoys in May 1857. Muslim sepoys, peasants, and discontented elites joined in. The rebels asserted old traditions: sepoy officers in Delhi proclaimed their loyalty to the Mughal emperor; others rallied behind the Maratha leader Nana Sahib. The rebellion was put down by March 1858, but it shook British India to its core.

Historians have attached different names and meanings to the events of 1857 and 1858. Seeing only an unlawful action by soldiers, nineteenth-century British historians labeled it the **"Sepoy Rebellion"** or the "Mutiny," names that are still commonly used. Seeing these events as the beginnings of the later movement for independence, some modern Indian historians have termed it the "Revolution of 1857."

Sepoy Rebellion The revolt of Indian soldiers in 1857 against certain practices that violated religious customs; also known as the Sepoy Mutiny.

Political Reform and Industrial Impact

Whatever its label, the rebellion of 1857–1858 was a historical turning point. In its wake, Indians gained a new centralized government, entered a period of rapid economic growth, and began to develop a new national consciousness.

The changes in government were immediate. In 1858, Britain eliminated the last traces of Mughal and EIC rule. In their place, a new secretary of state for India in London oversaw Indian policy, and a new governor-general in Delhi acted as the British monarch's viceroy on the spot. A proclamation by Queen Victoria in November 1858 guaranteed all Indians equal protection of the law and the freedom to practice their religions and social customs; it also assured Indian princes that so long as they were loyal to the queen, British India would respect their control of territories and "their rights, dignity and honour."[3]

A powerful and efficient bureaucracy controlled the Indian masses. Members of the elite **Indian Civil Service** (ICS), mostly graduates of Oxford and Cambridge Universities, held the senior administrative and judicial posts. Numbering only a thousand men at the end of the nineteenth century, they visited the villages in their

Indian Civil Service The elite professional class of officials who administered the government of British India. Originally composed exclusively of well-educated British men, it gradually added qualified Indians.

Delhi Durbar, January 1, 1903

The parade of Indian princes on ornately decorated elephants and accompanied by retainers fostered their sense of belonging to the vast empire of India that British rule had created. The durbar was meant to evoke the glories of India's earlier empires, but many of the details and ceremonies were nineteenth-century creations.   (British Empire and Commonwealth Museum, Bristol, UK/The Bridgeman Art Library)

HISTORY IN FOCUS   As the caption for this image suggests, the purpose of these parades was to showcase Indian princes. What evidence of British colonial power can you detect in this photo? In this context, does the date of the parade strike you as significant? *Find the answer online.*

districts, heard lawsuits and complaints, and passed judgments. A far greater number of Indian officials and employees served beneath them. Recruitment into the ICS was by open examination given only in England and thus inaccessible to most Indians. In 1870, only one Indian was a member of the ICS. Subsequent reforms led to fifty-seven Indian appointments by 1887, but there the process stalled.

British industry spurred a second transformation. The government invested millions of pounds sterling in harbors, cities, irrigation canals, and other public works. British interests felled forests to make way for tea plantations, persuaded Indian farmers to grow cotton and jute for export, and created great irrigation systems to alleviate the famines. As a result, India's trade expanded rapidly.

Most of the exports were agricultural commodities: cotton fiber, opium, tea, silk, and sugar. In return, India imported manufactured goods, including the flood of machine-made cotton textiles that undercut handloom weavers. Individual experiences varied enormously. Some women found jobs at very low pay on plantations or in the growing cities, where prostitution flourished. Others struggled to hold families together or ran away from abusive husbands. Everywhere in India, poverty remained the norm.

New technologies were introduced in India soon after their appearance in Britain. Beginning in the 1840s, after an earlier enthusiasm for canals and river steamers, a railroad boom (paid for out of government revenues) gave India a national transportation network, followed shortly by telegraph lines. Indeed, in 1870, India had the greatest rail network in Asia and the fourth largest in the world.

Easier movement and urbanization promoted the spread of cholera (KAHL-uhr-uh), a disease transmitted through water contaminated by human feces. In 1867, officials demonstrated the close connection between cholera and pilgrims who bathed in and drank from sacred pools and rivers. The installation of a new sewerage system (1865) and a filtered water supply (1869) in Calcutta dramatically reduced cholera deaths there. Similar measures in Bombay and Madras also led to great reductions, but most Indians lived in small villages, where famine and lack of sanitation kept cholera deaths high.

SECTION REVIEW

- British, Dutch, and French "Company Men" advanced European trade interests in India, with the British EIC winning major concessions in Bengal.

- The EIC fought French rivals and native rulers to establish bases at Madras and Bombay.

- EIC rulers undertook westernization, Anglicization, and modernization but also supported "traditions," all with mixed results.

- Discontent among the EIC's Indian soldiers erupted into the Sepoy Rebellion/Revolution.

- Direct British rule led to the creation of the Indian Civil Service and involvement with Britain's industrialization.

- British rule spurred the rise of Indian nationalism, from which emerged the secular, middle-class Indian National Congress.

Rising Indian Nationalism

Both the successes and the failures of British rule stimulated the development of Indian nationalism. The failure of the rebellion of 1857 led some thoughtful Indians to argue that the only way to regain control of their destiny was to reduce their country's social and ethnic divisions.

Individuals such as Rammohun Roy (1772–1833) had promoted pan-Indian nationalism a generation earlier. A Western-educated Bengali from a Brahmin family, Roy was a successful administrator for the EIC and a thoughtful student of comparative religion. His Brahmo Samaj (BRAH-moh suh-MAHJ) (Divine Society), founded in 1828, attracted Indians who sought to reconcile the values they found in the West with the ancient religious traditions of India. They backed the British outlawing of widow burning (*sati* [suh-TEE]) in 1829 and of slavery in 1834 and sought to correct other abuses of women and female infanticide. Roy and his followers advocated reforming the caste system and urged a return to the founding principles set out in the Upanishads, ancient sacred writings of Hinduism.

Indian Railroad Station, 1866
British India built the largest network of railroads in Asia. People of every social class traveled by train.   (Private Collection)

Although Brahmo Samaj remained an influential movement, a growing number of Indian intellectuals based their nationalism on secular values learned in Western schools. European and American missionaries played a prominent role in the spread of Western education. In 1870, there were 790,000 Indians in over 24,000 elementary and secondary schools, and India's three universities (established in 1857) awarded 345 degrees.

The Indian middle class produced many new nationalists. They convened the first **Indian National Congress** in 1885 and called for a larger Indian role in the civil service and for greater efforts to reduce poverty. The Indian National Congress effectively voiced the opinions of elite, Western-educated Indians, but it would need the support of the masses to challenge British rule.

Indian National Congress A movement and political party founded in 1885 to demand greater Indian participation in government. Its membership was middle class, and its demands were modest until World War I. Led after 1920 by Mohandas K. Gandhi, it appealed increasingly to the poor, and it organized mass protests demanding self-government and independence.

BRITAIN'S EASTERN EMPIRE

What role did the abolition of slavery and the continued growth of British overseas trade play in the immigration of peoples from Africa, India, and Asia?

Military victories over rival trading nations, policies favoring free trade over mercantilism, and shipbuilding improvements that increased the speed and volume of shipping transformed Britain into a colossus that straddled the world. Linked to these changes were new European settlements in southern Africa, Australia, and New Zealand and the growth of a new long-distance trade in indentured labor.

Colonies and Commerce

France was still a serious rival for dominion in the Indian Ocean at the end of the eighteenth century. However, Napoleon's dream of restoring French dominance overseas did not outlive his empire. Napoleon's wars also gutted the Dutch overseas empire. When French armies occupied the Netherlands, the Dutch ruler, who had fled to

Britain in January 1795, authorized the British to take over his overseas possessions to keep them out of French hands. During 1795 and 1796 British forces occupied the Cape Colony at the tip of southern Africa, the strategic Dutch port of Malacca on the strait between the Indian Ocean and the South China Sea, and the island of Ceylon (modern Sri Lanka).

Then the British occupied Dutch Guiana and Trinidad in the southern Caribbean. In 1811 they even seized the island of Java, the center of the Netherlands' East Indian empire. British forces also seized control of the French islands of Mauritius and Réunion in the southwestern Indian Ocean. At the end of the Napoleonic Wars in 1814, Britain returned Java to the Dutch and Réunion to the French but kept the Cape Colony, British Guiana (once part of Dutch Guiana), Trinidad, Ceylon, Malacca, and Mauritius.

The Cape Colony was valuable because of Cape Town's strategic importance as a supply station for ships making the long voyages between Britain and India. With the port city came some twenty thousand descendants of earlier Dutch and French settlers who occupied far-flung farms and ranches in its hinterland. Despite their European origins, these people thought of themselves as permanent residents of Africa and were beginning to refer to themselves as "Afrikaners" ("Africans" in their dialect of Dutch). British governors prohibited any expansion of the white settler frontier because such expansion invariably led to wars with indigenous Africans. This decision, along with the imposition of laws protecting African rights within Cape Colony (including the emancipation of slaves in 1834), alienated many Afrikaners.

Between 1836 and 1839 parties of Afrikaners embarked on a "Great Trek," leaving British-ruled Cape Colony for the fertile high *veld* (plateau) to the north that two decades of Zulu wars had depopulated. The Great Trek led to the foundation of three new settler colonies by 1850: the Afrikaners' Orange Free State and Transvaal on the high veld and the British colony of Natal on the Indian Ocean coast. Although firearms enabled the settlers to win some important battles against the Zulu and other Africans, they were still a tiny minority surrounded by populous and powerful African kingdoms that had grown up at the beginning of the century.

Britain established another strategic outpost in Southeast Asia. In 1824 Thomas Stamford Raffles, who had governed Java during the period of British occupation from 1811 to 1814, helped the British East India Company establish a new free port at Singapore, a small Malay fishing village with a superb harbor. British merchants and Chinese businessmen and laborers quickly made Singapore the center of trade and shipping between the Indian Ocean and China. Along with Malacca and other possessions on the strait, Singapore formed the "Straits Settlements," which British India administered until 1867.

Further British expansion in Malaya (now Malaysia) did not occur until after 1874, but it came more quickly in neighboring Burma. Burma had emerged as a powerful kingdom by 1750 and in 1785 tried to annex neighboring territories of Siam (now Thailand) to the east. Thwarted by a coalition of Thai leaders in 1802, Burma next attacked Assam to the west. This led to war with British India, which also bordered Assam. India annexed Assam in 1826 and occupied two coastal provinces of northern Burma. As rice and timber trade from these provinces grew, the occupation became permanent, and in 1852 British India annexed the port of Rangoon and the rest of coastal Burma.

Imperial Policies and Shipping

By 1870 Britain had added several dozen colonies to the twenty-six it had in 1792, after the loss of the thirteen in North America. Nevertheless, Britain appears in many histories as a reluctant empire builder, its leaders unwilling to acquire new outposts that could prove difficult and expensive to administer. This is not a contradiction. The underlying goal of most British imperial expansion was trade, not territory. Most of the new colonies served as ports for a shipping network that encircled the globe, or as production and distribution centers for that network.

Whether colonized or not, more and more African, Asian, and Pacific lands connected with the commercial networks created by British expansion and industrialization. Britain bought vegetable oils for industrial and domestic use and forest products for dyes and construction from uncolonized parts of West Africa. Uncolonized eastern Africa exported ivory for piano keys and household decorations. From the far corners of the world came coffee, cocoa, and tea (along with sugar to sweeten them) for the tables of the new industrial classes in Britain and other parts of Europe.

In return, the industrialized nations sold manufactured goods at attractive prices. Sales of cotton cloth to Africa increased 950 percent from the 1820s to the 1860s. British trade to India grew 350 percent between 1841 and 1870, while India's exports increased 400 percent. In most cases such trade benefited both sides, but there is no question that the industrial nations were the dominant partners.

A second impetus to global commercial expansion was the technological revolution in the construction of oceangoing ships. The middle decades of the century were a golden age for sailing ships. Using iron to fasten timbers together enabled shipbuilders to construct much larger vessels. Eighteenth-century merchant ships rarely exceeded 300 tons, but after 1850 swift American-built **clipper ships** of 2,000 tons set the standard. Ships from the East Indies or India had taken six months to reach Europe in the seventeenth century; ships built after 1850 could complete the voyage in three.

clipper ship Large, fast, streamlined sailing vessel, often American built, of the mid-to-late nineteenth century rigged with vast canvas sails hung from tall masts.

This increase in size and speed lowered shipping costs. The growth in size and numbers of ships increased the tonnage of British merchant shipping by 400 percent between 1778 and 1860. To extend the life of such ships in tropical lands, clippers intended for Eastern service generally were built of teak and other tropical hardwoods from new British colonies in South and Southeast Asia. Although tropical forests began to be cleared for rice and sugar plantations as well as for timbers, the effects on the environment and people of Southeast Asia came primarily after 1870.

Colonization of Australia and New Zealand

Rather than rule indigenous populations, as they did in India, or set up commercial outposts, as they did in Singapore and Cape Town, British settlers displaced indigenous populations in the new colonies of Australia and New Zealand, just as they had done in North America.

Portuguese mariners had sighted Australia in the early seventeenth century, but it was too remote to be of interest. However, after the English adventurer Captain James Cook systematically explored New Zealand and the fertile eastern coast of Australia between 1769 and 1778, expanding shipping networks brought in growing numbers of visitors and settlers.

The Australia Cook visited was home for about 650,000 hunting-and-gathering

The Aborigines of Australia

Native peoples had been thriving in Australia for tens of thousands of years when the British established their first colonies there in the nineteenth century. Since then they have been the victims of racism and political oppression, and most live on reservations distant from urban areas populated by the descendants of Caucasian and Asian immigrants. (AFP/Getty Images)

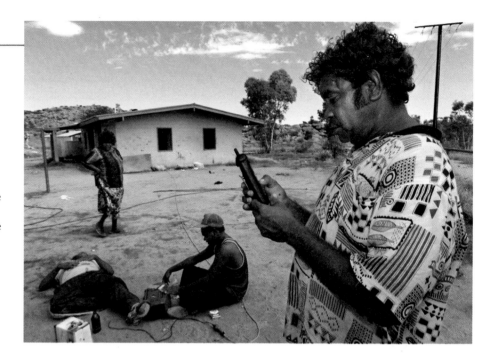

people, whose Melanesian (mel-uh-NEE-zhuhn) ancestors had arrived some forty thousand years earlier. About 250,000 Maori (MOW-ree [*ow* as in *cow*]) inhabited the two islands of New Zealand, lying 1,000 miles (1,600 kilometers) southeast of Australia. They practiced hunting, fishing, and simple forms of agriculture, which their Polynesian ancestors had introduced around 1200 C.E. These two populations were as vulnerable as the Amerindians had been to unfamiliar diseases introduced by overseas contacts. In the 1890s only 93,000 aboriginal Australians and 42,000 Maori had survived the exposure to Europeans. By then, British settler populations both outnumbered and dominated them.

The first permanent British settlers in Australia were 736 convicts, of whom 188 were women, sent into exile from British prisons in 1788. Australian penal colonies grew slowly and had only slight contact with the indigenous population, whom the British called "Aborigines." However, the discovery of gold in 1851 brought a flood of free European settlers (and some Chinese) and hastened the end of the penal colonies. When the gold rush subsided, government subsidies enabled tens of thousands of British settlers to settle "down under." Even with improved sailing ships it still took more than three months to reach Australia from Britain. By 1860 Australia had a million immigrants, and the settler population doubled during the next fifteen years.

British settlement in New Zealand proceeded more slowly. Initially a few temporary residents along the coast slaughtered seals and exported pelts to Western countries to be made into men's felt hats. A single ship in 1806 took away sixty thousand sealskins, and by the early 1820s overhunting had nearly exterminated the seal population. Sperm whales were also targeted; whalers hunted them near New Zealand for their oil, used for lubrication, soap, and lamps; ambergris (AM-ber-grees), an ingredient in perfume; and bone, used in women's corsets. Military suppression of Maori resistance, a brief gold rush, and the availability of faster ships and subsidized passages attracted more British immigrants after 1860. The colony especially courted women immigrants to offset the preponderance of single men. By the early 1880s the fertile agricultural lands of this most distant frontier of the British Empire had a settler population of 500,000.

Britain encouraged the settlers in Australia and New Zealand to become self-governing, following the 1867 model that had formed the Dominion of Canada out of the very diverse and thinly settled colonies of British North America. In 1901 a unified Australia emerged from the federation of six separate colonies. New Zealand became a self-governing dominion in 1907.

By gradually turning over governing power to the colonies' inhabitants, Britain accomplished three things. It satisfied the settlers' desire for greater local control; it muted demands for independence; and it made the colonial governments responsible for most of their own expenses. Indigenous peoples were outvoted by the settlers or even excluded from voting.

North American patterns also shaped the indigenous peoples' fate. An 1897 Australian law segregated the remaining Aborigines onto reservations, where they lacked the rights of Australian citizenship. The requirement that voters had to be able to read and write English kept Maori from voting in early New Zealand elections, but four seats in the lower house of the legislature were reserved for Maori from 1867 on.

In other ways the new settler colonies were more progressive. Australia developed very powerful trade unions, which improved the welfare of skilled and semiskilled urban white male workers, promoted democratic values, and exercised considerable political clout. In New Zealand, where sheep raising was the main occupation, populist and progressive sentiments promoted the availability of land for the common person. Australia and New Zealand were also among the first states in the world to grant women the right to vote, beginning in 1894.

New Labor Migrations

Between 1834 and 1870 many thousands of Indians, Chinese, and Africans responded to labor recruiters, especially to work overseas on sugar plantations. In the half-century after 1870 tens of thousands of Asians and Pacific islanders made similar voyages.

In part these migrations were linked to the end of slavery. After their emancipation in British colonies in 1834, freed slaves were no longer willing to put in the long hours they had been forced to work. Given freedom of movement, many left the plantations. To compete with slave-manned sugar plantations in Cuba, Brazil, and the French Caribbean, British colonies had to recruit new laborers.

India's poor provided one alternative. After planters on Mauritius, an Indian Ocean island, successfully introduced Indian laborers, the Indian labor trade moved to the British Caribbean in 1838. Three years later the British government allowed Caribbean planters to recruit Africans rescued from slave ships and liberated. By 1870 nearly 40,000 Africans had settled in British colonies, along with over 500,000 Indians and over 18,000 Chinese. After the French and Dutch abolished slavery in 1848, their colonies recruited over 150,000 new laborers from Asia and Africa.

Indentured Labor Register

This page comes from the passenger roster of the ship *Fatal Razack*, which brought the first Indian indentured laborers to Trinidad in 1845, five years after the final abolition of slavery there. The trip took 90 days. Over 140,000 more Indians followed these new arrivals, who are identified by name, father's name, sex, and age. (Courtesy, Indo-Caribbean Heritage)

SECTION REVIEW

- By the end of the Napoleonic Wars, Britain controlled most Dutch and French possessions in the Indian Ocean and the Caribbean.

- The Afrikaners' Great Trek resulted in three new colonies in southern Africa, and British expansion in Malaya added Singapore and Burma to the empire.

- Driven by free trade and technological innovation, Britain's overseas expansion drew more and more of the world into its commercial networks.

- New ships and shipping encouraged the colonization of Australia and New Zealand, where settlers displaced native peoples.

- To avoid the conflicts that led to the American Revolution, Britain encouraged self-government in Australia and New Zealand.

- The decline of slavery prompted migrations of indentured workers from Africa and Asia, mainly to agricultural colonies.

contract of indenture A voluntary agreement binding a person to work for a specified period of years in return for free passage to an overseas destination. Before 1800 most indentured servants were Europeans; after 1800 most indentured laborers were Asians.

Slavery continued in Cuba until 1886, but the rising cost of slaves led the sugar planters to recruit 138,000 new laborers from China between 1847 and 1873. Indentured labor recruits became the mainstay of new sugar plantations in places that had never known slave labor. After 1850 American planters in Hawaii recruited labor from China and Japan; British planters in Natal recruited from India; and those in Queensland (in northeastern Australia) relied on laborers from South Pacific islands.

Larger, faster ships made transporting such laborers affordable. Nevertheless, despite close regulation of shipboard conditions, crowded accommodations encouraged the spread of cholera and other contagious diseases.

All of these laborers served under **contracts of indenture**, which bound them to work for a specified period (usually from five to seven years) in return for free passage to their overseas destination. They were paid a small salary and provided with housing, clothing, and medical care. Indian indentured laborers also received free passage home if they worked a second five-year contract. To promote family life, British Caribbean colonies required forty women to be recruited for every hundred men. So many Indians chose to stay in Mauritius, Trinidad, British Guiana, and Fiji that they constituted a third or more of the total population by the early twentieth century.

Although many early recruits from China and the Pacific Islands were kidnapped or otherwise coerced into leaving home, in most cases the new indentured migrants had much in common with contemporary emigrants from Europe. Both groups hoped to improve their economic and social conditions. Both earned modest salaries. Many brought money back when they returned home, or used their earnings to buy land or to start a business in their new countries. One major difference was that people recruited as indentured laborers were generally so much poorer than emigrants from Europe that they had to accept lower-paying jobs in less desirable areas because they could not pay their own way. However, it is also true that many European immigrants into distant places like Australia and New Zealand had their passages subsidized but did not have to sign a contract of indenture. This shows that racial and cultural preferences, not just economics, shaped the flow of labor into European colonies.

A person's decision to accept an indentured labor contract could also be shaped by political circumstances. In India disruption brought by British colonial policies and the suppression of the 1857 rebellion contributed significantly to people's desire to emigrate. Poverty, famine, and warfare had not been strangers in precolonial India. Nor were these causes of emigration absent in China and Japan.

COMPARATIVE PERSPECTIVES

One perspective on the changes described in this chapter stresses the exploitation of the weak by the strong, of African, Asian, and Pacific peoples by aggressive Europeans. In this view, Britain's emergence as a dominant power in the Indian Ocean Basin and South Pacific continued the European expansion dating back to the Portuguese and the Spanish voyages of exploration and the subsequent conquest and colonization of the Americas.

From another perspective what was most important about this period was not the political and military strength of the Europeans but their growing commercial domination. In this view, the British, like other Europeans, were drawn to Africa and southern Asia by a desire to obtain new materials.

However, Britain's commercial expansion in the nineteenth century was also the product of non-European demand for industrial manufactures. The growing exchanges could be mutually beneficial. African and Asian consumers found industrial goods far cheaper and sometimes better than the handicrafts they replaced or supplemented. Industrialization also created new markets for African and Asian agricultural commodities. There were also negative impacts, as in the case of the displaced weavers of India.

Africa, Asia, and the Pacific did not become mere appendages of Europe. While the balance of military and economic power shifted in the Europeans' favor between 1750 and 1870, other cultures were still vibrant and local initiatives often dominant. Islamic reform movements and the rise of the Zulu nation had greater significance for their respective regions of Africa than did Western forces. Despite European inroads, Southeast Asians were still largely in control of their own destinies. Even in India, most people's lives and beliefs showed overwhelming continuity with the past.

Finally, it must not be imagined that Asians and Africans were powerless in dealing with European expansion. The Indian princes who extracted concessions from the British in return for their cooperation and the Indians who rebelled against the raj both forced the system to accommodate their needs. Moreover, some Asians and Africans were beginning to use European education, technology, and methods to transform their own societies. Leaders in Egypt, India, and other lands, like those in Russia, the Ottoman Empire, and China (see Chapter 21), were learning to challenge the power of the West on its own terms.

Chapter Review

 DOWNLOAD THE MP3 AUDIO FILE OF THE CHAPTER REVIEW TO LISTEN TO ON THE GO.

How did different African leaders react to modern times, and how did European nations' relationship to African peoples change during this period? (page 600)

New African states arose in this period: the Zulu, Swazi, and Lesotho kingdoms in the south, and the Sokoto Caliphate in the west. Some old states were also reinvigorated. In Egypt and Ethiopia enterprising rulers modernized their armies to consolidate power. Commerce between Europe and Africa grew enormously, owing first to the slave trade and then to trade in vegetable oils, gold, and ivory. No country enforced the abolition of slavery more effectively than Britain. British antislavery naval operations freed more than one hundred thousand captives, settling them in Freetown, the capital of Sierra Leone.

KEY TERMS

Zulu *(p. 600)*
Sokoto Caliphate *(p. 603)*
modernization *(p. 603)*
Muhammad Ali *(p. 603)*
"legitimate" trade *(p. 604)*
recaptives *(p. 605)*
sepoy *(p. 606)*
nawab *(p. 606)*
British raj *(p. 607)*
Sepoy Rebellion *(p. 610)*

(Continued)

How did Britain secure its hold on India, and what colonial policies led to the beginnings of Indian nationalism? (page 606)

The British East India Company, using negotiation or force in dealing with local princes, was able to secure control of the cities of Calcutta, Madras, and Bombay. The British instituted a powerful colonial government and skillfully exploited native traditions and local rulers. In 1857–1858 the Sepoy Rebellion prompted a wave of reforms: Queen Victoria promised all Indians freedom of religion and equal protection under the law, and great sums of money were invested in harbors, canals, trains, and telegraph lines. However, the profits from such enterprises remained in colonial hands, and the loss of manufacturing jobs, epidemics of cholera, and an increasingly educated middle class sparked the rise of Indian nationalism.

What role did the abolition of slavery and the continued growth of British overseas trade play in the immigration of peoples from Africa, India, and Asia? (page 613)

After Britain, France, and the Netherlands had abolished slavery, thousands of Indians, Chinese, Africans, and Pacific islanders immigrated to British colonies, above all to the Caribbean, under contracts of indenture. By 1778, when James Cook had explored New Zealand and eastern Australia, expanding shipping networks brought growing numbers of settlers there, displacing the native Maori and Australian peoples. Europeans brought new and devastating diseases, as they had done to Amerindian peoples two centuries before: over 80 percent of native New Zealanders and Australians perished in just over a century.

Indian Civil Service *(p. 611)*

Indian National Congress *(p. 613)*

clipper ship *(p. 615)*

contract of indenture *(p. 618)*

WEB RESOURCES

Pronunciation Guide

Primary Sources

The Interesting Narrative of Olaudah Equiano as Written by Himself

Answer to the History in Focus Question

See photo on page 611, "Delhi Durbar, January 1, 1903."

Plus

Chapter Objectives

ACE multiple-choice quiz

Flashcards

SUGGESTED READING

Bayly, C. A. *Indian Society and the Making of the British Empire.* 1987. Highlights India's centrality within the British Empire.

Bennett, Norman R. *Arab Versus European: Diplomacy and War in Nineteenth Century East Central Africa.* 1986. Studies eastern and northeastern Africa.

Bose, Sugata. *A Hundred Horizons: The Indian Ocean in the Age of Global Empire.* 2006. A broad view based on India.

Eltis, David. *Economic Growth and the Ending of the Transatlantic Slave Trade.* 1987. A good study of Atlantic relations.

Headrick, Daniel. *The Tentacles of Progress: Technology Transfer in the Age of Imperialism, 1850–1940.* 1988. Contains illuminating chapters on environmental and technological aspects of Indian history.

Hopkins, A. G. *An Economic History of West Africa.* 1973. Sticks to economic matters.

Hughes, Robert. *The Fatal Shore: The Epic of Australia's Founding.* 1988. A well-written popular account of Australian history.

Last, Murray. *The Sokoto Caliphate.* 1967. Examines Muslim states in West Africa.

Northrup, David. *Indentured Labor in the Age of Imperialism, 1834–1922.* 1995. Recent scholarship on the indentured labor trade.

Oliver, Roland, and Anthony Atmore. *Africa Since 1800.* 5th ed. 2005. Provides a brief introduction to Africa.

Omer-Cooper, J. D. *The Zulu Aftermath: A Nineteenth Century Revolution in Bantu Africa.* 1978. An excellent study of southern Africa.

SarDesai, D. R. *Southeast Asia: Past and Present.* 5th ed. 2004. A good introduction to a complex subject.

Sinclair, Keith, ed. *The Oxford Illustrated History of New Zealand.* 1996. Provides a wide-ranging introduction.

Wolpert, Stanley. *A New History of India.* 7th ed. 2004. A standard survey work.

Woodruff, William. *Impact of Western Man: A Study of Europe's Role in the World Economy, 1750–1960.* 1982. A broad overview.

NOTES

1. Quoted in P. J. Vatikiotis, *The History of Modern Egypt: From Muhammad Ali to Mubarak,* 4th ed. (Baltimore: Johns Hopkins University Press, 1991), 74.
2. David Eltis, "Precolonial Western Africa and the Atlantic Economy," in *Slavery and the Rise of the Atlantic Economy,* ed. Barbara Solow (New York: Cambridge University Press, 1991), table 1.

3. Quoted by Bernard S. Cohn, "Representing Authority in Victorian England," in *The Invention of Tradition,* ed. Eric Hobsbawm and Terence Ranger (Cambridge: Cambridge University Press, 1983), 165.

BETWEEN THE AMERICAN REVOLUTION and the last decades of the nineteenth century, Europe and the Americas were transformed. The ancient power of kings and the authority of religion were eclipsed by muscular new ways of organizing political, economic, and intellectual life. The Western world was vastly different in 1870 than it had been a century earlier. One of the less heralded but enduringly significant changes was the huge expansion of government statistical services.

The rise of the nation-state was associated with the development of modern bureaucratic departments that depended on reliable statistics to measure the nation's achievements and discover its failures. The nation-state, whether democratic or not, mobilized resources on a previously unimaginable scale. Modern states were more powerful and wealthier, and they were also more ambitious and more intrusive. The growth of their power can be seen in the modernization of militaries, the commitment to internal improvements such as railroads, and the growth in state revenues. In recent years historians have begun to examine a less visible but equally important manifestation of growing state power: census taking.

Governments and religious authorities have counted people since early times. Our best estimates of the Amerindian population of the Western Hemisphere in 1500 rest almost entirely on what were little more than missionaries' guesses about the numbers of people they baptized. Spanish and Portuguese kings were eager to count native populations, since "indios" (adult male Amerindians) were subject to special labor obligations and tribute payments. So, from the mid-sixteenth century onward, imperial officials conducted regular censuses of Amerindians, adapting practices already in place in Europe.

The effort to measure and categorize populations was transformed in the last decades of the eighteenth century when the nature of European governments began to change. The Enlightenment belief that the scientific method could be applied to human society proved to be attractive both to political radicals, like the French Revolutionaries, and to reforming monarchs like Maria Theresa of Austria. Enlightenment philosophers had argued that a science of government could remove the inefficiencies and irrationalities that had long subverted the human potential for prosperity and happiness. The French intellectual Condorcet wrote in 1782:

> Those sciences, created almost in our own days, the object of which is man himself, the direct goal of which is the happiness of man, will enjoy a progress no less sure than that of the physical sciences. . . . In meditating on the nature of the moral sciences [what we now call the social sciences], one cannot help seeing that, as they are based like the physical sciences on the observation of fact, they must follow the method, acquire a language equally exact and precise, attaining the same degree of certainty.[1]

State Power, the Census, and the Question of Identity

As confidence in this new "science" grew, the term previously used to describe the collection of numbers about society, *political arithmetic*, was abandoned by governments and practitioners in favor of *statistics*, a term that clearly suggests its close ties to the "state." In the nineteenth century the new objectives set out by Condorcet and others led to both the formal university training of statisticians and the creation of government statistical services.

The ambitions of governments in this new era were great. Nation-states self-consciously sought to transform society, sponsoring economic development, education, and improvements in health and welfare. They depended on statistics to measure the effectiveness of their policies and, as a result, were interested in nearly everything. They counted taverns, urban buildings, births and deaths, and arrests and convictions. They also counted their populations with a thoroughness never before seen. As statistical reporting became more uniform across Europe and the Americas, governments could measure not only their own progress but also that of their neighbors and rivals.

The revolutionary governments of France modernized the census practices of the overthrown monarchy. They spent much more money, hired many more census takers, and devoted much more energy to training the staff that designed censuses and analyzed results. Great Britain set up an official census in 1801 but established a special administrative structure only in the 1830s. In the Western Hemisphere nearly every independent nation provided for "scientific" censuses. In the United States the federal constitution required that a census be taken every ten years. Latin American nations, often torn by civil war in the nineteenth century, took censuses less regularly, but even the poorest nations took censuses when they could. It was as if the census itself confirmed the existence of the government, demonstrating its modernity and seriousness.

Until recently, historians who relied on these documents in their research on economic performance, issues of race and ethnicity, family life, and fertility and mortality asked few questions about the politics of census design. What could be more objective than rows of numbers? But the advocates of statistics who managed census taking were uninhibited in advertising the usefulness of reliable numbers to the governments that employed them. At the 1860 International Statistical Congress held in London one speaker said, "I think the true meaning to be attached to 'statistics' is not every collection of figures, but figures collected with the sole purpose of applying the principles deduced from them to questions of importance to the state."[2] The desire to be useful meant that statistics could not be fully objective.

Subjectivity was an unavoidable problem with censuses. Censuses identified citizens and foreign residents by place of residence, sex, age, and family relationships within households as well as profession and literacy. These determinations were sometimes subjective. Modern scholars have demonstrated that census takers also often undercounted the poor and those living in rural areas.

Because census takers, as agents of nation-states, were determined to be useful, they were necessarily concerned with issues of nationality and, in the Americas, with race because these characteristics commonly determined political rights and citizenship. The assessment and recording of nationality and race would prove to be among the most politically problematic objectives of the new social sciences.

Nationality had not been a central question for traditional monarchies. For the emerging nation-state, nationality was central. A nation's strength was assumed to depend in large measure on the growth of its population, a standard that, once articulated, suggested that the growth of minority populations was dangerous. Who was French? Who was Austrian or Hungarian? European statisticians relied on both *language of use* and *mother tongue* as proxies for *nationality,* the first term being flexible enough to recognize the assimilation of minorities, the second suggesting a more permanent identity based on a person's original language. Both terms forced bilingual populations to simplify their more complex identities. Ethnic minorities, once identified, were sometimes subject to discrimination such as exclusion from military careers or from universities. In parts of Spanish America language was used as a proxy for *race.* Those who spoke Spanish were citizens in the full sense, even if they were indistinguishable from Amerindians in appearance. Those who spoke indigenous languages were "indios" and therefore subject to special taxes and labor obligations and effectively denied the right to vote.

Beyond providing a justification for continuing discrimination, census categories compressed and distorted the complexity and variety of human society to fit the preconceptions of bureaucrats and politicians. Large percentages of the residents of Mexico, Peru, and

Bolivia, among other parts of the Americas, were descended from both Europeans and Amerindians and, in the Caribbean region, from Europeans and Africans. Census categories never adequately captured the complexities of these biological and cultural mixtures. We now know that the poor were often identified as "indios" or "blacks" and the better-off were often called something else, "Americanos," "criollos" (creoles), or even whites. Since this process flattened and streamlined the complexities of identity, censuses on their own are not reliable guides to the distribution of ethnicity and race in a population.

In Europe the issue of nationality proved similarly perplexing for census takers and similarly dangerous to those identified as minorities. Linguistic and ethnic minorities had always lived among the politically dominant majorities: Jewish and Polish minorities in areas controlled by German speakers, German speakers among the French, and Serbo-Croatian speakers among Hungarians, for example. The frontiers between these minority populations and their neighbors were always porous. Sexual unions and marriages were common, and two or more generations of a family often lived together in the same household, with the elder members speaking one language and the younger members another. Who was what? In a very real sense, nationality, like race in the Americas, was ultimately fixed by the census process, where the nation-state forced a limited array of politically utilitarian categories onto the rich diversity of ethnicity and culture.

Part Seven

Global Diversity and Dominance, 1850–1949

In 1850, the world still embraced a huge diversity of societies, cultures, and states. During the century that followed, European nations, the United States, and Japan dominated much of the world in a wave of conquest we call the New Imperialism and tried to convert their new subjects to their own cultures and ways of life.

In Europe, mounting tensions and the awesome power of modern armaments led to the devastating Great War of 1914–1918. Russia and China erupted in revolution. Soon after, the heartland of the Ottoman Empire became modern Turkey, while its Arab provinces were taken over by France and Britain.

The political and economic system the European powers crafted after the war fell apart in the 1930s. While the capitalist nations fell into a deep economic depression, the Soviet Union industrialized at breakneck speed. In Germany and Japan, extremists sought to solve their countries' grievances by military conquest.

In World War II nationalism and industrial warfare led to the massacre of millions of people and the destruction of countless cities. The war also weakened Europe's control of its overseas empires. Nationalists in Asia, Latin America, and Africa were inspired by Western ideas and by the desire to acquire the benefits of industrialization. India gained its independence in 1947. Two years later, Mao Zedong led the Chinese communists to victory. Latin American leaders embraced nationalist economic and social policies. Of all the once great powers, only the United States and the Soviet Union remained to compete for global dominance.

	1850	1870	1890
AMERICAS		**1861–1865** U.S. Civil War · **1867** Creation of Dominion of Canada	• **1880s** British build railroads in Brazil and Argentina **1880–1914** Immigration from southern and eastern Europe surges	• **1898** Spanish-American War
EUROPE	• **1851** Majority of British population living in cities · **1856** Transformation of steel and chemical industries begins	**1870–1914** Era of the New Imperialism • **1871** Unification of Germany, Italy	**1894–1906** Dreyfus affair in France
AFRICA	End of transatlantic slave trade **1867** •	West Africa conquered by France and Britain **1880s** •	**1884–1885** Berlin Africa Conference Nigeria becomes British protectorate **1899** •	• **1896** Ethiopians defeat Italian army at Adowa
MIDDLE EAST	**1863–1879** Ismail westernizes Egypt • **1869** Suez Canal opens	• **1882** British occupy Egypt • **1878** Ottoman Empire loses most of its European territories	
ASIA AND OCEANIA	• **1858** Direct British rule in India · **1868** Meiji Restoration in Japan • **1862** French conquer Indochina	First Indian National Congress **1885** •	• **1894** Sino-Japanese War Boxer Rebellion in China **1900** • **1884–1887** Russia conquers Central Asia

1910 **1930** **1950**

- **1906–1914** U.S. builds Panama Canal
- **1917** U.S. enters World War I
- **1911–1920** Mexican Revolution
- **1929** U.S. stock market crash leads to Great Depression
- **1938** Mexico nationalizes oil industry
- **1946** Juan Perón becomes president of Argentina

- **1905** Revolution of 1905 in Russia
- **1922–1945** Fascism in Italy
- **1917** Russian Revolutions
- **1933** Hitler takes power in Germany
- **1914–1918** World War I
- **1939–1945** World War II
- **1939–1945** A million Africans serve in World War II

- **1908** Congo annexed by Belgium
- **1909** African National Congress founded

- Balfour Declaration **1917**
- **1922–1938** Atatürk secularizes Turkey
- **1948** State of Israel founded
- **1904** Young Turk reforms in Ottoman Empire
- **1918** Breakup of Ottoman Empire
- **1915–1918** Arab Revolt against Ottomans

- **1904–1905** Russo-Japanese War
- **1910** Korea annexed by Japan
- **1911** Overthrow of Qing dynasty in China
- **1931** Japanese invasion of Manchuria
- **1941** Japan attacks U.S.
- **1945** U.S. atomic bombs force Japanese surrender
- **1947** India and Pakistan win independence
- **1949** Communists take power in China

college.cengage.com/pic/bullietbrief4e

The New Power Balance

CHAPTER **23**

1850–1900

CHAPTER PREVIEW

New Technologies and the World Economy *What new technologies and industries appeared between 1850 and 1900, and how did they affect the world economy?*

Social Changes *How did the societies of the industrial countries change during this period?*

Nationalism and the Rise of Italy, Germany, and Japan *How did industrialization contribute to the socialist and labor movements?*

The Great Powers of Europe, 1871–1900 *How was nationalism transformed from a revolutionary to a conservative ideology?*

China, Japan, and the Western Powers *How did the forces of nationalism affect the major powers of Europe?*

ENVIRONMENT AND TECHNOLOGY: Railroads and Immigration

MATERIAL CULTURE: Cotton Clothing

O n July 8, 1853, four American warships, two of them steam-powered, appeared in Edo Bay, close to the capital of Japan. The commander of the fleet, **Commodore Matthew Perry**, delivered a letter from President Millard Fillmore, demanding that Japan open its ports to foreign trade. Although foreign ships had occasionally appeared in Japanese waters, Perry's "black ships," as the Japanese called them, broke through the barriers that had kept Japan isolated from the rest of the world for two and a half centuries.

A year later, Perry returned with a fleet of seven ships to receive the answer from the Japanese government. The Americans also set up a track and a little steam locomotive, a short telegraph line, and other marvels of Western technology. For the next twenty years, Japanese society was torn between those who

626

 This icon will direct you to the website where you can Prepare for Class, Improve Your Grade, and Ace the Test: college.cengage.com/pic/bullietbrief4e

wanted to retreat into isolation and those who wished to embrace the foreign ways and acquire their machines and the industries that made them. For it soon became clear that industrialization gave power and that only by industrializing could Japan join the ranks of the powerful nations and escape the fate of weaker ones that were then being overwhelmed by imperialism.

Commodore Matthew Perry
A navy commander who, on July 8, 1853, became the first foreigner to break through the barriers that had kept Japan isolated from the rest of the world for 250 years.

NEW TECHNOLOGIES AND THE WORLD ECONOMY

What new technologies and industries appeared between 1850 and 1900, and how did they affect the world economy?

After 1850, industrialization took off in new directions. Germany and the United States surpassed Great Britain as the world's leading industrial powers by 1890. Small companies were overshadowed by large corporations owned by wealthy capitalists or (especially in Russia and Japan) by governments. New technologies based on advances in physics and chemistry revolutionized everyday life and transformed the world economy.

Railroads

By the mid-nineteenth century, steam engines had become the prime mover of industry and commerce. Nowhere was this more evident than in the spread of **railroads**. By 1850 the first railroads had proved so successful that every industrializing country, and many that aspired to become industrial, began to build lines. The next fifty years saw a tremendous expansion of the world's rail networks. After a rapid spurt of building new lines, British railroad mileage leveled off at around 20,000 miles (over 32,000 kilometers) in the 1870s. France and Germany built networks longer than Britain's, as did Canada and Russia. By the early twentieth century, rail lines reached every city and province in Japan (see Map 23.2).

railroads Networks of iron (later steel) rails on which steam (later electric or diesel) locomotives pulled long trains at high speeds. The first railroads were built in England in the 1830s. Their success caused a railroad-building boom throughout the world that lasted well into the twentieth century.

The American rail network was the largest by far. At the end of its Civil War in 1865 the United States already had 35,000 miles (over 56,000 kilometers) of track, three times as much as Britain. By 1915 the American network reached 390,000 miles (around 628,000 kilometers), more than the next seven longest networks combined.

Railroads were not confined to the industrialized nations; they could be constructed almost anywhere they would be of value to business or government. That included regions with abundant raw materials or agricultural products, like South Africa, Mexico, and Argentina, and densely populated countries like Egypt. The British built the fourth largest rail network in the world in India to reinforce their presence and develop trade with their largest colony. Until the opening of the Panama Canal in 1915, a railroad across the isthmus carried freight between the Atlantic and Pacific Oceans.

With one exception, European or American engineers built these railroads with equipment imported from the West. In 1855, barely a year after Commodore Perry's visit, the Japanese instrument maker Tanaka Hisashige built a model steam train that he demonstrated to an admiring audience. In the 1870s the Japanese government

Construction of the Trans-Siberian Railroad

Schemes to link Russia in Europe by rail to its eastern territories all the way to Vladivostok on the Pacific Ocean failed to gain government support before 1880 because of Siberia's low level of economic productivity. Construction finally began in 1891, in some places using convicts or soldiers as laborers. Industrial products traveling eastward and Siberian wheat traveling westward accounted for most of the transport capacity. (Hulton Archive/Getty Images)

hired British engineers to build the first line from Tokyo to Yokohama and sent them home again as soon as they had trained Japanese engineers. Within a few years, Japan began manufacturing its own equipment.

Railroads consumed huge amounts of land. Many old cities doubled in size to accommodate railroad stations, sidings, tracks, warehouses, and repair shops. In the countryside, railroads required bridges, tunnels, and embankments. Railroads also consumed vast quantities of timber for ties to hold the rails and for bridges, often using up whole forests for miles on either side of the tracks. Throughout the world, they opened new land to agriculture, mining, and other human exploitation of natural resources, whether for the benefit of the local inhabitants, as in Europe and North America, or for a distant power, as in the colonial empires.

Steamships and Telegraph Cables

Steam-powered ships dated back to the 1830s but were initially too costly for anything but first-class passenger traffic. Then, by midcentury, a series of developments radically transformed ocean shipping. First iron, then steel, replaced the wood that had been used for hulls since shipbuilding began. Propellers replaced paddle wheels, and engineers built more powerful and fuel-efficient engines. By the turn of the century a marine engine could convert the heat produced by burning a single sheet of paper into the power to move one ton over half a mile. The average size of freighters increased from 200 tons in 1850 to 7,500 tons in 1900. Coaling stations and ports able to handle large ships were built around the world. Most of all, the Suez Canal, constructed in 1869, shortened the distance between Europe and Asia and triggered a massive switch from sail power to steam (see Chapter 24).

The steamers of the turn of the century were so costly they had to be used as efficiently as possible. As the world's fleet of merchant ships grew from 9 million tons in 1850 to 35 million tons in 1910, new organizations developed to make the best use of them. Shipping lines, companies that offered fast and reliable service on a fixed schedule, transported passengers, mail, and perishable freight. Most ships, however, were tramp freighters that voyaged from one port to another under orders from their company headquarters in Europe or North America.

To control their ships around the globe, shipping companies used a new medium of communications: **submarine telegraph cables** laid on the ocean floor. Cables were laid across the Atlantic in 1866, to India in 1870, to China, Japan, and Australia in 1871 and 1872, to Latin America in 1872 and 1873, to East and South Africa in 1879, and to West Africa in 1886. By the turn of the century cables connected every country and almost every inhabited island. As cables became the indispensable tools of modern shipping and business, the public and the press extolled the "annihilation of time and space."

submarine telegraph cables Insulated copper cables laid along the bottom of a sea or ocean for telegraphic communication. The first short cable was laid across the English Channel in 1851; the first successful transatlantic cable was laid in 1866.

Chronology

	Europe	United States	East Asia
1850			
	1851 Majority of British population living in cities		
			1853 Commodore Perry "opens" Japan
	1859 Charles Darwin, *On the Origin of Species*		
	1861 Emancipation of serfs (Russia)		
		1865 Civil War ends; economic expansion begins	
		1865–1914 Surge of immigration from southern and eastern Europe	
	1866 Alfred Nobel develops dynamite		
	1867 Karl Marx, *Das Kapital*		
			1868 Meiji Restoration begins modernization drive in Japan
	1871 Unification of Germany; unification of Italy		
1875			
		1879 Thomas Edison develops incandescent lamp	
	1882 Married Women's Property Act (Britain)		
		1890s "Jim Crow" laws enforce segregation in southern states	
			1894 Sino-Japanese War
		1899 United States acquires Puerto Rico and the Philippines	
1900			**1900** Boxer uprising ends
			1904–1905 Russo-Japanese War
	1905 Revolution of 1905 (Russia)		
			1910 Japan annexes Korea

The Steel and Chemical Industries

Steel is a special form of iron, both hard and elastic. A series of inventions in the 1850s made steel the cheapest and most versatile metal ever known. As a result, world steel production rose from a half-million tons in 1870 to 28 million in 1900, of which the United States produced 10 million, Germany 8, and Britain 4.9. Steel became cheap and abundant enough to make rails, bridges, ships, and even "tin" cans meant to be used once and thrown away.

The new steel mills were hungry consumers of coal, iron ore, limestone, and other raw materials. They took up as much space as whole towns, belched smoke and

steel A form of iron that is both durable and flexible. It was first mass-produced in the 1860s and quickly became the most widely used metal in construction, machinery, and railroad equipment.

particulates night and day, and left behind huge hills of slag and other waste products. Environmental degradation affected steel-producing regions such as the English Midlands, the German Ruhr, parts of Pennsylvania, and the regions around Tokyo and Osaka in Japan.

The chemical industry followed a similar pattern. In the early nineteenth century, only soda, sulfuric acid, and chlorine bleach (used in the cotton industry) were manufactured on a large scale, especially in Britain. Then in 1856, the development of the first synthetic dye, aniline purple, from coal tar launched the mass production of organic chemicals—compounds containing carbon atoms. These bright, long-lasting colors delighted consumers but hurt tropical countries, such as India, that produced indigo, a blue vegetable dye.

Chemistry also advanced the manufacture of explosives. In 1866, the Swedish scientist Alfred Nobel found a way to turn nitroglycerin into a stable solid—dynamite. This and other new explosives were useful in mining and the construction of railroads and canals. They also enabled armies and navies to arm themselves with increasingly accurate and powerful rifles and cannon.

The growing complexity of industrial chemistry made it one of the first fields where science and technology interacted on a daily basis. This development gave a great advantage to Germany, which then had the most advanced engineering schools and scientific institutes. By the end of the nineteenth century, Germany was the world's leading producer of dyes, drugs, synthetic fertilizers, ammonia, and nitrates used in making explosives.

Electricity

electricity A form of energy used in telegraphy from the 1840s on and for lighting, industrial motors, and railroads beginning in the 1880s.

No innovation of the late nineteenth century changed people's lives as radically as **electricity**. At first, producing electric current cost so much that it was used only for electroplating and telegraphy. In 1831 the Englishman Michael Faraday showed that the motion of a copper wire through a magnetic field induced an electric current in the wire. Based on his discovery, inventors in the 1870s devised efficient generators that turned mechanical energy into electric current. Electricity was more flexible and much easier to use than waterpower or the stationary steam engine, which had powered industrialization until then.

Electricity opened the way to a host of new applications. Arc lamps lit up public squares, theaters, and stores. For a while, homes continued to rely on gas lamps, which produced a softer light. Then in 1879 in the United States **Thomas Edison** developed an incandescent lamp well suited to lighting small rooms. In 1882 Edison created the world's first electrical distribution network in New York City. By the turn of the century electric lighting was rapidly replacing dim and smelly gas lamps in the cities of Europe and North America.

Thomas Edison (1847–1931) American inventor best known for inventing the electric light bulb, acoustic recording on wax cylinders, and motion pictures.

Other uses of electricity quickly appeared. Electric streetcars and, later, subways helped reduce the traffic jams that clogged the large cities of Europe and North America. Electric motors replaced steam engines and power belts, increasing productivity and improving workers' safety. As demand for electricity grew, engineers learned to use waterpower to produce electricity, and hydroelectric plants were built. The plant at Niagara Falls, on the border between Ontario, Canada, and New York State, produced an incredible 11,000 horsepower when it opened in 1895. At the newly created Imperial College of Engineering in Japan, an Englishman, William Ayrton, became the first professor of electrical engineering anywhere in the world; his students later went on to found major corporations and government research institutes.

World Trade and Finance

Thanks to the growing speed and falling cost of transportation between 1850 and 1913, world trade expanded tenfold, transforming the economies of different parts of the world in different ways. The capitalist economies of western Europe and North America grew more prosperous and diversified, despite deep depressions in which workers lost their jobs and investors their fortunes.

Long after German and American industries surpassed the British, Britain continued to dominate the flow of trade, finance, and information. In 1900, two-thirds of the world's submarine cables were British or passed through Britain. Over half of the world's shipping was British owned. Britain invested one-fourth of its national wealth overseas, much of it in the United States and Argentina.

Nonindustrial areas were more vulnerable to changes in price and demand than were the industrialized nations, for many of them produced raw materials that could be replaced by synthetic substitutes or alternative sources of supply. Nevertheless, until World War I, the value of exports from the tropical countries generally remained high.

SECTION REVIEW

- As industrialization surged forward, the steel and chemical industries rose, creating important new products but at great environmental cost.

- Electricity became widely available for lighting and other uses, lessening some environmental problems and stimulating new demand for copper.

- New materials and mechanization expanded global shipping and the submarine telegraph cables used to control it.

- Railroads expanded rapidly after 1850, with the United States leading the world in track mileage in 1865.

- Propelled by improved transportation, international trade expanded, strengthening the Western capitalist economies.

SOCIAL CHANGES

How did the societies of the industrial countries change during this period?

The technological and economic changes of the late nineteenth century sparked profound social changes in the industrial nations. A fast-growing population swelled cities to unprecedented size, and millions of Europeans immigrated to the Americas. Workers spawned labor movements and new forms of radical policies, and women's lives were dramatically altered.

Population and Migrations

The population of Europe grew faster from 1850 to 1914 than ever before or since, almost doubling from 265 million to 468 million, despite mass migrations of Europeans to the United States, Canada, Australia, New Zealand, and Argentina. Between 1850 and 1900, on average, 400,000 Europeans migrated overseas every year; between 1900 and 1914, the flood rose to over 1 million a year (see Environment and Technology: Railroads and Immigration). People of European ancestry rose from one-fifth to one-third in the world's population.

Much of the increase came from a drop in the death rate, as epidemics and starvation became less common. The Irish famine of 1847–1848 was the last peacetime

Railroads and Immigration

Why did so many Europeans immigrate to North America in the late nineteenth and early twentieth centuries? The quick answer is that millions of people longed to escape the poverty or tyranny of their home countries and start new lives in a land of freedom and opportunity. Personal desire alone, however, does not account for the migrations. After all, poverty and tyranny existed long before the late nineteenth century. Two other factors helped determine when and where people migrated: whether they were allowed to migrate, and whether they were able to.

In the nineteenth century Asians were recruited to build railroads and work on farms. But from the 1890s on, the United States and Canada closed their doors to non-Europeans, so regardless of what they wanted, they could not move to North America. In contrast, emigrants from Europe were admitted until after the First World War.

The ability to travel was a result of improvements in transportation. Until the 1890s most immigrants came from Ireland, England, or Germany—countries with good rail transportation to their own harbors and low steamship fares to North America. As rail lines were extended into eastern and southern Europe, more and more immigrants came from Italy, Austria-Hungary, and Russia.

Similarly, until the 1870s most European immigrants to North America settled on the east coast. Then, as the railroads pushed west, more of them settled on farms in the central and western parts of the continent. The power of railroads moved people as much as their desires did.

EMIGRANT WAITING ROOM   The opening of the western region of the United States attracted settlers from the east coast and from Europe. These migrants are waiting for a train to take them to the Black Hills of Dakota during one of the gold rushes of the late nineteenth century.   (Library of Congress)

famine in European history. North American wheat supplemented Europe's food, and year-round supplies of meat, fruit, vegetables, and oils improved the diet of European and North American city dwellers.

Urbanization and Urban Environments

In 1851, Britain became the first nation to have a majority of its population living in towns and cities. By 1914, 80 percent of its population was urban, as were 60 percent of the German and 45 percent of the French populations. London grew from 2.7 million in 1850 to 6.6 million in 1900. New York reached 3.4 million by 1900, a fiftyfold increase in the century. In the English Midlands, in the German Ruhr, and around Tokyo Bay, towns fused into one another, filling in the fields and woods that once had separated them.

In early industrial cities, the poor crowded together in unsanitary tenements. New urban technologies transformed city life for most residents. Pipes brought in clean water and carried away sewage. First gas and then electric lighting made cities safer and more pleasant at night. By the end of the century, municipal governments provided police and fire departments, schools, parks, and other amenities unheard of a century earlier.

As sanitation improved, urban death rates fell below birthrates for the first time. Confident that their children would survive infancy, couples began to limit the number of children they had. To accommodate the growing population, planners laid out new cities on a rectangular grid, and middle-class families moved to new developments on the edges of cities. In Paris, older neighborhoods with narrow, crooked streets and rickety tenements were replaced with broad boulevards and modern apartment buildings. Brilliantly lit by gas and electricity, Paris became the "City of Lights," a

Paris Lit Up by Electricity, 1900

The electric light bulb was invented in the United States and Britain, but Paris made such extensive use of the new technology that it was nicknamed "City of Lights." To mark the Paris Exposition of 1900, the Eiffel Tower and all the surrounding buildings were illuminated with strings of light bulbs while powerful spotlights swept the sky. (Civiche Raccolte delle Stampe Achille Bertarelli, Milano) model for city planners from New Delhi to Buenos Aires. By 1900, electric streetcars and subways allowed working-class people to live miles from their workplaces.

In fast-growing cities such as London, New York, and Chicago, newcomers arrived so quickly that housing construction and municipal services could not keep up. Immigrants who saved their money to reunite their families could not afford costly municipal services. As a result, the poorest neighborhoods remained as overcrowded, unhealthy, and dangerous as they had been since the early decades of industrialization.

While urban environments improved in many ways, air quality worsened. Coal, burned to power steam engines and heat buildings, polluted the air, coating everything with a film of grimy dust. And the thousands of horses that pulled the carts and carriages covered the streets with their wastes, causing a terrible stench.

Victorian Age The reign of Queen Victoria of Great Britain (r. 1837–1901). The term is also used to describe late-nineteenth-century society, with its rigid moral standards and sharply differentiated roles for men and women and for middle-class and working-class people.

"separate spheres" Nineteenth-century idea in Western societies that men and women, especially of the middle class, should have clearly differentiated roles in society: women as wives, mothers, and homemakers; men as breadwinners and participants in business and politics.

Middle-Class Women's "Separate Sphere"

In English-speaking countries the period from about 1850 to 1901 is known as the **"Victorian Age."** The expression refers not only to the reign of Queen Victoria of England (r. 1837–1901) but also to rules of behavior and to an ideology surrounding the family and the relations between men and women. The Victorians contrasted the masculine ideals of strength and courage with the feminine virtues of beauty and kindness, and they idealized the home as a peaceful and loving refuge from the dog-eat-dog world of competitive capitalism.

Victorian morality claimed to be universal, yet it best fit upper- and middle-class European families. Men and women were thought to belong in **"separate spheres."** Successful businessmen spent their time at work or relaxing in men's clubs. They put their wives in charge of rearing the children, running the household, and spending the family money to enhance the family's social status.

Before electric appliances, maintaining a middle-class home involved enormous amounts of work. Families were larger, and middle-class couples entertained often and lavishly. Carrying out these tasks required servants. A family's status and the activities and lifestyle of the "mistress of the house" depended on the availability of servants to help with household tasks.

Toward the turn of the century modern technology began to transform middle-class homes. Plumbing eliminated the pump and the outhouse. Central heating replaced fireplaces, stoves, and endless dusting. Gas and electricity lit houses and cooked food without soot, smoke, and ashes. Vacuum cleaners and washing machines came in the early twentieth century. These technological advances did not mean less housework for women. As families acquired new household technologies, they raised their standards of cleanliness, thus demanding just as much labor as before.

Unlike the rich of previous eras who handed their children over to wet nurses and tutors, Victorian mothers nursed their own babies and showered their children with love and attention. Even those who could afford nannies and governesses remained personally involved in their children's education. Girls received an education very different from that of boys. While boys were being prepared for the business world or the professions, girls were taught embroidery, drawing, and music, which offered no monetary reward or professional preparation but enhanced their social graces and marriage prospects.

Victorian morality frowned on middle-class women working. Young women could work until they got married, but only in genteel places like stores and offices, never in factories. When the typewriter and telephone entered the business world in the 1880s, businessmen found that they could get better work at lower wages from educated young women than from men. Operating these machines became typecast as women's work.

Most professional careers were closed to women. Until late in the century few universities granted degrees to women. In the United States higher education was available to women only at elite colleges in the East and teachers' colleges in the Midwest. European women had fewer opportunities. Before 1914 very few women became doctors, lawyers, or professional musicians.

The first profession open to women was teaching, due to laws calling for universal compulsory education. By 1911, for instance, 73 percent of all teachers in England were women. They were considered well suited to teaching young children and girls—an extension of the duties of Victorian mothers. Teaching, however, was judged suitable only for single women. A married woman was expected to get pregnant right away and to stay home taking care of her own children rather than the children of other people.

A home life, no matter how busy, did not satisfy all middle-class women. Some became volunteer nurses or social workers, receiving little or no pay. Others organized to fight prostitution, alcohol, and child labor. By the turn of the century a few were challenging male domination of politics and the law. Women suffragists, led in Britain by Emmeline Pankhurst and in the United States by Elizabeth Cady Stanton and Susan B. Anthony, demanded the right to vote. By 1914 U.S. women had won the right to vote in twelve states. British women did not vote until 1918.

Working-Class Women

In the new industrial cities, men and women no longer worked together at home or in the fields. The separation of work and home affected women's lives even more than men's lives. Women formed a majority of the workers in the textile industries and in domestic service. Yet working-class women needed to keep homes and raise children as well as earn their living. As a result, they led lives of toil and pain, considerably harder than the lives of their menfolk. In Japan, as in Ireland and New England, tenant farmers, squeezed by rising taxes and rents, were forced to send their daughters to work in textile mills. Others became domestic servants, commonly working sixteen hours a day, six and a half days a week, for little more than room and board. Their living quarters, usually in attics or basements, contrasted with the luxurious quarters of their masters. Without appliances, much of their work was physically hard: hauling coal and water up stairs, washing laundry by hand.

Female servants were vulnerable to sexual abuse by their masters or their masters' sons. A well-known case is that of Helene Demuth, who worked for Karl and Jenny Marx all her life. At age thirty-one she bore a son by Karl Marx and put him with foster parents rather than leave the family. She was more fortunate than most; the majority of families fired servants who got pregnant, rather than embarrass the master of the house.

Young women often preferred factory work to domestic service. Here, too, Victorian society practiced a strict division of labor by gender. Men worked in construction, iron and steel, heavy machinery, or on railroads; women worked in textiles and the clothing trades, extensions of traditional women's household work (see Material Culture: Cotton Clothing). Appalled by the abuses of women and children in the early years of industrialization, most industrial countries passed protective legislation limiting the hours or forbidding the employment of women in the hardest and most dangerous occupations, such as mining and foundry work. Such legislation limited abuses but also reinforced gender divisions in industry, keeping women in low-paid, subordinate positions. Denied access to the better-paid jobs of foremen or machine repairmen, female factory workers earned between one-third and two-thirds of men's wages.

Married women with children were expected to stay home, even if their husbands did not make enough to support the family. Most working-class married women had double responsibilities within the home: not only the work of child rearing and housework but also that of contributing to the family's income. Families who had room to spare, even a bed or a corner in the kitchen, took in boarders. Many women did piecework such as sewing dresses, making hats or gloves, or weaving baskets. The hardest and worst-paid work was washing other people's clothes. Many women worked at home ten to twelve hours a day and enlisted the help of their small children, perpetuating practices long outlawed in factories.

Socialism and Labor Movements

Industrialization combined with the revolutionary ideas of the late eighteenth century to produce two kinds of movements—socialism and labor movements—calling for further changes. **Socialism** was an ideology developed by radical thinkers who questioned the sanctity of private property and argued in support of industrial workers against their employers. **Labor unions** were organizations formed by industrial workers to defend their interests in negotiations with employers. The socialist and labor movements were never identical. Most of the time they were allies; occasionally they were rivals.

Socialism began as an intellectual movement. By far the best-known socialist was **Karl Marx** (1818–1883), a German journalist and writer who spent most of his life in England and collaborated with another socialist, Friedrich Engels (1820–1895), author of *The Condition of the Working Class in England in 1844* (1845). Together, they combined German philosophy, French revolutionary ideas, and knowledge of British industrial conditions.

Marx expressed his ideas succinctly in the *Communist Manifesto* (1848) and in great detail in *Das Kapital* (DUSS cop-ee-TAHL) (1867). He saw history as a series of conflicts between social classes, the latest being between property owners (the bourgeoisie) and workers (the proletariat). He argued that the capitalist system allowed the bourgeoisie to extract the "surplus value" of workers' labor—that is, the difference between their wages and the value of the goods they manufactured. He saw business enterprises becoming larger and more monopolistic and workers growing more numerous and impoverished. He concluded that this conflict would inevitably lead to a revolutionary overthrow of the bourgeoisie, after which the workers would establish a communist society without classes.

What Marx called "scientific socialism" provided an intellectual framework for the growing dissatisfaction with raw industrial capitalism. In the late nineteenth

---

socialism A political ideology that originated in Europe in the 1830s. Socialists advocated government protection of workers from exploitation by property owners and government ownership of industries. This ideology led to the founding of socialist or labor parties throughout Europe in the second half of the nineteenth century.

labor union An organization of workers in a particular industry or trade, created to defend the interests of members through strikes or negotiations with employers.

Karl Marx (1818–1883) German journalist and philosopher, founder of the Marxist branch of socialism. He is known for two books: *The Communist Manifesto* (1848) and *Das Kapital* (Vols. I–III, 1867–1894).

MATERIAL CULTURE

Cotton Clothing

Of all the things that bring us comfort, nothing compares to cotton. For clothes, sheets, and towels, it is the world's favorite textile. And no wonder: cotton is cool next to the skin, can be dyed in bright colors, absorbs moisture, and, unlike other fabrics such as wool, can be washed easily.

The use of cotton for clothing has a long history dating back to 3000 B.C.E., when it was grown in the Indus River Valley. Originally, the cotton plant was grown and the cloth woven only in India, Mexico, Peru, and a few other places in the tropics. The Maya wove fine textiles from cotton and traded them with other parts of Mesoamerica. Indian cottons were particularly fine and exported as luxury items to China and Rome. Cotton replaced hemp clothing in China and was used extensively by the Mongols for turbans, pants, and other items of clothing. The Arabs spread cotton growing and weaving to the Middle East and Spain. By the tenth century, it was a major crop in Iran and elsewhere in the region. Many of our names for particular kinds of cotton fabric come from cities in India, like calico (from Calicut) or madras, or in the Middle East, like damask (from Damascus) or muslin (from Mosul in Iraq).

Around 800 C.E., Arab merchants brought cotton cloth to Europe, where it became as precious as silk. With the invention of machines like the spinning jenny and the water frame in the eighteenth century (see Chapter 20), cotton became less precious and more available. Cotton yarn and cloth were the first items to be mass-produced in the Industrial Revolution, with important consequences for India, the American South, and other countries.

Mass production means mass consumption. In the nineteenth century, for the first time, the poor could afford to wear bright, colorful clothes and—even more important—to wash them. These clothes were made almost exclusively by women. Wealthy European families hired seamstresses who came to the house, took measurements, and returned a few days later with finished clothes. Other women sewed clothes for themselves and their families.

Sewing by hand was very time-consuming and increasingly costly compared to the declining price of cloth. By the mid-nineteenth century, prosperity and a faster pace of life in Europe and America provided an incentive for inventors

THE SEWING MACHINE The Japanese imported many innovations from the West after the Meiji Restoration of 1868. Among the most popular were Western-style clothing and sewing machines. Sewing was a gendered activity in Japan as in the West, with the woman sewing and the man looking on. (Private Collection)

to devise a machine that could sew. In 1850, Isaac Singer manufactured the first practical machine for commercial use. A few years later, he designed the "Singer Family Sewing Machine" with an iron stand and a foot-treadle for home use. By 1891 Singer alone had manufactured 10 million machines in the United States and Europe. Some were industrial machines sold to makers of ready-to-wear clothes in the new garment districts. Others were home models, some inexpensive enough for the working class. There were even portable models that seamstresses could take with them to their clients' homes.

The combination of cotton cloth and sewing machines revolutionized clothing. A shirt that took fourteen and a half hours to sew by hand could be made in an hour and a quarter on a machine; an apron could be made in nine minutes instead of an hour and a half. Now the poor could afford to own several shirts, skirts, or pants, even underwear. Better-off homemakers subscribed to fashion magazines, bought patterns, and made blouses and dresses, even complicated items like crinolines and hoopskirts, which would once have been too tedious to sew by hand.

Today, the world uses more cotton than any other fiber. China is the largest producer (and consumer) of cotton, followed by the United States, India, and Pakistan. Almost all of the cotton clothing sold is produced on powerful computerized machines in the developing countries of Asia and Latin America.

century business tycoons spent money lavishly on mansions, yachts, private railroad cars, and other displays of wealth that contrasted sharply with the poverty of the workers. Even though industrial workers were not becoming poorer as Marx believed, the class struggle between workers and employers was brutally real. What Marx did was to offer a persuasive explanation of the causes of this contrast and the antagonisms it bred.

Marx was not just a philosopher; he also had a direct impact on politics. In 1864 he helped found the International Working Man's Association (later known as the First International), a movement he hoped would bring about the overthrow of the bourgeoisie. However, it attracted more intellectuals than workers. Workers found other means of redressing their grievances, such as the vote and labor unions.

Since the beginning of the nineteenth century, workers had united to create "friendly societies" for mutual assistance in times of difficulty. Anti-combination laws, however, forbade workers to strike. These laws were abolished in Britain in the 1850s and in the rest of Europe in subsequent decades. Labor unions sought better wages as well as improved working conditions and insurance against illness, disability, and old age. They grew slowly because they required a permanent staff and a great deal of money to sustain their members during strikes. By the end of the century British labor unions counted 2 million members, and German and American unions had 1 million members each.

The nineteenth century saw a gradual extension of the right to vote throughout Europe and North America. Universal male suffrage became law in the United States in 1870, in France and Germany in 1871, in Britain in 1885, and in the rest of Europe soon thereafter. Because there were so many newly enfranchised workers, universal male suffrage meant that socialist politicians could expect to capture many seats in their nations' parliaments. Unlike Marx, who predicted that workers would seize power through revolution, the socialists expected workers to use their voting power to obtain concessions from government and eventually even to form a government.

The Social Democratic Party of Germany was founded in 1875 with a revolutionary socialist program. Within two years it won a half-million votes and several seats in the Reichstag (RIKES-tog) (the lower house of the German parliament). Through superb organizing efforts and important concessions wrung from the government, the party grew fast, garnering 4.2 million votes in 1912 and winning more seats in the Reichstag than any other party. In pursuit of electoral success, the Social Democrats became more reformist and less radical. By joining the electoral process, they abandoned the idea of violent revolution.

Working-class women were not welcome in the male-dominated trade unions or radical political parties. A few radical women, such as the German socialist Rosa Luxemburg and Emma Goldman in the United States, an **anarchist** who believed in abolishing all governments, became famous but did not have large followings. It was never easy to reconcile the demands of workers and those of women. In 1889 the German socialist Clara Zetkin wrote: "Just as the male worker is subjected by the capitalist, so is the woman by the man, and she will always remain in subjugation until she is economically independent. Work is the indispensable condition for eco-

SECTION REVIEW

- Between 1850 and 1914, Europe's population nearly doubled, and millions migrated to North America, Argentina, Australia, and New Zealand.

- Urbanization accelerated in the industrial world, but new technologies, plans, and policies helped to reduce earlier urban problems.

- Victorian values idealized the home and divided upper- and middle-class men and women into separate spheres.

- Gender divisions widened between working-class men and women; women often worked in domestic service or their homes or were forced into prostitution.

- Industrialization and revolutionary ideologies prompted the rise of the labor and socialist movements, including Marxism.

- Expanding suffrage after 1870 enabled socialists to participate in electoral politics.

anarchists Revolutionaries who wanted to abolish all private property and governments, usually by violence, and replace them with free associations of groups.

nomic independence." Six years later, she recognized that the liberation of women would have to await a change in the position of the working class as a whole: "The proletarian woman cannot attain her highest ideal through a movement for the equality of the female sex, she attains salvation only through the fight for the emancipation of labor."[1]

NATIONALISM AND THE RISE OF ITALY, GERMANY, AND JAPAN

How did industrialization contribute to the socialist and labor movements?

The most influential idea of the nineteenth century was **nationalism**. The French revolutionaries had defined people, previously considered the subjects of a sovereign, as the citizens of a *nation*—a concept identified with a territory, the state that ruled it, and the culture of its people. While Italians and Germans looked inward to create unified nations, the Japanese would eventually look outward, embracing Western ideas and institutions as a way to protect and strengthen their country.

Language and National Identity in Europe Before 1871

Language was usually the crucial element in creating a feeling of national unity. It was important both as a way to unite the people of a nation and as the means of persuasion by which political leaders inspired their followers. Yet language and citizenship seldom coincided.

The fit between France and the French language was closer than in most large countries, though some French-speakers lived outside of France and some French people spoke other languages. Italian- and German-speaking people, however, were divided among many small states. Living in the Austrian Empire were peoples who spoke German, Czech, Slovak, Hungarian, Polish, and other languages. Even where people spoke a common language, they could be divided by religion or institutions. The Irish, though English-speaking, were mostly Catholic, whereas the English were primarily Protestant.

The idea of redrawing the boundaries of states to accommodate linguistic, religious, or cultural differences was revolutionary. In Italy and Germany it led to the forging of large new states out of many small ones in 1871. In central and eastern Europe, nationalism threatened to break up large states into smaller ones.

Until the 1860s nationalism was associated with **liberalism**, the revolutionary middle-class ideology that asserted the sovereignty of the people and demanded constitutional government, a national parliament, and freedom of expression. The most famous nationalist of the early nineteenth century was the Italian liberal Giuseppe Mazzini (jew-SEP-pay mots-EE-nee) (1805–1872), the leader of the failed revolution of 1848 in Italy. Mazzini not only sought to unify the Italian peninsula into one nation but also associated with like-minded revolutionaries elsewhere to bring nationhood and liberty to peoples oppressed by tyrants and foreigners. These new ideas could not be quashed. To staff bureaucracies and police forces needed to maintain

nationalism A political ideology that stresses people's membership in a nation—a community defined by a common culture and history as well as by territory. In the late eighteenth and early nineteenth centuries, nationalism was a force for unity in western Europe. In the late nineteenth century it hastened the disintegration of the Austro-Hungarian and Ottoman Empires. In the twentieth century it provided the ideological foundation for scores of independent countries emerging from colonialism.

liberalism A political ideology that emphasizes the civil rights of citizens, representative government, and the protection of private property. This ideology, derived from the Enlightenment, was especially popular among the property-owning middle classes of Europe and North America.

control, even conservative regimes like Russia, Prussia, and Austria required educated personnel, and education meant universities, the seedbeds of new ideas transmitted by a national language.

The Unification of Italy, 1860–1870

The Austrian statesman Prince Metternich once described Italy as "a geographical expression." By midcentury, however, popular sentiment was building throughout Italy for unification. Opposing it were Pope Pius IX, who abhorred everything modern, and Austria, which controlled two Italian provinces, Lombardy and Venetia. The prime minister of the Kingdom of Piedmont-Sardinia, Count Camillo Benso di Cavour, saw rivalry between France and Austria as an opportunity to unify Italy. He secretly formed an alliance with France and then instigated a war with Austria in 1858. The war triggered uprisings throughout northern and central Italy in favor of joining Piedmont-Sardinia, a moderate constitutional monarchy under King Victor Emmanuel.

If the conservative, top-down approach to unification prevailed in the north, a more radical approach arose in the south. In 1860 the fiery revolutionary **Giuseppe Garibaldi** (jew-SEP-pay gar-y-BAHL-dee) and a small band of followers landed in Sicily and then in southern Italy, overthrew the Kingdom of the Two Sicilies, and prepared to found a democratic republic. The royalist Cavour, however, took advantage of the unsettled situation to sideline Garibaldi and expand Piedmont-Sardinia into a new Kingdom of Italy. Unification was completed with the addition of Venetia in 1866 and the Papal States in 1870.

The process of unification illustrates the shift of nationalism from a radical democratic idea to a conservative method of building popular support for a strong centralized government, even an aristocratic and monarchical one.

Giuseppe Garibaldi (1807–1882) Italian nationalist and revolutionary who conquered Sicily and Naples and added them to a unified Italy in 1860.

The Unification of Germany

Some German nationalists wanted to unite all Germans under the Catholic Austrian throne. Others wanted to exclude Austria with its many non-Germanic peoples and unite all other German-speaking areas under Lutheran Prussia. The Prussian state had two advantages: (1) the newly developed industries of the Rhineland and (2) the first European army to make use of railroads, telegraphs, breechloading rifles, steel artillery, and other products of modern industry. The king of Prussia, Wilhelm I (r. 1861–1888), had entrusted the running of his government to his chancellor, the brilliant and authoritarian aristocrat **Otto von Bismarck** (1815–1898), who was determined to use Prussian military and German nationalism to advance the interests of the Prussian state.

In 1864, after a quick victory against Denmark, Bismarck set his sights on Austria, which surrendered in 1866. To everyone's surprise, Prussia took no Austrian territory. Instead, Prussia and some smaller states formed the North German Confederation, the nucleus of a future Germany. Then in 1870, Bismarck provoked a war with France. In this "Franco-Prussian War," German armies used their superior firepower and tactics to achieve a quick victory.

The spoils of victory included a large indemnity and two provinces of Alsace and Lorraine (see Map 23.1). To the Germans, this region was German because a major-

Otto von Bismarck (1815–1898) Chancellor (prime minister) of Prussia from 1862 until 1871, when he became chancellor of Germany. A conservative nationalist, he led Prussia to victory against Austria (1866) and France (1870) and was responsible for the creation of the German Empire in 1871.

Primary Source: Extracts from History of Germany in the Nineteenth Century and Historical and Political Writings *Learn why the image of the "hypocritical Englishman, with the Bible in one hand and a pipe of opium in the other," rang true for some Germans.*

Map 23.1   The Unification of Germany, 1866–1871

Germany was united after a series of short, successful wars by the kingdom of Prussia against Austria in 1866 and against France in 1871.

Legend:
- Prussia before 1866
- Conquered by Prussia in Austro-Prussian War, 1866
- Austrian territories excluded from North German Confederation, 1867
- Joined with Prussia to form North German Confederation, 1867
- South German states joining with Prussia to form German Empire, 1871
- Won by Prussia in Franco-Prussian War, 1871

✕ Major battles
— German Confederation boundary, 1815–1866
— Bismarck's German Empire, 1871

ity of its inhabitants spoke German. To the French, it was French because it had been so when the nation of France was forged in the Revolution and because most of its inhabitants considered themselves French. These two conflicting definitions of nationalism kept enmity between France and Germany smoldering for decades.

The West Challenges Japan

In Japan a completely different political organization was in place. The emperor was revered but had no power. Instead, Japan was governed by the Tokugawa Shogunate—a secular government under a military leader, or *shogun*, who had come to power in 1600 (see Chapter 18). Local lords, called *daimyo*, were permitted to control their lands and populations with very little interference from the shogunate.

Because this system did not permit the coordination of resources necessary to resist foreign invasion, the shoguns attempted to minimize exposure to foreigners. In the early 1600s they prohibited foreigners from entering Japan and Japanese from going abroad. The most flagrant violators of these rules were powerful lords in southern Japan who ran large pirate or black-market operations. These lords benefited from the decentralization of the shogunal political system. But when a genuine foreign threat was suggested—as when, in 1792, Russian and British ships were spotted off the Japanese coast—the local lords realized that Japan was perilously weak and decentralized. Some regional lords began to develop their own reformed armies, arsenals, and shipyards.

By the 1800s Satsuma (SAT-soo-mah) and Choshu (CHOE-shoo), two large domains in southern Japan, had become wealthy and ambitious. They enjoyed high rates of revenue and population growth. Their remoteness from the capital Edo (now Tokyo) and their economic vigor fostered a strong sense of local self-reliance.

In 1853, as mentioned earlier, the American commodore Matthew C. Perry arrived off the coast of Japan and demanded that Japan open its ports to trade and allow American ships to refuel and take on supplies. Perry's demands sparked a crisis in the shogunate. After consultation with the provincial daimyos, the shogun's advisers advocated capitulation to Perry. They pointed to China's humiliating defeats in the Opium and Arrow Wars (see Chapter 21). In 1854, when Perry returned, representatives of the shogun indicated their willingness to sign the Treaty of Kanagawa (KAH-nah-GAH-wah), modeled on the unequal treaties between China and the Western powers. Angry and disappointed, some provincial governors encouraged an underground movement calling for the destruction of the Tokugawa regime and the banning of foreigners from Japan.

Tensions between the shogunate and some provincial leaders, particularly in Choshu and Satsuma, increased in the early 1860s. When British and French ships shelled the southwestern coasts in 1864 to protest the treatment of foreigners, the action enraged the provincial samurai, who rejected the Treaty of Kanagawa. Young, ambitious, educated men who faced mediocre prospects under the rigid Tokugawa class system emerged as provincial leaders. In 1867 the Choshu leaders Yamagata Aritomo and Ito Hirobumi finally realized that they should stop warring with their rival province, Satsuma, and jointly rebel against the shogunate.

Meiji Restoration The political program that followed the destruction of the Tokugawa Shogunate in 1868, in which a collection of young leaders set Japan on the path of centralization, industrialization, and imperialism.

The Meiji Restoration and the Modernization of Japan, 1868–1894

The civil war was intense but brief. In 1868 provincial rebels overthrew the Tokugawa Shogunate and declared young emperor Mutsuhito (moo-tsoo-HE-toe) (r. 1868–1912) "restored." The new leaders called their regime the **"Meiji** (MAY-gee) **Restoration"** after Mutsuhito's reign name (*Meiji* means "enlightened rule"). The "Meiji oligarchs," as the new rulers were known, were extraor-

Japan's New Army

After the Meiji Restoration in 1868, the leaders of the new government set out to make Japan "a rich country with a strong army." They modeled the new army on the European armies of the time, with Western-style uniforms, rifles, cannon, and musical instruments.   (Tsuneo Tamba Collection/Laurie Platt Winfrey, Inc.)

dinarily talented and far-sighted. Though imposed from above, the Meiji Restoration marked as profound a change as the French Revolution (see Map 23.2).

The oligarchs knew they would have to transform their institutions and their society. In the Charter Oath issued in 1868, the young emperor included a prophetic phrase: "Knowledge shall be sought throughout the world and thus shall be strengthened the foundation of the imperial polity." It was to be the motto of a new Japan, which embraced all foreign ideas, institutions, and techniques that could strengthen the nation. The literacy rate in Japan was the highest in Asia at the time, and the oligarchs shrewdly exploited it in their introduction of new educational systems, a conscript army, and new communications. The government was able to establish heavy industry through the use of judicious deficit financing without extensive foreign debt, thanks to decades of experimentation with industrial development and financing in the provinces in the earlier 1800s.

The Meiji leaders copied the government structure of imperial Germany. They modeled the new Japanese navy on the British and the army on the Prussian. They introduced Western-style postal and telegraph services, railroads and harbors, banking, clocks, and calendars. To learn the secrets of Western strength, they sent hundreds of students to Britain, Germany, and the United States. Western-style hairstyles and clothing, including military and police uniforms, became popular. Even pastimes were affected, with garden parties and formal dances becoming common.

The government was especially interested in Western technology. It opened vocational, technical, and agricultural schools and founded four imperial universities. It brought in foreign experts to advise on medicine, science, and engineering. To encourage industrialization, the government set up state-owned enterprises to manufacture cloth and inexpensive consumer goods for sale abroad. The first Japanese industries, some of which had been founded in the early nineteenth century, exploited their workers ruthlessly, just as the first industries in Europe and America had done. In 1881, to pay off its debts, the government sold these enterprises to private investors, mainly large *zaibatsu* (zye-BOT-soo), or conglomerates. It encouraged individual technological innovation. Thus the carpenter Toyoda Sakichi founded the Toyoda Loom Works (now Toyota Motor Company) in 1906; ten years later he patented the world's most advanced automatic loom.

 Primary Source: Letter to Mitsubishi Employees

The responsibilities of the Mitsubishi company are "even greater than the full weight of Mt. Fuji thrust upon" its shoulders. Find out why.

Map 23.2   Expansion and Modernization of Japan, 1868–1918

As Japan acquired modern industry, it followed the example of the European powers in seeking overseas colonies. Its colonial empire grew at the expense of its neighbors: Taiwan was taken from China in 1895; Karafutu (Sakhalin) from Russia in 1905; and all of Korea became a colony in 1910.

Nationalism and Social Darwinism

In many countries, the dominant group used nationalism to justify the imposing of its language, religion, or customs on minority populations. The Russian Empire attempted to "Russify" its diverse ethnic populations. The Spanish government made the Spanish language compulsory in the schools, newspapers, and courts of its Basque- and Catalan-speaking provinces.

Some people looked to science for support of political dominance. One of the most influential scientists of the century, and the one whose ideas were most widely cited and misinterpreted, was the English biologist **Charles Darwin** (1809–1882),

Charles Darwin (1809–1882)
With Alfred Russell Wallace (1823–1913) he developed the theory of evolution through natural selection. Their work was first made known simultaneously in 1858.

Silk Factory in Japan

Silk manufacture, Japan's best-known industry, began to be mechanized in the 1870s. In this factory, as in most textile mills, the workers were women.   (The Metropolitan Museum of Art, gift of Lincoln Kirstein, 1959 [JP 3346]. Photograph by Otto E. Nelson. Photograph © 1986 The Metropolitan Museum of Art.)

HISTORY IN FOCUS Examine the image "Silk Factory in Japan," and then look back at the image "The Pit Head of a Coal Mine" in Chapter 20. Compare the two images. How do these representations of machines and workers resemble and differ from each other? What does the Japanese image suggest about the process of modernization in Japan? *Find the answer online.*

who based his theories on observations made during a research voyage in South America and by observing English livestock breeders. His famous book, *On the Origin of Species by Means of Natural Selection* (1859), argued that over hundreds of thousands of years, living beings had either evolved in the struggle for survival or become extinct. The philosopher Herbert Spencer (1820–1903) and others took up Darwin's ideas of "natural selection" and "survival of the fittest" and applied them to human society. Extreme Social Darwinists developed elaborate pseudo-scientific theories of racial differences, claiming that they were the result not of history but of biology.

THE GREAT POWERS OF EUROPE, 1871–1900

How was nationalism transformed from a revolutionary to a conservative ideology?

After 1871, politicians and journalists discovered how easily they could whip up popular frenzy against neighboring countries. Rivalries over colonial territories, ideological differences between liberal and conservative governments, and even minor border incidents or trade disagreements contributed to a growing atmosphere of international tension.

- The most influential nineteenth-century idea was nationalism, which was associated with revolutionary liberalism before the 1860s.

- After the 1848 revolutions, conservative governments adopted nationalism to preserve the status quo.

- Bismarck exploited German nationalism to unify Germany under militarist Prussia.

- In Japan power was in the hands of the Tokugawa Shogunate until, forced to open to foreign trade and influence, the shogunate fell to a rebellion of provincial leaders.

- The Meiji Restoration later brought to power reformers who modernized Japan's government, economy, education system, and military.

- Social Darwinism offered "scientific" support for policies of racial, political, and economic dominance.

Germany at the Center of Europe

International relations revolved around a united Germany, because Germany was located in the center of Europe and had the most powerful army on the European continent. After creating a unified Germany in 1871, Bismarck worked to maintain peace in Europe. To isolate France, he forged a loose coalition with Austria-Hungary and Russia, which he was able to keep together for twenty years.

Bismarck proved equally adept at manipulating mass politics at home. To weaken the influence of middle-class liberals, he extended the vote to all adult men. By imposing high tariffs on manufactured goods and wheat, he gained the support of both the wealthy industrialists of the Rhineland and the great landowners of eastern Germany. He stole the thunder of the socialists by introducing social legislation—medical, unemployment, and disability insurance and old-age pensions—long before other industrial countries did. Under his leadership, the German people developed a strong sense of national unity and pride in their industrial and military power.

In 1888, Wilhelm I was succeeded by his grandson Wilhelm II (r. 1888–1918), who dismissed Chancellor Bismarck. Wilhelm II talked about his "global policy" and demanded that Germany, with the mightiest army and the largest industrial economy in Europe, have a colonial empire, "a place in the sun."

The Liberal Powers: France and Great Britain

France had difficulty reconciling itself to being second to Germany. Its population and its army lagged far behind Germany's, and its industry was growing more slowly, thanks to the loss of the iron and coal mines of Lorraine. The French people were deeply divided politically: some were monarchists and Catholics; a growing number were republican and anticlerical. Despite these problems, a long tradition of popular participation in politics and a strong sense of nationhood, reinforced by a fine system of universal public education, gave the French people a deeper cohesion than appeared on the surface.

Great Britain was the only other country in Europe with a democratic tradition. The British government alternated smoothly between the Liberal and Conservative Parties, and the income gap between rich and poor gradually narrowed. Nevertheless, Britain had problems. One was Irish resentment of English rule as a foreign occupying force. Another was the British economy. Great Britain lagged behind the United States and Germany in iron and steel, chemicals, electricity, and textiles. Germany was even catching up in shipbuilding. Finally, Britain's far-flung empire was a constant drain on government finances.

The Conservative Powers: Russia and Austria-Hungary

The forces of nationalism weakened rather than strengthened Russia and Austria-Hungary. The reason for this effect was that their populations were far more divided, socially and ethnically, than were the German, French, or British peoples.

Nationalism was most divisive in the Austrian Empire. The decision to rename itself the Austro-Hungarian Empire in 1867 appeased its Hungarian critics but alienated its Slavic-speaking minorities. The Austro-Hungarian Empire still thought of itself as a great power and attempted to dominate the Balkans. This strategy irritated Russia, which thought of itself as the protector of Slavic peoples everywhere, and it eventually led to war.

Russia was the most misunderstood country in Europe. Its enormous size and population led many Europeans to exaggerate its military potential, but Russia was weakened by national and social divisions. All in all, only 45 percent of the peoples of the tsarist empire spoke Russian.

To strengthen the bonds between the monarchy and the Russian people and promote industrialization by enlarging the labor pool, the moderate conservative Tsar Alexander II (r. 1855–1881) emancipated the peasants from serfdom in 1861. That measure, however, did not create a modern society but only turned serfs into communal farmers with few skills and little capital. Though technically "emancipated," the great majority of Russians had little education, few legal rights, and no say in their government. After Alexander's assassination in 1881, his successors Alexander III (r. 1881–1894) and Nicholas II (r. 1894–1917) opposed all forms of social change. Industrialization consisted largely of state-sponsored projects, such as railroads, iron foundries, and armament factories, and led to social unrest among urban workers. Wealthy landowning aristocrats continued to dominate the Russian court and administration and succeeded in blocking most reforms.

The weaknesses in Russia's society and government became glaringly obvious after Russia's defeat in the Russo-Japanese War of 1904–1905 (see below). The shock of defeat caused a popular uprising, the Revolution of 1905, that forced Tsar Nicholas II to grant a constitution and an elected Duma (parliament). But as soon as he was able to rebuild the army and the police, he reverted to the traditional despotism of his forefathers. Small groups of radical intellectuals, angered by the contrast between the wealth of the elite and the poverty of the common people, began plotting the violent overthrow of the tsarist autocracy.

SECTION REVIEW

- Powerful unified Germany became the center of European politics, as Bismarck sought to maintain peace, isolate France, and strengthen authoritarian rule at home.

- Under Wilhelm II, Germany became more aggressive and pursued colonial expansion.

- Despite military defeat and social and political division, France maintained a strong sense of democratic national unity.

- In democratic Britain, the division between rich and poor narrowed, but ethnic and economic problems became increasingly apparent.

- Nationalism weakened ethnically diverse Austria-Hungary but drove it to continue trying to dominate Slavic minorities.

- Nationalism also undermined Russia, where traditional social divisions persisted and economic and military development lagged.

CHINA, JAPAN, AND THE WESTERN POWERS

How did the forces of nationalism affect the major powers of Europe?

After 1850 China and Japan—the two largest countries in East Asia—felt the influence of the Western powers as never before, but their responses were completely opposite. China resisted Western influence and became weaker, while Japan transformed itself into a major industrial and military power. One reason for this difference was the Western powers' heavy involvement in China. More important was the difference between the Chinese and Japanese elites' attitudes toward foreign cultures.

China in Turmoil

China had been devastated by the Taiping (tie-PING) Rebellion that raged from 1850 to 1864 (see Chapter 21). The French and British took advantage of China's weakness to demand treaty ports where they could trade at will. The British took over China's customs and allowed the free import of opium until 1917. A Chinese "self-strengthening

**Empress Dowager Cixi
(1835–1908)** Empress of China and mother of Emperor Guangxi. She put her son under house arrest, supported antiforeign movements, and resisted reforms of the Chinese government and armed forces.

**Yamagata Aritomo
(1838–1922)** One of the leaders of the Meiji Restoration.

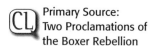

Primary Source:
Two Proclamations of the Boxer Rebellion

Find out how the supporters of the Boxer Rebellion planned to deal with Christian converts.

movement" tried in vain to bring about significant reforms by reducing government expenditures and eliminating corruption. The **Empress Dowager Cixi** (TSUH-shee) (r. 1862–1908), who had once encouraged the construction of shipyards, arsenals, and telegraph lines, opposed railways and other foreign technologies that could carry foreign influences to the interior. Government officials, who did not dare resist the Westerners outright, secretly encouraged crowds to attack and destroy the intrusive devices. They were able to slow the foreign intrusion, but in doing so, they denied themselves the best means of defense against foreign pressure.

Japan Confronts China

The motive for the transformation of Japan was defensive—to protect the nation from the Western powers—but the methods that strengthened Japan against the imperial ambitions of others could also be used offensively. Japan's path to imperialism was laid out by **Yamagata Aritomo**, a leader of the Meiji oligarchs. He believed that an independent Japan required a "sphere of influence" that included Korea, Manchuria, and part of China. If other countries controlled this sphere, Japan would be at risk. To protect this sphere of influence, Yamagata insisted, Japan must accelerate its military industrialization, culminating in the building of battleships.

As Japan grew stronger, China grew weaker. In 1894 the two nations went to war over Japanese encroachments in Korea. The Sino-Japanese War lasted less than six months, and it forced China to evacuate Korea, cede Taiwan and the Liaodong (li-AH-oh-dong) Peninsula, and pay a heavy indemnity. France, Germany, Britain, Russia, and the United States, upset at seeing a newcomer join the ranks of the imperialists, made Japan give up Liaodong in the name of the "territorial integrity" of China. In exchange for their "protection," the Western powers then made China grant them territorial and trade concessions, including ninety treaty ports.

Les Événements de Chine
MORT AUX ÉTRANGERS !

The Boxer Uprising

In 1900 a Chinese secret society, the Righteous Fists, rose up with the encouragement of the Empress Dowager Cixi and attacked foreigners and their establishments. In the Western press they were known as "Boxers" and shown in lurid poses, such as these men putting up a poster that reads "Death to Foreigners!"
(Mary Evans Picture Library/The Image Works)

In 1900 Chinese officials around the Empress Dowager Cixi encouraged a series of antiforeign riots known as the Boxer Uprising. Military forces from the European powers, Japan, and the United States put down the riots and occupied Beijing. Emboldened by China's obvious weakness, Japan and Russia competed for possession of the mineral-rich Chinese province of Manchuria.

Japan's participation in the suppression of the Boxer Uprising demonstrated its military power in East Asia. In 1905 Japan surprised the world by defeating Russia in the Russo-Japanese War. By the Treaty of Portsmouth that ended the war, Japan established a protectorate over Korea. In spite of Western attempts to restrict it to the role of junior partner, Japan continued to increase its influence. It gained control of southern Manchuria, with its industries and railroads. In 1910 it finally annexed Korea, joining the ranks of the world's colonial powers.

SECTION REVIEW

- The French and British became heavily involved in trade in China despite Chinese attempts to sabotage foreign enterprises.

- Chinese resistance to the new technologies of the West contributed to its decline in power and status.

- While the European powers were caught up in a rush to secure the world's remaining unclaimed territory, the United States and Japan were in the process of becoming great powers.

- After 1894, Japan began a program of imperial expansion, winning new territories through successful wars with China and Russia.

Chapter Review

 DOWNLOAD THE MP3 AUDIO FILE OF THE CHAPTER REVIEW TO LISTEN TO ON THE GO.

What new technologies and industries appeared between 1850 and 1900, and how did they affect the world economy? (page 627)

After World War I broke out in 1914, many people, especially in Europe, looked back on the period from 1850 to 1914 as a golden age. For some, and in certain ways, it was. Industrialization was a powerful torrent changing Europe, North America, and East Asia. While other technologies like shipping and railroads increased their global reach, new ones—electricity, the steel and chemical industries, and the global telegraph network—contributed to the enrichment and empowerment of the industrial nations. World trade increased tenfold during this period, and many countries' economies were transformed.

How did the societies of the industrial countries change during this period? (page 631)

With these new technologies, memories of the great scourges—famines, wars, and epidemics—faded. Clean water, electric lights, and railways began to improve the lives of city dwellers, even the poor. Municipal services made city life less dangerous and chaotic. Goods from distant lands, even travel to other continents, came within the reach of millions. While middle-class women continued

KEY TERMS

Commodore Matthew Perry *(p. 626)*
railroads *(p. 627)*
submarine telegraph cables *(p. 628)*
steel *(p. 629)*
electricity *(p. 630)*
Thomas Edison *(p. 630)*
Victorian Age *(p. 634)*
"separate spheres" *(p. 634)*
socialism *(p. 636)*
labor union *(p. 636)*
Karl Marx *(p. 636)*
anarchists *(p. 638)*
nationalism *(p. 639)*
liberalism *(p. 639)*
Giuseppe Garibaldi *(p. 640)*
Otto von Bismarck *(p. 640)*
Meiji Restoration *(p. 642)*
Charles Darwin *(p. 644)*
Empress Dowager Cixi *(p. 648)*
Yamagata Aritomo *(p. 648)*

to focus on domestic pursuits and lived in a "separate sphere" from men, many working-class women took jobs in the textile industry. Yet their work outside the home did not lessen their domestic and child-rearing responsibilities.

How did industrialization contribute to the socialist and labor movements? (page 639)

Industrialization created a large class of factory and railroad workers. Karl Marx predicted a class struggle between workers and employers, but socialism became more of an intellectual movement. Through labor unions, workers achieved some measure of recognition and security. By the turn of the century, liberal political reforms had taken hold in western Europe and seemed about to triumph in Russia as well. Universal male suffrage became law in the United States in 1870 and in various parts of Europe by the 1880s. Morality and legislation aimed at providing security for women and families, though equality between the sexes was still beyond reach.

How was nationalism transformed from a revolutionary to a conservative ideology? (page 645)

The framework for all these changes was the nation-state. Until the 1860s nationalism was associated with liberalism, but later generations of conservatives used public education, military service, and colonial conquests to build a sense of national unity. By 1871 both Italy and Germany had become unified states. In Japan, the Meiji Restoration restored power to the emperor and ushered in a period of Western influences. By the 1880s nationalist views had taken hold in many non-Western countries such as Egypt, India, and Japan.

How did the forces of nationalism affect the major powers of Europe? (page 647)

The world economy, international politics, and even cultural and social issues revolved around a handful of countries—the great powers—that believed they controlled the destiny of the world. These included the most powerful European nations of the previous century, as well as three newcomers—Germany, the United States, and Japan—that were to play important roles in the future. Under the leadership of Bismarck, the German people developed a strong sense of national pride. Religious differences proved to be a hindrance to nationalism in France. Great Britain's problems were due to Irish resentment of English rule and economic issues.

WEB RESOURCES

Pronunciation Guide

Primary Sources

Extracts from History of Germany in the Nineteenth Century and Historical and Political Writings

Letter to Mitsubishi Employees

Two Proclamations of the Boxer Rebellion

Answer to the History in Focus Question

See photo on p. 645, "Silk Factory in Japan."

Plus

Chapter Objectives

ACE multiple-choice quiz

Flashcards

SUGGESTED READING

Anderson, Benedict. *Imagined Communities: Reflections on the Origin and Spread of Nationalism.* 1991. A highly influential theory of nationalism by an anthropologist.

Blackbourne, David. *The Long Nineteenth Century: A History of Germany, 1780–1918.* 1998. An excellent survey.

Branca, Patricia. *Silent Sisterhood: Middle-Class Women in the Victorian Home.* 1975. Women's history in the Victorian era.

Duus, Peter. *The Rise of Modern Japan.* 2d ed. 1998. A solid survey.

Fairbank, John King. *The Great Chinese Revolution, 1800–1985.* 1987. Offers fine coverage of modern China.

Gottlieb, Beatrice. *The Family in the Western World from the Black Death to the Industrial Age.* 1993. A broad, inclusive history.

Hobsbawm, E. J. *Nation and Nationalism Since 1780.* 1990. An interpretation of nationalism by a noted historian.

McBride, Theresa. *The Domestic Revolution: The Modernization of Household Service in England and France, 1820–1920*. 1976. Discusses technology and everyday life.

Moore, Barrington. *The Social Origins of Dictatorship and Democracy*. 1966. A classic essay on European society.

Price, Roger. *A Social History of Nineteenth-Century France*. 1987. An excellent treatment of an important subject.

Read, Donald. *The Age of Urban Democracy: England, 1868–1914*. 1994. A solid survey.

Rogger, Hans. *Russia in the Age of Modernization and Revolution, 1881–1917*. 1983. A good introduction to the field.

Sked, Alan. *The Decline and Fall of the Habsburg Empire, 1815–1918*. 1989. Studies the history leading to the dissolution of the Austrian Empire.

Smil, Vaclav. *Creating the Twentieth Century: Technical Innovations of 1867–1914 and Their Lasting Impact*. 2005. Discusses the "second industrial revolution."

NOTES

1. Quoted in Bonnie S. Anderson and Judith P. Zinsser, *A History of Their Own: Women in Europe from Prehistory to the Present,* vol. 2 (New York: Harper & Row, 1988), 372, 387.

The New Imperialism

1869–1914

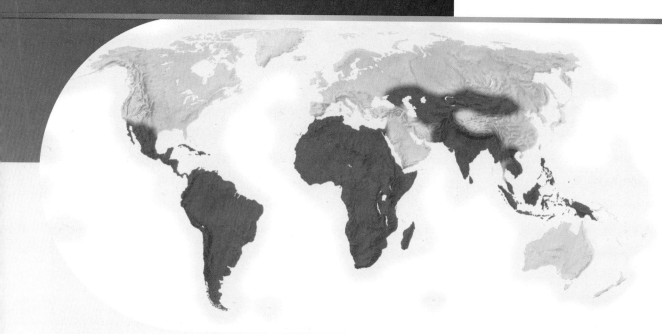

CHAPTER PREVIEW

In 1869 Ismail (is-mah-EEL), the khedive (kuh-DEEV) (ruler) of Egypt, invited all the Christian princes of Europe and all the Muslim princes of Asia and Africa—except the Ottoman sultan, his nominal overlord—to celebrate the inauguration of the greatest construction project of the century: the **Suez Canal**. Among the sixteen hundred dignitaries from the Middle East and Europe who assembled at Port Said (port sah-EED) were Emperor Francis Joseph of Austria-Hungary and Empress Eugénie of France. A French journalist wrote:

> This multitude, coming from all parts of the world, presented the most varied and singular spectacle. All races were represented. . . . We saw, coming to attend this festival of civilization, men of the Orient wearing clothes of dazzling colors, chiefs of African tribes wrapped in their

 This icon will direct you to the website where you can Prepare for Class, Improve Your Grade, and Ace the Test: college.cengage.com/pic/bullietbrief4e

Opening the Suez Canal
When the canal opened in 1869, thousands of dignitaries and ordinary people gathered to watch the ships go by.   (Bildarchiv Preussischer Kulturbesitz/Art Resource, NY)

great coats, Circassians in war costumes, officers of the British army of India with their shakos [hats] wrapped in muslin, Hungarian magnates wearing their national costumes.[1]

Ismail used the occasion to emphasize the harmony and cooperation between the peoples of Africa, Asia, and Europe and to show that Egypt was not only independent but was also an equal of the great powers. To bless the inauguration, Ismail had invited clergy of the Muslim, Orthodox, and Catholic faiths. A reporter noted: "The Khedive . . . wished to symbolize thereby the unity of men and their brotherhood before God, without distinction of religion; it was the first time that the Orient had seen such a meeting of faiths to celebrate and bless together a great event and a great work."[2]

The canal was a great success, but not in the way Ismail intended. Ships using it could travel between Europe and India in less than two weeks—much less time than the month or longer consumed by sailing around Africa and across the Indian Ocean. By lowering freight costs, the canal stimulated shipping and the construction of steamships, giving an advantage to nations that had heavy industry and a large maritime trade over land-based empires and countries with few merchant ships. Great Britain, which long opposed construction of the canal for fear that it might fall into enemy hands, benefited more than any other nation. France, which provided half the capital and most of the engineers, came in a distant second, for it had less trade with Asia than Britain did. Egypt, which contributed the other half of the money and most of the labor, was the loser. Instead of making Egypt powerful

Suez Canal Ship canal dug across the isthmus of Suez in Egypt, designed by Ferdinand de Lesseps. It opened to shipping in 1869 and shortened the sea voyage between Europe and Asia. Its strategic importance led to the British conquest of Egypt in 1882.

and independent, the Suez Canal provided the excuse for a British invasion and occupation of Egypt.

Far from inaugurating an era of harmony among the peoples of three continents and three faiths, the canal triggered a wave of European domination over Africa and Asia. Between 1869 and 1914 Germany, France, Britain, Russia, Japan, and the United States used industrial technology to impose their will on the nonindustrial parts of the world. Historians use the expression **New Imperialism** to describe this exercise of power.

New Imperialism Historians' term for the late-nineteenth- and early-twentieth-century wave of conquests by European powers, the United States, and Japan, which were followed by the development and exploitation of the newly conquered territories for the benefit of the colonial powers.

THE NEW IMPERIALISM: MOTIVES AND METHODS

What motivated the industrial nations to conquer new territories, and what means did they use?

The New Imperialism was characterized by an explosion of territorial conquests even more rapid than the Spanish conquests of the sixteenth century. Between 1869 and 1914, in a land grab of unprecedented speed, Europeans seized territories in Africa and Central Asia, and both Europeans and Americans took territories in Southeast Asia and the Pacific. Approximately 10 million square miles (26 million square kilometers) and 150 million people fell under the rule of Europe and the United States in this period.

The New Imperialism was more than a land grab. The imperial powers used economic and technological means to reorganize dependent regions and bring them into the world economy as suppliers of foodstuffs and raw materials and as consumers of industrial products. In Africa and other parts of the world, this was done by conquest and colonial administration. In the Latin American republics the same result was achieved indirectly. Even though they remained politically independent, they became economic dependencies of the United States and Europe.

What inspired Europeans and Americans to venture overseas and impose their will on other societies? There is no simple answer to this question. Economic, cultural, and political motives were involved in all cases.

Political Motives

The great powers of the late nineteenth century, as well as less powerful countries like Italy, Portugal, and Belgium, were competitive and hypersensitive about their status. France, humiliated by its defeat by Prussia in 1871 (see Chapter 23), sought to reestablish its prestige through territorial acquisitions overseas. Great Britain, already in possession of the world's largest and richest empire, felt the need to protect India, its "jewel in the crown," by acquiring colonies in East Africa and Southeast Asia. German chancellor Otto von Bismarck had little interest in acquiring colonies, but many Germans believed that a country as important as theirs deserved an overseas empire.

Political motives were not limited to statesmen in the capital cities. Colonial governors and political officers practiced their own diplomacy, often making a claim to a territory just to forestall some rival. Armies fighting frontier wars found it

Chronology

The Scramble for Africa	Asia and Western Dominance	Imperalism in Latin America
	1862–1895 French conquer Indochina	
	1865–1876 Russian forces advance into Central Asia	
1869 Opening of the Suez Canal		
1870		**1870–1910** Railroad building boom; British companies in Argentina and Brazil; U.S. companies in Mexico
1874 Warfare between the British and the Asante (Gold Coast)		
1877–1879 Warfare between the British and the Xhosa and between the British and the Zulu (South Africa)		
	1878 United States obtains Pago Pago Harbor (Samoa)	
1882 British forces occupy Egypt		
1884–1885 Berlin Conference; Leopold II obtains Congo Free State	**1885** Britain completes conquest of Burma	
	1887 United States obtains Pearl Harbor (Hawaii)	
1890	**1894–1895** China defeated in Sino-Japanese War	
	1895 France completes conquest of Indochina	**1895–1898** Cubans revolt against Spanish rule
1896 Ethiopians defeat Italian army at Adowa; warfare between the British and the Asante		
1898 Battle of Omdurman	**1898** United States annexes Hawaii and purchases Philippines from Spain	**1898** Spanish-American War; United States annexes Puerto Rico and Guam
1899–1902 South African War between Afrikaners and the British	**1899–1902** U.S. forces conquer and occupy Philippines	
		1901 United States imposes Platt Amendment on Cuba
1902 First Aswan Dam completed (Egypt)	**1903** Russia completes Trans-Siberian Railway	**1903** United States backs secession of Panama from Colombia
	1904–1905 Russia defeated in Russo-Japanese War	**1904–1907, 1916** U.S. troops occupy Dominican Republic
		1904–1914 United States builds Panama Canal
1908 Belgium annexes Congo		
1910		**1912** U.S. troops occupy Nicaragua and Honduras

easier to defeat their neighbors than to make peace with them. In response to border skirmishes with neighboring states, colonial agents were likely to send in troops, take over their neighbors' territories, and then inform their home governments. Governments felt obligated to back up their men-on-the-spot in order not to lose face. The great powers of Europe acquired much of West Africa, Southeast Asia, and the Pacific islands in this manner.

Cultural Motives   The late nineteenth century saw a Christian revival in Europe and North America, as both Catholics and Protestants founded new missionary societies. Their purpose was not only religious—to convert nonbelievers, whom they regarded as "heathen"—but also cultural in a broader sense. They sought to export their own norms of "civilized" behavior: they were determined to abolish slavery in Africa and bring Western education, medicine, hygiene, monogamous marriage, and modest dress to all the world's peoples.

Many women joined missionary societies to become teachers and nurses, sometimes attaining positions of greater authority than they could hope to find at home. Their influence often helped soften the harshness of colonial rule—for example, by calling attention to issues of maternity and women's health. Mary Slessor, a British missionary who lived for forty years among the people of southeastern Nigeria, campaigned against slavery, human sacrifice, and the killing of twins and, generally, for women's rights. In India missionaries denounced the customs of child marriages and *sati* (the burning of widows on their husbands' funeral pyres). Such views often clashed with the customs of the people among whom they settled.

The sense of moral duty and cultural superiority was not limited to missionaries. Many Europeans and Americans equated technological innovations with "progress." They believed that Western technology proved the superiority of Western ideas, customs, and culture. While some concluded that non-Western peoples could achieve, through education, the same cultural level as Europeans and Americans, many others espoused racist ideas that relegated non-Europeans to a status of permanent inferiority. Racists assigned different stages of biological development to the world's various peoples based on physical appearance and ranked these races in a hierarchy that ranged from "civilized" at the highest level down through "semibarbarous," "barbarian," and finally, at the bottom, "savage." Caucasians—whites—were always at the top of this ranking. Such ideas were often presented as an excuse for permanent rule over Africans and Asians.

Imperialism first interested small groups of explorers, clergy, and businessmen but soon attracted people from other walks of life. Young men, finding few opportunities for adventure and glory at home in an era of peace, sought them overseas as the Spanish conquistadors had done over three centuries earlier. At first, European people and parliaments were indifferent or hostile to overseas adventures, but a few easy victories in the 1880s helped to overcome their reluctance. The United States was fully preoccupied with its westward expansion until the 1880s, but in the 1890s popular attention shifted to lands outside U.S. borders. Newspapers, which achieved wide readership in the second half of the nineteenth century, discovered that they could boost circulation with reports of wars and conquests. By the 1890s imperialism was a popular cause; it was the overseas extension of the nationalism propelling the power politics of the time.

Economic Motives

The industrialization of Europe and North America stimulated the demand for minerals—copper for electrical wiring, tin for canning, chrome and manganese for the steel industry, coal for steam engines, and, most of all, gold and diamonds. The demand for such industrial crops as cotton and rubber and for stimulants such as sugar, coffee, tea, and tobacco also grew. These products were found in the tropics, but never in sufficient quantities.

An economic depression lasting from the mid-1870s to the mid-1890s caused European merchants, manufacturers, and shippers to seek protection against foreign competition (see below). They argued that their respective countries needed secure sources of tropical raw materials and protected markets for their industries. Declining business opportunities at home prompted entrepreneurs and investors to look for profits from mines, plantations, and railroads in Asia, Africa, and Latin America. Since these investments were often extremely risky, businessmen sought the backing of their governments, preferably with soldiers.

The sudden increase in the power that industrial peoples could wield over nonindustrial peoples and over the forces of nature underlay the new imperialism as much as cultural and political factors. Indeed, technological advances explain both the motives and the outcome of the New Imperialism.

The Tools of the Imperialists

To succeed, empire builders needed the means to achieve their objectives at a reasonable cost. The Industrial Revolution (see Chapter 20) provided these means. In the early part of the nineteenth century technological innovations began to tip the balance of power in favor of Europe.

Dominant at sea since about 1500, the Europeans increased their naval power still more with the introduction of steamships. The first steamer reached India in 1825; regular mail service followed in the 1830s. The long voyage around Africa was at first too costly for cargo steamers, for coal had to be shipped from England. The building of the Suez Canal and the development of increasingly efficient engines solved this problem and led to a boom in shipping to the Indian Ocean and East Asia. Whenever fighting broke out, passenger liners were requisitioned as troopships. This advantage in mobility was enhanced by the development of a global network of submarine telegraph cables connecting Europe with North America in the 1860s, with Latin America and Asia in the 1870s, with Africa in the 1880s, and finally across the Pacific in 1904.

Until the middle of the nineteenth century, western Europeans were much weaker on land than at sea. Thereafter, Europeans used gunboats with considerable success in China, Burma, Indochina, and the Congo Basin. Although gunboats opened the major river basins to European penetration, the invaders often found themselves hampered by other natural obstacles. *Falciparum* malaria, found only in Africa, was so deadly to Europeans that few explorers survived before the 1850s. In 1854 a British doctor discovered that the drug quinine, taken regularly during one's stay in Africa, could prevent the disease. This and a few sanitary precautions reduced the annual death rate among whites in West Africa from between 250 and 750 per thousand in the early nineteenth century to between 50 and 100 per thousand after 1850. This reduction was sufficient to open the continent to merchants, officials, and missionaries.

Muzzle-loading smoothbore muskets had been used in Europe, Asia, and the Americas since the late seventeenth century, and by the early nineteenth century they were also common in much of Africa. The development of new and much deadlier firearms in the 1860s and 1870s shifted the balance of power on land between Westerners and other peoples. One of these was the breechloading rifle: ten times faster to load and five or six times longer in range than a musket. By the 1870s all European and American armies had switched to these new rifles. The 1880s saw two more innovations, smokeless powder, which did not foul the gun or reveal the soldier's position, and repeating rifles, which could shoot fifteen rounds in fifteen seconds. Machine guns, which could fire eleven bullets per second, appeared a decade later.

In the course of the century Asians and Africans also acquired better firearms, mostly old weapons that European armies had discarded. As European firearms improved, however, the firepower gap widened, making colonial conquests easier than ever. By the 1880s and 1890s European-led forces of a few hundred could defeat non-European armies of thousands. Against the latest weapons, African and Asian soldiers armed with muskets or, in some cases, with spears did not stand a chance, no matter how numerous and courageous they were.

Battle of Omdurman British victory over the Mahdi in the Sudan in 1898. General Kitchener led a mixed force of British and Egyptian troops armed with rapid-firing rifles and machine guns.

At the **Battle of Omdurman** in Sudan, on September 2, 1898, forty thousand Sudanese attacked an Anglo-Egyptian expedition that had come up the Nile on six steamers and four other boats. General Horatio Kitchener's troops had twenty machine guns and four artillery pieces; the Sudanese were equipped with muskets and spears. Within a few hours eleven thousand Sudanese and forty-eight British lay dead. Winston Churchill, the future British prime minister, witnessed the battle and called it

> the most signal triumph ever gained by the arms of science over barbarians. Within the space of five hours the strongest and best-armed savage army yet arrayed against a modern European Power had been destroyed and dispersed, with hardly any difficulty, comparatively small risk, and insignificant loss to the victors.[3]

Colonial Agents and Administration

Once colonial agents took over a territory, their home government expected them to cover their own costs and, if possible, return some profit to the home country. The system of administering and exploiting territories for the benefit of the home country is known as **colonialism**. In some places, such as along the West African coast or in Indochina, there was already a considerable trade that could be taxed. In other places profits could come only from investments and a thorough reorganization of the indigenous societies. In applying modern scientific and industrial methods to their colonies, colonialists started the transformation of Asian and African societies and landscapes that has continued to our day.

colonialism Policy by which a nation administers a foreign territory and develops its resources for the benefit of the colonial power.

Legal experts and academics emphasized the differences between various systems of colonial government and debated whether colonies eventually should be as-

The Battle of Omdurman

In the late nineteenth century, most battles between European (or European-led) troops and African forces were one-sided encounters because of the disparity in the opponents' firearms and tactics. The Battle of Omdurman in Sudan in 1898 is a dramatic example. The forces of the Mahdi, some on horseback, were armed with spears and single-shot muskets. The British troops and their Egyptian allies, lined up in the foreground, used repeating rifles and machine guns able to shoot much farther than the Sudanese weapons. As a result, there were many Sudanese casualties but very few British or Egyptian casualties.   (The Art Archive)

CL   HISTORY IN FOCUS   Review the opening section of Chapter 24, "The New Imperialism: Motives and Methods," paying special attention to Winston Churchill's words quoted at the end of the section. Now examine the image "The Battle of Omdurman." Does the painting illustrate Churchill's pronouncement? Does it depict the battle from a European point of view? Why or why not? If so, how do you think the depiction would be different if an African Mahdi sympathizer had painted it? *Find the answer online.*

similated into the ruling nation, associated in a federation, or allowed to rule themselves. Colonies that were protectorates retained their traditional governments, even their monarchs, but had a European "resident" or "consul-general" to "advise" them. Other colonies were directly administered by a European governor. In fact, the impact of colonial rule depended much more on economic and social conditions than on narrow legal distinctions.

One important factor was the presence or absence of European settlers. In Canada, Australia, and New Zealand, whites were already in the majority by 1869, and their colonial "mother-country," Britain, encouraged them to elect parliaments and rule themselves. Where European settlers were numerous but still a minority of

SECTION REVIEW

- The political motives of the New Imperialism included European nationalism and the initiatives of colonial officials.

- Cultural motives included a Christian revival in the West, a sense of superiority born of technological advancement, and adventurism among young men.

- The economic motives were the demands of industrialization, the effects of a long depression, and a general sense of power bred by industrial might.

- Imperialists made good use of sea power, new drugs and sanitary methods, and advanced military technology.

- Colonies were expected to pay their own expenses and were administered in a variety of ways, depending on the number of European settlers.

the population, as in Algeria and South Africa, settlers and the home country contested for control over the indigenous population. In colonies with few white settlers, the European governors ruled autocratically.

In the early years of the New Imperialism, colonial administrations consisted of a governor and his staff, a few troops to keep order, and a small number of tax collectors and magistrates. The cooperation of indigenous elites was essential to the maintenance of order. In most cases the colonial governors exercised power through traditional rulers willing to cooperate. Areas governed indirectly in this fashion were called "Princely States." In addition, colonial governments educated a few local youths for "modern" jobs as clerks, policemen, customs inspectors, and the like. These individuals came in time to rival the traditional rulers.

Western women seldom took part in the early stages of colonial expansion. Once peace was achieved and steamships and railroads made travel less difficult, however, colonial officials and settlers began bringing their wives to the colonies. By the 1880s the British Women's Emigration Association was recruiting single women to go out to the colonies to marry British settlers. As one of its founders, Ellen Joyce, explained, "The possibility of the settler marrying his own countrywoman is of imperial as well as family importance."

The arrival of white women in Asia and Africa increased racial segregation. Sylvia Leith-Ross, wife of a colonial officer in Nigeria, explained: "When you are alone, among thousands of unknown, unpredictable people, dazed by unaccustomed sights and sounds, bemused by strange ways of life and thought, you need to remember who you are, where you come from, what your standards are." Many colonial wives found themselves in command of numerous servants and expected to follow the complex etiquette of colonial entertainment in support of their husbands' official positions. Occasionally they found opportunities to exercise personal initiatives, usually charitable work involving indigenous women and children. However well meaning, their efforts were always subordinate to the work of men.

THE SCRAMBLE FOR AFRICA

Why were imperialists drawn to the natural resources of Africa, and how did their presence on that continent change the environment?

Until the 1870s African history was largely shaped by internal forces and local initiatives (see Chapter 22). Outside Algeria and southern Africa, only a handful of Europeans had ever visited the interior of Africa, and European countries possessed only small enclaves on the coasts. As late as 1879 Africans ruled more than 90 percent of the continent. Then, within a decade, Africa was invaded and divided among the European powers in a movement often referred to as the **"scramble" for Africa** (see Map 24.1). This invasion affected all regions of the continent.

"scramble" for Africa Sudden wave of conquests in Africa by European powers in the 1880s and 1890s. Britain obtained most of eastern Africa, France most of northwestern Africa. Other countries (Germany, Belgium, Portugal, Italy, and Spain) acquired lesser amounts.

Egypt

Ironically, European involvement in Egypt resulted from Egypt's attempt to free itself from Ottoman Turkish rule. The khedives of Egypt, hereditary governors descended

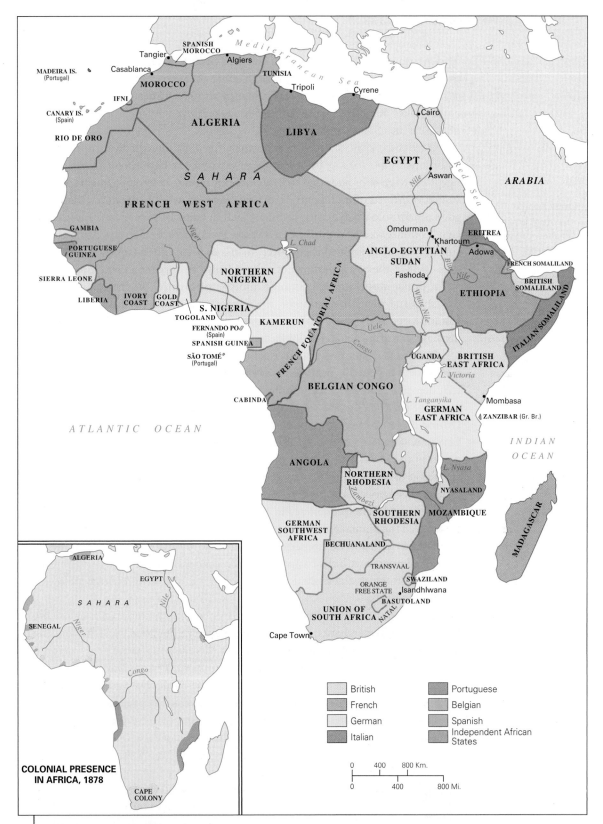

Map 24.1 shows the following labels:

Mediterranean Sea

SPANISH MOROCCO
Tangier
Algiers
MADEIRA IS. (Portugal)
Casablanca
TUNISIA
MOROCCO
Tripoli
Cyrene
IFNI
CANARY IS. (Spain)
Cairo
ALGERIA
LIBYA
RIO DE ORO
EGYPT
S A H A R A
Nile
Aswan
ARABIA
Red Sea
FRENCH WEST AFRICA
GAMBIA
Niger
L. Chad
Omdurman
ERITREA
PORTUGUESE GUINEA
Khartoum
Adowa
FRENCH SOMALILAND
ANGLO-EGYPTIAN SUDAN
SIERRA LEONE
NORTHERN NIGERIA
Blue Nile
BRITISH SOMALILAND
Fashoda
LIBERIA
IVORY COAST
GOLD COAST
S. NIGERIA
ETHIOPIA
TOGOLAND
FERNANDO PO (Spain)
KAMERUN
Uele
White Nile
ITALIAN SOMALILAND
SPANISH GUINEA
Congo
SÃO TOMÉ (Portugal)
FRENCH EQUATORIAL AFRICA
UGANDA
BRITISH EAST AFRICA
L. Victoria
CABINDA
BELGIAN CONGO
L. Tanganyika
Mombasa
ATLANTIC OCEAN
GERMAN EAST AFRICA
ZANZIBAR (Gr. Br.)
INDIAN OCEAN
ANGOLA
L. Nyasa
NORTHERN RHODESIA
NYASALAND
Zambezi
MOZAMBIQUE
GERMAN SOUTHWEST AFRICA
SOUTHERN RHODESIA
MADAGASCAR
BECHUANALAND
TRANSVAAL
SWAZILAND
ORANGE FREE STATE
Isandhlwana
BASUTOLAND
NATAL
UNION OF SOUTH AFRICA
Cape Town

Legend:
British
French
German
Italian
Portuguese
Belgian
Spanish
Independent African States

0   400   800 Km.
0   400   800 Mi.

COLONIAL PRESENCE IN AFRICA, 1878
ALGERIA
EGYPT
SAHARA
Nile
SENEGAL
Niger
Congo
CAPE COLONY

Map 24.1 Africa in 1878 and 1914

In 1878 the European colonial presence was limited to a few coastal enclaves, plus portions of Algeria and South Africa. By 1914, Europeans had taken over all of Africa except Ethiopia and Liberia.

CL Interactive Map

from Muhammad Ali (see Chapter 21), used profits from exporting cotton during the American Civil War to modernize their armed forces and build canals, harbors, railroads, and other public works. Their support for the Suez Canal project was part of this policy. Khedive Ismail even tried to make Egypt the center of an empire reaching south into Sudan and Ethiopia.

Once cotton prices returned to normal after 1865, the khedives supported their ambitions by borrowing from European creditors at high interest rates. By 1876 Egypt's foreign debt had risen to £100 million sterling. Interest payments alone consumed one-third of its foreign export earnings. To avoid bankruptcy the Egyptian government sold its shares in the Suez Canal to Great Britain and accepted four foreign "commissioners of the debt" to oversee its finances. French and British bankers, still not satisfied, lobbied their governments to secure the loans by stronger measures. In 1878 the two governments obliged Ismail to appoint a Frenchman as minister of public works and a Briton as minister of finance. When high taxes caused hardship and popular discontent, the French and British persuaded the Ottoman sultan to depose Ismail. This foreign intervention provoked a military uprising under Egyptian army colonel Arabi Pasha, which threatened the Suez Canal.

Fearing for their investments, the British sent an army into Egypt in 1882. They intended to occupy Egypt for only a year or two. But theirs was a seaborne empire that depended on secure communications between Britain and India. So important was the Suez Canal to their maritime supremacy that they stayed for seventy years. During those years the British ruled Egypt "indirectly"—that is, they maintained the Egyptian government and the fiction of Egyptian sovereignty but retained real power in their own hands.

Eager to develop Egyptian agriculture, especially cotton production, the British brought in engineers and contractors to build the first dam across the Nile, at Aswan in upper Egypt. When completed in 1902, it was one of the largest dams in the world. It captured the annual Nile flood and released its waters throughout the year, allowing farmers to grow two, sometimes three, crops a year. This doubled the effective acreage compared with the basin system of irrigation practiced since the time of the pharaohs, in which the annual floodwaters of the Nile were retained by low dikes around the fields.

The economic development of Egypt by the British enriched a small elite of landowners and merchants, many of them foreigners. Egyptian peasants got little relief from the heavy taxes collected to pay for their country's crushing foreign debt and the expenses of the British army of occupation. Western ways that conflicted with the teachings of Islam—such as the drinking of alcohol and the relative freedom of women—offended Muslim religious leaders. Most Egyptians found British rule more onerous than that of the Ottomans. By the 1890s Egyptian politicians and intellectuals were demanding that the British leave, to no avail.

CL Primary Source: Convention on Free Navigation of the Suez Canal Between the European Powers and the Ottoman Empire, October 29, 1888
Learn about the ways in which nations work together to ensure free travel along a key waterway.

Western and Equatorial Africa

While the British were taking over Egypt, the French were planning to extend their empire into the interior of West Africa. Starting from the coast of Senegal, which had been in French hands for centuries, they hoped to build a railroad from the upper Senegal River to the upper Niger to open the interior to French merchants. This in turn led the French military to undertake the conquest of western Sudan.

Meanwhile, the actions of three individuals, rather than a government, brought about the occupation of the Congo Basin, an enormous forested region in the heart of equatorial Africa (see Map 24.1). In 1879 the American journalist **Henry Morton Stanley**, who had explored the area, persuaded King **Leopold II** of Belgium to invest his personal fortune in "opening up" equatorial Africa. With Leopold's money, Stanley returned to Africa from 1879 to 1884 to establish trading posts along the southern bank of the Congo River. At the same time, **Savorgnan de Brazza**, an Italian officer serving in the French army, obtained from an African ruler living on the opposite bank a treaty that placed the area under the "protection" of France.

These events sparked a flurry of diplomatic activity. German chancellor Bismarck called the **Berlin Conference** on Africa of 1884 and 1885. There the major powers agreed that henceforth "effective occupation" would replace the former trading relations between Africans and Europeans. This meant that every country with colonial ambitions had to send troops into Africa and participate in the division of the spoils. As a reward for triggering the "scramble" for Africa, Leopold II acquired a personal domain under the name "Congo Free State," while France and Portugal took most of the rest of equatorial Africa. In this manner, the European powers and King Leopold managed to divide Africa among themselves, at least on paper.

"Effective occupation" required many years of effort. In the interior of West Africa, Muslim rulers resisted the French invasion for up to thirty years. The French advance encouraged the Germans to stake claims to parts of the region and the

Henry Morton Stanley (1841–1904) British-American explorer of Africa, famous for his expeditions in search of Dr. David Livingstone. Stanley helped King **Leopold II** establish the Congo Free State.

Leopold II (1835–1909) King of Belgium (r. 1865–1909). He was active in encouraging the exploration of Central Africa and became the ruler of the Congo Free State (to 1908).

Savorgnan de Brazza (1852–1905) Franco-Italian explorer sent by the French government to claim part of equatorial Africa for France. Founded Brazzaville, capital of the French Congo, in 1880.

Berlin Conference (1884–1885) Conference that German chancellor Otto von Bismarck called to set rules for the partition of Africa. It led to the creation of the Congo Free State under King **Leopold II** of Belgium.

A Steamboat for the Congo River

Soon after the Congo Basin was occupied by Europeans, the new colonial rulers realized they needed to improve transportation. Since access from the sea was blocked by rapids on the lower Congo River, steamboats had to be brought in sections, hauled from the coast by thousands of Congolese over very difficult terrain. This picture shows the pieces arriving at Stanley Pool, ready to be reassembled.   (From H. M. Stanley, *The Congo,* vol. 2, London, 1885)

British to move north from their coastal enclaves, until the entire region was occupied by Britain, France, and Germany.

Because West Africa had long had a flourishing trade, the new rulers took advantage of existing trade networks, taxing merchants and farmers, investing the profits in railroads and harbors, and paying dividends to European stockholders. In the Gold Coast (now Ghana) British trading companies bought the cocoa grown by African farmers at low prices and resold it for large profits. The interior of French West Africa lagged behind. Although the region could produce cotton, peanuts, and other crops, the difficulties of transportation limited its development before 1914.

Compared to West Africa, equatorial Africa had few inhabitants and little trade. Rather than try to govern these vast territories directly, authorities in the Congo Free State, the French Congo, and the Portuguese colonies of Angola and Mozambique granted huge pieces of land as concessions to private companies that thereby gained monopolies on natural resources and trade and the right to employ soldiers and impose taxes.

Freed from outside supervision, the companies forced the African inhabitants at gunpoint to produce cash crops and carry them, on their heads or backs, to the nearest railroad or navigable river. The worst abuses took place in the Congo Free State, where a rubber boom lasting from 1895 to 1905 made it profitable for private companies to coerce Africans to collect latex from vines that grew in the forests. One Congolese refugee told the British consul Roger Casement who investigated the atrocities:

> We begged the white men to leave us alone, saying we could get no more rubber, but the white men and their soldiers said: "Go. You are only beasts yourselves, you are only *nyama* (meat)." We tried, always going further into the forest, and when we failed and our rubber was short, the soldiers came to our towns and killed us. Many were shot, some had their ears cut off; others were tied up with ropes around their necks and bodies and taken away. [4]

After 1906 the British press began publicizing the horrors. The public outcry that followed, coinciding with the end of the rubber boom, convinced the Belgian government to take over Leopold's private empire in 1908.

Southern Africa

The history of white settlers in southern Africa between 1869 and 1914 differs from that of the rest of the continent. **Afrikaners**, descendants of Dutch settlers on the Cape of Good Hope, moved inland throughout the nineteenth century; British prospectors and settlers arrived later in the century; and, finally, Indians were brought over by the British and stayed.

Southern Africa attracted European settlers because of its good pastures and farmland and its phenomenal deposits of diamonds, gold, and copper, as well as coal and iron ore. This was the new El Dorado that imperialists had dreamed of since the heyday of the Spanish Empire in Peru and Mexico in the sixteenth century.

The discovery of diamonds at Kimberley in 1868 lured thousands of European prospectors as well as Africans looking for work. It also attracted the interest of Great Britain, colonial ruler of the Cape Colony, which annexed the diamond area in 1871, thereby angering the Afrikaners. Once in the interior, the British defeated the Xhosa (KOH-sah) people in 1877 and 1878. Then in 1879 they confronted the Zulu, militarily the most powerful of the African peoples in the region.

Afrikaners South Africans descended from Dutch and French settlers of the seventeenth century. Their Great Trek founded new settler colonies in the nineteenth century. Though a minority among South Africans, they held political power after 1910, imposing a system of racial segregation called apartheid after 1949.

Climate similior to Europe

The Zulu, led by their king Cetshwayo (set-SHWAH-yo), resented their encirclement by Afrikaners and British. A growing sense of nationalism and their proud military tradition led them into a war with the British in 1879. At first they held their own, defeating the British at Isandhlwana (ee-sawn-dull-WAH-nuh), but a few months later they were defeated. Cetshwayo was captured and sent into exile, and the Zulu lands were given to white ranchers. Yet throughout those bitter times, the Zulu's sense of nationhood remained strong.

Relations between the British and the Afrikaners, already tense as a result of British encroachment, took a turn for the worse when gold was discovered in the Afrikaner republic of Transvaal (trans-VAHL) in 1886. In the gold rush that ensued, the British soon outnumbered the Afrikaners.

Britain's invasion of southern Africa was driven in part by the ambition of **Cecil Rhodes** (1853–1902), who once declared that he would "annex the stars" if he could. Rhodes made his fortune in the Kimberley diamond fields, founding De Beers Consolidated, a company that has dominated the world's diamond trade ever since. He then turned to politics. He encouraged a concession company, the British South Africa Company, to push north into Central Africa, where he named two new colonies after himself: Southern Rhodesia (now Zimbabwe) and Northern Rhodesia (now Zambia). The Ndebele (en-duh-BELL-ay) and Shona peoples, who inhabited the region, resisted this invasion, but the machine guns of the British finally defeated them.

British attempts to annex the two Afrikaner republics, Transvaal and Orange Free State, and the inflow of English-speaking whites into the gold- and diamond-mining areas led to the South African War (also called the Boer War), which lasted from 1899 to 1902. At first the Afrikaners had the upper hand, for they were highly motivated, possessed modern rifles, and knew the land. In 1901, however, Great Britain brought in 450,000 troops and crushed the Afrikaner armies. Ironically, the Afrikaners' defeat in 1902 led to their ultimate victory. Wary of costly commitments overseas, the British government expected European settlers in Africa to manage their own affairs, as they were doing in Canada, Australia, and New Zealand. Thus, in 1910 the European settlers created the Union of South Africa, in which the Afrikaners eventually emerged as the ruling element.

Unlike Canada, Australia, and New Zealand, South Africa had a majority of indigenous inhabitants and substantial numbers of Indians and "Cape Coloureds" (people of mixed ancestry). Yet the Europeans were both numerous enough to demand self-rule and powerful enough to deny the vote and other civil rights to the majority. In 1913 the South African parliament passed the Natives Land Act, assigning Africans to reservations and forbidding them to own land elsewhere. This and other racial policies turned South Africa into a land of segregation, oppression, and bitter divisions.

Political and Social Consequences

Africa was home to a wide variety of indigenous societies, some of them long-established kingdoms with aristocracies or commercial towns dominated by a merchant class, others centered on agricultural villages without any outside government, and still others consisting of pastoral nomads organized along military lines. Not surprisingly, these societies responded in very different ways to the European invasion.

Some peoples welcomed the invaders as allies against local enemies. Once colonial rule was established, they sought work in government service or in European

Cecil Rhodes (1853–1902) British entrepreneur and politician involved in the expansion of the British Empire from South Africa into Central Africa. The colonies of Southern Rhodesia (now Zimbabwe) and Northern Rhodesia (now Zambia) were named after him.

Primary Source: His Story *Examine a first-person account of the arrival of the "white men" in southern Africa.*

Primary Source: Memorandum to Lord Selborne, High Commissioner of Transvaal, October 1905 *See how a British Indian in Potchefstroom attempts to speak up for himself and his fellow tradespeople before the British High Commissioner of Transvaal.*

firms and sent their children to mission schools. In exchange, they were often the first to receive benefits such as clinics and roads.

Others, especially peoples with a pastoral or a warrior tradition, fought tenaciously. Examples abound, from the Zulu and Ndebele of southern Africa to the pastoral Herero (hair-AIR-oh) people of Southwest Africa (now Namibia), who rose up against German invaders in 1904; in repressing their uprising, the Germans exterminated two-thirds of them. In the Sahel, a belt of grasslands south of the Sahara, charismatic leaders rose up in the name of a purified Islam, gathered a following of warriors, and led them on partly religious, partly empire-building campaigns called *jihads*. These leaders included Samori Toure in western Sudan (now Mali), Rabih in the Chad basin, and the Mahdi (MAH-dee) in eastern Sudan. All of them eventually came into conflict with European-led military expeditions and were defeated.

Some commercial states with long histories of contact with Europeans also fought back. The kingdom of **Asante** (uh-SAWN-tay) in Gold Coast rose up in 1874, 1896, and 1900 before it was finally overwhelmed. In the Niger Delta, the ancient city of Benin, rich with artistic treasures, resisted colonial control until 1897, when a British "punitive expedition" set it on fire and carted its works of art off to Europe.

One resistance movement succeeded, to the astonishment of Europeans and Africans alike. When **Menelik II** became emperor of Ethiopia in 1889 (see Chapter 22), his country was threatened by Sudanese Muslims to the west and by France and Italy, which controlled the Red Sea coast to the east. For many years, Ethiopia had been purchasing weapons. By the Treaty of Wichelle (1889), Italy agreed to sell more weapons to Ethiopia. Six years later, when Italians attempted to establish a protectorate over Ethiopia, they found the Ethiopians armed with thousands of rifles and even a few machine guns and artillery pieces. Although Italy sent twenty thousand troops to attack Ethiopia, in 1896 they were defeated at Adowa (AH-do-ah) by a larger and better-trained Ethiopian army.

Most Africans neither joined nor fought the European invaders but tried to continue living as before. They found this increasingly difficult because colonial rule disrupted every traditional society. The presence of colonial officials meant that rights to land, commercial transactions, and legal disputes were handled very differently and that traditional rulers lost all authority, except where Europeans used them as local administrators.

Changes in landholding were especially disruptive, for most Africans were farmers or herders for whom access to land was a necessity. In areas with a high population density, such as Egypt and West Africa, colonial rulers left peasants in place, encouraged them to grow cash crops, and collected taxes on the harvest. Elsewhere, the new rulers declared any land that was not farmed to be "waste" or "vacant" and gave it to private companies or to European planters and ranchers. In Kenya, Northern Rhodesia, and South Africa, Europeans found the land and climate to their liking, in contrast to other parts of Africa, where soldiers, officials, missionaries, or traders stayed only a few years. White settlers forced Africans to become squatters, sharecroppers, or ranch hands on land they had farmed for generations. In South Africa they forced many Africans off their lands and onto "reserves," much like the nomadic peoples of North America, Russia, and Australia.

The colonial rulers were even more interested in African labor than in the land. To get workers to take low-paid jobs on plantations, railroads, or other European enter-

Asante African kingdom on the Gold Coast that expanded rapidly after 1680. Asante participated in the Atlantic economy, trading gold, slaves, and ivory. It resisted British imperial ambitions for a quarter century before being absorbed into Britain's Gold Coast colony in 1902.

Menelik II (1844–1911) Emperor of Ethiopia (r. 1889–1911). He enlarged Ethiopia to its present dimensions and defeated an Italian invasion at Adowa (1896).

prises, they imposed various taxes, such as the hut tax and the head tax. To pay the tax, Africans had little choice but to accept whatever work the Europeans offered. In the South African mines Africans were paid, on average, one-tenth as much as Europeans.

Some Africans migrated great distances to the cities and mining camps in search of a better life. Most migrant workers were men who left their wives and children behind in villages and on reserves, sometimes for years. Only occasionally did the authorities allow them to bring their families and settle permanently. This caused great hardship for African women, who had to grow food for their families during the men's absences and care for sick and aged workers. Long separations between spouses also led to prostitution and the spread of sexually transmitted diseases.

Some African women welcomed colonial rule, for it brought an end to fighting and slave raiding, but others were led into captivity. A few succeeded in becoming wealthy traders or owners of livestock. On the whole, however, African women benefited less than men from the economic changes that colonialism introduced. Whenever colonial rulers replaced communal property (traditional in most of Africa) with private property, property rights were assigned to the head of the household—that is, to the man. Almost all the jobs open to Africans, even those considered "women's work" in Europe, such as nursing and domestic service, were reserved for men.

Cultural Responses

Africans came into contact with missionaries more than with any other Europeans. Mission schools taught reading, writing, and arithmetic to village children. Boys learned crafts like carpentry and blacksmithing, while girls were taught domestic skills.

The first generation of Africans educated in mission schools also acquired Western ideas of justice and progress. Samuel Ajayi Crowther, a Yoruba rescued from slavery as a boy and educated in mission schools in Sierra Leone, went on to become an Anglican minister and, in 1864, the first African bishop. Crowther thought that Africa needed European assistance in achieving both spiritual and economic development:

> Africa has neither knowledge nor skill . . . to bring out her vast resources for her own improvement. . . . Therefore to claim Africa for the Africans alone, is to claim for her the right of a continued ignorance. . . . For it is certain, unless help [comes] from without, a nation can never rise above its present state.[5]

After the first generation, many mission teachers were themselves African, the products of a mission education. They discovered that Christian ideals clashed with the reality of colonial exploitation. One convert wrote in 1911:

> There is too much failure among all Europeans in Nyasaland. The three combined bodies—Missionaries, Government and Companies or gainers of money—do form the same rule to look upon the native with mockery eyes. . . . If we had enough power to communicate ourselves to Europe, we would advise them not to call themselves Christendom, but Europeandom. Therefore the life of the three combined bodies is altogether too cheaty, too thefty, too mockery. Instead of "Give," they say "Take away from." There is too much breakage of God's pure law.[6]

SECTION REVIEW

- Financial crisis and threats to the Suez Canal led to Britain's occupation, indirect rule, and economic development of Egypt.

- While France expanded into West Africa, the actions of a few individuals in equatorial Africa precipitated the Berlin Conference, at which it was decided that France, Britain, Germany, and Portugal would divide up West and equatorial Africa.

- Attracted by valuable resources, Britain expanded deeper into southern Africa, subduing indigenous peoples and white Afrikaners.

- Some Africans welcomed Europeans and others resisted, but most continued to live as they had, even as colonial rule disrupted traditional ways.

- Christian missionaries converted and educated many followers of traditional religions, and Islam, which successfully resisted change, spread southward from northern and eastern Africa.

Missionaries were not the only ones to bring religious change to Africa. In southern and Central Africa indigenous preachers adapted Christianity to African values and customs and founded new denominations known as "Ethiopian" churches.

Christianity proved successful in converting followers of traditional religions but made no inroads among Muslims. Instead, Islam, long predominant in northern and eastern Africa, spread southward as Muslim teachers established Quranic schools and founded Muslim brotherhoods. European colonialism unwittingly helped the diffusion of Islam. By building cities and increasing trade, colonial rule permitted Muslims to settle in new areas. As Islam—a universal religion untainted by colonialism—became increasingly relevant to Africans, the number of Muslims in sub-Saharan Africa probably doubled between 1869 and 1914.

IMPERIALISM IN ASIA AND THE PACIFIC

What were the social and cultural effects of imperialism in Asia?

From 1869 to 1914 the pressure of the industrial powers was felt throughout Asia, the East Indies, and the Pacific islands (see Map 24.2). As trade with these regions grew in the late nineteenth century, so did their attractiveness to imperialists eager for economic benefits and national prestige.

By 1869 Britain already controlled most of India and Burma; Spain occupied the Philippines; and the Netherlands held large parts of the East Indies (now Indonesia). Between 1862 and 1895 France conquered Indochina (now Vietnam, Kampuchea, and Laos).

Central Asia

Farther north, Russia continued its colonial expansion, aided by the acquisition of modern rifles and artillery. Between 1865 and 1876 Russian forces advanced into Central Asia. Nomads like the Kazakhs, who lived east of the Caspian Sea, resisted; but soon Kazakhstan became home to 200,000 Russian settlers. Although the governments of Tsar Alexander II (r. 1855–1881) and Tsar Alexander III (r. 1881–1894) claimed not to interfere in indigenous customs, they declared communally owned grazing lands "waste" or "vacant" and turned them over to farmers from Russia. By the end of the century the nomads were fenced out and reduced to starvation. An eminent Russian jurist declared: "International rights cannot be taken into account when dealing with semibarbarous peoples."

South of the Kazakh steppe the fabled cities of Tashkent, Bukhara, and Samarkand served the caravan trade between China and the Middle East. By the 1860s and 1870s the Qing Empire was losing control over Central Asia, so it was fairly easy for Russian expeditions to conquer the indigenous peoples. Russia thereby acquired land suitable for cotton, along with a large Muslim population.

The Russians abolished slavery, built railroads to link the region with Europe, and planted hundreds of thousands of acres of cotton. Unlike the British in India, however, they did not attempt to change the customs, languages, or religious beliefs of their subjects.

Map 24.2 Asia in 1914

By 1914, much of Asia was claimed by colonial powers. The southern rim, from the Pacific Gulf to the Pacific, was occupied by Great Britain, France, the Netherlands, and the United States. Central Asia had been incorporated into the Russian Empire. Japan, now industrialized, had joined the Western imperialist powers in expanding its territory and influence at the expense of China.

Great Britain
France
Japan
United States
Netherlands
Russia
Independent Asian states

Southeast Asia and Indonesia

Until the mid-nineteenth century, independent kingdoms ruled most of the Southeast Asian peninsula and the Indonesian archipelago. As in Africa, colonialism varied considerably from region to region. Burma (now Myanmar), nearest India, was gradually taken over by the British, the last piece being annexed in 1885. Indochina fell under French control bit by bit until it was finally subdued in 1895. Similarly, Malaya (now Malaysia) came under British rule in stages during the 1870s and 1880s. By the early 1900s the Dutch had subdued northern Sumatra, the last part of the Dutch East Indies to be conquered. Only Siam (now Thailand) remained independent, although it lost several border provinces.

Despite their varied political histories, all these regions had features in common: fertile soil, constant warmth, and heavy rains along with a long tradition of intensive gardening, irrigation, and terracing. Where the population was sparse, Europeans imported landless laborers from China and India. The climate favored the transfer of commercially valuable plants from other parts of the world. Tobacco, cinchona (sin-CHO-nah) (an antimalarial drug), manioc (an edible root crop), maize (corn), and natural rubber came from the Americas; sugar from India; tea from China; and coffee and oil palms from Africa. By 1914 much of the world's supply of these valuable products—in the case of rubber, almost all—came from Southeast Asia and Indonesia (see Environment and Technology: Imperialism and Tropical Ecology).

Europe and North America formed the export market for most of these products. In exchange, the inhabitants of the region benefited from peace and a reliable food supply. As a result, their numbers increased at an unprecedented rate. For instance, the population of Java (an island the size of Pennsylvania) doubled from 16 million in 1870 to over 30 million in 1914.

Colonialism and population growth spurred many social changes. Agricultural and commercial peoples gradually moved into mountainous and forested areas, displacing groups that practiced hunting and gathering or shifting agriculture and had not experienced as much population growth. Javanese migrating to Borneo and Sumatra are but one example. Immigrants from China and India changed the ethnic composition and culture of every country in the region. Thus the

A Rubber Plantation

As bicycles and automobiles proliferated in the early twentieth century, the demand for rubber outstripped the supply available from wild rubber trees in the Amazon forest. Rubber grown on plantations in Southeast Asia came on the market from 1910 on. The rubber trees had to be tapped very carefully and on a regular schedule to obtain the latex or sap from which rubber was extracted. In this picture a woman and a boy perform this operation on a plantation in British Malaya. (Mary Evans Picture Library/The Image Works)

Imperialism and Tropical Ecology

Like all conquerors before them, the European imperialists of the nineteenth century exacted taxes and rents from the peoples they conquered. But they also sent botanists and agricultural experts to their tropical colonies to increase the production of commercial crops, radically changing the landscapes.

The most dramatic effects were brought about by the deliberate introduction of new crops—an acceleration of the Columbian Exchange that had begun in the fifteenth century. In the early nineteenth century tea was transferred from China to India and Ceylon. In the 1850s British and Dutch botanists smuggled seeds of the cinchona tree from the Andes in South America to India and Java. They had to operate in secret because the South American republics, knowing the value of this crop, prohibited the export of seeds. With the seeds, the British and Dutch established cinchona plantations in Ceylon and Java, respectively, to produce quinine, which was essential as an antimalarial drug and a flavoring for tonic water. Similarly, in the 1870s British agents stole seeds of rubber trees from the Amazon rain forest and transferred them to Malaya and Sumatra.

Before these transfers, vast forests covered the highlands of India, Southeast Asia, and Indonesia, precisely the lands where the new plants grew best. So European planters had the forests cut down and replaced with thousands of acres of commercially profitable trees and bushes, all lined up in perfect rows and tended by thousands of indigenous laborers to satisfy the demands of customers in faraway lands. The crops that poured forth from the transformed environments brought great wealth to the European planters and the imperial powers. In 1909 the British botanist John Willis justified the transformation in these terms:

> Whether planting in the tropics will always continue to be under European management is another question, but the northern powers will not permit that the rich and as yet comparatively undeveloped countries of the tropics should be entirely wasted by being devoted merely to the supply of the food and clothing wants of their own people,

BRANCH OF A CINCHONA TREE The bark of the cinchona tree was the source of quinine, the only antimalarial drug known before the 1940s. Quinine made it much safer for Europeans to live in the tropics. (From Bentley & Trimen's Medicinal Plants. Hunt Institute for Botanical Documentation, Carnegie Mellon University)

> when they can also supply the wants of the colder zones in so many indispensable products.

This quotation raises important questions about trade versus self-sufficiency. If a region's economy supplies the food and clothing wants of its own people, is its output "entirely wasted"? What is the advantage of trading the products of one region (such as the tropics) for those of another (such as the colder zones)? Is this trade an obligation? Should one part of the world (such as the "northern powers") let another refuse to develop and sell its "indispensable products"? Can you think of a case where a powerful country forced a weaker one to trade?

Source: The quotation is from John Christopher Willis, *Agriculture in the Tropics: An Elementary Treatise* (Cambridge: Cambridge University Press, 1909), 38–39.

population of the Malay Peninsula became one-third Malay, one-third Chinese, and one-third Indian.

As in Africa, European missionaries spread Christianity under the colonial umbrella. Islam, however, was much more successful in gaining new converts, for it had been established in the region for centuries and people did not consider it a religion imposed on them by foreigners.

Education and European ideas had an impact on the political perceptions in Southeast Asia and Indonesia, as did events in neighboring Asian countries: in India, where a nationalist movement arose in the 1880s; in China, where modernizers were undermining the authority of the Qing; and especially in Japan, whose rapid industrialization culminated in its brilliant victory over Russia in the Russo-Japanese War (1904–1905). A young Vietnamese writing soon after the Russo-Japanese War expressed the spirit of a rising generation:

CL **Primary Source: Letter to the French Chamber of Deputies** *Learn how a Vietnamese citizen defends his attempts to rid his country of the French Indochinese government.*

> I, . . . an obscure student, having had occasion to study new books and new doctrines, have discovered in a recent history of Japan how they have been able to conquer the impotent Europeans. This is the reason why we have formed an organization. . . . We have selected from young Annamites [Vietnamese] the most energetic, with great capacities for courage, and are sending them to Japan for study. . . . Several years have passed without the French being aware of the movement. . . . Our only aim is to prepare the population for the future.[7]

Hawaii and the Philippines, 1878–1902

By the 1890s the United States had a fast-growing population and industries that produced more manufactured goods than they could sell at home. Merchants and bankers began to look for export markets. The political mood was also expansionist, and many echoed the feelings of the naval strategist Alfred T. Mahan (mah-HAHN): "Whether they will or no, Americans must now begin to look outward. The growing production of the country requires it."

Some Americans had been looking outward for quite some time, especially across the Pacific to China and Japan. In 1878 the United States obtained the harbor of Pago Pago in Samoa as a coaling and naval station, and in 1887 it secured the use of Pearl Harbor in Hawaii for the same purpose. Six years later American settlers in Hawaii deposed Queen Liliuokalani (1838–1917) and offered the Hawaiian Islands to the United States. At the time President Grover Cleveland (1893–1897) was opposed to annexation, and the settlers had to content themselves with an informal protectorate. By 1898, however, the United States under President William McKinley (1897–1901) had become openly imperialistic, and it annexed Hawaii as a stepping-stone to Asia. As the United States became ever more involved in Asian affairs, Hawaii's strategic location brought an inflow of U.S. military personnel, and its fertile land caused planters to import farm laborers from Japan, China, and the Philippines. These immigrants soon outnumbered the native Hawaiians.

While large parts of Asia were falling under colonial domination, the people of the Philippines were chafing under their Spanish rulers. The movement for independence began among young Filipinos studying in Europe. José Rizal, a young doctor working in Spain, was arrested and executed in 1896 for writing anti-Spanish and anticlerical novels. Thereafter, the center of resistance shifted to the Philippines, where **Emilio Aguinaldo**, leader of a secret society, rose in revolt and proclaimed a republic in 1899. The revolutionaries had a good chance of winning independence, for Spain had its hands full with a revolution in Cuba (see below).

Unfortunately for Aguinaldo and his followers, the United States went to war against Spain in April 1898 and quickly overcame Spanish forces in the Philippines and Cuba. President McKinley had not originally intended to acquire the Philippines; but after the Spanish defeat, he realized that a weakened Spain might lose the islands to another imperialist power. Japan, having recently defeated China in the Sino-Japanese War (1894–1895) and annexed Taiwan, was eager to expand. So was Germany, which had taken over parts of New Guinea and Samoa and several Pacific archipelagoes during the 1880s. To forestall them, McKinley purchased the Philippines from Spain for $20 million.

The Filipinos were not eager to trade one master for another. For a while, Aguinaldo cooperated with the Americans in the hope of achieving full independence. When his plan was rejected, he rose up again in 1899 and proclaimed the independence of his country. In spite of protests by anti-imperialists in the United States, the U.S. government decided that its global interests outweighed the interests of the Filipino people. In rebel areas, a U.S. army of occupation tortured prisoners, burned villages and crops, and forced the inhabitants into "reconcentration camps." Many American soldiers tended to look on Filipinos with the same racial contempt with which Europeans viewed their colonial subjects. By the end of the insurrection in 1902, the war had cost the lives of 5,000 Americans and 200,000 Filipinos.

After the insurrection ended, the United States attempted to soften its rule with public works and economic development projects. New buildings went up in the city of Manila; roads, harbors, and railroads were built; and the Philippine economy was tied ever more closely to that of the United States. In 1907 Filipinos were allowed to elect representatives to a legislative assembly, but ultimate authority remained in the hands of a governor appointed by the president of the United States. An American promise of independence made in 1916 was not fulfilled until thirty years later.

Emilio Aguinaldo (1869–1964)
Leader of the Filipino independence movement against Spain (1895–1898). He proclaimed the independence of the Philippines in 1899, but his movement was crushed and he was captured by the United States Army in 1901.

SECTION REVIEW

- Russia steadily expanded into Central Asia, abolishing slavery and building railroads but leaving local customs and languages in place.

- Britain and France took Southeast Asia, except for Siam, and the Dutch added to their East Indian holdings.

- Southeast Asian colonial economies grew around cash crops, while social change resulted from immigration, missionary work, and Islam.

- An imperialist United States annexed Hawaii and occupied the Philippines, rejecting Filipino independence.

IMPERIALISM IN LATIN AMERICA

What were the economic motives behind imperialism in Latin America?

Nations in the Americas followed two divergent paths. In Canada and the United States manufacturing industries, powerful corporations, and wealthy financial institutions arose. By contrast, Latin America and the Caribbean exported raw materials and imported manufactured goods. The poverty of their people, the preferences of their elites, and the pressures of the world economy made them increasingly dependent on the industrialized countries. Instead of suffering outright annexation by the colonial empires, they experienced manipulation by the industrial powers, including the United States, in a form of economic dependence called **free-trade imperialism**.

In the Western Hemisphere, therefore, the New Imperialism manifested itself not by a "scramble" for territories but in two other ways. In the larger republics of

free-trade imperialism Economic dominance of a weaker country by a more powerful one, while maintaining the legal independence of the weaker state. In the late nineteenth century, free-trade imperialism characterized the relations between the Latin American republics, on the one hand, and Great Britain and the United States, on the other.

South America, the pressure was mostly financial and economic. In Central America and the Caribbean, it also included military intervention by the United States.

Railroads and the Imperialism of Free Trade

Latin America's economic potential was huge, for the region could produce many agricultural and mineral products in demand in the industrial countries. What was needed was a means of opening the interior to development. Railroads seemed the perfect answer.

Foreign merchants and bankers as well as Latin American landowners and politicians embraced the new technology. Starting in the 1870s almost every country in Latin America acquired railroads, usually connecting mines or agricultural regions with the nearest port rather than linking up the different parts of the interior. Since Latin America did not have any steel or mechanical industries, railroad equipment and building materials came from Britain or the United States. So did the money to build the networks, the engineers who designed and maintained them, and the managers who ran them.

Argentina, a rich source of wheat, beef, and hides, gained the longest and best-developed rail network south of the United States. By 1914, British firms owned 86 percent of the railroads in Argentina; 40 percent of the employees were British; and the official railroad language was English, not Spanish. Similar situations arose elsewhere throughout Latin America. The Argentine nationalist Juan Justo saw a parallel with Ireland:

> English capital has done what English armies could not do. Today our country is tributary to England . . . the gold that the English capitalists take out of Argentina or carry off in the form of products does us no more good than the Irish get from the revenues that the English lords take out of Ireland.[8]

The Irish, however, had little say in the matter because they were under British rule. But in Latin America the political elites encouraged foreign companies with generous concessions as the most rapid way to modernize their countries and enrich the property owners. In countries where the majority of the poor were Indians (as in Mexico and Peru) or of African origin (as in Brazil), they were neither consulted nor allowed to benefit from the railroad boom.

American Expansionism and the Spanish American War, 1898

After 1865 Europeans used their financial power to penetrate Latin America. But they avoided territorial acquisitions for four reasons: (1) they were overextended in Africa and Asia; (2) there was no need, because the Latin American governments provided the political backing for their economic penetration; (3) Mexico's resistance to the French in the 1860s had shown that invasion would not be easy; and (4) the United States claimed to defend the entire Western Hemisphere against all outside intervention. This claim, made in the Monroe Doctrine (1823), did not prevent the United States itself from intervening in Latin American affairs.

The United States had long had interests in Cuba, the closest and richest of the Caribbean islands and a Spanish colony. American businesses had invested great sums of money in Cuba's sugar and tobacco industries, and tens of thousands of Cubans had migrated to the United States. In 1895 the Cuban nationalist José Martí started a revolution against Spanish rule. American newspapers thrilled readers with lurid stories of Spanish atrocities; businessmen worried about their investments; and politicians demanded that the U.S. government help liberate Cuba.

On February 15, 1898, the U.S. battleship *Maine* accidentally blew up in Havana harbor, killing 266 American sailors. The U.S. government immediately blamed Spain and issued an ultimatum that the Spanish evacuate Cuba. Spain agreed to the ultimatum, but the American press and Congress were eager for war, and President McKinley did not restrain them.

The Spanish-American War was over quickly. On May 1, 1898, U.S. warships destroyed the Spanish fleet at Manila in the Philippines. Two months later the United States Navy sank the Spanish Atlantic fleet off Santiago, Cuba. By mid-August Spain was suing for peace. U.S. secretary of state John Hay called it "a splendid little war." The United States purchased the Philippines from Spain but took over Puerto Rico and Guam as war booty. The two islands remain American possessions to this day. Cuba became an independent republic, subject, however, to intense interference by the United States.

American Intervention in the Caribbean and Central America, 1901–1914

The nations of the Caribbean and Central America were small and poor, and their governments were corrupt, unstable, and often bankrupt. They seemed to offer an open invitation to foreign interference. A government would borrow money to pay for railroads, harbors, electric power, and other symbols of modernity. When it could not repay the loan, the lending banks in Europe or the United States would ask for assistance from their home governments. To ward off European intervention, the United States sent in the marines on more than one occasion.

Presidents Theodore Roosevelt (1901–1909), William Taft (1909–1913), and Woodrow Wilson (1913–1921) felt impelled to intervene in the region, though they differed sharply on the proper policy the United States should follow toward the small nations to the south. Roosevelt encouraged regimes friendly to the United States, like Porfirian Mexico; Taft sought to influence them through loans from American banks; and the moralist Wilson tried to impose clean governments through military means.

Having "liberated" Cuba from Spain, the United States forced the Cuban government to accept the Platt Amendment in 1901. This gave the United States the "right to intervene" to maintain order on the island. The United States used this excuse to occupy Cuba militarily from 1906 to 1909, in 1912, and again from 1917 to 1922. In all but name Cuba became an American protectorate. U.S. troops also occupied the Dominican Republic from 1904 to 1907 and again in 1916, Nicaragua and Honduras in 1912, and Haiti in 1915. They brought sanitation and material progress but no political improvements.

The United States was especially forceful in Panama, which was a province of Colombia. Here the issue was not corruption or debts but the construction of a canal to speed shipping between the east and west coasts

SECTION REVIEW

- In Latin America, industrial powers pursued free-trade imperialism to control agricultural and mineral resources.

- To tap these resources, foreign interests, with the support of Latin American elites, financed, built, and maintained railroads.

- Avoiding territorial expansion, Europeans relied instead on financial power.

- Through the Spanish-American War, the United States gained territories from Spain and guarded commercial interests in Cuba.

- The United States repeatedly intervened in Central America and the Caribbean, supporting Panamanian rebels to gain rights to build the Panama Canal.

Building the Panama Canal

When it opened in 1914, after ten years of construction, the canal shortened the sailing distance between San Francisco and New York from 14,000 miles (22,500 kilometers) to 6,000 miles (9,500 kilometers). With two sets of locks and numerous artificial lakes and channels, the canal is 47.9 miles (77.1 kilometers) long and today takes about nine hours to sail through. This picture shows dredges working to deepen a channel through the mountains. (Underwood & Underwood/Corbis)

of the United States. In 1878 the Frenchman Ferdinand de Lesseps, builder of the Suez Canal, had obtained a concession from Colombia to construct a canal across the isthmus of Panama, which lay in Colombian territory. Financial scandals and yellow fever, however, doomed his project.

When the United States acquired Hawaii and the Philippines, it recognized the strategic value of a canal that would allow warships to move quickly between the Atlantic and Pacific Oceans. The main obstacle was Colombia, whose senate refused to give the United States a piece of its territory. In 1903 the U.S. government supported a Panamanian rebellion against Colombia and quickly recognized the independence of Panama. In exchange, it obtained the right to build a canal and to occupy a zone 5 miles (8 kilometers) wide on either side of it. Work began in 1904, and the **Panama Canal** opened on August 15, 1914.

Panama Canal Ship canal cut across the isthmus of Panama by United States Army engineers; it opened in 1914. It greatly shortened the sea voyage between the east and west coasts of North America. The United States turned the canal over to Panama on January 1, 2000.

THE WORLD ECONOMY AND THE GLOBAL ENVIRONMENT

How did imperialism contribute to the growth and globalization of the world economy?

The New Imperialists were not traditional conquerors or empire builders like the Spanish conquistadors. Their aim was not just to extend their power over new territories and peoples but also to control both natural resources and indigenous societies and put them efficiently to work. Both their goals and their methods were industrial. A railroad, for example, was an act of faith as well as a means of transportation. The imperialists expressed their belief in progress and their good intentions in the clichés of the time: "the conquest of nature," "the annihilation of time and space," "the taming of the wilderness," and "our civilizing mission."

Expansion of the World Economy

The Industrial Revolution vastly expanded the traditional demand for tropical products. Imports of foods and stimulants such as tea, coffee, and cocoa increased substantially during the nineteenth century. The trade in industrial raw materials, whether agricultural (cotton, jute for bags, and palm oil for soap and lubricants) or mineral (diamonds, gold, and copper), grew even faster. Wild forest products came only later to be cultivated: timber for buildings and railroad ties, cinchona bark, rubber for rainwear and tires, and gutta-percha (gut-tah-PER-cha) to insulate electric cables.

The growing needs of the industrial world could not be met by the traditional methods of production and transportation of the nonindustrial world. When the U.S. Civil War interrupted the export of cotton to England in the 1860s, the British turned to India, only to find that Indian cotton was ruined by exposure to rain and dust while being carted from interior regions to the harbors. To prevent such technological backwardness in the colonies from stifling the expansion of industry, the imperialists made every effort to bring those territories into the mainstream of the world market.

Transportation was key. The Suez and Panama Canals cut travel time and lowered freight costs dramatically. Steamships became more numerous, and as their size increased, deeper harbors were needed. As for railroads, India alone had 37,000 miles (nearly 60,000 kilometers) of track by 1915, almost as much as Germany or Russia. Railroads reached into the interior of Latin America, Canada, China, and Australia. In 1903 the Russians completed the Trans-Siberian Railway from Moscow to Vladivostok on the Pacific. Visionaries even made plans for railroads from Europe to India and from Egypt to South Africa.

Transformation of the Global Environment

The economic changes brought by Europeans and Americans altered environments around the world. The British, whose craving for tea could not be satisfied with the limited exports available from China, introduced tea into the warm, rainy hill country of Ceylon and northeastern India. In those areas and in Java thousands of square miles of tropical rain forests were felled to make way for tea plantations.

Economic botany and agricultural science were applied to every promising plant species. European botanists had long collected and classified exotic plants from around the world. In the nineteenth century they founded botanical gardens in Java, India, Mauritius (maw-REE-shuss), Ceylon, Jamaica, and other tropical colonies. These gardens not only collected local plants but also exchanged plants with other gardens. They were especially active in systematically transferring commercially valuable plant species from one tropical region to another. Cinchona, tobacco, sugar, and other crops

SECTION REVIEW

- To feed their industries, the New Imperialists strove for efficient control of natural resources and peoples.

- The Industrial Revolution increased demand for tropical products and raw materials, a demand that could not be met by traditional means in nonindustrial countries.

- Economic changes in colonized territories led to the transformation of environments.

- Economic botany and agricultural science improved crops and thus expanded their cultivation.

- Railroad building and mineral extraction scarred the land even as they moved, employed, and enriched people.

South African Diamond Mine

When diamonds were found in Kimberley, South Africa, in 1868, the discovery precipitated a rush of prospectors from Europe and America. As soon as surface deposits were exhausted, their claims were bought by large companies that could afford the heavy equipment needed to mine deep underground. By the early twentieth century, diamonds came from major industrial mines like the Premier Mine shown here.   (Corbis)

were introduced, improved, and vastly expanded in the colonies of Southeast Asia and Indonesia. Cocoa and coffee growing spread over large areas of Brazil and Africa; oil-palm plantations were established in Nigeria and the Congo Basin. Rubber originally came from the latex of *Hevea* trees growing wild in the Brazilian rain forest. Then, in the 1870s, British agents smuggled seedlings from Brazil to the Royal Botanic Gardens at Kew near London, and from there to the Botanic Garden of Singapore. These plants formed the nucleus of the enormous rubber economy of Southeast Asia.

Throughout the tropics forests and lands devoted to shifting slash-and-burn agriculture gave way to permanent farms and plantations. Even in areas not developed to export crops, growing populations put pressure on the land. In Java and India farmers felled trees to obtain arable land and firewood. They terraced hillsides, drained swamps, and dug wells.

Irrigation and water control transformed the dry parts of the tropics as well. In the 1830s British engineers in India had restored ancient canals that had fallen into disrepair. Their success led them to build new irrigation canals, turning thousands of previously barren acres into well-watered, densely populated farmland. The migration of European experts spread the newest techniques of irrigation engineering around the world. By the turn of the century irrigation projects were under way wherever rivers flowed through dry lands. In Egypt and Central Asia irrigation brought more acres under cultivation in one forty-year span than in all previous history.

Railroads had voracious appetites for land and resources. They cut into mountains, spanned rivers and canyons with trestles, and covered as much land with their freight yards as whole cities had needed in previous centuries. They also consumed vast quantities of iron, timber for ties, and coal or wood for fuel. Most important of all, railroads brought people and their cities, farms, and industries to areas previously occupied by small, scattered populations.

Prospectors looking for valuable minerals opened the earth to reveal its riches: gold in South Africa, Australia, and Canada; tin in Nigeria, Malaya, and Bolivia; copper in Chile and Central Africa; iron ore in northern India; and much else. Where mines were dug deep inside the earth, the dirt and rocks brought up with the ores formed huge mounds near mine entrances. Open mines dug to obtain ores lying close to the surface created a landscape of lunar craters, and runoff from the minerals poisoned the water for miles around. Refineries that processed the ores fouled the environment with slag heaps and more toxic runoff.

The transformation of the land by human beings, a constant throughout history, accelerated sharply. Only the changes occurring since 1914 can compare with the transformation of the global environment that took place between 1869 and 1914.

Chapter Review

 DOWNLOAD THE MP3 AUDIO FILE OF THE CHAPTER REVIEW
TO LISTEN TO ON THE GO.

*What motivated the industrial nations to conquer new territories, and
what means did they use? (page 654)*

European and American imperial powers were driven by economic, cultural,
and political motives. Many governments used overseas colonies as a way to help
reestablish their nations' prestige and power. Catholic and Protestant missionaries sought not only to convert the native peoples to their religious beliefs but
also to "civilize" their behavior. This sense of moral and cultural superiority was
common among the colonizing nations. Finally, colonizing nations were led by
the demand for minerals and natural resources. The imperialists used tools provided by the Industrial Revolution, such as steamships, gunboats, and improved
firearms, to build their empires.

*Why were imperialists drawn to the natural resources of Africa, and how
did their presence on that continent change the environment? (page 660)*

Africans ruled over 90 percent of the continent until the European "scramble" for Africa began after the 1870s. Europeans took control of African resources
to further their own military and economic power. After the Egyptians secured
the Suez Canal, they constructed a dam across the Nile to help develop agriculture. In other parts of the continent, European companies took over profits
from local trade in rubber, diamonds, and other resources. Local reaction to
colonial rule varied greatly, traditional land use patterns were disrupted, and all
Africans were affected by changes in social and cultural customs.

What were the social and cultural effects of imperialism in Asia? (page 668)

The effects of colonialism varied throughout Asia, although in all regions the
economic profits benefited the Europeans rather than the indigenous workers.
Southeast Asia's fertile soil and heavy rains made farming of various crops, most
importantly rubber, quite profitable. As laborers were brought in from overseas,
they gradually displaced the earlier inhabitants. A similar situation occurred in
Hawaii, where U.S. military personnel and foreign farm laborers eventually outnumbered the native Hawaiians. Europeans differed in their approach to indigenous cultures and religions. In Central Asia, the Russians did not attempt to impose
their customs, language, or religious beliefs on their subjects. Christian missionaries in Southeast Asia, meanwhile, worked to spread their beliefs. Their efforts gained
only limited success in a land in which Islam had been dominant for centuries.

*What were the economic motives behind imperialism in Latin America?
(page 673)*

Latin America had great economic potential because of its wealth of agricultural and mineral products. The construction of railroads, using equipment,

KEY TERMS

Suez Canal *(p. 652)*
New Imperialism *(p. 654)*
Battle of Omdurman *(p. 658)*
colonialism *(p. 658)*
"scramble" for Africa *(p. 660)*
Henry Morton Stanley *(p. 663)*
Leopold II *(p. 663)*
Savorgnan de Brazza *(p. 663)*
Berlin Conference *(p. 663)*
Afrikaners *(p. 664)*
Cecil Rhodes *(p. 665)*
Asante *(p. 666)*
Menelik II *(p. 666)*
Emilio Aguinaldo *(p. 673)*
free-trade imperialism *(p. 673)*
Panama Canal *(p. 676)*

WEB RESOURCES

Pronunciation Guide
Interactive Maps
   MAP 24.1 Africa in 1878 and 1914
Primary Sources
   Convention on Free Navigation of
   the Suez Canal Between the Euro-
   pean Powers and the Ottoman
   Empire, October 29, 1888
   His Story
   Memorandum to Lord Selborne,
   High Commissioner of Transvaal,
   October 1905
   Letter to the French Chamber of
   Deputies

(Continued)

labor, and funding from Britain and the United States, helped to connect the interior regions with the coastal ports. Americans also saw economic potential in Cuba and invested heavily in the sugar and tobacco industries there. After the Spanish-American War, they issued the Platt Amendment to maintain their influence in the region. The United States also became involved in another war of independence in 1903, this time supporting a Panamanian rebellion against Colombia. Again, there was an economic motivation behind the American involvement: the Panama Canal.

Answer to the History in Focus Question

See photo on page 659, "The Battle of Omdurman."

Plus

Chapter Objectives

ACE multiple-choice quiz

Flashcards

How did imperialism contribute to the growth and globalization of the world economy? (page 676)

Imperialism, both formal and informal, opened up the world to increased trade and communication. Shipping, canals, and railroads were the most visible means of globalization. Other activities—farming, mining, labor migrations, and urbanization—were profoundly affected as well. In the process, natural environments were transformed as never before. Forests were replaced by plantations. Irrigation schemes opened dry lands to agriculture. And railroads and mines cut into the landscape, leaving scars and pollution.

SUGGESTED READING

Baumgart, Winfried. *Imperialism.* 1982. Presents the debate on theories of imperialism.

Bushnell, David, and Neill Macauley. *The Emergence of Latin America in the Nineteenth Century.* 1994. A historical overview.

Cook, Scott B. *Colonial Encounters in the Age of High Imperialism.* 1996. A good introduction to imperialism.

Davis, Mike. *Late Victorian Holocausts: El Niño Famines and the Making of the Third World.* 2001. Argues that imperialism exacerbated the social and demographic impact of climate fluctuation.

Drayton, Richard. *Nature's Government: Science, Imperial Britain, and the "Improvement" of the World.* 2000. Juxtaposes the histories of Britain, Western science, and imperialism with a focus on the Royal Botanic Gardens at Kew.

Fanon, Franz. *The Wretched of the Earth.* 1966. Classic analysis of colonialism from the point of view of the colonized.

Headrick, Daniel R. *The Tools of Empire: Technology and European Imperialism in the Nineteenth Century.* 1981; and *The Tentacles of Progress: Technology Transfer in the Age of Imperialism, 1850–1940.* 1988. Studies on the impact of technology on the New Imperialism.

Healy, David. *Drive to Hegemony: The United States in the Caribbean, 1898–1917.* 1989. Studies the American effort to dominate its maritime neighbors.

Hochschild, Adam. *King Leopold's Ghost: A Story of Greed, Terror, and Heroism in Colonial Africa.* 1998. A very readable account of imperialism in the Belgian Congo.

Hopkirk, Peter. *The Great Game: The Struggle for Empire in Central Asia.* 1994. Studies a crucible of great power rivalry.

Iriye, Akira. *Across the Pacific: An Inner History of American–East Asian Relations.* Rev. ed. 1992. Discusses imperial rivalries in Asia.

Karnow, Stanley. *In Our Image: America's Empire in the Philippines.* 1989. A view of American imperialism.

Mostert, Noel. *Frontiers: The Epic of South Africa's Creation and the Tragedy of the Xhosa People.* 1992. Examines race relations in the colonial world.

Pakenham, Thomas. *The Scramble for Africa.* 1991. A readable account of the European conquest of Africa.

Porter, Bernard. *The Lion's Share: A Short History of British Imperialism, 1850–1970.* 1976. A general overview.

NOTES

1. *Journal Officiel* (November 29, 1869), quoted in Georges Douin, *Histoire du Règne du Khédive Ismaïl* (Rome: Reale Società di Geografia d'Egitto, 1933), 453.

2. E. Desplaces in *Journal de l'Union des Deux Mers* (December 15, 1869), quoted in ibid., 453.

3. Winston Churchill, *The River War: An Account of the Reconquest of the Soudan* (New York: Charles Scribner's Sons, 1933), 300.

4. "Correspondence and Report from His Majesty's Consul at Boma respecting the Administration of the Independent State of the Congo," *British Parliamentary Papers, Accounts and Papers,* 1904 (Cd. 1933), lxii, 357.

5. Robert W. July, *A History of the African People,* 3d ed. (New York: Charles Scribner's Sons, 1980), 323.

6. George Shepperson and Thomas Price, *Independent African* (Edinburgh: University Press, 1958), 163–164, quoted in Roland Oliver and Anthony Atmore, *Africa Since 1800,* 4th ed. (Cambridge: Cambridge University Press, 1994), 150.

7. Thomas Edson Ennis, *French Policy and Development in Indochina* (Chicago: University of Chicago Press, 1936), 178, quoted in K. M. Panikkar, *Asia and Western Dominance* (New York: Collier, 1969), 167.

8. Quoted in Stanley J. Stein and Barbara H. Stein, *The Colonial Heritage of Latin America* (New York: Oxford University Press, 1970), 151.

The Crisis of the Imperial Order

1900–1929

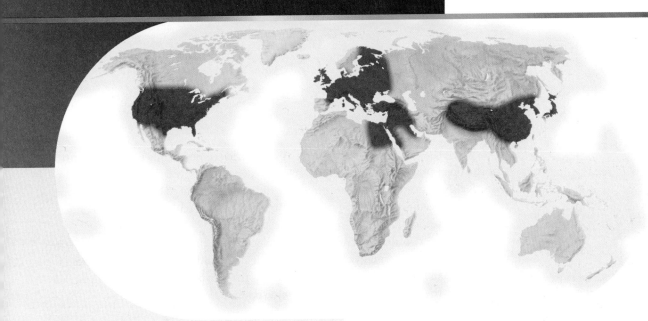

CHAPTER PREVIEW

On June 28, 1914, Archduke Franz Ferdinand, heir to the throne of Austria-Hungary, was riding in an open carriage through Sarajevo, capital of the province of Bosnia-Herzegovina, which Austria had annexed six years before. When the carriage stopped momentarily, Gavrilo Princip, a member of a pro-Serbian conspiracy, fired his pistol twice, killing the archduke and his wife.

Those shots ignited a war that spread throughout Europe and then turned into a global war as the Ottoman Empire fought against Britain in the Middle East and Japan attacked German positions in China. France and Britain involved their empires in the war and brought Africans, Indians, Australians,

 This icon will direct you to the website where you can Prepare for Class, Improve Your Grade, and Ace the Test: college.cengage.com/pic/bullietbrief4e

and Canadians to Europe to fight and labor on the front lines. Finally, in 1917, the United States entered the fray.

This chapter looks at the causes of war between the great powers; the consequences of that conflict in Europe, the Middle East, and Russia; and the upheavals in China and Japan. It also reviews the accelerating rate of technological change that made the first half of the twentieth century so violent and so hopeful. Entirely new technologies made war more dangerous yet allowed far more people to live healthier, more comfortable, and more interesting lives than ever before.

ORIGINS OF THE CRISIS IN EUROPE AND THE MIDDLE EAST

What led to the outbreak of the First World War?

When the twentieth century opened, the world seemed firmly under the control of the great powers. Its first decade saw peace, economic growth, and the spread of new technologies: airplanes, automobiles, radio, and cinema. The only international war of the period, the Russo-Japanese War (1904–1905), ended quickly with a decisive Japanese victory.

However, two major changes were undermining the apparent stability of the world. In Europe, Germany challenged Britain at sea and France in Morocco. And in the Ottoman Empire, government weakness in the face of chaos in the Balkans gradually drew the European powers into a whirlpool.

The Ottoman Empire and the Balkans

By 1900, the once-great Ottoman Empire had become the "sick man of Europe" and was losing its outlying provinces. Between 1902 and 1913, Macedonia rebelled, Austria-Hungary annexed Bosnia, Crete merged with Greece, Italy conquered Libya, and Albania became independent. In 1912–1913, Serbia, Bulgaria, Romania, and Greece chased the Turks out of the Balkans, except for a small enclave around Constantinople. Russia and Austria-Hungary competed to become the protector of the Slavic peoples of the Balkans. France and Britain, the empire's creditors, controlled Ottoman finances, taxes, railroads, mines, and public utilities.

In reaction, Turks began to assert themselves against rebellious minorities and meddling foreigners. In 1908–1909, the revolutionary group known as the Young Turks overthrew the sultan and replaced him with his brother. The new regime began to reform the police, the bureaucracy, and the education system and hired a German general to modernize Turkey's armed forces. At the same time, it cracked down on Greek and Armenian minorities.

Nationalism, Alliances, and Military Strategy

Nationalism united the citizens of France, Britain, Italy, and Germany behind their respective governments and gave them tremendous cohesion and strength of purpose. But nationalism could divide as well as unify. In the large

Chronology

	Europe and North America	Middle East	East Asia
1900			**1900** Boxer Rebellion in China
			1904–1905 Russo-Japanese War
	1907 British-French-Russian Entente		
		1909 Young Turks overthrow Sultan Abdul Hamid	
1910			
			1911 Chinese revolutionaries led by Sun Yat-sen overthrow Qing dynasty
	1912–1913 Balkan Wars		
	1914 Assassination of Archduke Franz Ferdinand sparks World War I		
			1915 Japan presents Twenty-One Demands to China
	1916 Battles of Verdun and the Somme	**1916** Arab Revolt in Arabia	
	1917 Russian Revolutions; United States enters the war	**1917** Balfour Declaration	
	1918 Armistice ends World War I		
	1919 Treaty of Versailles		**1919** May Fourth Movement in China
1920	**1920** First commercial radio broadcast (United States)		
	1921 New Economic Policy in Russia		
		1922 Egypt nominally independent	
		1923 Mustafa Kemal proclaims Turkey a republic	
	1927 Charles Lindbergh flies alone across the Atlantic		**1927** Guomindang forces occupy Shanghai and expel communists

but fragile multinational empires—Russia, Austria-Hungary, and the Ottoman Empire—ethnic and religious minorities were stirring. The easy victories in the wars of the New Imperialism (see Chapter 24) led some in power to believe that only war could heal the divisions in their societies.

What turned assassination of the Archduke Franz Ferdinand into a conflict involving all the great powers was the system of alliances that had accumulated over the previous decades. Germany stood at Europe's center as the most heavily industrialized country in Europe. Its army was the best trained and equipped, and its battleships were challenging Great Britain's naval supremacy. Germany joined Austria-Hungary and Italy in the Triple Alliance in 1882. When in 1907 Britain, France, and Russia

Map 25.1   The First World War in Europe

Most of the fighting in World War I took place on two fronts. After an initial surge through Belgium into northern France, the German offensive bogged down for four years along the Western Front. To the east, the German armies conquered a large part of Russia during 1917 and early 1918. Despite spectacular victories in the east, Germany lost the war because its armies collapsed along the strategically important Western Front.

formed an Entente (on-TONT) ("understanding"), Europe was divided into two blocs of roughly equal power (see Map 25.1).

The alliance system was cursed by inflexible military planning. Anticipating possible war, military planners in France and Germany had worked out elaborate railroad timetables to mobilize their respective armies in a few days. Other countries were less well prepared. Russia with its underdeveloped rail system needed several weeks to mobilize. Britain, with only a tiny volunteer army, had no mobilization plans. German generals, believing that the British would stay out of a European war, made plans to defeat France in a matter of days and then transport their entire army by train across Germany to the Russian border before Russia could fully mobilize.

On July 28, 1914, emboldened by the backing of Germany, Austria-Hungary declared war on Serbia, triggering mobilization plans in Russia, France, and Germany. The next day, Russia ordered general mobilization to force Austria to back down. On August 1, France honored its treaty obligation to Russia and ordered general mobilization. Minutes later, Germany did the same. War was now unavoidable.

The German General Staff expected France to capitulate before the British could get involved. But on August 3, when German troops entered Belgium, Britain demanded their withdrawal. When Germany refused, Britain declared war on Germany.

SECTION REVIEW

- Ottoman decline and German self-assertion undermined European stability.

- The weakening Ottoman Empire lost outlying provinces, and newly independent Balkan states pushed it to the edge of Europe.

- European powers meddled in Ottoman affairs, provoking the coup led by the Young Turks.

- Nationalism, the alliance system, and inflexible military plans drove the European powers into war after the assassination of Archduke Franz Ferdinand.

THE "GREAT WAR" AND THE RUSSIAN REVOLUTIONS, 1914–1918

How did the war lead to revolution in Russia?

Throughout Europe, people greeted the outbreak of war with parades and hopes for a quick victory. The German sociologist Max Weber wrote: "This war, with all its ghastliness, is nevertheless grand and wonderful. It is worth experiencing." Very few imagined that their side might not win, and no one foresaw that everyone would lose.

Stalemate, 1914–1917

The generals' carefully drawn-up plans went awry from the start. Believing that a spirited attack would always prevail, French generals hurled their troops against the well-defended German border and suffered a crushing defeat. By early September, the German armies held Belgium and northern France and were fast approaching Paris.

German victory seemed assured. But when Russia attacked, German troops needed for the final push into France were shifted to the eastern front. A gap opened between two German armies along the Marne River, into which France's last reserves moved. At the Battle of the Marne, the Germans were thrown back several miles.

During the next month, both sides spread out until they formed an unbroken battleline extending over 300 miles (some 500 kilometers) from the North Sea to the border of Switzerland. All along this **Western Front**, machine guns provided an almost impenetrable defense against advancing infantry but were useless for the offensive because they were too heavy for one man to carry and took too much time to

Western Front A line of trenches and fortifications in World War I that stretched without a break from Switzerland to the North Sea. Scene of most of the fighting between Germany, on the one hand, and France and Britain, on the other.

Trench Warfare in World War I

German and Allied soldiers on the Western Front faced each other from elaborate networks of trenches. Attacking meant jumping out of the trenches and racing across a no man's land of mud and barbed wire. Here we see Princess Patricia's Canadian Light Infantry repelling a German attack near Ypres, in northern France, in March 1915, using machine guns, rifles, and hand grenades. (Courtesy, The Princess Patricia's Canadian Light Infantry, Regimental Museum and Archives)

set up. To escape the deadly streams of bullets, soldiers dug holes for themselves in the ground, connected the holes to form shallow trenches, and then dug communications trenches to the rear. Within weeks, the battlefields were scarred with lines of trenches several feet deep, their tops protected by sandbags and their floors covered with planks.

For four years, generals on each side again and again ordered thousands of young men to climb out of their trenches, race across the open fields, and be mowed down by enemy machine-gun fire. Poison gas added to the horror of battle.

The year 1916 saw the bloodiest and most futile battles of the war. The Germans attacked French forts at Verdun, losing 281,000 men and causing 315,000 French casualties. In retaliation, the British attacked the Germans at the Somme River and suffered 420,000 casualties—60,000 on the first day alone—while the Germans lost 450,000 and the French 200,000.

This was not warfare as it had ever been waged before; it was mass slaughter. Neither side could win, for the armies were stalemated by trenches and machine guns. During four years of the bloodiest fighting the world had ever seen, the Western Front moved no more than a few miles one way or another.

At sea, the war was just as inconclusive. As soon as the war broke out, the British cut the German overseas telegraph cables, blockaded the coasts of Germany and Austria-Hungary, and set out to capture or sink all enemy ships still at sea. The German High Seas Fleet, built at enormous cost, seldom left port. Only once, in May 1916, did it confront the British Grand Fleet. At the Battle of Jutland, off the coast of Denmark, the two fleets lost roughly equal numbers of ships, and the Germans escaped back to their harbors.

In early 1915, in retaliation for the British naval blockade, Germany announced a blockade of Britain by submarines. German submarines attacked every vessel they could. One attack sank the British ocean liner *Lusitania,* killing 1,198 people, 139 of them Americans. When the United States protested, Germany ceased its submarine campaign, hoping to keep America neutral.

The Home Front and the War Economy

The war economy transformed civilian life. In France and Britain, food rations were allocated according to need, improving nutrition among the poor. Unemployment vanished. Thousands of Africans, Indians, and Chinese were recruited for heavy labor in Europe. Employers hired women to fill jobs in steel mills, mines, and munitions plants. Women became streetcar drivers, mail carriers, and police or found work in government bureaucracies. Many joined auxiliary military services as doctors, nurses, mechanics, and ambulance drivers. These positions gave thousands of women a sense of participation and a taste of independence.

The British naval blockade punished Germany's civilians. German chemists developed synthetic explosives and fuel, but synthetic food was not an option. Wheat flour disappeared, replaced first by rye, then by potatoes and turnips, then by acorns and chestnuts, and finally by sawdust. After the failure of the potato crop in 1916 came the "turnip winter," when people had to survive on 1,000 calories per day, half of the normal adult amount. Women, children, and the elderly were especially hard hit.

Abroad the British and French overran all of Germany's African colonies except German East Africa, which remained undefeated until the end of the war (see Map 24.1). In many African colonies, war policies imposed heavy taxes, low prices for requisitioned supplies, and military recruitment. Many Europeans stationed in Africa left to join the war, leaving large areas with little or no European presence. Over a million Africans served in the various armies, and perhaps three times that number were drafted as porters to carry army equipment. In some places, these impositions provoked African uprisings that lasted for years.

One country grew rich during the war: the United States, which for two and a half years stayed technically neutral while companies engaging in war production did a roaring business supplying France and Britain. After the United States entered the war in 1917, civilians were exhorted to help the war effort by investing their savings in war bonds and growing food in backyard "victory gardens." Employment created by the war opened up jobs for women and African Americans.

The Ottoman Empire at War

On August 2, 1914, the Turks signed a secret alliance with Germany. In November, they joined the fighting, hoping to gain land at Russia's expense. But the campaign in the

Primary Source: Letter from Turkey, Summer 1915
Read a detailed account of one Armenian woman's ghastly experiences on the forced march away from her homeland.

Faisal I (1885–1933) Arab prince, leader of the Arab Revolt in World War I. The British made him king of Iraq in 1921, and he reigned under British protection until 1933.

Balfour Declaration Statement issued by Britain's Foreign Secretary Arthur Balfour in 1917 favoring the establishment of a Jewish national homeland in Palestine.

Primary Source: The Balfour Declaration
Read the Balfour Declaration and follow the discussion it engendered regarding the establishment of a Jewish homeland in Palestine.

Bolsheviks Radical Marxist political party founded by Vladimir Lenin in 1903. Under Lenin's leadership, the Bolsheviks seized power in November 1917 during the Russian Revolution.

Caucasus proved disastrous for both sides. Suspecting the local Armenian population of being pro-Russian, the Turks forced them to march from their homelands across the mountains in the winter. Hundreds of thousands of Armenians died of hunger and exposure. Famine stalked the empire.

The Turks also closed the Dardanelles, the strait between the Mediterranean and Black Seas (see Map 25.1). When a British attack on the Dardanelles failed disastrously, they tried to subvert the Ottoman Empire from within by promising the emir (governor) of Mecca, Hussein ibn Ali, a kingdom of his own. In 1916, Hussein started an Arab revolt against the Turks. His son **Faisal I** (fie-SAHL) led an Arab army into Palestine and Syria in support of the British advance from Egypt, thereby contributing to the Ottoman defeat.

The British made promises to Chaim Weizmann (hi-um VITES-mun), leader of the British Zionists, that a Jewish homeland in Palestine would be carved out of the Ottoman Empire and placed under British protection. In November, as British armies were advancing on Jerusalem, Foreign Secretary Sir Arthur Balfour wrote that "His Majesty's Government view with favor the establishment in Palestine of a national home for the Jewish people and will use their best endeavours to facilitate the achievement of that object, it being clearly understood that nothing shall be done which may prejudice the civil and religious rights of existing non-Jewish communities in Palestine." The British did not foresee that this statement, known as the **Balfour Declaration**, would lead to conflicts between Palestinians and Jewish settlers.

Double Revolution in Russia, 1917

Russia began the war with the largest army in the world, but its generals were incompetent, supplies were lacking, and soldiers were poorly trained and equipped. In August 1914, two Russian armies were thrown back in eastern Germany. Russia did better against the Austro-Hungarian army. In 1916, after a string of defeats, the Russian army ran out of ammunition and other essential supplies. Soldiers were ordered into battle unarmed and told to pick up the rifles of fallen comrades.

With so many men in the army, railroads broke down for lack of fuel and parts, and crops rotted in the fields. Civilians faced shortages and widespread hunger. In the cities, food and fuel became scarce. During the bitterly cold winter of 1916–1917, factory workers and housewives had to line up in front of grocery stores before dawn to get something to eat. The court of Tsar (zahr) Nicholas II, however, remained as extravagant and corrupt as ever.

When food ran out in Petrograd, the capital, in early March 1917, housewives and women factory workers staged mass demonstrations. Soldiers mutinied and joined striking workers to form soviets (councils) to take over factories and barracks. A few days later, the tsar abdicated, and leaders of the parliamentary parties formed a Provisional Government. Thus began what Russians called the "February Revolution" because their calendar was two weeks behind the one in use elsewhere.

Revolutionary groups came out of hiding. Most numerous were the Social Revolutionaries, who advocated redistributing land to the peasants. The Social Democrats, a Marxist party, were divided. The Mensheviks, who advocated electoral politics and reform in the tradition of European Socialists, had a large following among intellectuals and factory workers. The rival **Bolsheviks** were a small but tightly disci-

Lenin the Orator

The leader of the Bolshevik revolutionaries was a spellbinding orator. Here Lenin is addressing Red Army soldiers in Sverdlov Square, Moscow, in 1920. (Trotsky, who originally appeared in this picture, was airbrushed out.) At the time, the Bolsheviks were mopping up the last anti-Bolshevik forces and were fully engaged in a war with Poland. The fate of the Revolution depended on the fighting spirit of the Red Army soldiers and on their loyalty to Lenin.
(David King Collection)

plined group dedicated to revolution. **Vladimir Lenin** (1870–1924), the Bolshevik leader, became a revolutionary in his teens when his older brother was executed for plotting to kill the tsar. His goal was to create a party that would lead the revolution rather than wait for it.

In early April 1917, the German government, hoping to destabilize Russia, allowed Lenin to travel from exile in Switzerland to Russia in a sealed railway car. As soon as he arrived in Petrograd, he announced his program: immediate peace, all power to the soviets, and transfers of land to the peasants and factories to the workers. This plan proved immensely popular among the soldiers and workers exhausted by the war.

When the Provisional Government ordered another offensive against the Germans a few months later, Russian soldiers deserted by the hundreds of thousands, throwing away their rifles and walking back to their villages. The Bolsheviks, meanwhile, were gaining support among the workers of Petrograd and the soldiers and sailors stationed there. On November 6, 1917 (October 24 in the Russian calendar), they rose up and took over the city. This "October Revolution" overthrew the Provisional Government and arrested Mensheviks, Social Revolutionaries, and other rivals.

Vladimir Lenin (1870–1924)
Leader of the Bolshevik (later Communist) Party. He lived in exile in Switzerland until 1917, then returned to Russia to lead the Bolsheviks to victory during the Russian Revolution and the civil war that followed.

The Bolsheviks nationalized all private land and ordered the peasants to hand over their crops without compensation. The peasants, having seized their landlords' estates, resisted. In the cities, the Bolsheviks took over the factories and drafted the workers into compulsory labor brigades. To enforce his rule, Lenin created the Cheka, a secret police force with powers to arrest and execute opponents. The Bolsheviks also sued for peace with Germany and Austria-Hungary. By the Treaty of Brest-Litovsk, signed on March 3, 1918, Russia forfeited territories containing a third of its population and wealth.

Woodrow Wilson (1856–1924)
President of the United States (1913–1921) and the leading figure at the Paris Peace Conference of 1919. He was unable to persuade the U.S. Congress to ratify the Treaty of Versailles or join the League of Nations.

The End of the War in Western Europe, 1917–1918

Like many Americans, President **Woodrow Wilson** wanted to stay out of the European conflict. For nearly three years, he kept the United States neutral and tried to persuade the belligerents to compromise. But in late 1916, Germany's decision to starve the British by using submarines to sink food ships risked bringing the United States into the war. German leaders were willing to gamble that Britain and France would collapse before the United States could send a decisive number of troops.

The German gamble failed. The British organized their merchant ships into convoys protected by destroyers, and on April 6, 1917, President Wilson asked the United States Congress to declare war on Germany.

On the Western Front, the two sides were so evenly matched in 1917 that the war seemed unlikely to end until one side or the other ran out of young men. Losing hope of winning, soldiers began to mutiny. In May 1917, before the arrival of U.S. forces, fifty-four of one hundred French divisions along the Western Front refused to attack. At Caporetto, Italian troops were so demoralized that 275,000 were taken prisoner.

Between March and August 1918, General Erich von Ludendorff launched a series of surprise attacks that broke through the front at several places and pushed to within 40 miles (64 kilometers) of Paris. But victory eluded him. Meanwhile, every month was bringing another 250,000 American troops to the front. In August, the Allies counterattacked, and the Germans began a retreat that could not be halted, for German soldiers, many of them sick with the flu, had lost the will to fight.

In late October, Ludendorff resigned, and sailors in the German fleet mutinied. Two weeks later, Kaiser Wilhelm fled to Holland as a new German government signed an armistice. On November 11 at 11 A.M., the guns on the Western Front went silent.

SECTION REVIEW

- During the stalemate of trench warfare, indecisive battles were fought at Verdun and the Somme, while German submarine warfare prompted American protests.

- The war economy brought both greater employment and privation, drew upon far-flung colonial resources, and enriched the United States.

- Allied with Germany, the Ottoman Empire persecuted Armenians and repulsed a British invasion.

- Britain sought to undermine the Ottomans by supporting the Arab Revolt and backing the Balfour Declaration, which promised a Jewish homeland.

- In Russia, the February Revolution replaced the tsar with a Provisional Government, which later fell to the Bolshevik-led October Revolution.

- In 1917–1918, U.S. troops reinvigorated the Allies and the German offensives failed, forcing Germany to sign an armistice.

PEACE AND DISLOCATION IN EUROPE, 1919–1929

What role did the war play in eroding European dominance in the world?

The Great War lasted four years. It took almost twice as long for Europe to recover. Millions of people had died or been disabled, political tensions lingered, and national economies remained depressed until the mid-1920s. The return of peace and prosperity in the late 1920s soon proved illusory.

The Impact of the War

It is estimated that between 8 million and 10 million people died, almost all of them young men. Perhaps twice that many returned home wounded, gassed, or shell-shocked, many of them disabled for life. In addition, the war created millions of refugees.

France welcomed 1.5 million refugees, but the preferred destination was the United States. About 800,000 immigrants succeeded in reaching it before U.S. immigration laws passed in 1921 and 1924 closed the door to eastern and southern Europeans. Canada, Australia, and New Zealand adopted similar restrictions on immigration. The Latin American republics welcomed European refugees, but their poverty discouraged potential immigrants.

One unexpected disaster was the great influenza epidemic of 1918–1919, which started among soldiers heading for the Western Front. This was no ordinary flu but a virulent strain that infected almost everyone on earth and killed one person in every forty. Half a million Americans perished in the epidemic—five times as many as died in the war. Worldwide, some 30 million people died, 20 million in India alone.

The war also seriously damaged the environment. No place on earth was ever so completely devastated as the scar across France and Belgium known as the Western Front. The fighting ravaged forests and demolished towns. The earth was gouged by trenches, pitted with craters, and littered with ammunition, broken weapons, chunks of concrete, and the bones of countless soldiers. After the war, it took a decade to clear away the debris and create military cemeteries with neat rows of crosses stretching for miles.

The Peace Treaties

In early 1919, delegates of the victorious Allies met in Paris. The defeated powers were kept out until the treaties were ready for signing. Russia, in the throes of counter-revolutionary civil war, was not invited.

From the start, three men dominated the Paris Peace Conference: President Wilson, British prime minister David Lloyd George, and French premier Georges Clemenceau (zhorzh cluh-mon-SO). They ignored the Italians, who had joined the Allies in 1915, and paid even less attention to the smaller European nations. They rejected the Japanese proposal that all races be treated equally and ignored the call of the Pan-African Congress for attention to the concerns of Africans. They also ignored delegates who did not represent sovereign states and who came to Paris to lobby for their causes—the Arab leader Faisal, the Zionist Chaim Weizmann, and several Armenian delegations.

Each man had his own agenda. Wilson wanted to apply the principle of self-determination, by which he meant creating nations that reflected European ethnic or linguistic divisions. He proposed a **League of Nations**, a world organization to safeguard the peace and foster international cooperation. His idealism clashed with the more hardheaded and self-serving nationalism of the Europeans. Lloyd George insisted that Germany pay a heavy indemnity. Clemenceau wanted Germany to give back Alsace and Lorraine, cede the industrial Saar region to France, and make the Rhineland a buffer state.

 Primary Source: Mud and Khaki, Memoirs of an Incomplete Soldier *Follow a day in the life of a soldier fighting in the trenches during World War I.*

Primary Source: The Zionist Organization's Memorandum . . . State in Palestine *Read how the Zionist Organization presented its case in 1919 for the establishment of a Jewish state in Palestine.*

League of Nations International organization founded in 1919 to promote world peace and cooperation but greatly weakened by the refusal of the United States to join. It proved ineffectual in stopping aggression by Italy, Japan, and Germany in the 1930s, and it was superseded by the United Nations in 1945.

The result was a series of compromises that satisfied no one. The European powers formed a League of Nations, but the United States Congress, reflecting the isolationist feelings of the American people, refused to join. France recovered Alsace and Lorraine but was unable to detach the Rhineland and had to content itself with vague promises of British and American protection if Germany ever rebuilt its army. Britain acquired new territories in Africa and the Middle East but was greatly weakened by human losses and the disruption of its trade.

On June 28, 1919, the German delegates reluctantly signed the **Treaty of Versailles** (vuhr-SIGH). Germany was forbidden to have an air force and was permitted only a token army and navy. It gave up large parts of its eastern territory to a newly reconstituted Poland. The Allies made Germany promise to pay reparations, but they did not set a figure or a period of time for payment. A "guilt clause," which was to rankle for years to come, obliged the Germans to accept "responsibility for causing all the loss and damage" of the war. The Treaty of Versailles left Germany humiliated but largely intact and potentially the most powerful nation in Europe. Establishing a peace neither of punishment nor of reconciliation, the treaty was one of the great failures in history.

In eastern Europe, the Allies created new national states in the lands lost by the old Russian, German, and Austro-Hungarian Empires. Austria and Hungary became separate states; Poland was resurrected after over a century; Czechoslovakia and Yugoslavia were created from parts of Austria-Hungary. These small nations all contained disaffected minorities and were safe only so long as Germany and Russia remained weak.

Russian Civil War and the New Economic Policy

Fighting continued in Russia for another three years after the end of the Great War. The Bolshevik Revolution had provoked Allied intervention, and, in December 1918, civil war broke out in Russia. The communists, as the Bolsheviks now called themselves, held central Russia, but all the surrounding provinces rose up against them. Counterrevolutionary armies led by former tsarist officers obtained weapons and supplies from the Allies. However, by 1921, the superior discipline of the Red Army, led by Leon Trotsky, gave the communists victory.

Gradually, the communists reunited the old Russian Empire. In 1920, Ukrainian communists declared the independence of a Soviet republic of Ukraine; then, in 1922, this merged with Russia to create the Union of Soviet Socialist Republics (USSR), or Soviet Union. In 1920–1921, the Red Army reconquered the oil-rich Caucasus and reestablished Soviet control of Central Asia. In 1922, the new Soviet republics of Georgia, Armenia, and Azerbaijan joined the USSR.

The Russian economy was in a state of ruin. Factories and railroads had shut down. Farmland had been devastated and livestock killed. Lenin decided to release the economy from party and government control. In March 1921, he announced the **New Economic Policy** (NEP), which allowed peasants to own land and sell their crops, private merchants to trade, and private workshops to produce goods and sell them on the free market. Only the biggest businesses, such as banks, railroads, and factories, remained under government ownership.

The relaxation of controls had an immediate effect. Production began to climb, and food and other goods became available. In the cities, food remained scarce be-

---

Treaty of Versailles (1919) The treaty imposed on Germany by France, Great Britain, the United States, and other Allied Powers after World War I. It demanded that Germany dismantle its military and give up some lands to Poland. It was resented by many Germans.

 Primary Source: Comments of the German Delegation . . . October 1919 *Read about the innate rights and responsibilities of nations in times of war and peace, from the perspective of the German Delegation after World War I.*

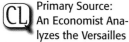 **Primary Source: An Economist Analyzes the Versailles Treaty and Finds It Lacking** *Find out what a noted economist thinks of the Treaty of Versailles and the situation of the world in 1919.*

New Economic Policy Policy proclaimed by Vladimir Lenin in 1921 to encourage the revival of the Soviet economy by allowing small private enterprises. Joseph Stalin ended the NEP in 1928 and replaced it with a series of Five-Year Plans.

cause farmers used their crops to feed their livestock rather than sell them. But the NEP reflected no change in the communist goal of creating a modern industrial economy without private property. It merely provided breathing space—what Lenin called "one step back to advance two steps forward." This meant investing in heavy industry and electrification, moving farmers to the new industries, and providing food for the urban workers. In other words, it meant making the peasants, the great majority of the Soviet people, pay for the industrialization of Russia.

When Lenin died in January 1924, his associates jockeyed for power. Leon Trotsky, commander of the Red Army, had the support of many "Old Bolsheviks" who had joined the party before the Revolution, but Joseph Stalin, general secretary of the Communist Party, got the support of the majority and filled the party bureaucracy with individuals loyal to himself. In January 1929, he forced Trotsky to flee the country. Then, as absolute master of the party, he prepared to industrialize the Soviet Union at breakneck speed.

An Ephemeral Peace

After the war came five years of painful recovery and readjustment (1919–1923), followed by six years of growing peace and prosperity (1924–1929). One of the big adjustments in many Western societies was granting political rights to women (see "Class and Gender" below). Changes in international politics and economics were more upsetting. In the first period, the German government had printed money recklessly to fund reparations payments, causing devastating inflation. As Germany teetered on the brink of civil war, radical nationalists called for revenge and tried to overthrow the government. Finally, the German government issued a new currency and promised to resume reparations payments, and the French agreed to withdraw their troops from the Ruhr.

Then in 1924, the vexed issue of reparations vanished as Germany borrowed money from New York banks to make its payments to France and Britain, which used the money to repay their wartime loans from the United States. This triangular flow of money stimulated the rapid recovery of the European economies. France began rebuilding its war-torn northern zone, Germany recovered from its hyperinflation and joined the League of Nations, and in the United States a boom began that was to last over five years.

While their economies flourished, governments grew more cautious and businesslike. Yet Germany and the Soviet Union did not accept their borders with the small nations that had arisen between them. In 1922, they signed a secret pact allowing the German army to conduct maneuvers in Russia (in violation of the Versailles treaty) in exchange for German help in building up Russian industry.

For a time, the League of Nations proved adept at resolving issues pertaining to health, labor relations, and postal and telegraph communications. But without U.S. participation, sanctions against states that violated League rules carried little weight.

SECTION REVIEW

- The Great War left millions dead or disabled, caused environmental devastation, and sparked the influenza epidemic of 1918–1919.

- The Paris Peace Conference redrew the map of Europe, ignored many international concerns, and humiliated Germany with the Treaty of Versailles.

- After winning the Russian civil war, Lenin's communist government initiated the New Economic Policy to rebuild Russia.

- Lenin's death provoked a power struggle between Trotsky and Stalin, from which Stalin emerged victorious.

- Between 1919 and 1923, the new peace appeared fleeting, but from 1924 to 1929 peace and prosperity, even in Germany, seemed lasting.

CHINA AND JAPAN: CONTRASTING DESTINIES

Why did China and Japan follow such divergent paths in this period?

China and Japan took different directions in the early twentieth century. Still in need of deep internal reform, giant China went through a revolution but soon collapsed into chaos. Japan's reforms before 1900 had gained it industry and a powerful military, which it used to take advantage of China's weakness.

Revolution in China

China's population—about 400 million in 1900—was the largest in the world and growing fast. Most Chinese worked incessantly, survived on a diet of grain and vegetables, and spent their lives in fear of floods, bandits, and tax collectors. Peasant plots averaged half what they had been two generations earlier. Landowners lived off the rents of their tenants. Officials, chosen through an elaborate examination system, enriched themselves from taxes and the government's monopolies on salt, iron, and other products. Wealthy merchants handled China's growing import-export trade in collaboration with foreign companies. The contrast between the squalor in which most urban residents lived and the luxury of the foreigners' enclaves in the treaty ports sharpened the resentment of educated Chinese.

When China's **Empress Dowager Cixi** (TSUH-shee) died in 1908, eight years after the Boxer Rebellion that she had encouraged (see Chapter 23), the Revolutionary Alliance led by **Sun Yat-sen** (soon yot-SEN) (Sun Zhongshan, 1867–1925) prepared to take over. Sun had spent much of his life in Japan, England, and the United States, plotting the overthrow of the Qing dynasty. His tenacious spirit and his ideas, a mixture of nationalism, socialism, and Confucian philosophy, attracted a large following. A revolutionary assembly elected Sun president of China in December 1911, and the last Qing ruler, the boy-emperor Puyi, abdicated the throne. But Sun had no military forces at his command. To avoid a clash with the army, he resigned after a few weeks, and a new national assembly elected **Yuan Shikai** (you-AHN she-KIE), the most powerful of the regional generals, president of the new Chinese republic.

Yuan was an able military leader, but he had no political program. When Sun reorganized his followers into a political party called **Guomindang** (gwo-min-dong) (National People's Party), Yuan quashed every attempt at creating a Western-style government and harassed Sun's followers.

Japan and World War I

Japan's population reached 60 million in 1925 and was increasing by a million a year. The crash program of industrialization begun in 1868 by the Meiji oligarchs (see Chapter 23) accelerated during the First World War when the Japanese suddenly found their textiles, consumer goods, and munitions in great demand.

The Japanese economy grew four times faster than western Europe's and eight times faster than China's. Blessed with a rainy climate and many fast-flowing rivers, Japan expanded its hydroelectric capacity. By the mid-1930s, 89 percent of Japanese households had electric lights, compared with 44 percent of British households.

Empress Dowager Cixi, (1835–1908) Empress of China and mother of Emperor Guangxi. She put her son under house arrest, supported antiforeign movements, and resisted reforms of the Chinese government and armed forces.

Sun Yat-sen (1867–1925) Chinese nationalist revolutionary, founder and leader of the Guomindang until his death. He attempted to create a liberal democratic political movement in China but was thwarted by military leaders.

Yuan Shikai (1859–1916) Chinese general and first president of the Chinese Republic (1912–1916). He stood in the way of the democratic movement led by Sun Yat-sen.

Guomindang Nationalist political party founded on democratic principles by Sun Yat-sen in 1912. After 1925, the party was headed by Chiang Kai-shek, who turned it into an increasingly authoritarian movement.

The *zaibatsu* (zie-BOT-soo), four giant corporations—Mitsubishi, Sumitomo, Ya-suda, and Mitsui—that controlled most of Japan's industry and commerce profited the most. Farmers, who constituted half the population, remained poor; some, in desperation, sold their daughters to textile mills or into domestic service, where young women formed the bulk of the labor force. Labor unions were weak and repressed by the police.

Japan was quick to join the Allied side in World War I. Japanese forces soon conquered the German colonies in the northern Pacific and on the coast of China, and then turned their attention to the rest of China. In 1915, Japan presented China with Twenty-One Demands, which would have turned it into a virtual protectorate. Britain and the United States persuaded Japan to soften the demands but could not prevent it from keeping the German coastal enclaves and extracting railroad and mining concessions at China's expense. Thus began a bitter struggle that was to last for thirty years.

Primary Source: The Three People's Principles and the Future of the Chinese People
Discover the motivation behind Chinese revolutionary Sun Yat-sen's efforts to end taxation in China and to adopt a constitution.

China in the 1920s

To many educated Chinese, the great powers' decision at the Paris Peace Conference to go along with Japan's seizure of the German enclaves in China was a cruel insult. On May 4, 1919, students demonstrated in front of the Forbidden City of Beijing. Despite a government ban, the May Fourth Movement spread to other parts of China.

China's regional generals—the warlords—still supported their armies through plunder and arbitrary taxation, frightening off trade and investment. While neglecting the dikes and canals on which Chinese farmers depended, they fought one another and protected the gangsters who ran the opium trade. During the warlord era, China grew poorer. Only the treaty ports prospered.

Sun Yat-sen tried to make a comeback in Canton (Guangzhou) in the early 1920s. Though not a communist, he was impressed with the efficiency of Lenin's revolutionary tactics and let a Soviet adviser reorganize the Guomindang along Leninist lines. He also welcomed members of the newly created Chinese Communist Party into the Guomindang.

When Sun died in 1925, the leadership of his party passed to Chiang Kai-shek (chang kie-shek) (1886–1975). An officer and director of the military academy, Chiang trained several hundred young officers, who remained loyal to him thereafter. In 1927, he determined to crush the regional warlords. Moving north from his base in Canton, he briefly formed an alliance with the communists. Once Shanghai was occupied, however, he allied himself with local gangsters to crush the labor unions and decimate the communists, whom he considered a threat. He then defeated or co-opted most of the other warlords and established a dictatorship.

Chiang's government issued ambitious plans to revitalize the economy, but his followers were neither competent administrators like the Japanese officials of the Meiji Restoration nor ruthless modernizers like the Russian Bolsheviks. Instead, the government attracted thousands of opportunists whose goal was to "become an official and get rich" by taxing and plundering businesses. In the countryside, tax collectors and landowners squeezed the peasants ever harder.

SECTION REVIEW

- By 1900, the Qing presided over corruption and economic stagnation.

- Sun Yat-sen's Revolutionary Alliance overthrew the Qing, but the military thwarted Guomindang attempts to set up a Western-style government.

- During World War I and after Japanese industry boomed, the *zaibatsu* corporations benefited most from the growing prosperity.

- Japan joined the Allies, captured German colonies, and tried to impose the Twenty-One Demands on China.

- In the 1920s, warlords controlled China, though the May Fourth Movement rose to challenge them.

- To subdue the warlords, Chiang Kai-shek allied with the communists, and his government then crushed the communists and attempted top-down modernization.

THE NEW MIDDLE EAST

How did the Middle East change as a result of the war?

At the Paris Peace Conference, France, Britain, Italy, and Japan proposed to divide the territories of the Ottoman Empire among themselves, but their ambitions clashed with President Wilson's ideal of national self-determination. Turkish nationalists fought for and achieved independence. The Arab-speaking territories of the old Ottoman Empire became part of the League of Nations' new **mandate system**, run by French and British administrations charged with promoting "the material and moral well-being and the social progress of the inhabitants" (see Diversity and Dominance: The Middle East After World War I). In Palestine, Zionists accelerated Jewish immigration (see Map 25.2).

mandate system Allocation of former German colonies and Ottoman possessions to the victorious powers after World War I, to be administered under League of Nations supervision.

The Rise of Modern Turkey

At war's end, Allied forces occupied the Ottoman Empire and made the sultan give up most of his lands. But they had to reckon with Mustafa Kemal, a war hero who formed a nationalist government in central Anatolia with the backing of fellow army officers. His armies defeated a Greek army of occupation in western Anatolia in 1922. An ensuing population exchange moved hundreds of thousands of Greeks to Greece and brought Muslims from that country to Turkey.

As a war hero proclaimed savior of his country, Kemal was able to impose wrenching changes on his people. An outspoken modernizer, he was eager to bring Turkey closer to Europe as quickly as possible. He abolished the sultanate, declared Turkey a secular republic in 1923, and introduced European laws. In a radical break with Islamic tradition, he suppressed Muslim courts, schools, and religious orders and replaced the Arabic alphabet with the Latin alphabet.

Women received civil equality, including the right to vote and to be elected to the national assembly. Kemal forbade polygamy and instituted civil marriage and divorce. He even changed people's clothing, strongly discouraging women from veiling their faces and ordering Turkish men to wear European brimmed hats instead of the fez. He ordered everyone to take a family name, choosing the name Atatürk ("father of the Turks") for himself.

Mustafa Kemal Atatürk

After World War I, Mustafa Kemal was determined to modernize Turkey on the Western model. Here he is shown wearing a European-style suit and teaching the Latin alphabet.   (Stock Montage)

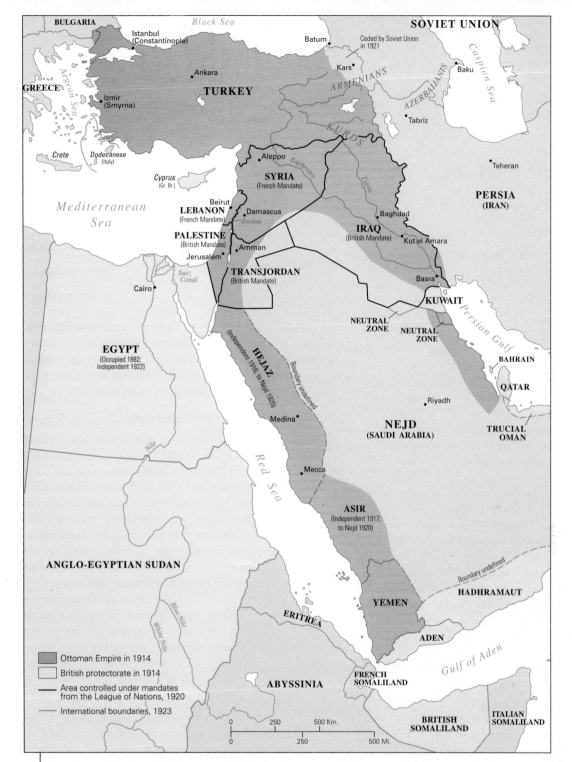

Map 25.2   Territorial Changes in the Middle East After World War I

The defeat and dismemberment of the Ottoman Empire at the end of World War I resulted in an entirely new political map of the region. The Turkish Republic inherited Anatolia and a small piece of Europe, while the Ottoman Empire's Arab provinces were divided between France and Great Britain as "Class A Mandates." The French acquired Syria and Lebanon, and the British got Palestine (now Israel, Jordan, and the Occupied Territories) and Iraq.

 Interactive Map

college.cengage.com/pic/bullietbrief4e

The Middle East After World War I

*D*uring the First World War, Entente forces invaded the Arab provinces of the Ottoman Empire and occupied Palestine, Mesopotamia, and Syria. This raised the question of what to do with these territories after the war. The following documents illustrate the diversity of opinions among various groups planning the postwar settlement: Great Britain concerned with defeating Germany and maintaining its empire; the United States, basing its policies on lofty principles; and Arab spokesmen seeking self-determination.

In the early twentieth century, in response to the rise of anti-Semitism in Europe, a movement called Zionism had arisen among European Jews. Zionists, led by Theodore Herzl, hoped for a return to Israel, the ancestral homeland of the Jewish people. For two thousand years this land had been under a variety of rulers. Its population was Arabic-speaking and mostly Muslim.

During the war the British government eagerly sought the support of the American Jewish community to balance the hostility of Irish-Americans and German-Americans toward the British war effort. It was therefore receptive to the idea of establishing a Jewish homeland in Palestine. The result was a policy statement, sent by Foreign Secretary Arthur James Balfour to Baron Rothschild, a prominent supporter of the Zionist movement in England. This statement, called the "Balfour Declaration," has haunted the Middle East ever since.

The Balfour Declaration of 1917

Foreign Office
November 2nd, 1917

Dear Lord Rothschild:

I have much pleasure in conveying to you, on behalf of His Majesty's Government, the following declaration of sympathy with Jewish Zionist aspirations which have been submitted to, and approved by, the Cabinet:

> His Majesty's Government view with favor the establishment in Palestine of a national home for the Jewish people, and will use their best endeavors to facilitate the achievement of this object, it being clearly understood that nothing shall be

done which may prejudice the civil and religious rights of existing non-Jewish communities in Palestine, or the rights and political status enjoyed by Jews in any other country.

I should be grateful if you would bring this declaration to the knowledge of the Zionist Federation.

Yours,
Arthur James Balfour

*O*n January 8, 1918, the American president Woodrow Wilson issued his famous Fourteen Points proposal to end the war. Much of his speech was devoted to European affairs or to international relations in general, but two of his fourteen points were understood as referring to the Arab world.

Woodrow Wilson's Fourteen Points

We entered this war because violations of right had occurred which touches us to the quick and made the life of our own people impossible unless they were corrected and the world secured once for all against their recurrence. What we demand in this war, therefore, is nothing peculiar to ourselves. It is that the world be made fit and safe to live in; and particularly that it be made safe for every peace-loving nation which, like our own, wishes to live its own life, determine its own institutions, be assured of justice and fair dealing by the other peoples of the world as against force and selfish aggression. All the peoples of the world are in effect partners in this interest, and for our own part we see very clearly that unless justice be done to others it will not be done to us. The programme of the world's peace, therefore, is our programme; and that programme, the only possible programme, as we see it, is this:

V. A free, open-minded, and absolutely impartial adjustment of all colonial claims, based upon a strict observance of the principle that in determining all such questions of sovereignty the interests of the populations concerned must have equal weight with the equitable claims of the government whose title is to be determined.

XII. The Turkish portions of the present Ottoman Empire should be assured a secure sovereignty, but the other nationalities which are now under Turkish rule should be assured an undoubted security of life and an absolutely unmolested opportunity of autonomous development. . . .

*W*hen the war ended, the victorious Allies assembled in Paris to determine, among other things, the fate of the former Arab provinces of the Ottoman Empire. This was a matter of grave concern to both Zionists and leaders of the Arab populations. Arab leaders, in particular, had reason to doubt the intentions of the great powers, especially Britain and France. When the Allies decided to create mandates in the Arab territories on the grounds that the Arab peoples were not ready for independence, Arab leaders expressed their misgivings, as the following statement shows:

Memorandum of the General Syrian Congress, July 2, 1919

We the undersigned members of the General Syrian Congress, meeting in Damascus on Wednesday, July 2nd, 1919, made up of representatives from the three Zones, viz., The Southern, Eastern, and Western, provided with credentials and authorizations by the inhabitants of our various districts, Moslems, Christians, and Jews, have agreed upon the following statement of the desires of the people of the country who have elected us. . . .

1. We ask absolutely complete political independence for Syria. . . .
2. We ask that the government of this Syrian country should be a democratic civil constitutional Monarchy on broad decentralization principles, safeguarding the rights of minorities, and that the King be the Emir Feisal, who carried on a glorious struggle in the cause of our liberation and merited our full confidence and entire reliance.
3. Considering the fact that the Arabs inhabiting the Syrian area are not naturally less gifted than other more advanced races and that they are by no means less developed than the Bulgarians, Serbians, Greeks, and Roumanians at the beginning of their independence, we protest against Article 22 of the Covenant of the League of Nations, placing us among the nations in their middle stage of development which stand in need of a mandatory power.
4. In the event of the rejection of the Peace Conference of this just protest for certain considerations that we may not understand, we, relying on the declarations of President Wilson that his object in waging war was to put an end to the ambition of conquest and colonization, we can only regard the mandate mentioned in the Covenant of the League of Nations as equivalent to the rendering of economical and technical assistance that does not prejudice our complete independence. And desiring that our country should not fall a prey to colonization and believing that the American Nation is furthest from any thought of colonization and has no political ambition in our country, we will seek the technical and economic assistance from the United States of America, provided that such assistance does not exceed 20 years.

5. In the event of America not finding herself in a position to accept our desire for assistance, we will seek this assistance from Great Britain, also provided that such does not prejudice our complete independence and unity of our country and that the duration of such assistance does not exceed that mentioned in the previous article.
6. We do not acknowledge any right claimed by the French Government in any part whatever of our Syrian country and refuse that she should assist us or have a hand in our country under any circumstances and in any place.
7. We opposed the pretensions of the Zionists to create a Jewish commonwealth in the southern part of Syria, known as Palestine, and oppose Zionist migration to any part of our country; for we do not acknowledge their title but consider them a grave peril to our people from the national, economical, and political points of view. Our Jewish compatriots shall enjoy our common rights and assume our common responsibilities.

QUESTIONS FOR ANALYSIS

1. **Was there a contradiction between Balfour's proposal to establish "a national home for the Jewish people" and the promise "that nothing shall be done which may prejudice the civil and religious rights of existing non-Jewish communities in Palestine"?**
2. **How would Woodrow Wilson's statements about "the interests of the populations concerned" and "an absolutely unmolested opportunity of autonomous development" apply to Palestine?**
3. **Why did the delegates to the Syrian General Congress object to the plan to create mandates in the former Ottoman provinces? What alternatives did they offer?**
4. **Why did the delegates object to the creation of a Jewish commonwealth?**

Source: The Balfour Declaration, *The Times* (London), November 9, 1917. Memorandum of the General Syrian Congress, *Foreign Relations of the United States: Paris Peace Conference*, vol. 12 (Washington, DC: Government Printing Office, 1919), 780–781.

The Jewish Settlement of Palestine
The Jewish population of Israel originated with the immigration to Palestine of thousands of Jews fleeing persecution and discrimination in Europe. Many settled on the land and founded kibbutzim, or collective farms. In this picture taken in 1912, an eighty-four-year-old immigrant from Russia learns to plow the land.   (Hulton Archive/Getty Images)

SECTION REVIEW

- Wilson's self-determination principle clashed with British, French, Italian, and Japanese attempts to partition the Ottoman Empire.

- After World War I, Mustafa Kemal led Turkish nationalists against European occupiers and expelled Greeks from Turkey.

- Kemal declared Turkey a secular republic and, as Atatürk, westernized Turkey's economy and society.

- In Arab lands under the mandate system, Britain and France used military force to crush nationalist uprisings.

- In Egypt, Britain substituted phony independence for colonialism.

- Jewish immigration to Palestine created tension, often erupting into violence, between Jews and Palestinian Arabs.

Arab Lands and the Question of Palestine

Among the Arab people, the thinly disguised colonialism of the mandate system set off protests and rebellions. Arabs viewed the European presence not as "liberation" from Ottoman "oppression" but as foreign occupation.

The British attempted to control the Middle East with a mixture of bribery and intimidation. They helped Faisal, leader of the Arab Revolt, become king of Syria. When the French ousted him, the British made him king of Iraq and used aerial bombing to quell the resulting rural insurrections. In 1931, Britain granted Iraq official independence in exchange for the right to keep two air bases, a military alliance, and an assured flow of petroleum. France, meanwhile, sent thousands of troops to Syria and Lebanon to crush nationalist uprisings.

In Egypt as in Iraq, the British substituted a phony independence for official colonialism. They declared Egypt independent in 1922 but reserved the right to station troops along the Suez Canal to secure their link with India. Despite nationalist opposition, Britain was successful in keeping Egypt in limbo—neither independent nor a colony—thanks to an alliance with King Farouk (sultan 1917–1922; king 1922–1936) and conservative Egyptian politicians who feared both secular and religious radicalism.

As soon as Palestine became a British mandate in 1920, Jewish immigrants, encouraged by the Balfour Declaration of 1917, arrived to join the small community that had immigrated in the nineteenth century. Most settled in the cities, but some purchased land to establish *kibbutzim*, communal farms. The purchases of land by Jewish agencies angered the indigenous Palestinians, especially tenant farmers who had been evicted to make room for settlers. In 1920–1921, riots erupted between Jews and Arabs. When far more Jewish immigrants arrived than they had anticipated, the British tried to limit immigration, thereby alienating the Jews without mollifying the Arabs. Increasingly, Jews arrived without papers, smuggled in by militant Zionist organizations. In the 1930s, the country was torn by strikes and guerrilla warfare that the British could not control. In the process, Britain earned the hatred of both sides.

SOCIETY, CULTURE, AND TECHNOLOGY IN THE INDUSTRIALIZED WORLD

How did European and North American society and technology change in the aftermath of the war?

Advances in science offered astonishing new insights into the mysteries of nature and the universe. New technologies, many of them pioneered in the

United States, promised to change the daily lives of millions of people. At the same time, new cultural trends developed that had profound effects.

Class and Gender   After the war, class distinctions began to fade. Many European aristocrats had died on the battlefields, and with them went their class's long domination of the army, the diplomatic corps, and other elite sectors of society. On both sides of the Atlantic, engineers, businessmen, lawyers, and other professionals rose to prominence, increasing the relative importance of the middle class.

The activities of governments had expanded during the war and continued to grow. Governments provided housing, highways, schools, public health facilities, broadcasting, and other services. This growth of government influence created a need for thousands more bureaucrats. Department stores, banks, insurance companies, and other businesses also increased the white-collar work force.

In contrast with the middle class, the working class did not expand. The introduction of new machines and new ways of organizing work, such as the automobile assembly line that Henry Ford devised, increased workers' productivity so that greater outputs could be achieved without a larger labor force.

Women's lives changed more rapidly in the 1920s than in any previous decade. Although the end of the war marked a retreat from wartime job opportunities, some women remained in the work force as wage earners and salaried professionals. The young and wealthy enjoyed new personal freedoms; they drove cars, played sports, traveled alone, and smoked in public. For others the upheavals of war brought more suffering than liberation. Millions of women had lost their fathers, brothers, sons, husbands, and fiancés in the war or in the great influenza epidemic. The shortage of young men caused many single women to lead lives of loneliness and destitution.

In Europe and North America advocates of women's rights had been demanding the vote for women since the 1890s. Before the twentieth century, only New Zealand granted women the vote. Norway followed in 1915, Russia in 1917, and Canada and Germany in 1918. Britain gave the vote to women over thirty in 1918 and later extended it to younger women. The Nineteenth Amendment to the U.S. Constitution granted suffrage to American women in 1920. Women in Turkey began voting in 1934. Most other countries withheld suffrage until after 1945.

CL Primary Source: Women and the Vote in Syria . . . in the Proposed State *Follow along as members of the Syrian parliament debate whether or not to grant Syrian women the right to vote.*

In dictatorships voting rights for women made no difference, and in democratic countries women tended to vote like their male relatives. In the British elections of 1918—the first to include women—they overwhelmingly voted for the Conservative Party. Everywhere, their influence on politics was less radical than feminists had hoped and conservatives had feared.

On both sides of the Atlantic women participated in social reform movements to prevent mistreatment of women, children, and industrial workers. In the United States such reforms were championed by Progressives such as Jane Addams (1860–1935), who founded a settlement house in a poor neighborhood and received the Nobel Peace Prize in 1931. In Europe reformers were generally aligned with Socialist or Labour Parties.

Since 1874 the Women's Christian Temperance Union had campaigned against alcohol and taverns. In the early twentieth century the American Carrie Nation (1846–1911) became famous for destroying saloons and lecturing in the United

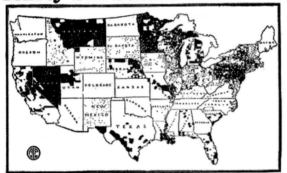

MAKE THE MAP ALL WHITE
By Constitutional Amendment
Thirty-Six States Can Do It

Wet ▪   Dry ☐

Over 52,000,000 of the population of the United States live under Prohibition.

Over 71 per cent of the area is prohibition territory. This area will be increased 14 per cent when the constitutional amendments adopted by five states in the Fall of 1914 become effective.

One-half of all the people now living in license territory, *live in four states*—New York, Pennsylvania, Illinois and New Jersey.

One-fourth of all the people in the United States who live in saloon territory, *live in six cities*—New York, Chicago, Philadelphia, St. Louis, Boston, Cleveland.

There are fewer saloons south of the Mason and Dixon line than there are in the city of Chicago.

The fourteen Prohibition States are: Maine, Kansas, North Dakota, Oklahoma, Mississippi, Georgia, North Carolina, Tennessee, West Virginia, Virginia, Colorado, Oregon, Washington, and Arizona.

Since this map was revised, January 1, 1915, Alabama and Idaho have adopted Statutory Prohibition by an overwhelming vote in the Legislature.

Thirty-six states can be selected that have a total number of saloons less than New York City, and

Thirty-Six States Can Adopt the National Prohibition Amendment

Copyright, 1915   The Anti-Saloon League of America, Westerville, Ohio

Margaret Sanger (1883–1966)
American nurse and author; pioneer in the movement for family planning; organized conferences and established birth control clinics.

Max Planck (1858–1947)
German physicist who developed quantum theory and was awarded the Nobel Prize for physics in 1918.

Albert Einstein (1879–1955)
German physicist who developed the theory of relativity, which states that time, space, and mass are relative to each other and not fixed.

Flyer in Support of Prohibition

The constitutional amendments adopted in the wake of World War I represented the successful outcome of long moral campaigns. National Prohibition was established by the Eighteenth Amendment in 1919, and women gained the vote a year later through the Nineteenth Amendment. Though the former was judged a failure in practice and was repealed by the Twenty-first Amendment in 1933, it originally had powerful support from the country's Protestant majority and reflected disapproval of the lifestyles of big cities with sizable immigrant populations.

States and Europe against the evils of liquor. As a result of this campaign, the Eighteenth Amendment imposed prohibition in the United States from 1919 until it was revoked by the Twenty-First Amendment fourteen years later.

Among the most controversial, and eventually most effective, of the reformers were those who advocated contraception, such as the American **Margaret Sanger** (1883–1966). Her campaign brought her into conflict with the authorities, who equated birth control with pornography. Finally, in 1923 she was able to found a birth control clinic in New York. In France, however, the government prohibited contraception and abortion in 1920 in an effort to increase the birthrate and make up for the loss of so many young men in the war. Only the Russian communists allowed abortion, for ideological reasons.

Revolution in the Sciences

At the end of the nineteenth century, a revolution in physics undermined all the old certainties about nature. Physicists discovered that atoms, the building blocks of matter, are not indivisible but consist of far smaller subatomic particles. In 1900, the German physicist **Max Planck** (1858–1947) found that light and energy do not flow in a continuous stream but travel in small units, which he called *quanta*. These findings seemed strange enough, but what really undermined Newtonian physics was the theory of relativity developed by **Albert Einstein** (1879–1955), another German physicist. In 1916, Einstein announced that not only is matter made of insubstantial particles, but also that time, space, and mass are not fixed but are relative to one another.

To nonscientists, it seemed as though theories expressed in arcane mathematical formulas were replacing truth and common sense. Far from being mere speculation, however, the new physics promised to unlock the secrets of matter and provide humans with plentiful—and potentially dangerous—new sources of energy.

The new social sciences were even more unsettling than the new physics, for they challenged Victorian morality, middle-class values, and notions of Western superiority. Sigmund Freud (1856–1939), a Viennese physician, developed a technique—psychoanalysis—to probe the minds of his patients. He found not only rationality but also hidden layers of emotion and desire repressed by social restraints. "The primitive, savage and evil impulses have not vanished from any individual, but continue their existence, although in a repressed state," he warned. Meanwhile, sociologists and anthropologists had begun the empirical study of societies, both Western and non-Western. Before the war, the French sociologist Emile Durkheim (1858–1917) had come to the then-shocking conclusion that "there are no religions that are false. All are true in their own fashion."

If the words *primitive* and *savage* applied to Europeans as well as to other peoples, and if religions were all equally "true," then what remained of the superiority of Western civilization? Cultural relativism, as the new approach to human societies was called, was as unnerving as relativity in physics.

The New Technologies of Modernity

In North America, even working-class people could afford some of the new products of scientific research, inventors' ingenuity, and industrial production. Mass consumption lagged in Europe, but science and technology were just as advanced, and public fascination with the latest inventions—the cult of the modern—was just as strong.

No innovation attracted more public interest than the airplane. In 1903, two young American mechanics, Wilbur and Orville Wright, built the first aircraft that was heavier than air and could be maneuvered in flight. From that moment on, wherever they appeared, airplanes fascinated people. During the war, the exploits of air aces relieved the tedium of news from the front. In the 1920s, aviation became a sport and a form of entertainment. Among the most celebrated pilots were three Americans: Amelia Earhart, the first woman to fly across the Atlantic Ocean; Richard Byrd, the first to fly over the North Pole, in 1926; and Charles Lindbergh, the first person to fly alone across the Atlantic, in 1927. The heroic age of flight lasted until the late 1930s, when aviation became a means of transportation.

Electricity's impact on home life was more sweeping. The first home use of electricity was for lighting, thanks to the economical and long-lasting incandescent bulb. Then electrical utilities joined manufacturers in advertising electric irons, fans, washing machines, hot plates, radios, and other electric appliances. After the war, radio moved from the battlefield into the home. The first commercial station began broadcasting in Pittsburgh in 1920. By 1930, hundreds of stations were broadcasting news, sports, soap operas, and advertising to 12 million homes in North America. In Europe, radio spread more slowly because governments reserved the airwaves for cultural and official programs and taxed radio owners to pay for the service.

Another medium that spread explosively in the 1920s was film. Motion pictures had begun in France in 1895 and flourished in Europe. In the United States, filmmaking started at almost the same time, but American filmmakers saw the medium's potential to entertain audiences rather than preserve outstanding theatrical performances. After World War I, filmmaking took root and flourished in Japan, India, Turkey, Egypt, and a suburb of Los Angeles, California, called Hollywood. American and European movie studios were both successful in exporting films, since silent movies presented no language problems. Then in 1927 the United States introduced the first "talking" motion picture, *The Jazz Singer,* which changed all the

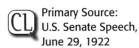

Primary Source: U.S. Senate Speech, June 29, 1922
Read one of the earliest arguments for censorship in the motion picture industry.

rules. Hollywood studios began the diffusion of American culture that has continued to this day.

Advances in medicine—some learned in the war—were another important technology. Wounds were regularly disinfected, and x-ray machines diagnosed fractures. After the war, cities built costly water supply and sewage treatment systems. By the 1920s, indoor plumbing and flush toilets penetrated even working-class neighborhoods. Interest in cleanliness altered private life. Soap and appliance manufacturers filled women's magazines with advertisements for products to help housewives keep their family's homes and clothing spotless and their meals fresh and wholesome. The decline in infant mortality and the improvements in general health and life expectancy in this period owe as much to the cult of cleanliness as to advances in medicine.

Technology and the Environment

Two new technologies—the skyscraper and the automobile—transformed the urban environment. At the end of the nineteenth century, architects had begun to design ever-higher buildings using load-bearing steel frames and passenger elevators. Major corporations in Chicago and New York competed to build the most daring buildings in the world, such as New York's 55-story Woolworth Building (1912) and Chicago's 34-story Tribune Tower (1923). A building boom in the late 1920s produced dozens of skyscrapers, culminating with the 86-story, 1,239-foot (377-meter) Empire State Building in New York City, completed in 1932.

European cities restricted the height of buildings to protect their architectural heritage; Paris forbade buildings over 56 feet (17 meters) high. In innovative designs, however, European architects led the way. In the 1920s, the Swiss architect known as Le Corbusier (luh cor-booz-YEH) outlined a new approach to architecture that featured simplicity of form, absence of surface ornamentation, easy manufacture, and inexpensive materials. Other architects—including the Finn Eero Saarinen, the Germans Ludwig Mies van der Rohe (LOOD-vig MEES fon der ROW-uh) and Walter Gropius, and the American Frank Lloyd Wright—advanced his lines of thought and added their own to create what became known as the International Style.

While central business districts were reaching for the sky, outlying areas were spreading into the countryside, thanks to the automobile. The assembly line pioneered by Henry Ford mass-produced vehicles in ever-greater volume and at falling prices. By 1929, the United States had one car for every five people, five-sixths of the world's automobiles. Far from being blamed for their exhaust emissions, automobiles were praised as the solution to urban pollution. As cars replaced carts and carriages, horses disappeared from city streets, as did tons of manure.

The most important environmental effect of automobiles was suburban sprawl. Middle-class families could now live in single-family homes that were too far apart to be served by public transportation. As middle- and working-class families bought cars, cities acquired rings of automobile suburbs. Los Angeles, the first true automobile city, consisted of suburbs spread over hundreds of square miles and linked together by broad avenues. In those sections of the city where streetcar lines went out of business, the automo-

SECTION REVIEW

- After the war, class distinctions loosened and governments and businesses grew, encouraging the expansion of the middle class.

- Women's lives changed as many gained the right to vote, remained in the work force, and participated in social reform movements.

- Modern physicists challenged Newtonian physics, while social scientists undermined Victorian values and ideas of Western superiority.

- New technologies, such as aircraft, motion pictures, and advances in medicine, transformed daily life in the industrialized world.

- Skyscrapers transformed urban environments, and modern architects developed the International Style.

- Mass-produced automobiles offered low-cost transportation and encouraged suburban sprawl and the expansion of road systems.

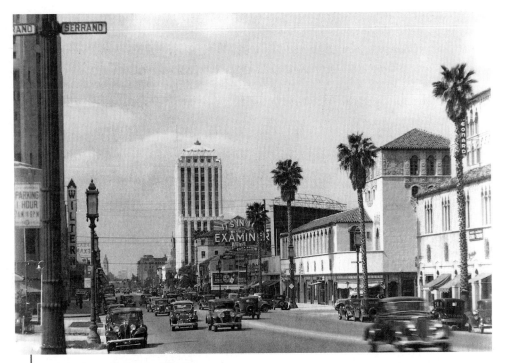

The Archetypal Automobile City

As Los Angeles grew from a modest town into a sprawling metropolis, broad avenues, parking lots, and garages were built to accommodate automobiles. By 1929, most families owned a car, and streetcar lines had closed for lack of passengers. This photograph shows a street in the downtown business district. (Ralph Morris Archives/Los Angeles Public Library)

 HISTORY IN FOCUS   The skyscraper and the automobile transformed the twentieth-century urban environment. The photo, "The Archetypal Automobile City," clearly illustrates the effect of the automobile on Los Angeles. Does the skyscraper appear to have had the same effect? Why or why not? *Find the answer online.*

bile became a necessity for commuters. Many Americans saw Los Angeles as the portent of a glorious future when everyone would have a car; only a few foresaw the congestion and pollution that would ensue.

COMPARATIVE PERSPECTIVES

The Great War caused a major realignment among the nations of the world. France and Britain, the two leading colonial powers, emerged economically weakened despite their victory. The war brought defeat and humiliation to Germany but did not reduce its military or industrial potential. It destroyed the old regime of Russia, leading to civil war and revolution from which the victorious powers sought to isolate themselves. Two other old empires—the Austro-Hungarian and the Ottoman—were divided into many smaller and weaker nations.

Only two countries benefited from the war. Japan took advantage of the European conflict to develop its industries and press its demands on a China weakened by domestic turmoil. The United States emerged as the most prosperous and potentially most powerful nation, restrained only by strong isolationist sentiments.

In the Middle East, the fall of the Ottoman Empire awakened aspirations for nationhood among various ethnic groups. These aspirations were thwarted when France and Great Britain tried to impose their rule upon the former Ottoman lands, causing conflicts and bitter enmities.

Chapter Review

 DOWNLOAD THE MP3 AUDIO FILE OF THE CHAPTER REVIEW TO LISTEN TO ON THE GO.

What led to the outbreak of the First World War? (page 682)

In 1914 the great powers of Europe had not had a major conflict in decades and believed a war would be quick and victorious. Each of the two alliances they formed—the Central Powers and the Entente—was locked into a rigid timetable of mobilizations and railroad schedules. When competing nationalisms in the Balkans triggered a conflict between Serbia and Austria-Hungary, the alliances quickly drew Russia, Germany, France, and Britain into the conflict.

How did the war lead to revolution in Russia? (page 685)

Russia was the least prepared for war. Chaotic mobilization and a string of defeats disrupted the economy, causing severe shortages. As the war progressed, soldiers began to desert, and the government lost control of the army and the population. The moderate government that replaced the tsar in March 1917 could neither satisfy the people nor pursue the war. Its failure allowed the Bolsheviks to overthrow it in a second revolution.

What role did the war play in eroding European dominance in the world? (page 690)

France, Great Britain, and Italy expected to reap the benefits of victory and expand their empires at the expense of the defeated powers. However, with the exception of the United States, which withdrew to the Western Hemisphere, the victors were exhausted and impoverished by the war and had lost the will to fight in colonial wars. Meanwhile, the idea of self-determination had spread to the Middle East and Asia, where nationalist politicians and their followers were determined to resist European dominance.

Why did China and Japan follow such divergent paths in this period? (page 694)

After 1868, Japan established a strong government and built an industrial economy comparable to those of Europe. Meanwhile China, long ruled by the

KEY TERMS

Western Front *(p. 685)*
Faisal I *(p. 688)*
Balfour Declaration *(p. 688)*
Bolsheviks *(p. 688)*
Vladimir Lenin *(p. 689)*
Woodrow Wilson *(p. 690)*
League of Nations *(p. 691)*
Treaty of Versailles *(p. 692)*
New Economic Policy *(p. 692)*
Empress Dowager Cixi *(p. 694)*
Sun Yat-sen *(p. 694)*
Yuan Shikai *(p. 694)*
Guomindang *(p. 694)*
mandate system *(p. 696)*
Margaret Sanger *(p. 702)*
Max Planck *(p. 702)*
Albert Einstein *(p. 702)*

WEB RESOURCES

Pronunciation Guide
Interactive Maps
   MAP 25.2 Territorial Changes in the Middle East After World War I
Primary Sources
   Letter from Turkey, Summer 1915

Qing dynasty, erupted after 1911 in civil wars in which warlords and political factions vied for power. The Japanese military and major industries seized the opportunity of Europe's involvement in the Great War to build up Japan's economy at China's expense.

How did the Middle East change as a result of the war? (page 696)

In Anatolia, the heartland of the Ottoman Empire, a movement for national unity led by Kemal Atatürk fought for and achieved Turkish independence. In the predominantly Arab lands, nationalist leaders decried European domination. Jewish immigration into Palestine provoked a violent reaction from the Palestinians, which their British overlords found hard to control.

How did European and North American society and technology change in the aftermath of the war? (page 700)

Many women who had participated in the war effort remained in the work force and demanded voting and other rights. Governments took on new responsibilities for education, public health, and social welfare. Automobiles, movies, and radio broadcasts were eagerly adopted. Advances in the sciences, especially in physics and psychology, undermined the old cultural certainties, while birth control and family planning provoked considerable opposition from traditionalists.

The Balfour Declaration

Mud and Khaki, Memoirs of an Incomplete Soldier

The Zionist Organization's Memorandum . . . State in Palestine

Comments of the German Delegation . . . October 1919

An Economist Analyzes the Versailles Treaty and Finds It Lacking

The Three People's Principles and the Future of the Chinese People

Women and the Vote in Syria . . . in the Proposed State

U.S. Senate Speech, June 29, 1922

Answer to the History in Focus Question

See photo on page 705, "The Archetypal Automobile City."

Plus

Chapter Objectives

ACE multiple-choice quiz

Flashcards

SUGGESTED READING

Bianco, Lucien. *Origins of the Chinese Revolution, 1915–1949.* 1971. Covers the warlord and Guomindang periods.

Ellis, John. *The Social History of the Machine Gun.* 1975. Looks at a key technology in the development of modern warfare.

Figes, Orlando. *A People's Tragedy: The Russian Revolution, 1891–1924.* 1996. A sweeping and vivid account.

Fritzsche, Peter. *A Nation of Fliers: German Aviation and the Popular Imagination.* 1992. A readable and nontechnical account of German popular enthusiasm for aviation.

Fromkin, David. *A Peace to End All Peace.* 1989. A readable general account of the post–World War I period in the Middle East.

Geiss, Imanuel. *July 1914: The Outbreak of the First World War.* 1967. Argues that Germany caused the conflict.

Goldman, Wendy. *Women, the State, and Revolution: Soviet Family Policy and Social Life, 1917–1936.* 1993. Gender issues in early Soviet history.

Higonnet, Margaret, et al., eds. *Behind the Lines: Gender and the Two World Wars.* 1987. Essays on women and the home front.

Hughes, H. Stuart. *Consciousness and Society: The Reorientation of European Social Thought, 1890–1930.* 1958. An influential analysis of the cultural transformation of Europe.

Hughes, Thomas. *American Genesis: A Century of Invention and Technological Enthusiasm, 1870–1970.* 1989. A sweeping overview.

Kamamura, Noriko. *Turbulence in the Pacific: Japanese-U.S. Relations During World War I.* 2000. Studies the beginnings of estrangement between Japan and the United States.

Keegan, John. *The First World War.* 1999. A readable overview.

Pipes, Richard. *The Russian Revolution.* 1990. A long, comprehensive history.

Rowbotham, Sheila. *A Century of Women: The History of Women in Britain and the United States.* 1997. A monumental history with a feminist perspective.

Von Laue, Theodore. *Why Lenin? Why Stalin?* 2d ed. 1971. Studies the background to the Russian Revolution.

The Collapse
of the Old Order

CHAPTER PREVIEW

Before the First World War, the Italian futurist poets exalted violence as a noble and manly idea. Filippo Marinetti defined their creed in these words: "We want to glorify war, the world's only hygiene— militarism, deed, destroyer of anarchisms, the beautiful ideas that are death-bringing, and the subordination of women." His friend Gabriele d'Annunzio said: "If it is a crime to incite citizens to violence, I shall boast of this crime."

The war taught most survivors to abhor violence. During the 1920s, the world seemed to return to what United States president Warren Harding called "normalcy": prosperity in Europe and America, European colonialism in Asia and Africa, paternalistic U.S. domination of Latin America, and peace almost everywhere. But for a few, war and domination became a creed and a goal.

 This icon will direct you to the website where you can Prepare for Class, Improve Your Grade, and Ace the Test: college.cengage.com/pic/bullietbrief4e

In 1929, the artificial normalcy of the 1920s began to come apart. The Great Depression caused governments to turn against one another in a desperate attempt to protect their people's livelihood. As the economic crisis spread around the world, businesses went bankrupt, prices fell, factories closed, and workers were laid off. Even wholly agricultural nations and colonies suffered as markets for their exports shriveled.

Some countries chose to solve their problems by violent means. When nations shut their doors to Japan's products, the Japanese military tried to save their country by conquering China. In Germany, the Depression reawakened resentments against the victors of the Great War; people who feared communism or blamed Jews for their troubles turned to Hitler and the Nazis, who promised to save their society by dominating others. In the Soviet Union, Stalin used energetic and murderous means to force his country into a communist version of the Industrial Revolution.

The result was war. The Second World War engulfed more lands and peoples and caused far more death and destruction than any previous conflict. At the end of it, much of Europe and East Asia lay in ruins, and millions of destitute refugees sought safety in other lands. The European colonial powers were either defeated or so weakened that they could no longer hold on to their empires when Asian and African peoples asserted their desire for independence.

THE STALIN REVOLUTION

How did the Soviet Union change under Stalin, and at what cost?

After **Joseph Stalin** (1879–1953) achieved total mastery over the USSR in early 1929 (see Chapter 25), he led it through another revolution: an economic and social transformation that turned it into a great industrial and military power and intensified both admiration for and fear of communism throughout the world.

Joseph Stalin (1879–1953)
Bolshevik revolutionary, head of the Soviet Communist Party after 1924, and dictator of the Soviet Union from 1929 to 1953. He led the Soviet Union with an iron fist, using **Five-Year Plans** to increase industrial production and terror to crush all opposition.

Five-Year Plans

Stalin's ambition to turn the USSR into an industrial nation was not intended initially to produce consumer goods for a mass market, much less enrich individuals as in Britain and the United States. Instead, his aim was to increase the power of the Communist Party domestically and the power of the Soviet Union in relation to other countries. By building up Russia's industry, Stalin was determined to prevent a repetition of the humiliating defeat Russia had suffered at the hands of Germany in 1917.

Stalin encouraged rapid industrialization through a series of **Five-Year Plans**, a system of centralized control copied from the German experience of World War I. The goal of the first Five-Year Plan was to quintuple the output of electricity and double that of heavy industry: iron, steel, coal, and machinery. Beginning in October 1928, the communist government created whole industries and cities from scratch, then recruited millions of peasants and trained them to work in the new factories and mines and offices. In every way except actual fighting, Stalin's Russia resembled a nation at war.

Rapid industrialization hastened environmental changes. Hydroelectric dams turned rivers into strings of reservoirs. Roads, canals, and railroad tracks cut the

Five-Year Plans Plans that Joseph Stalin introduced to industrialize the Soviet Union rapidly, beginning in 1928. They set goals for the output of steel, electricity, machinery, and most other products and were enforced by the police powers of the state. They succeeded in making the Soviet Union a major industrial power before World War II.

landscape. Forests and grassland were turned into farmland. From an environmental perspective, the outcome of the Five-Year Plans resembled the transformation that had occurred in the United States and Canada a few decades earlier.

Collectivization of Agriculture

Since the Soviet Union was still a predominantly agrarian country, the only way to pay for these massive investments, provide the labor, and feed the millions of new industrial workers was to squeeze the peasantry. Stalin therefore proceeded with the most radical social experiment conceived up to that time: the collectivization of agriculture.

Collectivization meant consolidating small private farms into vast collectives and making the farmers work together in commonly owned fields. Each collective was expected to supply the government with a fixed amount of food and distribute what was left among its members. Collectives were to become outdoor factories through the use of machinery and techniques of mass production. Collectivization was expected to bring the peasants once and for all under government control so they never again could withhold food supplies as they had done during the period of Lenin's New Economic Policy (see Chapter 25).

The government mounted a massive propaganda campaign to enlist the farmers' support. At first, all seemed to go well, but soon *kulaks* (COO-lox) ("fists"), the better-off peasants, began to resist giving up all their property. When soldiers came to force them into collectives at gunpoint, the kulaks burned their own crops, smashed their own equipment, and slaughtered their own livestock. Within a few months, they slaughtered half of the Soviet Union's horses and cattle and two-thirds of its sheep and goats. In retaliation, Stalin ruthlessly ordered the "liquidation of kulaks as a class" and incited the poor peasants to attack their wealthier neighbors. Over 8 million kulaks were arrested. Many were executed, and the rest were sent to slave labor camps, where most starved to death.

The peasants who were left had been the least successful before collectivization and proved to be the least competent after. Many were sent to work in factories. The rest were forbidden to leave their farms. With half of their draft animals gone, they

The Collectivization of Soviet Agriculture

One of the goals of collectivization was to introduce modern farm machinery. This poster shows delighted farmers operating new tractors and threshers.   (David King Collection)

Chronology

	Europe and North Africa	Asia and the Pacific
1930		
	1931 Great Depression reaches Europe	**1931** Japanese forces occupy Manchuria
	1933 Hitler comes to power in Germany	
1935		
	1936 Hitler invades the Rhineland	
		1937 Japanese troops invade China, conquer coastal provinces; Chiang Kai-shek flees to Sichuan
		1937–1938 Japanese troops take Nanjing
	1939 (Sept. 1) German forces invade Poland	
1940	**1940 (March–April)** German forces conquer Denmark, Norway, the Netherlands, and Belgium	
	1940 (May–June) German forces conquer France	
	1940 (June–Sept.) Battle of Britain	
	1941 (June 21) German forces invade USSR	**1941 (Dec. 7)** Japanese aircraft bomb Pearl Harbor
	1942–1943 Allies and Germany battle for control of North Africa; Soviet victory in Battle of Stalingrad (1943)	**1942 (Jan–March)** Japanese conquer Thailand, Philippines, Malaya
		1942 (June) United States Navy defeats Japan at Battle of Midway
	1943–1944 Red Army slowly pushes Wehrmacht back to Germany	
	1944 (June 6) D-day: U.S., British, and Canadian troops land in Normandy	
1945	**1945 (May 7)** Germany surrenders	**1945 (Aug. 6)** United States drops atomic bomb on Hiroshima
		1945 (Aug. 14) Japan surrenders
		1945–1949 Civil war in China
		1949 Communists defeat Guomindang; Mao proclaims People's Republic (Oct. 1)

could not plant or harvest enough to meet the swelling demands of the cities. Yet government agents took whatever they could find, leaving little or nothing for the farmers themselves. After bad harvests in 1933 and 1934, a famine swept through the countryside, killing some 5 million people, about one in every twenty farmers.

Stalin's second Five-Year Plan, designed to run from 1933 to 1937, was originally intended to increase the output of consumer goods. But when the Nazis took over Germany in 1933 (see below), Stalin changed the plan to emphasize heavy industries that could produce armaments. Between 1927 and 1937, the Soviet output of metals and machines increased fourteen-fold while consumer goods became scarce and food was rationed. After a decade of Stalinism, the Soviet people were more poorly clothed, fed, and housed than they had been during the years of the New Economic Policy.

Terror and Opportunities

The 1930s brought both terror and new opportunities to the Soviet people. The forced pace of industrialization, the collectivization of agriculture, and the uprooting of millions of people could be accomplished only under duress. To prevent any possible resistance or rebellion, the NKVD, Stalin's secret police force, created a climate of suspicion and fear. The terror that pervaded the country was a reflection of Stalin's own paranoia, for he distrusted everyone and feared for his life.

First "Old Bolsheviks" and high officials were put on trial; then the terror spread steadily downward. The government regularly made demands on people that they could not meet, so everyone was guilty of breaking some regulation. People from all walks of life were arrested—sometimes on a mere suspicion or because of a false accusation by a jealous coworker or neighbor, sometimes for expressing a doubt or working too hard or not hard enough, sometimes for being related to someone previously arrested, sometimes for no reason at all. Millions of people were sentenced without a trial. At the height of the terror, some 8 million were sent to *gulags* (GOO-log) (labor camps), where perhaps a million died each year of exposure or malnutrition. To its victims, the terror seemed capricious and random.

Yet Stalin's regime received the support of many Soviet citizens. Suddenly, with so many people gone and new industries and cities being built everywhere, there were opportunities for those who remained, especially the poor and the young. Women entered careers and jobs previously closed to them, becoming steelworkers, physicians, and office managers; but they retained their household and child-rearing duties, receiving little help from men. People who moved to the cities, worked enthusiastically, and asked no questions could hope to rise into the upper ranks of the Communist Party, the military, the government, or the professions, where the privileges and rewards were many.

Stalin's brutal methods helped the Soviet Union industrialize faster than any country had ever done. By the late 1930s, the USSR was the world's third largest industrial power, after the United States and Germany. To foreign observers, it seemed to be booming with construction projects, production increases, and labor shortages. Even anti-communist observers admitted that only a planned economy subject to strict government control could avoid the Depression. To millions of Soviet citizens who took pride in the new strength of their country, and to many foreigners who contrasted conditions in the Soviet Union with the unemployment and despair in the West, Stalin's achievement seemed worth any price.

SECTION REVIEW

- To build Russian industry, Stalin initiated the Five-Year Plans.

- To support industrialization and control the peasantry, Stalin ordered the collectivization of agriculture.

- Stalin prevented resistance through terror, purging Old Bolsheviks and arresting millions.

- Stalin's regime offered new opportunities to many, especially women, and succeeded in making the USSR a world industrial power.

THE DEPRESSION

What caused the Depression, and what effects did it have on the world?

On October 24, 1929—"Black Thursday"—the New York stock market went into a dive. Within days, stocks lost half their value, and their value continued to fall for three years. Thousands of banks and businesses collapsed. Millions of workers lost their jobs. The stock market crash started the deepest and most widespread depression in history.

Economic Crisis

As consumers reduced their purchases, businesses cut production. General Motors, for example, saw its sales drop by half between 1929 and 1931. Companies laid off thousands of workers, throwing them onto public charity. Business and government agencies replaced their women workers with men, arguing that men had to support their families, whereas women worked only for "pin money." Jobless men deserted their families. As farm prices fell, small farmers went bankrupt and lost their land. By mid-1932, the American economy had fallen by half, and 25 percent of the work force was unemployed. Government spending on welfare and public works was unable to restore prosperity. Many observers thought the free-enterprise system would be replaced by bread lines, soup kitchens, men selling apples on street corners, and hoboes riding freight trains.

Frightened by the stock market collapse, the New York banks called in their loans to Germany and Austria. Without American money, Germany and Austria stopped paying reparations to France and Britain, which then could not repay their war loans to America. By 1931, the Depression had spread to Europe. Governments canceled both reparations payments and war loans, but it was too late to save the world economy.

In 1930, the U.S. government, hoping to protect domestic industries from foreign competition, imposed the highest import duty in American history. In retaliation, other countries raised their tariffs. As a result, global industrial production declined by 36 percent between 1929 and 1932, while world trade dropped by a breathtaking 62 percent.

Depression in Industrial Nations

This massive economic upheaval had profound political repercussions. In the United States, Franklin D. Roosevelt was elected president in 1932 on a "New Deal" platform of government programs to stimulate and revitalize the economy. British and French governments also intervened in their economies and escaped the worst of the Depression by making their colonial empires purchase their products. In the Soviet Union, the Five-Year Plans continued to provide jobs and economic growth.

Nations that relied on exports to pay for imported food and fuel, in particular Japan and Germany, suffered much more. In Germany, unemployment reached 6 million by 1932, twice as high as in Britain. Half the German population lived in poverty. In Japan, the burden of the Depression fell on the farmers and fishermen, who saw their incomes drop sharply. Some, in desperation, revived the ancient practice of

SECTION REVIEW

- The 1929 stock market crash provoked a worldwide economic crisis in which domestic unemployment rose, financial networks collapsed, and world trade dropped.

- Governments of industrial nations intervened in their economies, but countries that relied on exports suffered acutely.

- The Depression affected nonindustrial countries differently; those dependent on exports endured the greatest hardships.

- Many of the hardest-hit nations saw the rise of radical military regimes.

selling their daughters. As economic grievances worsened, radical politicians took over the governments in Germany and Japan, manipulated the economies, and turned their nations' military might to acquiring empires large enough to support a self-sufficient economy.

Depression in Nonindustrial Regions

The Depression affected Asia, Africa, and Latin America in different ways. A wall of new import duties protected India's infant industries from foreign competition; living standards stagnated but did not drop. The Depression added little to China's problems, except in coastal regions.

Countries that depended on exports were hard hit by the Depression. When automobile production dropped by half in the United States and Europe, so did imports of rubber, devastating the economies of Southeast Asia. When the Depression hit, American tourists vanished from Cuba's beaches and bars, and with them went Cuba's prosperity. The industrialization of Argentina and Brazil was set back a decade or more by the loss of their export markets. In response, military officers seized power in several Latin American countries, consciously imitating dictatorships emerging in Europe.

Southern and Central Africa recovered from the Depression quickly, because falling prices made their gold and other minerals more valuable. But this mining boom benefited only a small number of mine owners and investors. For Africans, it was at best a mixed blessing, for mining offered jobs and cash wages to men, while women had to manage without them in the villages.

THE RISE OF FASCISM

How did fascism in Italy and Germany lead to the Second World War?

The Depression sharpened the polarization of European society that had been under way for decades. Many underpaid or unemployed workers saw in the seeming collapse of the capitalist economy an opportunity as well as temporary suffering. They urged the establishment of a socialist society through the ballot box and strikes instead of the violent revolution that had torn Russia apart.

Frightened investors and factory owners, along with conservative elements in society such as the church and the military, feared the consequences of this political shift to the left. In the democracies of western Europe and North America, middle-income voters kept politics in balance. But in some societies, the war and the Depression left people vulnerable to the appeals of ultranationalist politicians who became adept at using propaganda to appeal to people's fears. They promised to bring back full employment, stop the spread of communism, and achieve the territorial conquests that World War I had denied them.

Mussolini's Italy

The first country to seek radical answers was Italy. World War I, which had never been popular, left thousands of veterans who found neither pride in their victory nor jobs in the postwar economy. Unemployed veterans and violent youths banded together into *fasci di combattimento* (fighting units) to demand action and intimidate politicians. When socialist unions threatened to strike, factory and property owners hired gangs of these *fascisti* to defend them.

Benito Mussolini (1883–1945), a spellbinding orator, quickly became the leader of the **Fascist Party**, which glorified warfare and the Italian nation. By 1921, the party had 300,000 members, many of whom used violent methods to repress strikes, intimidate voters, and seize municipal governments. A year later, when the fascists failed to win an election, Mussolini threatened to march on Rome if he was not appointed prime minister. The government gave in.

Mussolini proceeded to install Fascist Party members in all government jobs, crush all opposition parties, and jail anyone who criticized him. The party took over the press, public education, and youth activities and gave employers control over their workers. The fascists lowered living standards but reduced unemployment and provided social security and public services. On the whole, they proved to be neither ruthless radicals nor competent administrators.

What Mussolini and the fascist movement really excelled at was publicity: bombastic speeches, spectacular parades, news bulletins full of praise for *Il Duce* (eel DOO-chay) ("the leader"), and signs everywhere proclaiming "Il Duce is always right!" Mussolini's genius was to apply the techniques of modern mass communications and advertisement to political life. Billboards, movie footage, and radio news bulletins galvanized the masses in ways never before seen in peacetime. Although his rhetoric was filled with words like *war, violence,* and *struggle,* his foreign policy was cautious. But his techniques of whipping up public enthusiasm were not lost on other radicals. By the 1930s, fascist movements had appeared in most European countries, as well as in Latin America, China, and Japan.

Benito Mussolini (1883–1945) fascist dictator of Italy (1922–1943). He led Italy to conquer Ethiopia (1935), joined Germany in the Axis pact (1936), and allied Italy with Germany in World War II. He was overthrown in 1943 when the Allies invaded Italy.

Fascist Party Italian political party created by Benito Mussolini during World War I. It emphasized aggressive nationalism and was Mussolini's instrument for the creation of a dictatorship in Italy from 1922 to 1943.

Hitler's Germany

Like Mussolini, **Adolf Hitler** (1889–1945) had served in World War I and looked back fondly on the clear lines of authority and the camaraderie he had experienced in battle. After the war, he too recreated that experience in a paramilitary group, the National Socialist German Workers' Party—**Nazis** for short. Hitler used his gifts as an orator to appeal to Germans disappointed at Germany's humiliation after the war and the hyperinflation of 1923. In 1924, he too led an uprising, but the attempted seizure of Munich was a failure. Germany was not yet ready to follow Italy's path.

The Depression changed that. While serving a jail sentence for the coup attempt, Hitler wrote *Mein Kampf* (mine compf) (*My Struggle*), but when it was published in 1925, no one took the book or its author's extreme nationalist, racist, and anti-Jewish ideas seriously. Hitler believed that Germany should incorporate all German-speaking people, even those who lived in neighboring countries. He distinguished among a "master race" of Aryans (he meant Germans, Scandinavians, and Britons), a degenerate "Alpine" race of French and Italians, and an inferior race of Russian and eastern European Slavs, who, he believed, were fit only to be slaves of the master race. He reserved his most intense hatred for Jews, on whom he blamed every disaster that had befallen Germany, especially the defeat of 1918. He glorified violence, which would enable the "master race" to defeat and subjugate all others.

Adolf Hitler (1889–1945) Born in Austria, Hitler became a radical German nationalist during World War I. He led the National Socialist German Workers' Party—the **Nazis**—in the 1920s and became dictator of Germany in 1933. He led Europe into World War II.

Nazis German political party joined by Adolf Hitler, emphasizing nationalism, racism, and war. When Hitler became chancellor of Germany in 1933, the Nazis became the only legal party and an instrument of Hitler's absolute rule. The party's formal name was National Socialist German Workers' Party.

A Nazi Rally

In the years leading up to World War II, Hitler organized mass rallies at Nurem-berg to whip up popular support for his regime and to indoctrinate young Germans with martial spirit. Thousands of men in uniform marched in torch-lit parades before Hitler and his top officials.   (AP Images/Wide World Photos)

CL Primary Source: The Centerpiece of Nazi Racial Legisla-tion: The Nuremberg Laws
Find out how the Nazis defined what it was to be a Jew.

CL Primary Source: Speech to the National Socialist Women's Association
Learn about efforts to inspire German women to stand along-side German men in supporting the Nazi cause.

When the Depression hit, the Nazis gained supporters among the unemployed who believed Nazi promises of jobs for all and among property owners frightened by the growing popularity of communists. In March 1933, as leader of the largest party in Germany, Hitler became chancellor.

Once in office, he quickly assumed dictatorial power, just as Mussolini had done. He expelled the Communist Party from the Reichstag (RIKES-tog) (parliament), intimidated it to give him dictatorial powers, and then put Nazis in charge of all government agencies, educational institutions, and professional organizations. He banned all other political parties and threw their leaders into concentration camps. The Nazis deprived Jews of their citizenship and civil rights, prohibited them from marrying "Aryans," ousted them from the professions, and confiscated their property. In August 1934, Hitler proclaimed himself *Führer* (FEW-rer) ("leader") and called Germany the "Third Reich" (empire)—the third after the Holy Roman Empire and the German Empire of 1871 to 1918.

The Nazis' economic and social policies were spectacularly effective. The government undertook massive public works projects. Businesses got contracts to manufacture weapons for the armed forces. Women, who had entered the work force during and after World War I, were urged to return to *"Kinder, Kirche, Küche"* (children, church, kitchen), releasing jobs for men. By 1936, business was booming, unemployment was at its lowest level since the 1920s, and living standards were rising. Hitler's popularity soared because most Germans believed their economic well-being outweighed the loss of liberty.

The Road to War, 1933–1939

Hitler sought not prosperity or popularity, but conquest. As soon as he came to office, he began to build up the armed forces with conquest in mind. Meanwhile, he tested the reactions of the other powers through a series of surprise moves followed by protestations of peaceful intent.

In 1933, Hitler withdrew Germany from the League of Nations. France and Britain hesitated to retaliate by blockading or invading Germany. Two years later, he announced that Germany was going to introduce conscription, build up its army, and create an air force—in violation of the Versailles treaty. Instead of protesting, Britain signed a naval agreement with Germany. The message was clear: neither Britain nor France was willing to risk war by standing up to Germany. The United States, absorbed in its own domestic economic problems, had reverted to isolationism.

Emboldened by the weakness of the democracies, Italy in 1935 invaded Ethiopia, one of only two independent states in Africa and a member of the League of Nations. The League and the democracies protested but refused to close the Suez Canal to Italian ships or impose an oil embargo. The following year, when Hitler sent troops into the Rhineland on the borders of France and Belgium, the other powers merely protested.

By 1938, Hitler decided his rearmament plans were far enough advanced that he could escalate his demands. In March, Germany invaded and soon annexed Austria, with little protest from its German-speaking citizens. Then came the turn of Czechoslovakia. Hitler demanded autonomy for its German-speaking borderlands, then their annexation. At the Munich Conference of September 1938, the leaders of France, Britain, and Italy gave Hitler everything he wanted to keep him from starting a war. Once again, Hitler learned that aggression paid off and that the democracies always gave in.

The democracies' policy of "appeasement" ran counter to the European balance-of-power tradition for three reasons. The first was the deep-seated fear of war among all people who had lived through World War I. The second was fear of communism. The conservative politicians who ruled France and Britain were more afraid of Stalin than of Hitler, for Hitler claimed to respect Christianity and private property. Rather than revive the pre–World War I alliance of Britain, France, and Russia, they sold out the Czechs. The third cause was the very novelty of fascist tactics. Britain's prime minister, Neville Chamberlain, assumed that political leaders (other than the Bolsheviks) were honorable men and that an agreement was as valid as a business contract. Thus, when Hitler said he had "no further territorial demands," Chamberlain believed him.

After Munich, it was too late to stop Hitler, short of war. Germany and Italy were now united in an alliance called the Axis. In March 1939, Germany invaded what was left of Czechoslovakia. Belatedly realizing that Hitler could not be trusted, France and Britain sought Soviet help. Stalin,

SECTION REVIEW

- In Italy, Mussolini exploited postwar frustrations and fears of communism to lead his Fascist Party to power.
- Although authoritarian rulers, the Fascists were poor administrators who were only adept at political theater.
- In Germany, Hitler also played upon postwar fears and resentments, promoting extreme nationalism and vicious anti-Semitism.
- The Depression enabled the Nazis to seize power, after which they initiated new economic and social policies, including the systematic persecution of Jews.
- Italian and German aggression and the democracies' appeasement policy pushed Europe toward war.
- War broke out with Germany's invasion of Poland in September 1939.

however, distrusted the "capitalists" as much as they distrusted him. Hitler, meanwhile, offered to divide Poland between Germany and the Soviet Union. On August 23, Stalin accepted. The Nazi-Soviet Pact freed Hitler from the fear of a two-front war and gave Stalin two more years of peace to build up his armies. One week later, on September 1, 1939, German forces swept into Poland across the Eastern Front. The war was on.

East Asia, 1931–1945

What were the economic reasons behind Japan's invasion of Manchuria?

When the Depression ruined Japan's export trade, ultranationalists, including young army officers, resented their country's dependence on foreign trade. If only Japan had a colonial empire, they thought, it would not be beholden to the rest of the world. But Europeans and Americans had already taken most potential colonies in Asia. Japan had only Korea, Taiwan, and a railroad in Manchuria. Japanese nationalists saw China, with its vast population and resources, as the solution to their country's problems.

The Manchurian Incident of 1931

Meanwhile, the Guomindang (gwo-min-dong) was becoming stronger in China and preparing to challenge the Japanese presence in Manchuria, a province rich in coal and iron ore. Junior officers in the Japanese army guarding the South Manchurian Railway, frustrated by the caution of their superiors, determined to take action. In September 1931, an explosion on a railroad track, probably staged, gave them an excuse to conquer the entire province. In Tokyo, weak civilian ministers acquiesced to the attack to avoid losing face and shortly recognized the "independence" of Manchuria under the name *Manchukuo* (man-CHEW-coo-oh).

The U.S. government condemned the Japanese conquest. The League of Nations refused to recognize Manchukuo and urged the Japanese to remove their troops from China. Persuaded that the Western powers would not fight, Japan resigned from the League.

During the next few years, the Japanese built railways and heavy industries in Manchuria and northeastern China and sped up their rearmament. The government grew more authoritarian, jailing thousands of dissidents. On several occasions, superpatriotic junior officers who mutinied or assassinated leading political figures received mild punishments, and generals and admirals sympathetic to their views replaced more moderate civilian politicians.

Chiang Kai-shek (1886–1975) Chinese military and political leader. He succeeded Sun Yat-sen as head of the Guomindang in 1925; headed the Chinese government from 1928 to 1948; fought against the Chinese communists and Japanese invaders. After 1949 he headed the Chinese Nationalist government in Taiwan.

The Chinese Communists and the Long March

Until the Japanese seized Manchuria, the Chinese government seemed to be consolidating its power and creating the conditions for a national recovery. The main challenge to the government of **Chiang Kai-shek** (chang kie-shek) came from the Chinese communists, who were organizing industrial workers and

Mao Zedong Addressing His Followers on the Long March

At the age of 40, Mao led his forces on the Long March from southern China to a safer location in the remote northwestern province of Shaanxi. Though only a small fraction of those who began the trek made it to the end, the ordeal kept the movement from being destroyed by the nationalist forces of Chiang Kai-shek and laid the groundwork for the communists' eventual takeover of the country after World War II.   (Bettmann/Corbis)

who worked in alliance with the Nationalists until 1927, when Chiang Kai-shek arrested and executed communists and labor leaders alike.

The few communists who escaped the mass arrests fled to the remote mountains of Jiangxi (jang-she), in southeastern China. Among them was **Mao Zedong** (ma-oh zay-dong) (1893–1976), a farmer's son who had left home to study philosophy.

In the early 1920s, Mao discovered the works of Karl Marx, joined the Communist Party, and soon became one of its leaders. In Jiangxi, Mao began studying conditions among the peasants, in whom communists had previously shown no interest. He planned to redistribute land from the wealthier to the poorer peasants, thereby gaining adherents for the coming struggle with the Guomindang army.

Mao's reliance on the peasantry was a radical departure from Marxist-Leninist ideology, which stressed the backwardness of the peasants and pinned its hopes on industrial workers. Mao was also an advocate of women's equality. Before 1927, the communists had organized the women who worked in Shanghai's textile mills, the most exploited of all Chinese workers. Later, in their mountain stronghold in Jiangxi, they organized women farmers, allowed divorce, and banned arranged marriages and footbinding.

Mao Zedong (1893–1976)
Leader of the Chinese Communist Party (1927–1976). He led the communists on the Long March (1934–1935) and rebuilt the Communist Party and Red Army during the Japanese occupation of China (1937–1945). After World War II, he led the communists to victory over the Guomindang. He ordered the Cultural Revolution in 1966.

The Guomindang army pursued the communists into the mountains, building small forts throughout the countryside. Rather than risk direct confrontations, Mao responded with guerrilla warfare. Government troops often mistreated civilians, but Mao insisted that his soldiers help the peasants, pay a fair price for food and supplies, and treat women with respect. In spite of their good relations with the peasants of Jiangxi, the communists decided to break out of the southern mountains and trek to Shaanxi (SHAWN-she), an even more remote province in northwestern China. The so-called **Long March** took them 6,000 miles (nearly 9,700 kilometers) in one year, 17 miles (27 kilometers) a day over desolate mountains and through swamps and deserts, pursued by the army and bombed by Chiang's aircraft. Of the 100,000 communists who left Jiangxi in October 1934, only 4,000 reached Shaanxi a year later.

Long March (1934–1935) The 6,000-mile (9,600-kilometer) flight of Chinese communists from southeastern to northwestern China. The communists, led by Mao Zedong, were pursued by the Chinese army under orders from Chiang Kai-shek. The four thousand survivors of the march formed the nucleus of a revived communist movement that defeated the Guomindang after World War II.

The Sino-Japanese War, 1937–1945

On July 7, 1937, Japanese troops attacked Chinese forces near Beijing. As in 1931, the junior officers who ordered the attack quickly obtained the support of their commanders and then, reluctantly, of the government. By November, Japanese troops had seized Beijing, Tianjin, Shanghai, and other coastal cities, and the Japanese navy had blockaded the entire coast of China.

Once again, the United States and the League of Nations denounced the Japanese atrocities. Yet the Western powers were too preoccupied with events in Europe and with their own economic problems to risk a military confrontation in Asia. When the Japanese sank a U.S. gunboat and shelled a British ship on the Yangzi River, the U.S. and British governments responded only with righteous indignation and pious resolutions.

The large Chinese armies were poorly led and armed and lost every battle. Within a year, Japan controlled the coastal provinces of China and the lower Yangzi and Yellow River Valleys, China's richest and most populated regions, but the Chinese people continued to resist, either in the army or, increasingly, with the communist guerrilla forces. Japan's periodic attempts to turn the tide by conquering one more piece of China only pushed Japan deeper into the quagmire.

Warfare between the Chinese and Japanese was incredibly violent. In the winter of 1937–1938, Japanese troops took Nanjing, raped 20,000 women, killed 200,000 prisoners and civilians, and looted and burned the city. To slow them down, Chiang ordered the Yellow River dikes blasted open, causing a flood that destroyed 4,000 villages, killed 890,000 people, and made 12.5 million homeless. Two years later, when the communists ordered a massive offensive, the Japanese retaliated with a "kill all, burn all, loot all" campaign, destroying hundreds of villages down to the last person, building, and farm animal.

The Chinese government, led by Chiang Kai-shek, escaped to the mountains of Sichuan in the center of the country. There he built up a huge army, both to fight Japan and to prepare for a future confrontation with the communists. The army drafted over 3 million men, even though it had only a million rifles and could not provide food or clothing for all its soldiers. The Guomindang raised farmers' taxes, even when famine forced farmers to eat

SECTION REVIEW

- The collapse of Japan's export trade prompted ultranationalists into imperialist designs on China.

- Japanese officers in Manchuria used a railway incident to conquer the resource-rich province.

- Using Manchurian resources, Japan rearmed, and in the process became more militaristic and authoritarian.

- Chinese communists fled Guomindang attacks and, under Mao, won the support of peasants and women.

- During their guerrilla war against the Guomindang, Mao's communists undertook the Long March.

- Japanese aggression sparked the brutal Sino-Japanese War, during which the Chinese communists offered the most effective resistance.

the bark of trees. Such taxes were not enough to support both a large army and the thousands of government officials and hangers-on who had fled to Sichuan. To avoid taxing its wealthy supporters, the government printed money, causing inflation, hoarding, and corruption.

From his capital of Yan'an in Shaanxi province, Mao also built up his army and formed a government. Unlike the Guomindang, the communists listened to the grievances of the peasants, especially the poor, to whom they distributed land confiscated from wealthy landowners. Because they could present themselves as the only group in China that was serious about fighting the Japanese, the communists obtained support and intelligence from farmers in Japanese-occupied territory.

THE SECOND WORLD WAR

How was the war fought, and why did Japan and Germany lose?

The Second World War was much bigger and deadlier than the first in every way. It was fought around the world, from Norway to New Guinea, from Hawaii to Egypt, and on every ocean. It was a total war that showed how effectively industry, science, and nationalism could be channeled into mass destruction.

The War of Movement Defensive maneuvers had dominated in World War I. In World War II, motorized weapons gave back the advantage to the offensive. Opposing forces moved fast, their victories hinging as much on the aggressive spirit of their commanders and the military intelligence they obtained as on numbers of troops or firepower.

The Wehrmacht (VAIR-mokt), or German armed forces, was the first to learn this lesson. It not only had tanks, trucks, and fighter planes but also had perfected their combined use in a tactic called *blitzkrieg* (BLITS-creeg) (lightning war): fighter planes scattered enemy troops and disrupted communications, and tanks punctured the enemy's defenses and then, with the help of the infantry, encircled and captured enemy troops. At sea, the navies of both Japan and the United States had developed aircraft carriers that could launch planes against targets hundreds of miles away.

The very size and mobility of the opposing forces made the fighting far different from any the world had ever seen. Countries were conquered in a matter of days or weeks. The belligerents mobilized the economies of entire continents, squeezing them for every possible resource. They tried not only to defeat their enemies' armed forces but—by means of blockades, submarine attacks on shipping, and bombing raids on industrial areas—to damage the economies that supported those armed forces. They thought of civilians not as innocent bystanders but as legitimate targets and, later, as vermin to be exterminated.

War in Europe and North Africa It took less than a month for the Wehrmacht to conquer Poland. Britain and France declared war on Germany but took no military action. Meanwhile, the Soviet Union invaded eastern Poland and the Baltic republics of Lithuania, Latvia, and Estonia. Although the Poles fought bravely, the Polish infantry and cavalry were no match for German or Russian tanks. During the winter of 1939–1940, Germany and the Western democracies faced each other in what soldiers called a "phony war" and watched as the Soviet Union attacked Finland, which resisted for many months.

In April 1940, Hitler went on the offensive again, conquering Denmark, Norway, the Netherlands, and Belgium in less than two months. In May, he attacked France. Although the French army had as many soldiers, tanks, and aircraft as the Wehrmacht, its morale was low, and it quickly collapsed. By the end of June, Hitler was master of all of Europe between Russia and Spain.

Germany still had to face one enemy: Britain. The British had no army to speak of, but they had other assets: the English Channel, the Royal Navy and Air Force, and a tough new prime minister, Winston Churchill. The Germans knew they could invade Britain only by gaining control of the airspace over the Channel, so they launched a massive air attack—the Battle of Britain—lasting from June through September. They failed, however, because the Royal Air Force had better fighters and used radar and code breaking to detect approaching German planes (see Environment and Technology: The Enigma Machine).

Frustrated, Hitler turned his attention eastward against the Soviet Union. Within five months, the Wehrmacht conquered the Baltic states, Ukraine, and half of European Russia; captured a million prisoners of war; and stood at the very gates of Moscow and Leningrad (now St. Petersburg). The USSR seemed on the verge of collapse when suddenly the weather turned cold, machines froze, and the fighting came to a halt. Like Napoleon, Hitler had ignored the environment of Russia at his peril.

The next spring, the Wehrmacht renewed its offensive. It surrounded Leningrad in a siege that was to cost a million lives. Leaving Moscow aside, it turned toward the Caucasus and its oil wells. In August, the Germans attacked **Stalingrad** (now Volgograd), the key to the Volga River and the supply of oil. For months, German and Soviet soldiers fought over every street and every house. When winter came, the Red Army counterattacked and encircled the city. In February 1943, the remnants of the German army in Stalingrad surrendered. Hitler had lost his greatest gamble (see Map 26.1).

From Europe, the war spread to Africa. During 1941, British forces conquered Italian East Africa and invaded Libya as well. The Italian rout in North Africa brought the Germans to their rescue. During 1942, the German army and the forces of the British Empire seesawed back and forth across the deserts of Libya and Egypt. Because the British could decode German messages and had more weapons and supplies, they were finally able to expel the Germans from Africa in May 1943.

Stalingrad City in Russia, site of a Red Army victory over the German army in 1942–1943. The Battle of Stalingrad was the turning point in the war between Germany and the Soviet Union. Today it is known as Volgograd.

War in Asia and the Pacific

The war presented Japan with the opportunity to take over European colonies in Southeast Asia, with their abundant oil, rubber, and other strategic materials. After Japanese forces occupied French Indochina in September 1940, the United States and Britain cut off shipments of steel, scrap iron, oil, and other products that Japan desperately needed. This left Japan with three alternatives: accept the shame and humiliation of giving up its conquests, as the Americans insisted; face economic ruin; or widen the war. Japan chose war.

ENVIRONMENT + TECHNOLOGY

The Enigma Machine

Since ancient times, governments and armies have used various methods of encrypting messages, that is, making them unreadable to people who do not possess the proper code (words replaced by other words using a codebook) or cipher (letters replaced by numbers). The introduction of radio, which could be easily monitored by agents of foreign powers, turned cryptography (secret writing) into a necessity of diplomacy and war. Yet encrypting and decrypting messages required expert code clerks and took time. Furthermore, since each nation used several codes and ciphers and changed them periodically, a breakthrough in one code or cipher did not necessarily make other messages easier to decrypt.

After World War I, inventors in several countries set out to create machines that could encrypt and decrypt messages automatically while also making them harder to crack than manual codes and ciphers. The invention that was most successful was the Enigma, first produced by a German company in 1923. It consisted of a typewriter keyboard, a set of rotors containing electrical wires and contacts, and a series of lights marked with letters. When the operator entered a letter on the keyboard, an electrical current went through the rotors and lit up a letter different from the one entered. With each keystroke, the rotors also turned, so that the next time the same key was pushed, a different light went on. At the receiving end, if the operator had set his rotors in the same pattern as the sender, entering the encrypted letters on the keyboard lit up the letters of the original plaintext. Anyone who had an Enigma but was not privy to the rotor settings and attempted to read an encrypted message would have to try an almost infinite number of settings. This might take months or years, by which time the information would no longer have any value.

As war approached, the German armed forces purchased thousands of Enigma machines, each the size of a portable typewriter. They accompanied ships at sea, frontline troops, and squadrons of airplanes. The Germans considered their cipher unbreakable and their secrets safe from enemy eyes. They were wrong. Before the war began, Polish cryptanalysts had figured out how the Enigma worked and built some replicas. They also devised an electromechanical device they called "bomba" that went through rotor settings at blazing speed until it encountered an expres-

sion, such as "Heil Hitler," that often appeared in German messages. When the war broke out, they fled to France. From there, the secret of the bomba passed to British cryptanalysts at a secret installation at Bletchley Park, north of London.

With this breakthrough, the British were able to read many Luftwaffe signals during the Battle of Britain in 1940. Cracking the German navy and army Enigmas proved to be much more difficult, for the other services used more rotors, changed the settings more frequently, and, most importantly, learned to avoid stock phrases. Nonetheless, by the spring of 1942, Bletchley Park had a staff of 1,500 handling some 40,000 German military messages a month. Their ability to read German messages was instrumental in the Allied victories against General Rommel in North Africa in 1942 and against the German U-boats in the Battle of the Atlantic in 1943.

THE ENIGMA MACHINE During World War II, German armed forces used Enigma machines like the one seen here in the vehicle of a German tank commander. With Enigmas, they could encrypt and decrypt radio messages, keeping them secret (they believed) from enemy code-breakers.
(Courtesy, Brian Johnson)

723

Map 26.1   World War II in Europe and North Africa

In a series of quick and decisive campaigns from September 1939 to December 1941, German forces overran much of Europe and North Africa. There followed three years of bitter fighting as the Allies slowly pushed the Germans back. This map shows the maximum extent of Germany's conquests and alliances, as well as the key battles and the front lines at various times.   **CL** Interactive Map

Legend:
- Hitler's Greater Germany
- Allied with Germany
- Occupied by Germany and its allies
- Grand Alliance
- Neutral nations
- X Major battles

Map labels:

Battle of Britain, fall 1940

German surrender: Reims, May 7, 1945; Berlin, May 8, 1945

Battle of the Bulge, Dec. 1944

Invasion of Normandy, June 6, 1944

Western front, Feb. 1945

Rhine Crossing, March 7, 1945

Axis troops occupy Vichy France, Nov. 10 and 11, 1942

Allies land in Provence, Aug. 15, 1944

Russian front, Feb. 1945

Siege of Leningrad, Sept. 1941–Jan. 1944

Russian front, spring 1944

Russian front, Dec. 1941

Russian front, Nov. 1942

Siege of Stalingrad, Aug. 21, 1942–Jan. 31, 1943

Italian front, Feb. 1945

Monte Casino, May 1944

Salerno, Sept. 1943

Sicily, July 1943

Allies invade Sicily and Italy, July–Sept. 1943

Rommel defeated in Tunisia; Axis troops evacuated, May 1943

El Alamein, summer 1942

Casablanca, Nov. 1942

400 Mi.
400 Km.
200
0

German Dive-Bomber over Eastern Europe

In this painting, a German ME-100 fighter plane attacks a Soviet troop convoy on the Eastern Front.   (akg-images)

 HISTORY IN FOCUS What does this image tell you about the effect—material and psychological—of the German blitzkrieg tactics? *Find the answer online.*

On December 7, 1941, Japanese planes bombed the U.S. naval base at **Pearl Harbor**, Hawaii, sinking or damaging scores of warships. Then, between December 1941 and March 1942, the Japanese bombed Singapore and occupied Thailand, the Philippines, and Malaya. Within a few months, they occupied all of Southeast Asia and the Dutch East Indies. The Japanese claimed to be liberating the inhabitants of these lands from European colonialism. But they soon began to confiscate food and raw materials and demand heavy labor from the inhabitants, whom they treated with contempt. Those who protested were brutally punished.

The entry of the United States into the war, in alliance with Britain and the Soviet Union, challenged Japan's dream of an East Asian empire. In April 1942, American planes bombed Tokyo. In May, the United States Navy defeated a Japanese fleet in the Coral Sea, ending Japanese plans to conquer Australia. A month later, at the **Battle of Midway**, Japan lost four of its six largest aircraft carriers. Japan did not have enough industry to replace them, for its war production was only one-tenth that of the United States. In the vastness of the Pacific Ocean, aircraft carriers held the key to victory, and without them, Japan faced a long and hopeless war (see Map 26.2).

Pearl Harbor Naval base in Hawaii attacked by Japanese aircraft on December 7, 1941. The sinking of much of the U.S. Pacific Fleet brought the United States into World War II.

Battle of Midway U.S. naval victory over the Japanese fleet in June 1942, in which the Japanese lost four of their best aircraft carriers. It marked a turning point in World War II.

The End of the War

Its new American ally also helped the Soviet Union capitalize on the advantage it had won in the Battle of Stalingrad. Aided by a growing stream of supplies from factories in

Map 26.2   World War II in Asia and the Pacific

Interactive Map

After having conquered much of China between 1937 and 1941, Japanese forces launched a sudden attack on Southeast Asia, Indonesia, and the Pacific in late 1941 and early 1942. American forces slowly reconquered the Pacific islands and the Philippines until August 1945, when the atomic bombing of Hiroshima and Nagasaki forced Japan's surrender.

the United States, the Red Army began pushing the Wehrmacht back toward Germany.

The Western powers, meanwhile, staged two invasions of Europe. Beginning in July 1943, they captured Sicily and invaded Italy. Mussolini resigned, and Italy signed an armistice, but German troops held off the Allied advance for two years. Then on D-day (June 6, 1944), 156,000 British, American, and Canadian troops landed on the coast of Normandy in western France. Within a week, the Allies had more troops in France than Germany did. To meet this growing force, Hitler had to transfer part of

Hiroshima After the Atomic Bomb
On August 6, 1945, an atomic bomb destroyed the city, killing over fifty thousand people. This photo shows the devastation of the city center, where only a few concrete buildings remained standing.   (Bettmann/Corbis)

the Wehrmacht from the Eastern Front. Despite advancing armies on three sides, Germany held out for almost a year. On May 7, 1945, a week after Hitler committed suicide, German military leaders surrendered.

By June 1944, U.S. bombers were also attacking Japan from newly captured island bases in the Pacific, and U.S. submarines were sinking larger numbers of Japanese merchant ships, gradually cutting off Japan's oil and other raw materials. After May 1945, with the Japanese air force grounded for lack of fuel, U.S. planes began destroying Japanese shipping, industries, and cities at will.

On August 6, 1945, the United States dropped an atomic bomb on **Hiroshima**, killing some 80,000 people in a flash and leaving about 120,000 more to die agonizing deaths from burns and radiation. Three days later, another atomic bomb destroyed Nagasaki. On August 14, Japan offered to surrender, and Emperor Hirohito gave the order to lay down arms. Two weeks later, Japanese leaders signed the terms of surrender. The war was officially over.

CL Primary Source: The Decision to Use the Atomic Bomb   *Learn about some of the considerations that went into the U.S. decision to use the atomic bomb and reflections on that decision after the fact.*

Hiroshima City in Japan, the first to be destroyed by an atomic bomb, on August 6, 1945. The bombing hastened the end of World War II.

Chinese Civil War and Communist Victory

The Japanese surrender also meant the end of Japanese occupation of much of China, but instead of bringing peace, it marked an intensification of the contest between the Guomindang and the communists. Guomindang forces started with many advantages: more troops and weapons, U.S. support, and control of China's cities. But

SECTION REVIEW

- Unlike World War I, World War II was a mobile, offensive war, of which Germany was the first effective practitioner.

- Germany quickly conquered most of continental Europe but failed to subdue Britain.

- Soviet troops halted Germany's invasion at Stalingrad, and Britain drove German forces from North Africa.

- Despite initial successes, Japan lost critical battles, particularly Midway, and never could match U.S. war production.

- With the help of vital U.S. resources, the Western powers defeated Germany, while the United States pressed Japan, dropping two atomic bombs to force its surrender.

- In China, Mao's communists won the civil war with the Guomindang by gaining support from the people.

their behavior eroded whatever popular support they had. They taxed the people they "liberated" more heavily than the Japanese had, looted businesses, confiscated supplies, and enriched themselves at the expense of the population. To pay its bills, Chiang's government printed money so fast that it soon lost all its value, ruining merchants and causing hoarding and shortages. In the countryside, the Guomindang's brutality alienated the peasants.

In contrast, the communists' land reform programs had won them popular support, which was even more important than the heavy equipment brought by Guomindang soldiers, who began deserting by the thousands, and the Japanese equipment seized by the Soviets in the last weeks of the war. By 1949, the Guomindang armies were collapsing everywhere, defeated more by their own greed and ineptness than by the communists. As the communists advanced, high-ranking members of the Guomindang fled to Taiwan, protected from the mainland by the United States Navy. On October 1, 1949, Mao Zedong announced the founding of the People's Republic of China.

THE CHARACTER OF WARFARE

How did science and technology change the nature of warfare?

The war left an enormous death toll. Recent estimates place the figure at close to 60 million deaths, six to eight times more than in World War I. Over half of the dead were civilian victims of massacres, famines, or bombs. The Soviet Union lost between 20 and 25 million people, more than any other country. China suffered 15 million deaths; Poland lost some 6 million, of whom half were Jewish; the Jewish people lost another 3 million outside Poland. Over 4 million Germans and over 2 million Japanese died. In much of the world, almost every family mourned one or more of its members. In contrast, Great Britain lost 400,000 people, the United States 300,000.

One reason for the terrible toll in human lives and suffering was a change in moral values, as belligerents identified not just soldiers but entire peoples as enemies. Another reason for the devastation was the appearance of new technologies that carried destruction deep into enemy territory far beyond the traditional battlefields.

The War of Science   Scientists made many contributions to the technology of warfare. Chemists found ways to make synthetic rubber from coal or oil. Physicists perfected radar, which warned of approaching enemy aircraft and submarines. Others broke enemy codes and developed antibiotics that saved the lives of countless wounded soldiers.

Aircraft development was especially striking. As war approached, German, British, and Japanese aircraft manufacturers developed fast, maneuverable fighter planes. U.S. industry produced aircraft of every sort but was especially noted for its heavy bombers designed to fly in huge formations and drop tons of bombs on enemy cities. The Japanese developed the Mitsubishi "Zero" fighter plane—light, fast, and agile.

Unable to produce heavy planes in large numbers, Germany responded with radically new designs, including the first jet fighters, low-flying buzz bombs, and fearful V-2 missiles.

In October 1939, President Roosevelt received a letter from physicist Albert Einstein, a Jewish refugee from Nazism, warning of the dangers of nuclear power. Fearing that Germany might develop a nuclear bomb first, Roosevelt placed the vast resources of the U.S. government at the disposal of physicists and engineers, both Americans and refugees from Europe. By 1945, they had built two atomic bombs, each one powerful enough to annihilate an entire city.

Bombing Raids

The Germans began the war from the air, but it was the British and Americans who excelled at large-scale urban bombardment. Since it was very hard to pinpoint individual buildings, especially at night, such raids were aimed at weakening the morale of the civilian population.

In May 1942, 1,000 British planes dropped incendiary bombs on Cologne, setting fire to most of the old city. Between July 24 and August 2, 1943, 3,330 British and Americans bombers set fire to Hamburg, killing 50,000 people. Later raids destroyed Berlin, Dresden, and other German cities. All in all, the bombing raids against Germany killed 600,000 people—more than half of them women and children—and injured 800,000. If the air strategists had hoped thereby to break the morale of the German people, they failed. The only effective bombing raids were those directed against oil depots and synthetic fuel plants; by early 1945, they had almost brought the German war effort to a standstill.

American bombing raids on Japanese cities were even more devastating than the fire-bombing of German cities, for Japanese cities were built of wood. In March 1945, a large raid set Tokyo ablaze, killing 80,000 people and leaving a million homeless. Five months later, single atomic bombs did something similar.

The Holocaust

The Nazis killed defenseless civilians on an even larger scale. Their murders were not the byproducts of some military goal but a calculated policy of extermination.

Their first targets were Jews. Soon after Hitler came to power, he deprived German Jews of their citizenship and legal rights. When eastern Europe fell under Nazi rule, the Nazis herded its large Jewish population into ghettos in the major cities, where many died of starvation and disease. Then, in early 1942, the Nazis decided to carry out Hitler's "final solution to the Jewish problem" by applying modern industrial methods to the slaughter of human beings. German companies built huge extermination camps in eastern Europe. Every day, trainloads of cattle cars arrived at the camps and disgorged thousands of captives and the corpses of those who had died of starvation or asphyxiation along the way. The strongest survivors were put to work and fed almost nothing until they died. Women, children, the elderly, and the sick were shoved into gas chambers and asphyxiated with poison gas. **Auschwitz**, the biggest camp, was a giant industrial complex designed to kill up to twelve thousand people a day. Most horrifying of all were the tortures inflicted on prisoners

Primary Source: Memoirs *Read the words of Rudolph Hoss, commandant at Auschwitz, as he describes his initial reaction to the order to "annihilate all the Jews" and his feelings as the process commenced, progressed, and finally came to an end.*

Auschwitz Nazi extermination camp in Poland, the largest center of mass murder during the Holocaust. Close to a million Jews, Gypsies, Communists, and others were killed there.

U.S. Army Medics and Holocaust Victims
At the end of World War II, Allied troops entered the Nazi concentration camps, where they found the bodies of thousands of victims of the Holocaust. In this picture, taken at Dachau in southern Germany, two U.S. Army medics are overseeing a truckload of corpses to be taken to a burial site.   (Hulton-Deutsch Collection/Corbis)

selected by Nazi doctors for "medical experiments." This mass extermination, now called the **Holocaust** ("burning"), claimed some 6 million Jewish lives.

Besides the Jews, the Nazis also killed 3 million Polish Catholics—especially professionals, army officers, and the educated—in an effort to reduce the Polish people to slavery. They also exterminated homosexuals, Jehovah's Witnesses, Gypsies, the disabled, and the mentally ill—all in the interests of "racial purity." Whenever a German was killed in an occupied country, the Nazis retaliated by burning a village with all its inhabitants. After the invasion of Russia, the Wehrmacht was given orders to execute all captured communists, government employees, and officers. They also worked millions of prisoners of war to death or let them die of starvation.

Holocaust Nazis' program during World War II to kill people they considered undesirable. Some 6 million Jews perished during the Holocaust, along with millions of Poles, Gypsies, communists, socialists, and others.

The Home Front

Rapid military movements and air power carried the war to people's homes in China, Japan, Southeast Asia, and Europe. Armies swept through the land, confiscating food, fuel, and anything else of value. Bombers and heavy artillery pounded cities into rubble, leaving only the skeletons of buildings, while survivors cowered in cellars. Air-raid sirens awakened people throughout the night. Millions fled their homes in terror. Of all the major belligerents, only Americans escaped such nightmares, and war production ended the deprivations of the Depression years.

The war demanded an enormous production effort from civilians. In the face of advancing Germans in 1941, the Soviets dismantled over fifteen hundred factories and rebuilt them in the Ural Mountains and Siberia, where workers soon turned out more tanks and artillery than the Axis. American factories produced an unending supply of ships, aircraft, trucks, tanks, and other materiel for the Allied effort. The Axis powers could not compete with this vast outpouring.

With so many men mobilized for war, women were responsible for much of this production. For example, 6 million women entered the American labor force during the war, 2.5 million of them in manufacturing jobs previously considered "men's work." Soviet women took over half of all industrial and three-quarters of all agricultural jobs. In the other belligerent countries, women also played a major role in the war effort, replacing men in fields, factories, and offices. The Nazis, in contrast, believed that German women should stay home and bear children, and they imported 7 million "guest workers"—a euphemism for war prisoners and captured foreigners.

War and the Environment

As in World War I, battles scarred the landscape, leaving behind spent ammunition and damaged equipment. Retreating armies flooded large areas of China and the Netherlands. The bombing of cities left ruins that remained visible for a generation or more. The main cause of environmental stress, however, was not the fighting but the economic development that sustained it.

As war industries boomed—the United States increased its industrial production fourfold during the war—so did the demand for raw materials. Mining companies opened new mines and towns in Central Africa to supply strategic minerals. Brazil, Argentina, and other Latin American countries deprived of manufactured imports began building their own steel mills, factories, and shipyards. In India, China, and Europe, timber felling accelerated far beyond forest regrowth.

We must keep the environmental effects of the war in perspective. From the vantage point of the present, the environmental impact of the war seems quite modest in comparison with the damage inflicted on the earth by the long consumer boom that began in the post–World War II years.

SECTION REVIEW

- New technologies and shifts in moral values were responsible for the war's huge death toll.
- Scientists pioneered many military technologies, including new aircraft and nuclear weapons.
- Britain and the United States perfected the large-scale bombing raid, devastating German and Japanese cities.
- The Nazis carried out programs of systematic extermination, killing mainly Jews but also members of other groups deemed inferior.
- Civilian populations, particularly women, endured both the horrors of warfare and the demands of wartime production.
- Battles and growing war industries scarred the environment; the demand for raw materials reached into Africa and Latin America.

Chapter Review

 DOWNLOAD THE MP3 AUDIO FILE OF THE CHAPTER REVIEW TO LISTEN TO ON THE GO.

How did the Soviet Union change under Stalin, and at what cost? *(page 709)*

After the Great War ended, the world seemed to return to its prewar state, but it was an illusion. In the Soviet Union, Joseph Stalin was determined to turn his country into a modern industrial state at breakneck speed, regardless of the human cost. Several million people—most of them peasants—died and millions more were enslaved during the Five-Year Plans and the collectivization of agriculture, and by 1941 Soviet industry was much better prepared for a war with Germany than it had been in 1914–1917.

What caused the Depression, and what effects did it have on the world? *(page 713)*

In 1929, after a few years of prosperity, excessive speculation based on shaky loans caused the New York stock market to collapse; within a few months, the

KEY TERMS

Joseph Stalin *(p. 709)*
Five-Year Plans *(p. 709)*
Benito Mussolini *(p. 715)*
Fascist Party *(p. 715)*
Adolf Hitler *(p. 715)*
Nazis *(p. 715)*
Chiang Kai-shek *(p. 718)*
Mao Zedong *(p. 719)*
Long March *(p. 720)*
Stalingrad *(p. 722)*
Pearl Harbor *(p. 725)*
Battle of Midway *(p. 725)*
Hiroshima *(p. 727)*
Auschwitz *(p. 729)*
Holocaust *(p. 730)*

world economy fell into the Great Depression, which threw millions out of work, not only in the industrial nations but also throughout the world. Countries such as France and Britain survived the Depression by making their colonial empires purchase their products. Countries that were dependent on exports, such as Germany and Japan, suffered more. Only the USSR and southern Africa, where gold became more valuable, boomed during the 1930s.

How did fascism in Italy and Germany lead to the Second World War? (page 714)

In Italy, the government that was already fascist became more tyrannical. Mussolini installed Fascist Party members in all government jobs and jailed anyone who criticized him. In Germany, economic collapse led people to entrust their government to Adolf Hitler and his Nazi followers, who quickly set to work establishing a totalitarian government. Nazi Germany's rebuilding of its military and its invasion of Austria and Czechoslovakia were greeted with a policy of appeasement by Western democracies, until finally they could no longer overlook Germany's intentions.

What were the economic reasons behind Japan's invasion of Manchuria? (page 718)

The Depression hit Japan hard because the worldwide demand for silk and rice collapsed. Japan saw China as a potential new colony with a vast population and resources to help solve its economic problems. In 1931, Japan conquered Manchuria and proceeded to build railways and heavy industries there. The United States and the League of Nations protested but did little else. The Sino-Japanese War, which began with the Japanese invasion of Beijing in 1937, was a long and brutal war that became a drain on the Japanese economy and resources. Meanwhile, the communists, led by Mao Zedong, were slowly gaining support in the Chinese countryside.

How was the war fought, and why did Japan and Germany lose? (page 721)

Italy conquered Ethiopia in 1935, and Japan attacked China in 1937, while the Western democracies disapproved but took no action. The war spread to Europe in 1939 when Germany conquered Poland, then Denmark, Norway, the Low Countries, and, in 1940, France. The war turned global when Germany invaded the Soviet Union and Japan attacked the United States in 1941. The Allies won because of Russia's hard fighting and its victory at Stalingrad; the Allies' overwhelming materiel resources, especially those of the United States; the invasion of D-Day, which put enough men on the European continent to finally drive back Germany; and U.S. naval victories in the Pacific and its use of atomic weapons against Japan.

How did science and technology change the nature of warfare? (page 728)

The Second World War was by far the deadliest and most horrific in history. Modern mechanized forces swept across entire nations and oceans. Their tar-

WEB RESOURCES

Pronunciation Guide

Interactive Maps

MAP 26.1 World War II in Europe and North Africa

MAP 26.2 World War II in Asia and the Pacific

Primary Sources

The Centerpiece of Nazi Racial Legislation: The Nuremberg Laws

Speech to the National Socialist Women's Association

The Decision to Use the Atomic Bomb

Memoirs

Answer to the History in Focus Question

See photo on page 725, "German Dive-Bomber over Eastern Europe."

Plus

Chapter Objectives

ACE multiple-choice quiz

Flashcards

gets were not only each other's armed forces, but their civilian populations as well. Though Germany had considerable scientific and technical talent, the war favored the nations with the most heavy industries, namely, the United States and the Soviet Union. The Allies destroyed German and Japanese cities with fire-bombs, and the United States dropped atomic bombs on Hiroshima and Nagasaki. Of the roughly 60 million people who died in the war, most of them were civilians.

SUGGESTED READING

Bianco, Lucien. *Origins of the Chinese Revolution, 1915–1949.* 1971. Covers the warlord and Guomindang periods.

Burleigh, Michael. *Third Reich: A New History.* 2000. An excellent recent interpretation.

Conquest, Robert. *The Great Terror: A Reassessment.* 1990. Describes the purges of the 1930s.

Dawidowicz, Lucy. *The War Against the Jews, 1933–1945.* 2d ed. 1986. A study of the Holocaust.

De Grand, Alexander. *Italian Fascism: Its Origins and Development.* 2d ed. 1989. Provides an excellent interpretation of fascism.

Dower, John. *War Without Mercy: Race and Power in the Pacific War.* 1987. A seminal work on the war with Japan.

Fitzpatrick, Sheila. *Stalin's Peasants: Resistance and Survival in the Russian Village After Collectivization.* 1994. Agriculture under Stalin.

Higonnet, Margaret, et al., eds. *Behind the Lines: Gender and the Two World Wars.* 1987. Discusses the role of women in the war.

Irokawa, Daikichi. *The Age of Hirohito: In Search of Modern Japan.* 1995. The best recent book on Japan in the twentieth century.

Kotkin, Stephen. *Magnetic Mountain: Stalinism as Civilization.* 1995. The Stalin era as seen from an industrial city.

Latham, A. J. H. *The Depression and the Developing World, 1914–1939.* 1981. Offers a global perspective on economic history.

McElvaine, Robert. *The Great Depression: America, 1929–1941.* 1984. Sophisticated economic analyses of the Depression.

Medvedev, Roy. *Let History Judge: The Origins and Consequences of Stalinism.* 1989. On the transformation of the USSR.

Rhodes, Richard. *The Making of the Atomic Bomb.* 1986. A long but fascinating account of the scientific side of warfare.

Spector, Ronald. *Eagle Against the Sun.* 1988. A highly readable account of the war in Asia and the Pacific.

Weinberg, Gerhard. *A World at Arms: A Global History of World War II.* 1994. A recent detailed treatment.

CHAPTER 27

Striving for Independence: India, Africa, and Latin America

1900–1949

CHAPTER PREVIEW

The Indian Independence Movement, 1905–1947
Why did the educated elites of India want independence? What were ordinary Indians hoping for?

Sub-Saharan Africa, 1900–1945
What changes did foreign rule bring to Africa, and how did Africans respond?

Mexico, Argentina, and Brazil, 1900–1949
What could Latin Americans do to achieve social justice and economic development? Were these two goals compatible?

Comparative Perspectives

DIVERSITY AND DOMINANCE: A Vietnamese Nationalist Denounces French Colonialism

Modern technologies, such as mass transit, airlines, and radio systems, first appeared in the wealthier countries of Europe and North America. When they were transferred to Asia, Africa, and Latin America, they reinforced the dependence of these less developed parts of the world on the industrialized countries and widened the gap between their social classes. The tensions of modernization contributed to popular movements for independence and social justice.

The previous two chapters focused on a world convulsed by war and revolution. The world wars involved Europe, East Asia, the Middle East, and the United States, and they sparked violent revolutions in Russia and China. They accelerated the development of aviation, electronics, nuclear power, and other technologies. Although these momentous events dominate

 This icon will direct you to the website where you can Prepare for Class, Improve Your Grade, and Ace the Test: college.cengage.com/pic/bullietbrief4e

the history of the first half of the twentieth century, parts of the world that were little touched by war also underwent profound changes in this period, partly for internal reasons and partly because of the warfare and revolution in other parts of the world.

In this chapter we examine the changes that took place in India, in sub-Saharan Africa, and in three major countries of Latin America—Mexico, Brazil, and Argentina. These three regions represent three very distinct cultures, yet they had much in common. India and Africa were colonies of Europe, both politically and economically. Though politically independent, the Latin American republics were dependent on Europe and the United States for the sale of raw materials and commodities and for imports of manufactured goods, technology, and capital. In all three regions independence movements tried to wrest control from distant foreigners and improve the livelihood of their peoples. Their success was partial at best.

THE INDIAN INDEPENDENCE MOVEMENT, 1905–1947

Why did the educated elites of India want independence? What were ordinary Indians hoping for?

Under British rule the Indian subcontinent acquired many of the trappings of Western-style economic development, such as railroads, harbors, modern cities, and cotton and steel mills, as well as an active and worldly middle class. The economic transformation of the region awakened in this educated middle class a sense of national dignity that demanded political fulfillment. In response, the British gradually granted India limited political autonomy while maintaining overall control. Religious and communal tensions among the Indian peoples were carefully papered over under British rule. Violent conflicts tore India apart after the withdrawal of the British in 1947.

The Land and the People

Despite periodic famines, notably between 1896 and 1900 when 2 million people died of starvation, the Indian population grew from 250 million in 1900 to 319 million in 1921 and 389 million in 1941. This growth caused landless young men to converge on the cities, exceeding the number of jobs available in the slowly expanding industries. To produce timber for construction and railroad ties, and to clear land for tea and rubber plantations, government foresters cut down most of the tropical hardwood forests that had covered the subcontinent in the nineteenth century. In spite of deforestation and extensive irrigation, the amount of land available per peasant family shrank with each successive generation.

Economic development—what the British called the "moral and material progress of India"—hardly benefited the average Indian. Peasants, always the great majority, paid rents to the landowner, interest to the village moneylender, and taxes to the government and had little left to improve their land or raise their standard of living. The government protected property owners, from village moneylenders all the way up to the maharajahs (mah-huh-RAH-juh), or ruling princes, who owned huge tracts of land. The cities were crowded with craftsmen, traders, and workers of all sorts, most very poor. Although the British had banned the burning of widows on their husbands' funeral pyres, in other respects women's lives changed little under British rule.

The peoples of India spoke many different languages: Hindi in the north, Tamil in the south, Bengali in the east, Gujerati around Bombay, Urdu in the northwest, and dozens of others. As a result of British rule and increasing trade and travel, English became, like Latin in medieval Europe, the common medium of communication of the Western-educated middle class. This new class of English-speaking government bureaucrats, professionals, and merchants was to play a leading role in the independence movement.

The majority of Indians practiced Hinduism and were subdivided into hundreds of castes, each affiliated with a particular occupation. Hinduism discouraged intermarriage and other social interactions among the castes and with people who were not Hindus. Muslims constituted one-quarter of the people of India but formed a majority in the northwest and in eastern Bengal. Muslim rulers had dominated northern and central India until they were displaced by the British in the eighteenth century. More reluctant than Hindus to learn English, Muslims felt discriminated against by both British and Hindus.

British Rule and Indian Nationalism

Colonial India was ruled by a viceroy appointed by the British government and administered by a few thousand members of the highly dutiful Indian Civil Service. Drawn mostly from the English gentry, they liked to think of India as a land of lords and peasants. They believed it was their duty to protect the Indian people from the dangers of industrialization, while defending their own positions from Indian nationalists.

As Europeans they admired modern technology but tried to control its introduction into India so as to maximize the benefits to Britain and to themselves. For example, they encouraged railroads, harbors, telegraphs, and other communications technologies, as well as irrigation and plantations, because these increased India's foreign trade and strengthened British control. At the same time, they discouraged the cotton and steel industries and limited the training of Indian engineers, ostensibly to spare India the social upheavals that had accompanied the Industrial Revolution in Europe, while actually protecting British industry from Indian competition.

At the turn of the century the majority of Indians accepted British rule. But the Europeans' racist attitude toward dark-skinned people increasingly offended a limited number of Indians who had learned English and absorbed English ideas of freedom and representative government, only to discover that thinly disguised racial quotas excluded them from the Indian Civil Service, the officer corps, and prestigious country clubs.

In 1885 a small group of English-speaking Hindu professionals founded a political organization called the **Indian National Congress**. For twenty years its members respectfully petitioned the government for access to the higher administrative positions and for a voice in official decisions, but they had little influence outside intellectual circles. Then, in 1905, Viceroy Lord Curzon divided the province of **Bengal** in two to improve the efficiency of its administration. This decision, made without consulting anyone, angered not only educated Indians, who saw it as a way to lessen

Indian National Congress A movement and political party founded in 1885 to demand greater Indian participation in government. Its membership was middle class, and its demands were modest until World War I. Led after 1920 by Mohandas K. Gandhi, it appealed increasingly to the poor, and it organized mass protests demanding self-government and independence.

Bengal Region of northeastern India. It was the first part of India to be conquered by the British in the eighteenth century and remained the political and economic center of British India throughout the nineteenth century. The 1905 split of the province into predominantly Hindu West Bengal and predominantly Muslim East Bengal (now Bangladesh) sparked anti-British riots.

Chronology

	India	Africa	Latin America
1900		**1900s** Railroads connect ports to the interior	**1876–1910** Porfirio Diaz, dictator of Mexico
	1905 Viceroy Curzon splits Bengal; mass demonstrations		
	1906 Muslims found All-India Muslim League		
	1911 British transfer capital from Calcutta to Delhi		**1911–1919** Mexican Revolution; Emiliano Zapata and Pancho Villa against the Constitutionalists
		1912 African National Congress founded	
			1917 New constitution proclaimed in Mexico
	1919 Amritsar Massacre		
1920		**1920s** J. E. Casely Hayford organizes political movement in British West Africa	
			1928 Plutarco Elías Calles founds Mexico's National Revolutionary Party
	1929 Gandhi leads Walk to the Sea		
	1930s Gandhi calls for independence; he is repeatedly arrested		
			1930–1945 Getulio Vargas, dictator of Brazil
			1934–1940 Lázaro Cárdenas, president of Mexico
			1938 Cárdenas nationalizes Mexican oil industry; Vargas proclaims Estado Novo in Brazil
	1939 British bring India into World War II	**1939–1945** A million Africans serve in World War II	
1940	**1940** Muhammad Ali Jinnah demands a separate nation for Muslims		
			1943 Juan Perón leads military coup in Argentina
			1946 Perón elected president of Argentina
	1947 Partition and independence of India and Pakistan		

their influence, but also millions of uneducated Hindu Bengalis, who suddenly found themselves outnumbered by Muslims in East Bengal. Soon Bengal was the scene of demonstrations, boycotts of British goods, and incidents of anti-British violence.

Muslims, fearful of Hindu dominance elsewhere in India, founded the **All-India Muslim League** in 1906. The government responded to the political agitation by granting Indians a limited franchise based on wealth. Muslims, however, were on average poorer than Hindus, for many poor and low-caste Hindus had converted to Islam to escape caste discrimination. Accordingly, the British instituted separate representation and different voting qualifications for Hindus and Muslims. Then, in 1911, the British transferred the capital of India from Calcutta to Delhi (DEL-ee), the former Mughal (MOO-guhl) capital. These changes raised the political consciousness of Indians of all classes and religions, giving rise to two mass movements: one by Hindus and one by Muslims.

Fearful of social upheavals, the British resisted the idea that India could, or should, industrialize. Their geologists looked for minerals, such as coal or manganese, that British industry required. However, when the only Indian member of the Indian Geological Service, Pramatha Nath Bose, wanted to prospect for iron ore, he had to resign because the government wanted no part of an Indian steel industry that could compete with that of Britain. Bose joined forces with Jamsetji Tata, a Bombay textile magnate who decided to produce steel anyway. With the help of German and American engineers and equipment, Tata's son Dorabji opened the first steel mill in India in 1911, in a town called Jamshedpur in honor of his father. Although it produced only a fraction of the steel that India required, Jamshedpur became a powerful symbol of Indian national pride.

During World War I Indians supported Britain enthusiastically; 1.2 million men volunteered for the army, and millions more voluntarily contributed money to the government. Many expected the British to reward their loyalty with political concessions. Others organized to demand concessions and a voice in the government. Responding to the agitation, the British announced in 1917 "the gradual development of self-governing institutions with a view to the progressive realization of responsible government in India as an integral part of the British Empire." This sounded like a promise of self-government, but the timetable was so vague that nationalists denounced it as a devious postponement of India's independence.

In late 1918 and early 1919 the great influenza pandemic began in the war zone of northern France (see Chapter 25). Of the 30 million people who died around the world, two out of three were Indian. This dreadful toll increased the mounting political tensions. Leaders of the Indian National Congress declared that the British reform proposals were too little, too late.

On April 13, 1919, in the city of Amritsar in Punjab, General Reginald Dyer ordered his troops to fire into a peaceful crowd of some 10,000 demonstrators, killing at least 379 and wounding 1,200. Waves of angry demonstrations swept over India, but the government waited six months to appoint a committee to investigate the massacre. After General Dyer retired, the British House of Lords voted to approve his actions, and a fund was raised in appreciation of his services. Indians interpreted these gestures as showing British contempt for their colonial subjects, effectively bringing to a close the period of gradual accommodation between the British and the Indians.

All-India Muslim League
Political organization founded in India in 1906 to defend the interests of India's Muslim minority. Led by Muhammad Ali Jinnah, it attempted to negotiate with the Indian National Congress. In 1940, the League began demanding a separate state for Muslims, to be called Pakistan.

Mahatma Gandhi and Militant Nonviolence

For the next twenty years violent uprisings and harsh repression, possibly even war, seemed imminent. That the worst did not come to pass was due to **Mohandas K. Gandhi** (GAHN-dee) (1869–1948), a man known to his followers as "Mahatma," the "great soul."

Gandhi began life with every advantage. His wealthy family sent him to England for his education. After his studies he lived in South Africa and practiced law for the small Indian community there. During World War I he returned to India and was one of many Western-educated Hindu intellectuals who joined the Indian National Congress.

Gandhi had some unusual political ideas. Unlike many radical political thinkers of his time, he denounced the popular ideals of power, struggle, and combat. Instead, inspired by both Hindu and Christian concepts, he preached the virtues of *ahimsa* (uh-HIM-sah) (nonviolence) and *satyagraha* (suh-TYAH-gruh-huh) (the search for truth). He refused to countenance violence among his followers, and he called off several demonstrations when they turned violent.

Gandhi had an affinity for the poor that was unusual even among socialist politicians. In 1921 he gave up both Western-style suits and the finery of wealthy Indians and henceforth wore simple peasant garb: a length of homespun cloth below

Mohandas K. (Mahatma) Gandhi (1869–1948) Leader of the Indian independence movement and advocate of nonviolent resistance. After being educated as a lawyer in England, he returned to India and became leader of the Indian National Congress in 1920. He appealed to the poor, led nonviolent demonstrations against British colonial rule, and was jailed many times. Soon after independence he was assassinated for attempting to stop Hindu-Muslim rioting.

Gandhi's "Walk to the Sea"

Mahatma Gandhi brilliantly publicized his disregard for British rule by leading a group of followers on a march to the seashore to collect salt, a product over which the government had established a monopoly. Shown here bare-headed with a walking stick at the shore, Gandhi also displays his large pocket watch, which seemingly contradicts his insistence that Indians stick to simple native technologies.   (Time Life Pictures/Getty Images) his waist and a shawl to cover his torso. He spoke for the farmers and the outcasts, whom he called *harijan* (HAH-ree-jahn), "children of God." He attracted ever-larger numbers of followers among the poor and the illiterate, who soon began to revere him; and he transformed the cause of Indian independence from an elite movement of the educated into a mass movement with a quasi-religious aura.

Gandhi was a brilliant political tactician and a master of public relations gestures. In 1929, for instance, he led a few followers on an 80-mile (129-kilometer) walk, camped on a beach, and gathered salt from the sea in a well-publicized act of civil disregard for the government's monopoly on salt. But he discovered that unleashing the power of popular participation was one thing and controlling its direction was quite another. Within days of his "Walk to the Sea," demonstrations of support broke out all over India, in which the police killed a hundred demonstrators and arrested over sixty thousand.

Many times during the 1930s Gandhi threatened to fast "unto death," and several times he did come close to death, to protest the violence of both the police and his followers and to demand independence. He was repeatedly arrested and spent a total of six years in jail. But arrest made him more popular. He became an iconic figure not only in his own country but also in the Western media. In the words of historian Percival Spear, he made the British "uncomfortable in their cherished field of moral rectitude," and he gave Indians the feeling that theirs was the ethically superior cause.

India Moves Toward Independence

In the 1920s, the British slowly began to give in to the pressure of the Indian National Congress and the Muslim League. They handed over control of "national" areas such as education, the economy, and public works. They also admitted more Indians into the Civil Service and the officer corps.

Economically, Indian politicians obtained the right to erect high tariff barriers against imports to protect India's infant industries. Behind these barriers, Indian entrepreneurs built plants to manufacture iron and steel, cement, paper, cotton and jute textiles, and sugar. While these manufactures did not improve the lives of the peasants or urban poor, they helped create a class of wealthy Indian businessmen who supported the Indian National Congress and its demands for independence. Though paying homage to Gandhi, they preferred his designated successor as leader of the Indian National Congress, **Jawaharlal Nehru** (NAY-roo) (1889–1964). A highly educated nationalist and subtle thinker, Nehru, unlike Gandhi, looked forward to creating a modern industrial India.

Congress politicians won regional elections but continued to be excluded from the viceroy's cabinet, the true center of power. When World War II began in September 1939, Viceroy Lord Linlithgow declared war without consulting a single Indian. The Congress-dominated provincial governments resigned in protest and found that boycotting government office increased their popular support. When the British offered to give India its independence once the war ended, Gandhi called the offer a "postdated cheque on a failing bank" and demanded full independence immediately. His "Quit India" campaign aroused popular demonstrations against the British and provoked a wave of arrests. Nehru remarked: "I would fight Japan sword in hand, but I can only do so as a free man."

Jawaharlal Nehru (1889–1964) Indian statesman. He succeeded Mohandas K. Gandhi as leader of the Indian National Congress. He negotiated the end of British colonial rule in India and became India's first prime minister (1947–1964).

Most Indian soldiers felt they were fighting to defend their country rather than to support the British Empire. As in World War I, Indians contributed heavily to the Allied war effort, supplying 2 million soldiers and enormous amounts of resources. A small number of Indians, however, were so anti-British that they joined the Japanese side.

India's subordination to British interests was vividly demonstrated in the famine of 1943 in Bengal. Unlike previous famines, this one was caused not by drought but by the Japanese conquest of Burma, which cut off imports of Burmese rice. Although food was available elsewhere in India, the British army had requisitioned the railroads to transport troops and equipment in preparation for a Japanese invasion. As a result, supplies ran short in Bengal and surrounding areas, while speculators hoarded whatever they could find. Some 2 million people starved to death before the army was ordered to supply food.

Partition and Independence

When the war ended, Britain's new Labour Party government prepared for Indian independence, but deep suspicions between Hindus and Muslims complicated the process. The break between the two communities had started in 1937, when the Indian National Congress won provincial elections and refused to share power with the Muslim League. In 1940 the leader of the League, **Muhammad Ali Jinnah** (jee-NAH) (1876–1948), demanded what many Muslims had long dreamt of: a country of their own, to be called Pakistan (from "Punjab-Afghans-Kashmir-Sind" plus the Persian suffix -*stan* meaning "home of").

As independence approached, talks between Jinnah and Nehru broke down. Violent rioting between Hindus and Muslims broke out in Bengal and Bihar. Gandhi's appeals for tolerance and cooperation fell on deaf ears. In despair, he retreated to his home near Ahmedabad. The British made frantic proposals to keep India united, but their authority was waning fast.

By early 1947 the Indian National Congress had accepted the idea of a partition of India into two states, one secular but dominated by Hindus, the other Muslim. In June Lord Mountbatten, the last viceroy, decided that independence must come immediately. On August 15 British India gave way to a new India and Pakistan. The Indian National Congress, led by Nehru, formed the first government of India; Jinnah and the Muslim League established a government for the provinces that made up Pakistan.

Violent clashes between Muslims and Hindus marred any celebration of independence. Throughout the land, Muslim and Hindu neighbors turned on one another, and armed members of one faith hunted down people of the other faith. For centuries Hindus and Muslims had intermingled throughout most of India. Now, leaving most of their possessions behind, Hindus fled from predominantly Muslim areas, and Muslims fled from Hindu areas. Trainloads of desperate refugees were attacked and massacred by members of the opposite faith. Within a few months some 12 million people had abandoned their ancestral homes and a half-million lay dead. In January 1948 Gandhi died too, gunned down by an angry Hindu refugee.

When the dust cleared, few Hindus remained in Pakistan, and Muslims were a minority in all but one state of India. That state was Kashmir, a strategically important region in the foothills of the Himalayas. India

Muhammad Ali Jinnah (1876–1948) Indian Muslim politician who founded the state of Pakistan. A lawyer by training, he joined the All-India Muslim League in 1913. As leader of the League from the 1920s on, he negotiated with the British and the Indian National Congress for Muslim participation in Indian politics. From 1940 on, he led the movement for the independence of India's Muslims in a separate state of Pakistan, founded in 1947.

SECTION REVIEW

- The inequities of British rule caused the rising class of English-speaking Indian professionals to create an independence movement.

- Changes in colonial administration and voting rights played upon religious divisions and created parallel Hindu and Muslim political movements.

- World War I and its aftermath stimulated nationalist agitation, which turned violent after the Amritsar Massacre.

- Employing militant nonviolence, Gandhi built a morally charged mass independence movement.

- Under Nehru's leadership, industrializing India pushed for greater independence, but World War II subordinated India to British interests.

- After gaining independence, India split into two states, and violence erupted between Hindus and Muslims.

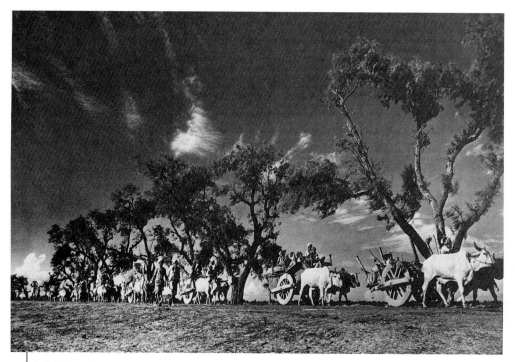

The Partition of India

When India became independent, Muslims fled from Hindu regions, and Hindus fled from Muslim regions. Margaret Bourke-White photographed a long line of refugees, with their cows, carts, and belongings, trudging down a country road toward safety.   (Time Life Pictures/Getty Images)

annexed Kashmir because the local maharajah was Hindu and because the state held the headwaters of the rivers that irrigated millions of acres of Indian farmland. The majority of the inhabitants of Kashmir were Muslims, however, and would probably have joined Pakistan if they had been allowed to choose. Partition and the Kashmir question turned India and Pakistan into bitter enemies that have fought several wars in the past half-century.

SUB-SAHARAN AFRICA, 1900–1945

What changes did foreign rule bring to Africa, and how did Africans respond?

The first half of the twentieth century, the time when nationalist movements threatened European rule in Asia (see Diversity and Dominance: A Vietnamese Nationalist Denounces French Colonialism), was Africa's period of classic colonialism. After World War I Britain, France, Belgium, and South Africa divided Germany's African colonies among themselves. In the 1930s Italy invaded Ethiopia. The colonial empires reached their peak shortly before World War II.

A Vietnamese Nationalist Denounces French Colonialism

The regions described in this chapter were not the only ones whose inhabitants chafed at the dominance of the great powers and sought more control over their own national destinies. Movements for independence were a worldwide phenomenon. The tactics that different peoples used to achieve their goals differed widely. French Indochina is a case in point.

Indochina, comprising the countries we now call Vietnam, Kampuchea, and Laos, was conquered piecemeal by the French from 1862 to 1895. Thereafter, France modernized the cities and irrigation systems and transformed the country into a leading producer of tea, rice, and natural rubber. This meant transferring large numbers of landless peasants to new plantations and destroying the traditional social structure. To govern Indochina, the French brought in more soldiers and civil administrators than the British had in all of India, a far larger colony. Though they succeeded in crushing the resistance of the peasants and the old Confucian elites, the French began educating a new elite in the French language. These newly educated youths, inspired by French ideas of liberty and nationhood and by the examples of the Guomindang and the Communist Party in neighboring China, formed the core of two revolutionary movements.

The Vietnamese Revolutionary Youth League was founded by Ho Chi Minh (1890–1969) in 1925. It later became the Indochinese Communist Party. The other movement, the Viet Nam Quoc Dan Dang, or Vietnamese Nationalist Party, was modeled after Sun Yat-sen's Guomindang. Founded in 1927 by a schoolteacher named Nguyen Thai Hoc (1904–1930), it attracted low-level government employees, soldiers, and small businessmen. At first Nguyen Thai Hoc lobbied the colonial government for reforms, but in vain. Two years later he turned to revolutionary action. In February 1930 he led an uprising at Yen Bay that the French quickly crushed. He and many of his followers were executed four months later, leaving Ho Chi Minh's communists as the standard-bearers of nationalist revolution in Vietnam.

While awaiting his execution, Nguyen Thai Hoc wrote the following letter to the French Chamber of Deputies.

Gentlemen:

I, the undersigned, Nguyen Thai Hoc, a Vietnamese citizen, twenty-six years old, chairman and founder of the Vietnamese Nationalist Party, at present arrested and imprisoned at the jail of Yen Bay, Tongking, Indochina, have the great honor to inform you of the following facts:

According to the tenets of justice, everyone has the right to defend his own country when it is invaded by foreigners, and according to the principles of humanity, everyone has the duty to save his compatriots when they are in difficulty or in danger. As for myself, I have assessed the fact that my country has been annexed by you French for more than sixty years. I realize that under your dictatorial yoke, my compatriots have experienced a very hard life, and my people will without doubt be completely annihilated, by the naked principle of natural selection. Therefore, my right and my duty have compelled me to seek every way to defend my country which has been invaded and occupied, and to save my people who are in great danger.

At the beginning, I had thought to cooperate with the French in Indochina in order to serve my compatriots, my country and my people, particularly in the areas of cultural and economic development. As regards economic development, in 1925 I sent a memorandum to Governor General Varenne, describing to him all our aspirations concerning the protection of local industry and commerce in Indochina. I urged strongly in the same letter the creation of a Superior School of Industrial Development in Tongking. In 1926 I again addressed another letter to the then Governor General of Indochina in which I included some explicit suggestions to relieve the hardships of our poor people. In 1927, for a third time, I sent a letter to the Résident Supérieur [provincial administrator] in Tongking, requesting permission to publish a weekly magazine with the aim of safeguarding and encouraging local industry and commerce. With regard to the cultural domain, I sent a letter to the Governor General in 1927, requesting (1) the privilege of opening tuition-free schools for the children of the lower classes, particularly children of workers and peasants; (2) freedom to open popular publishing houses and libraries in industrial centers.

It is absolutely ridiculous that every suggestion has been rejected. My letters were without answer; my plans have not been considered; my requests have been ignored; even the articles that I sent to newspapers have been censored and rejected. From the experience of these rejections, I have come to the conclusion that the French have no sincere intention of helping my country or my people. I also concluded that we have to expel France. For this reason, in 1927, I began to organize a revolutionary party, which I named the Vietnamese Nationalist Party, with the aim of overthrowing the dictatorial and oppressive administration of our country. We aspire to create a Republic of Vietnam, composed of persons sincerely concerned with the happiness of the people. My party is a clandestine organization, and in February 1929, it was uncovered by the security police. Among the members of my party, a great number have been arrested. Fifty-two persons have been condemned to forced labor ranging from two to twenty years. Although many have been detained and many others unjustly condemned, my party has not ceased its activity. Under my guidance, the Party continues to operate and progress towards its aim.

During the Yen Bay uprising someone succeeded in killing some French officers. The authorities accused my party of having organized and perpetrated this revolt. They have accused me of having given the orders for the massacre. In truth, I have never given such orders, and I have presented before the Penal Court of Yen Bay all the evidence showing the inanity of this accusation. Even so, some of the members of my party completely ignorant of that event have been accused of participating in it. The French Indochinese government burned and destroyed their houses. They sent French troops to occupy their villages and stole their rice to divide it among the soldiers. Not just members of my party have been suffering from this injustice—we should rather call this cruelty rather than injustice—but also many simple peasants, interested only in their daily work in the rice fields, living miserable lives like buffaloes and horses, have been compromised in this reprisal. At the present time, in various areas there are tens of thousands of men, women, and children, persons of all ages, who have been massacred. They died either of hunger or exposure because the French Indochinese government burned their homes. I therefore beseech you in tears to redress this injustice which otherwise will annihilate my people, which will stain French honor, and which will belittle all human values.

I have the honor to inform you that I am responsible for all events happening in my country under the leadership of my party from 1927 until the present. You only need to execute me. I beg your indulgence for all the others who at the present time are imprisoned in various jails. I am the only culprit, all the others are innocent. They are innocent because most of them are indeed members of my party, and have joined it only because I have succeeded in convincing them of their duties as citizens of this country, and of the humiliations of a slave with a lost country. Some of them are not even party members. They have been wrongly accused by their enemy or by the security police; or they simply are wrongly accused by their friends who have not been able to bear the tortures inflicted by the security police. I have the honor to repeat once again that you need execute only me. If you are not satisfied with killing one man, I advise you to kill also the members of my family, but I strongly beg your indulgence towards those who are innocent.

Finally, I would like to declare in conclusion: if France wants to stay in peace in Indochina, if France does not want to have increasing troubles with revolutionary movements, she should immediately modify the cruel and inhuman policy now practiced in Indochina. The French should behave like friends to the Vietnamese, instead of being cruel and oppressive masters. They should be attentive to the intellectual and material sufferings of the Vietnamese people, instead of being harsh and tough. Please, Gentlemen, receive my gratitude.

QUESTIONS FOR ANALYSIS

1. **When he first became involved in politics, what were Nguyen Thai Hoc's views of French colonialism?**
2. **What were his first initiatives, and what response did he get from the French colonial administration?**
3. **What motivated Nguyen Thai Hoc to organize an uprising, and what was the response of the French?**
4. **Compare Nguyen Thai Hoc's views and methods and the French response with the situation in India.**

Source: Harry Benda and John Larkin, *The World of Southeast Asia* (New York: Harper & Row, 1967), 182–185. Reprinted by permission of the author.

Colonial Africa: Economic and Social Changes

Outside of Algeria, Kenya, and South Africa, few Europeans lived in Africa. In 1930 Nigeria, with a population of 20 million, was ruled by 386 British officials and by 8,000 policemen and military, of whom 150 were European. Yet even such a small presence stimulated deep social and economic changes.

Since the turn of the century the colonial powers had built railroads from coastal cities to mines and plantations in the interior in order to access raw materials. The economic boom of the interwar years benefited few Africans. Colonial governments took lands that Africans owned communally and sold or leased them to European companies or, in eastern and southern Africa, to white settlers. Large European companies dominated wholesale commerce, while immigrants from various countries—Indians in East Africa, Greeks and Syrians in West Africa—handled much of the retail trade.

Where land was divided into small farms, some Africans benefited from the boom. Farmers in the Gold Coast (now Ghana [GAH-nuh]) profited from the high price of cocoa, as did palm-oil producers in Nigeria and coffee growers in East Africa. In most of Africa women played a major role in the retail trades, selling pots and pans, cloth, food, and other items in the markets. Many maintained their economic independence and kept their household finances separate from those of their husbands, following a custom that predated the colonial period.

African Farmers in the Gold Coast

African farmers in the Gold Coast (now Ghana) sold their cocoa beans to government agents. The government kept the prices artificially low in order to profit on the transactions.   (Popperfoto/Getty Images)

For many Africans, however, economic development meant working in European-owned mines and plantations, often under compulsion. Colonial governments were eager to develop the resources of their territories but could not afford to pay high enough wages to attract workers. Instead, they used police power to force Africans to work under harsh conditions for little or no pay. In the 1920s, when the government of French Equatorial Africa decided to build a railroad from Brazzaville to the Atlantic coast, a distance of 312 miles (502 kilometers), it drafted 127,000 men to carve a roadbed across mountains and through rain forests. Lacking adequate food, clothing, and medical care, 20,000 of them died, an average of 64 deaths per mile of track.

Europeans prided themselves on bringing modern health care to Africa; yet before the 1930s there was too little of it to help the majority of Africans, and other aspects of colonialism actually worsened public health. Migrants to cities, mines, and plantations and soldiers moving from post to post spread syphilis, gonorrhea, tuberculosis, and malaria. Sleeping sickness and smallpox epidemics raged throughout Central Africa. In recruiting men to work, colonial governments depleted rural areas of farmers needed to plant and harvest crops. Forced requisitions of food to feed the workers left the remaining populations undernourished and vulnerable to diseases. Not until the 1930s did colonial governments realize the negative consequences of their labor policies and begin to invest in agricultural development and health care for Africans.

In 1900 Ibadan (ee-BAH-dahn) in Nigeria was the only city in sub-Saharan Africa with more than 100,000 inhabitants; fifty years later, dozens of cities had reached that size, including Nairobi (nie-ROE-bee) in Kenya, Johannesburg in South Africa, Lagos in Nigeria, Accra in Gold Coast, and Dakar in Senegal. Africans migrated to cities for jobs, excitement, and, for a few, the chance to become wealthy.

However, migrations damaged family life, for almost all the migrants were men leaving women in the countryside to farm and raise children. Cities built during the colonial period had racially segregated housing, clubs, restaurants, hospitals, and other institutions. Racial discrimination was most rigid in the white-settler colonies of eastern and southern Africa.

SECTION REVIEW

- Colonial empires in Africa reached their peak just before World War II.

- In general, interwar economic development benefited European residents, owners of small farms, and women.

- Urbanization damaged traditional family life, and colonial labor policies caused severe health problems.

- Many Africans turned to Christianity and Islam for solace and education, and educated Africans joined nationalist movements.

- Urbanization, economic development, and involvement in World War II all contributed to the postwar independence movements.

Religious and Political Changes

Traditional religious belief could not explain the dislocations that foreign rule, migrations, and sudden economic changes brought to the lives of Africans. Many therefore turned to one of the two universal religions, Christianity and Islam, for guidance.

Christianity, introduced by Western missionaries, except in Ethiopia, where it was indigenous, met its greatest success in the coastal regions of West and South Africa, where European influence was strongest. Mission schools, which taught both craft skills and basic literacy, provided access to employment as minor functionaries, teachers, and shopkeepers. These schools also imparted Western political ideas to a new educated elite. Many Africans read the suffering of their own peoples into the biblical stories of Moses and the parables of Jesus. The churches trained some of the brighter pupils to become catechists, teachers, and clergymen. A few rose to high positions, such as James Johnson, a Yoruba who became the Anglican bishop of the Niger Delta

CL Primary Source: Education, Civilization, and "Foreignization" in Buganda   *Find out how one man views his country's wholesale acquisition of Western education and customs.*

Pastorate. Independent Christian churches—known as "Ethiopian" churches—associated Christian beliefs with radical ideas of racial equality and political participation.

Through the influence and example of Arab and African merchants, Islam spread inland from the East African coast and southward from the Sahel (SAH-hel) toward the West African coast. Islam also emphasized literacy—in Arabic through Quranic schools rather than in a European language—and was less disruptive of traditional African customs such as polygamy.

In a few places, such as Dakar in Senegal and Cape Town in South Africa, small numbers of Africans could obtain secondary education. Even smaller numbers went on to college in Europe or America. Though few in number, they became the leaders of political movements. The contrast between the liberal ideas imparted by Western education and the realities of racial discrimination under colonial rule contributed to the rise of nationalism among educated Africans. In Senegal **Blaise Diagne** (dee-AHN-yuh) agitated for African participation in politics and fair treatment in the French army. In the 1920s J. E. Casely Hayford began organizing a movement for greater autonomy in British West Africa. In South Africa Western-educated lawyers and journalists founded the **African National Congress** in 1912 to defend the interests of Africans. These nationalist movements were partly inspired by the ideas of Pan-Africanists from America such as W. E. B. Du Bois and Marcus Garvey, who advocated the unity of African peoples around the world. Before World War II, however, they were small and had little influence.

During the Second World War increased forced labor, inflation, and requisitions of raw materials had a profound effect even on Africans who were far removed from the theaters of war. Yet the war also brought hope. During the campaign to oust the Italians from Ethiopia, Emperor **Haile Selassie** (HI-lee seh-LASS-ee) (r. 1930–1974) led his own troops into Addis Ababa, his capital, and reclaimed his title. A million Africans served as soldiers and porters in Burma, North Africa, and Europe. They listened to Allied propaganda in favor of European liberation movements and against Nazi racism, and they returned to their countries with new and radical ideas.

After the Second World War the building of cities, railroads, and other enterprises brought Africa into the global economy, often at great human cost. Colonialism also brought changes to African culture and religion, hastening the spread of Christianity and Islam. And the foreign occupation awakened political ideas that inspired the next generation of Africans to demand independence (see Chapter 28).

MEXICO, ARGENTINA, AND BRAZIL, 1900–1949

What could Latin Americans do to achieve social justice and economic development? Were these two goals compatible?

In the nineteenth century Latin America achieved independence from Spain and Portugal but did not industrialize. Most of the new states suffered from ideological divisions, unstable governments, and violent upheavals. Foreign investment and the exchange of raw materials and agricultural products for foreign manufactured goods made them economically dependent on the wealthier countries to the north, especially the United States and Great Britain. Their societies remained deeply split between wealthy landowners and desperately poor peasants.

Blaise Diagne (1872–1934) Senegalese political leader. He was the first African elected to the French National Assembly. During World War I, in exchange for promises to give French citizenship to Senegalese, he helped recruit Africans to serve in the French army. After the war, he led a movement to abolish forced labor in Africa.

African National Congress An organization dedicated to obtaining equal voting and civil rights for black inhabitants of South Africa. Founded in 1912 as the South African Native National Congress, it changed its name in 1923. Though it was banned and its leaders were jailed for many years, it eventually helped bring majority rule to South Africa.

Primary Source: London Manifesto *Hear an argument for Pan-Africanism as expressed by the Pan-African Congress of 1921.*

Primary Source: Parable of the Eagle, Limbo, Prayer for Peace, Vultures *Find out why an eagle will always remain an eagle even when it has been trained to be a chicken.*

Haile Selassie (1892–1975) Emperor of Ethiopia (r. 1930–1974) and symbol of African independence. He fought the Italian invasion of his country in 1935 and regained his throne during World War II, when British forces expelled the Italians. He ruled Ethiopia as a traditional autocracy until he was overthrown in 1974.

Mexico, Brazil, and Argentina contained well over half of Latin America's land, population, and wealth, and their relations with other countries and their economies were similar. Mexico, however, underwent a traumatic social revolution, while Argentina and Brazil evolved more peaceably.

Background to Revolution: Mexico in 1910

A Mexican saying observed wryly: "Poor Mexico: so far from God, so close to the United States." In Mexico the chasm between rich and poor was so deep that only a revolution could move the country toward prosperity and democracy.

Mexico was the Latin American country most influenced by the Spanish during three centuries of colonial rule. After independence in 1821 it suffered from a half-century of political turmoil. At the beginning of the twentieth century Mexican society was divided into rich and poor and into persons of Spanish, Indian, and mixed ancestry. A few very wealthy families of Spanish origin, less than 1 percent of the population, owned 85 percent of Mexico's land, mostly in huge *haciendas* (estates). A handful of American and British companies closely tied to this elite controlled most of Mexico's railroads, silver mines, and plantations. At the other end of the social scale were Indians, many of whom did not speak Spanish. *Mestizos* (mess-TEE-zoh), people of mixed Indian and European ancestry, were only slightly better off; most of them were peasants who worked on the haciendas or farmed small communal plots near their ancestral villages.

The urban middle class was small and had little political influence. Few professional and government positions were open to them, and foreigners owned most businesses. Industrial workers also were few in number; the only significant groups were textile workers in the port of Veracruz on the Gulf of Mexico and railroad workers spread throughout the country.

During the colonial period, the Spanish government had made halfhearted efforts to defend Indians and mestizos from the land-grabbing tactics of the haciendas. After independence in 1821 wealthy Mexican families and American companies used bribery and force to acquire millions of acres of good agricultural land from villages in southern Mexico. Peasants lost not only their fields but also access to firewood and pasture for their animals. Sugar, cotton, and other commercial crops replaced corn and beans. To survive, the peasants had to buy food and other necessities on credit from the hacienda owner's store. Eventually, they fell permanently into debt.

In the 1880s American investors purchased from the Mexican government dubious claims to more than 2.5 million acres (1 million hectares) traditionally held by the Yaqui people of Sonora, in northern Mexico. When the Yaqui resisted the expropriation of their lands, they were brutally repressed by the Mexican army.

Northern Mexicans had no peasant tradition of communal ownership, for the northern half of the country was too dry for farming, unlike the tropical and densely populated south. The north was a region of silver mines and cattle ranches, some of them enormous. It was thinly populated by cowboys and miners. The harshness of their lives and the vast inequities in the distribution of income made northern Mexicans as resentful as people in the south.

Despite many upheavals in Mexico in the nineteenth century, in 1910 the government seemed in control. For thirty-four years General Porfirio Díaz (DEE-as) (1830–1915) had ruled Mexico under the motto "Liberty, Order, Progress." To Díaz "liberty" meant freedom for rich hacienda owners and foreign investors to acquire more land. The government imposed "order" through rigged elections and a policy of *pan o palo* (bread or the stick)—that is, bribes for Díaz's supporters and summary justice for those who opposed him. "Progress" meant mainly the importing of foreign capital, machinery, and technicians to take advantage of Mexico's labor, soil, and natural resources.

During the Díaz years (1876–1910) Mexico City—with paved streets, streetcar lines, electric street lighting, and public parks—became a showplace, and new telegraph and railroad lines connected cities and towns throughout Mexico. But this material progress benefited only a handful of well-connected businessmen. The boom in railroads, agriculture, and mining at the turn of the century actually caused a decline in the average Mexican's standard of living.

Though a mestizo himself, Díaz discriminated against the nonwhite majority of Mexicans. He and his supporters tried to eradicate what they saw as Mexico's embarrassingly rustic traditions. On many middle- and upper-class tables French cuisine replaced traditional Mexican dishes. The wealthy replaced sombreros and ponchos with European garments. Though bullfighting and cock-fighting remained popular, the well-to-do preferred horse racing and soccer. To the educated middle class—the only group with a strong sense of Mexican nationhood—this devaluation of Mexican culture became a symbol of the Díaz regime's failure to defend national interests against foreign influences.

Revolution and Civil War in Mexico

Unlike the independence movement in India, the Mexican Revolution was a social revolution and was not the work of one party with a well-defined ideology. Instead, it developed haphazardly, led by a series of ambitious but limited leaders, each representing a different segment of Mexican society.

The first was Francisco I. Madero (1873–1913), the son of a wealthy landowning and mining family, educated in the United States. When minor uprisings broke out in 1911, the government collapsed and Díaz fled into exile. The Madero presidency was welcomed by some, but it aroused opposition from peasant leaders like **Emiliano Zapata** (sah-PAH-tah) (1879–1919). In 1913, after two years as president, Madero was overthrown and murdered by one of his former supporters, General Victoriano Huerta. Woodrow Wilson (1856–1924), president of the United States, showed his displeasure by sending the United States Marines to occupy Veracruz.

The inequities of Mexican society and foreign intervention in Mexico's affairs angered Mexico's middle class and industrial workers. They found leaders in Venustiano Carranza, a landowner, and in Alvaro Obregón (oh-bray-GAWN), a schoolteacher. Calling themselves Constitutionalists, Carranza and Obregón organized private armies and succeeded in overthrowing Huerta in 1914. By then, the revolution had spread to the countryside.

As early as 1911 Zapata, an Indian farmer, had led a revolt against the haciendas in the mountains of Morelos, south of Mexico City (see Map 27.1). His soldiers were peasants, some of them women, mounted on horseback and armed with pistols and rifles. For several years they periodically came down from the mountains, burned hacienda buildings, and returned land to the Indian villages to which it had once belonged.

Primary Source: The Plan of Ayala
Examine the Mexican revolutionaries' call for the overthrow of the established government and the return of Mexico to her people.

Emiliano Zapata (1879–1919) Revolutionary and leader of peasants in the Mexican Revolution. He mobilized landless peasants in south-central Mexico in an attempt to seize and divide the lands of the wealthy landowners. Though successful for a time, he was ultimately defeated and assassinated.

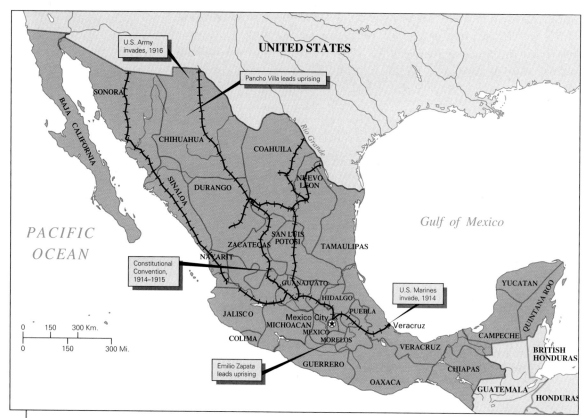

Map 27.1   The Mexican Revolution

The Mexican Revolution began in two distinct regions of the country. One was the mountainous and densely populated area south of Mexico City, particularly Morelos, homeland of Emiliano Zapata. The other was the dry and thinly populated ranch country of the north, such as Chihuahua, home of Pancho Villa. The fighting that ensued crisscrossed the country along the main railroad lines, shown on the map.

 Interactive Map

Francisco "Pancho" Villa (1877–1923) A popular leader during the Mexican Revolution. An outlaw in his youth, when the revolution started, he formed a cavalry army in the north of Mexico and fought for the rights of the landless in collaboration with Emiliano Zapata. He was assassinated in 1923.

Another leader appeared in Chihuahua, a northern state where seventeen individuals owned two-fifths of the land and 95 percent of the people had no land at all. Starting in 1913 **Francisco "Pancho" Villa** (1877–1923), a former ranch hand, mule driver, and bandit, organized an army of three thousand men, most of them cowboys. They too seized land from the large haciendas, not to rebuild traditional communities as in southern Mexico but to create family ranches.

Zapata and Villa were part agrarian rebels, part social revolutionaries. They enjoyed tremendous popular support but could never rise above their origins and lead a national revolution. The Constitutionalists had fewer soldiers than Zapata and Villa, but they held the major cities, controlled the country's oil exports, and used the proceeds to buy modern weapons. Gradually the Constitutionalists took over most of Mexico. In 1919 they defeated and killed Zapata; Villa was assassinated four years later. An estimated 2 million people lost their lives in the civil war, and much of Mexico lay in ruins.

The Constitutionalists adopted many of their rivals' agrarian reforms, such as restoring communal lands to the Indians of Morelos. They also proposed social programs aimed at workers and the middle class. The Constitution of 1917 promised universal suffrage and a one-term presidency; state-run education; the end of debt peonage; restrictions on foreign ownership of property; and laws specifying minimum wages and maximum hours to protect laborers. Though not immediately implemented, these reforms carried symbolic meaning. They enshrined the dignity of Mexicans and the equality of Indians, mestizos, and whites, as well as of peasants and city people.

In the early 1920s, after years of violence that exhausted all classes, the Mexican Revolution lost momentum. Only in Morelos did peasants receive land, and President Obregón and his closest associates made all the important decisions. In 1928 Obregón was assassinated. His successor, Plutarco Elías Calles (KAH-yace), founded the National Revolutionary Party, or PNR (the abbreviation of its name in Spanish). The PNR was a forum where all the pressure groups and vested interests—labor, peasants, businessmen, landowners, the military—worked out compromises. The establishment of the PNR gave the Mexican Revolution a second wind.

Lázaro Cárdenas (LAH-sah-roe KAHR-dih-nahs), chosen by Calles to be president in 1934, brought peasants' and workers' organizations into the party, renamed it the Mexican Revolutionary Party (PRM), and removed the generals from government positions. Then he set to work implementing the reforms promised in the Constitution. Cárdenas redistributed 44 million acres (17.6 million hectares) to peasant communes, replaced church-run schools with government schools, and nationalized the railroads and other businesses.

Most dramatic was the expropriation of foreign-owned oil companies. In the early 1920s Mexico was the world's leading producer of oil, but a handful of American and British companies exported almost all of it. In 1938 Cárdenas seized the foreign-owned oil industry, more as a matter of national pride than of economics. The oil companies expected the governments of the United States and Great Britain to come to their rescue, perhaps with military force. But Mexico and the United States chose to resolve the issue through negotiation, and Mexico retained control of its oil industry.

When Cárdenas's term ended in 1940, Mexico, like India, was still a land of poor farmers with a small industrial base. Yet the political system was free of both chaos and dictatorships, and land and other resources were no longer monopolized by a small group of people. The military was tamed; the Catholic Church no longer controlled education; and the nationalization of oil had demonstrated Mexico's independence.

In the arts the Mexican Revolution sparked a surge of creativity. The political murals of José Clemente Orozco and Diego Rivera and the paintings of Frida Kahlo focused on social themes, showing peasants, workers, and soldiers in scenes from the Revolution. These works of art gave Mexicans a sense of national unity and pride in the achievements of the Revolution that lasted long after the revolutionary fervor had dissipated.

What did the Mexican Revolution accomplish? It did not fulfill the democratic promise of Madero's campaign, for it brought to power a party that monopolized the government for eighty years. However, it allowed far wider participation in politics and promised far-reaching social reforms. These long-delayed reforms began to be implemented during the Cárdenas administration. They fell short of the ideals expressed by the revolutionaries, but they laid the foundation for Mexico's later industrialization.

CL Primary Source: Speech to the Nation
Hear Mexican president Lázaro Cárdenas explain to his country and the world that he intends to take control of the foreign-owned oil industry in Mexico.

Lázaro Cárdenas (1895–1970)
President of Mexico (1934–1940). He brought major changes to Mexican life by distributing millions of acres of land to the peasants, bringing representatives of workers and farmers into the inner circles of politics, and nationalizing the oil industry.

The Agitator, *a Mural by Diego Rivera*

Diego Rivera (1886–1957) was politically committed to the Mexican Revolution and widely admired as an artist. This mural, painted at the National Agricultural School at Chapingo near Mexico City, shows a political agitator addressing peasants and workers. With one hand, the speaker points to miners laboring in a silver mine; with the other, to a hammer and sickle.   (© Banco de Mexico, Diego Rivera & Frida Kahlo Museums)

HISTORY IN FOCUS   Notice the differences between the agitator and his audience and the mine workers in this image. Why do you think Rivera had the agitator pointing to the miners? What do you suppose he wants his viewers to think about these groups of laborers in Mexico and their role in the revolution? *Find the answer online.*

The Transformation of Argentina

Most of Argentina consists of *pampas* (POM-pus), flat, fertile land that is easy to till, much like the prairies of the midwestern United States and Canada. Throughout the nineteenth century Argentina's economy was based on two exports: the hides of longhorn creole cattle and the wool of merino sheep, which roamed the pampas in huge herds.

At the end of the nineteenth century railroads and refrigerator ships that transported meat safely changed not only the composition of Argentina's exports but also the way they were produced. European consumers preferred the soft flesh of Lincoln sheep and Hereford cattle to the tough, sinewy meat of creole cattle and merino sheep. The valuable Lincolns and Herefords, however, were carefully bred and received a diet of alfalfa and oats. To safeguard them, the pampas had to be divided, plowed, cultivated, and fenced with barbed wire. Once fenced, the land could be used to produce wheat as well as beef and mutton. Within a few years grasslands that had stretched to the horizon were transformed into farmland. Like the North American Midwest, the pampas became one of the world's great producers of wheat and meat.

Argentina's government represented the interests of the *oligarquía* (oh-lee-gar-KEE-ah), a very small group of wealthy hacienda owners. They also owned fine homes in Buenos Aires (BWAY-nihs AIR-eze), a city that was built to look like Paris. They traveled frequently to Europe and spent so lavishly that the French coined the superlative "rich as an Argentine." Being focused on wheat and meat, they were content to let foreign companies, mainly British, build Argentina's railroads, processing plants, and public utilities. In exchange for its agricultural exports Argentina imported almost all its manufactured goods from Europe and the United States. So important were British interests in the Argentinean economy that English, not Spanish, was used on the railroads, and the biggest department store in Buenos Aires was a branch of Harrods of London.

Brazil and Argentina, to 1929

Before the First World War Brazil produced most of the world's coffee and cacao, grown on vast estates, and natural rubber, gathered by Indians from rubber trees growing wild in the Amazon rain forest. Planters and rubber exporters made up Brazil's elite. Like their Argentinean counterparts, they spent their money lavishly, building palaces in Rio de Janeiro (REE-oh day zhuh-NAIR-oh) and one of the world's most beautiful opera houses in Manaus (meh-NOWSE), deep in the Amazon. As in Argentina, British companies built railroads, harbors, and other infrastructure and imported most manufactured goods.

Both Argentina and Brazil had small but outspoken middle classes that demanded a share in government and looked to Europe as a model. Beneath each middle class were the poor. In Argentina these were mainly Spanish and Italian immigrants who had ended up as landless farm laborers or workers in urban packing plants. In Brazil there was a large class of sharecroppers and plantation workers, many of them descendants of slaves.

Rubber exports collapsed after 1912, replaced by cheaper plantation rubber from Southeast Asia. The outbreak of war in 1914 put an end to imports from Europe as Britain and France focused all their industries on war production and Germany was cut off entirely. These disruptions weakened the landowning class. In Argentina the urban middle class obtained the secret ballot and universal male suffrage in 1916 and elected a liberal politician, **Hipólito Irigoyen** (ee-POH-lee-toe ee-ree-GO-yen), as president. To a certain extent, the United States replaced the European countries as suppliers of machinery and consumers of coffee. European immigrants built factories to manufacture textiles and household goods. Desperate for money to pay for the war, Great Britain sold many of its railroad, streetcar, and other companies to the governments of Argentina and Brazil.

South America prospered during the postwar years. Trade with Europe resumed; export prices remained high; and both Argentina and Brazil used accumulated profits to industrialize and improve their transportation systems and public utilities. Nevertheless, workers and middle-class professionals demanded social reforms and a larger voice in politics. In Argentina students' and workers' demonstrations were brutally crushed. In Brazil junior officers rebelled several times, calling for universal suffrage, social reforms, and freedom for labor unions. Though they accomplished little, they laid the groundwork for later reformist movements. In neither country did the urban middle class take power away from the wealthy landowners. Instead, the two classes shared power at the expense of both the landless peasants and the urban workers.

Though Argentina and Brazil moved forward, new technologies again left them dependent on the advanced industrial countries. Brazilians are justly proud that the first person to fly an airplane outside the United States was Alberto Santos-Dumont,

Hipólito Irigoyen (1850–1933)
Argentine politician, president of Argentina from 1916 to 1922 and 1928 to 1930. The first president elected by universal male suffrage, he began his presidency as a reformer, but later became conservative.

a Brazilian. He did so in 1906 in France, where he lived most of his life and had access to engine manufacturers and technical assistance. Aviation reached Latin America after World War I, when European and American companies such as Aéropostale and Pan American Airways introduced airmail service between cities and linked Latin America with the United States and Europe.

Before and during World War I radio, then called "wireless telegraphy," was used not for broadcasting but for point-to-point communications. Transmitters powerful enough to send messages across oceans or continents were extraordinarily complex and expensive: their antennas covered many acres; they used as much electricity as a small town; and they cost tens of thousands of pounds sterling (millions of dollars in today's money).

Right after the war, the major powers scrambled to build powerful transmitters on every continent to compete with the telegraph cable companies and take advantage of the boom in international business and news reporting. However, no Latin American country possessed the knowledge or funds to build its own transmitters. In 1919, therefore, President Irigoyen of Argentina granted a radio concession to a German firm. France and Britain protested this decision, and eventually four powerful radio companies—one British, one French, one German, and one American—formed a cartel to control all radio communications in Latin America. This cartel set up a national radio company in each republic, installing a prominent local politician as its president. But the cartel held all the stock and therefore received all the profits.

The Depression and the Vargas Regime in Brazil

The Depression hit Latin America as hard as Europe and the United States; in many ways, it marks a more important turning point for the region than either of the world wars. As long-term customers cut back their orders, the value of agricultural and mineral exports fell by two-thirds between 1929 and 1932. Argentina and Brazil could no longer afford to import manufactured goods. An imploding economy also undermined their shaky political systems. Like European countries, Argentina and Brazil veered toward authoritarianism.

In 1930 **Getulio Vargas** (jay-TOO-lee-oh VAR-gus) (1883–1954), a state governor, staged a coup and proclaimed himself president of Brazil. He proved to be a masterful politician. He wrote a new constitution that broadened the franchise and limited the president to one term. He raised import duties and promoted national firms and state-owned enterprises, culminating in the construction of the Volta Redonda steel mill in the 1930s. By 1936 industrial production had doubled, especially in textiles and small manufactures. Brazil was on its way to becoming an industrial country. Vargas's policy, called **import-substitution industrialization**, became a model for other Latin American countries as they attempted to break away from neocolonial dependency.

The industrialization of Brazil brought all the familiar environmental consequences. Powerful new machines allowed the reopening of old mines and the digging of new ones. Cities grew as poor peasants looking for work arrived from the countryside. Around the older neighborhoods of Rio de Janeiro and São Paulo (sow PAL-oh), the poor turned steep hillsides and vacant lands into immense *favelas* (feh-VEL-luh) (slums) of makeshift shacks.

Getulio Vargas (1883–1954) Dictator of Brazil from 1930 to 1945 and from 1951 to 1954. Defeated in the presidential election of 1930, he overthrew the government and created a dictatorship that emphasized industrialization and helped the urban poor but did little to alleviate the problems of the peasants.

import-substitution industrialization An economic system aimed at building a country's industry by restricting foreign trade. It was especially popular in Latin American countries such as Mexico, Argentina, and Brazil in the mid-twentieth century. It proved successful for a time but could not keep up with technological advances in Europe and North America.

The countryside also was transformed. Scrubland was turned into pasture, and new acreage was planted in wheat, corn, and sugar cane. Even the Amazon rain forest—half the land area of Brazil—was affected. In 1930 American industrialist Henry Ford invested $8 million to clear land along the Tapajós River and prepare it to become the site of the world's largest rubber plantation. Ford encountered opposition from Brazilian workers and politicians; the rubber trees proved vulnerable to diseases; and he had to abandon the project—but not before leaving 3 million acres (1.2 million hectares) denuded of trees. The ecological changes of the Vargas era were but a tiny forerunner of the degradation of the Brazilian environment that was to take place later in the century.

Vargas's reforms brought labor unions, pension plans, and disability insurance to urban workers, but he refused to take measures to help the millions of landless peasants or harm the interests of the great landowners. Although the Brazilian economy recovered from the Depression, the benefits of recovery were so unequally distributed that communist and fascist movements demanded even more radical changes.

Constitutionally prohibited from being reelected in 1938, Vargas staged another coup, abolished the constitution, and instituted the Estado Novo (esh-TAH-doe NO-vo), or "New State," with himself as supreme leader. He banned political parties,

Rush Hour in Brazil

In Latin American countries, modern conveniences, when first introduced, were often insufficient to meet the demand from eager customers. Here the Sao Januario streetcar in Rio de Janeiro carries twice as many passengers as it was designed for.   (Genevieve Naylor, photographer/Reznikoff Artistic Partnership, NY)

SECTION REVIEW

- By 1910, Mexico was sharply divided along ethnic and class lines, with most of its wealth controlled by elites and foreign businesses.

- Elites and foreigners enjoyed the support of Díaz's government, which also tried to impose European cultural values.

- After Díaz's fall, local revolutionary leaders emerged, including the Constitutionalists, Zapata, and Villa; they initiated reforms and fought among themselves, but some changes occurred.

- Cárdenas and the PRM expanded party representation, implemented reforms, and nationalized foreign-owned oil companies.

- Both Argentina and Brazil developed agricultural economies dependent on European technology, consumer demand, and manufactured goods.

- In both countries, wealthy elites dominated small middle classes and large working classes composed mainly of agricultural laborers.

- World War I prompted economic and political changes, especially in Argentina.

- During the interwar years, both countries enjoyed prosperity but remained dependent on industrialized nations for new technologies.

- The hardships of the Depression caused political instability, from which emerged authoritarian regimes devoted to rapid industrialization.

Juan Perón (1895–1974) President of Argentina (1946–1955, 1973–1974). As a military officer, he championed the rights of labor. Aided by his wife Eva Duarte Perón, he was elected president in 1946. He built up Argentinean industry, became very popular among the urban poor, but harmed the economy.

Eva Duarte Perón (1919–1952) Wife of Juan Perón and champion of the poor in Argentina. She was a gifted speaker and popular political leader who campaigned to improve the life of the urban poor by founding schools and hospitals and providing other social benefits.

jailed opposition leaders, and turned Brazil into a fascist state. When the Second World War broke out, however, Vargas aligned Brazil with the United States and contributed troops and ships to the Allied war effort.

Despite his economic achievements, Vargas harmed Brazil. By running roughshod over laws, constitutions, and rights, he infected not only Brazil but all of South America with the temptations of political violence. It is ironic, but not surprising, that Vargas was overthrown in 1945 by a military coup.

Argentina After 1930

Economically, the Depression hurt Argentina badly. Politically, however, the consequences were delayed. In 1930 General José Uriburu (hoe-SAY oo-ree-BOO-roo) overthrew the popularly elected President Irigoyen. The Uriburu government represented the large landowners and big business interests. For thirteen years the generals and the oligarquía ruled, doing nothing to lessen the poverty of the workers or the frustrations of the middle class. When World War II broke out, Argentina sympathized with the Axis but remained officially neutral.

In 1943 another military revolt flared, this one among junior officers angry at conservative politicians. It was led by Colonel **Juan Perón** (hoo-AHN pair-OWN) (1895–1974). The intentions of the rebels were clear:

Civilians will never understand the greatness of our ideal; we shall therefore have to eliminate them from the government and give them the only mission which corresponds to them: work and obedience.[1]

Once in power the officers took over the highest positions in government and business and began to lavish money on military equipment and their own salaries. Their goal, inspired by Nazi victories, was nothing less than the conquest of South America.

As the war turned against the Nazis, the officers saw their popularity collapse. Perón, however, had other plans. Inspired by his charismatic wife **Eva Duarte Perón** (AY-vuy doo-AR-tay pair-OWN) (1919–1952), he appealed to the urban workers. Eva Perón became the champion of the *descamisados* (des-cah-mee-SAH-dohs), or "shirtless ones," and campaigned tirelessly for social benefits and for the cause of women and children. With his wife's help, Perón won the presidency in 1946 and created a populist dictatorship in imitation of the Vargas regime in Brazil.

Like Brazil, Argentina industrialized rapidly under state sponsorship. Perón spent lavishly on social welfare projects as well as on the military, depleting the capital that Argentina had earned during the war. Though a skillful demagogue who played off the army against the navy and both against the labor unions, Perón could not create a stable government out of the chaos of coups and conspiracies. He had to back down from a plan to make Eva his vice president. When she died in 1952, he lost his political skills (or perhaps they were hers), and soon thereafter he was overthrown in yet another military coup.

COMPARATIVE PERSPECTIVES

The wars and revolutions that engulfed the Northern Hemisphere between 1900 and 1949 affected India, sub-Saharan Africa, and Latin America by placing heavy demands on their peoples and raising their hopes for a better life. Sub-Saharan Africa and India were still under colonial rule. Political life revolved around the desire of their elites for political independence while ordinary people yearned for social justice. Mexico, Argentina, and Brazil were politically independent, but their economies, like those of Africa and India, were closely tied to the economies of the industrial nations. When the Depression hit, all three turned to state intervention and import-substitution industrialization. Like all industrializing countries, they did so by mining, farming, ranching, cutting down forests, and irrigating land, all at the expense of the natural environment.

In Mexico social stresses brought about a long and violent revolution, out of which Mexicans forged a lasting sense of national identity. Argentina and Brazil moved toward greater economic independence, but the price was social unrest, militarism, and dictatorship. They languished under conservative regimes devoted to the interests of wealthy landowners, sporadically interrupted by military coups and populist demagogues. In India growing expectations conflicted with the reality of colonial rule. A movement for independence and an ethnic split tore the nation apart. In sub-Saharan Africa demands for national self-determination and economic development were only beginning to be voiced by 1949 and did not come to fruition until the second half of the century.

Nationalism and the yearning for social justice were the two most powerful forces for change in the early twentieth century. These ideas originated in the industrialized countries but resonated in the independent countries of Latin America as well as in colonial regions such as the Indian subcontinent and sub-Saharan Africa. However, they did not always unite people against their colonial rulers or foreign oppressors; instead, they often divided them along social, ethnic, or religious lines. Western-educated elites looked to industrialization as a means of modernizing their country and ensuring their position in it, while peasants and urban workers supported nationalist and revolutionary movements in the hope of improving their lives. Often these goals were not compatible.

Chapter Review

DOWNLOAD THE MP3 AUDIO FILE OF THE CHAPTER REVIEW TO LISTEN TO ON THE GO.

Why did the educated elites of India want independence? What were ordinary Indians hoping for? (page 735)

In the late nineteenth century, educated Indians began to resent the racist condescension with which they were treated by their colonial masters. They believed that they could govern India and develop its economy better than the British could. Poorer Indians were persuaded by Mahatma Gandhi, the Indian

KEY TERMS

Indian National Congress *(p. 736)*
Bengal *(p. 736)*
All-India Muslim League *(p. 738)*
Mohandas K. Gandhi *(p. 739)*
Jawaharlal Nehru *(p. 740)*
(Continued)

National Congress, and the Muslim League that national independence would alleviate their poverty.

What changes did foreign rule bring to Africa, and how did Africans respond? (page 742)

Sub-Saharan Africa was radically transformed by its colonial rulers, who built cities, railroads, harbors, mines, and plantations. Africans were forced to provide the labor for these projects and received few benefits from them. Many turned to Christianity or Islam for spiritual guidance during these upheavals.

What could Latin Americans do to achieve social justice and economic development? Were these two goals compatible? (page 747)

Decades of modernization had left most Mexicans poorer than before. The revolution that broke out in 1911 promised to repair the injustices of the past, but it fell short of the ideals for which it was fought. Brazil and Argentina avoided a revolution but remained dependent on Britain and the United States. In both countries, as in Mexico, economic growth was difficult to achieve, democracy was fragile and often repressed by dictators, and social justice proved just as elusive as in earlier centuries.

SUGGESTED READING

Adelman, Jeremy. *Frontier Development: Land, Labour and Capital on the Wheatlands of Argentina and Canada, 1890–1914.* 1994. Describes the transformation of the Argentinean environment.

Burns, E. Bradford. *A History of Brazil.* 3d ed. 1993. A standard general survey.

Collins, Larry, and Dominique Lapierre. *Freedom at Midnight.* 1975. A readable account of India's transition from colonialism to partition and independence.

Crosby, Alfred W. *America's Forgotten Pandemic: The Influenza of 1918.* 1989. Where history of medicine intersects world history.

Dean, Warren. *Brazil and the Struggle for Rubber: A Study in Environmental History.* 1987. An important contribution to environmental history.

Gadgil, M., and R. Guha. *This Fissured Land: An Ecological History of India.* 1993. A pioneering work of environmental history.

Herskovits, Melville. *The Human Factor in Changing Africa.* 1958. A classic overview of Africa under colonial rule.

Knight, Alan. *The Mexican Revolution.* 2 vols. 1986. A recent thorough study.

Krauze, Enrique. *Mexico: Biography of Power: A History of Modern Mexico, 1810–1996.* 1997. A good general overview of modern Mexican history.

Oliver, Roland, and Anthony Atmore. *Africa Since 1800.* 4th ed. 1994. An excellent general introduction.

Rock, David. *Argentina, 1517–1987: From Spanish Colonization to Alfonsín.* 1987. The history of modern Argentina ably treated.

Sarkar, Sumit. *Modern India, 1885–1947.* 8th ed. 2002. A general introduction with an emphasis on history from below.

Skidmore, Thomas, and Peter Smith. *Modern Latin America.* 3d ed. 1992. The best brief introduction.

Spear, Percival. *India: A Modern History.* Rev. ed. 1972. A standard survey.

NOTES

1. George Blankstein, *Perón's Argentina* (Chicago: University of Chicago Press, 1953), 37.

WEB RESOURCES

Pronunciation Guide

Interactive Map

MAP 27.1 The Mexican Revolution

Primary Sources

Education, Civilization, and "Foreignization" in Buganda

London Manifesto

Parable of the Eagle, Limbo, Prayer for Peace, Vultures

The Plan of Ayala

Speech to the Nation

Answer to the History in Focus Question

See photo on page 752, "*The Agitator,* a Mural by Diego Rivera."

Plus

Chapter Objectives

ACE multiple-choice quiz

Flashcards

NATURE IS NEVER RELIABLE, and all living things periodically suffer from a catastrophic drop in food supplies. Human history is filled with tales of famines—times when crops failed, food supplies ran out, and people starved.

NATURAL FAMINES

India, dependent on the monsoon rains, has been particularly prone to such calamities, with famines striking two to four times a century, whenever the rains failed for several years in succession. Three times in the eighteenth century (1702–1704, 1769–1770, and 1790–1792) famines killed several million people in different parts of the subcontinent. The nineteenth century was worse, with famines in 1803–1804, 1837–1838, 1868–1870, and 1876–1878. The last famine also afflicted northern China, causing between 9 and 13 million deaths from hunger and from the diseases of malnutrition. There were even incidents of cannibalism, as starving adults killed and ate starving children.

When a drought hit a region, it decimated not only the human population but also the animals they relied on to transport goods and plow the land. Likewise, droughts lowered the water levels in rivers and canals, so food could not be moved from one place to another.

COMMERCIAL FAMINES

That all changed in the nineteenth century. Railroads and steamships could transport foodstuffs across great distances in a matter of days or weeks, regardless of drought or heavy rains. Great Britain became dependent on imports of wheat from Russia and the American Midwest, and later of beef from Argentina. Yet famines were worse than ever, and the global death toll from starvation has been far higher since the mid-nineteenth century than it ever was in earlier times. Why?

Consider the Irish famine of 1845–1848. By the early nineteenth century the potato had become the main source of nutrition for the Irish people. Potatoes grew abundantly in the cool, moist climate of Ireland and produced more calories per acre than any other crop. Most of the Irish were poor tenant farmers, and potatoes had allowed their population to increase far more than wheat or rye could have.

In fall 1845 the blight turned the potatoes in the fields black, mushy, and inedible. The harvest was ruined the following year as well. It recovered slightly in 1847, but was bad again in 1848. Tens of thousands died of starvation, while hundreds of thousands died from the diseases that strike malnourished people, especially dysentery, typhus, and cholera. Travelers saw corpses rotting in their hovels or on the sides of roads. Altogether, a million or more people died, while another million managed to emigrate, reducing the population of Ireland by half.

Throughout those years, wheat grew in Ireland, but much of it was exported to England, where customers had money to pay for it. Like any other commodity, food cost money. The Irish farmers, poor even before the famines, were destitute and could not afford to buy the wheat. The British government, wedded to the ideology of laissez faire, was convinced that interfering with the free market would only make things worse. Relief efforts were half-hearted at best; the official responsible for Irish affairs preferred to leave the situation to "the operation of natural causes."

The same held true in India, like Ireland a colony of Great Britain. The drought of 1876–1878 killed over 5 million Indians in the Deccan region, while British officials were helpless or indifferent. Part of the problem was transportation. In the 1870s only a few railway lines connected major cities. Most goods were still transported in bullock carts, but the bullocks also starved during the drought. Another obstacle was political. The idea that a government should be responsible

Famines and Politics

for feeding the population was unthinkable at the time. And so, while millions were starving in the Deccan, the Punjab region was exporting wheat to Britain.

Over the next twenty years so-called famine railways were built in the regions historically most affected by the failures of the monsoon. When drought struck again at the end of the century, the railways were ready to transport food to areas that had previously been accessible only by bullock carts. However, the inhabitants of the affected regions had no money with which to buy what little food there was, and the government was still reluctant to interfere with free enterprise. Grain merchants bought all the stocks, hoarded them until the price rose, then used the railways to transport them out of the famine regions to regions where the harvests were better and people had more money.

In the twentieth century commercial famines became rare, as governments have come to realize that they have a responsibility for food supplies not only for their own people, but for people in other countries as well. Yet commercial famines have not entirely disappeared. In 1974, when a catastrophic flood covered half of Bangladesh, the government was too disorganized to distribute its stocks of rice, while merchants bought what they could and exported it to India. Thousands died, and thousands more survived only because of belated shipments of food from donor countries.

POLITICAL FAMINES

To say that governments are responsible for food supplies does not mean that they exercise that responsibility for the good of the people. Some do, but in many instances food is used as a weapon. In the twentieth century global food supplies were always adequate for the population of the world, and transportation was seldom a problem. Yet the century witnessed the most murderous famines ever recorded.

War-induced famines were not new. In 1812, as the Russian army retreated, it practiced a "scorched-earth" policy of burning food stocks to prevent them from falling into the hands of Napoleon's army. In doing so, it also caused a famine among Russian peasants.

Similar famines resulted from the destruction or requisitioning of crops in the Russian civil war of 1921–1922, the Japanese occupation of Indochina in 1942–1945, and the Biafran war in Nigeria in 1967–1969.

The Bengal famine of 1943 was also war-related. In 1942 the Japanese army had conquered Burma, a rich rice-producing colony. Food supplies in Bengal, which imported rice from Burma, dropped by 5 percent. As prices began to rise, merchants bought stocks of rice and held them in the hope that prices would continue to increase. Sharecroppers sold their stocks to pay off their debts to landlords and village moneylenders. Meanwhile, the railroads that in peacetime would have carried food from other parts of India were fully occupied with military traffic. In October 1943, when a new viceroy, Lord Wavell, arrived in India and ordered the army to transport food to Bengal, food prices dropped to a level that the poor could afford. By then, however, between 1.5 and 2 million Bengalis had starved to death.

Worst of all were the famines that happened in peacetime as a result of the deliberate decisions of governments. The most famous of these political famines was caused by Stalin's collectivization of agriculture in 1932–1934. The Communist Party tried to force the peasants to give up their land and livestock and join collectives, where they could be made to work harder and provide food for the growing cities and industries. When they resisted, their crops were seized. Millions were sent to prison camps and millions of others died of starvation. Stalin chided the overly enthusiastic party members who had caused the famine for being "dizzy with success."

An even worse famine took place in China from 1958 to 1961 during the "Great Leap Forward" (see Chapter 28). Communist Party chairman Mao Zedong decided to hasten the transformation of China into a communist state and industrial power by relying not on the expertise of economists and technocrats but on the enthusiasm of the masses. All farms were consolidated into huge communes. Peasants were mobilized to work on giant construction projects or to make steel out of household utensils and tools in backyard furnaces. The harvest of 1959 was poor, and later ones were even worse. The amount of grain per person declined from 452 pounds (205 kilograms) in 1957 to 340 pounds (154 kilograms) in 1961. Since the Central Statistical Bureau had been shut down, the central government was unaware of the shortages and demanded ever-higher requisitions of food to feed the army and urban and industrial workers and to export to the Soviet Union to pay off China's debts. The amount of food left to the farmers was between one-fifth and one-half of their usual subsistence diet. From 1958 to 1961 between 20 and 30 million Chinese are estimated to have starved or died of the diseases of malnutrition in the most catastrophic famine in the history of the world. The leaders of the Communist Party either were unaware of its extent or, if they knew, did not dare mention it for fear of displeasing Mao, who denied its existence.

Nothing quite as horrible has happened since the Great Leap Forward. During the droughts in Africa in the 1970s and 1980s, most people in the affected regions received international food aid, but the governments of Ethiopia and Sudan either denied that their people were hungry or prevented food shipments from reaching drought victims in order to crush rebellions.

In the world today, natural disasters are as frequent as ever, and many countries are vulnerable to food shortages. No one now claims, as many did in the nineteenth century, that governments have no business providing free food to the starving. Though food is not equitably distributed, there is enough for all human beings now, and there will be enough for the foreseeable future. However, humanitarian feelings compete with other political agendas, and the specter of politically motivated famines still stalks the world.

Issues in World History

Perils and Promises of a Global Community, 1945 to the Present

An increasingly interconnected world faced new hopes and fears after World War II. The United Nations promoted peace, international cooperation, and human rights. Colonized peoples gained independence, and global trade expanded.

However, Cold War rhetoric and nuclear stalemate dispelled dreams of world peace. Wars in Korea and Vietnam, as well as proxy conflicts from Nicaragua to Afghanistan, pitted the United States against communist regimes. Following the Cold War nuclear proliferation and terrorism became top concerns. The 9/11 attacks by Muslim zealots on the World Trade Center and the Pentagon triggered an American "global war on terrorism." The ensuing invasions of Afghanistan and Iraq made the Middle East a top danger spot.

The industrialized nations, including Germany and Japan, recovered well from World War II. Elsewhere economic development came slowly, except in a handful of countries: South Korea, Taiwan, Brazil, Argentina, and, after 2000, China and India. In Africa and other poor regions, population growth usually offset economic gains.

Although the Green Revolution of the 1960s and genetic engineering thirty years later alleviated much world hunger, industrial growth and automobile use increased pollution and competition for petroleum supplies. Global warming became an international concern, along with overfishing, deforestation, and endangerment of wild species.

Globalization affected culture as well. Transnational corporations selling uniform products threatened localized economic enterprises, and Western popular culture aroused fears of cultural imperialism. The Internet and the emergence of English as the global language improved international communication but also stimulated fears that cultural diversity would be lost.

1950 | 1960 | 1970

- **1945** United Nations charter signed in San Francisco
- Military takes power in Brazil **1964**
- Military coup overthrows Allende in Chile **1973**
- **1946** International Monetary Fund and World Bank founded
- Cuban Revolution **1959**
- **1962** Cuban missile crisis
- **1952** U.S. tests first hydrogen bomb
- Neil Armstrong walks on moon **1969**

- **1948–1952** Marshall Plan helps rebuild western Europe
- **1961** Berlin Wall built
- **1949** NATO founded
- **1955** Warsaw Pact formed
- **1968** Student uprising in France
- Soviet troops crush revolt in Hungary **1956**
- **1957** Common Market founded

- Apartheid becomes official in South Africa **1948**
- Guinea wins independence from France **1958**
- Ghana first British colony in West Africa to win independence **1957**
- **1960** Nigeria, Congo, Somalia, Togo win independence
- **1963** Kenya independent
- **1970–1980** White domination of Rhodesia yields to international pressure

- **1948** State of Israel founded; first Arab-Israeli War
- **1956** Suez crisis
- **1960** Organization of Petroleum Exporting Countries founded
- **1967** Six Day Arab-Israeli War
- **1954–1962** Algerian war for Independence
- October Arab-Israeli War leads to oil embargo, price hikes **1973**

- Communist Revolution in China **1949**
- **1949** Indonesia wins independence from Netherlands
- **1951–1953** Korean War
- **1954–1975** Vietnam War
- **1966–1969** Cultural Revolution in China
- **1971** Independence of Bangladesh
- Japan becomes world economic power **1970s**

1980 **1990** **2000**

- **1976** Military takes power in Argentina
- **1983–1989** Democracy restored in Brazil, Argentina, Chile
- **1994** NAFTA agreement among Canada, U.S., Mexico
- **1994** Maya uprising in southern Mexico
- **2001** Terrorists attack New York, Washington, D.C.

- **1975** Helsinki Accords
- **1980** Solidarity union founded in Poland
- Fall of communist regimes in eastern Europe **1989**
- **1990** Reunification of Germany
- Introduction of euro **1999**
- End of USSR **1991**
- **1992–2000** Disintegration of Yugoslavia
- European Union admits ten new members **2004**
- **2005** Terrorists bomb London buses

- **1975** Angola and Mozambique win independence from Portugal
- **1985** Africa equals Europe in population
- **1994–1999** Nelson Mandela president of South Africa
- **1999** Democracy restored in Nigeria

- **1979** Islamic Revolution overthrows shah of Iran
- **1980–1988** Iran-Iraq War
- **1991** Persian Gulf War
- **2003** U.S., Britain invade, occupy Iraq
- **2006** Israel and Hezbollah war in Lebanon

- **1979** USSR enters war in Afghanistan
- **1980s** Taiwan, South Korea, Singapore industrialize
- **1989** Chinese troops suppress Tiananmen Square protest
- **1997** Asian financial crisis starts in Thailand
- **1999** East Timor wins independence from Indonesia

CHAPTER 28

The Cold War and Decolonization

1945–1975

CHAPTER PREVIEW

In 1946, in a speech at Fulton, Missouri, Great Britain's wartime leader Winston Churchill declared that "an iron curtain has descended across the Continent [of Europe]. . . . I am convinced there is nothing they [the communists] so much admire as strength, and there is nothing for which they have less respect than weakness, especially military weakness." The phrase **"iron curtain"** became a watchword of the **Cold War**, the state of political tension and military rivalry that was then beginning between the United States and its allies and the Soviet Union and its allies.

In the early years of World War II, Churchill and President Franklin Roosevelt had looked forward to a postwar world of economic cooperation and restoration of sovereignty to peoples suffering Axis occupation and, above all, to a world where war and territorial

CL This icon will direct you to the website where you can Prepare for Class, Improve Your Grade, and Ace the Test: college.cengage.com/pic/bullietbrief4e conquest would not be tolerated. By the time Churchill delivered his "iron curtain" speech, however, Britain's electorate had voted him out of power, Harry S Truman had succeeded to the presidency after Roosevelt's death, and the Soviet Union was dominating eastern Europe and supporting communist movements in China, Iran, Turkey, Greece, and Korea. Although Soviet diplomats sat with their former allies in the newly founded United Nations Organization, confrontation rather than cooperation was the hallmark of relations between East and West.

The intensity of the Cold War sometimes obscured a postwar phenomenon of even greater importance. Western domination of Asia, Africa, and Latin America was largely ended, and the colonial empires of the New Imperialism were gradually dismantled. A new generation of national leaders sometimes skillfully played Cold War antagonism to their own advantage. Their real business, however, was the difficult task of nation building.

Each land freeing itself from imperialism had its own specific history and conditions. After independence, some new nations sided openly with the United States and some with the Soviet Union. Others banded together in a posture of neutrality and spoke with one voice about their need for economic and technical assistance and the obligation of the wealthy nations to satisfy those needs.

The Cold War military rivalry stimulated extraordinary advances in weaponry and associated technologies, but many new nations struggled to educate their citizens, nurture industry, and escape the economic constraints imposed by their former imperialist masters. The environment suffered severe pressures, whether from oil exploration and transport to feed the growing economies of the wealthy nations or from deforestation in poor regions challenged by the need for cropland. Neither rich nor poor realized the costs associated with environmental change.

THE COLD WAR

What were the major threats to world peace during the Cold War?

The wartime alliance between the United States, Great Britain, and the Soviet Union had been an uneasy one. Fear of working-class revolution, which the Nazis had played on in their rise to power, was not confined to Germany. For more than a century political and economic leaders committed to free markets and untrammeled capital investment had loathed socialism in its several forms. After World War II, the iron curtain in Europe and communist insurgencies in China and elsewhere seemed to confirm the threat of worldwide revolution.

To protect themselves from the Soviet Union, which they perceived as the nerve center of world revolution and as a military power capable of launching a terrible new war, the United States and the countries of western Europe established the **North Atlantic Treaty Organization (NATO)** military alliance in 1949. Soviet leaders felt themselves surrounded by hostile forces just when they were trying to recover from the terrible losses sustained in the war. The distrust and suspicion between the two sides played out on a worldwide stage. The United Nations provided the venue for face-to-face debate.

iron curtain Winston Churchill's term for the Cold War division between the Soviet-dominated East and the U.S.-dominated West.

Cold War (1945–1991) The ideological struggle between communism (Soviet Union) and capitalism (United States) for world influence. The Soviet Union and the United States came to the brink of actual war during the Cuban missile crisis but never attacked one another. The Cold War came to an end when the Soviet Union dissolved in 1991.

North Atlantic Treaty Organization (NATO) Organization formed in 1949 as a military alliance of western European and North American states against the Soviet Union and its east European allies.

The Founding of the United Nations
This photograph shows the arrival of President Harry S Truman's motorcade at the Fairmount Hotel in San Francisco for the signing of the United Nations Charter in June 1945. Though the war in the Pacific had not yet ended, delegates from fifty countries signed the treaty that idealistically promised an end to wars of aggression.   (McCreary/UN Photo)

United Nations International organization founded in 1945 to promote world peace and cooperation. It replaced the League of Nations.

The United Nations

In 1944, representatives from the United States, Great Britain, the Soviet Union, and China met and drafted specific charter proposals that finally bore fruit in the United Nations Charter, a treaty ratified on October 24, 1945. Like the League of Nations, the **United Nations** had two main bodies: the General Assembly, with representatives from all member states; and the Security Council, with five permanent members—China, France, Great Britain, the United States, and the Soviet Union—and seven rotating members. Various United Nations agencies focused on specialized international problems—for example, UNICEF (United Nations Children's Emergency Fund), FAO (Food and Agriculture Organization), and UNESCO (United Nations Educational, Scientific and Cultural Organization) (see Environment and Technology: The Green Revolution). The United Nations operated by majority vote, except that the five permanent members of the Security Council had veto power in that chamber.

All signatories to the United Nations Charter renounced war and territorial conquest. Nevertheless, peacekeeping, the sole preserve of the Security Council, became a vexing problem. The permanent members often exercised their veto to protect their friends and interests, though from time to time they authorized the United Nations to send observers or peacekeeping forces to monitor truces or agreements.

The decolonization of Africa and Asia greatly swelled the size of the General Assembly but not the Security Council. Many of the new nations looked to the United Nations for material assistance and access to a wider political world. While the vetoes of the Security Council's permanent members often stymied actions touching

Chronology

Cold War	Decolonization
	1947 Partition of India
1948–1949 Berlin airlift	
1949 NATO formed	**1949** Dutch withdraw from Indonesia
1950–1953 Korean War	
1952 United States detonates first hydrogen bomb	
	1954 CIA intervention in Guatemala; defeat at Dienbienphu ends French hold on Vietnam
1955 Warsaw Pact concluded	**1955** Bandung Conference
1956 Soviet Union suppresses Hungarian revolt	
1957 Soviet Union launches first artificial satellite into earth orbit	**1957** Ghana becomes first British colony in Africa to gain independence
	1959 Fidel Castro leads revolution in Cuba
	1960 Shootings in Sharpeville intensify South African struggle against apartheid; Nigeria becomes independent
1961 East Germany builds Berlin Wall	
1962 Cuban missile crisis	**1962** Algeria wins independence
	1971 Bangladesh secedes from Pakistan
1975 Helsinki Accords; end of Vietnam War	

(Time markers: 1945, 1955, 1965, 1975)

even indirectly on Cold War concerns, the General Assembly became an arena for expressing opinions on many issues involving decolonization, a movement that the Soviet Union strongly encouraged but the Western colonial powers resisted.

In the early years of the United Nations, General Assembly resolutions carried great weight. An example is a 1947 resolution that sought to divide Palestine into sovereign Jewish and Arab states. Gradually, though, the flood of new members produced a voting majority concerned more with poverty, racial discrimination, and the struggle against imperialism than with the Cold War. As a result, the Western powers increasingly disregarded the General Assembly, allowing the new nations of the world to have their say but not to act collectively.

Capitalism and Communism

In July 1944, with Allied victory a forgone conclusion, economic specialists representing over forty countries met at Bretton Woods, a New Hampshire resort, to devise a new international monetary system. The signatories eventually agreed to fix exchange

ENVIRONMENT + TECHNOLOGY

The Green Revolution

Concern about world food supplies grew directly out of serious shortages caused by the devastation and trade disruptions of World War II. The Food and Agriculture Organization of the United Nations, the Rockefeller Foundation, and the Ford Foundation took leading roles in fostering crop research and educating farmers about agricultural techniques. In 1966 the International Rice Research Institute (established in 1960–1962) began distributing seeds for an improved rice variety known as IR-8. Crop yields from this and other new varieties, along with improved farming techniques, were initially so impressive that the term *Green Revolution* was coined to describe a new era in agriculture.

On the heels of the successful new rice strains, new varieties of corn and wheat were introduced. Building on twenty years of Rockefeller-funded research in Mexico, the Centro Internacional de Mejoramiento de Maiz y Trigo (International Center for the Improvement of Maize and Wheat) was established in 1966 under Norman Borlaug, who was awarded the Nobel Peace Prize four years later. This organization distributed short, stiff-strawed varieties of wheat that were resistant to disease and responsive to fertilizer.

By 1970 other centers for research on tropical agriculture had been established in Ibadan, Nigeria, and Cali, Colombia. But the success of the Green Revolution and the growing need for its products called for a more comprehensive effort. The Consultative Group on International Agricultural Research brought together World Bank expertise, private foundations, international organizations, and national foreign aid agencies to undertake worldwide support of efforts to increase food productivity and improve natural resource management. More recently, the optimism that followed these innovations has been muted by the realization that population growth, soil depletion, the costs of irrigation and fertilizer, and the growing concentration of land in the export sector combined to reduce the effects of improved crop technology in poor countries.

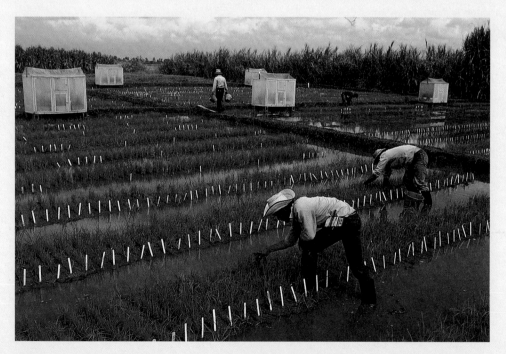

MIRACLE RICE New strains of so-called miracle rice made many nations in South and Southeast Asia self-sufficient in food production after decades of worry that population growth would outstrip agricultural productivity.
(Victor Englebert)

rates. They also created the International Monetary Fund (IMF) to use currency reserves from member nations to finance temporary trade deficits and the **World Bank** to provide funds for reconstructing Europe and helping needy countries.

The Soviet Union attended the Bretton Woods Conference and signed the agreements, but by 1946, suspicion between the Soviet Union and the United States and Britain had deepened. While the rest of the world moved to a monetary system that relied for stability on most countries holding reserves of dollars and the United States holding reserves of gold, the Soviet Union established a closed monetary system for itself and the new communist regimes in eastern Europe. In the Western countries, supply and demand determined prices; in the Soviet command economy, government priorities and agencies allocated goods and set prices, irrespective of market forces.

Many leaders from the newly independent states preferred the Soviet Union's socialist example to the capitalism of their former colonizers. Thus, the relative success of economies patterned on Eastern or Western models became an element in the Cold War rivalry. Each side trumpeted economic successes measured by such things as industrial output, changes in per capita income, and productivity gains as evidence of its superiority.

During World War II, increased military spending and the draft brought full employment and high wages to the United States. With peace, the United States enjoyed prosperity and an international competitive advantage, while European economies were still heavily damaged from the war. To support European reconstruction, the U.S. **Marshall Plan** provided $12.5 billion to friendly countries between 1948 and 1952. By 1963, a resurgent European economy had doubled 1940 output.

Western European governments generally increased their role in economic management during this period. In Great Britain, the Labour Party government of the 1950s nationalized coal, steel, railroads, and health care. The French government nationalized public utilities; the auto, banking, and insurance industries; and parts of the mining industry.

In 1948, European governments also promoted economic cooperation and integration with the creation of the Organization of European Economic Cooperation (OEEC). After cooperative policies on coal and steel proved successful, some OEEC countries were ready to begin lowering tariffs to encourage the movement of goods and capital. In 1957, France, West Germany, Italy, the Netherlands, Belgium, and Luxembourg signed a treaty creating the European Economic Community, also known as the Common Market. The word *economic* was dropped from the group's title in 1967, making it simply the **European Community (EC)**. By the 1970s, the EC nations had nearly overtaken the United States in industrial production. The economic alliance expanded after 1970, as Great Britain, Denmark, Greece, Ireland, Spain, Portugal, Finland, Sweden, and Austria joined.

Prosperity brought dramatic changes to European society. Average wages increased, unemployment fell, and social welfare benefits were expanded. Governments increased spending on health care, unemployment benefits, old-age pensions, public housing, and grants to poor families with children. The combination of economic growth and income redistribution raised living standards and fueled demand for consumer goods.

The Soviet experience provided a dramatic contrast. The economy of the Soviet Union was just as devastated at the end of the Second World War as those of western

World Bank A specialized agency of the United Nations that makes loans to countries for economic development, trade promotion, and debt consolidation. Its formal name is the International Bank for Reconstruction and Development.

Marshall Plan U.S. program to support the reconstruction of western Europe after World War II. By 1961 more than $20 billion in economic aid had been dispersed.

European Community (EC) An organization promoting economic unity in Europe formed in 1967 by consolidation of earlier, more limited, agreements. It was replaced by the European Union (EU) in 1993.

Europe. However, with enormous natural resources, a large population, and abundant energy at its disposal, Soviet recovery was rapid at first. Moreover, Soviet planners had made large investments in technical and scientific education, and the Soviet state had developed heavy industry in the 1930s and during the war years. But as the postwar period progressed, bureaucratic control of the economy grew less efficient. In the 1970s, the gap with the West widened. The Soviet economy failed to meet domestic demand for clothing, housing, food, automobiles, and consumer electronics. Agricultural inefficiency forced the Soviet Union to rely on food imports.

The socialist nations of eastern Europe were compelled to follow the Soviet economic model, although some national differences appeared. Poland and Hungary, for example, implemented agricultural collectivization more slowly than did Czechoslovakia. Significant growth occurred among the socialist economies, but the inefficiencies and failures that plagued the Soviet economy troubled them as well.

The United States and the Soviet Union competed in providing loans and grants and in supplying arms (at bargain prices) to countries willing to align with them politically. Thus, the relative success or failure of capitalism and communism in Europe and the United States was not necessarily the strongest consideration in other parts of the world when the time came to construct new national economies.

West Versus East in Europe and Korea

For Germany, Austria, and Japan, peace brought foreign military occupation and new governments that were initially controlled by the occupiers. When relations with the Western powers cooled at the end of the war, the Soviet Union sought to prevent the reappearance of hostile regimes on its borders. Initially, the Soviet Union seemed willing to accept governments in neighboring states that included a mix of parties as long as they were not hostile to local communist groups or to the Soviets. The nations of central and eastern Europe were deeply split by the legacies of the war, and many were willing to embrace the communists as a hedge against those who had supported fascism or cooperated with the Germans. As relations between the Soviets and the West worsened in the late 1940s, local communists, their strength augmented by Soviet military occupation, gained victories across eastern Europe. Western leaders saw the rapid emergence of communist regimes in Poland, Czechoslovakia, Hungary, Bulgaria, Romania, Yugoslavia, and Albania as a threat.

For the United States, the shift from viewing the Soviet Union as an ally against Germany to seeing it as a worldwide enemy took two years. In the waning days of World War II, the United States had seemed amenable to the Soviet desire for freer access to the Mediterranean through Turkish straits. But in July 1947, the **Truman Doctrine** offered military aid to help both Turkey and Greece resist Soviet military pressure and subversion. In 1951, Greece and Turkey were admitted to NATO. NATO's Soviet counterpart, the **Warsaw Pact**, emerged in 1955 in response to the Western powers' decision to allow West Germany to rearm within limits set by NATO.

The Soviet Union tested Western resolve in 1948–1949 by blockading the areas of Berlin occupied by British, French, and American forces, which were surrounded by Soviet-controlled East Germany. Airlifts of food and fuel defeated the blockade. In 1961, the East German government accentuated Germany's political division by building the Berlin Wall, as much to prevent its citizens from fleeing to the noncom-

Truman Doctrine Foreign policy initiated by U.S. president Harry Truman in 1947. It offered military aid to help Turkey and Greece resist Soviet military pressure and subversion.

Warsaw Pact The 1955 treaty binding the Soviet Union and countries of eastern Europe in an alliance against the North Atlantic Treaty Organization.

munist western part of that city as to keep Westerners from entering East German territory. The West tested the East, in turn, by encouraging a rift between the Soviet Union and Yugoslavia. Western aid and encouragement resulted in Yugoslavia's signing a defensive treaty with Greece and Turkey (but not with NATO) and deciding against joining the Warsaw Pact.

Soviet power set clear limits on how far any eastern European country might stray from Soviet domination. In 1956, Soviet troops crushed an anti-Soviet revolt in Hungary. Czechoslovakia suffered Hungary's fate in 1968. The West, a passive onlooker, had no recourse but to acknowledge that the Soviet Union had the right to intervene in the domestic affairs of any Soviet-bloc nation whenever it wished.

A more explosive crisis erupted in Korea, where the Second World War had left Soviet troops in control north of the thirty-eighth parallel and American troops in control to the south. When no agreement could be reached on holding countrywide elections, communist North Korea and noncommunist South Korea became independent states in 1948. Two years later, North Korea invaded South Korea. The United Nations Security Council, in the absence of the Soviet delegation, voted to condemn the invasion and called on members of the United Nations to come to the defense of South Korea. The United States was the primary ally of South Korea. The People's Republic of China supported North Korea. The **Korean War** lasted until 1953, when the two sides eventually agreed to a truce along the thirty-eighth parallel, but no peace treaty was concluded.

Korean War (1950–1953) Conflict that began with North Korea's invasion of South Korea and came to involve the United Nations (primarily the United States) allying with South Korea and the People's Republic of China allying with North Korea.

Japan benefited from the Korean War in an unexpected way. Massive purchases of supplies by the United States and spending by American servicemen on leave provided a financial stimulus to the Japanese economy similar to the stimulus that Europe received from the Marshall Plan.

U.S. Defeat in Vietnam

A shooting war also developed in Vietnam. In 1954, United States president Dwight D. Eisenhower (1953–1961) and his foreign policy advisers decided not to aid France in its effort to sustain colonial rule in Vietnam, perceiving that the days of the European colonial empires were numbered. After winning independence, however, communist North Vietnam supported a guerrilla movement—the Viet Cong—against the noncommunist government of South Vietnam.

When John F. Kennedy became president (1961–1963), he and his advisers decided to support the South Vietnamese government of President Ngo Dinh Diem (dee-EM). They realized that the Diem government was corrupt and unpopular, but they feared that a communist victory would encourage communist movements throughout Southeast Asia and alter the Cold War balance of power. Kennedy steadily increased the number of American military advisers from 685 to almost 16,000 while secretly encouraging the overthrow and execution of Diem in hopes of seeing a more popular and honest government come to power.

Lyndon Johnson, who became president (1963–1969) after Kennedy was assassinated, gained support from Congress for unlimited expansion of U.S. military deployment. By the end of 1966, 365,000 U.S. troops were engaged in the **Vietnam War**. Nothing the Americans tried, however, succeeded in stopping the Viet Cong guerrillas and their North Vietnamese allies. Diem's successors turned out to be just

Vietnam War (1954–1975) Conflict pitting North Vietnam and South Vietnamese communist guerrillas against the South Vietnamese government, aided after 1961 by the United States.

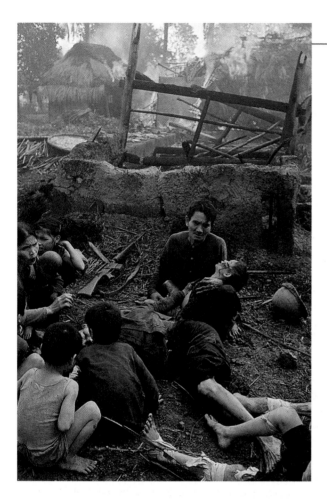

The Vietnamese People at War
American and South Vietnamese troops burned many villages to deprive the enemy of civilian refuges. This policy undermined support for the South Vietnamese government in the countryside. (Dana Stone/stockphoto.com)

HISTORY IN FOCUS To what extent do you think communist ideology motivated many South Vietnamese to support the northern side? *Find the answer online.*

as corrupt and unpopular as he was, and the heroic nationalist image of North Vietnam's leader, Ho Chi Minh, evoked strong sympathies among many South Vietnamese.

In 1973, a treaty between North Vietnam and the United States ended U.S. involvement in the war and promised future elections. Two years later, in violation of the treaty, Viet Cong and North Vietnamese troops overran the South Vietnamese army and captured the southern capital of Saigon, renaming it Ho Chi Minh City. The two parts of Vietnam were reunited in a single state ruled from the north. The war was bloody and traumatic. The Vietnamese had over a million casualties. The deaths of fifty-eight thousand Americans overseas and the vigorous antiwar movement at home ensured that the United States would not easily be drawn into another shooting war.

The Race for Nuclear Supremacy

Fear of nuclear warfare affected strategic decisions in the Korean and Vietnam Wars. It also affected all other aspects of Cold War confrontation. The devastation of Hiroshima and Nagasaki by atomic weapons (see Chapter 26) had ushered in a new era. Nuclear weapons fed into a logic of total war that was already reaching a peak in Nazi genocide and terror bombing and in massive Allied air raids on large cities. After the Soviet Union exploded its first nuclear device in 1949, fears of a worldwide holocaust grew. Fears increased when the United States exploded a far more powerful weapon, the hydrogen bomb, in 1952 and the Soviet Union followed suit less than a year later. The possibility of the theft of nuclear secrets by Soviet spies fostered paranoia in the United States, and the conviction that the nuclear superpowers were willing to use their terrible weapons if their vital interests were threatened spread despair around the world.

In 1954, President Eisenhower warned Soviet leaders against attacking western Europe. In response to such an attack, he said, the United States would reduce the Soviet Union to "a smoking, radiating ruin at the end of two hours." A few years later, the Soviet leader Nikita Khrushchev (KROOSH-chof) offered an equally stark promise: "We will bury you." His reference was to economic competition, but the image produced in Americans was of literal burial.

Everyone's worst fears seemed about to be realized in the **Cuban missile crisis** of 1962. When the Soviet Union deployed nuclear-tipped missiles in Cuba in response to the U.S. installation of similar missiles in Turkey, the world held its breath. Confronted by unyielding diplomatic pressure and military threats from President Kennedy, Khrushchev backed down and pulled the missiles from Cuba. Subsequently, the United States removed its missiles from Turkey.

Arms limitation also saw progress. In 1963, Great Britain, the United States, and the Soviet Union agreed to ban the testing of nuclear weapons in the atmosphere, in space, and under water, thus reducing the environmental danger of radioactive fallout. In 1968, the United States and the Soviet Union together proposed a world treaty against further proliferation of nuclear weapons. It was signed by 137 countries. Not until 1972, however, did the two superpowers truly recognize the futility of squandering their wealth on ever-larger missile forces.

In Europe, the Soviet-American arms race outran the economic ability of atomic powers France and Britain to keep pace. Instead, the European states sought to relax tensions. Between 1972 and 1975, the Conference on Security and Cooperation in Europe (CSCE) brought delegates from thirty-seven European states, the United States, and Canada to Helsinki. The goal of the Soviet Union was to gain European acceptance of the political boundaries of the Warsaw Pact nations. The **Helsinki Accords** affirmed that no boundaries should be changed by military force. It also contained formal (but nonbinding) declarations calling for economic, social, and governmental contacts across the iron curtain, and for cooperation in humanitarian fields, a provision that paved the way for dialogue about human rights.

Space exploration was another offshoot of the nuclear arms race. The contest to build larger and more accurate missiles for delivery of warheads prompted the superpowers to prove their skills in rocketry by launching space satellites. The Soviet Union placed a small *Sputnik* satellite into orbit around the earth in October 1957. The United States responded with its own satellite three months later. The space race was on, a contest in which accomplishments in space were understood to signify equivalent achievements in the military sphere. *Sputnik* administered a deep shock to American pride and confidence, but in 1969 two Americans, Neil A. Armstrong and Edwin E. "Buzz" Aldrin, became the first humans to walk on the moon.

Despite rhetorical Cold War saber-rattling by Soviet and American leaders, the threat of nuclear war forced a measure of restraint on the superpower adversaries. Because fighting each other directly would have risked escalation to the level of nuclear exchange, they carefully avoided crises that might provoke such confrontations.

Cuban missile crisis (1962) Brink-of-war confrontation between the United States and the Soviet Union over the latter's placement of nuclear-armed missiles in Cuba.

Helsinki Accords (1975) Political and human rights agreement signed in Helsinki, Finland, by the Soviet Union and western European countries.

SECTION REVIEW

- At the outset of the Cold War, the United States established NATO, thus fueling Soviet fear and suspicion.

- The structure of the United Nations created problems with peacekeeping and managing the conflicting aims of member nations.

- After the war, the United States, the USSR, and their respective allies and supporters formed competing economic systems.

- European countries prospered through government management and economic integration, but the Soviet economy steadily lagged behind.

- Superpower rivalry divided Europe and fueled the Korean War, while the Vietnam War resulted in a U.S. defeat.

- The superpower nuclear rivalry culminated with the Cuban missile crisis, after which the superpowers practiced restraint and engaged in arms limitation negotiations.

DECOLONIZATION AND NATION BUILDING

How were the experiences of Asia, Africa, and Latin America similar in this period?

Whereas the losing countries in World War I were stripped of colonies, it was primarily countries on the winning side in World War II that ended up losing their colonies (see Map 28.1).

Circumstances differed profoundly from place to place. In some Asian countries, where colonial rule was of long standing, newly independent states found themselves in possession of viable industries, communications networks, and education systems. In other countries, notably in Africa, decolonization gave birth to nations facing dire economic problems and internal disunity. In Latin America, where political independence already had been achieved, the quest was for freedom from foreign economic domination, particularly by the United States.

New Nations in Southern Asia

Newly independent India and Pakistan were strikingly dissimilar. Muslim Pakistan defined itself according to religion and quickly fell under the control of military leaders. Though 90 percent Hindu, the much larger republic of India, led by Prime Minister Jawaharlal Nehru, was secular. It inherited most of the considerable industrial and educational resources the British had developed, along with the larger share of trained civil servants and military officers.

The decision of the Hindu ruler of the northwestern state of Jammu and Kashmir to join India without consulting his overwhelmingly Muslim subjects led to a war between India and Pakistan in 1947 that ended with an uneasy truce, only to resume briefly in 1965. Though Kashmir remains a flashpoint of patriotic feeling, the two countries managed to avoid further warfare.

Despite recurrent predictions that multilingual India might break up into a number of linguistically homogeneous states, most Indians recognized that unity benefited everyone; and the country pursued a generally democratic and socialist line of development. Pakistan, in contrast, did break up. In 1971, its Bengali-speaking eastern section seceded to become the independent country of Bangladesh.

Elsewhere in the region, nationalist movements won independence as well. Britain granted independence to Burma (now Myanmar [myahn-MAH]) in 1948 and established the Malay Federation that same year. (Singapore, once a member of the federation, became an independent city-state itself in 1965.) In 1946, the United States kept its promise of postwar independence for the Philippine Islands but retained close economic ties and leases on military bases. In the Dutch East Indies, Sukarno (1901–1970) had cooperated with the Japanese occupation in hopes that the Dutch would never return. After a military confrontation, Dutch withdrawal was finally negotiated in 1949, and Sukarno went on to become the dictator of his resource-rich but underdeveloped nation of Indonesia.

In all these cases, communist insurgents plagued the departing colonial powers and the newly formed governments. The most important postwar communist movement arose in the part of Southeast Asia known as French Indochina. There, Ho Chi

Map 28.1 Decolonization, 1947–1999

Notice that independence came a decade or so earlier in South and Southeast Asia than in Africa. Numerous countries that gained independence after World War II in the Caribbean, in South and Central America, and in the Pacific are not shown.

Interactive Map

Date is year independence was achieved. Shading indicates former ruler.

Great Britain	Belgium
France	Portugal
Netherlands	United States
Italy	Other

Minh (hoe chee min) (1890–1969), who had spent several years in France during World War I, played the pivotal role. After training in Moscow, he returned to Vietnam to found the Indochina Communist Party in 1930.

Ho Chi Minh's nationalist coalition, then called the Viet Minh, fought the French with help from the People's Republic of China. After a brutal struggle, the French stronghold of Dienbienphu (dyen-byen-phu) fell in 1954, marking the doom of France's colonial enterprise. Ho's Viet Minh government took over in the north, and a noncommunist nationalist government ruled in the south. As already described, fighting between North and South Vietnam eventually became a major Cold War conflict (see "U.S. Defeat in Vietnam" above).

The Struggle for Independence in Africa

In the quarter-century between 1955 and 1980, African nationalists succeeded in ending European colonial rule. Mostly they gained their independence peacefully, but where European settlers were numerous, violence became the norm.

Algeria rebelled in 1954. The French government was as determined to hold on to Algeria as it had been to keep Vietnam. Ten percent of the Algerian population was European, and Algeria's economy was strongly oriented toward France. Both sides pursued the revolt with great brutality. When the Algerians finally won independence in 1962, the flood of angry colonists returning to France undermined the Algerian economy because very few Arabs had received technical training or acquired management experience.

None of the independence movements in sub-Saharan Africa matched the Algerian struggle in scale. Some of the politicians who led the nationalist movements had devoted their lives to ridding their homelands of foreign occupation. An example is Kwame Nkrumah (KWAH-mee nn-KROO-muh) (1909–1972), who in 1957 became prime minister of Ghana (formerly the Gold Coast), the first British colony in Africa to achieve independence. Only a few hundred Ghanaian children of Nkrumah's generation had graduated each year from the seven-year elementary schools, and he was one of only a handful who made it through teacher training college. After graduation, he spent a decade reading philosophy and theology in the United States and absorbing ideas about black pride and independence then being propounded by black leaders W. E. B. Du Bois and Marcus Garvey.

After a brief stay in Britain, Nkrumah returned in 1947 to the Gold Coast to work for independence. The time was right. Great Britain had already freed its Asian colonies, and Nkrumah quickly united the people of Ghana behind him. Independence thus came without war or protracted bloodshed. Nkrumah turned out to be more effective internationally as a spokesman for colonized peoples than he was at home as an administrator. In 1966, a group of army officers ousted him.

Jomo Kenyatta (ca. 1894–1978) traveled a more difficult road in Kenya, where a substantial number of European coffee planters strengthened Britain's desire to retain control. A movement the settlers called Mau Mau, formed mostly by the Kikuyu (kih-KOO-you) people, became active in 1952. As violence between settlers and movement fighters escalated, British troops hunted down the leaders and resettled the Kikuyu. The British charged Kenyatta with being a Mau Mau leader and held him in prison and then in internal exile for eight years during a declared state of

CL **Primary Source: Comments on Algeria** *Find out why Charles de Gaulle believes Algeria is more trouble to France than it is worth.*

Jomo Kenyatta

Jomo Kenyatta, newly elected premier, is cheered by crowds in Nairobi in 1963. Kenyatta (waving ceremonial "whisk") had led the struggle to end British colonial rule in Kenya.   (Bettmann/Corbis)

emergency. They released him in 1961, and negotiations with the British to write a constitution for an independent Kenya followed. In 1964, Kenyatta was elected the first president of the Republic of Kenya. He proved to be an effective, though autocratic, ruler.

In contrast, African leaders in the French colonies of sub-Saharan Africa were slow to call for independence. They visualized change in terms of promises of greater political and civil rights made in 1944 by the Free French movement of General Charles de Gaulle at a conference in Brazzaville. This Brazzaville Conference also had promised to expand French education at the village level, to improve health services, and to open more lower-level administrative positions to Africans, but the word *independence* was never mentioned.

African politicians also realized that some French colonies—such as Ivory Coast with its coffee and cacao exports, fishing, and hardwood forests—had good economic prospects and others, such as land-locked, desert Niger, did not. As a Malagasy politician said in 1958, "When I let my heart talk, I am a partisan of total and immediate independence [for Madagascar]; when I make my reason speak, I realize that it is impossible." Ultimately, however, the heart prevailed everywhere. Guinea, under the dynamic leadership of Sékou Touré (SAY-koo too-RAY), led the way in 1958. By the time Nigeria, the most populous West African state, achieved independence from Great Britain in 1960, the leaders of many former French colonies in West Africa could attend the celebrations as independent heads of state.

European settlers fought hard to hold on in southern Africa. The African struggle against Portuguese rule in Angola and Mozambique dragged on until frustrated Portuguese military commanders overthrew the government of Portugal in 1974 and granted the African colonies independence the following year. After a ten-year fight, European settlers in the British colony of Southern Rhodesia ceded power in 1980 to the African majority, who renamed the country Zimbabwe. The change had been swift; a century after the "scramble" for Africa began, European colonial rule in Africa had ended.

Only South Africa and neighboring Southwest Africa remained in the hands of European minorities. After World War II, the white minority government had reconstructed South Africa according to extreme racial separation, or *apartheid* (uh-PART-hate). The cities, the best jobs, and most of the land were reserved for Europeans. Africans and others classified as "nonwhites" were subjected to strict limitations on place of residence, right to travel, and access to jobs and public facilities.

CL Primary Source:
The Rivonia Trial
Speech to the Court
*Find out why Nelson Mandela
decided that violence was the
only way out for Africans.*

The African National Congress (ANC), formed in 1912, led the fight against apartheid and in favor of a nonracial society. After police fired on demonstrators in the African town of Sharpeville in 1960, an African lawyer named Nelson Mandela (b. 1918) organized guerrilla resistance by the ANC. Mandela was sentenced to life in prison in 1964, and the government outlawed the ANC and other opposition organizations. For a time, things were quiet, but in 1976 young students reignited the bloody and prolonged struggle that would force an end to apartheid.

The Quest for Economic Freedom in Latin America

In Latin America, the postwar decades saw continuing struggles over foreign ownership and social inequality. American and European companies dominated Chile's copper, Cuba's sugar and resort hotels, Colombia's coffee, Guatemala's bananas, and the communications networks of several countries. Even in a country like Mexico, where the ruling Institutional Revolutionary Party, or PRI, was officially committed to revolutionary independence and economic development, a yawning gulf between rich and poor, urban and rural, persisted. According to one estimate from the mid-1960s, not more than 300 foreign and 800 Mexican companies dominated the country, and some 2,000 families made up the industrial-financial elite. At the other end of the economic scale were peasants and the 14 percent of the population classified as Indian.

Jacobo Arbenz Guzmán, elected president of Guatemala in 1951, was typical of Latin American leaders who tried to confront the power of foreign interests. His expropriation of large estates angered the United Fruit Company, a U.S. corporation that dominated banana exports and held vast tracts of land in reserve. Reacting to reports that Arbenz was becoming friendly toward communism, the United States Central Intelligence Agency (CIA) prompted a takeover by the Guatemalan military in 1954. CIA intervention removed Arbenz from the scene; it also condemned Guatemala to decades of governmental instability and growing violence between leftist and rightist elements in society.

In Cuba, U.S. companies owned 40 percent of raw sugar production, 23 percent of nonsugar industry, 90 percent of telephone and electrical services, and 50 percent of public service railways. The needs of the U.S. economy largely determined Cuban foreign trade and held back development. Profits went north to the United States or to a small class of wealthy Cubans, many of foreign origin. Cuba's ruler during that period, Fulgencio Batista, became a symbol of corruption, repression, and foreign economic domination.

In 1959, a popular rebellion forced Batista to flee the country. Fidel Castro, the lawyer leader of the rebels, his brother Raoul Castro, and Ernesto "Che" Guevara (chay guh-VAHR-uh), who was the main theorist of communist revolution in Latin America, created a new regime. Within a year, Fidel Castro's government had redistributed land, lowered urban rents, and raised wages, effectively transferring 15 percent of the national income from rich to poor. Within twenty-two months, the Castro government seized almost all U.S. property in Cuba and most Cuban corporations. This action resulted in a blockade by the United States, the flight of middle-class and technically trained Cubans, a drop in foreign investment, and the beginning of chronic food shortages.

Little evidence supports the view that Castro undertook his revolution to install a communist government. But at that time, the East-West rivalry of the Cold War was increasingly influencing international politics, and Castro soon turned to the Soviet Union for economic aid. In doing so, he unwittingly committed his nation to economic stagnation and dependence on a foreign power as damaging as the previous relationship with the United States had been.

In April 1961, some fifteen hundred Cuban exiles, whom the CIA had trained for a year in Guatemala, landed at the Bay of Pigs in an effort to overthrow Castro. The Cuban army defeated the attempted invasion in a matter of days, partly because the new U.S. president, John F. Kennedy, decided not to provide all the air support that the plan originally called for. The failure of the Bay of Pigs invasion tarnished the reputation of the United States and the CIA and provoked Castro into declaring that he and his revolution were and always had been Marxist-Leninist.

Challenges of Nation Building

Decolonization occurred on a vast scale. Fifty-one nations signed the United Nations Charter in the closing months of 1945. During the United Nations' first decade, twenty-five new members joined, a third of them upon gaining independence. During the next decade forty-six more new members were admitted, nearly all of them former colonial territories.

Each of these nations had to organize and institute some form of government. Comparatively few were able to do so without experiencing coups, rewritten constitutions, or regional rebellions. Leaders did not always agree on the form independence should take. In the absence of established constitutional traditions, leaders frequently tried to impose their own visions by force. Most of the new nations, while trying to establish political stability, also faced severe economic challenges, including foreign ownership and operation of key resources and the need to build infrastructure. Overdependence on world demand for raw materials and on imported manufactured goods persisted in many places long after independence.

Because the achievement of political and economic goals called for educated and skilled personnel, education was another common concern in newly emerging nations. Addressing that concern required more than building and staffing schools. In some countries, leaders had to decide which language to teach and how to inculcate a sense of national unity in students from different—and sometimes historically antagonistic—ethnic, religious, and linguistic groups. Another problem was how to provide satisfying jobs for new graduates, many of whom had high expectations because of their education.

Only rarely were the new nations able to surmount these hurdles. Even the most economically and educationally successful, such as South Korea, suffered from tendencies toward authoritarian rule. Costa Rica, a country with a remarkably stable parliamentary regime from 1949 onward and a literacy rate of 90 percent, remained heavily dependent on world prices for agricultural commodities and on importation of manufactured goods.

SECTION REVIEW

- British India split into secular, multilingual India and its rival, Muslim Pakistan, a military state that inherited few British-built resources.
- Nationalists won independence in Burma, the Malay Federation, the Philippines, and Indonesia, while Vietnamese communists fought to control their country.
- African colonies achieved independence peacefully except for those with significant numbers of European settlers.
- Latin American struggles for economic independence often flared into violence and revolution and provoked U.S. intervention.
- Decolonization occurred rapidly and often yielded political, social, and economic instability.

BEYOND A BIPOLAR WORLD

How did the rivalry between the Cold War superpowers affect the rest of the world?

Although the East-West superpower rivalry dominated world affairs, newly independent states had concerns that were primarily domestic and regional. The challenge they faced was to find a way to pursue their ends within the bipolar structure of the Cold War—and possibly to take advantage of the East-West rivalry. In short, the superpowers dominated the world but did not control it. And as time progressed, they dominated it less and less.

The Third World

As one of the most successful leaders of the decolonization movement, Indonesia's President Sukarno was an appropriate figure to host a meeting in 1955 of twenty-nine African and Asian countries at Bandung, Indonesia. The conferees proclaimed solidarity among all peoples fighting against colonial rule. The Bandung Conference marked the beginning of an effort by the many new, poor, mostly non-European nations emerging from colonialism to gain more weight in world affairs by banding together. The terms **nonaligned nations** and **Third World**, which became commonplace in the following years, signaled these countries' collective stance toward the rival sides in the Cold War. If the West, led by the United States, and the East, led by the Soviet Union, represented two worlds locked in mortal struggle, the Third World consisted of everyone else.

nonaligned nations Developing countries that announced their neutrality in the Cold War.

Third World Term applied to a group of developing countries who professed nonalignment during the Cold War.

Leaders of the so-called Third World countries preferred the label *nonaligned,* which signified freedom from membership on either side. However, because the Soviet Union supported national liberation movements and the nonaligned movement included communist countries such as China and Yugoslavia, many Western leaders did not take the term *nonaligned* seriously. They saw Sukarno, Nehru, Nkrumah, and Egypt's Gamal Abd al-Nasir (gah-MAHL AHB-d al–NAH-suhr) as stalking horses for a communist takeover of the world. This may also have been the hope of some Soviet leaders, who were quick to offer some of these countries military and financial aid.

For the movement's leaders, however, nonalignment was a means to extract money and support from one or both superpowers. By flirting with the Soviet Union, the United States, or the People's Republic of China, a country could get military and economic aid.

Some skillful nonaligned leaders were able to gain from both sides. Nasir, who ruled Egypt from 1952 to 1970, and his successor, Anwar Sadat (seh-DAT), played the game well. The United States offered to build a dam at Aswan (AS-wahn), on the Nile River, to increase Egypt's electrical generating and irrigation capacity. When Egypt turned to the Soviet Union for arms, the United States reneged on the dam project in 1956. The Soviet Union then picked it up and in the 1960s brought it to conclusion. In 1956, Israel, Great Britain, and France conspired to invade Egypt. Their objective was to overthrow Nasir, regain the Suez Canal (he had recently nationalized it), and secure Israel from any Egyptian threat. The invasion succeeded militarily, but both the United States and the Soviet Union pressured the invaders to withdraw, thus saving Nasir's government. In 1972, Sadat evicted his Soviet military advisers but a year later used his Soviet weapons to attack Israel. After he lost that war, he announced his faith in the power of the United States to solve Egypt's political and economic problems.

Numerous other countries adopted similar balancing strategies. In each case, local leaders were trying to develop their nation's economy and assert or preserve their nation's interests. Manipulating the superpowers was simply a means toward those ends and implied very little about true ideological orientation.

Japan and China

No other countries took better advantage of the opportunities presented by the superpowers' preoccupation than did Japan and China. Japan signed a peace treaty with most of its former enemies in 1951 and regained independence from American occupation the following year. Renouncing militarism and its imperialist past, Japan remained on the sidelines throughout the Korean War. Its new constitution, written under American supervision in 1946, allowed only a limited self-defense force, banned the deployment of Japanese troops abroad, and gave the vote to women.

The Japanese turned their talents and energies to rebuilding their industries and engaging in world commerce. By isolating Japan from most world political issues, the Cold War provided an exceptionally favorable environment for Japan to develop its economic strength.

Three industries that took advantage of government aid and the newest technologies paved the way for Japan's emergence as an economic superpower after 1975. Projects producing 60 million kilowatts of electricity were completed between 1951 and 1970, almost a third through dams on Japan's many rivers. Between 1960 and 1970, steel production more than quadrupled, reaching 15.7 percent of the total capacity of countries outside the Soviet bloc. The shipbuilding industry produced six times as much tonnage in 1970 as in 1960, almost half of the new tonnage produced outside the Soviet bloc.

While Japan benefited from being outside the Cold War, China was deeply involved in Cold War politics. When Mao Zedong (maow dzuh-dong) and the communists defeated the nationalists in 1949 and established the People's Republic of China (PRC), their main ally and source of arms was the Soviet Union. By 1956, however, the PRC and the Soviet Union were beginning to diverge politically, partly in reaction to the Soviet rejection of Stalinism and partly because of China's reluctance to be cast forever in the role of student. Mao had his own notions of communism, focusing strongly on the peasantry, whom the Soviets ignored in favor of the industrial working class.

Mao's Great Leap Forward in 1958 was supposed to vault China into the ranks of world industrial powers by maximizing the use of labor in small-scale, village-level industries. The policy failed but demonstrated Mao's willingness to carry out massive economic and social projects of his own devising.

In 1966, Mao instituted another radical nationwide program, the **Cultural Revolution**. He ordered the mass mobilization of Chinese youth into Red Guard units. His goal was to kindle revolutionary fervor in a new generation and to ward off the stagnation and bureaucratization he saw in the Soviet Union. Red Guard units criticized and purged teachers, party officials, and intellectuals for "bourgeois values." Internal party conflict continued until 1971, when Mao admitted that attacks

Cultural Revolution (China) (1966–1969) Campaign in China ordered by Mao Zedong to purge the Communist Party of his opponents and instill revolutionary values in the younger generation.

Chinese Red Guards
During the Cultural Revolution young Chinese militants joined the Red Guards, identifying enemies of the Communist Party and Chairman Mao. They also turned on their teachers and sometimes their parents and neighbors, labeling them enemies of the people or members of the bourgeoisie. Here a victim is paraded wearing a dunce cap on which his crimes are written.   (AP Images/Wide World Photos)

Primary Source: One Hundred Items for Destroying the Old and Establishing the New *Would you be willing to give up your blue jeans for the Cultural Revolution? Find out what following Mao Zedong required.*

on individuals had gotten out of hand. Meanwhile, small-scale industrialization resulted in record levels of agricultural and industrial production. The last years of the Cultural Revolution were dominated by radicals led by Mao's wife, Jiang Qing (jyahn ching), who focused on restrictions on artistic and intellectual activity.

In the meantime, the rift between the PRC and the Soviet Union had opened so wide that United States President Richard Nixon (1969–1974), by reputation a staunch anticommunist, dropped objections to the PRC's joining the United Nations. In 1971, the PRC occupied China's permanent seat on the Security Council, displacing the Chinese nationalist government on Taiwan. The following year, Nixon visited Beijing, making dramatically clear the new cooperation between the People's Republic of China and the United States.

The Middle East

Independence had come gradually to the Arab countries of the Middle East. Britain granted Syria and Lebanon independence after World War II. Other Arab countries— Iraq, Egypt, Jordan—enjoyed nominal independence during the interwar period but remained under indirect British control until the 1950s.

Overshadowing all Arab politics, however, was the struggle with the new state of Israel. British policy on Palestine between the wars oscillated between favoring Zionist Jewish immigrants and the indigenous Palestinian Arabs. After the war, under intense pressure to resettle European Jewish refugees, Britain turned the Palestine problem over to the United Nations. In November 1947, the General Assembly voted in favor of partitioning Palestine into two states, one Jewish and one Arab. The Jewish community made plans to declare independence, while the Palestinians, who felt the proposed land division was unfair, reacted in horror and took up arms. When Israel declared its independence in May 1948, neighboring Arab countries sent armies to help the Palestinians crush the newborn state.

Israel, however, prevailed on all fronts. Some 700,000 Palestinians became refugees. They found shelter in United Nations refugee camps in Jordan, Syria, Lebanon, and the Gaza Strip (a bit of coastal land on the Egyptian-Israeli border). The right of these refugees to return home remains a focal point of Arab politics. In 1967, Israel responded to threatening military moves by Egypt's Nasir by preemptively attacking Egyptian and Syrian air bases. In six days, Israel won a smashing victory. Israel won control of Jerusalem (previously split with Jordan), the West Bank, the Gaza Strip, the strategic Golan Heights in southern Syria, and the entire Sinai Peninsula (see Map 28.2). Acquiring all of Jerusalem satisfied Jews' deep longing to return to their holiest city, but Palestinians continued to regard Jerusalem as their destined capital, and Muslims in many countries protested Israeli control of the Dome of the Rock, a revered Islamic shrine located in the city. These acquisitions resulted in a new wave of Palestinian refugees.

The rival claims to Palestine continued to plague Middle Eastern politics. The Palestine Liberation Organization (PLO), headed by Yasir Arafat (AR-uh-fat), waged guerrilla war against Israel, frequently engaging in acts of terrorism. The militarized Israelis were able to blunt or absorb these attacks and launch counterstrikes that likewise involved assassinations and bombings. Though the United States proved a firm friend of Israel and the Soviet Union armed the Arab states, neither superpower saw the struggle between Zionism and Palestinian nationalism as a vital concern—until oil became a political issue.

The phenomenal concentration of oil wealth in the Persian Gulf states—Iran, Iraq, Kuwait, Saudi Arabia, Qatar, Bahrain, and the United Arab Emirates—was not fully realized until after World War II when demand for oil rose sharply as civilian economies recovered. As a world oversupply diminished in the face of rising demand, oil-producing states in 1960 formed the **Organization of Petroleum Exporting Countries (OPEC)** to promote their collective interest in higher revenues.

Oil politics and the Arab-Israeli conflict intersected in October 1973. A surprise Egyptian attack across the Suez Canal threw the Israelis into temporary disarray. Within days, the war turned in Israel's favor, and an Egyptian army was trapped at the canal's southern end. The United States then arranged a cease-fire and the disengagement of forces. But before that could happen, the Arab oil-producing countries voted to embargo oil shipments to the United States and the Netherlands as punishment for their support of Israel.

The implications of oil as an economic weapon profoundly disturbed the worldwide oil industry. Prices rose—along with feelings of insecurity. In 1974, OPEC responded to the turmoil in the oil market by quadrupling prices, setting the stage for massive transfers of wealth to the producing countries and provoking a feeling of crisis throughout the consuming countries.

Organization of Petroleum Exporting Countries (OPEC) Organization formed in 1960 by oil-producing states to promote their collective interest in generating revenue from oil.

The Emergence of Environmental Concerns

Skyrocketing oil prices focused new attention on natural resource issues. Before the mid-1960s, only a few people noticed that untested technologies and all-out drives for industrial productivity were rapidly degrading the environment. The superpowers were particularly negligent of the environmental impact of pesticide and herbicide use, automobile exhaust, industrial waste disposal, and radiation hazards.

New youth activism focused awareness on environmental problems. In 1968, a wave of student unrest swept many parts of the world. Earth Day was first celebrated

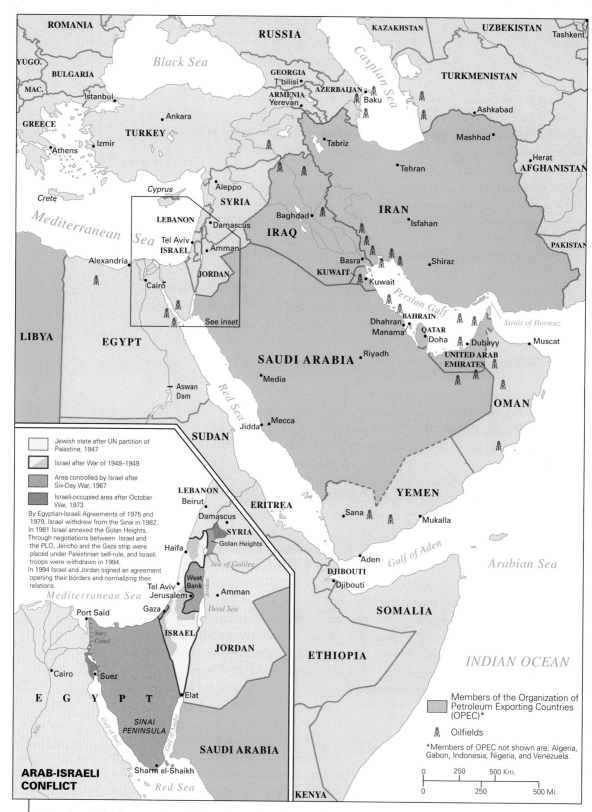

Map 28.2   Middle East Oil and the Arab-Israeli Conflict, 1947–1973

Oil resources were long controlled by private European and American companies. In the 1960s most countries, guided by OPEC, negotiated agreements for sharing control, eventually leading to national ownership. This set the stage for the use of oil as a weapon in the 1973 Arab-Israeli war and for subsequent price increases.

in 1970, the year in which the United States established its Environmental Protection Agency.

After 1974, making gasoline engines and home heating systems more efficient and lowering highway speed limits to conserve fuel became matters of national debate in the United States while poorer countries struggled to find the money to import oil. A widely read 1972 study, *The Limits of Growth,* forecast a need to cut back on consumption of natural resources in the twenty-first century. Thus, as the most dangerous moments of the Cold War seemed to be passing, ecological and environmental problems of worldwide impact vied with the superpower rivalry and Third World nation building for public attention.

COMPARATIVE PERSPECTIVES

The alliance between the Soviet Union and the Western democracies led by the United States did not survive into the post–World War II era. Shortly after the war both sides began to prepare for a new round of hostilities, establishing competing military alliances and attempting to influence the new governments of nations formerly occupied by the Axis. Each side portrayed this tension as a struggle between irreconcilably different social and economic systems, and each side emphasized the corruption, injustice, and unfairness of its opponent. When Winston Churchill spoke in 1946 of Soviet control in eastern Europe as an iron curtain, he suggested that the Soviet system was, in effect, a prison.

The boundary that separated the United States and its allies and the Soviet Union and its allies was soon defended by massive armies armed with increasingly sophisticated weapons, including nuclear weapons that were far more destructive than those dropped on Japan. This Cold War quickly became global in character as distant civil wars, regional conflicts, and nationalist revolutions were transformed by support provided by these contestants for global ascendancy.

Many of the flash points in this war were provided by the desire of colonized peoples to throw off imperial controls and establish independent nations. The Western nations had defined World War II as a war for freedom and self-determination. The Free French had promised greater autonomy to African colonies, the United States had used nationalist forces to fight against the Japanese in the Philippines and in Vietnam, and the British also had used forces recruited throughout its empire to fight the war. Once organized and set in motion, these nationalist energies could not be easily contained again in the confines of traditional colonial rule. The most powerful force in the postwar era was nationalism, the desire of peoples to control their own destinies. This reality, clear now, was obscured by the global contest of the Cold War.

In Africa, the Middle East, South Asia, and Latin America this desire to throw off foreign controls would lead to the creation of scores of new nations by the 1970s. Each nation's struggle had its own character. While in India these passions led to independence, similar sentiments led in China to the overthrow of a government seen as weak and subordinate to foreign powers and to the creation of a communist dictatorship. In much of Africa, the Middle East, and the Caribbean, nationalism was manifested as traditional anticolonial struggles, not unlike the conflict that gave birth to

SECTION REVIEW

- Many developing nations joined the nonaligned movement to achieve national goals by manipulating superpower rivalry.

- Japan rebuilt its economy by remaining outside Cold War politics, while Mao's China broke with the Soviet Union to follow its own communist path.

- The politics of the postwar Middle East came to be dominated by the Arab-Israeli conflict and oil.

- In the 1970s, environmental concerns joined superpower rivalry and Third World nation building as a major global issue.

the United States. In the Middle East the desire for self-government was complicated by the creation of the state of Israel. In Latin America, where most nations had been independent for well over a century, the era's nationalist sentiment manifested itself as a desire for economic independence and an end to foreign interventions. For this reason Castro found it easy to connect his revolutionary ambitions to anticolonial movements elsewhere.

The end of Japanese control in Korea and Vietnam led to territorial partitions that separated Soviet-leaning and Western-allied polities. Civil war and foreign interventions soon followed. In both cases the Soviet Union and China supported communist forces. The United States committed large military forces to protect the anticommunist governments, gaining a stalemate in Korea and eventually losing in Vietnam. While the outcomes were mixed for the superpowers, the wars were contained and managed so as to prevent direct engagement and nuclear conflict.

Chapter Review

DOWNLOAD THE MP3 AUDIO FILE OF THE CHAPTER REVIEW
TO LISTEN TO ON THE GO.

What were the major threats to world peace during the Cold War? (page 765)

The arms race associated with the rivalry between the West and the Soviets produced the largest peacetime militaries in world history. The reliance of both sides on large inventories of nuclear weapons meant that any direct conflict had the potential of provoking massive retaliation. For more than fifty years massed armies faced each other across Europe. In the end this confrontation was projected into space, as each side sought to advertise its technological capacity through satellite launches and finally a moon landing. During the Cold War leaders of the opposing alliances viewed their struggle as a global conflict between irreconcilable systems. This meant that every popular movement, revolution, or civil war was strategically important and could involve the superpowers or their allies.

How were the experiences of Asia, Africa, and Latin America similar in this period? (page 774)

Africa, Asia, and Latin America were all powerfully affected by nationalism in the postwar period. In Africa and South Asia nationalist forces gathered strength and swept away colonial rule. In China nationalist frustration with the weak and corrupt government, viewed as incapable of defending national sovereignty, helped to propel communist revolutionaries led by Mao Zedong to power. Latin American nationalists aimed for economic independence and an end to foreign intervention, and Fidel Castro identified these goals with those

KEY TERMS

iron curtain *(p. 764)*
Cold War *(p. 764)*
North Atlantic Treaty Organization (NATO) *(p. 765)*
United Nations *(p. 766)*
World Bank *(p. 769)*
Marshall Plan *(p. 769)*
European Community (EC) *(p. 769)*
Truman Doctrine *(p. 770)*
Warsaw Pact *(p. 770)*
Korean War *(p. 771)*
Vietnam War *(p. 771)*
Cuban missile crisis *(p. 773)*
Helsinki Accords *(p. 773)*
nonaligned nations *(p. 780)*
Third World *(p. 780)*
Cultural Revolution (China) *(p. 781)*
Organization of Petroleum Exporting Countries (OPEC) *(p. 783)*

of countries struggling for independence in Asia and Africa. Many newly installed nationalist governments experimented with forms of state-directed economic development, nationalizing important industries and seizing natural resources. Even while rejecting communism, these nationalist governments adapted Soviet economic institutions and policies, such as five-year plans and central planning, to their own purposes. While some new governments supported the Soviets and others supported the United States, there was broad agreement on the importance of political and economic self-determination.

How did the rivalry between the Cold War superpowers affect the rest of the world? (page 780)

The Cold War rivalry never led to direct conflict between the major powers. Emerging nations were sometimes able to use this rivalry to gain foreign aid for development projects or infrastructure projects such as roads and schools. More typically, military aid flowed to political allies, leading to destructive and bloody conflicts. Both the West and the Soviets armed and trained contestants in civil wars, revolutions, and regional conflicts. The independence of the Congo turned into a protracted civil war financed in part by this rivalry, and a series of wars between Israel and its Arab neighbors were made possible by the transfer of massive amounts of military equipment. In the wake of the communist success in China, the United States went to war twice in Asia—in Korea and in Vietnam—to prevent further communist advances. The United States also supported the overthrow of the Guatemalan government in 1954 and attempted in 1961 to overthrow Castro as well. The Soviet Union crushed Hungarian nationalists in 1956 and Czechoslovakian patriots in 1968. No region of the world completely escaped the costs associated with the Cold War.

WEB RESOURCES

Pronunciation Guide

Interactive Map
MAP 28.1 Decolonization, 1947–1999

Primary Sources
Comments on Algeria

The Rivonia Trial Speech to the Court

One Hundred Items for Destroying the Old and Establishing the New

Answer to the History in Focus Question
See photo on page 772, "The Vietnamese People at War."

Plus
Chapter Objectives

ACE multiple-choice quiz

Flashcards

SUGGESTED READING

Allison, Graham. *Essence of Decision: Explaining the Cuban Missile Crisis.* 1971. An influential study of decision making in a time of crisis.

Barraclough, Geoffrey. *An Introduction to Contemporary History.* 1964. A remarkable early effort at understanding the broad sweep of ongoing history.

Chamberlain, M. E. *Decolonization: The Fall of the European Empires.* 2d ed. 1999. A comprehensive overview.

Dower, John. *Embracing Defeat: Japan in the Wake of World War II.* 1999. An excellent history of the American occupation of Japan.

Karnow, Stanley. *Vietnam: A History.* 2d ed. 1997. A detailed and balanced history.

Kyle, Keith. *Suez 1956.* 1991. Examines the international complications of a brief war.

Lapping, Brian. *End of Empire.* 1985. Covers the dissolution of the British Empire.

Leffler, Melvyn P., and David S. Painter, eds. *Origins of the Cold War: An International History.* 1994. Offers reconsiderations of earlier historical viewpoints.

MacDougall, Walter. *The Heavens and the Earth: A Political History of the Space Age.* 1985. Looks at the intersection of politics, technology, and international competition.

Mazower, Mark. *Dark Continent.* 1999. An outstanding reappraisal of Europe's twentieth-century history.

Meisner, Maurice. *Mao's China and After: A History of the People's Republic.* 3d ed. 1999. A highly regarded survey.

Merrill, John. *Korea: The Peninsular Origins of the War.* 1989. Presents the Korean War as a civil and revolutionary conflict as well as part of the Cold War.

Nakamura, Takafusa. *A History of Showa Japan, 1926–1989.* 1998. A solid Japanese study of the reign of Emperor Hirohito.

Smith, Charles D. *Palestine and the Arab-Israeli Conflict.* 6th rev. ed. 2007. Comprehensive coverage of an ongoing crisis.

Walker, Martin. *The Cold War: A History.* 1993. A good general history.

CHAPTER 29

The End of the Cold War and the Challenge of Economic Development and Immigration

1975–2000

CHAPTER PREVIEW

China began an ambitious program of economic reforms at the end of the 1970s. Until then China, with the world's largest population, lagged far behind the mature industrialized nations of Europe and North America in economic performance, as well as behind neighboring nations like Japan and South Korea. Since the reforms, China has experienced rapid economic growth and has become one of the few socialist nations to make the transition from a socialist to a market economy. Nevertheless, as many as 100 million Chinese still lived in poverty in 2000. Ancient technology and poverty still existed in close proximity with modernity and affluence. These same problems of poverty and inequality are found across the globe. In an era of astounding technological change and spreading prosperity, 1.2 billion of the world's population live on less than a dollar per day.

 This icon will direct you to the website where you can Prepare for Class, Improve Your Grade, and Ace the Test: college.cengage.com/pic/bullietbrief4e

At the end of the twentieth century many of the nations of the developing world found that population growth continued to outstrip economic resources. In wealthy industrialized nations as well, politicians and social reformers still worry about the effects of unemployment, family breakdown, substance abuse, and homelessness. As had been true during the Industrial Revolution in the eighteenth century (see Chapter 20), dramatic economic expansion, increased global economic integration, and rapid technological progress in the last decades of the twentieth century coincided with problems of social dislocation and inequality.

POSTCOLONIAL CRISES AND ASIAN ECONOMIC EXPANSION

How did the Cold War affect politics in Latin America and the Middle East in the 1970s and 1980s?

Between 1975 and the end of the century, wars and revolutions provoked by a mix of ideology, nationalism, ethnic hatred, and religious fervor spread death and destruction through many of the world's least developed regions. Although often tied to earlier colonialism and foreign intervention, each conflict reflected a specific set of historical experiences. In many cases, conflicts provoked by local and regional causes tended to become more deadly and long lasting because the United States and the Soviet Union intervened. Conflicts in which the rival superpowers financed and armed competing factions or parties were called **proxy wars.**

In Latin America superpower rivalry helped transform conflicts over political rights, social justice, and economic policies into a cycle of revolution, military dictatorship, and foreign meddling. In Iran and Afghanistan resentment against foreign intrusion and a growing religious hostility to secular culture led to revolutionary transformations. Here again superpower ambitions played a role. These experiences were not universal. Some Asian nations experienced rapid transformation. Japan became one of the world's leading industrial powers, and a small number of other Asian economies entered the ranks of industrial and commercial powers.

The collapse of the Soviet system in eastern Europe at the end of the 1980s ended the Cold War and undermined socialist economies elsewhere. As developing and former socialist nations opened their markets to foreign investment and competition, economic transformation was often accompanied by wrenching social change. The world's growing economic interconnectedness coincided with increased inequality. Yet some developing nations also reaped substantial benefits from rapid technological change and world economic integration.

This period also witnessed soaring world population and increased international migration. Population growth and increased industrialization degraded the global environment. Every continent felt the destructive effects of forest depletion, soil erosion, and pollution. Wealthy nations with slow population growth found it easier to respond to these environmental challenges than did poor nations with rapidly growing populations.

proxy wars During the Cold War, local or regional wars in which the superpowers armed, trained, and financed the combatants.

Revolutions, Repression, and Democratic Reform in Latin America

In the 1970s Latin America entered a dark era of political violence. Revolutionary movements challenged the established order in many nations; democratic governments were overturned by military revolts. A region of weak democracy in 1960 became a region of military dictatorships fifteen years later. The new authoritarian leaders had little patience with civil liberties and human rights.

The ongoing confrontation between Fidel Castro and the government of the United States (see Chapter 28) helped propel the region toward crisis. The fact that Cuba's communist government survived opposition from the United States energized the revolutionary left throughout Latin America. In response, the United States increased support for its political and military allies. Many of the military leaders who would come to power in this period were trained by the United States.

Brazil was the first nation to experience fully the conservative reaction to the Cuban Revolution. Claiming that Brazil's civilian political leaders could not protect against communist subversion, the army overthrew the government of President João Goulart (ju-wow go-LARHT) in 1964. The military suspended the constitution, outlawed political parties, and exiled former presidents and opposition leaders. Death squads—illegal paramilitary organizations sanctioned by the government—detained, tortured, and executed thousands of citizens. The dictatorship also undertook an ambitious economic program that promoted industrialization through import substitution, using tax and tariff policies to compel foreign-owned companies to increase investment in manufacturing.

This combination of dictatorship, violent repression, and government promotion of industrialization was called the "Brazilian Solution." Elements of this "solution" spread across much of the region in the 1970s and early 1980s. In 1970 Chile's new president, **Salvador Allende** (sal-vah-DOR ah-YEHN-day), undertook ambitious socialist reforms. He also nationalized most of Chile's heavy industry and mines, including the American-owned copper companies that dominated the Chilean economy. From the beginning of Allende's presidency the administration of President Richard Nixon (1969–1973) opposed his reforms. Amidst inflation, mass consumer protests, and declining foreign trade, a military uprising led by General Augusto Pinochet (ah-GOOS-toh pin-oh-CHET) and supported by the United States overthrew Allende in 1973. President Allende and thousands of Chileans died in the uprising. Thousands more were illegally seized, tortured, and imprisoned. Pinochet rolled back Allende's social reforms, reduced state participation in the economy, and encouraged foreign investment.

In 1976 Argentina followed Brazil and Chile into dictatorship. Isabel Martínez de Perón (EES-ah-bell mar-TEEN-ehz deh pair-OWN) became president after the death of her husband Juan Perón in 1974 (see Chapter 27). Argentina was wracked by inflation, terrorism, and labor protests. Losing trust in the president, the military seized power and suspended the constitution. During the next seven years the military fought what it called the **Dirty War** against terrorism. More than nine thousand Argentines lost their lives; thousands of others endured arrest, torture, and the loss of property.

Yet some revolutionary movements persisted, reaching a peak in 1979 in Nicaragua with the overthrow of the corrupt dictatorship of Anastasio Somoza. The

Salvador Allende (1908–1973) Socialist politician elected president of Chile in 1970 and overthrown by the military in 1973. He died during the military attack.

Dirty War War waged by the Argentine military (1976–1983) against leftist groups. It was marked by the use of illegal imprisonment, torture, and executions by the military.

Chronology

	The Americas	Middle East	Asia	Europe
1970	**1964** Military takeover in Brazil **1970** Salvador Allende elected president of Chile **1973** Allende overthrown **1976** Military takeover in Argentina		**1975** Vietnam War ends **1978** China opens its economy	
1980	**1979** Sandinistas overthrow Anastasio Somoza in Nicaragua **1983–1990** Democracy returns in Argentina, Brazil, and Chile	**1979** Islamic Revolution overthrows shah of Iran **1980–1988** Iran-Iraq War		**1979** USSR sends troops to Afghanistan **1985** Mikhail Gorbachev becomes Soviet head of state
			1986 Average Japanese income overtakes income in United States **1989** Tiananmen Square confrontation	**1989** USSR withdraws troops from Afghanistan; Berlin Wall falls **1989–1991** End of communism in eastern Europe
1990	**1990** Sandinistas defeated in elections in Nicaragua	**1990** Iraq invades Kuwait **1991** Persian Gulf War		**1990** Reunification of Germany

broad alliance of revolutionaries and reformers that took power called themselves **Sandinistas** (sahn-din-EES-tahs). They took their name from Augusto César Sandino, who had led Nicaraguan opposition to U.S. military intervention between 1927 and 1932. The Sandinistas sought to imitate the command economies of Cuba and the Soviet Union, nationalizing properties owned by members of the Nicaraguan elite and U.S. citizens.

President Jimmy Carter (1977–1980) championed human rights in the hemisphere and stopped the flow of U.S. arms to regimes with the worst records. Carter also agreed to the reestablishment of Panamanian sovereignty in the Canal Zone at the end of 1999, but his effort to find common ground with the Sandinistas failed.

Sandinistas Members of a leftist coalition that overthrew the Nicaraguan dictatorship of Anastasio Somoza in 1979 and attempted to install a socialist economy. The United States financed armed opposition by the Contras. The Sandinistas lost national elections in 1990.

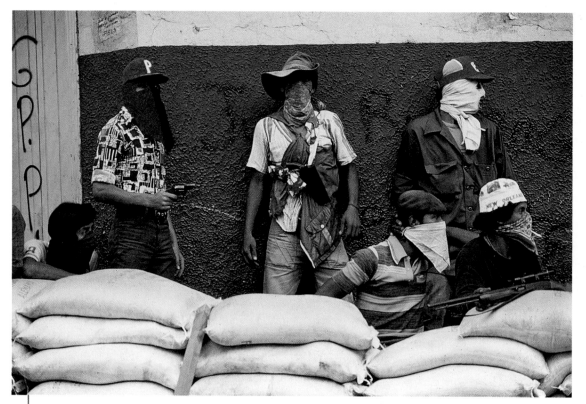

The Nicaraguan Revolution Overturns Somoza

A revolutionary coalition that included Marxists drove the dictator Anastasio Somoza from power in 1979. The Somoza family had ruled Nicaragua since the 1930s and maintained a close relationship with the United States.   (Susan Meiselas/ Magnum Photos, Inc.)

 HISTORY IN FOCUS   How and why did the Sandinistas succeed in taking power from the Nicaraguan government? What kind of change did they seek to implement? *Find the answer online.*

In 1981 Ronald Reagan became president. He was committed to reversing the results of the Nicaraguan Revolution and defeating a revolutionary movement in neighboring El Salvador. His options, however, were limited by the U.S. Congress, which resisted sending troops and put strict limits on military aid. The Reagan administration resorted to punitive economic measures against the Sandinistas and to the recruitment and arming of anti-Sandinista Nicaraguans, called Contras (counterrevolutionaries).

Confident that they were supported by the majority of Nicaraguans and assured that the U.S. Congress would soon cut off aid to the Contras, the Sandinistas called for free elections in 1990. But they miscalculated. Exhausted by more than a decade of violence, a majority of Nicaraguan voters rejected the Sandinistas and elected a middle-of-the-road coalition led by Violeta Chamorro (vee-oh-LET-ah cha-MOR-roe).

The revolutionaries of El Salvador hoped to imitate the initial success of the Sandinistas of Nicaragua. Taking their name from a martyred leftist leader of the 1930s, the FMLN (Farabundo Martí [fah-rah-BOON-doh mar-TEE] National Liberation Front) organized an effective guerrilla force. The United States responded by providing hundreds of millions of dollars in military assistance and by training units of the El Salvadoran army.

When government death squads assassinated Archbishop Oscar Romero and other members of the Catholic clergy and military units murdered thousands of noncombatants, the Reagan administration encountered growing opposition in the U.S. Congress. Eventually, external events brought peace to El Salvador. With the electoral defeat of the Sandinistas in Nicaragua and the collapse of the Soviet Union (see below), popular support for armed struggle waned and the FMLN rebels negotiated an end to the war, transforming themselves into a civilian political party.

The military dictatorships established in Brazil, Chile, and Argentina came to an end between 1983 and 1990. In each case, reports of kidnappings, tortures, and government corruption sapped public support. In Argentina the military junta's foolish decision in 1982 to seize the Falkland Islands—the Argentines called them the "Malvinas"—from Great Britain ended in an embarrassing military defeat and precipitated the return to civilian rule. In Chile and Brazil the military dictatorships ended less dramatically. Despite significant economic growth under Pinochet, Chileans resented the violence and corruption of the military. In 1988 Pinochet called a plebiscite to extend his authority, but the majority voted against him. A year later Chile elected its first civilian president in eighteen years. Brazil's military initiated a gradual transition to civilian rule in 1985 and four years later had its first popular presidential election. By 2000 nearly 95 percent of Latin America's population lived under civilian rule.

Despite these changes, Latin America was even more dominated by the United States than it had been in 1975. Antileftist actions in Nicaragua and El Salvador and an invasion of the tiny Caribbean nation of Grenada in 1983 demonstrated U.S. willingness to interfere. In 1989, when the United States overthrew and arrested dictator General Manuel Noriega (MAN-wel no-ree-EGG-ah) of Panama, Latin Americans were reminded of prior interventions.

With its influence uncontested, the United States urged Latin American nations to reform their economies by reducing the role of the state. Called **neo-liberalism** in Latin America and other developing regions, these free-market policies reduced protections for local industries, government social welfare policies, and public-sector employment. Public-sector industries, like national airlines, manufacturing facilities, and public utilities, were sold to foreign corporations, but political scandals and a slowing economy eroded popular support. Between 2001 and 2002 Argentina, which had ambitiously pursued neo-liberal reforms, experienced an economic and political meltdown, after which a nationalist left reappeared in the region and began to roll back those reforms (see Diversity and Dominance: The Struggle for Women's Rights in an Era of Global Political and Economic Change). The most vocal critic of neo-liberalism and American influence was Hugo Chávez (HUGH-go SHAH-vez), elected president of Venezuela in 1998.

neo-liberalism The term used in Latin America and other developing regions to describe free-market policies that include reducing tariff protection for local industries; the sale of public-sector industries, like national airlines and public utilities, to private investors or foreign corporations; and the reduction of social welfare policies and public-sector employment.

Islamic Revolutions in Iran and Afghanistan

Although the Arab-Israeli conflict and the oil crisis (see Chapter 28) concerned both superpowers, the prospect of direct military involvement remained remote. When

The Struggle for Women's Rights in an Era of Global Political and Economic Change

The struggle for women's rights was one of the most important social movements of the twentieth century. Although their objectives were fundamentally similar, women in less-developed nations recognized that their strategies must take into account international inequalities in power and wealth. In this section Gladys Acosta, a militant Peruvian feminist, discusses the appropriate agenda for this struggle in the era after the fall of the Soviet Union and the rise of neo-liberalism, which many Latin Americans believe was a new form of imperialism.

No one can abstain from the debate about the great historical systems of our time. Not even those of us who are trying to change the complex web of human relationships from a feminist perspective. Everywhere people are talking about the end of ideologies. But before we can grasp the significance of current events and their consequences, we need to pinpoint our various doubts and blank spots. Capitalism is the main pivot of our lives because we were born under its influence. It [has] hegemony. . . .

Gender, the main distinction between all people, is ignored in most philosophical, political or economic discussions. The reason for this lies partly in the low level of women's participation, but not entirely, because women are not always aware of the system of submission and repression to which we are subjected against our will. We need to find something which unites women in a gender-specific manner. That doesn't mean sweeping under the carpet all the differences between us, like social position, culture or age. . . .

Neo-Liberalism in Action

For those of us who live under the influence of the capitalist system, the situation is different. When I talk of neo-liberalism, I mean austerity measures, foreign debts, and increased liberties for all those who have the power of money at their disposal and the power of repression over those who make demands. We have now reached a new form of capitalist accumulation. The world's economic system is in a state of change and capital has become more concentrated and centralised. I would not go as far as to say countries don't exist anymore but national identities do certainly play a different role now. It is important to understand the dynamics because otherwise historical responsibilities are obscured and we no longer know whom we're fighting against. If we look at the bare face of neo-liberalism from a woman's point of view, we cannot fail to notice its murderous consequences. To create a more humane society we must continue to reject neo-liberalism here and now in the hope of being able to change the dead present into a living future. Under neo-liberalism there is a breathtaking circulation of commodities, but also an exchange of ideas, illusions and dreams. At the moment we're experiencing capitalism's greatest ideological offensive. It's all business: everything is bought and sold and everything has its price.

The Consequences of Neo-Liberal Politics

We women play an important role in this ever-more internationalized economy because we represent, as ever, a particularly exploitable workforce. A number of studies have revealed the existence of subcontractor chains who work for transnational companies "informally" and mainly employ women. Basically we are dealing with a kind of integration into the world market which often uses our own homes as its outlet. Obviously, this work is badly paid and completely unprotected and has to be done without any of those social rights which were formerly achieved by trade union struggles. The most important thing for us is to keep hold of just one thread of the enterprise so we can show how the commodities make their way to their final destination. As it advances worldwide, this capitalism also encourages the expansion of certain kinds of tourism. A visible increase in prostitution is part of this, whereby women from poor countries are smuggled into large, internationally-operated rings which exploit them. The reports of Filipina women traded on the West German market send shivers down our spines. . . . What kind of freedom are you talking about there?

How the Adoption of Austerity Measures Affects Women's Lives

It is obvious that foreign debt is one of the most inhuman forms of exploitation in our countries when one considers the ratio between work necessary for workers' needs and work producing profit for employers. The experts have already explained how the prevailing exchange and investment structures have created international finance systems which keep whole populations in inhuman conditions. Although many people might think it crazy, the development model of the global economy has a marked relation to gender. As long as prices were slapped on some luxury consumer items there weren't any serious problems; but now the snares have been set around basic commodities. Women in every household are suffering every day as a result of impoverished economies and those who are most exposed to the effects of foreign debt are women.

When it comes to shopping, caring for sick children or the impossibility of meeting their schooling costs, the illusion of "leaving poverty behind" evaporates. Yet the problem is not only of an economic nature because under such circumstances the constant tension leads to grave, often lasting exhaustion. The psychosocial damage is alarming. The situation is ready to explode, so to speak. . . . The adoption of austerity measures means a curtailment of the state's commitment to social services with a direct effect on women. Daily life becomes hell for them. The lack of even minimal state welfare presents women (and obviously children too) with crushing working days. There is a constant expenditure of human energy without any hope of rest! No relaxation, no breaks. . . . And if we consider what happens within the family, we notice that women keep the smallest portion of the meagre family income. They give everything to their children or those adults who bring home a pay packet. As a result malnutrition among women is increasing at an alarming rate and their frequent pregnancies represent a superhuman physical achievement.

Women's valiant achievements in defending life and survival are not acknowledged by society. The efforts of women's organisations, whether it be communal kitchens, the glass-of-milk committees [milk distribution among the poor] or health services don't get the appropriate social esteem. The social value of women cannot be calculated. Perhaps in years to come the fate of millions of women who sacrifice everything to support the children and youth of Peru and other countries in Latin America will be acknowledged. We should not ignore the fact that violence of every form . . . goes hand-in-hand with the difficult situation I have described.[1] It's nothing new for women because the open wounds of sexual violence, abuse at home and the contempt of this *machista* culture, have always featured in our lives and our mothers' lives. The challenge is to prevent these from also affecting our future generations.

And the Future?

The neo-liberal offensive is international and demands international opposition strategies combined with political proposals by new social forces which address women's problems. We want to change estimations of our worth and achieve society's acknowledgement of what has been belittled until now as "women's affairs." Such important decisions as the right to the termination of unwanted pregnancies can no longer be ignored on the political stage. We want our place in the political decision-making process; we want to have a say in all problems which concern the Peruvian people and the whole world. We want to be informed so as not to be deceived by those who are used to practising politics for a flock of sheep. This road will be difficult but at least we shall regain the strengths of socialism and create social alternatives which are aimed at changing the destructive technological order as well as eliminating the international division of labour and the sexual hierarchy inherent within it. In so doing we shall try to create democratic structures which include the people in the decision-making process. The barriers thrown up by formal representative structures must be overcome urgently. A new democracy should be founded as the basic prerequisite for the society of the future.

QUESTIONS FOR ANALYSIS

1. **What is neo-liberalism?**
2. **According to Acosta, how does global economic integration fostered by neo-liberalism affect the lives of women as workers?**
3. **Acosta claims that indebtedness to foreign lenders leads to austerity measures. How does this situation impact families in poor countries?**
4. **What does Acosta advocate?**

Source: Excerpt from Gladys Acosta, "The View of a Peruvian Militant," in *Compañeras: Voices from the Latin American Women's Movement,* edited by Gaby Küppers (London: Latin American Bureau, 1994), 167–172. Copyright 1994 by Mr. Press. Reprinted by permission of Monthly Review Foundation.

[1] In the last Report of the Comisaria de mujeres in Lima (the only one in the country at present) 4,800 rapes were filed for 1990, of which 4,200 went to trial. The police commissioner, in reading the document, personally acknowledged the alarming social problem which is posed by the violence of men who are connected to their victims in some way and which, indeed, persists throughout all levels of society.

unexpected crises developed in Iran and Afghanistan, however, significant strategic issues came to the foreground. Both countries adjoined Soviet territory. Exercising post-Vietnam War caution, the United States reacted with restraint. The Soviet Union chose a bolder and ultimately disastrous course.

Muhammad Reza Pahlavi (REH-zah PAH-lah-vee) succeeded his father as shah of Iran in 1941. In 1953, covert intervention by the United States Central Intelligence Agency (CIA) helped the shah retain his throne in the face of a movement to usurp royal power. Even after nationalizing the foreign-owned oil industry, the shah continued to enjoy American support. When oil income mushroomed following the price increases of 1973–1974, the United States encouraged the shah to spend his nation's growing wealth on advanced American weaponry. By the mid-1970s, popular resentment against the shah's dependence on the United States, the ballooning wealth of the elite families that supported him, and the brutality, inefficiency, malfeasance, and corruption of his government grew into mass opposition.

Ayatollah Ruhollah Khomeini (eye-uh-TOLL-uh ROOH-ol-LAH ko-MAY-nee), a Shi'ite (SHE-ite) philosopher-cleric who had spent most of his eighty-plus years in religious and academic pursuits, became the voice and symbolic leader of the opposition. Massive street demonstrations and crippling strikes forced the shah to flee Iran and ended the monarchy in 1979. In the Islamic Republic of Iran, which replaced the monarchy, Ayatollah Khomeini was supreme arbiter of disputes and guarantor of religious legitimacy. Elections were held, but monarchists, communists, and other groups opposed to the idea of an Islamic Republic were barred from office. Shi'ite clerics with little training for government service emerged in many of the highest posts, and stringent measures were taken to replace Western styles and culture with Islamic norms. Universities temporarily closed as their faculties were purged of secularists and monarchists. Women were compelled to wear modest Islamic garments outside the house while semi-official vigilante committees policed public morals and cast a pall over entertainment and social life.

The United States under President Carter had criticized the shah's repression, but the overthrow of a long-standing ally and the creation of the Islamic Republic were blows to American prestige. Khomeini saw the United States as a "Great Satan" and encouraged Islamic revolutionary movements elsewhere, to the distress of both the United States and Israel. In November 1979, Iranian radicals seized the U.S. embassy in Tehran and then held fifty-two diplomats hostage for 444 days. Americans felt humiliated by their inability to do anything, particularly after the failure of a military rescue attempt.

In the fall of 1980, shortly after negotiations for release of the hostages began, **Saddam Husayn** (sah-DAHM who-SANE), the ruler of neighboring Iraq, invaded Iran to topple the Islamic Republic. His own dictatorial rule rested on a secular Arab nationalist philosophy and long-standing friendship with the Soviet Union, which supplied his army. He feared that Iran's revolutionary fervor would infect his own country's Shi'ite majority and threaten his power. While the war pitted American weapons in Iranian hands against Soviet weapons in Iraqi hands, the superpowers avoided overt involvement. Covertly, however, the Reagan administration sent arms via Israel to Iran, hoping to gain the release of other American hostages held by Muslim radicals in Lebanon and to secretly finance the Contra war against the Sandinista government of Nicaragua. When this deal came to light in 1986, the resulting

Ayatollah Ruhollah Khomeini (1900?–1989) Shi'ite philosopher and cleric who led the overthrow of the shah of Iran in 1979 and created an Islamic republic.

Primary Source: Islamic Government
Read Ayatollah Khomeini's rationale for overthrowing the Shah of Iran.

Saddam Husayn (1937-2007) President of Iraq from 1979 until overthrown by an American-led invasion in 2003. Waged war on Iran from 1980 to 1988. His invasion of Kuwait in 1990 was repulsed in the Persian Gulf War in 1991.

political scandal intensified American hostility toward Iran. Openly tilting toward Iraq, President Reagan sent the United States Navy to the Persian Gulf, ostensibly to protect nonbelligerent shipping. This threatening move helped persuade Iran to accept a cease-fire in 1988.

While the United States experienced anguish and frustration in Iran, the Soviet Union found itself facing even more serious problems in neighboring Afghanistan. In 1978 a Marxist party with a secular reform agenda seized power in Afghanistan. Offended by these efforts to reform education and grant rights to women, traditional ethnic and religious leaders led a successful rebellion. In 1979, the Soviet Union responded by sending its army to Afghanistan to bolster communist rule.

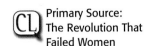

Primary Source: The Revolution That Failed Women

Discover why many women in Iran initially embraced the ideology of the Ayatollah.

With the United States, Saudi Arabia, and Pakistan paying, equipping, and training the Afghan rebels, the Soviet Union found itself in the same kind of unwinnable war the United States had stumbled into in Vietnam. Unable to justify the continuing drain on manpower, morale, and economic resources and facing widespread domestic discontent, Soviet leaders finally withdrew their troops in 1989. The Afghan communists held on for another three years, and then rebel groups took control of the entire country and began to fight among themselves over who should rule.

Asian Transformation

Japan has few mineral resources and is dependent on oil imports, but the Japanese economy weathered the oil price shocks of the 1970s better than did the economies of Europe and the United States. In fact, Japan's economy grew at the stupendous rate of about 10 percent a year during the 1970s and 1980s. Average income also increased rapidly, overtaking that of the United States in 1986.

The Japanese industrial model differed from the American and European models. During the American occupation, Japanese industrial conglomerates, *zaibatsu* (see Chapter 25), were broken up. Although ownership of major industries became less concentrated, new industrial alliances appeared. There are now six major **keiretsu** (kay-REHT-soo) that each include firms in industry, commerce, and construction tied together with a major bank in an interlocking ownership structure. Minor keiretsu may form around a major corporation, like Toyota, and its major suppliers. These industrial combinations have close relationships with government, which imposes tariffs and import regulations to inhibit foreign competition. Such support was crucial in fostering the development of Japan's automobile and semiconductor industries.

keiretsu Alliances of corporations and banks that dominate the Japanese economy.

Through the 1970s and 1980s, the Japanese ability to export manufactured goods produced huge trade surpluses. Attempts by the United States and the European Community to pry open the Japanese market through negotiation had only limited success. In 1990, Japan's trade surplus was double that of 1985. Many experts assumed that the competitive advantages that Japan enjoyed in the 1980s would propel Japan past the United States as the world's preeminent industrial economy. But the Japanese economy began to stall at the end of the decade.

A few other Asian states imitated the Japanese model of close cooperation between government and industry. South Korea overcame the devastation of the Korean War in little more than a decade through a combination of inexpensive labor, strong technical education, and substantial domestic capital reserves. It developed heavy industries like steel and shipbuilding, as well as consumer industries like automobiles and consumer electronics. Japanese investment and technology transfers accelerated this process.

Taiwan, Hong Kong, and Singapore moved so rapidly in the same direction that these three nations and South Korea were often called the **Asian Tigers.** Taiwan suffered a number of political reverses, including the loss of its United Nations seat to the People's Republic of China in 1971 and the withdrawal of diplomatic recognition by the United States. Nevertheless, it achieved remarkable economic progress, based on smaller, more specialized companies and investment in the People's Republic of China.

Hong Kong and Singapore were former British colonies with limited resources. Singapore's economy rested on its busy port and on banking and commercial services. After separating from Malaysia in 1965, this society of around 4 million people diversified by building textile and electronics industries. Hong Kong's economic prosperity, based on its port as well as its banking and commercial services, was increasingly tied to China's growing economy. Worried about Hong Kong's reintegration into the People's Republic of China in 1997, local capitalists moved significant amounts of capital to safe havens like the United States and Canada, but in recent years Hong Kong has regained its dynamism and is now even more closely tied to the rapidly expanding Chinese economy.

These **newly industrialized economies (NIEs)** all had disciplined and hardworking labor forces and invested heavily in education. As early as 1980 Korea had as many engineering graduates as Germany, Britain, and Sweden combined. These countries also emphasized outward-looking export strategies and had high rates of personal saving—about 35 percent of GDP—that allowed them to fund investment in new technology. Like Japan, they practiced government sponsorship and protection.

Despite this momentum the region was shaken by a deep crisis that began in 1997. Like the recession that had already afflicted Japan, the Asian financial crisis stemmed from bad loans, weak banks, and the international effects of currency speculation. The situation was stabilized by relief efforts of the United States, Japan, and the International Monetary Fund.

China Rejoins the World Economy

In China after Mao Zedong's death in 1976, the communist leadership introduced a comprehensive economic reform that allowed more individual initiative and permitted individuals to accumulate wealth. Beginning in 1978, the Communist Party in Sichuan province freed more than six thousand firms to compete for business outside the state planning process. The results were remarkable. Under China's leader, **Deng Xiaoping** (dung show-ping), these reforms were expanded across the nation. China also began to permit foreign investment for the first time since the communists came to power in 1949. Between 1978 and the end of the 1990s, foreign investors committed more than $180 billion to the Chinese economy, and McDonald's, Coca-Cola, Airbus, and other foreign companies opened for business. But more than 100 million workers were still employed in state-owned enterprises, and most foreign-owned companies were segregated in special economic zones. The result was a dual industrial sector—one modern and efficient and connected to international markets, the other dominated by government and directed by political decisions.

In the countryside, Deng Xiaoping permitted the contracting of land to individuals and families, who were free to consume or sell whatever they produced. By 1984,

Asian Tigers Collective name for South Korea, Taiwan, Hong Kong, and Singapore—nations that became economic powers in the 1970s and 1980s.

newly industrialized economies (NIEs) Rapidly growing, new industrial nations of the late twentieth century, including the Asian tigers.

Deng Xiaoping (1904–1997) Communist Party leader who forced Chinese economic reforms after the death of Mao Zedong.

93 percent of China's agricultural land was in effect in private hands and producing for the market, tripling agricultural output.

Perhaps the best measure of the success of Deng's reforms is that between 1980 and 1993 China's per capita output more than doubled, averaging more than 8 percent growth per year in comparison with the world average of slightly more than 1 percent and Japan's average of 3.3 percent. This growth was overwhelmingly the result of exports to the developed nations of the West, especially the United States. Nevertheless, per capita measures of wealth indicated that China remained a poor nation. China's per capita GDP was roughly the same as Mexico's—about $3,600 per year. By comparison, Taiwan had a per capita GDP of $14,700.

Much of China's command economy remained in place, and the leadership of the Chinese Communist Party resisted serious political reform. Deng Xiaoping's strategy of balancing change and continuity avoided some of the social and political costs experienced by Russia and other socialist countries that abruptly embraced capitalism and democracy. However, the nation's leadership faced a major challenge in 1989. Responding to inflation and to worldwide mass movements in favor of democracy, Chinese students and intellectuals, many of whom had studied outside China, led a series of protests demanding more democracy and an end to corruption. This movement culminated in **Tiananmen** (tee-yehn-ahn-men) **Square,** in the heart of Beijing, where hundreds of thousands of protesters gathered and refused to leave. After weeks of standoff, tanks pushed into the square, killing hundreds and arresting thousands.

China's continuing economic growth is sustained by direct foreign investment and by one of the world's highest savings rates. China's industries are modern and compete with more established industries in Japan and the West. But there are challenges. Increasing inequality, high levels of migration from the countryside to the cities, relatively weak infrastructure, poor protection of intellectual property rights, and corruption could retard future growth.

SECTION REVIEW

- The Cuban Revolution provoked a conservative reaction throughout Latin America, and democratic governments fell to U.S.-supported military coups.

- The 1980s saw the end of Sandinista rule in Nicaragua and of military dictatorships elsewhere in Latin America.

- Islamic revolutionaries seized power in Iran, thwarting U.S. intervention and prompting war with Iraq.

- The Soviet Union invaded Afghanistan to support the communist government against Islamic rebels.

- Japan's economy thrived through trade surpluses and close relationships between government and industry.

- The Asian Tigers adapted the Japanese model to their economies, and China implemented economic reforms while resisting democracy.

Tiananmen Square Site in Beijing where Chinese students and workers gathered to demand greater political openness in 1989. The demonstration was crushed by Chinese military with great loss of life.

THE END OF THE BIPOLAR WORLD

What forces led to the collapse of the Soviet Union?

Few in 1980 predicted the startling collapse of the Soviet Union and the socialist nations of the Warsaw Pact. The once-independent nations and ethnic groups that had been brought within the Soviet Union and the eastern European nations seemed securely transformed by the experiences and institutions of communism. By 1990, however, nationalism was resurgent, and communism was nearly finished.

Crisis in the Soviet Union

Under United States president Ronald Reagan and the Soviet Union's general secretary, Leonid Brezhnev (leh-oh-NEED BREZH-nef), the rhetoric of the Cold War remained intense. Massive new U.S. investments in armaments placed heavy burdens on a Soviet economy unable to absorb the cost of developing similar weapons. Soviet economic problems were systemic; shortages had become a part of Soviet life. Obsolete industrial plants and centralized planning that stifled initiative led to a declining standard of living relative to the West, while the arbitrariness of the bureaucracy, the cynical manipulation of information, and deprivations created a generalized crisis in morale.

Despite the unpopularity of the war in Afghanistan and growing discontent, Brezhnev refused to modify his rigid and unsuccessful policies. But he was unable to contain an underground current of protest. In a series of powerful books, the writer Alexander Solzhenitzyn (sol-zhuh-NEET-sin) castigated the Soviet system and particularly the Stalinist prison camps. He won a Nobel Prize in literature but was charged with treason and expelled from the country in 1974. Self-published underground writings (*samizdat* [sah-meez-DAHT]) by critics of the regime circulated widely despite government efforts to suppress them.

By the time **Mikhail Gorbachev** (GORE-beh-CHOF) took up the reins of the Soviet government in 1985, war weariness, economic decay, and vocal protest had reached critical levels. Casting aside Brezhnev's hard line, Gorbachev authorized major reforms in an attempt to stave off total collapse. His policy of political openness (*glasnost*) permitted criticism of the government and the Communist Party. His policy of **perestroika** (per-ih-STROY-kuh) ("restructuring") was an attempt to address long-suppressed economic problems by moving away from central state planning and toward a more open economic system. In 1989 he ended the unpopular war in Afghanistan.

Primary Source: Letter to Comrades Brezhnev, Kosygin, and Podgorny
Examine a letter urging the Soviet government to turn to democracy in order to save itself from decline.

Mikhail Gorbachev (b. 1931)
Head of the Soviet Union from 1985 to 1991. His liberalization effort improved relations with the West, but he lost power after his reforms led to the collapse of communist governments in eastern Europe.

perestroika Policy of "openness" that was the centerpiece of Mikhail Gorbachev's efforts to liberalize communism in the Soviet Union.

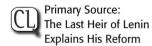

Primary Source: The Last Heir of Lenin Explains His Reform Plans: Perestroika and Glasnost *Find out why Mikhail Gorbachev believes the essence of perestroika lies in the union of socialism and democracy.*

Solidarity Polish trade union created in 1980 to protest working conditions and political repression. It began the nationalist opposition to communist rule that led in 1989 to the fall of communism in eastern Europe.

The Collapse of the Socialist Bloc

Events in eastern Europe were very important in forcing change on the Soviet Union. In 1980, protests by Polish shipyard workers in the city of Gdansk led to the formation of **Solidarity,** a labor union that soon enrolled 9 million members. The Roman Catholic Church in Poland, strengthened by the elevation of a Pole, Karol Wojtyla (KAH-rol voy-TIL-ah), to the papacy as John Paul II in 1978, gave strong moral support to the protest movement. As Gorbachev loosened political controls in the Soviet Union after 1985, communist leaders elsewhere lost confidence in Soviet resolve, and critics and reformers in Poland and throughout the rest of eastern Europe were emboldened (see Map 29.1).

Beleaguered Warsaw Pact governments vacillated between relaxation of control and the suppression of dissent. As the Catholic clergy in Poland had supported Solidarity, Protestant and Orthodox religious leaders aided the rise of opposition groups elsewhere. This combination of nationalism and religion provided a powerful base for opponents of the communist regimes. Threatened by these forces, communist governments sought to quiet the opposition by seeking solutions to their severe economic problems. They turned to the West for trade and financial assistance and opened their nations to travelers, ideas, styles, and money from Western countries, all of which accelerated the demand for change.

By the end of 1989, communist governments across eastern Europe had fallen. The dismantling of the Berlin Wall, the symbol of a divided Europe and the bipolar world, vividly represented this transformation. In Poland, Hungary, Czechoslovakia, and Bulgaria, communist leaders decided that change was inevitable and initiated

Map 29.1   The End of Soviet Domination in Eastern Europe

The creation of new countries out of Yugoslavia and Czechoslovakia and the reunification of Germany marked the most complicated changes of national borders since World War I. The Czech Republic and Slovakia separated peacefully, but Slovenia, Croatia, Macedonia, and Bosnia and Herzegovina achieved independence only after bitter fighting.

 Interactive Map

political reforms. When Romanian dictator Nicolae Ceausescu (neh-koh-LIE chow-SHES-koo) refused to surrender power, he provoked a rebellion that ended with his arrest and execution. The comprehensiveness of these changes became clear in 1990, when Solidarity leader Lech Walesa (leck wah-LEN-suh) was elected president of Poland and dissident playwright Vaclav Havel (vahc-SLAV hah-VEL) was elected president of Czechoslovakia. That same year, East and West Germany were reunited, and the eastern Baltic states of Lithuania, Estonia, and Latvia declared their independence from the Soviet Union.

The end of the Soviet Union came suddenly in 1991. Gorbachev's efforts to transform the Soviet system could not keep up with the tide of change sweeping through the region. After communist hardliners botched a poorly conceived coup against Gorbachev, disgust with communism boiled over. Boris Yeltsin, the president of the Russian Republic and long-time member of the Communist Party, led popular resistance to the coup in Moscow and emerged as the most powerful leader

The Fall of the Berlin Wall

The Berlin Wall was the most important symbol of the Cold War. Constructed to keep residents of East Germany from fleeing to the West and defended by armed guards and barbed wire, for many in the West it was the public face of communism. As the Soviet system fell apart, the residents of East and West Berlin broke down sections of the wall. Here young people straddle the wall, signaling the end of an era.   (Bossu Regis/Corbis Sygma)

in the country. Russia, the largest republic in the Soviet Union, was effectively taking the place of the disintegrating USSR. In September 1991, the Congress of People's Deputies voted to dissolve the union. Mikhail Gorbachev went into retirement.

The ethnic and religious passions that fueled the breakup of the Soviet Union soon overwhelmed the Balkan state of Yugoslavia. In 1991 it dissolved into a morass of separatism and warring ethnic and religious groups. Slovenia and Croatia, the most westerly provinces, both heavily Roman Catholic, became independent states in 1992. Reflecting centuries of Muslim, Catholic, and Orthodox competition in the Balkans, the people of the province of Bosnia and Herzegovina were more mixed: 40 percent were Muslims, 30 percent Serbian Orthodox, and 18 percent Catholics. Following the declaration of Bosnian national independence in 1992, the Orthodox Serbs attempted to rid the state of Muslims, a violent campaign identified as **ethnic cleansing** in the international press. At first, no European power acted to stop this tragedy. Finally, after extensive television coverage of atrocities and wanton destruction seemed to force the issue, the United States intervened and eventually brokered a settlement in 1995.

In 1999 new fighting and a new round of ethnic cleansing occurred in the southernmost Yugoslavian province of Kosovo. Once the ancient homeland of the Serbs, Kosovo now had a predominantly Muslim and Albanian population. When NATO's warnings went unheeded, the United States, Britain, and France launched an aerial war against Serbia that forced the withdrawal of Serbian forces from Kosovo. While attention was focused on the Balkans, destructive ethnic and religious conflict also characterized the transitional period in Armenia, Georgia, and Chechnya.

ethnic cleansing Effort to eradicate a people and its culture by means of mass killing and the destruction of historical buildings and cultural materials. Ethnic cleansing was used by both sides in the conflicts that accompanied the disintegration of Yugoslavia in the 1990s.

Progress and Conflict in Africa

Since independence democracy has had mixed results in sub-Saharan Africa. Many elected leaders have used their offices to enrich themselves and limit or eliminate political opposition. Military coups and conflicts over resources such as diamonds have also been distressingly common. Southern Africa, however, has seen democratic progress and a steady decline in armed conflicts since 1991. A key change came in South Africa in 1994, when long-time political prisoner Nelson Mandela and his African National Congress (ANC) won the first national elections in which the African majority could participate equally. Since then, the lively politics of this ethnically diverse country have been a model of how democracy can resolve conflicts. Also hopeful has been the return to democracy of Nigeria, Africa's most populous state, after decades of military rulers. In 1999, after a succession of military governments, Nigerians elected President Olusegun Obasanjo (oh-LOO-she-gun oh-BAH-san-jo) (a former coup leader), and a 2003 vote renewed his term, despite serious voting irregularities. Similarly, in 2002 Kenyans voted out the party that had held power for thirty-nine years.

Unfortunately, Africa was also the scene of ethnic cleansing. In 1994 the political leaders of the Central African nation of Rwanda incited Hutu people to massacre their Tutsi neighbors. The major powers avoided characterizing the slaughter as genocide because an international agreement mandated intervention to stop genocide. Without action by foreign powers, the carnage continued until some 750,000 people were dead and millions of refugees had fled into neighboring states. Finally, the United States and other powers intervened and the United Nations set up a tribunal to try those responsible for the genocide. In 1998 violence spread from Rwanda to neighboring Congo, where growing opposition and ill health had forced President Joseph Mobutu from office after over three decades of dictatorial misrule. Various peacemaking attempts failed to restore order. By mid-2003 more than 3 million Congolese had died from disease, malnutrition, and injuries related to the fighting.

The Persian Gulf War

The first significant conflict to occur after the breakup of the Soviet Union and the end of the Cold War was the Persian Gulf War. The immediate causes were local and bilateral. Iraq's ruler, Saddam Husayn, had borrowed a great deal of money from neighboring Kuwait and sought unsuccessfully to get Kuwait's royal family to reduce the size of this debt. He was also eager to gain control of Kuwait's oil fields. Husayn believed that the smaller and militarily weaker nation could be quickly defeated, and he suspected, as a result of a conversation with an American diplomat, that the United States would not react. The invasion came in August 1990.

The United States convinced the government of Saudi Arabia that it was a possible target of Iraq's aggression. Saudi Arabia, an important regional ally of the United States and a major oil producer, was the key to any military action by the United States. The United States and its allies concentrated an imposing military force of 500,000 in the region. With his intention to use force endorsed by the United Nations and with many Islamic nations supporting military action, President George H. W. Bush ordered an attack in early 1991. Iraq proved incapable of countering the sophisticated weaponry of the coalition. The missiles and bombs of the United States not only destroyed military targets but also "relegated [Iraq] to a pre-industrial age," the United Nations reported after the war. Although Iraq's military defeat was comprehensive, Husayn remained in power, and the country was not occupied. In fact, Husayn crushed an uprising in the months following this defeat. The United States and its key allies then imposed "no-fly" zones that

SECTION REVIEW

- Soviet dissidents protested economic deprivation and government repression, inefficiency, and arbitrariness.
- Gorbachev attempted to reform the system through *glasnost* and *perestroika*.
- Beginning in Poland, the Soviet-bloc governments fell to the combined pressure of nationalism and religion.
- In 1991, the Soviet Union dissolved, driven partly by ethnic/religious tensions that later challenged Czechoslovakia and Yugoslavia.
- A U.S.-led coalition defeated Iraq in the Persian Gulf War, but Saddam Husayn remained in power.

denied Iraq's military aircraft access to the northern and southern regions of the country. As a result, military tensions and periodic armed confrontations continued.

In the United States the results of the Persian Gulf War were interpreted to mean that the U.S. military defeat in the Vietnam War could be forgotten and that U.S. military capability was unrivaled. Unable to deter military action by the U.S.-led coalition or to meaningfully influence the diplomacy that surrounded the war, Russia had been of little use to its former ally Iraq, and its impotence was clear.

THE CHALLENGE OF POPULATION GROWTH

What explains differences in the rate of population growth among the world's cultural regions?

For most of human history, population growth was viewed as beneficial, and human beings were seen as a source of wealth. Since the late eighteenth century, however, population growth has been viewed with increasing alarm. Some feared that food supplies could not keep up with population growth. Others foresaw class and ethnic struggle as numbers overwhelmed resources. By the second half of the twentieth century, population growth was increasingly seen as a threat to the environment.

Demographic Transition

Thomas Malthus (1766–1834) Eighteenth-century English intellectual who warned that population growth threatened future generations because, in his view, population growth would always outstrip increases in agricultural production.

demographic transition A change in the rates of population growth. Before the transition, both birthrates and death rates are high, resulting in a slowly growing population; then the death rate drops but the birthrate remains high, causing a population explosion; finally the birthrate drops and the population growth slows down. This transition took place in Europe in the late nineteenth and early twentieth centuries, in North America and East Asia in the mid-twentieth century and, most recently, in Latin America and South Asia.

The population of Europe almost doubled between 1850 and 1914, putting enormous pressure on rural land and urban housing and overwhelming fragile public institutions that provided some crisis assistance (see Chapter 23). This dramatic growth forced a large wave of immigration across the Atlantic, helping to develop the Western Hemisphere and invigorating the Atlantic economy. Population growth also contributed to Europe's Industrial Revolution by lowering labor costs and increasing consumer demand.

Educated Europeans of the nineteenth century were ambivalent about the rapid increase in human population. Some saw it as a blessing that would promote economic well-being. Others warned that the seemingly relentless increase would bring disaster. The best-known pessimist was the English cleric **Thomas Malthus,** who in 1798 argued that unchecked population growth would outstrip food production. When Malthus looked at Europe's future, he used a prejudiced image of China to terrify his European readers. A visitor to China, he claimed, "will not be surprised that mothers destroy or expose many of their children; that parents sell their daughters for a trifle; . . . and that there should be such a number of robbers. The surprise is that nothing still more dreadful should happen."[1]

The generation that came of age in the years immediately following World War II inherited a world in which the views of Malthus were casually dismissed. Industrial and agricultural productivity had multiplied supplies of food and other necessities. Cultural changes associated with expanded female employment, older age at marriage, and more effective family planning had combined to slow the rate of population increase. And by the late 1960s Europe and other industrial societies had made what was called the **demographic transition** to lower fertility rates (average number of births per woman) and reduced mortality. The number of births in the developed nations was just adequate for the maintenance of current population levels.

By the late 1970s, however, the demographic transition had not occurred in the Third World, and the issue of population growth had become politicized. The leaders of some developing nations actively promoted large families, arguing that larger populations would increase national power. These arguments remained a persistent part of the debate between developed and developing nations. Industrialized, mostly white, nations raised concerns about rapid population growth in Asia, Africa, and Latin America. Populist political leaders in those regions asked whether these concerns were not fundamentally racist.

The question exposed the influence of racism in the population debate and temporarily disarmed Western advocates of birth control. However, once the economic shocks of the 1970s and 1980s revealed the vulnerability of developing economies, governments in the developing world jettisoned policies that promoted population growth. Mexico is a good example. In the1970s the government had encouraged high fertility, and population growth rose to 3 percent per year. In the 1980s Mexico rejected these policies and promoted birth control. As a result Mexico's annual population growth fell to 2.3 percent per year by the end of the decade and in the 1990s to 1.7 percent.

World population exploded in the twentieth century. Although the rate of growth has slowed since the 1980s, world population still increases by a number equal to the total population of the United States every three years. If fertility remains constant from today, with a world average of 2.5 children per woman, world population will reach nearly 30 billion in 2150, more than three times the 2050 projection found in Table 29.1.

This is not likely. Fertility is already declining in many developing nations, and many scholars see world population in 2150 in the 10 to 15 billion range. Mortality rates have also increased in some areas as immigration, commercial expansion, and improved transportation facilitate the transmission of disease. The rapid spread of HIV/AIDS is an example of this phenomenon. Less-developed regions with poorly funded public health institutions and with few resources to invest in prevention and treatment experience the highest rates of infection and the greatest mortality. In Russia, for example, new HIV infections rose from under five thousand in 1997 to over ninety thousand in 2001. AIDS has spread at a similar pace in China. But the disease has developed most quickly and with the most devastating results in Africa, the home of 28 million of the world's 40 million infected people.

Unlike population growth in the eighteenth and nineteenth centuries, when much of the increase occurred in the wealthiest nations, population growth at the end of the twentieth century was overwhelmingly in the poorest nations. Although fertility rates dropped in most developing nations, they remained much higher than rates in the industrialized nations. At the same time, improvements in hygiene and medical treatment caused mortality rates to fall, despite recent catastrophes, such as HIV/AIDS. The result has been rapid population growth.

The Industrialized Nations

In much of Europe and Japan at the beginning of the twenty-first century, fertility levels are so low that population will fall unless immigration increases. In Japan,

TABLE 29.1 | POPULATION FOR WORLD AND MAJOR AREAS, 1750–2050

POPULATION SIZE (MILLIONS) (ESTIMATED)

MAJOR AREA	1750	1800	1850	1900	1950	1995	2050
World	791	978	1,262	1,650	2,521	5,666	8,909
Africa	106	107	111	133	221	697	1,766
Asia	502	635	809	947	1,402	3,437	5,268
Europe	163	203	276	408	547	728	628
Latin America and the Caribbean	16	24	38	74	167	480	809
North America	2	7	26	82	172	297	392
Oceania	2	2	2	6	13	28	46

PERCENTAGE DISTRIBUTION (ESTIMATED)

MAJOR AREA	1750	1800	1850	1900	1950	1995	2050
World	100.0	100.0	100.0	100.0	100.0	100.0	100.0
Africa	13.4	10.9	8.8	8.1	8.8	12.0	19.8
Asia	63.5	64.9	64.1	57.4	55.6	61.0	59.1
Europe	20.6	20.8	21.9	24.7	21.7	13.0	7.0
Latin America and the Caribbean	2.0	2.5	3.0	4.5	6.6	8.0	9.1
North America	0.3	0.7	2.1	5.0	6.8	5.0	4.4
Oceania	0.3	0.2	0.2	0.4	0.5	1.0	0.5

Source: J. D. Durand, "Historical Estimates of World Population: An Evaluation" (Philadelphia: University of Pennsylvania, Population Studies Center, 1974, mimeographed); United Nations, *The Determinants and Consequences of Population Trends,* vol. 1 (New York: United Nations, 1973); United Nations, *World Population Prospects as Assessed in 1963* (New York: United Nations, 1966); United Nations, *World Population Prospects: The 1998 Revision* (New York: United Nations, forthcoming); United Nations Population Division, Department of Economic and Social Affairs, http://www.popin.org/pop1998/4.htm.

women have an average of 1.39 children; in Italy, the number is 1.2. Sweden provides cash payments, tax incentives, and job leaves to families with children, but the average number of births there fell to 1.4 in recent years. The low fertility found in mature industrial nations is tied to higher levels of female education and employment, the material values of consumer culture, and access to contraception and abortion. Educated women now defer marriage and child rearing until they are established in careers.

As fertility has declined in the industrialized nations of western Europe, life expectancy has improved because of more abundant food, improved hygiene, and better medical care. Italy, for example, soon will have more than twenty adults fifty years old or over for each five-year-old child. Japan faces an even more drastic aging of its population. This demographic transformation presents a challenge very different from the one foreseen by Malthus. These nations generally offer a broad array of social services, including retirement income, medical services, and housing supplements for the elderly. As the number of retirees increases relative to the number of people who are employed, the costs of these services may become unsustainable.

In contrast, in Russia and some former socialist nations, life expectancy and birthrates have both fallen. Life expectancy for Russian men is now only fifty-seven years, down almost ten years since 1980. In the Czech Republic, Hungary, and Poland, life expectancy is improving in response to improved economic conditions, but most of the rest of eastern Europe follows the Russian pattern of declining life expectancy. High unemployment, low incomes, food shortages, and the dismantling of the social welfare system of the communist era have all contributed to this decline.

The Developing Nations

At current rates, 95 percent of all future population growth will be in developing nations (see Table 29.1). A comparison between Europe and Africa illustrates these changes. In 1950, Europe had twice the population of Africa. By 1985, Africa had drawn even. According to projections, by 2025 Africa's population will be three times larger than Europe's.

As the 1990s ended, the populations of Latin America and Asia also were expanding dramatically, but at rates slower than those in sub-Saharan Africa and the Muslim world. In Asia, the populations of India and China continued to grow despite government efforts to reduce family size. In China, efforts to enforce a limit of one child per family led to large-scale female infanticide as rural families sought to produce male heirs. India's policies of forced sterilization created widespread outrage and led to the electoral defeat of the ruling Congress Party. Yet both countries achieved some successes. Between 1960 and 1982, India's birthrate fell from 48 to 34 per thousand, while China's rate declined even more sharply—from 39 to 19. Still, by 2025, China and India will each have some 1.5 billion people.

Old and Young Populations

Population pyramids generated by demographers clearly illustrate the profound transformation in human reproductive patterns and life expectancy in the years since

Chinese Family-Planning Campaign

Hoping to slow population growth, the Chinese government has sought to limit parents to a single child. Billboards and other forms of mass advertising have been an essential part of the campaign to gain compliance with national family-planning directives. (Picard/Sipa Press)

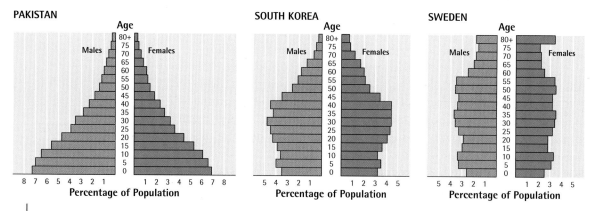

Figure 29.1   Age Structure Comparison

Islamic Nation (Pakistan), Non-Islamic Developing Nation (South Korea), and Developed Nation (Sweden), 2001.
Source: U.S. Bureau of the Census, International Database, 2001.

World War II. Figure 29.1 shows the 2001 age distributions in Pakistan, South Korea, and Sweden—nations at three different stages of economic development. Sweden is a mature industrial nation. South Korea is rapidly industrializing and has surpassed many European nations in both industrial output and per capita wealth. Pakistan is a poor, traditional Muslim nation with rudimentary industrialization, low educational levels, and little effective family planning.

In 2001 nearly 50 percent of Pakistan's population was under age sixteen. The resulting pressures on the economy have been extraordinary. Every year approximately 150,000 men reach age sixty-five—and another 1.2 million turn sixteen. Pakistan, therefore, has to create more than a million new jobs a year or face steadily growing unemployment and steadily declining wages. Sweden confronts a different problem. Sweden's aging population, growing demand for social welfare benefits, and declining labor pool means that its industries may become less competitive and living standards may decline. In South Korea, a decline in fertility dramatically altered the ratio of children to adults, creating an age distribution similar to that of western Europe earlier in the twentieth century. South Korea does not face Pakistan's impossible task of creating new jobs or Sweden's growing demands for welfare benefits for the aged.

The demographic problem and potential technological adjustments are most clearly visible in Japan. Japan has the oldest population in the world, with a current median age of forty-one. Whereas large numbers of young immigrants from poorer nations are entering the work forces of Canada, Germany, the United States, and most other industrialized nations, slowing the aging of these populations, Japan has resisted immigration, instead investing heavily in technological solutions to the problems created by its aging labor force. As of 1994 Japan had 75 percent of the world's industrial robots. Although Japanese industries are able to produce more goods with fewer workers, Japan will still face long-term increases in social welfare payments.

SECTION REVIEW

- In the twentieth century, populations exploded in the world's poorest nations.

- The demographic transition of the industrialized nations failed to occur in the Third World, politicizing the population issue.

- Economic hardships of the 1970s and 1980s forced developing nations to discourage population growth.

- In Japan and much of industrialized Europe, low fertility rates and higher life expectancy have effected a demographic transformation.

- Populations continue to expand in the developing world.

UNEQUAL DEVELOPMENT AND THE MOVEMENT OF PEOPLES

How does wealth inequality among nations impact international migration patterns?

Two characteristics of the postwar world should now be clear. First, despite decades of experimentation with state-directed economic development, most nations that were poor in 1960 were as poor or poorer at the end of the 1990s. The only exceptions were a few rapidly developing Asian industrial nations and an equally small number of oil-exporting nations. Second, world population increased to startlingly high levels, and most of the increase was in the poorest nations.

The combination of intractable poverty and growing population generated a surge in international immigration, both legal and illegal. Few other issues stirred more controversy. Even moderate voices sometimes framed the discussion of immigration as a competition among peoples. One commentator summarized his analysis this way: "As the better-off families of the northern hemisphere individually decide that having only one or at the most two children is sufficient, they may not recognize that they are in a small way vacating future space (that is, jobs, parts of inner cities, shares of population, shares of market preferences) to faster-growing ethnic groups both inside and outside their boundaries. But that, in fact, is what they are doing."[3]

The Problem of Growing Inequality

Since 1945, global economic productivity has expanded more rapidly than at any other time in the past. Faster, cheaper communications and transportation have combined with improvements in industrial and agricultural technologies to create levels of material abundance that would have amazed those who experienced the first Industrial Revolution (see Chapter 20). Despite this remarkable economic expansion and growing market integration, the majority of the world's population remains in poverty. The industrialized nations of the Northern Hemisphere now enjoy a larger share of the world's wealth than they did a century ago. As a result, the gap between rich and poor nations has grown much wider. The thousands of homeless street children who live among the gleaming glass and steel towers of Rio's banking district can be seen as a metaphor for the social consequences of postwar economic development.

Wealth inequality within nations also grew. In the United States, for example, the South and Southwest grew richer in the past three decades relative to the older industrial regions of the Midwest. Regional inequalities also appeared in developing nations. Generally, capital cities such as Buenos Aires, in Argentina, and Lagos, in Nigeria, attracted large numbers of migrants from rural areas because they offer more opportunities, even if those opportunities could not compare to the ones available in developed nations.

Even in the industrialized world people were divided into haves and have-nots. During the presidency of Ronald Reagan (1981–1989), wealth inequality in the United States reached its highest level since the 1929 stock market crash. Some scholars estimated that the wealthiest 1 percent of households in the United States controlled more than 30 percent of the nation's total wealth. Even in Europe, where tax and inheritance laws redistributed wealth, unemployment, homelessness, and substandard housing were increasingly common.

Internal Migration: The Growth of Cities

Migration from rural areas to urban centers in developing nations increased threefold from 1925 to 1950. After that, the pace accelerated (see Table 29.2). Shantytowns sprawling around major cities in developing nations are commonly seen as signs of social breakdown and economic failure. Nevertheless, even in the shantytowns city life was generally better than life in the countryside. A World Bank study estimated that three out of four migrants to cities made economic gains. Residents of cities in sub-Saharan Africa, for example, were six times more likely than rural residents to have safe water. An unskilled migrant from the depressed northeast of Brazil could triple his or her income by moving to Rio de Janeiro.

As the scale of rural-to-urban migration grew, these benefits proved more elusive, however. In many West African cities, basic services were crumbling under the pressure of rapid population growth. In 1990 in Mexico City, one of the world's largest cities, more than thirty thousand people lived in garbage dumps, where they scavenged for food and clothing.

TABLE 29.2 | THE WORLD'S LARGEST METROPOLITAN AREAS (POPULATION OF 10 MILLION OR MORE)

CITY	1950	CITY	1975	CITY	2000	CITY	2015
1 New York	12.3	1 Tokyo	19.8	1 Tokyo	26.4	1 Tokyo	26.4
		2 New York	15.9	2 Mexico City	18.1	2 Bombay	26.1
		3 Shanghai	11.4	3 Bombay	18.1	3 Lagos	23.2
		4 Mexico City	11.2	4 Sao Paulo	17.8	4 Dhaka	21.1
		5 São Paulo	10.0	5 New York	16.6	5 Sao Paulo	20.4
				6 Lagos	13.4	6 Karachi	19.2
				7 Los Angeles	13.1	7 Mexico City	19.2
				8 Calcutta	12.9	8 New York	17.4
				9 Shanghai	12.9	9 Jakarta	17.3
				10 Buenos Aires	12.6	10 Calcutta	17.3
				11 Dhaka	12.3	11 Delhi	16.8
				12 Karachi	11.8	12 Metro Manila	14.8
				13 Delhi	11.7	13 Shanghai	14.6
				14 Jakarta	11.0	14 Los Angeles	14.1
				15 Osaka	11.0	15 Buenos Aires	14.1
				16 Metro Manila	10.9	16 Cairo	13.8
				17 Beijing	10.8	17 Istanbul	12.5
				18 Rio de Janeiro	10.6	18 Beijing	12.3
				19 Cairo	10.6	19 Rio de Janeiro	11.9
						20 Osaka	11.0
						21 Tianjin	10.7
						22 Hyderabad	10.5
						23 Bangkok	10.1

Source: International Migration Report 2002, United Nations, Department of Economic and Social Affairs, Population Division, "World Urbanization Prospects: The 1999 Revision," p. 6. The United Nations is the author of the original material. Reprinted by permission of United Nations Publications.

Worsening conditions and the threat of crime and political instability led many governments to try to slow migration to cities and, in some cases, to return people to the countryside. Indonesia, for example, has relocated more than half a million urban residents since 1969. Despite some successes with slowing the rate of internal migration, nearly every poor nation still faces the challenge of rapidly growing cities.

Global Migration

Each year, hundreds of thousands of men and women leave the developing world to emigrate to industrialized nations. After 1960, this movement increased in scale, and ethnic and racial tensions in the host nations worsened. By the 1990s, levels of immigration posed daunting social and cultural challenges for both host nations and immigrants.

When an expanding European economy first confronted labor shortages in the 1960s, many European nations actively promoted guest worker programs and other inducements to immigration. However, attitudes toward immigrants changed as the size of the immigrant population grew and as European economies slowed in the 1980s. Facing higher levels of unemployment, native-born workers saw immigrants as competitors willing to work for lower wages and less likely to support unions.

Because immigrants generally are young adults and commonly retain the positive attitudes toward early marriage and large families dominant in their native cultures, immigrant communities in Europe and the United States tended to have fertility rates higher than the rates of the host populations. In Germany in 1975, for example, immigrants made up about 7 percent of the population but accounted for nearly 15 percent of all births. Although the fertility of the Hispanic population in the United States is lower than the rates in Mexico and other Latin American nations, Hispanic groups will contribute well over 20 percent of all population growth in the United States during the next twenty-five years.

As the Muslim population in Europe and the Asian and Latin American populations in the United States expand in the twenty-first century, cultural conflicts will test definitions of citizenship and nationality. The United States will have some advantages in meeting these challenges because of long experience with immigration and relatively open access to citizenship. Yet in the 1990s, the United States was moving slowly in the direction of European efforts to restrict immigration and defend a culturally conservative definition of nationality.

SECTION REVIEW

- Despite rapid postwar economic growth, most of the world remains impoverished.
- Wealth inequality within nations and between industrialized and developing nations continues to grow.
- Cities in developing nations have grown rapidly since World War II.
- Migrants initially made economic gains, but their numbers are overwhelming limited urban resources.
- Migration from developing to industrialized nations has created growing social and cultural tensions in host countries.

TECHNOLOGICAL AND ENVIRONMENTAL CHANGE

How has technological change affected the global environment in the recent past?

Technological innovation powered the economic expansion that began after World War II by increasing productivity and disseminating human creativity. Because most of the economic benefits were concentrated in the advanced industrialized nations, technology increased the power of those nations relative to the developing world. Even within developed nations, postwar technological innovations did not benefit all classes, industries, and regions equally.

The multiplication of farms and factories intensified environmental threats. Loss of rain forest, soil erosion, global warming, pollution of air and water, and extinction of species imperiled human societies. Environmental protection measures, like the acquisition of new technology, progressed furthest in societies with the most economic resources.

New Technologies and the World Economy

Nuclear energy, jet engines, radar, and tape recording were among the many World War II developments that later had an impact on consumers' lives. When applied to industry, new technology increased productivity, reduced labor requirements, and improved the flow of information. As the Western economies recovered from the war and incomes rose, consumers purchased new products that reduced their workloads or provided entertainment.

Improvements in existing technologies accounted for much of the developed world's productivity increases during the 1950s and 1960s. Larger and faster trucks, trains, and airplanes cut transportation costs. Both capitalist and socialist governments expanded highway systems, improved railroad track, and constructed airports and nuclear power plants.

No other technology had greater significance in this period than the computer. Only large corporations, governments, and universities could afford the first computers. But by the mid-1980s, desktop computers had replaced typewriters in most of the developed world's offices, and technological advances continued. Each new generation of computers was faster and more powerful than the one before.

Computers also altered manufacturing. Small dedicated computers were used to control and monitor machinery in some industries. European and Japanese companies were the first to introduce such robots into the factory. The United States introduced robots more slowly because it enjoys lower labor costs.

The transnational corporation became the primary agent of these technological changes. In the post–World War II years, many companies with multinational ownership and management invested in and marketed products throughout the world. International trade agreements and open markets furthered the process.

As transnational manufacturers, agricultural conglomerates, and financial giants became wealthier and more powerful, they increasingly escaped the controls imposed by national governments. If labor costs were too high in Japan, antipollution measures too intrusive in the United States, or taxes too high in Great Britain, transnational companies relocated—or threatened to do so. Governments in the developing world were often hard-pressed to control the actions of these powerful enterprises. As a result, the worst abuses of labor or of the environment usually occurred in poor nations.

Conserving and Sharing Resources

In the 1960s, environmental activists and political leaders began warning about the devastating environmental consequences of population growth, industrialization, and the expansion of agriculture onto marginal lands. Assaults on rain forests and red-woods, the disappearance of species, and the poisoning of streams and rivers raised public consciousness. Environmental damage occurred in the advanced industrial economies and in the poorest of the developing nations. Perhaps the worst environmental record was achieved in the former Soviet Union, where industrial and nuclear wastes were often dumped with little concern for environmental consequences. The accumulated effect of scientific studies and public debate led to national and international efforts to slow, if not undo, damage to the environment.

The expanding global population required increasing quantities of food, housing, energy, and other resources as the twentieth century ended (see Map 29.2). In the developed world, the consumer-driven economic expansion of the post–World War II years became an obstacle to addressing environmental problems. How could the United States, Germany, or Japan change consumption patterns to protect the environment without endangering corporate profits, wages, and employment levels?

Many developing countries saw exploitation of their environmental resources and industrialization as the solution to their rapidly growing populations. The results were predictable: erosion and pollution.

Responding to Environmental Threats

Despite the gravity of environmental threats, there were many successful efforts to preserve and protect the environment. The Clean Air Act, the Clean Water Act, and the Endangered Species Act were passed in the United States in the 1970s as part of an environmental effort that included the nations of the European Community and Japan. Environmental awareness spread by means of the media and grassroots political movements, and most nations in the developed world enforced strict antipollution laws and sponsored massive recycling efforts. Many also encouraged resource conservation by rewarding energy-efficient factories and the manufacturers of fuel-efficient cars and by promoting the use of alternative energy sources such as solar and wind power.

These efforts produced significant results. In western Europe and the United States, air quality improved dramatically. In the United States, smog levels were down nearly a third from 1970 to 2000 even though the number of automobiles increased more than 80 percent. Emissions of lead and sulfur dioxide were down as well. The Great Lakes, Long Island Sound, and Chesapeake Bay were all much cleaner at the end of the century than they had been in 1970. The rivers of North America and Europe also improved. Still, more than thirty thousand deaths each year in the United States are attributed to exposure to pesticides and other chemicals.

New technologies made much of this improvement possible. Pollution controls on automobiles, planes, and factory smokestacks reduced harmful emissions. Similar progress was made in the chemical industry. Scientists identified the chemicals that threaten the ozone layer, and the phase-out of their use in new appliances and cars began.

Clearly the desire to preserve the natural environment was growing around the world. In the developed nations, continued political organization and enhanced awareness of environmental issues seemed likely to lead to step-by-step improvements in environmental policy. In the developing world

SECTION REVIEW

- Innovative and improved technologies, especially the computer, helped to drive postwar economic expansion in the industrialized world.

- Transnational corporations emerged as powerful institutions, often able to elude government controls.

- Since the 1960s, national and international efforts to address environmental damage have increased.

- Global population growth has placed increasing pressure on the world environment, requiring nations to address consumption patterns and resource use.

- Many industrialized nations have introduced successful antipollution laws and recycling and resource-conservation programs.

- Developing nations and the former Soviet bloc face many obstacles to similar initiatives.

Map 29.2   Fresh Water Resources

This map links population density and the availability of water. Red areas are highly stressed environments where populations use at least 40 percent or more of available water. Less stressed environments are blue. The deeper the shade of red or blue the greater the environmental stress.   *Source:* From "Global Water Stress," *National Geographic,* September 2002, pp. 14–16. NGS/National Geographic Image Collection. Reprinted by permission of the National Geographic Society.

and most of the former Soviet bloc, however, population pressures and weak governments were major obstacles to effective environmental policies. In China, for example, respiratory disease caused by pollution was the leading cause of death. Thus, it was likely that the industrialized nations would have to fund global improvements, and the cost was likely to be high.

Chapter Review

 DOWNLOAD THE MP3 AUDIO FILE OF THE CHAPTER REVIEW TO LISTEN TO ON THE GO.

How did the Cold War affect politics in Latin America and the Middle East in the 1970s and 1980s? (page 789)

During the Cold War the United States and the Soviet Union were engaged in a global contest for dominance. While the superpowers avoided direct conflict, they both were drawn into revolutions, civil wars, and regional conflicts when they found opportunities to undercut each other. Fear that the Cuban (1959) and later Nicaraguan (1979) revolutions would spread across Latin America led the United States to support the rise of military dictatorships across the region. In the Middle East, the United States and the Soviet Union both armed and trained the militaries of Israel and the Arab nations. Earlier U.S. support for the government of the shah of Iran helped to produce a religious and nationalist uprising that overthrew the shah and led to a long confrontation with the United States. The Soviet Union, pursuing the establishment of friendly regimes on its borders, sent an army into Afghanistan and set up a puppet government. However, with the United States, Saudi Arabia, and Pakistan supplying the insurgency, the Soviet Union was forced to withdraw.

What forces led to the collapse of the Soviet Union? (page 799)

The Soviet Union ultimately collapsed at the end of the 1980s. Although its economy had made great strides in the decades immediately after World War II, central planning proved uncompetitive with the West, especially in meeting demands for consumer products and technological innovation. The Soviets also found it increasingly difficult to control the nationalist passions that circulated below the surface of its constituent republics. Nationalism was more dangerous still in the satellite nations. Use of military force to crush uprisings in Hungary in 1956 and Czechoslovakia in 1968 were the clearest indications that the Soviet empire was based on force. As the cost of the Cold War grew in the 1980s, the Soviet system began to crumble. Between 1989 and 1991 the socialist bloc and then the Soviet Union itself dissolved.

KEY TERMS

proxy wars *(p. 789)*

Salvador Allende *(p. 790)*

Dirty War *(p. 790)*

Sandinistas *(p. 791)*

neo-liberalism *(p. 793)*

Ayatollah Ruhollah Khomeini *(p. 796)*

Saddam Husayn *(p. 796)*

keiretsu *(p. 797)*

Asian Tigers *(p. 798)*

newly industrialized economies (NIEs) *(p. 798)*

Deng Xiaoping *(p. 798)*

Tiananmen Square *(p. 799)*

Mikhail Gorbachev *(p. 800)*

perestroika (p. 800)

Solidarity *(p. 800)*

ethnic cleansing *(p. 802)*

Thomas Malthus *(p. 804)*

demographic transition *(p. 804)*

WEB RESOURCES

Pronunciation Guide

Interactive Maps

MAP 29.1 The End of Soviet Domination in Eastern Europe

(Continued)

What explains differences in the rate of population growth among the world's cultural regions? (page 804)

In the mature industrial nations and Japan, fertility declined in the period after 1945. Populations in the developed world have grown slowly or not at all, largely because women are better educated and have entered the work force in larger numbers. As a result, they marry later and have fewer children. The effects are mitigated by longer life expectations. A more extreme pattern is found in Russia and the other nations of the old Soviet Union. In these nations birthrates have crashed and life expectancy has declined as well, leading to falling population levels. In the developing world the educational levels and work force participation rates of women are more traditional. Birthrates remain high while life expectancy has generally improved. As a result, population is growing rapidly. While in Korea, China, and other newly industrialized economies birthrates are now close to those in the developed world, birthrates remain high in sub-Saharan Africa and the Muslim world. As a result, more than 95 percent of the world's future population growth will occur in the poorest developing nations.

How does wealth inequality among nations impact international migration patterns? (page 809)

With population growing most rapidly in the world's poorest nations and the richest nations producing fewer children and growing older, people have begun to migrate from poorer nations to richer nations, especially to the United States and Canada, Australia and New Zealand, and western Europe. In addition, within developing nations migrants leave the poorest agricultural regions to seek opportunities in slightly-better-off urban centers. These patterns were growing in strength at the end of the twentieth century.

How has technological change affected the global environment in the recent past? (page 811)

Growing population and the development process have forced marginal lands into production and stimulated the exploitation of new resources. The need to feed a rapidly growing world population has also pressured ocean resources. As the world's population has reached 6 billion and the largest cities have reached 20 million, the need to produce and deliver raw materials and finished goods has put tremendous stress on the environment. In the 1990s these pressures were compounded with the rapid development of the Chinese and Indian economies.

At the same time, new technologies and the wealth produced by economic expansion have allowed the world's richest nations to implement ambitious programs of environmental protection. As a result, pollution produced by automobiles and factories has actually declined in the richest nations. The question that remains is whether rapidly developing nations, such as China and India, will move more quickly than the mature industrial nations did to introduce these new technologies.

Primary Sources

Islamic Government

The Revolution That Failed Women

Letter to Comrades Brezhnev, Kosygin, and Podgorny

The Last Heir of Lenin Explains His Reform Plans: Perestroika and Glasnost

Answer to the History in Focus Question

See photo on page 792, "The Nicaraguan Revolution Overturns Somoza."

Plus

Chapter Objectives

ACE multiple-choice quiz

Flashcards

SUGGESTED READING

Bakhash, Shaul. *The Reign of the Ayatollahs: Iran and the Iranian Revolution.* 1990. Account of the Iranian Revolution and the early days of the Islamic Republic of Iran.

Berry, John A., and Carol Pott Berry, eds. *Genocide in Rwanda: A Collective Memory.* 1999. Covers a major calamity too readily forgotten.

Dyson, Tim, et al., eds. *Twenty-first Century India: Population, Economy, Human Development, and the Environment.* 2005. Culmination of a large research project.

Gaddis, John Lewis. *The Cold War: A New History.* 2005. A solid overview.

Kenez, Peter. *A History of the Soviet Union from the Beginning to the End.* 2006. Explains the demise of the USSR.

Kennedy, Paul M. *Preparing for the Twenty-first Century.* 1993. Asks whether world resources can cope with future population growth.

Lardy, Nicholas R. *China's Unfinished Economic Revolution.* 1998. A well-researched study of economic changes.

Maier, Charles. *Dissolution: The Crisis of Communism and the End of East Germany.* 1997. Covers the collapse of the Soviet empire in Europe.

McNeill, John R. *Something New Under the Sun: An Environmental History of the Twentieth-Century World.* 2000. A survey coverage of a rising field of historical study.

Meredith, Martin. *The Fate of Africa: From the Hopes of Freedom to the Heart of Despair.* 2005. An overview of recent African history.

Rubin, Barnett. *The Fragmentation of Afghanistan.* 1995. Provides excellent coverage of the struggle between Soviet forces and the Muslim resistance.

Shenkar, Oded. *The Chinese Century: The Rising Chinese Economy and Its Impact on the Global Economy, the Balance of Power, and Your Job.* 2004. A business-oriented appraisal of the surging Chinese economy.

Skidmore, Thomas E., and Peter H. Smith. *Modern Latin America.* 4th ed. 1996. Provides an excellent general introduction to the period 1975 to 1991.

Stiglitz, Joseph E. *Globalization and Its Discontents.* 2003. An overview by a major economic thinker.

Thompson, Leonard. *A History of South Africa.* 3d ed. 2005. Looks at a key African country.

NOTES

1. Quoted in Antony Flew, "Introduction," in Thomas Robert Malthus, *An Essay on the Principle of Population and a Summary View of the Principle of Population* (New York: Penguin Books, 1970), 30

2. Paul Kennedy, *Preparing for the Twenty-First Century* (New York: Random House, 1993), 45.

CHAPTER 30

Globalization in the New Millennium

CHAPTER PREVIEW

Global Economic and Political Currents
What are the main benefits and dangers of growing political, economic, and cultural integration?

Trends and Visions
What roles do religious beliefs and secular ideologies play in the contemporary world?

Global Culture
How has technology contributed to the process of global interaction?

ENVIRONMENT AND TECHNOLOGY: Global Warming

MATERIAL CULTURE: Fast Food

The workday began normally at the World Trade Center in lower Manhattan on the morning of September 11, 2001. The 50,000 people who work there were making their way to the two 110-story towers, as were some 140,000 others who visited on a typical day. Suddenly, at 8:46 A.M., an American Airlines Boeing 767 with 92 people on board, traveling at a speed of 470 miles per hour (756 kilometers per hour), crashed into floors 94 to 98 of the north tower, igniting the 10,000 gallons (38,000 liters) of fuel in its tanks. Just before 9:03 A.M. a United Airlines flight with 65 people on board and a similar fuel load hit floors 78 to 84 of the south tower.

As the burning jet fuel engulfed the collision areas, the buildings' surviving occupants struggled through smoke-filled corridors and down dozens of flights of stairs. Many of those trapped above the crash sites

This icon will direct you to the website where you can Prepare for Class, Improve Your Grade, and Ace the Test: college.cengage.com/pic/bullietbrief4e

used cell phones to say good-bye to loved ones. Rather than endure the flames and fumes, a few jumped to their deaths.

Just before 10 o'clock, temperatures that had risen to 2,300° Fahrenheit (1,260° Celsius) caused the steel girders in the impacted area of the south tower to give way. The collapsing upper floors crushed the floors underneath one by one, engulfing lower Manhattan in a dense cloud of dust. Twenty-eight minutes later the north tower pancaked in a similar manner. Miraculously, most of the buildings' occupants had escaped before the towers collapsed. Besides the people on the planes, more than 2,700 lost their lives, including some 200 police officers and firefighters helping in the evacuation.

That same morning another American Airlines jet crashed into the Pentagon, killing all 64 people on board and 125 others inside the military complex near Washington, D.C. Passengers on a fourth plane managed to overpower their hijackers, and the plane crashed in rural Pennsylvania, killing all 45 on board.

The four planes had been hijacked by teams of Middle Eastern men who slit the throats of service and flight personnel and seized control. Of the nineteen hijackers, fifteen were from Saudi Arabia. All had links to an extremist Islamic organization, al-Qaeda (ahl–KAW-eh-duh) (the base or foundation), commanded by a rich Saudi named **Usama bin Laden** (oo-SAH-mah bin LAH-din), who was incensed with American political, military, and cultural influence in the Middle East. The men were educated and well traveled, had lived in the United States, and spoke English. Some had trained as pilots so that they could fly the hijacked aircraft.

The hijackers left few records of their personal motives, but the acts spoke for themselves. The Pentagon was the headquarters of the American military, the most technologically sophisticated and powerful fighting force the world had ever seen. The fourth plane was probably meant to hit the Capitol or the White House, the legislative and executive centers of the world's only superpower. The Twin Towers may have been targeted because they were the tallest buildings in New York, but they were not just American targets. The World Trade Center housed 430 companies involved in international commerce and finance. Among the dead were people from more than half the countries in the world. New York was the site of the attack, but the World Trade Center was a powerful symbol of the international economy.

The events of September 11, which became commonly referred to as 9/11, can be understood on many levels. The hijackers and their supporters saw themselves as engaged in a holy struggle against economic, political, and military institutions they believed to be evil. They believed so deeply in their mission that they were willing to give their lives for it and to take as many other lives as they could. People directly affected and political leaders around the world tended to describe the attacks as evil acts against innocent victims.

To understand why the nineteen attackers were heroes to some and terrorists to others, one needs to explore the historical context of global changes at the turn of the millennium and the ideological tensions they have generated. While the advancing economic, political, and cultural integration of the world is welcomed by some, it seems threatening to others. The unique prominence of the United States in every major aspect of global integration, as well as its support for pro-American governments overseas, also elicits sharply divergent views.

Usama bin Laden Saudi-born Muslim extremist who founded the al-Qaeda organization that was responsible for several terrorist attacks, including those on the World Trade Center and the Pentagon in 2001.

CL **Primary Source: The Last Night** *Read the directions Mohammad Atta prepared for himself prior to the September 11 attack.*

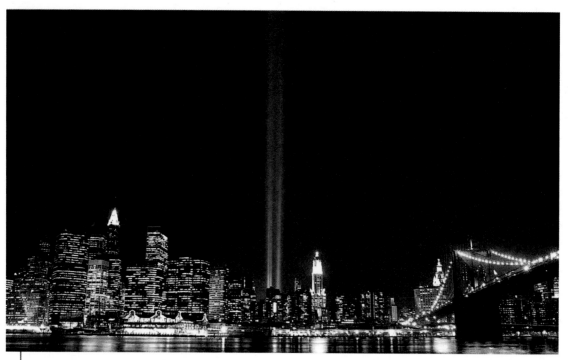

Lower Manhattan, March 11, 2002
Six months after the terrorist attacks, beams of light commemorated the destroyed twin towers of the World Trade Center and those who perished in them.
(AFP Photo/Doug Kanter/Getty Images)

GLOBAL ECONOMIC AND POLITICAL CURRENTS

What are the main benefits and dangers of growing political, economic, and cultural integration?

globalization The economic, political, and cultural integration and interaction of all parts of the world brought about by increasing trade, travel, and technology.

The turn of the millennium saw the intensification of **globalization** trends that had been building since the 1970s. Growing trade and travel and new technologies were bringing all parts of the world into closer economic, political, and cultural integration and interaction. The collapse of the Soviet Union had completed the dissolution of territorial empires that had been under way throughout the twentieth century. Autonomous national states (numbering about two hundred) became an almost universal norm, and a growing number of them had embraced democratic institutions. The rapid integration of world trade and markets had convinced world leaders of the need to balance national autonomy with international agreements and associations.

An Interconnected Economy

The heated expansion of trade, global interconnections, and privatization of government enterprises that gained momentum with the dismantling of Soviet-style socialist

Chronology

Politics	Economics and Society
2000 Al-Qaeda attacks American destroyer *USS Cole* in Yemen	
2001 Terrorists destroy the World Trade Center and damage the Pentagon on September 11	**2001–2003** Terrorist attacks trigger global recession **2001** Shanghai Cooperation Organization formed **2001** U.S. withdraws from Kyoto Protocol on global warming **2001** Al-Jazeera television in Qatar begins broadcasting statements by Usama bin Laden
2002 United Nations weapons inspectors return to Iraq	**2002** Euro currency adopted in twelve European countries
2003 United States and Britain invade and occupy Iraq	
2004 Terrorists bomb Spanish trains	
2004 Hamid Karzai becomes first democratically elected president of Afghanistan	**2004** Ten new members admitted to European Union
2005 Terrorists bomb London transit system	
2005 Iraqis adopt new constitution	
2005 Anti-American president Mahmoud Ahmadinejad elected president of Iran	
2006 Iran announces ability to enrich uranium	
2006 Iraqis elect new government	
2006 Hamas movement defeats PLO in Palestinian election	
2006 Israel attacks Hezbollah in Lebanon in response to its seizure of Israeli soldiers	
2006 In midterm elections, American voters reject Bush policies.	

Left column year markers: 2000, 2001, 2002, 2003, 2004, 2005, 2006

economies in the 1990s cooled abruptly in the wake of 9/11. The rate of growth in world trade fell from 13 percent in 2000 to only 1 percent in 2001. The United States, and therefore its economic and foreign policies, were crucial to the world economic system. The gigantic U.S. economy, larger than the economies of the next five countries combined—Japan, Germany, Great Britain, China (including Hong Kong), and France—also consumed by far the largest portion of the world's natural resources, including over a quarter of annual global oil production.

Economic growth in China and India resumed quickly after the shock of 2001, and the very large populations of these two countries marked them as future world economic powers. Their growth put particular pressure on world energy supplies.

OPEC's manipulation of world oil prices, combined with political events like the Iranian Revolution of 1979 and Iraq's ensuing invasion of Iran, had caused crude oil prices to soar between 1973 and 1985. But aside from those years, the average price of oil remained consistently below $20 per barrel (adjusted for inflation) throughout the second half of the twentieth century. In the year 2000, however, oil prices began a new period of increase caused not by OPEC but by rising demand, especially in the United States and Asia, and by political turmoil in the Middle East (see below). By the middle of 2006, the price of a barrel of crude had crept past $70. A year and a half later it hit $100. This increase not only boosted the national incomes of major producing countries such as Russia, Iran, and Saudi Arabia, but it also caused energy security to overtake the formation of international trade associations as a matter of global economic concern.

Among the regional trade associations that had come into being to promote growth, reduce the economic vulnerability of member states, and, less explicitly, balance American economic dominance, the European Union (EU) was the most successful (see Map 30.1). Twelve member states adopted a new common currency, the euro, in 2002, making the Euro-bloc a formidable competitor with the United States for investment and banking. Ten new members from eastern Europe and the Mediterranean were admitted to the EU in May 2004, and other countries, including Turkey, Bulgaria, and Romania, have aspirations to join.

Despite the EU's expansion, the North American Free Trade Agreement (NAFTA), which eliminated tariffs among the United States, Canada, and Mexico in 1994, governed the world's largest free-trade zone. However, a heated debate in the United States over illegal immigration across the Mexican border, as well as conservative fears that Spanish speakers might somehow dilute American culture and identity, limited popular enthusiasm for the agreement. The third largest free-trade zone, Mercosur, created by Argentina, Brazil, Paraguay, and Uruguay in 1991, decided in 2002 to allow the free movement of people within its area and gave equal employment rights to the citizens of all member states. Other free-trade associations operated in West Africa, southern Africa, Southeast Asia, Central America, the Pacific Basin, and the Caribbean.

The Shanghai Cooperation Organization (SCO), which formed in 2001 with China, Russia, and four former parts of the USSR—Kazakhstan (KAH-zahk-stahn), Kyrgyzstan (KER-gihz-stahn), Tajikistan (tah-JEHK-ih-stahn), and Uzbekistan (ooz-BEHK-ih-stahn)—as members, originally pursued common security interests, such as combating separatist movements and terrorism. But its announced twenty-year plan for reducing barriers to trade and population movements took a step forward in 2006 when Mahmoud Ahmadinejad, the president of Iran, a country with observer status, signaled Iran's desire to expand relations with the SCO. Bringing Iran's oil-rich economy into alignment with a rapidly developing China and a similarly oil-rich Russia, then recovering from the period of post-Soviet economic turmoil, promised to complicate the world economic and political picture.

Because of the inequalities and downturns that are intrinsic to free economic markets, the global bodies that tried to manage world trade and finance found it hard to convince poorer nations that they were not concerned only with the welfare of richer countries. In 1995 the world's major trading powers established the **World Trade Organization (WTO).** The WTO encourages reduced trading barriers and

World Trade Organization (WTO) An international body established in 1995 to foster and bring order to international trade.

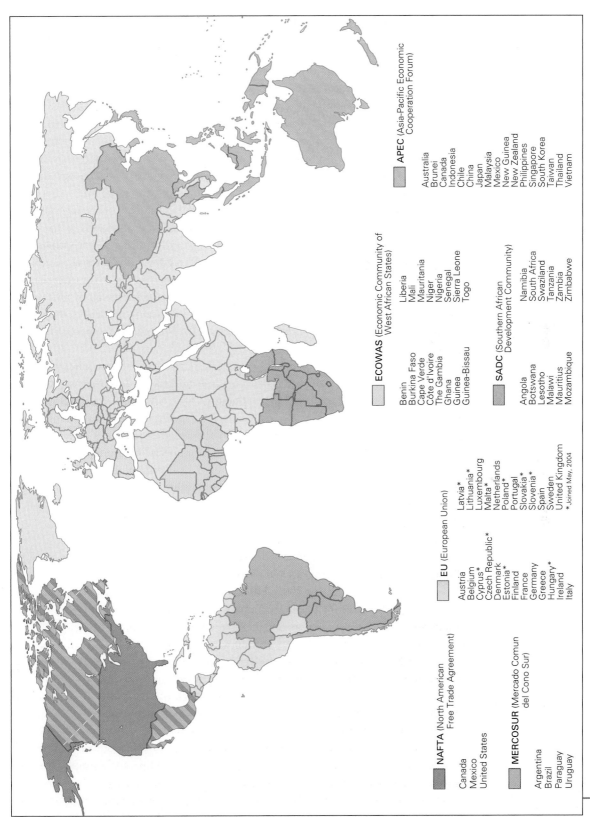

APEC (Asia-Pacific Economic Cooperation Forum)

Australia
Brunei
Canada
Indonesia
Chile
China
Japan
Malaysia
Mexico
New Guinea
New Zealand
Philippines
Singapore
South Korea
Taiwan
Thailand
Vietnam

ECOWAS (Economic Community of West African States)

Benin
Burkina Faso
Cape Verde
Côte d'Ivoire
The Gambia
Ghana
Guinea
Guinea-Bissau
Liberia
Mali
Mauritania
Niger
Nigeria
Senegal
Sierra Leone
Togo

SADC (Southern African Development Community)

Angola
Botswana
Lesotho
Malawi
Mauritius
Mozambique
Namibia
South Africa
Swaziland
Tanzania
Zambia
Zimbabwe

EU (European Union)

Austria
Belgium
Cyprus*
Czech Republic*
Denmark
Estonia*
Finland
France
Germany
Greece
Hungary*
Ireland
Italy
Latvia*
Lithuania*
Luxembourg
Malta*
Netherlands
Poland*
Portugal
Slovakia*
Slovenia*
Spain
Sweden
United Kingdom
*Joined May, 2004

NAFTA (North American Free Trade Agreement)

Canada
Mexico
United States

MERCOSUR (Mercado Comun del Cono Sur)

Argentina
Brazil
Paraguay
Uruguay

Map 30.1   Regional Trade Associations, 2004

International trade and development are major concerns of governments in developed and developing countries. NAFTA, Mercosur, and the EU are free-trade areas. The other associations promote trade and development.

enforces international trade agreements. Despite a membership of 150 nations by 2007, the WTO had many critics and regularly encountered street protests during its ministerial meetings. Some protesters feared that low-cost foreign manufacturers would shrink the job opportunities in richer states; others demanded continuing tariff protection for local farmers.

Countries in economic trouble had little choice but to turn to the international financial agencies for funds to keep things from getting worse. The International Monetary Fund (IMF) and World Bank (see Chapter 28) made their assistance conditional on internal economic reforms that were often politically unpopular, such as terminating government subsidies for basic foodstuffs, cutting social programs, and liberalizing investment. The bitter pill of economic reform sometimes paid off in long-term improvement, but it could also fuel popular criticism of the international economic system and of the governments that acceded to its demands.

The emphasis on free trade led to changes in government-to-government aid programs. During the Cold War countries had often gained funds for economic development by allying themselves with one of the superpowers. Not surprisingly, when the Cold War ended, foreign economic aid to poor nations fell by a third. On an African tour in 2000 President Bill Clinton told African countries that the days of large handouts were over and that they would have to rely on their own efforts to expand their economies.

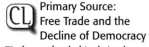

Primary Source: Free Trade and the Decline of Democracy
Find out what babies being born without brains in record numbers has to do with free trade.

In the face of rising criticism at home and protests at international meetings, however, world leaders rethought their positions and pledged to increase attention to the problem of economic despair, especially in Africa. At a Millennium Summit in September 2000 the states of the United Nations agreed to make sustainable development and the elimination of world poverty their highest priorities. A 2002 United Nations meeting in Monterrey, Mexico, called for special commitments to Africa. Late in 2002 President George W. Bush proposed a substantial increase in American foreign aid. In practice, however, special consideration of Africa's economic plight seldom resulted in major increases in support.

Globalization and Democracy

The last decades of the twentieth century saw rapid increases in democratic institutions and personal freedom. In 2003, 140 countries regularly held elections; people in 125 had access to free (or partly free) presses; and most people lived in fully democratic states.[1]

The great appeal of democracy in modern times has been that elections offer a peaceful way to settle the inevitable differences among a country's social classes, cultural groups, and regions. Although majority votes swing from one part of the political spectrum to another, democracies tend to encourage political moderation. Moreover, wars between fully democratic states are extremely rare.

Democratic gains were made especially in the nations of eastern Europe that had been under Soviet control, though some newly democratic states became subject to great mood swings among the electorate. In Ukraine, for example, the election in 1999 of Viktor Yushchenko, a reform-minded prime minister, came undone a year and a half later when a no-confidence vote supported by communist hardliners and big business interests removed him from office. Violent demonstrations followed in which protesters demanded the impeachment of the authoritarian president Leonid Kuchma. Kuchma yielded in 2004, and his hand-picked candidate seemingly outpolled Yushchenko in the election to succeed him. But when international monitors presented evidence of massive electoral fraud, pro-Yushchenko demonstrations, designated "the Orange Revolution," led to the Supreme Court invalidating the results. After a new election in 2005, Yushchenko finally became president. This experience, which had parallels in other former Soviet territories, demonstrated that working democracies can be hard to establish in countries with a history of authoritarianism.

Asian democracies proved somewhat more stable. Beginning with free parliamentary elections in 1999, the populous state of Indonesia moved from years of authoritarian and corrupt rule toward more open political institutions. The following years witnessed many problems: a violent independence movement of the Acheh district of northern Sumatra, the secession in 2002 of East Timor after years of brutal Indonesian military occupation, terrorist bombings on the island of Bali in 2004, and a devastating earthquake and tsunami in 2004. But democratic elections were regularly held. The losing candidates left office peacefully, and the populace at large accepted the results.

In India a major political shift occurred in 1998 when the Bharatiya Janata Party (BJP) secured an electoral victory that ended four decades of Congress Party rule. The BJP success came through blatant appeals to Hindu nationalism, the condoning of violence against India's Muslims, and opposition to the social and economic progress of the Untouchables (those traditionally confined to the dirtiest jobs). In 2004, however, in a major upset, the BJP lost a national election to the Congress Party and peacefully handed over power.

In sub-Saharan Africa, democracy had mixed results. Nelson Mandela, the leader of the African National Congress (ANC) who had become the first postapartheid president of South Africa in 1994 (see Chapter 29), left office in 1999 and was succeeded by the deputy president and ANC leader Thabo Mbeki. Mbeki was reelected in 2004. The lively politics of this ethnically diverse country have been a model of how democracy can resolve conflicts. Nigeria, Africa's most populous state, also tried democracy in 1999 when General Olusegun Obasanjo (oh-LOO-say-goon oh-bah-SAHN-joh), running on an anticorruption and reform platform, was elected president after decades of military rule. However, his reelection in 2003 was tainted by voting irregularities, and a campaign by his supporters to amend the constitution so he could run for a third term failed in 2006. In the meantime, Nigeria was wracked by periodic Muslim-Christian violence in the cities of the north and east, and a guerrilla movement in the Niger Delta aimed at sabotaging and threatening the oil industry in order to gain more of its benefits for local communities.

Regime Change in Iraq and Afghanistan The most closely watched experiments in democratization took place in Iraq and Afghanistan, countries that the United States invaded in response to the terrorist attacks of 9/11. While the use of Afghanistan as a safe haven for Usama bin Laden and his al-Qaeda organization was the unequivocal justification given for the overthrow in December 2001 of the militantly religious Taliban regime that protected him, the

CL Primary Source: Islamic Fundamentalist Usama bin Laden Calls on Muslims to Take Up Arms Against America
Find out why Usama bin Laden has singled out America as a target for Muslims.

weapons of mass destruction
Nuclear, chemical, and biological devices that are capable of injuring and killing large numbers of people.

CL Primary Source: Declaration of Jihad Against Americans Occupying the Land of the Two Holy Mosques *Follow along with an argument in defense of a declaration of jihad.*

rationale for invading Iraq underwent a change. During the leadup to the war the American government contended that Iraq was a clear and present danger to the United States because it possessed **weapons of mass destruction** (WMDs), nuclear, chemical, and biological weapons that it might supply to terrorists like bin Laden. In November 2002 the Bush administration persuaded the United Nations Security Council to pass a resolution ordering the return of United Nations weapons inspectors to Iraq and requiring the Iraqi government to specify what WMDs it still possessed. When the new United Nations inspectors failed to find any evidence of banned weapons, a split widened between those nations wanting to continue inspections and those, led by the United States and Britain, wanting to intervene militarily. Abandoning efforts to gain explicit Security Council authorization, an American-led "coalition of the willing" began the invasion of Iraq with a massive aerial bombardment of Baghdad on March 20, 2003. Twenty-five days later the United States declared that "major fighting" had ended, little realizing that a guerrilla insurgency would continue for years.

Though Iraq then fell into a deep state of turmoil because the coalition army was too small or otherwise unprepared to prevent the looting and destruction of government facilities and other lawlessness, a thorough search was launched for prohibited weapons. This search failed to turn up any WMDs, just as intelligence analysis failed to uncover any evidence that Saddam Husayn, Iraq's fallen dictator, had been in league with Usama bin Laden or had played a role in the 9/11 attacks.

However, American concern for WMDs was not eliminated. North Korea had an open program to build nuclear weapons, and Iran was suspected of having a covert plan based in part on technological aid secretly given by the head of Pakistan's successful nuclear arms program. Iran's outspokenly anti-American and anti-Israeli president, Mahmoud Ahmadinejad, elected in 2005, and North Korea's dictator Kim Jong-il presented the United States with difficult challenges, but the military invasion option chosen for Iraq was seldom talked of.

The failure to find Iraqi WMDs having become an embarrassment to the United States, President George W. Bush declared that the rationale for invading Iraq had actually been to liberate the Iraqi people and substitute democracy for oppression. Though an intense debate followed within the United States about whether the Bush administration had used deception in leading the nation into war, the question of whether the war would ultimately be termed a success or a failure came to hinge on the establishment of democratic institutions in both Afghanistan and Iraq.

Though Afghanistan had a far less developed economy and was suffering from the devastation caused by years of guerrilla war against the Soviet Union and from the harsh and stifling rule of the Taliban, the democratic process started well with an assembly of traditional tribal leaders selecting Hamid Karzai as interim president in 2002. Two years later Karzai was elected president in Afghanistan's first democratic elections.

Unfortunately, the power of the new Afghan government did not extend effectively over the entire country. Traditional warlords retained control in some areas, and in 2007 an effort by the Taliban to regain power gave rise to assassinations and guerrilla warfare in various parts of the country. Though the United States was able to enlist the participation of NATO forces in helping to police Afghanistan, the number of foreign troops and the amount of monetary aid made available to the

Iranian President Mahmoud Ahmadinejad

After two terms under the comparatively liberal, but ineffective, government of President Mohammad Khatami, voters in the Islamic Republic of Iran elected a relatively unknown conservative in 2005. President Ahmadinejad took confrontational positions on international affairs, notably denying Israel's legitimacy as a state and asserting Iran's right to develop nuclear technology. This enhanced his domestic popularity, while convincing many analysts that with the American defeat of Saddam Husayn, Iran had become a major power in the Middle East and the Islamic world.   (IRNA/Reuters/Corbis)

 HISTORY IN FOCUS   How are people both inside and outside of Iran reacting to President Ahmadinejad's stance on international affairs? How might the view of the United States be different from that of the Middle East? *Find the answer online.*

Karzai government were insufficient to ensure either security or economic recovery. To the frustration of the countries trying to help Afghanistan with its many problems, opium produced for the world drug trade remained a mainstay of the country's farm income.

When the "major fighting" ended in Iraq, the United States and its allies established a Coalition Provisional Authority to govern the country while democratic institutions were being designed. After sixteen months of American direct rule, the authority appointed an Iraqi Governing Council composed mostly of Iraqi exiles who had opposed Saddam Husayn's dictatorship. The council adopted a Transitional Administrative Law to serve as a temporary constitution and then passed authority on to an Iraqi Interim Government, which in turn gave way to an Iraqi Transitional Government elected in January 2006. This election, the first under a constitution adopted three months earlier, marked the culmination of the democratization process.

At every turning point along this twisting path to democratic rule, the United States declared that Iraq was finally emerging from chaos and anarchy, but in fact the growth of democracy was mirrored by the spread of a lethal resistance movement that attacked coalition forces and Iraqis who were helping them, especially newly recruited soldiers and police. When the elections produced a parliament in which Shi'ite political parties, representing the country's majority population and closely aligned with Iran, formed the largest bloc of votes, the insurgency increasingly targeted Shi'ite civilians and mosques. In response, Shi'ite militiamen, some of them incorporated within the government's security forces, attacked Sunni Arabs in Baghdad and elsewhere. The question was soon being asked whether Iraq was on the verge of, or already in the midst of, a civil war. Though the Bush administration continued to claim that, despite the violence, democracy would eventually succeed in both Iraq and Afghanistan, public opinion polls showed that most Americans had doubts about this and worried about how and when American troops might be able to return home. In the 2006 midterm elections, opposition to the war led to Democrats capturing both the U.S. Senate and House of Representatives. In 2007 President Bush decided to push on toward what he considered victory by ordering a "surge" that committed thousands more American soldiers to the struggle for internal security in Baghdad and the country at large.

With the democratization process in Afghanistan and Iraq in question, other Middle Eastern countries hesitated to follow American urgings to liberalize their political systems. Though some small oil-producing countries in the Persian Gulf took cautious steps toward democratization and Kuwait for the first time allowed women to vote in 2006, large countries like Egypt and Syria talked about liberalization but continued to suppress most critics. These countries were fearful that free elections would lead to Islamic political parties gaining a share of power, or even forming a new government, as the religious Shi'ite parties had in Iraq. The capture of 23 out of 128 seats in the Lebanese parliament by the Lebanese Shi'ite movement Hezbollah in 2005 and the absolute majority of seats won by the militantly anti-Israeli Hamas movement in elections for the Palestine Governing Authority in 2006 seemed to confirm this fear, since both movements were strongly religious in their goals and policies. Attacks launched by Israel against both Hamas and Hezbollah in response to kidnappings of Israeli soldiers in 2006 suggested that fear of domination by Islamic movements might in the future become more important than democratization in the Middle East, regardless of American policies. In 2007 the elected Hamas government succeeded in driving its Palestinian rivals of the al-Fath faction out of the Gaza Strip, triggering violent exchanges there with Israeli troops. On the West Bank, Israel and the United States decided to support the al-Fath faction as a counterweight to Hamas.

SECTION REVIEW

- Since the Cold War, global politics has been defined largely by the problem of international intervention.
- To manage economic change, many nations have joined a variety of trade organizations, and free-trade policies have caused widespread controversy.
- Since 1991, the global economy has expanded rapidly, especially in developing countries, but historic disparities still persist.
- Poorer countries have had to turn to international financial agencies for help but have had to agree to unpopular economic reforms in return for assistance.
- Since 1991, democracy has spread throughout the world, often resulting in major political shifts, but it remains exceptional in Africa and the Middle East.
- U.S. intervention in Iraq and Afghanistan has shown that the promotion of democracy in some countries faces stiff resistance.

TRENDS AND VISIONS

What roles do religious beliefs and secular ideologies play in the contemporary world?

As people around the world faced the opportunities and problems of globalization, they tried to make sense of these changes in terms of their own cultures and beliefs. With 6 billion people, the world was big enough to include many different approaches, whether religious or secular, local or international, traditional or visionary. In some cases, however, conflicting visions fed violence.

Faith and Politics

Religious beliefs increasingly inspired political actions during the second half of the twentieth century, and the trend intensified as the new century began. Though for Americans this change reversed two centuries of growing secularism, Western analysts did not agree on the cause of the religious revival.

Evangelical Protestants became a powerful conservative political force in the United States, particularly during the presidency of George W. Bush. Catholic conservatives led by Pope John Paul II, who died in 2005, and his successor Pope Benedict XVI forcefully reiterated politically sensitive teachings, such as opposition to abortion, homosexuality, marriage of priests, and admission of women to the priesthood. In Israel, hyperorthodox Jews known as *haredim* played a leading role in settling the West Bank and Gaza, the Palestinian territories captured by Israel in 1967, and vehemently resisted both Israel's unilateral withdrawal from Gaza in 2005 and subsequent plans for withdrawal from parts of the West Bank. And in India, Hindu zealots made the BJP party a powerful political force (see above).

Yet Islam became the focus of most discussions of faith and politics. The birth of the Islamic Republic of Iran in the revolution of 1979 made the current of Muslim political assertiveness, which had been building in several Muslim countries for twenty years, visible to all. But by the year 2000 acts of **terrorism** perpetrated by non-Iranian Muslim groups claiming to be acting for religious reasons were capturing the headlines.

Terrorism as a political tactic by which comparatively weak militants used grotesquely inhumane and lethal acts to convince a frightened public that danger is everywhere and the government is incapable of protecting them has a long history. But the instantaneous media links made possible by satellite communications, and the tradition in the news business of publicizing violence, increased its effectiveness from the 1980s onward.

Bombings, kidnappings, and assassinations made political sense to all sorts of political groups: secular Palestinians confronting Israel; national separatists like the Tamils in Sri Lanka, Basques in Spain, and Chechens in Russia; Catholic and Protestant extremists in Northern Ireland; and racialist militias in Rwanda and Darfur, to name a few. But Muslim groups gained the lion's share of attention because they targeted the United States and Europe, concentrated on spectacular attacks, drew from Muslim populations all over the world, and made effective use of video and audio communications from their charismatic leader, Usama bin Laden.

terrorism Political belief that extreme and seemingly random violence will destabilize a government and permit the terrorists to gain political advantage. Though an old technique, terrorism gained prominence in the late twentieth century with the growth of worldwide mass media that, through their news coverage, amplified public fears of terrorist acts.

Born into a wealthy Saudi family and educated as an engineer, bin Laden fought against the Soviet Union in Afghanistan and there recruited and trained a core group of fighters called al-Qaeda. Though his family disowned him and Saudi Arabia stripped him of his citizenship, his calls for a holy war (*jihad*) and his portrayal of the United States as an evil puppet-master manipulating both non-Muslim (e.g., Israel, India, Russia) and Muslim (e.g., Egypt, Algeria, Saudi Arabia) governments to murder and oppress innocent Muslims made sense to millions of Muslims, even if only a very few committed themselves to follow him into battle.

Al-Qaeda blew up the American embassies in Kenya and Tanzania in 1998, crippled the U.S. Navy destroyer *Cole* while it was making a port call in Yemen in 2000, and then capped everything by crashing hijacked jetliners into the World Trade Center and the Pentagon in 2001. Though the "global war on terrorism" declared in response by President Bush successfully destroyed the Afghan government that had given bin Laden safe haven as well as the dictatorship of Saddam Husayn that the United States claimed was a real or potential supporter of terrorism, bin Laden and his primary deputy, the Egyptian Ayman Zawahiri, could not be found. Further terrorist attacks—by Indonesians on tourists on the island of Bali in 2002, by North Africans on commuter trains servicing Madrid in 2004, and by English-born Muslims on the London transit system in 2005—made it clear that the current of violence unleashed by al-Qaeda had become decentralized and that recruits and cells might no longer be taking orders from bin Laden. In the meantime, the primary center of terrorist activity had shifted to Iraq, where suicide bombings became commonplace and a growing insurgency attacked coalition soldiers, the Iraqi citizens who worked for them, and Iraqis who belonged to opposing Muslim sects.

In trying to explain a current of violence that could strike anywhere in the world but seemed to be centered on Muslims, some analysts argued that the religion of Islam encouraged violence against non-Muslims. The counterargument pointed out that terrorists came from many backgrounds and that the vast majority of Muslims saw their religion as one of peace. Others maintained that rigidly conservative Muslims like Usama bin Laden were blindly opposed to freedom and modernity. The counterargument pointed out that al-Qaeda used modern military and propaganda techniques and that many of its operatives, like bin Laden himself, graduated from modern technical programs. A third school of thought felt that the United States instigated al-Qaeda's wrath through policies like supporting Israel and stationing troops in Saudi Arabia. The counterargument pointed out that the United States had also championed the Muslim cause in Bosnia and driven the secular dictator Saddam Husayn out of Kuwait, an act that most Arab governments supported.

Whether Islam and the West were destined to fight one another in a "clash of civilizations," as political scientist Samuel Huntington predicted, or whether their differences would eventually be resolved within a common "Islamo-Christian civilization," as Richard W. Bulliet maintained in response to Huntington, fear of terrorism became pervasive throughout the world, and many peaceful Muslims found themselves suspect because of their beliefs.

CL Primary Source: Lebanese Author Elias Khoury Argues for Democracy, Demilitarization, and Cultural Pluralism in the Middle East and North Africa *Find out what Elias Khoury considers "the greatest cultural tragedy in history."*

Universal Rights and Values

Alongside the growing influence of religion on politics, efforts to promote adherence to universal standards of human rights also expanded. Religious leaders had been the first to voice the notion that all people are equal, but the modern human rights movement grew out of the secular statements of the French Declaration of the Rights of Man (1789) and the U.S. Constitution (1788) and Bill of Rights (1791). Over the next century, the logic of universal rights moved Westerners to undertake international campaigns to end slave trading and slavery throughout the world and to secure equal legal rights (and eventually voting rights) for women.

International organizations in the twentieth century secured agreement on labor standards, the rules of war, and the rights of refugees. The pinnacle of these efforts was the **Universal Declaration of Human Rights**, passed by the United Nations General Assembly in 1948, which proclaimed itself "a common standard of achievement for all peoples and nations." Its thirty articles condemned slavery, torture, cruel and inhuman punishment, and arbitrary arrest, detention, and exile. The Declaration called for freedom of movement, assembly, and thought. It asserted rights to life, liberty, and security of person; to impartial public trials; and to education, employment, and leisure. The principle of equality was most fully articulated in Article 2:

> Everyone is entitled to all the rights and freedoms set forth in this Declaration, without distinction of any kind, such as race, color, sex, language, religion, or political or other opinion, national or social origin, property, birth or other status.[2]

Universal Declaration of Human Rights A 1948 United Nations covenant binding signatory nations to the observance of specified rights.

This passage reflected an international consensus against racism and imperialism and a growing acceptance of the importance of social and economic equality. Most newly independent countries joining the United Nations willingly signed the Declaration because it implicitly condemned European colonial regimes.

The idea of universal human rights has not gone unchallenged. Some have asked whether a set of principles whose origins are so clearly Western can be called universal. Others have been uneasy with the idea of subordinating the traditional values of their culture or religion to a broader philosophical standard. Despite these objections, important gains have been made in implementing these standards.

Besides the official actions of the United Nations and various national governments, individual human rights activists, often working through international philanthropic bodies known as **nongovernmental organizations (NGOs),** have been important forces for promoting human rights. Amnesty International, founded in 1961 and numbering 1.8 million members in 162 countries by the 1990s, concentrates on gaining the freedom of people who have been tortured or imprisoned without trial and campaigns against summary execution by government death squads or other gross violations of rights. Arguing that no right is more fundamental than the right to life, other NGOs have devoted themselves to famine relief, refugee assistance, and health care around the world. Médecins Sans Frontières (Doctors Without Borders), founded in 1971, was awarded the Nobel Peace Prize for 1999 for the medical assistance it offered in scores of crisis situations.

nongovernmental organizations (NGOs) Nonprofit international organizations devoted to investigating human rights abuses and providing humanitarian relief. Two NGOs won the Nobel Peace Prize in the 1990s: International Campaign to Ban Landmines (1997) and Doctors Without Borders (1999).

While NGOs often worked on individual situations in specific countries, other universal goals became enshrined in international agreements. Such agreements have made genocide a crime and have promoted environmental protection of the seas, of Antarctica, and of the atmosphere. The United States and a few other nations were greatly concerned that such treaties would unduly limit their sovereignty or threaten their national interests. For this reason the U.S. Congress delayed ratifying the 1949 convention on genocide until 1986. More recently the United States drew widespread international criticism for demanding exemption for Americans from the jurisdiction of the International Criminal Court, created in 2002 to try international criminals, and for declaring that "enemy combatants" taken prisoner during the "global war on terrorism" should not be treated in accordance with the Third Geneva Convention (1950) on humane treatment of prisoners of war. While these two actions grew out of America's acknowledged role as the one superpower capable of intervening in military crises anywhere in the world, the American withdrawal in 2001 from the 1997 Kyoto Protocol requiring industrial nations to sharply reduce emissions of pollutants that damage the atmosphere (see Environment and Technology: Global Warming) reflected a purely economic interest, namely, a fear that curbing emissions would impose great cost on power producers, vehicle makers, and manufacturers.

Women's Rights

The women's rights movement, which began on both sides of the North Atlantic in the nineteenth century, became an important human rights issue in the twentieth century. Rights for women became accepted in Western countries and were enshrined in the constitutions of many nations newly freed from colonial rule. In 1979 the United Nations General Assembly adopted the Convention on the Elimination of All Forms of Discrimination Against Women, and in 1985 the first international conference on the status of women, sponsored by the United Nations Division for the Advancement of Women, was held in Nairobi, Kenya. A second conference in Beijing ten years later added momentum to the women's rights movement. By 2007, 183 countries had endorsed the 1979 convention.

Besides highlighting the similarity of the problems women face around the world, international conferences have also revealed great variety in the views and concerns of women. Feminists from the West, who had been accustomed to dictating the agenda and who had pushed for the liberation of women in other parts of the world, sometimes found themselves accused of having narrow concerns and condescending attitudes. Some non-Western women complained about Western feminists' endorsement of sexual liberation and about the deterioration of family life in the West. They found Western feminists' concern with matters such as comfortable clothing misplaced and trivial compared to the issues of poverty and disease.

Other cultures came in for their share of criticism. Western women and many secular leaders in Muslim countries protested Islam's requirement that a woman cover her head and wear loose-fitting garments to conceal the shape of her body, practices enforced by law in countries such as Iran and Saudi Arabia. Nevertheless, many outspoken Muslim women voluntarily donned concealing garments as expressions of personal belief, statements of resistance to secular dictatorship, or defense against coarse male behavior. Much Western criticism focused on the African custom of circumcising girls, a form of genital mutilation that can cause chronic infections or permanently impair sexual enjoyment. While not denying the problems this practice can lead to, many African women saw deteriorating economic conditions, rape, and AIDS as more important issues (see Figure 30.1).

The conferences were more important for the attention they focused on women's issues than for the solutions they generated. The search for a universally

SECTION REVIEW

- The second half of the twentieth century has seen an increase in political action inspired by religious belief.

- Militant Islam has risen in response to hardships in many Muslim countries and to U.S. international influence.

- Universal standards of human rights have gained wider acceptance and underlie the work of the United Nations, individual states, and NGOs.

- Concepts of human rights have expanded to include health care, and new standards have emerged to address genocide and environmental protection.

- Global debates on women's rights have addressed a variety of economic, political, and social problems but have also involved clashes over cultural values.

ENVIRONMENT + TECHNOLOGY

Global Warming

Until the 1980s environmental alarms focused mainly on localized episodes of air and water pollution, exposure to toxic substances, waste management, and the disappearance of wilderness. The development of increasingly powerful computers and complex models of ecological interactions in the 1990s, however, made people aware of the global scope of certain environmental problems.

Many scientists and policymakers came to perceive global warming, the slow increase of the temperature of the earth's lower atmosphere, as an environmental threat requiring preventive action on an international scale. The warming is caused by a layer of atmospheric gases (carbon dioxide, methane, nitrous oxide, and ozone) that allow solar radiation to reach earth and warm it but that keep infrared energy (heat) from radiating from earth's surface into space. Called the *greenhouse effect*, this process normally keeps the earth's temperature at a level suitable for life. However, increases in greenhouse-gas emissions—particularly from the burning of fossil fuels in industry and transportation—have added to this insulating atmospheric layer.

Recent events have confirmed predictions of global temperature increases and melting glaciers and icecaps. Globally, the five warmest years on record were 1995, 1997, 1998, 2001, and 2002. Record heat hit northern Europe in the summer of 2003. Greenland glaciers and Arctic Ocean sea ice melted at record rates during 2002, and a huge section of the Antarctic ice shelf broke up and floated away. Andean glaciers are shrinking so fast they could disappear in a decade, imperiling water supplies for drinking, irrigation, and hydroelectric production. Drought has affected much of the United States in recent years, and in 2002 Australia experienced the "Big Dry," its worst drought in a century.

Despite this evidence, governments of the industrialized countries that produce the most greenhouse gases have been slow to adopt measures stringent enough to reduce emissions because of the negative effects they believe this could have on their economies. There is also fear that it may be already too late to reverse global warming. The pledges that representatives from 178 countries made at the first Earth Summit in Rio de Janeiro in 1992 to limit their *increase* in greenhouse-gas production have so far been ineffective. Fearing limits on gas emissions could cripple their plans for industrial and economic expansion, many nations hesitated to sign the 1997 Kyoto Protocol, the first international agreement to impose penalties on countries that failed to cut greenhouse-gas emissions. It was a major environmental victory when Japan added its signature in March 2001, but to the consternation of many world leaders President George W. Bush rejected the agreement. Ostensibly, he acted because he was unconvinced by the scientific evidence for global warming and reluctant to impose burdens on American businesses, but global security concerns also made the environment a lower American priority. Until the destructive effects of global warming, such as the inundation of coastal regions and large cities by rising sea levels, match the destruction of terrorists, the political focus is unlikely to shift.

FLOODING IN BANGLADESH Typhoon-driven floods submerge the low-lying farmlands of Bangladesh with tragic regularity. Any significant rise in the sea level will make parts of the country nearly uninhabitable. (Dominique Aubert/Corbis Sygma)

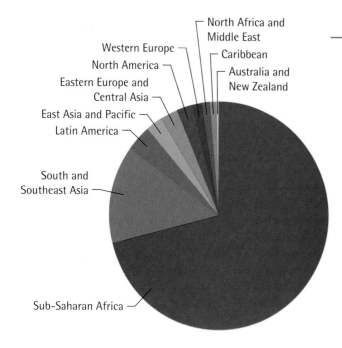

North Africa and
Middle East

Western Europe

North America

Eastern Europe and
Central Asia

East Asia and Pacific

Latin America

South and
Southeast Asia

Sub-Saharan Africa

Caribbean

Australia and
New Zealand

Figure 30.1   World Distribution of HIV/AIDS Cases (2001 estimates)   *Source:* United Nations AIDS and World Health Organization, *Report on the Global HIV/AIDS Epidemic* (June 2000).

accepted women's rights agenda proved elusive because of local concerns and strong disagreement on abortion and other issues. Nevertheless, increases in women's education, access to employment, political participation, and control of fertility augured well for the eventual achievement of gender equality.

Such efforts raised the prominence of human rights as a global concern and put pressure on governments to consider human rights when making foreign policy decisions. Skeptics observed, however, that a Western country could successfully prod a non-Western country to improve its human rights performance—for example, by granting women more equal access to education and careers—but that reverse criticism of a Western country often fell on deaf ears—for example, condemnation of the death penalty in the United States. For such critics the human rights movement was seen not as an effort to make the world more humane but as another form of Western cultural imperialism, a club with which to beat former colonial societies into submission. Still, support for universal rights has grown, especially because increasing globalization has made common standards of behavior more important.

GLOBAL CULTURE

How has technology contributed to the process of global interaction?

Along with the human rights movement, other kinds of cultural globalization were also proceeding rapidly at the turn of the millennium. A global language, a global educational system, and global forms of artistic expression have all come into being. Trade, travel, and migration have made a common culture necessary. Electronic communications that were once confined to members of a jet-setting elite have enabled global cultural influences to move deeper into many societies, and a sort of global popular culture has also emerged. These changes have angered some and delighted others.

cultural imperialism Domination of one culture over another by a deliberate policy or by economic or technological superiority.

The Media and the Message

Although cultural influences from every continent travel around the world, the fact that the most pervasive elements of global culture have their origins in the West raises concerns in many quarters about **cultural imperialism.** Critics complain that entertainment conglomerates are flooding the world's movie theaters and television screens with Western tastes and styles and that manufacturers are flooding world markets with Western goods—both relying on sophisticated advertising techniques that promote consumption and cultural conformity. In this view, global marketing is an especially insidious effort not only to overwhelm the world with a single Western outlook shaped by capitalist ideology, but also to suppress or devalue traditional cultures and alternative ideologies. As the leader of the capitalist world, the United States is seen as the primary culprit.

But in truth, technology plays a more central role than ideology in spreading Western culture. Even though imperialist forces old and new shape choices, strongly democratic forces are also at work as people around the world make their selections in the cultural marketplace. Thus, a diversity of voices is more characteristic of cultural globalization than the cultural imperialism thesis maintains.

The pace of cultural globalization began to quicken during the economic recovery after World War II. The Hollywood films and American jazz recordings that had become popular in Europe and parts of Asia continued to spread. But the birth of electronic technology opened contacts with large numbers of people who could never have afforded to go to a movie or buy a record.

The first step was the development of cheap transistor radios that could run for months on a couple of small batteries. Perfected by American scientists at Bell Telephone Laboratories in 1948, solid-state electronic transistors replaced power-hungry and less reliable electron tubes in radios and a wide array of other devices. Just as tube radios had spread in Europe and America in the decades before the war, small portable transistor radios, most made in Japan and elsewhere in Asia, spread rapidly in parts of the world where homes lacked electricity.

Because the transistor radios sold in Asia and Africa were designed to receive shortwave broadcasts, they brought people in remote villages the news, views, and music that American, European, Soviet, and Chinese transmitters beamed to the world. For the first time in history, the whole world could learn of major political and cultural events simultaneously. Although such broadcasts came in local and regional languages, many were in English. Electronic audiotape and CD players added to the diversity of music available to individuals everywhere.

Television, made possible by the invention of an electron-scanning gun in 1928, became widely available to consumers in Western countries in the 1950s. In poorer parts of the world TVs were not common until the 1980s and 1990s, after mass production and cheap transistors made sets more affordable and reliable. Outside the United States, television broadcasting was usually a government monopoly at first, following the pattern of telegraph and postal service and radio broadcasting. Governments expected news reports and other programming to disseminate a unified national viewpoint.

Government monopolies eroded as the high cost of television production opened up global markets for rebroadcasts of American soap operas, adventure series, and situation comedies. By the 1990s a global network of satellites brought privately owned television broadcasting to even remote areas of the world, and the VCR (videocassette recorder) brought an even greater variety of programs to people everywhere. In the following decade DVD players continued the trend. British programs found a secondary market in the United States, Canada, Australia, and other countries. As a result of wider circulation of programming, people often became familiar with different dialects of English and other languages. People in Portugal, for example, who in the 1960s had found it difficult to understand Brazilian Portuguese, have become avid fans of Brazilian soap operas. Immigrants from Albania and North Africa often arrive in Italy with a command of Italian learned from Italian stations whose signals they could pick up at home.

Further internationalization of culture resulted from satellite transmission of TV signals. Specializing in rock music videos aimed at a youth audience, MTV (Music Television) became an international enterprise offering special editions in different parts of the world. Music videos shown in Uzbekistan, for example, often featured Russian bands, and Chinese groups appeared in MTV programs shown in Singapore. CNN (Cable News Network) expanded its international market after becoming the most-viewed and informative news source during the 1991 Persian Gulf War, when it broadcast live from Baghdad. CNN's fundamentally American view of the news stimulated broadcasters in other countries to develop their own round-the-clock coverage. Al-Jazeera, based in the Persian Gulf emirate of Qatar, broadcast various statements by Usama bin Laden from 2001 onward and offered video footage and interpretation that differed greatly from American news coverage after the war in Iraq began in 2003.

The Internet, a linkage of academic, government, and business computer networks developed in the 1960s, began to transform world culture in the early years of the twenty-first century. Personal computers proliferated in the 1980s, and with the establishment of the easy-to-use graphic interface of the World Wide Web in 1994, the number of Internet users skyrocketed. Myriad new companies formed to exploit "e-commerce," the commercial dimension of the Internet, and college students were soon spending less time studying conventional books and scholarly resources than they were exploring the Web for information and entertainment. Blogs, or weblogs, offered a vehicle for anyone in the world to place his or her opinions, experiences, and creative efforts before anyone with access to a computer.

As had happened so often throughout history, technological developments had unanticipated consequences. Although the new telecommunications and entertainment technologies derived disproportionately from American invention, industry, and cultural creativity, Japan and other East Asian nations came to dominate the manufacture and refinement of computer devices. In the 1990s Japan introduced digital television broadcasting at about the time that disks containing digitized movies and computer programs with movielike action became increasingly available. High-definition television (HDTV), mostly in digital format, debuted in the first decade of the twenty-first century and seemed destined to become the global standard. At the miniaturized end of the visual scale, cell phones became increasingly used for taking and transmitting pictures and connecting to the Internet.

Primary Source: Internet Discussion of Marriage and Education for Saudi Women
Follow a lively online discussion in which people with a wide variety of beliefs participate.

The Spread of Pop Culture

New technologies changed perceptions of culture as well as its distribution around the world and among different social classes. For most of history, popular culture was folk culture, highly localized ways of dress, food, music, and expression. Only the educated and urban few had access to the riches of a broader "great tradition," such as

Confucianism in East Asia or Western culture in Europe and the Americas. The schools of modern nation-states promoted national values and beliefs, as well as tastes in painting, literature, and art. Governments also promoted a common language or dialect and frequently suppressed local traditions and languages. In a more democratic way, the transistor helped break down barriers and create a global popular culture that transcended regional great traditions and national cultures.

Initially, the content of **global pop culture** was heavily American. Singer Michael Jackson was almost as well known to the youth of Dar-es-Salaam (Tanzania) and Bangkok (Thailand) as to American fans. Basketball star Michael Jordan became a worldwide celebrity, heavily promoted by Nike, McDonald's, and television. American television programs such as Wheel of Fortune and Friends acquired immense followings and inspired local imitations. American movies, which had long had great popular appeal, steadily increased their share of world markets.

But the United States did not have a lock on global pop culture. Latin American soap operas, *telenovelas*, had a vast following in the Americas, eastern Europe, and elsewhere. Bombay, India, long the largest producer of films in the world, began to make more films for an international audience, rather than just for the home market. And the highly successful martial arts filmmakers of Hong Kong saw their style flourish in high-budget international spectaculars like director Ang Lee's Academy Award–winning *Crouching Tiger, Hidden Dragon* (2000) and the *Matrix* trilogy (1999–2003), which relied heavily on the skills of Hong Kong fight choreographers.

> **global pop culture** Popular cultural practices and institutions that have been adopted internationally, such as music, the Internet, television, food, and fashion.

Emerging Global Culture

While the globalization of popular culture has been criticized, cultural links across national and ethnic boundaries at a more elite level have generated little controversy. The end of the Cold War reopened intellectual and cultural contacts between former adversaries, making possible such things as Russian-American collaboration on space missions and extensive business contacts among former rivals. The English language, modern science, and higher education became the key elements of this **global elite culture.**

The emergence of English as the first global language depended on developments that had been building for centuries. The British Empire introduced the language to far-flung colonies. When the last parts of the empire gained independence after World War II, most former colonies chose to continue using English as an official language because it provided national unity and a link to the outside world that the dozens or hundreds of local languages could not. After independence, representatives of former British colonies formed the Commonwealth on the basis of their shared language and commercial ties. Newly independent countries that made a local language official for nationalist reasons often found the decision counterproductive. Indian nationalists had pushed for Hindi to be India's official language, but they found that students taught in Hindi were unable to compete internationally because of poor knowledge of English. Sri Lanka, which had made Sinhala its official language in 1956, reversed itself after local reporters revealed in 1989 that prominent officials were sending their children to English-medium private schools.

The use of English as a second language was greatly stimulated by the importance of the United States in postwar world affairs. Individuals recognized the importance

> **global elite culture** At the beginning of the twenty-first century, the attitudes and outlook of well-educated, prosperous, Western-oriented people around the world, largely expressed in European languages, especially English.

of mastering English for successful business, diplomatic, and military careers. After the collapse of Soviet domination, students in eastern Europe flocked to study English instead of Russian. Ninety percent of students in Cambodia (a former French colony) chose to study English, even though a Canadian agency offered a sizable cash bonus if they would study French. In the 1990s China made the study of English as a second language nearly universal from junior high school onwards, but it also forced an English-medium school in Hong Kong to teach most subjects in Chinese.

English has become the language of choice for most international academic conferences, business meetings, and diplomatic gatherings. International organizations that provide equal status to many languages, such as the United Nations and the European Union, tend to conduct all informal committee meetings in English. English has even replaced Latin as the working language for international consultations in the Catholic Church. In cities throughout the world, signs and notices are now posted in the local language and English.

The utility of English as a global language is also evident in the emergence of an international literature in English. The trend has been evident for decades in former British colonies in Africa, where most writers use English to reach both a national audience and an international one. Wole Soyinka, the first sub-Saharan African to win the Nobel Prize in literature for 1986, wrote in English, the national language of Nigeria, rather than his native Yoruba. When Arundhati Roy won the prestigious Booker Prize in 1997 for *The God of Small Things,* a novel set in her native state of Kerala in southwest India, she was part of an English-language literary tradition that has been growing in India for a century. V. S. Naipaul of Trinidad, winner of the Nobel Prize in literature for 2001, is a good example of the way global migration has fostered the use of English. Naipaul's ancestors had emigrated from India in the nineteenth century.

World literature remains highly diverse in form and language, but science and technology have become standardized components of global culture. Though imperialism helped spread the Western disciplines of biology, chemistry, and physics around the world, their popularity continued to expand even after imperial systems ended because they worked so much better than other approaches to the natural world. Their truth was universal even if plants and animals continue to be classified in Latin and the less common elements are called by names originally derived from Latin and Greek. Global manufacturing could not function without a common system of applied science. Because of their scientific basis Western medicine and drugs are increasingly accepted as the best treatments, even though many cultures also use traditional remedies.

The third pillar of global elite culture is the university. The structure and curricula of modern universities are nearly indistinguishable around the world, permitting students today to cross national boundaries as freely as students in the Latin West or the Muslim world did in medieval times. Instruction in the pure sciences varies little from place to place, and standardization is nearly as common in social science and applied sciences such as engineering and medicine. There may be more diversity in the humanities, but professors and students around the world pay attention to the latest literary theories and topics of historical interest.

While university subjects are taught in many languages, instruction in English is spreading rapidly. Because discoveries are often first published in English, advanced students in science, business, and international relations need to know that language to keep up with the latest developments. The global mobility of professors and students also promotes classroom instruction in the most global language. Many courses in the Netherlands and in Scandinavian countries have long been offered in English, and elsewhere in Europe offering more courses in English was the obvious way to facilitate the EU's efforts to encourage students to study outside their countries of origin. When South Africa ended the apartheid educational systems that had required people to study in their own languages, most students chose to study in English.

Because global elite culture is so deeply rooted in years of training, complex institutions, and practical utility, it is less subject to fads and commercial promotion than is global pop culture. Because such elite culture is confined to a distinct minority in most places, it poses little threat to national and folk cultures and, therefore, is much less controversial.

Enduring Cultural Diversity

Although protesters regularly denounce the "Americanization" of the world, a closer look suggests that cultural globalization is more complex and multifaceted. Just as English has largely spread as a second language, so global culture is primarily a second culture that dominates some contexts but does not displace other traditions. From this perspective, American music, fast food, and fashions are more likely to add to a society's options than to displace local culture (see Material Culture: Fast Food).

Japan first demonstrated that a country with a non-Western culture could perform at a high industrial level. Individuality was less valued in Japan than the ability of each person to fit into a group, whether as an employee, a member of an athletic team, or a student in a class. Moreover, the Japanese considered it unmannerly to directly contradict, correct, or refuse the request of another person. From a Western point of view, these Japanese customs seemed to discourage individual initiative and personality development and to preserve traditional hierarchies. Japanese women, for example, even though they often worked outside the home, responded only slowly to the American and European feminist advocacy of equality in economic and social relations. However, the Japanese approach to social relations was well suited to an industrial economy. The efficiency, pride in workmanship, and group solidarity of Japanese workers, supported by closely coordinated government and corporate policies, played a major role in transforming Japan from a defeated nation with a demolished industrial base in 1945 to an economic power by the 1980s.

Japan's success in the modern industrial world called into question the older assumption that successful industrialization required the adoption of Western culture. As awareness of the economic impact of Japanese culture and society began to spread, it became apparent that Taiwan and South Korea, along with Singapore and Hong Kong (a British colony before being reunited with China in 1997), were developing dynamic industrial economies of their own. The prospect of India and the People's Republic of China following the same path led many observers to surmise that by the end of the twenty-first century the United States and Europe would no longer dominate the globe in industrial creativity and might.

CL Primary Source: Selections from a Roundtable Discussion of Globalization and Its Impact on Arab Culture, October 26, 2000 *Find out why national cultures, if they are to successfully participate in the culture of globalization, need wings as much as they need roots.*

SECTION REVIEW

- The global pervasiveness of Western culture has provoked charges of U.S. cultural imperialism.

- Technology has been largely responsible for the spread of Western culture since World War II.

- Technology has also contributed to the emergence of a global pop culture that blends a variety of cultural elements.

- A global elite culture has also developed combining the English language, science, and higher education.

- Despite globalizing forces, cultural diversity remains strong, if not completely secure.

MATERIAL CULTURE

Fast Food

Since early times foods and beverages have been moved across national borders and cultural boundaries by empires and commercial enterprises. The list of examples is very long. Sugar, coffee, tea, chocolate, corn, manioc, potatoes, wheat, wine, beer, distilled alcohols, tomatoes, and bananas are a small number of the foods and beverages carried from their origins to new continents and new peoples. In each case, host cultures accepted these additions to the indigenous cuisine while at the same time changing their preparation and altering their cultural meanings. Chocolate, a bitter ritual beverage consumed by the Aztec elite, for example, was sweetened with sugar and became a beverage of mass consumption in Europe.

Though street vendors of prepared foods have played an important role in many societies, in modern industrialized nations uniform meals prepared by worldwide fast food franchises have appeared everywhere to meet the needs of populations transformed by cultural changes. Women and men in these societies marry later or not at all, and families have fewer meals together because of the schedules of school and work. The traditional boundaries between work and family life have been blurred. Individuals work long hours, travel long distances, and eat on the run. In 2003 there were 1.9 billion fast food outlets worldwide, with annual sales of $282 billion.

With globalization, increased immigration and travel, and greater cultural connectivity promoted by films, television, and the Web, cuisine and associated ideas about preparation and delivery have been internationalized. McDonald's now operates more than 30,000 restaurants in 119 countries. When a new franchise opened in Kuwait City, the drive-through line was over 10 kilometers long. Generally meals cost the same in each cultural setting. In the United States, one of the richest countries in the world, McDonald's provides low-cost food to the masses, while in Pakistan, one of the poorest, the meals are luxuries. What is the attraction? For many in the developing world the fast food cuisines, restaurant designs, and styles of preparation represent the world of modernity and sophistication, not unlike the enthusiasm in the developed world for Mexican, Thai, or Ethiopian restaurants and cuisines.

Indeed, McDonald's is merely one of numerous examples of fast food globalization. The one-thousandth KFC outlet

PIZZA HUT IN INDIA   The booming, cosmopolitan city of Mumbai hosts India's most modern industries and many of the country's strictest vegetarians, as seen by the vegetarian menu advertised by this Pizza Hut restaurant.   (AP Images/Aiaz Rahi)

opened recently in China, surpassing McDonald's presence in this dynamic economy. Papa John's opened its fortieth outlet in Seoul and its twentieth outlet in Shanghai. Wendy's, Dominos, Cinnabon, and Subway have followed. Even Brazilian brands like Habib's and British brands like Dixy Chicken have expanded into the Middle East and India, respectively.

Many have condemned this process as Yankee imperialism and as the unwanted homogenization of global culture. Tens of thousands have demonstrated, and some have gone to jail as a result of attacks on these symbols of foreign cultural penetration. Yet, as in earlier examples of unequal cultural exchange, local cultures have found ways to impose their tastes and values on these powerful international businesses. In Singapore McDonald's serves its signature hamburger on rice cakes instead of buns, and in Israel McDonald's has established Kosher outlets. KFC, the most successful American chain in China, serves a Beijing Duck Wrap with spring onions and rice gruel for breakfast. In India, with its large vegetarian population, McDonald's, Pizza Hut, and other successful franchises devote as much as 75 percent of their menu to vegetarian foods. Not only have menus been altered, but local preferences for a more leisurely style of dining have also forced chains like Pizza Hut and KFC to modify restaurant design to provide more seating and table service.

Societies produce an enormous range of products that serve as class and culture markers and as forms of self-expression. In the modern world food helps mark consumers as "traditional" or "sophisticated" and as "rich" or "poor." Both the global success of fast food companies and the popular protests against them suggest the complexity of this form of cultural transmission.

This does not mean that the world's cultural diversity is secure. Every decade a number of minority languages cease to be spoken, usually as the result of the spread of national languages. Many religious practices are also disappearing in the face of the successful expansion of Islam, Christianity, and other religions, although secular values also play a role. Televised national ceremonies or performances for tourists may prevent folk customs and costumes from dying out, but they also tend to standardize rituals that once had many local variations. While it was possible to recognize the nationality of people from their clothing and grooming a century ago, today most urban men dress the same the world over, although women's clothing shows much greater variety. As much as one may regret the disappearance or commercialization of some folkways, most anthropologists would agree that change is characteristic of all healthy cultures. What doesn't change risks extinction.

Chapter Review

 DOWNLOAD THE MP3 AUDIO FILE OF THE CHAPTER REVIEW TO LISTEN TO ON THE GO.

What are the main benefits and dangers of growing political, economic, and cultural integration? (page 820)

The turn of the millennium has been a time of important global changes. The Iron Curtain that had divided Europe since the end of the Second World War fell, taking with it the tensions and risks of the Cold War. The great Soviet Empire broke up, while dozens of countries joined new economic coalitions. The bastions of communism embraced capitalism with varying degrees of enthusiasm. As trading barriers tumbled, world trade surged, creating new wealth and new inequalities in its distribution. Yet international terrorism and the proliferation of nuclear weapons cast shadows on the future, and the aggressive response of the United States to the attacks of 9/11 caused some people to worry about a new form of superpower imperialism.

What roles do religious beliefs and secular ideologies play in the contemporary world? (page 829)

Globalization has generated a wide range of religious and secular responses. Western commentators have recognized the emergence of a new age but have differed over whether globalizing forces or cultural and religious differences will define it. The pervasiveness of millennial ideas since the Iranian Revolution attests to the continuing power of religious belief. Militant Islam has emerged as an especially potent force, a response to economic and political conditions in Muslim countries and to the perceived evils of U.S. policy and influence. In addition to religious visions, broad standards of human rights have gained wide acceptance, particularly those embodied in the United Nations Universal Declaration of Human Rights. As well as informing United Nations actions, such

KEY TERMS

Usama bin Laden *(p. 819)*

globalization *(p. 820)*

World Trade Organization (WTO) *(p. 822)*

weapons of mass destruction *(p. 826)*

terrorism *(p. 829)*

Universal Declaration of Human Rights *(p. 831)*

nongovernmental organizations (NGOs) *(p. 831)*

cultural imperialism *(p. 834)*

global pop culture *(p. 837)*

global elite culture *(p. 837)*

WEB RESOURCES

Pronunciation Guide

Primary Sources

The Last Night

Free Trade and the Decline of Democracy

(Continued)

standards also underlie the activities of individual states and NGOs devoted to a variety of social, political, and economic causes. Recent international agreements addressing genocide and environmental protection exemplify the power of these standards. The work of the United Nations Division for the Advancement of Women has helped to make women's rights a global concern. However, while the movement has won many victories, it has also had to deal with significant clashes over cultural values.

How has technology contributed to the process of global interaction? (page 834)

The spread of Western culture after World War II, largely through American capitalism, has prompted accusations of U.S. cultural imperialism. Not ideology, however, but technology bears primary responsibility for the globalization of culture. Devices such as transistor radios, televisions, CD players, cell phones, satellites, and the Internet have diffused Western, especially American, cultural forms throughout the world. One effect of this diffusion has been the rise of a global pop culture, but rather than being dominated by American forms, it blends a diverse range of American, European, Latin American, and Asian elements. At the same time a global elite culture has risen on the foundations of the English language, the standardized concepts and practices of science, and higher education. Global pop culture in particular has provoked controversy over the fate of local cultural traditions. However, as the examples of Japan and other Asian nations suggest, cultural diversity remains strong as peoples choose and adapt global cultural forms to their own values. Even so, local traditions continue to fall to globalization, demonstrating that cultural diversity is not completely secure.

Islamic Fundamentalist Usama bin Laden Calls on Muslims to Take Up Arms Against America

Declaration of Jihad Against Americans Occupying the Land of the Two Holy Mosques

Lebanese Author Elias Khoury Argues for Democracy, Demilitarization, and Cultural Pluralism in the Middle East and North Africa

Internet Discussion of Marriage and Education for Saudi Women

Selections from a Roundtable Discussion of Globalization and Its Impact on Arab Culture, October 26, 2000

Answer to the History in Focus Question

See photo on page 827, "Iranian President Mahmoud Ahmadinejad."

Plus

Chapter Objectives

ACE multiple-choice quiz

Flashcards

SUGGESTED READING

Appadurai, Arjun. *Modernity at Large: Cultural Dimensions of Globalization.* 1996. Treats the interrelationships between high culture and popular culture.

Barber, Benjamin R. *Jihad vs. McWorld: How Globalism and Tribalism Are Reshaping the World.* 1995. A widely read attempt to describe the world at the turn of the millennium.

Bulliet, Richard W. *The Case for Islamo-Christian Civilization.* 2004. Takes issue with Samuel Huntington's "clash of civilizations" theory.

Chua, Amy. *World on Fire: How Exporting Free Market Democracy Breeds Ethnic Hatred and Global Instability.* 2003. A pessimistic perspective on globalization and world trade.

Devine, Carol, and Carol Rae Hansen. *Human Rights: The Essential Reference.* 1999. A standard work on the subject.

Friedman, Thomas L. *The Lexus and the Olive Tree.* 1999. A readable and influential analysis of alternative pathways to the future.

Hoffman, Bruce. *Inside Terrorism.* 2d ed. 2006. A well-regarded work on a complex topic.

Huntington, Samuel P. *The Clash of Civilizations and the Remaking of the World Order.* 1996. A controversial thesis that Islam and the West are destined for irresolvable conflict.

Kaplan, Robert. *Of Paradise and Power: America and Europe in the New World Order.* 2002. Examines the growing gulf between the United States and Europe.

Kupchan, Charles A. *The End of the American Era: U.S. Foreign Policy and the Geopolitics of the Twenty-first Century.* 2002. A realist perspective on the world balance of power.

Mamdani, Mahmood. *Good Muslim, Bad Muslim: America, the Cold War, and the Roots of Terror.* 2004. Explores the origins of Muslim militancy in opposition to the West.

Moore, Mike. *A World Without Walls: Freedom, Development, Free Trade and Global Governance.* 2003. A view of the global economy from a former director-general of the World Trade Organization.

Norris, Pippa. *Rising Tide: Gender Equality and Cultural Change Around the World.* 2003. Surveys the condition of women.

Pennycock, Alistaire. *The Cultural Politics of English as an International Language.* 1994. The rise of English as a global means of communication.

Priest, Dana. *Mission: Waging War and Keeping Peace with America's Military.* 2003. A critique of American military policies in the twenty-first century.

NOTES

1. "Liberty's Great Advance," *The Economist,* June 28–July 4, 2003, pp. 5–6.

2. "Universal Declaration of Human Rights," in *Twenty-five Human Rights Documents* (New York: Center for the Study of Human Rights, Columbia University, 1994), 6.

Glossary

The glossary for *The Earth and Its Peoples, Brief 4/e* is for the complete text, Chapters 1 through 30.

Abbasid Caliphate Descendants of the Prophet Muhammad's uncle, al-Abbas, the Abbasids overthrew the **Umayyad Caliphate** and ruled an Islamic empire from their capital in Baghdad (founded 762) from 750 to 1258. (*p. 210*)

abolitionists Men and women who agitated for a complete end to slavery. Abolitionist pressure ended the British transatlantic slave trade in 1808 and slavery in British colonies in 1834. In the United States the activities of abolitionists were one factor leading to the Civil War (1861–1865). (*p. 542*)

Acheh Sultanate Muslim kingdom in northern Sumatra. Main center of Islamic expansion in Southeast Asia in the early seventeenth century, it declined after the Dutch seized **Malacca** from Portugal in 1641. (*p. 489*)

Aden Port city in the modern south Arabian country of Yemen. It has been a major trading center in the Indian Ocean since ancient times. (*p. 355*)

African National Congress An organization dedicated to obtaining equal voting and civil rights for black inhabitants of South Africa. Founded in 1912 as the South African Native National Congress, it changed its name in 1923. Though it was banned and its leaders were jailed for many years, it eventually helped bring majority rule to South Africa. (*p. 747*)

Afrikaners South Africans descended from Dutch and French settlers of the seventeenth century. Their Great Trek founded new settler colonies in the nineteenth century. Though a minority among South Africans, they held political power after 1910, imposing a system of racial segregation called apartheid after 1949. (*p. 664*)

Agricultural Revolutions (ancient) The change from food gathering to food production that occurred between ca. 8000 and 2000 B.C.E. Also known as the Neolithic Revolution. (*p. 8*)

agricultural revolution (eighteenth century) The transformation of farming that resulted in the eighteenth century from the spread of new crops, improvements in cultivation techniques and livestock breeding, and the consolidation of small holdings into large farms from which tenants and sharecroppers were forcibly expelled. (*p. 552*)

Aguinaldo, Emilio (1869–1964) Leader of the Filipino independence movement against Spain (1895–1898). He proclaimed the independence of the Philippines in 1899, but his movement was crushed and he was captured by the United States Army in 1901. (*p. 673*)

Akbar (1542–1605) Most illustrious sultan of the **Mughal Empire** in India (r. 1556–1605). He expanded the empire and pursued a policy of conciliation with Hindus. (*p. 486*)

Akhenaten Egyptian pharaoh (r. 1353–1335 B.C.E.). He built a new capital at Amarna, fostered a new style of naturalistic art, and created a religious revolution by imposing worship of the sun-disk. The Amarna letters, largely from his reign, preserve official correspondence with subjects and neighbors. (*p. 74*)

Alexander (356–323 B.C.E.) King of Macedonia in northern Greece. Between 334 and 323 B.C.E. he conquered the Persian Empire, reached the Indus Valley, founded many Greek-style cities, and spread Greek culture across the Middle East. Later known as Alexander the Great. (*p. 126*)

Alexandria City on the Mediterranean coast of Egypt founded by Alexander. It became the capital of the Hellenistic kingdom of the **Ptolemies.** It contained the famous Library and the Museum—a center for leading scientific and literary figures. Its merchants engaged in trade with areas bordering the Mediterranean and the Indian Ocean. (*p. 128*)

Allende, Salvador (1908–1973) Socialist politician elected president of Chile in 1970 and overthrown by the military in 1973. He died during the military attack. (*p. 790*)

All-India Muslim League Political organization founded in India in 1906 to defend the interests of India's Muslim minority. Led by Muhammad Ali Jinnah, it attempted to negotiate with the **Indian National Congress.** In 1940, the League began demanding a separate state for Muslims, to be called Pakistan. (See also **Jinnah, Muhammad Ali.**) (*p. 738*)

altepetl An ethnic state in ancient Mesoamerica, the common political building block of that region. (*p. 289*)

amulet Small charm meant to protect the bearer from evil. Found frequently in archaeological excavations in Mesopotamia and Egypt, amulets reflect the religious practices of the common people. (*p. 22*)

Amur River This river valley was a contested frontier between northern China and eastern Russia until the settlement arranged in the Treaty of Nerchinsk (1689). (*p. 507*)

anarchists Revolutionaries who wanted to abolish all private property and governments, usually by violence, and replace them with free associations of groups. (*p. 638*)

Anasazi Important culture of what is now the southwest United States (700–1200 C.E.). Centered on Chaco Canyon in New Mexico and Mesa Verde in Colorado, the Anasazi culture built multistory residences and worshiped in subterranean buildings called kivas. (*p. 292*)

aqueduct A conduit, either elevated or underground, using gravity to carry water from a source to a location—usually a city—that needed it. The Romans built many aqueducts in a period of substantial urbanization. (*p. 159*)

Arawak Amerindian peoples who inhabited the Greater Antilles of the Caribbean at the time of Columbus. (*p. 390*)

Armenia One of the earliest Christian kingdoms, situated in eastern Anatolia and the western Caucasus and occupied by speakers of the Armenian language. (*p. 193*)

Asante African kingdom on the **Gold Coast** that expanded rapidly after 1680. Asante participated in the Atlantic economy, trading gold, slaves, and ivory. It resisted British imperial ambitions for a quarter century before being absorbed into Britain's Gold Coast colony in 1902. (*p. 666*)

Ashikaga Shogunate (1338–1573) The second of Japan's military governments headed by a shogun (a military ruler). Sometimes called the Muromachi Shogunate. *(p. 335)*

Ashoka Third ruler of the **Mauryan Empire** in India (r. 270–232 B.C.E.). He converted to Buddhism and broadcast his precepts on inscribed stones and pillars, the earliest surviving Indian writing. *(p. 139)*

Ashurbanipal The seventh century B.C.E. Assyrian ruler who assembled a large collection of writings drawn from the ancient literary, religious, and scientific traditions of Mesopotamia. The many tablets unearthed by archaeologists constitute one of the most important sources of present-day knowledge of the long literary tradition of Mesopotamia. *(p. 84)*

Asian Tigers Collective name for South Korea, Taiwan, Hong Kong, and Singapore—nations that became economic powers in the 1970s and 1980s. *(p. 798)*

Atahualpa (1502?–1533) Last ruling Inca emperor of Peru. He was executed by the Spanish. *(p. 405)*

Atlantic system The network of trading links after 1500 that moved goods, wealth, people, and cultures around the Atlantic Ocean Basin. *(p. 443)*

Augustus (63 B.C.E.–14 C.E.) Honorific name of Octavian, founder of the **Roman Principate,** the military dictatorship that replaced the failing rule of the **Roman Senate.** After defeating all rivals, between 31 B.C.E. and 14 C.E. he laid the groundwork for several centuries of stability and prosperity in the Roman Empire. *(p. 155)*

Auschwitz Nazi extermination camp in Poland, the largest center of mass murder during the **Holocaust.** Close to a million Jews, Gypsies, Communists, and others were killed there. *(p. 729)*

ayllu Andean lineage group or kin-based community. *(p. 295)*

Aztecs Also known as Mexica, the Aztecs created a powerful empire in central Mexico (1325–1521 C.E.). They forced defeated peoples to provide goods and labor as a tax. *(p. 289)*

Babylon The largest and most important city in Mesopotamia. It achieved particular eminence as the capital of the Amorite king **Hammurabi** in the eighteenth century B.C.E. and the Neo-Babylonian king Nebuchadnezzar in the sixth century B.C.E. *(p. 15)*

balance of power The policy in international relations by which, beginning in the eighteenth century, the major European states acted together to prevent any one of them from becoming too powerful. *(p. 436)*

Balfour Declaration Statement issued by Britain's Foreign Secretary Arthur Balfour in 1917 favoring the establishment of a Jewish national homeland in Palestine. *(p. 688)*

Bannermen Hereditary military servants of the **Qing Empire,** in large part descendants of peoples of various origins who had fought for the founders of the empire. *(p. 587)*

Bantu Collective name of a large group of sub-Saharan African languages and of the peoples speaking these languages. *(p. 191)*

Batavia Fort established ca. 1619 as headquarters of Dutch East India Company operations in Indonesia; today the city of Jakarta. *(p. 492)*

Battle of Midway U.S. naval victory over the Japanese fleet in June 1942, in which the Japanese lost four of their best aircraft carriers. It marked a turning point in World War II. *(p. 725)*

Battle of Omdurman British victory over the Mahdi in the Sudan in 1898. General Kitchener led a mixed force of British and Egyptian troops armed with rapid-firing rifles and machine guns. *(p. 658)*

Beijing China's northern capital, first used as an imperial capital in 906 and now the capital of the People's Republic of China. *(p. 326)*

Bengal Region of northeastern India. It was the first part of India to be conquered by the British in the eighteenth century and remained the political and economic center of British India throughout the nineteenth century. The 1905 split of the province into predominantly Hindu West Bengal and predominantly Muslim East Bengal (now Bangladesh) sparked anti-British riots. *(p. 736)*

Berlin Conference (1884–1885) Conference that German chancellor Otto von Bismarck called to set rules for the partition of Africa. It led to the creation of the Congo Free State under King **Leopold II** of Belgium. (See also **Bismarck, Otto von.**) *(p. 663)*

Bhagavad-Gita The most important work of Indian sacred literature, a dialogue between the great warrior Arjuna and the god Krishna on duty and the fate of the spirit. *(p. 140)*

bin Laden, Usama Saudi-born Muslim extremist who funded the al Qaeda organization that was responsible for several terrorist attacks, including those on the World Trade Center and the Pentagon in 2001. *(p. 819)*

Bismarck, Otto von (1815–1898) Chancellor (prime minister) of Prussia from 1862 until 1871, when he became chancellor of Germany. A conservative nationalist, he led Prussia to victory against Austria (1866) and France (1870) and was responsible for the creation of the German Empire in 1871. *(p. 640)*

Black Death An outbreak of **bubonic plague** that spread across Asia, North Africa, and Europe in the mid-fourteenth century, carrying off vast numbers of persons. *(p. 364)*

Bolívar, Simón (1783–1830) The most important military leader in the struggle for independence in South America. Born in Venezuela, he led military forces there and in Colombia, Ecuador, Peru, and Bolivia. *(p. 539)*

Bolsheviks Radical Marxist political party founded by Vladimir Lenin in 1903. Under Lenin's leadership, the Bolsheviks seized power in November 1917 during the Russian Revolution. (See also **Lenin, Vladimir.**) *(p. 688)*

Bonaparte, Napoleon. See **Napoleon I.**

bourgeoisie In early modern Europe, the class of well-off town dwellers whose wealth came from manufacturing, finance, commerce, and allied professions. *(p. 424)*

Brazza, Savorgnan de (1852–1905) Franco-Italian explorer sent by the French government to claim part of equatorial Africa for France. Founded Brazzaville, capital of the French Congo, in 1880. *(p. 663)*

British raj The rule over much of South Asia between 1765 and 1947 by the East India Company and then by the British government. *(p. 607)*

bubonic plague A bacterial disease of fleas that can be transmitted by flea bites to rodents and humans; humans in late stages of the illness can spread the bacteria by coughing. Because of its very high mortality rate and the difficulty of preventing its spread, major outbreaks have created crises in many parts of the world. (See also **Black Death.**) *(p. 318)*

Buddha (563–483 B.C.E.) An Indian prince named Siddhartha Gautama, who renounced his wealth and social position. After becoming "enlightened" (the meaning of *Buddha*) he enunciated the principles of Buddhism. This doctrine evolved and spread throughout India and to Southeast, East, and Central Asia. (See also **Mahayana Buddhism; Theravada Buddhism.**) *(p. 135)*

Byzantine Empire Historians' name for the eastern portion of the Roman Empire from the fourth century onward, taken from "Byzantion," an early name for Constantinople, the Byzantine capital city. The empire fell to the Ottomans in 1453. (See also **Ottoman Empire.**) *(p. 228)*

caliphate Office established in succession to the Prophet **Muhammad,** to rule the Islamic empire; also the name of that empire. (See also **Abbasid Caliphate; Sokoto Caliphate; Umayyad Caliphate.**) *(p. 208)*

calpolli A group of up to a hundred families that served as a social building block of an **altepetl** in ancient Mesoamerica. *(p. 289)*

capitalism The economic system of large financial institutions—banks, stock exchanges, investment companies—that first developed in early modern Europe. *Commercial capitalism,* the trading system of the early modern economy, is often distinguished from *industrial capitalism,* the system based on machine production. *(p. 461)*

caravel A small, highly maneuverable three-masted ship used by the Portuguese and Spanish in the exploration of the Atlantic. *(p. 393)*

Cárdenas, Lázaro (1895–1970) President of Mexico (1934–1940). He brought major changes to Mexican life by distributing millions of acres of land to the peasants, bringing representatives of workers and farmers into the inner circles of politics, and nationalizing the oil industry. *(p. 751)*

Carthage City located in present-day Tunisia, founded by **Phoenicians** ca. 800 B.C.E. It became a major commercial center and naval power in the western Mediterranean until defeated by Rome in the third century B.C.E. *(p. 94)*

Catholic Reformation Religious reform movement within the Latin Christian Church, begun in response to the **Protestant Reformation.** It clarified Catholic theology and reformed clerical training and discipline. *(p. 418)*

Celts Peoples sharing a common language and culture that originated in central Europe in the first half of the first millennium B.C.E. After 500 B.C.E. they spread as far as Anatolia in the east, Spain and the British Isles in the west, and later were overtaken by Roman conquest and Germanic invasions. Their descendants survive on the western fringe of Europe (Brittany, Wales, Scotland, Ireland). *(p. 57)*

Champa rice Quick-maturing rice that can allow two harvests in one growing season. Originally introduced into Champa from India, it was later sent to China as a tribute gift by the Champa state. (See also **tributary system.**) *(p. 279)*

Chang'an City in the Wei Valley in eastern China. It became the capital of the Qin and early Han Empires. Its main features were imitated in the cities and towns that sprang up throughout the Han Empire. *(p. 166)*

Charlemagne (742–814) King of the Franks (r. 768–814); emperor (r. 800–814). Through a series of military conquests he established the Carolingian Empire, which encompassed all of Gaul and parts of Germany and Italy. Though illiterate himself, he sponsored a brief intellectual revival. *(p. 228)*

chartered companies Groups of private investors who paid an annual fee to France and England in exchange for a monopoly over trade to the West Indies colonies. *(p. 461)*

Chavín The first major urban civilization in South America (900–250 B.C.E.). Its capital, Chavín de Huántar, was located high in the Andes Mountains of Peru. Chavín became politically and economically dominant in a densely populated region that included two distinct ecological zones, the Peruvian coastal plain and the Andean foothills. *(p. 64)*

Chiang Kai-shek (1887–1975) Chinese military and political leader. Succeeded Sun Yat-sen as head of the **Guomindang** in 1925; headed the Chinese government from 1928 to 1948; fought against the Chinese Communists and Japanese invaders. After 1949 he headed the Chinese Nationalist government in Taiwan. *(p. 718)*

chiefdom Form of political organization with rule by a hereditary leader who held power over a collection of villages and towns. Less powerful than kingdoms and empires, chiefdoms were based on gift giving and commercial links. *(p. 294)*

Chimú Powerful Peruvian civilization based on conquest. Located in the region earlier dominated by **Moche.** Conquered by **Inca** in 1465. *(p. 297)*

chinampas Raised fields constructed along lake shores in Mesoamerica to increase agricultural yields. *(p. 284)*

city-state A small independent state consisting of an urban center and the surrounding agricultural territory. A characteristic political form in early Mesopotamia, Archaic and Classical Greece, Phoenicia, and early Italy. (See also **polis.**) *(p. 17)*

civilization An ambiguous term often used to denote more complex societies but sometimes used by anthropologists to describe any group of people sharing a set of cultural traits. *(p. 5)*

Cixi, Empress Dowager (1835–1908) Empress of China and mother of Emperor Guangxi. She put her son under house arrest, supported antiforeign movements, and resisted reforms of the Chinese government and armed forces. *(pp. 648, 694)*

clipper ship Large, fast, streamlined sailing vessel, often American built, of the mid-to-late nineteenth century rigged with vast canvas sails hung from tall masts. *(p. 615)*

Cold War (1945–1991) The ideological struggle between communism (Soviet Union) and capitalism (United States) for world influence. The Soviet Union and the United States came to the brink of actual war during the **Cuban missile crisis** but never attacked one another. The Cold War came to an end when the Soviet Union dissolved in 1991. (See also **North Atlantic Treaty Organization; Warsaw Pact.**) *(p. 764)*

colonialism Policy by which a nation administers a foreign territory and develops its resources for the benefit of the colonial power. *(p. 658)*

Columbian Exchange The exchange of peoples, plants, animals, diseases, and technologies between the Americas and the rest of the world following Columbus's voyages. *(p. 466)*

Columbus, Christopher (1451–1506) Genoese mariner who in the service of Spain led expeditions across the Atlantic, reestablishing contact between the peoples of the Americas and the Old World and opening the way to Spanish conquest and colonization. *(p. 395)*

Confucius Western name for the Chinese philosopher Kongzi (551–479 B.C.E.). His doctrine of duty and public service had a great influence on subsequent Chinese thought and served as a code of conduct for government officials. *(p. 51)*

Congress of Vienna (1814–1815) Meeting of representatives of European monarchs called to reestablish the old order after the defeat of **Napoleon I.** *(p. 535)*

conquistadors Early-sixteenth-century Spanish adventurers who conquered Mexico, Central America, and Peru. (See **Cortés, Hernán; Pizarro, Francisco.**) *(p. 403)*

Constantine (285–337 C.E.) Roman emperor (r. 306–337). After reuniting the Roman Empire, he moved the capital to Constantinople and made Christianity a favored religion. *(p. 160)*

Constitutional Convention Meeting in 1787 of the elected representatives of the thirteen original states to write the Constitution of the United States. *(p. 530)*

contract of indenture A voluntary agreement binding a person to work for a specified period of years in return for free passage to an overseas destination. Before 1800 most **indentured servants** were Europeans; after 1800 most indentured laborers were Asians. *(p. 618)*

Cortés, Hernán (1485–1547) Spanish explorer and conquistador who led the conquest of Aztec Mexico in 1519–1521 for Spain. *(p. 404)*

Cossacks Peoples of the Russian Empire who lived outside the farming villages, often as herders, mercenaries, or outlaws. Cossacks led the conquest of Siberia in the sixteenth and seventeenth centuries. *(p. 514)*

Council of the Indies The institution responsible for supervising Spain's colonies in the Americas from 1524 to the early eighteenth century, when it lost all but judicial responsibilities. *(p. 444)*

creole In colonial Spanish America, term used to describe someone of European descent born in the New World. Elsewhere in the Americas, the term is used to describe all nonnative peoples. *(p. 448)*

Crimean War (1853–1856) Conflict between the Russian and Ottoman Empires fought primarily in the Crimean Peninsula. To prevent Russian expansion, Britain and France sent troops to support the Ottomans. *(p. 579)*

Crusades (1095–1204) Armed pilgrimages to the Holy Land by Christians determined to recover Jerusalem from Muslim rule. The Crusades brought an end to western Europe's centuries of intellectual and cultural isolation. *(p. 250)*

Crystal Palace Building erected in Hyde Park, London, for the Great Exhibition of 1851. Made of iron and glass, like a gigantic greenhouse, it was a symbol of the industrial age. *(p. 556)*

Cuban missile crisis (1962) Brink-of-war confrontation between the United States and the Soviet Union over the latter's placement of nuclear-armed missiles in Cuba. *(p. 773)*

cultural imperialism Domination of one culture over another by a deliberate policy or by economic or technological superiority. *(p. 834)*

Cultural Revolution (China) (1966–1969) Campaign in China ordered by **Mao Zedong** to purge the Communist Party of his opponents and instill revolutionary values in the younger generation. *(p. 781)*

culture Socially transmitted patterns of action and expression. *Material culture* refers to physical objects, such as dwellings, clothing, tools, and crafts. Culture also includes arts, beliefs, knowledge, and technology. *(p. 6)*

cuneiform A system of writing in which wedge-shaped symbols represented words or syllables. It originated in Mesopotamia and was used initially for Sumerian and Akkadian but later was adapted to represent other languages of western Asia. Because so many symbols had to be learned, literacy was confined to a relatively small group of administrators and **scribes.** *(p. 25)*

Cyrus (600–530 B.C.E.) Founder of the Achaemenid Persian Empire. Between 550 and 530 B.C.E. he conquered Media, Lydia, and Babylon. Revered in the traditions of both Iran and the subject peoples, he employed Persians and Medes in his administration and respected the institutions and beliefs of subject peoples. *(p. 108)*

czar See **tsar.**

daimyo Literally, "great name(s)." Japanese warlords and great landowners, whose armed **samurai** gave them control of the Japanese islands from the eighth to the later nineteenth century. Under the **Tokugawa Shogunate** they were subordinated to the imperial government. *(p. 496)*

Daoism Chinese school of thought, originating in the Warring States Period with Laozi (604–531 B.C.E.). Daoism offered an alternative to the Confucian emphasis on hierarchy and duty. Daoists believe that the world is always changing and is devoid of absolute morality or meaning. They accept the world as they find it, avoid futile struggles, and deviate as little as possible from the *Dao*, or "path" of nature. (See also **Confucius.**) *(p. 52)*

Darius I (ca. 558–486 B.C.E.) Third ruler of the Persian Empire (r. 522–486 B.C.E.). He crushed the widespread initial resistance to his rule and gave all major government posts to Persians rather than to Medes. He established a system of provinces and tribute, began construction of Persepolis, and expanded Persian control in the east (Pakistan) and west (northern Greece). *(p. 110)*

Darwin, Charles (1809–1882) With Alfred Russell Wallace (1823–1913) he developed the theory of evolution through natural selection. Their work was first made known simultaneously in 1858. *(p. 644)*

Decembrist revolt Abortive attempt by army officers to take control of the Russian government upon the death of Tsar Alexander I in 1825. *(p. 584)*

Declaration of the Rights of Man (1789) Statement of fundamental political rights adopted by the French **National Assembly** at the beginning of the French Revolution. *(p. 532)*

deforestation The removal of trees faster than forests can replace themselves. *(p. 427)*

Delhi Sultanate (1206–1526) Centralized Indian empire of varying extent, created by Muslim invaders. *(p. 344)*

democracy A system of government in which all "citizens" (however defined) have equal political and legal rights, privileges, and protections, as in the Greek city-state of Athens in the fifth and fourth centuries B.C.E. *(p. 116)*

demographic transition A change in the rates of population growth. Before the transition, both birthrates and death rates are high, resulting in a slowly growing population; then the death rate drops but the birthrate remains high, causing a population explosion; finally the birthrate drops and the population growth slows down. This transition took place in Europe in the late nineteenth and early twentieth centuries, in North America and East Asia in the mid-twentieth, and, most recently, in Latin America and South Asia. *(p. 804)*

Deng Xiaoping (1904–1997) Communist Party leader who forced Chinese economic reforms after the death of **Mao Zedong.** *(p. 798)*

Diagne, Blaise (1872–1934) Senegalese political leader. He was the first African elected to the French National Assembly. During World War I, in exchange for promises to give French citizenship to Senegalese, he helped recruit Africans to serve in the French army. After the war, he led a movement to abolish forced labor in Africa. *(p. 747)*

Dias, Bartolomeu (1450?–1500) Portuguese explorer who in 1488 led the first expedition to sail around the southern tip of Africa from the Atlantic and sight the Indian Ocean. *(p. 395)*

Diaspora A Greek word meaning "dispersal," used to describe the communities of a given ethnic group living outside their homeland. Jews, for example, spread from Israel to western Asia and Mediterranean lands in antiquity and today can be found throughout the world. *(p. 91)*

Dirty War War waged by the Argentine military (1976–1983) against leftist groups. Characterized by the use of illegal imprisonment, torture, and executions by the military. *(p. 790)*

division of labor A manufacturing technique that breaks down a craft into many simple and repetitive tasks that can be performed by unskilled workers. Pioneered in the pottery works of Josiah Wedgwood and in other eighteenth-century factories, it greatly increased the productivity of labor and lowered the cost of manufactured goods. (See also **Wedgwood, Josiah.**) *(p. 553)*

driver A privileged male slave whose job was to ensure that a slave gang did its work on a plantation. *(p. 459)*

Druids The class of religious experts who conducted rituals and preserved sacred lore among some ancient Celtic peoples. They provided education, mediated disputes between kinship groups, and were suppressed by the Romans as a potential focus of opposition to Roman rule. (See also **Celts.**) *(p. 58)*

Dutch West India Company (1621–1794) Trading company chartered by the Dutch government to conduct its merchants' trade in the Americas and Africa. *(p. 461)*

Edison, Thomas (1847–1931) American inventor best known for inventing the electric light bulb, acoustic recording on wax cylinders, and motion pictures. *(p. 630)*

Einstein, Albert (1879–1955) German physicist who developed the theory of relativity, which states that time, space, and mass are relative to each other and not fixed. *(p. 702)*

electricity A form of energy used in telegraphy from the 1840s on and for lighting, industrial motors, and railroads beginning in the 1880s. *(p. 630)*

electric telegraph A device for rapid, long-distance transmission of information over an electric wire. It was introduced in England and North America in the 1830s and 1840s and replaced telegraph systems that utilized visual signals such as semaphores. (See also **submarine telegraph cables.**) *(p. 558)*

encomienda A grant of authority over a population of Amerindians in the Spanish colonies. It provided the grant holder with a supply of cheap labor and periodic payments of goods by the Amerindians. It obliged the grant holder to Christianize the Amerindians. *(p. 448)*

English Civil War (1642–1648) A conflict over royal versus parliamentary rights, caused by King Charles I's arrest of his parliamentary critics and ending with his execution. Its outcome checked the growth of royal absolutism and, with the Glorious Revolution of 1688 and the English Bill of Rights of 1689, ensured that England would be a constitutional monarchy. *(p. 433)*

Enlightenment A philosophical movement in eighteenth-century Europe that fostered the belief that one could reform society by discovering rational laws that governed social behavior and were just as scientific as the laws of physics. *(pp. 423, 525)*

equites In ancient Italy, prosperous landowners second in wealth and status to the senatorial aristocracy. The Roman emperors allied with this group to counterbalance the influence of the old aristocracy and used the *equites* to staff the imperial civil service. *(p. 155)*

Estates General France's traditional national assembly with representatives of the three estates, or classes, in French society: the clergy, nobility, and commoners. The calling of the Estates General in 1789 led to the French Revolution. *(p. 531)*

Ethiopia East African highland nation lying east of the Nile River. (See also **Menelik II; Selassie, Haile.**) *(p. 193)*

ethnic cleansing Effort to eradicate a people and its culture by means of mass killing and the destruction of historical buildings and cultural materials. Ethnic cleansing was used by both sides in the conflicts that accompanied the disintegration of Yugoslavia in the 1990s. *(p. 802)*

European Community (EC) An organization promoting economic unity in Europe formed in 1967 by consolidation of earlier, more limited, agreements. Replaced by the European Union (EU) in 1993. *(p. 769)*

extraterritoriality The right of foreign residents in a country to live under the laws of their native country and disregard the laws of the host country. In the nineteenth and early twentieth centuries, European and American nationals living in certain areas of Chinese and Ottoman cities were granted this right. *(p. 580)*

Faisal I (1885–1933) Arab prince, leader of the Arab Revolt in World War I. The British made him king of Iraq in 1921, and he reigned under British protection until 1933. *(p. 688)*

Fascist Party Italian political party created by Benito Mussolini during World War I. It emphasized aggressive nationalism and was Mussolini's instrument for the creation of a dictatorship in Italy from 1922 to 1943. (See also **Mussolini, Benito.**) *(p. 715)*

fief In medieval Europe, land granted in return for a sworn oath to provide specified military service. *(p. 240)*

First Temple A monumental sanctuary built in Jerusalem by King Solomon in the tenth century B.C.E. to be the religious center for the Israelite god Yahweh. The Temple priesthood conducted sacrifices, received a tithe or percentage of agricultural revenues, and became economically and politically powerful. The First Temple was destroyed by the Babylonians in 587 B.C.E., rebuilt on a modest scale in the late sixth century B.C.E., and replaced by King Herod's Second Temple in the late first century B.C.E. (destroyed by the Romans in 70 C.E.). *(p. 88)*

Five-Year Plans Plans that Joseph Stalin introduced to industrialize the Soviet Union rapidly, beginning in 1928. They set goals for the output of steel, electricity, machinery, and most other products and were enforced by the police powers of the state. They succeeded in making the Soviet Union a major industrial power before World War II. (See also **Stalin, Joseph.**) *(p. 709)*

foragers People who support themselves by hunting wild animals and gathering wild edible plants and insects. *(p. 6)*

free-trade imperialism Economic dominance of a weaker country by a more powerful one, while maintaining the legal independence of the weaker state. In the late nineteenth century, free-trade imperialism characterized the relations between the Latin American republics, on the one hand, and Great Britain and the United States, on the other. *(p. 673)*

Fujiwara Aristocratic family that dominated the Japanese imperial court between the ninth and twelfth centuries. *(p. 277)*

Gama, Vasco da (1460?–1524) Portuguese explorer. In 1497–1498 he led the first naval expedition from Europe to sail to India, opening an important commercial sea route. *(p. 395)*

Gandhi, Mohandas K. (Mahatma) (1869–1948) Leader of the Indian independence movement and advocate of nonviolent resistance. After being educated as a lawyer in England, he returned to India and became leader of the **Indian National Congress** in 1920. He appealed to the poor, led nonviolent demonstrations against British colonial rule, and was jailed many times. Soon after independence he was assassinated for attempting to stop Hindu-Muslim rioting. *(p. 739)*

Garibaldi, Giuseppe (1807–1882) Italian nationalist and revolutionary who conquered Sicily and Naples and added them to a unified Italy in 1860. *(p. 640)*

Genghis Khan (ca. 1167–1227) The title of Temüjin when he ruled the Mongols (1206–1227). It means the "oceanic" or "universal" leader. Genghis Khan was the founder of the Mongol Empire. *(p. 310)*

gens de couleur Free men and women of color in Haiti. They sought greater political rights and later supported the Haitian Revolution. (See also **L'Ouverture, Toussaint.**) *(p. 537)*

gentry The term *gentry* denotes the class of landholding families in England and France below the aristocracy. In China, the class of prosperous families, next in wealth below the rural aristocrats, from which the emperors drew their administrative personnel. Respected for their education and expertise, these officials became a privileged group and made the government more efficient and responsive than in the past. *(pp. 167, 426)*

Ghana First known kingdom in sub-Saharan West Africa between the sixth and thirteenth centuries C.E. Also the modern West African country once known as the Gold Coast. *(p. 213)*

global elite culture At the beginning of the twenty-first century, the attitudes and outlook of well-educated, prosperous, Western-oriented people around the world, largely expressed in European languages, especially English. *(p. 837)*

global pop culture Popular cultural practices and institutions that have been adopted internationally, such as music, the Internet, television, food, and fashion. *(p. 837)*

globalization The economic, political, and cultural integration and interaction of all parts of the world brought about by increasing trade, travel, and technology. *(p. 820)*

Gold Coast (Africa) Region of the Atlantic coast of West Africa occupied by modern Ghana; named for its gold exports to Europe from the 1470s onward. *(p. 395)*

Golden Horde Mongol khanate founded by Genghis Khan's grandson Batu. It was based in southern Russia and quickly adopted both the Turkic language and **Islam.** Also known as the Kipchak Khanote. *(p. 318)*

Gorbachev, Mikhail (b. 1931) Head of the Soviet Union from 1985 to 1991. His liberalization effort improved relations with the West, but he lost power after his reforms led to the collapse of communist governments in eastern Europe. *(p. 800)*

Gothic cathedrals Large churches originating in twelfth-century France; built in an architectural style featuring pointed arches, tall vaults and spires, flying buttresses, and large stained-glass windows. *(p. 373)*

Grand Canal The 1,100-mile (1,771-kilometer) waterway linking the Yellow and the Yangzi Rivers. It was begun in the **Han** period and completed during the Sui Empire. *(p. 257)*

"great traditions" Anthropologists' term for a literate, well-institutionalized complex of religious and social beliefs and practices adhered to by diverse societies over a broad geographical area. (See also **"small traditions."**) *(p. 189)*

Great Western Schism A division in the Latin (Western) Christian Church between 1378 and 1415, when rival claimants to the papacy existed in Rome and Avignon. *(p. 380)*

Great Zimbabwe City, now in ruins (in the modern African country of Zimbabwe), whose many stone structures were built between about 1250 and 1450, when it was a trading center and the capital of a large state. *(p. 354)*

guild In medieval Europe, an association of men (rarely women), such as merchants, artisans, or professors, who worked in a particular trade and banded together to promote their economic and political interests. Guilds were also important in other societies, such as the Ottoman and Safavid Empires. *(p. 370)*

Gujarat Region of western India famous for trade and manufacturing; the inhabitants are called Gujarati. *(p. 350)*

gunpowder A mixture of saltpeter, sulfur, and charcoal, in-various proportions. The formula, brought to China in the 400s or 500s, was first used to make fumigators to keep away insect pests and evil spirits. In later centuries it was used to make explosives and grenades and to propel can-nonballs, shot, and bullets. *(p. 270)*

Guomindang Nationalist political party founded on demo-cratic principles by **Sun Yat-sen** in 1912. After 1925, the party was headed by **Chiang Kai-shek,** who turned it into an increasingly authoritarian movement. *(p. 694)*

Gupta Empire (320–550 C.E.) A powerful Indian state based, like its Mauryan predecessor, on a capital at Patal-iputra in the Ganges Valley. It controlled most of the In-dian subcontinent through a combination of military force and its prestige as a center of sophisticated culture. (See also **theater-state.**) *(p. 141)*

Habsburg A powerful European family that provided many Holy Roman Emperors, founded the Austrian (later Aus-tro-Hungarian) Empire, and ruled sixteenth- and seven-teenth-century Spain. *(p. 430)*

hadith A tradition relating the words or deeds of the Prophet **Muhammad;** next to the **Quran,** the most im-portant basis for Islamic law. *(p. 217)*

Hammurabi Amorite ruler of **Babylon** (r. 1792–1750 B.C.E.). He conquered many city-states in southern and northern Mesopotamia and is best known for a code of laws, inscribed on a black stone pillar, illustrating the prin-ciples to be used in legal cases. *(p. 18)*

Han A term used to designate (1) the ethnic Chinese people who originated in the Yellow River Valley and spread throughout regions of China suitable for agriculture and (2) the dynasty of emperors who ruled from 206 B.C.E. to 220 C.E. *(p. 166)*

Hanseatic League An economic and defensive alliance of the free towns in northern Germany, founded about 1241 and most powerful in the fourteenth century. *(p. 368)*

Harappa Site of one of the great cities of the Indus Valley civilization of the third millennium B.C.E. It was located on the northwest frontier of the zone of cultivation (in mod-ern Pakistan), and may have been a center for the acquisi-tion of raw materials, such as metals and precious stones, from Afghanistan and Iran. *(p. 36)*

Hatshepsut Queen of Egypt (r. 1473–1458 B.C.E.). She dis-patched a naval expedition down the Red Sea to Punt (possibly northeast Sudan or Eretrea), the faraway source of myrrh. There is evidence of opposition to a woman as ruler, and after her death her name and image were fre-quently defaced. *(p. 74)*

Hebrew Bible A collection of sacred books containing di-verse materials concerning the origins, experiences, beliefs, and practices of the Israelites. Most of the extant text was compiled by members of the priestly class in the fifth cen-tury B.C.E. and reflects the concerns and views of this group. *(p. 85)*

Hellenistic Age Historians' term for the era, usually dated 323–30 B.C.E., in which Greek culture spread across west-ern Asia and northeastern Africa after the conquests of **Alexander** the Great. The period ended with the fall of the last major Hellenistic kingdom to Rome, but Greek cul-tural influence persisted until the spread of **Islam** in the seventh century C.E. *(p. 127)*

Helsinki Accords (1975) Political and human rights agree-ment signed in Helsinki, Finland, by the Soviet Union and western European countries. *(p. 773)*

Henry the Navigator (1394–1460) Portuguese prince who promoted the study of navigation and directed voyages of exploration down the western coast of Africa. *(p. 392)*

Herodotus (ca. 485–425 B.C.E.) Heir to the technique of *his-toria*—"investigation"—developed by Greeks in the late Ar-chaic period. He came from a Greek community in Anatolia and traveled extensively, collecting information in western Asia and the Mediterranean lands. He traced the antecedents of and chronicled the **Persian Wars** be-tween the Greek city-states and the Persian Empire, thus originating the Western tradition of historical writing. *(p. 117)*

Hidalgo y Costilla, Miguel (1753–1811) Mexican priest who led the first stage of the Mexican independence war in 1810. He was captured and executed in 1811. *(p. 541)*

Hidden Imam Last in a series of twelve descendants of Muhammad's son-in-law Ali, whom **Shi'ites** consider di-vinely appointed leaders of the Muslim community. In oc-clusion since ca. 873, he is expected to return as a messiah at the end of time. *(p. 482)*

hieroglyphics A system of writing in which pictorial sym-bols represented sounds, syllables, or concepts. It was used for official and monumental inscriptions in ancient Egypt. Because of the long period of study required to master this system, literacy in hieroglyphics was confined to a rela-tively small group of **scribes** and administrators. Cursive symbol-forms were developed for rapid composition on other media, such as **papyrus.** *(p. 30)*

Hinduism A general term for a wide variety of beliefs and ritual practices that have developed in the Indian subcon-tinent since antiquity. Hinduism has roots in ancient Vedic, Buddhist, and south Indian religious concepts and practices. It spread along the trade routes to Southeast Asia. *(p. 137)*

Hiroshima City in Japan, the first to be destroyed by an atomic bomb, on August 6, 1945. The bombing hastened the end of World War II. *(p. 727)*

history The study of past events and changes in the devel-opment, transmission, and transformation of cultural practices. *(p. 6)*

Hitler, Adolf (1889–1945) Born in Austria, Hitler became a radical German nationalist during World War I. He led the National Socialist German Workers' Party—the **Nazis**—in the 1920s and became dictator of Germany in 1933. He led Europe into World War II. *(p. 715)*

Hittites A people from central Anatolia who established an empire in Anatolia and Syria in the Late Bronze Age. With wealth from the trade in metals and military power based on chariot forces, the Hittites vied with New Kingdom Egypt for control of Syria-Palestine before falling to unidentified attackers ca. 1200 B.C.E. (See also **Ramesses II.**) *(p. 72)*

Holocaust Nazis' program during World War II to kill people they considered undesirable. Some 6 million Jews perished during the Holocaust, along with millions of Poles, Gypsies, Communists, Socialists, and others. *(p. 730)*

Holocene The geological era since the end of the Great Ice Age about 13,000 years ago. *(p. 11)*

Holy Roman Empire Loose federation of mostly German states and principalities, headed by an emperor elected by the princes. It lasted from 962 to 1806. *(pp. 242, 430)*

hoplite A heavily armored Greek infantryman of the Archaic and Classical periods who fought in the close-packed phalanx formation. Hoplite armies—militias composed of middle- and upper-class citizens supplying their own equipment—were for centuries superior to all other military forces. *(p. 114)*

horse collar Harnessing method that increased the efficiency of horses by shifting the point of traction from the animal's neck to the shoulders; its adoption favors the spread of horse-drawn plows and vehicles. *(p. 249)*

House of Burgesses Elected assembly in colonial Virginia, created in 1618. *(p. 453)*

humanists (Renaissance) European scholars, writers, and teachers associated with the study of the humanities (grammar, rhetoric, poetry, history, languages, and moral philosophy), influential in the fifteenth century and later. *(p. 376)*

Hundred Years War (1337–1453) Series of campaigns over control of the throne of France, involving English and French royal families and French noble families. *(p. 380)*

Husayn, Saddam (b. 1937) President of Iraq from 1979 until overthrown by an American-led invasion in 2003. Waged war on Iran from 1980 to 1988. His invasion of Kuwait in 1990 was repulsed in the Persian Gulf War in 1991. *(p. 796)*

Ibn Battuta (1304–1369) Moroccan Muslim scholar, the most widely traveled individual of his time. He wrote a detailed account of his visits to Islamic lands from China to Spain and the western Sudan. *(p. 341)*

Il-khan A "secondary" or "peripheral" khan based in Persia. The Il-khans' khanate was founded by Hülegü, a grandson of **Genghis Khan,** and was based at Tabriz in modern Azerbaijan. It controlled much of Iran and Iraq. *(p. 318)*

import-substitution industrialization An economic system aimed at building a country's industry by restricting foreign trade. It was especially popular in Latin American countries such as Mexico, Argentina, and Brazil in the mid-twentieth century. It proved successful for a time but could not keep up with technological advances in Europe and North America. *(p. 754)*

Inca Largest and most powerful Andean empire. Controlled the Pacific coast of South America from Ecuador to Chile from its capital of Cuzco. *(p. 299)*

indentured servant A migrant to British colonies in the Americas who paid for passage by agreeing to work for a set term ranging from four to seven years. *(p. 453)*

Indian Civil Service The elite professional class of officials who administered the government of British India. Originally composed exclusively of well-educated British men, it gradually added qualified Indians. *(p. 611)*

Indian National Congress A movement and political party founded in 1885 to demand greater Indian participation in government. Its membership was middle class, and its

demands were modest until World War I. Led after 1920 by Mohandas K. Gandhi, it appealed increasingly to the poor, and it organized mass protests demanding self-government and independence. (See also **Gandhi, Mohandas K.**) *(pp. 613, 736)*

Indian Ocean Maritime System In premodern times, a network of seaports, trade routes, and maritime culture linking countries on the rim of the Indian Ocean from Africa to Indonesia. *(p. 181)*

indulgence The forgiveness of the punishment due for past sins, granted by the Catholic Church authorities as a reward for a pious act. Martin Luther's protest against the sale of indulgences is often seen as touching off the **Protestant Reformation.** *(p. 416)*

Industrial Revolution The transformation of the economy, the environment, and living conditions, occurring first in England in the eighteenth century, that resulted from the use of steam engines, the mechanization of manufacturing in factories, and innovations in transportation and communication. *(p. 550)*

investiture controversy Dispute between the popes and the Holy Roman Emperors over who held ultimate authority over bishops in imperial lands. *(p. 242)*

Irigoyen, Hipólito (1850–1933) Argentine politician, president of Argentina from 1916 to 1922 and 1928 to 1930. The first president elected by universal male suffrage, he began his presidency as a reformer, but later became conservative. *(p. 753)*

Iron Age Historians' term for the period during which iron was the primary metal for tools and weapons. The advent of iron technology began at different times in different parts of the world. *(p. 70)*

iron curtain Winston Churchill's term for the Cold War division between the Soviet-dominated East and the U.S.-dominated West. *(p. 764)*

Iroquois Confederacy An alliance of five northeastern Amerindian peoples (six after 1722) that made decisions on military and diplomatic issues through a council of representatives. Allied first with the Dutch and later with the English, the Confederacy dominated the area from western New England to the Great Lakes. *(p. 454)*

Islam Religion expounded by the Prophet **Muhammad** (570–632 C.E.) on the basis of his reception of divine revelations, which were collected after his death into the **Quran.** In the tradition of Judaism and Christianity, and sharing much of their lore, Islam calls on all people to recognize one creator god—Allah—who rewards or punishes believers after death according to how they led their lives. (See also **hadith.**) *(p. 207)*

Israel In antiquity, the land between the eastern shore of the Mediterranean and the Jordan River, occupied by the Israelites from the early second millennium B.C.E. The modern state of Israel was founded in 1948. *(p. 85)*

Janissaries Infantry, originally of slave origin, armed with firearms and constituting the elite of the Ottoman army from the fifteenth century until the corps was abolished in 1826. *(pp. 475, 573)*

jati. See **varna.**

Jesus (ca. 5 B.C.E.–34 C.E.) A Jew from Galilee in northern Israel who sought to reform Jewish beliefs and practices. He was executed as a revolutionary by the Romans. Hailed as the Messiah and son of God by his followers, he became the central figure in Christianity, a belief system that developed in the centuries after his death. *(p. 157)*

Jinnah, Muhammad Ali (1876–1948) Indian Muslim politician who founded the state of Pakistan. A lawyer by training, he joined the **All-India Muslim League** in 1913. As leader of the League from the 1920s on, he negotiated with the British and the **Indian National Congress** for Muslim participation in Indian politics. From 1940 on, he led the movement for the independence of India's Muslims in a separate state of Pakistan, founded in 1947. *(p. 741)*

joint-stock company A business, often backed by a government charter, that sold shares to individuals to raise money for its trading enterprises and to spread the risks (and profits) among many investors. *(p. 425)*

junk A very large flatbottom sailing ship produced in the **Tang, Ming,** and **Song Empires,** specially designed for long-distance commercial travel. *(p. 269)*

Kamakura Shogunate The first of Japan's decentralized military governments (1185–1333). *(p. 278)*

kamikaze The "divine wind," which the Japanese credited with blowing Mongol invaders away from their shores in 1281. *(p. 335)*

Kangxi (1654–1722) Qing emperor (r. 1662–1722). He oversaw the greatest expansion of the **Qing Empire.** *(p. 507)*

karma In Indian tradition, the residue of deeds performed in past and present lives that adheres to a "spirit" and determines what form it will assume in its next life cycle. The doctrines of karma and reincarnation were used by the elite in ancient India to encourage people to accept their social position and do their duty. *(p. 134)*

keiretsu Alliances of corporations and banks that dominate the Japanese economy. *(p. 797)*

khipu System of knotted colored cords used by preliterate Andean peoples to transmit information. *(p. 295)*

Khomeini, Ayatollah Ruhollah (1900?–1989) Shi'ite philosopher and cleric who led the overthrow of the shah of Iran in 1979 and created an Islamic republic. *(p. 796)*

Khubilai Khan (1215–1294) Last of the Mongol Great Khans (r. 1260–1294) and founder of the **Yuan Empire.** Original architect of the Forbidden City. *(p. 325)*

Kievan Russia State established at Kiev in Ukraine ca. 822 by Scandinavian adventurers asserting authority over a mostly Slavic farming population. *(p. 228)*

Korean War (1950–1953) Conflict that began with North Korea's invasion of South Korea and came to involve the United Nations (primarily the United States) allying with South Korea and the People's Republic of China allying with North Korea. *(p. 771)*

Koryo Korean kingdom founded in 918 and destroyed by a Mongol invasion in 1259. *(p. 275)*

Kush An Egyptian name for Nubia, the region alongside the Nile River south of Egypt, where an indigenous kingdom with its own distinctive institutions and cultural traditions arose beginning in the early second millennium B.C.E. It was deeply influenced by Egyptian culture and at times under the control of Egypt, which coveted its rich deposits of gold and luxury products from sub-Saharan Africa carried up the Nile corridor. *(p. 55)*

labor union An organization of workers in a particular industry or trade, created to defend the interests of members through strikes or negotiations with employers. *(p. 636)*

laissez faire The idea that government should refrain from interfering in economic affairs. The classic exposition of laissez-faire principles is Adam Smith's *Wealth of Nations* (1776). *(p. 563)*

lama In Tibetan Buddhism, a teacher. *(p. 326)*

Las Casas, Bartolomé de (1474–1566) First bishop of Chiapas, in southern Mexico. He devoted most of his life to protecting Amerindian peoples from exploitation. His major achievement was the New Laws of 1542, which limited the ability of Spanish settlers to compel Amerindians to labor for them. (See also **encomienda.**) *(p. 444)*

Latin West Historians' name for the territories of Europe that adhered to the Latin rite of Christianity and used the Latin language for intellectual exchange in the period ca. 1000–1500. *(p. 363)*

League of Nations International organization founded in 1919 to promote world peace and cooperation but greatly weakened by the refusal of the United States to join. It proved ineffectual in stopping aggression by Italy, Japan, and Germany in the 1930s, and it was superseded by the **United Nations** in 1945. *(p. 691)*

Legalism In China, a political philosophy that emphasized the unruliness of human nature and justified state coercion and control. The **Qin** ruling class invoked it to validate the authoritarian nature of their regime and its profligate expenditure of subjects' lives and labor. It was superseded in the **Han** era by a more benevolent Confucian doctrine of governmental moderation. *(p. 51)*

"legitimate" trade Exports from Africa in the nineteenth century that did not include the newly outlawed slave trade. *(p. 604)*

Lenin, Vladimir (1870–1924) Leader of the Bolshevik (later Communist) Party. He lived in exile in Switzerland until 1917, then returned to Russia to lead the Bolsheviks to victory during the Russian Revolution and the civil war that followed. *(p. 689)*

Leopold II (1835–1909) King of Belgium (r. 1865–1909). He was active in encouraging the exploration of Central Africa and became the ruler of the Congo Free State (to 1908). *(p. 663)*

liberalism A political ideology that emphasizes the civil rights of citizens, representative government, and the protection of private property. This ideology, derived from the **Enlightenment,** was especially popular among the property-owning middle classes of Europe and North America. *(p. 639)*

Linear B A set of syllabic symbols, derived from the writing system of **Minoan** Crete, used in the Mycenaean palaces of the Late Bronze Age to write an early form of Greek. It was used primarily for palace records, and the surviving Linear B tablets provide substantial information about the economic organization of Mycenaean society and tantalizing clues about political, social, and religious institutions. *(p. 79)*

Li Shimin (599–649) One of the founders of the **Tang Empire** and its second emperor (r. 626–649). He led the expansion of the empire into Central Asia. *(p. 258)*

Little Ice Age A century-long period of cool climate that began in the 1590s. Its ill effects on agriculture in northern Europe were notable. *(p. 427)*

llama A hoofed animal indigenous to the Andes Mountains in South America. It was the only domesticated beast of burden in the Americas before the arrival of Europeans. It provided meat and wool. The use of llamas to transport goods made possible specialized production and trade among people living in different ecological zones and fostered the integration of these zones by **Chavín** and later Andean states. *(p. 65)*

loess A fine, light silt deposited by wind and water. It constitutes the fertile soil of the Yellow River Valley in northern China. Because loess soil is not compacted, it can be worked with a simple digging stick, but it leaves the region vulnerable to devastating earthquakes. *(p. 46)*

Long March (1934–1935) The 6,000-mile (9,700-kilometer) flight of Chinese Communists from southeastern to northwestern China. The Communists, led by **Mao Zedong,** were pursued by the Chinese army under orders from **Chiang Kai-shek.** The four thousand survivors of the march formed the nucleus of a revived Communist movement that defeated the **Guomindang** after World War II. *(p. 720)*

L'Ouverture, Toussaint (1743–1803) Leader of the Haitian Revolution. He freed the slaves and gained effective independence for Haiti despite military interventions by the British and French. *(p. 538)*

ma'at Egyptian term for the concept of divinely created and maintained order in the universe. Reflecting the ancient Egyptians' belief in an essentially beneficent world, the divine ruler was the earthly guarantor of this order. (See also **pyramid.**) *(p. 29)*

Macartney mission (1792–1793) The unsuccessful attempt by the British Empire to establish diplomatic relations with the **Qing Empire.** *(p. 510)*

Magellan, Ferdinand (1480?–1521) Portuguese navigator who led the Spanish expedition of 1519–1522 that was the first to sail around the world. *(p. 398)*

Mahabharata A vast epic chronicling the events leading up to a cataclysmic battle between related kinship groups in early India. It includes the **Bhagavad-Gita,** the most important work of Indian sacred literature. *(p. 140)*

Mahayana Buddhism "Great Vehicle" branch of Buddhism followed in China, Japan, and Central Asia. The focus is on reverence for **Buddha** and for bodhisattvas, enlightened persons who have postponed nirvana to help others attain enlightenment. *(p. 136)*

Malacca Port city in the modern Southeast Asian country of Malaysia, founded about 1400 as a trading center on the Strait of Malacca. Also spelled Melaka. *(p. 356)*

Mali Empire created by indigenous Muslims in western Sudan of West Africa from the thirteenth to fifteenth century. It was famous for its role in the trans-Saharan gold trade. (See also **Mansa Kankan Musa, Timbuktu.**) *(p. 345)*

Malthus, Thomas (1766–1834) Eighteenth-century English intellectual who warned that population growth threatened future generations because, in his view, population growth would always outstrip increases in agricultural production. *(p. 804)*

mamluks Under the Islamic system of military slavery, Turkic military slaves who formed an important part of the armed forces of the **Abbasid Caliphate** of the ninth and tenth centuries. Mamluks eventually founded their own state, ruling Egypt and Syria (1250–1517). *(p. 212)*

Manchu Federation of Northeast Asian peoples who founded the **Qing Empire.** *(p. 496)*

Mandate of Heaven Chinese religious and political ideology developed by the **Zhou,** according to which it was the prerogative of Heaven, the chief deity, to grant power to the ruler of China and to take away that power if the ruler failed to conduct himself justly and in the best interests of his subjects. *(p. 49)*

mandate system Allocation of former German colonies and Ottoman possessions to the victorious powers after World War I, to be administered under League of Nations supervision. *(p. 696)*

manor In medieval Europe, a large, self-sufficient landholding consisting of the lord's residence (manor house), outbuildings, peasant village, and surrounding land. *(p. 237)*

mansabs In India, grants of land given in return for service by rulers of the **Mughal Empire.** *(p. 486)*

Mansa Kankan Musa Ruler of **Mali** (r. 1312–1337). His pilgrimage through Egypt to **Mecca** in 1324–1325 established the empire's reputation for wealth in the Mediterranean world. *(p. 346)*

Mao Zedong (1893–1976) Leader of the Chinese Communist Party (1927–1976). He led the Communists on the **Long March** (1934–1935) and rebuilt the Communist Party and Red Army during the Japanese occupation of China (1937–1945). After World War II, he led the Communists to victory over the **Guomindang.** He ordered the **Cultural Revolution** in 1966. *(p. 719)*

maroon A slave who ran away from his or her master. Often a member of a community of runaway slaves in the West Indies and South America. *(p. 460)*

Marshall Plan U.S. program to support the reconstruction of western Europe after World War II. By 1961 more than $20 billion in economic aid had been disbursed. *(p. 769)*

Marx, Karl (1818–1883) German journalist and philosopher, founder of the Marxist branch of **socialism.** He is known for two books: *The Communist Manifesto* (1848) and *Das Kapital* (Vols. I–III, 1867–1894). *(p. 636)*

mass deportation The forcible removal and relocation of large numbers of people or entire populations. The mass deportations practiced by the Assyrian and Persian Empires were meant as a terrifying warning of the consequences of rebellion. They also brought skilled and unskilled labor to the imperial center. *(p. 82)*

mass production The manufacture of many identical products by the division of labor into many small repetitive tasks. This method was introduced into the manufacture of pottery by Josiah Wedgwood and into the spinning of cotton thread by Richard Arkwright. (See also **Industrial Revolution; Wedgwood, Josiah.**) *(p. 553)*

Mauryan Empire The first state to unify most of the Indian subcontinent. It was founded by Chandragupta Maurya in 324 B.C.E. and survived until 184 B.C.E. From its capital at Pataliputra in the Ganges Valley it grew wealthy from taxes on agriculture, iron mining, and control of trade routes. (See also **Ashoka.**) *(p. 139)*

Maya Mesoamerican civilization concentrated in Mexico's Yucatán Peninsula and in Guatemala and Honduras but never unified into a single empire. Major contributions were in mathematics, astronomy, and development of the calendar. *(p. 284)*

Mecca City in western Arabia; birthplace of the Prophet **Muhammad,** and ritual center of the Islamic religion. *(p. 204)*

mechanization The application of machinery to manufacturing and other activities. Among the first processes to be mechanized were the spinning of cotton thread and the weaving of cloth in late-eighteenth- and early-nineteenth-century England. *(p. 554)*

medieval Literally "middle age," a term that historians of Europe use for the period ca. 500 to ca. 1500, signifying its intermediate point between Greco-Roman antiquity and the Renaissance. *(p. 228)*

Medina City in western Arabia to which the Prophet **Muhammad** and his followers emigrated in 622 to escape persecution in **Mecca.** *(p. 207)*

megaliths Structures and complexes of very large stones constructed for ceremonial and religious purposes in **Neolithic** times. *(p. 12)*

Meiji Restoration The political program that followed the destruction of the **Tokugawa Shogunate** in 1868, in which a collection of young leaders set Japan on the path of centralization, industrialization, and imperialism. (See also **Yamagata Aritomo.**) *(p. 642)*

Memphis The capital of Old Kingdom Egypt, near the head of the Nile Delta. Early rulers were interred in the nearby **pyramids.** *(p. 30)*

Menelik II (1844–1911) Emperor of Ethiopia (r. 1889–1911). He enlarged Ethiopia to its present dimensions and defeated an Italian invasion at Adowa (1896). *(p. 666)*

mercantilism European government policies of the sixteenth, seventeenth, and eighteenth centuries designed to promote overseas trade between a country and its colonies and accumulate precious metals by requiring colonies to trade only with their motherland country. The British system was defined by the Navigation Acts, the French system by laws known as the *Exclusif.* *(p. 461)*

Meroë Capital of a flourishing kingdom in southern Nubia from the fourth century B.C.E. to the fourth century C.E. In this period Nubian culture shows more independence from Egypt and the influence of sub-Saharan Africa. *(p. 55)*

Ming Empire (1368–1644) Empire based in China that Zhu Yuanzhang established after the overthrow of the **Yuan Empire.** The Ming emperor **Yongle** sponsored additions to the Forbidden City and the voyages of **Zheng He.** The later years of the Ming saw a slowdown in technological development and economic decline. *(pp. 328, 502)*

Minoan Prosperous civilization on the Aegean island of Crete in the second millennium B.C.E. The Minoans engaged in far-flung commerce around the Mediterranean and exerted powerful cultural influences on the early Greeks. *(p. 76)*

mit'a Andean labor system based on shared obligations to help kinsmen and work on behalf of the ruler and religious organizations. *(p. 296)*

Moche Civilization of the north coast of Peru (200–700 C.E.). An important Andean civilization that built extensive irrigation networks as well as impressive urban centers dominated by brick temples. *(p. 296)*

Moctezuma II (1466?–1520) Last Aztec emperor, overthrown by the Spanish conquistador **Hernán Cortés.** *(p. 404)*

modernization The process of reforming political, military, economic, social, and cultural traditions in imitation of the early success of Western societies, often with regard for accommodating local traditions in non-Western societies. *(p. 603)*

Mohenjo-Daro Largest of the cities of the Indus Valley civilization. It was centrally located in the extensive floodplain of the Indus River in contemporary Pakistan. Little is known about the political institutions of Indus Valley communities, but the large-scale of construction at Mohenjo-Daro, the orderly grid of streets, and the standardization of building materials are evidence of central planning. *(p. 36)*

moksha The Hindu concept of the spirit's "liberation" from the endless cycle of rebirths. There are various avenues—such as physical discipline, meditation, and acts of devotion to the gods—by which the spirit can distance itself from desire for the things of this world and be merged with the divine force that animates the universe. *(p. 135)*

monasticism Living in a religious community apart from secular society and adhering to a rule stipulating chastity, obedience, and poverty. It was a prominent element of medieval Christianity and Buddhism. Monasteries were the primary centers of learning and literacy in medieval Europe. *(p. 243)*

Mongols A people of this name is mentioned as early as the records of the **Tang Empire,** living as nomads in northern Eurasia. After 1206 they established an enormous empire under **Genghis Khan,** linking western and eastern Eurasia. *(p. 310)*

monotheism Belief in the existence of a single divine entity. Some scholars cite the devotion of the Egyptian pharaoh **Akhenaten** to Aten (sun-disk) and his suppression of traditional gods as the earliest instance. The Israelite worship of Yahweh developed into an exclusive belief in one god, and this concept passed into Christianity and **Islam.** *(p. 91)*

monsoon Seasonal winds in the Indian Ocean caused by the differences in temperature between the rapidly heating and cooling landmasses of Africa and Asia and the slowly changing ocean waters. These strong and predictable winds have long been ridden across the open sea by sailors, and the large amounts of rainfall that they deposit on parts of India, Southeast Asia, and China allow for the cultivation of several crops a year. *(pp. 132, 341)*

most-favored-nation status A clause in a commercial treaty that awards to any later signatories all the privileges previously granted to the original signatories. *(p. 587)*

movable type Type in which each individual character is cast on a separate piece of metal. It replaced woodblock printing, allowing for the arrangement of individual letters and other characters on a page, rather than requiring the carving of entire pages at a time. It may have been invented in Korea in the thirteenth century. (See also **printing press.**) *(p. 271)*

Mughal Empire Muslim state (1526–1857) exercising dominion over most of India in the sixteenth and seventeenth centuries. *(p. 486)*

Muhammad (570–632 C.E.) Arab prophet; founder of religion of **Islam.** *(p. 206)*

Muhammad Ali (1769–1849) Leader of Egyptian modernization in the early nineteenth century. He ruled Egypt as an Ottoman governor, but had imperial ambitions. His descendants ruled Egypt until overthrown in 1952. *(pp. 572, 603)*

mummy A body preserved by chemical processes or special natural circumstances, often in the belief that the deceased will need it again in the afterlife. In ancient Egypt the bodies of people who could afford mummification underwent a complex process of removing organs, filling body cavities, dehydrating the corpse with natron, and then wrapping the body with linen bandages and enclosing it in a wooden sarcophagus. *(p. 34)*

Muscovy Russian principality that emerged gradually during the era of Mongol domination. The Muscovite dynasty ruled without interruption from 1276 to 1598. *(p. 512)*

Muslim An adherent of the Islamic religion; a person who "submits" (in Arabic, *Islam* means "submission") to the will of God. *(p. 207)*

Mussolini, Benito (1883–1945) Fascist dictator of Italy (1922–1943). He led Italy to conquer Ethiopia (1935), joined Germany in the Axis pact (1936), and allied Italy with Germany in World War II. He was overthrown in 1943 when the Allies invaded Italy. *(p. 715)*

Mycenae Site of a fortified palace complex in southern Greece that controlled a Late Bronze Age kingdom. In Homer's epic poems Mycenae was the base of King Agamemnon, who commanded the Greeks besieging Troy. Contemporary archaeologists call the complex Greek society of the second millennium B.C.E. "Mycenaean." *(p. 78)*

Napoleon I (1769–1821) Overthrew French Directory in 1799 and became emperor of the French in 1804. Failed to defeat Great Britain and abdicated in 1814. Returned to power briefly in 1815 but was defeated and died in exile. *(p. 534)*

Nasir al-Din Tusi (1201–1274) Persian mathematician and cosmologist whose academy near Tabriz provided the model for the movement of the planets that helped to inspire the Copernican model of the solar system. *(p. 321)*

National Assembly French Revolutionary assembly (1789–1791). Called first as the Estates General, the three estates came together and demanded radical change. It passed the **Declaration of the Rights of Man** in 1789. *(p. 531)*

nationalism A political ideology that stresses people's membership in a nation—a community defined by a common culture and history as well as by territory. In the late eighteenth and early nineteenth centuries, nationalism was a force for unity in western Europe. In the late nineteenth century it hastened the disintegration of the Austro-Hungarian and Ottoman Empires. In the twentieth century it provided the ideological foundation for scores of independent countries emerging from **colonialism.** *(p. 639)*

nawab A Muslim prince allied to British India; technically, a semi-autonomous deputy of the Mughal emperor. *(p. 606)*

Nazis German political party joined by Adolf Hitler, emphasizing nationalism, racism, and war. When Hitler became chancellor of Germany in 1933, the Nazis became the only legal party and an instrument of Hitler's absolute rule. The party's formal name was National Socialist German Workers' Party. (See also **Hitler, Adolf.**) *(p. 715)*

Nehru, Jawaharlal (1889–1964) Indian statesman. He succeeded **Mohandas K. Gandhi** as leader of the **Indian National Congress.** He negotiated the end of British colonial rule in India and became India's first prime minister (1947–1964). *(p. 740)*

Neo-Assyrian Empire An empire extending from western Iran to Syria-Palestine, conquered by the Assyrians of northern Mesopotamia between the tenth and seventh centuries B.C.E. They used force and terror and exploited the wealth and labor of their subjects. They also preserved and continued the cultural and scientific developments of Mesopotamian civilization. *(p. 81)*

Neo-Babylonian kingdom Under the Chaldaeans (nomadic kinship groups that settled in southern Mesopotamia in the early first millennium B.C.E.), **Babylon** again became a major political and cultural center in the seventh and sixth centuries B.C.E. After participating in the destruction of Assyrian power, the monarchs Nabopolassar and Nebuchadnezzar took over the southern portion of the Assyrian domains. By destroying the **First Temple** in Jerusalem and deporting part of the population, they initiated the **Diaspora** of the Jews. *(p. 98)*

neo-Confucianism Term used to describe new approaches to understanding classic Confucian texts that became the basic ruling philosophy of China from the **Song** period to the twentieth century. *(p. 270)*

neo-liberalism The term used in Latin America and other developing regions to describe free-market policies that include reducing tariff protection for local industries; the sale of public-sector industries, like national airlines and public utilities, to private investors or foreign corporations; and the reduction of social welfare policies and public-sector employment. *(p. 793)*

Neolithic The period of the Stone Age associated with the ancient **Agricultural Revolution(s).** It follows the **Paleolithic** period. *(p. 6)*

Nevskii, Alexander (1220–1263) Prince of Novgorod (r. 1236–1263). He submitted to the invading Mongols in 1240 and received recognition as the leader of the Russian princes under the **Golden Horde.** *(p. 323)*

New Economic Policy Policy proclaimed by Vladimir Lenin in March 1921 to encourage the revival of the Soviet economy by allowing small private enterprises. Joseph Stalin ended the N.E.P. in 1929 and replaced it with a series of **Five-Year Plans.** (See also **Lenin, Vladimir.**) *(p. 692)*

New France French colony in North America, with a capital in Quebec, founded 1608. New France fell to the British in 1763. *(p. 454)*

New Imperialism Historians' term for the late-nineteenth- and early-twentieth-century wave of conquests by European powers, the United States, and Japan, which were followed by the development and exploitation of the newly conquered territories for the benefit of the colonial powers. *(p. 654)*

newly industrialized economies (NIEs) Rapidly growing, new industrial nations of the late twentieth century, including the **Asian Tigers.** *(p. 798)*

new monarchies Historians' term for the monarchies in France, England, and Spain from 1450 to 1600. The centralization of royal power was increasing within more or less fixed territorial limits. *(p. 382)*

nomadism A way of life, forced by a scarcity of resources, in which groups of people continually migrate to find pastures and water. *(p. 311)*

nonaligned nations Developing countries that announced their neutrality in the **Cold War.** *(p. 780)*

nongovernmental organizations (NGOs) Nonprofit international organizations devoted to investigating human rights abuses and providing humanitarian relief. Two NGOs won the Nobel Peace Prize in the 1990s: International Campaign to Ban Landmines (1997) and Doctors Without Borders (1999). *(p. 831)*

North Atlantic Treaty Organization (NATO) Organization formed in 1949 as a military alliance of western European and North American states against the Soviet Union and its east European allies. (See also **Warsaw Pact.**) *(p. 765)*

Olmec The first Mesoamerican civilization. Between ca. 1200 and 400 B.C.E., the Olmec people of central Mexico created a vibrant civilization that included intensive agriculture, wide-ranging trade, ceremonial centers, and monumental construction. The Olmec had great cultural influence on later Mesoamerican societies, passing on artistic styles, religious imagery, sophisticated astronomical observation for the construction of calendars, and a ritual ball game. *(p. 62)*

Oman Arab state based in Musqat, the main port in the southeastern region of the Arabian peninsula. Oman succeeded Portugal as a power in the western Indian Ocean in the eighteenth century. *(p. 491)*

Opium War (1839–1842) War between Britain and the **Qing Empire** that was, in the British view, occasioned by the Qing government's refusal to permit the importation of opium into its territories. The victorious British imposed the one-sided **Treaty of Nanking** on China. *(p. 587)*

Organization of Petroleum Exporting Countries (OPEC) Organization formed in 1960 by oil-producing states to promote their collective interest in generating revenue from oil. *(p. 783)*

Ottoman Empire Islamic state founded by Osman in northwestern Anatolia ca. 1300. After the fall of the **Byzantine Empire,** the Ottoman Empire was based at Istanbul (formerly Constantinople) from 1453 to 1922. It encompassed lands in the Middle East, North Africa, the Caucasus, and eastern Europe. *(pp. 325, 472)*

Paleolithic The period of the Stone Age associated with the evolution of humans. It predates the **Neolithic** period. *(p. 6)*

Pan-Slavism Movement among Russian intellectuals in the second half of the nineteenth century to identify culturally and politically with the Slavic peoples of eastern Europe. *(p. 582)*

Panama Canal Ship canal cut across the isthmus of Panama by United States Army engineers; it opened in 1914. It greatly shortened the sea voyage between the east and west coasts of North America. The United States turned the canal over to Panama on January 1, 2000. *(p. 676)*

papacy The central administration of the Roman Catholic Church, of which the pope is the head. *(pp. 241, 415)*

papyrus A reed that grows along the banks of the Nile River in Egypt. From it was produced a coarse, paper-like writing medium used by the Egyptians and many other peoples in the ancient Mediterranean and Middle East. *(p. 30)*

Parthians Iranian ruling dynasty between ca. 250 B.C.E. and 226 C.E. *(p. 177)*

patron/client relationship In ancient Rome, a fundamental social relationship in which the patron—a wealthy and powerful individual—provided legal and economic protection and assistance to clients, men of lesser status and means, and in return the clients supported the political careers and economic interests of their patron. *(p. 150)*

Paul (ca. 5–65 C.E.) A Jew from the Greek city of Tarsus in Anatolia, he initially persecuted the followers of **Jesus** but, after receiving a revelation on the road to Syrian Damascus, became a Christian. Taking advantage of his Hellenized background and Roman citizenship, he traveled throughout Syria-Palestine, Anatolia, and Greece, preaching the new religion and establishing churches. Finding his greatest success among pagans ("gentiles"), he began the process by which Christianity separated from Judaism. *(p. 158)*

pax romana Literally, "Roman peace," it connoted the stability and prosperity that Roman rule brought to the lands of the Roman Empire in the first two centuries C.E. The movement of people and trade goods along Roman roads and safe seas allowed for the spread of cultural practices, technologies, and religious ideas. *(p. 156)*

Pearl Harbor Naval base in Hawaii attacked by Japanese aircraft on December 7, 1941. The sinking of much of the U.S. Pacific Fleet brought the United States into World War II. *(p. 725)*

Peloponnesian War A protracted (431–404 B.C.E.) and costly conflict between the Athenian and Spartan alliance systems that convulsed most of the Greek world. The war was largely a consequence of Athenian imperialism. Possession of a naval empire allowed Athens to fight a war of attrition. Ultimately, Sparta prevailed because of Athenian errors and Persian financial support. *(p. 123)*

perestroika Policy of "openness" that was the centerpiece of Mikhail Gorbachev's efforts to liberalize communism in the Soviet Union. (See also **Gorbachev, Mikhail.**) *(p. 800)*

Pericles (ca. 495–429 B.C.E.) Aristocratic leader who guided the Athenian state through the transformation to full participatory democracy for all male citizens, supervised construction of the Acropolis, and pursued a policy of imperial expansion that led to the **Peloponnesian War.** He formulated a strategy of attrition but died from the plague early in the war. *(p. 119)*

Perón, Eva Duarte (1919–1952) Wife of **Juan Perón** and champion of the poor in Argentina. She was a gifted speaker and popular political leader who campaigned to improve the life of the urban poor by founding schools and hospitals and providing other social benefits. *(p. 756)*

Perón, Juan (1895–1974) President of Argentina (1946–1955, 1973–1974). As a military officer, he championed the rights of labor. Aided by his wife **Eva Duarte Perón,** he was elected president in 1946. He built up Argentinean industry, became very popular among the urban poor, but harmed the economy. *(p. 756)*

Perry, Commodore Matthew A navy commander who, on July 8, 1853, became the first foreigner to break through the barriers that had kept Japan isolated from the rest of the world for 250 years. *(p. 626)*

Persepolis A complex of palaces, reception halls, and treasury buildings erected by the Persian kings **Darius I** and Xerxes in the Persian homeland. It is believed that the New Year's festival was celebrated here, as well as the coronations, weddings, and funerals of the Persian kings, who were buried in cliff-tombs nearby. *(p. 111)*

Persian Wars Conflicts between Greek city-states and the Persian Empire, ranging from the Ionian Revolt (499–494 B.C.E.) through Darius's punitive expedition that failed at Marathon (490 B.C.E.) and the defeat of Xerxes' massive invasion of Greece by the Spartan-led Hellenic League (480–479 B.C.E.). This first major setback for Persian arms launched the Greeks into their period of greatest cultural productivity. **Herodotus** chronicled these events in the first "history" in the Western tradition. *(p. 120)*

Peter the Great (1672–1725) Russian tsar (r. 1689–1725). He enthusiastically introduced Western languages and technologies to the Russian elite, moving the capital from Moscow to the new city of St. Petersburg. *(p. 515)*

pharaoh The central figure in the ancient Egyptian state. Believed to be an earthly manifestation of the gods, he used his absolute power to maintain the safety and prosperity of Egypt. *(p. 29)*

Phoenicians Semitic-speaking Canaanites living on the coast of modern Lebanon and Syria in the first millennium B.C.E. From major cities such as Tyre and Sidon, Phoenician merchants and sailors explored the Mediterranean, engaged in widespread commerce, and founded **Carthage** and other colonies in the western Mediterranean. *(p. 92)*

pilgrimage Journey to a sacred shrine by Christians seeking to show their piety, fulfill vows, or gain absolution for sins. Other religions also have pilgrimage traditions, such as the Muslim pilgrimage to **Mecca** and the pilgrimages made by early Chinese Buddhists to India in search of sacred Buddhist writings. *(p. 251)*

Pilgrims Group of English Protestant dissenters who established Plymouth Colony in Massachusetts in 1620 to seek religious freedom after having lived briefly in the Netherlands. *(p. 453)*

Pizarro, Francisco (ca. 1478–1541) Spanish explorer who led the conquest of the **Inca** Empire of Peru in 1531–1533. *(p. 405)*

Planck, Max (1858–1947) German physicist who developed quantum theory and was awarded the Nobel Prize for physics in 1918. *(p. 702)*

polis The Greek term for a **city-state,** an urban center and the agricultural territory under its control. It was the characteristic form of political organization in southern and central Greece in the Archaic and Classical periods. Of the hundreds of city-states in the Mediterranean and Black Sea regions settled by Greeks, some were oligarchic, others democratic, depending on the powers delegated to the Council and the Assembly. *(p. 114)*

positivism A philosophy developed by the French count of Saint-Simon. Positivists believed that social and economic problems could be solved by the application of the scientific method, leading to continuous progress. Their ideas became popular in France and Latin America in the nineteenth century. *(p. 564)*

Potosí Located in Bolivia, one of the richest silver mining centers and most populous cities in colonial Spanish America. *(p. 447)*

printing press A mechanical device for transferring text or graphics from a woodblock or type to paper using ink. Presses using movable type first appeared in Europe in about 1450. See also **movable type.** *(p. 377)*

Protestant Reformation Religious reform movement within the Latin Christian Church beginning in 1519. It resulted in the "protesters" forming several new Christian denominations, including the Lutheran and Reformed Churches and the Church of England. *(p. 416)*

proxy wars During the **Cold War,** local or regional wars in which the superpowers armed, trained, and financed the combatants. *(p. 789)*

Ptolemies The Macedonian dynasty, descended from one of Alexander the Great's officers, that ruled Egypt for three centuries (323–30 B.C.E.). From their magnificent capital at Alexandria on the Mediterranean coast, the Ptolemies largely took over the system created by Egyptian pharaohs to extract the wealth of the land, rewarding Greeks and Hellenized non-Greeks serving in the military and administration. *(p. 128)*

Puritans English Protestant dissenters who believed that God predestined souls to heaven or hell before birth. They founded Massachusetts Bay Colony in 1629. *(p. 453)*

pyramid A large, triangular stone monument, used in Egypt and Nubia as a burial place for the king. The largest pyramids, erected during the Old Kingdom near **Memphis** with stone tools and compulsory labor, reflect the Egyptian belief that the proper and spectacular burial of the divine ruler would guarantee the continued prosperity of the land. (See also **ma'at.**) *(p. 30)*

Qin A people and state in the Wei Valley of eastern China that conquered rival states and created the first Chinese empire (221–206 B.C.E.). The Qin ruler, Shi Huangdi, standardized many features of Chinese society and ruthlessly marshaled subjects for military and construction projects, engendering hostility that led to the fall of his dynasty shortly after his death. The Qin framework was largely taken over by the succeeding **Han** Empire. *(p. 164)*

Qing Empire Empire established in China by Manchus who overthrew the **Ming Empire** in 1644. At various times the Qing also controlled Manchuria, Mongolia, Turkestan, and Tibet. The last Qing emperor was overthrown in 1911. *(p. 503)*

Quran Book composed of divine revelations made to the Prophet **Muhammad** between ca. 610 and his death in 632; the sacred text of the religion of **Islam.** *(p. 208)*

railroads Networks of iron (later steel) rails on which steam (later electric or diesel) locomotives pulled long trains at high speeds. The first railroads were built in England in the 1830s. Their success caused a railroad-building boom throughout the world that lasted well into the twentieth century. *(p. 627)*

Rajputs Members of a mainly Hindu warrior caste from northwest India. The Mughal emperors drew most of their Hindu officials from this caste, and **Akbar** married a Rajput princess. *(p. 486)*

Ramesses II A long-lived ruler of New Kingdom Egypt (r. 1290–1224 B.C.E.). He reached an accommodation with the **Hittites** of Anatolia after a standoff in battle at Kadesh in Syria. He built on a grand scale throughout Egypt. *(p. 75)*

Rashid al-Din (d. 1318) Adviser to the **Il-khan** ruler Ghazan, who converted to **Islam** on Rashid's advice. *(p. 320)*

recaptives Africans rescued by Britain's Royal Navy from the illegal slave trade of the nineteenth century and restored to free status. *(p. 605)*

reconquest of Iberia Beginning in the eleventh century, military campaigns by various Iberian Christian states to recapture territory taken by Muslims. In 1492 the last Muslim ruler was defeated, and Spain and Portugal emerged as united kingdoms. *(p. 382)*

Renaissance (European) A period of intense artistic and intellectual activity, said to be a "rebirth" of Greco-Roman culture. Usually divided into an Italian Renaissance, from roughly the mid-fourteenth to mid-fifteenth century, and a Northern (trans-Alpine) Renaissance, from roughly the early fifteenth to early seventeenth century. *(pp. 375, 414)*

Revolutions of 1848 Democratic and nationalist revolutions that swept across Europe. The monarchy in France was overthrown. In Germany, Austria, Italy, and Hungary the revolutions failed. *(p. 537)*

Rhodes, Cecil (1853–1902) British entrepreneur and politician involved in the expansion of the British Empire from South Africa into Central Africa. The colonies of Southern Rhodesia (now Zimbabwe) and Northern Rhodesia (now Zambia) were named after him. *(p. 665)*

Romanization The process by which the Latin language and Roman culture became dominant in the western provinces of the Roman Empire. The Roman government did not actively seek to Romanize the subject peoples, but indigenous peoples in the provinces often chose to Romanize because of the political and economic advantages that it brought, as well as the allure of Roman success. *(p. 157)*

Roman Principate A term used to characterize Roman government in the first three centuries C.E., based on the ambiguous title *princeps* ("first citizen") adopted by Augustus to conceal his military dictatorship. *(p. 155)*

Roman Republic The period from 507 to 31 B.C.E., during which Rome was largely governed by the aristocratic **Roman Senate.** *(p. 149)*

Roman Senate A council whose members were the heads of wealthy, landowning families. Originally an advisory body to the early kings, in the era of the **Roman Republic** the Senate effectively governed the Roman state and the growing empire. Under Senate leadership, Rome conquered an empire of unprecedented extent in the lands surrounding the Mediterranean Sea. In the first century B.C.E. quarrels among powerful and ambitious senators and failure to address social and economic problems led to civil wars and the emergence of the rule of the emperors. *(p. 150)*

Royal African Company Trading company chartered by England to conduct all trade with West Africa. *(p. 461)*

sacrifice A gift given to a deity, often with the aim of creating a relationship, gaining favor, and obligating the god to provide some benefit to the sacrificer, sometimes in order to sustain the deity and thereby guarantee the continuing vitality of the natural world. The object devoted to the deity could be as simple as a cup of wine poured on the ground, a live animal slain on the altar, or, in the most extreme case, the ritual killing of a human being. *(p. 116)*

Safavid Empire Iranian kingdom (1502–1722) established by Ismail Safavi, who declared Iran a Shi'ite state. *(p. 481)*

Sahel Belt south of the Sahara; literally, "the coast" in Arabic. *(p. 188)*

samurai Literally, "those who serve." The hereditary military elite of the **Tokugawa Shogunate.** *(p. 496)*

Sandinistas Members of a leftist coalition that overthrew the Nicaraguan dictatorship of Anastasio Somoza in 1979 and attempted to install a socialist economy. The United States financed armed opposition by the Contras. The Sandinistas lost national elections in 1990. *(p. 791)*

Sanger, Margaret (1883–1966) American nurse and author; pioneer in the movement for family planning; organized conferences and established birth control clinics. *(p. 702)*

Sasanid Empire Iranian empire, established ca. 224, with a capital in Ctesiphon, Mesopotamia. The Sasanid emperors established **Zoroastrianism** as the state religion. Islamic Arab armies overthrew the empire ca. 651. *(p. 179)*

satrap The governor of a province in the Achaemenid Persian Empire, often a relative of the king. He was responsible for protecting the province and for forwarding tribute to the central administration. Satraps in outlying provinces enjoyed considerable autonomy. *(p. 110)*

savanna Tropical or subtropical grassland, either treeless or with occasional clumps of trees. Most extensive in **sub-Saharan Africa** but also present in South America. *(p. 188)*

schism A formal split within a religious community. See **Great Western Schism.** *(p. 231)*

scholasticism A philosophical and theological system, associated with Thomas Aquinas, devised to reconcile Aristotelian philosophy and Roman Catholic theology in the thirteenth century. *(p. 376)*

Scientific Revolution The intellectual movement in Europe, initially associated with planetary motion and other aspects of physics, that by the seventeenth century had laid the groundwork for modern science. *(p. 421)*

"scramble" for Africa Sudden wave of conquests in Africa by European powers in the 1880s and 1890s. Britain obtained most of eastern Africa, France most of northwestern Africa. Other countries (Germany, Belgium, Portugal, Italy, and Spain) acquired lesser amounts. *(p. 660)*

scribe In the governments of many ancient societies, a professional position reserved for men who had undergone the lengthy training required to be able to read and write using **cuneiforms, hieroglyphics,** or other early, cumbersome writing systems. *(p. 20)*

seasoning An often difficult period of adjustment to new climates, disease environments, and work routines, such as that experienced by slaves newly arrived in the Americas. *(p. 459)*

Selassie, Haile (1892–1975) Emperor of Ethiopia (r. 1930–1974) and symbol of African independence. He fought the Italian invasion of his country in 1935 and regained his throne during World War II, when British forces expelled the Italians. He ruled **Ethiopia** as a traditional autocracy until he was overthrown in 1974. *(p. 747)*

Semitic Family of related languages long spoken across parts of western Asia and northern Africa. In antiquity these languages included Hebrew, Aramaic, and Phoenician. The most widespread modern member of the Semitic family is Arabic. *(p. 16)*

"separate spheres" Nineteenth-century idea in Western societies that men and women, especially of the middle class, should have clearly differentiated roles in society: women as wives, mothers, and homemakers; men as breadwinners and participants in business and politics. *(p. 634)*

sepoy A soldier in South Asia, especially in the service of the British. *(p. 606)*

Sepoy Rebellion The revolt of Indian soldiers in 1857 against certain practices that violated religious customs; also known as the Sepoy Mutiny. *(p. 610)*

Serbia The Ottoman province in the Balkans that rose up against **Janissary** control in the early 1800s. After World War II the central province of Yugoslavia. Serb leaders struggled to maintain dominance as the Yugoslav federation dissolved in the 1990s. *(p. 573)*

serf In medieval Europe, an agricultural laborer legally bound to a lord's property and obligated to perform set services for the lord. In Russia some serfs worked as artisans and in factories; serfdom was not abolished there until 1861. *(pp. 237, 515)*

shaft graves A term used for the burial sites of elite members of Mycenaean Greek society in the mid-second millennium B.C.E. At the bottom of deep shafts lined with stone slabs, the bodies were laid out along with gold and bronze jewelry, implements, weapons, and masks. *(p. 78)*

Shah Abbas I (r. 1587–1629) The fifth and most renowned ruler of the **Safavid** dynasty in Iran. Abbas moved the royal capital to Isfahan in 1598. *(p. 482)*

shamanism The practice of identifying special individuals (shamans) who will interact with spirits for the benefit of the community. Characteristic of the Korean kingdoms of the early medieval period and of early societies of Central Asia. *(p. 274)*

Shang The dominant people in the earliest Chinese dynasty for which we have written records (ca. 1750–1027 B.C.E.). Ancestor worship, divination by means of oracle bones, and the use of bronze vessels for ritual purposes were major elements of Shang culture. *(p. 46)*

Shi Huangdi Founder of the short-lived **Qin** dynasty and creator of the Chinese Empire (r. 221–210 B.C.E.). He is remembered for his ruthless conquests of rival states, stan-

dardization of practices, and forcible organization of labor for military and engineering tasks. His tomb, with its army of life-size terracotta soldiers, has been partially excavated. *(p. 165)*

Shi'ites Muslims belonging to the branch of **Islam** believing that God vests leadership of the community in a descendant of Muhammad's son-in-law Ali. Shi'ism is the state religion of Iran. (See also **Sunnis.**) *(pp. 208, 481)*

Siberia The extreme northeastern sector of Asia, including the Kamchatka Peninsula and the present Russian coast of the Arctic Ocean, the Bering Strait, and the Sea of Okhotsk. *(p. 512)*

Silk Road Caravan routes connecting China and the Middle East across Central Asia and Iran. *(p. 175)*

Slavophiles Russian intellectuals in the early nineteenth century who favored resisting western European influences and taking pride in the traditional peasant values and institutions of the Slavic people. *(p. 582)*

"small traditions" Anthropologists' term for a localized, usually nonliterate, set of customs and beliefs adhered to by a single society, often in conjunction with a **"great tradition."** *(p. 189)*

socialism A political ideology that originated in Europe in the 1830s. Socialists advocated government protection of workers from exploitation by property owners and government ownership of industries. This ideology led to the founding of socialist or labor parties throughout Europe in the second half of the nineteenth century. (See also **Marx, Karl.**) *(p. 636)*

Socrates Athenian philosopher (ca. 470–399 B.C.E.) who shifted the emphasis of philosophical investigation from questions of natural science to ethics and human behavior. He attracted young disciples from elite families but made enemies by revealing the ignorance and pretensions of others, culminating in his trial and execution by the Athenian state. *(p. 121)*

Sokoto Caliphate A large Muslim state founded in 1809 in what is now northern Nigeria. *(p. 603)*

Solidarity Polish trade union created in 1980 to protest working conditions and political repression. It began the nationalist opposition to communist rule that led in 1989 to the fall of communism in eastern Europe. *(p. 800)*

Song Empire Empire in central and southern China (960–1126) while the Liao people controlled the north. Empire in southern China (1127–1279; the "Southern Song") while the Jin people controlled the north. Distinguished for its advances in technology, medicine, astronomy, and mathematics. *(p. 267)*

Stalin, Joseph (1879–1953) Bolshevik revolutionary, head of the Soviet Communist Party after 1924, and dictator of the Soviet Union from 1929 to 1953. He led the Soviet Union with an iron fist, using **Five-Year Plans** to increase industrial production and terror to crush all opposition. *(p. 709)*

Stalingrad City in Russia, site of a Red Army victory over the German army in 1942–1943. The Battle of Stalingrad was the turning point in the war between Germany and the Soviet Union. Today Volgograd. *(p. 722)*

Stanley, Henry Morton (1841–1904) British-American explorer of Africa, famous for his expeditions in search of Dr. David Livingstone. Stanley helped King **Leopold II** establish the Congo Free State. *(p. 663)*

steam engine A machine that turns the energy released by burning fuel into motion. Thomas Newcomen built the first crude but workable steam engine in 1712. **James Watt** vastly improved his device in the 1760s and 1770s. Steam power was later applied to moving machinery in factories and to powering ships and locomotives. *(p. 556)*

steel A form of iron that is both durable and flexible. It was first mass-produced in the 1860s and quickly became the most widely used metal in construction, machinery, and railroad equipment. *(p. 629)*

stirrup Device for securing a horseman's feet, enabling him to wield weapons more effectively. First evidence of the use of stirrups was among the Kushan people of northern Afghanistan in approximately the first century C.E. *(p. 180)*

stock exchange A place where shares in a company or business enterprise are bought and sold. *(p. 425)*

Stone Age The historical period characterized by the production of tools from stone and other nonmetallic substances. It was followed in some places by the Bronze Age and more generally by the Iron Age. *(p. 6)*

submarine telegraph cables Insulated copper cables laid along the bottom of a sea or ocean for telegraphic communication. The first short cable was laid across the English Channel in 1851; the first successful transatlantic cable was laid in 1866. (See also **electric telegraph.**) *(p. 628)*

sub-Saharan Africa Portion of the African continent lying south of the Sahara. *(p. 188)*

Suez Canal Ship canal dug across the isthmus of Suez in Egypt, designed by Ferdinand de Lesseps. It opened to shipping in 1869 and shortened the sea voyage between Europe and Asia. Its strategic importance led to the British conquest of Egypt in 1882. *(p. 652)*

Suleiman the Magnificent (1494–1566) The most illustrious sultan of the **Ottoman Empire** (r. 1520–1566); also known as Suleiman Kanuni, "The Lawgiver." He significantly expanded the empire in the Balkans and eastern Mediterranean. *(p. 475)*

Sumerians The people who dominated southern Mesopotamia through the end of the third millennium B.C.E. They were responsible for the creation of many fundamental elements of Mesopotamian culture—such as irrigation technology, **cuneiform,** and religious conceptions—taken over by their **Semitic** successors. *(p. 16)*

Sunnis Muslims belonging to the branch of **Islam** believing that the community should select its own leadership. The majority religion in most Islamic countries. (See also **Shi'ites.**) *(p. 209)*

Sun Yat-sen (1867–1925) Chinese nationalist revolutionary, founder and leader of the **Guomindang** until his death. He attempted to create a liberal democratic political movement in China but was thwarted by military leaders. *(p. 694)*

Swahili Bantu language with Arabic loanwords spoken in coastal regions of East Africa. *(p. 491)*

Swahili Coast East African shores of the Indian Ocean between the Horn of Africa and the Zambezi River; from the Arabic *sawahil,* meaning "shores." *(p. 352)*

Taiping Rebellion (1850–1864) The most destructive civil war before the twentieth century. A Christian-inspired rural rebellion threatened to topple the **Qing Empire.** *(p. 589)*

Tamil kingdoms The kingdoms of southern India, inhabited primarily by speakers of Dravidian languages, which developed in partial isolation, and somewhat differently, from the Aryan north. They produced epics, poetry, and performance arts. Elements of Tamil religious beliefs were merged into the Hindu synthesis. *(p. 141)*

Tang Empire Empire unifying China and part of Central Asia, founded 618 and ended 907. The Tang emperors presided over a magnificent court at their capital, Chang'an. *(p. 258)*

Tanzimat "Restructuring" reforms by the nineteenth-century Ottoman rulers, intended to move civil law away from the control of religious elites and make the military and the bureaucracy more efficient. *(p. 574)*

Tenochtitlan Capital of the Aztec Empire, located on an island in Lake Texcoco. Its population was about 150,000 on the eve of Spanish conquest. Mexico City was constructed on its ruins. *(p. 290)*

Teotihuacan A powerful **city-state** in central Mexico (100 B.C.E.–750 C.E.). Its population was about 150,000 at its peak in 600. *(p. 283)*

terrorism Political belief that extreme and seemingly random violence will destabilize a government and permit the terrorists to gain political advantage. Though an old technique, terrorism gained prominence in the late twentieth century with the growth of worldwide mass media that, through their news coverage, amplified public fears of terrorist acts. *(p. 829)*

theater-state Historians' term for a state that acquires prestige and power by developing attractive cultural forms and staging elaborate public ceremonies (as well as redistributing valuable resources) to attract and bind subjects to the center. The **Gupta Empire** is an example of such a state. *(p. 141)*

Thebes Capital city of Egypt and home of the ruling dynasties during the Middle and New Kingdoms. Amon, patron deity of Thebes, became one of the chief gods of Egypt. Monarchs were buried across the river in the Valley of the Kings. *(p. 30)*

Theravada Buddhism "Teachings of the Elders" branch of Buddhism followed in Sri Lanka and much of Southeast Asia. Theravada remains close to the original principles set forth by the **Buddha;** it downplays the importance of gods and emphasizes austerity and the individual's search for enlightenment. *(p. 137)*

third-century crisis Historians' term for the political, military, and economic turmoil that beset the Roman Empire during much of the third century C.E.: frequent changes of ruler, civil wars, barbarian invasions, decline of urban centers, and near-destruction of long-distance commerce and the monetary economy. After 284 C.E. Diocletian restored order by making fundamental changes. *(p. 159)*

Third World Term applied to a group of developing countries that professed nonalignment during the **Cold War.** *(p. 780)*

three-field system A rotational system for agriculture in which one field grows grain, one grows legumes, and one lies fallow. It gradually replaced the two-field system in medieval Europe. *(p. 364)*

Tiananmen Square Site in Beijing where Chinese students and workers gathered to demand greater political openness in 1989. The demonstration was crushed by Chinese military with great loss of life. *(p. 799)*

Tibet Country centered on the high, mountain-bounded plateau north of India. Tibetan political power occasionally extended farther to the north and west between the seventh and thirteenth centuries. *(p. 265)*

Timbuktu City on the Niger River in the modern country of Mali. It was founded by the Tuareg as a seasonal camp sometime after 1000. As part of the **Mali** empire, Timbuktu became a major terminus of the trans-Saharan trade and a center of Islamic learning. *(p. 358)*

Timur (1336–1405) Member of a prominent family of the Mongols' Jagadai Khanate, Timur through conquest gained control over much of Central Asia and Iran. He consolidated the status of Sunni Islam as orthodox, and his descendants, the Timurids, maintained his empire for nearly a century and founded the **Mughal Empire** in India. *(p. 320)*

Tiwanaku Name of capital city and empire centered on the region near Lake Titicaca in modern Bolivia (375–1000 C.E.). *(p. 298)*

Tokugawa Shogunate (1603–1868) The last of the three shogunates of Japan. *(p. 498)*

Toltecs Powerful postclassic empire in central Mexico (900–1156 C.E.). It influenced much of Mesoamerica. Aztecs claimed ties to this earlier civilization. *(p. 289)*

trans-Saharan caravan routes Trading network linking North Africa with **sub-Saharan Africa** across the Sahara. *(p. 184)*

Treaty of Nanking (1842) The treaty that concluded the **Opium War.** It awarded Britain a large indemnity from the **Qing Empire,** denied the Qing government tariff control over some of its own borders, opened additional ports of residence to Britons, and ceded the island of Hong Kong to Britain. *(p. 587)*

Treaty of Versailles (1919) The treaty imposed on Germany by France, Great Britain, the United States, and other Allied Powers after World War I. It demanded that Germany dismantle its military and give up some lands to Poland. It was resented by many Germans. *(p. 692)*

treaty ports Cities opened to foreign residents as a result of the forced treaties between the **Qing Empire** and foreign signatories. In the treaty ports, foreigners enjoyed **extraterritoriality.** *(p. 587)*

tributary system A system in which, from the time of the **Han** Empire, countries in East and Southeast Asia not under the direct control of empires based in China nevertheless enrolled as tributary states, acknowledging the superiority of the emperors in China in exchange for trading rights or strategic alliances. *(p. 262)*

tribute system A system in which defeated peoples were forced to pay a tax in the form of goods and labor. This forced transfer of food, cloth, and other goods subsidized the development of large cities. An important component of the Aztec and Inca economies. *(p. 290)*

trireme Greek and Phoenician warship of the fifth and fourth centuries B.C.E. It was sleek and light, powered by 170 oars arranged in three vertical tiers. Manned by skilled sailors, it was capable of short bursts of speed and complex maneuvers. *(p. 121)*

tropical rain forest High-precipitation forest zones of the Americas, Africa, and Asia lying between the Tropic of Cancer and the Tropic of Capricorn. *(p. 188)*

tropics Equatorial region between the Tropic of Cancer and the Tropic of Capricorn. It is characterized by generally warm or hot temperatures year-round, though much variation exists due to altitude and other factors. Temperate zones north and south of the tropics generally have a winter season. *(p. 341)*

Truman Doctrine Foreign policy initiated by U.S. president Harry Truman in 1947. It offered military aid to help Turkey and Greece resist Soviet military pressure and subversion. *(p. 770)*

tsar (czar) From Latin *caesar,* this Russian title for a monarch was first used in reference to a Russian ruler by Ivan III (r. 1462–1505). *(pp. 324, 512)*

Tulip Period (1718–1730) Last years of reign Ottoman sultan Ahmed III, during which European styles and attitudes became briefly popular in Istanbul. *(p. 479)*

tyrant The term the Greeks used to describe someone who seized and held power in violation of the normal procedures and traditions of the community. Tyrants appeared in many Greek **city-states** in the seventh and sixth centuries B.C.E., often taking advantage of the disaffection of the emerging middle class and, by weakening the old elite, unwittingly contributing to the evolution of **democracy.** *(p. 116)*

Uighurs A group of Turkic-speakers who controlled their own centralized empire from 744 to 840 in Mongolia and Central Asia. *(p. 264)*

ulama Muslim religious scholars. From the ninth century onward, the primary interpreters of Islamic law and the social core of Muslim urban societies. *(p. 214)*

Umayyad Caliphate First hereditary dynasty of Muslim caliphs (661 to 750). From their capital at Damascus, the Umayyads ruled an empire that extended from Spain to India. Overthrown by the **Abbasid Caliphate.** *(p. 208)*

umma The community of all Muslims. A major innovation against the background of seventh-century Arabia, where traditionally kinship rather than faith had determined membership in a community. *(p. 207)*

United Nations International organization founded in 1945 to promote world peace and cooperation. It replaced the **League of Nations.** *(p. 766)*

Universal Declaration of Human Rights A 1948 United Nations covenant binding signatory nations to the observance of specified rights. *(p. 831)*

universities Degree-granting institutions of higher learning. Those that appeared in the Latin West from about 1200 onward became the model of all modern universities. *(p. 375)*

Ural Mountains This north-south range separates Siberia from the rest of Russia. It is commonly considered the boundary between the continents of Europe and Asia. *(p. 512)*

Urdu A Persian-influenced literary form of Hindi written in Arabic characters and used as a language since the 1300s. Today the national language of Pakistan. *(p. 358)*

utopian socialism A philosophy introduced by the Frenchman Charles Fourier in the early nineteenth century. Utopian socialists hoped to create humane alternatives to industrial capitalism by building self-sustaining communities whose inhabitants would work cooperatively. (See also **socialism.**) *(p. 564)*

Vargas, Getulio (1883–1954) Dictator of Brazil from 1930 to 1945 and from 1951 to 1954. Defeated in the presidential election of 1930, he overthrew the government and created a dictatorship that emphasized industrialization and helped the urban poor but did little to alleviate the problems of the peasants. *(p. 754)*

varna/jati Two categories of social identity of great importance in Indian history. *Varnas* are the four major social divisions: the *Brahmin* priest class, the *Kshatriya* warrior/administrator class, the *Vaishya* merchant/farmer class, and the *Shudra* laborer class. Within the system of *varna* are many *jatis*, regional groups of people who have a common occupational sphere, and who marry, eat, and generally interact with other members of their group. *(p. 134)*

vassal In medieval Europe, a sworn supporter of a king or lord committed to rendering specified military service to that king or lord. *(p. 240)*

Vedas Early Indian sacred "knowledge"—the literal meaning of the term—long preserved and communicated orally by Brahmin priests and eventually written down. These religious texts, including the thousand poetic hymns to various deities contained in the Rig Veda, are our main source of information about the Vedic period (ca. 1500–500 B.C.E.). *(p. 132)*

Versailles The huge palace built for French King Louis XIV south of Paris in the town of the same name. The palace symbolized the preeminence of French power and architecture in Europe and the triumph of royal authority over the French nobility. *(p. 434)*

Victorian Age The reign of Queen Victoria of Great Britain (r. 1837–1901). The term is also used to describe late-nineteenth-century society, with its rigid moral standards and sharply differentiated roles for men and women and for middle-class and working-class people. (See also **"separate spheres."**) *(p. 634)*

Vietnam War (1954–1975) Conflict pitting North Vietnam and South Vietnamese communist guerrillas against the South Vietnamese government, aided after 1961 by the United States. *(p. 771)*

Villa, Francisco "Pancho" (1877–1923) A popular leader during the Mexican Revolution. An outlaw in his youth, when the revolution started, he formed a cavalry army in the north of Mexico and fought for the rights of the landless in collaboration with **Emiliano Zapata.** He was assassinated in 1923. *(p. 750)*

Wari Andean civilization culturally linked to **Tiwanaku,** perhaps beginning as a colony of Tiwanaku. *(p. 297)*

Warsaw Pact A defense alliance formed in 1955 that bound the Soviet Union and countries of eastern Europe in an alliance against the **North Atlantic Treaty Organization.** *(p. 770)*

Washington, George (1732–1799) Military commander of the American Revolution. He was the first elected president of the United States (1789–1797). *(p. 529)*

water wheel A mechanism that harnesses the energy in flowing water to grind grain or to power machinery. It was used in many parts of the world but was especially common in Europe from 1200 to 1900. *(p. 367)*

Watt, James (1736–1819) Scot who invented the condenser and other improvements that made the **steam engine** a practical source of power for industry and transportation. The watt, an electrical measurement, is named after him. *(p. 556)*

weapons of mass destruction Nuclear, chemical, and biological devices that are capable of injuring and killing large numbers of people. *(p. 826)*

Wedgwood, Josiah (1730–1795) English industrialist whose pottery works were the first to produce fine-quality pottery by industrial methods. *(p. 553)*

Western Front A line of trenches and fortifications in World War I that stretched without a break from Switzerland to the North Sea. Scene of most of the fighting between Germany, on the one hand, and France and Britain, on the other. *(p. 685)*

Wilson, Woodrow (1856–1924) President of the United States (1913–1921) and the leading figure at the Paris Peace Conference of 1919. He was unable to persuade the U.S. Congress to ratify the **Treaty of Versailles** or join the **League of Nations.** *(p. 690)*

witch-hunt The pursuit of people suspected of witchcraft, especially in northern Europe in the late sixteenth and seventeenth centuries. *(p. 418)*

Women's Rights Convention An 1848 gathering of women angered by their exclusion from an international antislavery meeting. They met at Seneca Falls, New York, to discuss women's rights. *(p. 543)*

World Bank A specialized agency of the United Nations that makes loans to countries for economic development, trade promotion, and debt consolidation. Its formal name is the International Bank for Reconstruction and Development. *(p. 769)*

World Trade Organization (WTO) An international body established in 1995 to foster and bring order to international trade. *(p. 822)*

Xiongnu A confederation of nomadic peoples living beyond the northwest frontier of ancient China. Chinese rulers tried a variety of defenses and stratagems to ward off these "barbarians," as they called them, and finally succeeded in dispersing the Xiongnu in the first century C.E. *(p. 170)*

Yamagata Aritomo (1838–1922) One of the leaders of the **Meiji Restoration.** *(p. 648)*

Yi (1392–1910) The Yi dynasty ruled Korea from the fall of the **Koryo** kingdom to the colonization of Korea by Japan. *(p. 333)*

yin/yang In Chinese belief, complementary factors that help to maintain the equilibrium of the world. Yin is associated with feminine, dark, and passive qualities; yang with masculine, light, and active qualities. *(p. 53)*

Yongle Reign of Zhu Di (1360–1424), the third emperor of the **Ming Empire** (r. 1403–1424). He sponsored further work on the Forbidden City, a huge encyclopedia project, the expeditions of **Zheng He,** and the reopening of China's borders to trade and travel. *(p. 330)*

Young Ottomans Movement of young intellectuals to institute liberal reforms and build a feeling of national identity in the Ottoman Empire in the second half of the nineteenth century. *(p. 580)*

Yuan Empire (1271–1368) Empire created in China and Siberia by **Khubilai Khan.** *(p. 314)*

Yuan Shikai (1859–1916) Chinese general and first president of the Chinese Republic (1912–1916). He stood in the way of the democratic movement led by **Sun Yat-sen.** *(p. 694)*

Zapata, Emiliano (1879–1919) Revolutionary and leader of peasants in the Mexican Revolution. He mobilized landless peasants in south-central Mexico in an attempt to seize and divide the lands of the wealthy landowners. Though successful for a time, he was ultimately defeated and assassinated. *(p. 749)*

Zen The Japanese word for a branch of **Mahayana Buddhism** based on highly disciplined meditation. It is known in Sanskrit as *dhyana*, in Chinese as *chan*, and in Korean as *son*. *(p. 271)*

Zheng He (1371–1435) An imperial eunuch and Muslim, entrusted by the Ming emperor **Yongle** with a series of state voyages that took his gigantic ships through the Indian Ocean, from Southeast Asia to Africa. *(pp. 330, 389)*

Zhou The people and dynasty that took over the dominant position in north China from the **Shang** and created the concept of the **Mandate of Heaven** to justify their rule. The Zhou era, particularly the vigorous early period (1027–771 B.C.E.), was remembered in Chinese tradition as a time of prosperity and benevolent rule. In the later Zhou period (771–221 B.C.E.), centralized control broke down, and warfare among many small states became frequent. *(p. 48)*

ziggurat A massive pyramidal stepped tower made of mudbricks. It is associated with religious complexes in ancient Mesopotamian cities, but its function is unknown. *(p. 22)*

Zoroastrianism A religion originating in ancient Iran with the prophet Zoroaster. It centered on a single benevolent deity—Ahuramazda—who engaged in a twelve-thousand-year struggle with demonic forces before prevailing and restoring a pristine world. Emphasizing truth-telling, purity, and reverence for nature, the religion demanded that humans choose sides in the struggle between good and evil. Those whose good conduct indicated their support for Ahuramazda would be rewarded in the afterlife. Others would be punished. The religion of the Achaemenid and Sasanid Persians, Zoroastrianism may have spread within their realms and influenced Judaism, Christianity, and other faiths. *(p. 111)*

Zulu A people of modern South Africa whom King Shaka united in 1818. *(p. 600)*

and, 769–770; Cuban, 779; government role in, 712, 769; Latin American, 757; nation building and, 779; Asian tigers, 797–798; China (1980s–1990s), 798–799; Soviet reforms, 800; age distribution and, 808; environment and, 813
Ecuador: colonial, 449–450; independence of, 539, 540(map)
Edict of Nantes, 433
Edison, Thomas, 630
Edo. See Tokyo (Edo)
Education (educational institutions): See also Colleges and universities; Schools; in Ottoman Empire, 476, 576, 577; Latin American church and, 447; Chinese reforms, 595; gas light and, 562; in Russia, 516, 584; in Victorian Age, 634; of military, in Egypt, 572; of women, 429, 544, 595, 634–635, 806; conservatism and, 640; in British India, 613, 735; in France, 646; in Japan, 643; in Southeast Asia, 672; in colonial Africa, 605, 667, 747; state-run, in Mexico, 751; in Soviet Russia, 770; nation building and, 779; in Korea, 797, 798
Egypt, 828; Ottoman Empire and, 401, 402, 475, 479, 566, 567, 571, 572, 660; mamluks in, 472, 481, 571; Britain and, 566, 567, 658, 700; industrialization in, 550, 566; irrigation in, 662, 678; modernization in, 603–604, 662; under Muhammad Ali, 566–567, 574, 578, 599; Napoleon's invasion of, 566, 572, 599; foreign debt of, 662; railroads in, 627; Suez Canal and, 580, 628, 652–654 and illus., 662, 700; cotton production in, 566, 567, 580, 604; World War II and, 722; Aswan dam and, 662, 780; filmmaking in, 703; Israeli-Arab wars and, 780–781, 782, 783
Eiffel Tower, 633(illus.)
Einstein, Albert, 702, 729
Eisenhower, Dwight D., 771, 772
Elections: See also Voting rights; in Latin America, 793; in Ukraine, 825
Electricity: home use of, 630, 634, 703; in Paris, 633–634 and illus.; telegraph and, 558; in Japan, 694, 781; lighting, 630, 633–634 and illus., 703
Elephants, 605. See also Ivory trade; in Indian ceremonials, 609, 611(illus.)
Elite class: See also Aristocracy; Warrior elite; colonial Latin America, 443, 444, 451; China, 502; Revolutionary era, 545; Ottoman, 574; British India, 608, 613; Latin American, 674; New Imperialism and, 660, 662; colonial Africa, 746; Mexican, 748; Iranian, 796; global culture and, 837–839
Elizabeth I (England), 432
El Salvador, 792–793
Emancipation Proclamation (1863), 543
Embargo, oil (1973), 783

Empires. See Colonies; Expansion; Imperialism; New Imperialism, and specific empires and emperors
Empire State Building (New York City), 704
Enclosure movement (England), 552
Encomienda, 448, 451
Enfranchisement. See Voting rights
Engels, Friedrich, 550, 636
Engineering: foreign, in Russia, 581; Industrial Revolution, 552, 562; colleges for, 630, 631; foreign, in Japan, 627–628; Suez Canal, 653; Aswan dam, 662; foreign, in Argentina, 674; in British India, 678, 736, 738
England: See also British Empire; Great Britain; chartered companies, 425, 461; financial revolution in, 438; iron industry in, 427, 436; merchant fleet of, 438; monarchy in, 432, 433, 434(table); science in, 422; war with France, 455; emigration from, 453, 456, 632; Irish in, 565; population growth in, 551; Victorian "separate spheres," 635; women teachers in, 635; Protestantism in, 639 (See also Anglicanism)
English language: Argentine railroads and, 674, 753; in India, 736; as global second language, 835, 837–839; world literature in, 838
Enigma machine, 723 and illus.
Enlightenment, the, 423; intellectuals of, 525–526; legacy of, 545, 621; reforms of, 517, 526
Entente (France, Great Britain, and Russia), 684(map), 685
Entrepreneurs: See also Business; Industrial Revolution and, 558, 563, 564, 567; New Imperialism and, 657, 740; in British India, 567, 740
Environment, the (environmental stress). See also Climate and weather; Deforestation; Natural disasters; Pollution; Europe (1500s–1755), 417; mining and, 447, 678; African enslavement and, 465; soil erosion and, 459, 511; sugar plantation, 458–459; industrialization and, 550, 559, 560; in Qing China, 511, 585; urbanization and, 633–634; steel industry and, 630; tropical ecology, imperialism and, 671 and illus.; world economy and, 677–678; World War I and, 691; Soviet industrialization and, 709–710; World War II and, 731; Cold War and, 765; emergence of concern over (1970s), 783, 785; population growth and, 789, 813; sharing and conserving resources, 812–813; world economy and, 789, 813; global water resources, 814(map); industrial nations and, 813, 815, 832; Kyoto treaty and, 832, 833
Environmental Protection Agency (United States), 785

Environment and technology: 811–815; tobacco and waterpipes, 480 and illus.; gas lighting, 562 and illus.; railroads and immigration, 632 and illus.; imperialism and tropical ecology, 671 and illus.; post-World War I, 704–705; enigma machine and, 723 and illus.; Green Revolution, 768 and illus.; global warming, 833 and illus.
Epidemics. See also Disease; African slaves and, 448; Amerindians and, 403, 404, 406, 407, 442–443, 444, 448, 455; in China, 502, 503; influenza (1918–1919), 690, 691, 701, 738; smallpox, 404, 406, 442, 746
Equality principle, 545, 831, 839. See also Inequality; women's rights and, 544
Equatorial Africa, French, 661(map), 663–664, 746. See also Sub-Saharan Africa
Ericsson, Leif, 390
Erie Canal, 557
Erosion, soil, 459, 511
Estado Nuovo (New State; Brazil), 755–756
Estates General (France), 434, 531, 537
Estonia: 722; independence of, 801 and map
Ethiopia, 602(map), 662; alliance with Portugal, 401; Christianity in, 401, 667, 746, 747; cannon in, 603(illus.); modernization in, 604; defeat of Italian invasion by (1895), 666; Italian invasion of (1935), 717, 747; famine and drought in, 761
Ethnic cleansing: See also Genocide; in Balkans, 802; in Rwanda, 803
Ethnic minorities: See also Racism; specific minority; organizations for, 566; census and, 622–623; nationalism and, 682–683
Eugénie (France), 652
Eunuchs, in harems, 483
Eurasia, population changes in, 571
Euro (currency), launch of, 822
Europe (1500–1750), 414–439; bourgeoisie, 424–426; African trade and, 464–465; coffee in, 479; Columbian exchange and, 466, 467; Enlightenment, 423; expansion of, 407; Indian Ocean colonies, 490(illus.); Japan and, 499–500; peasants and laborers, 426–428; political craft, 431–432; political innovations, 429–438; religious policies, 430; Religious Reformation in, 416–418, 419(map); Scientific Revolution in, 420–422, 525; social and economic life, 423–429; state development in, 430; taxation in, 436, 438; warfare and diplomacy in, 435–436; women and family, 428–429; China trade and, 509
Europe, great powers of (1740), 437(map)
Europe, great powers of (1871–1900), 645–647; conservative countries, 646–647; Germany, 646; liberal countries, 646; New Imperialism and, 656; Russia and, 581–582, 647
European Community (EC), 769, 797, 813

India, under British rule, 606–613, 619, 654; (1707–1805), 607(map); administration, 608; Assam and, 608, 614; cholera in, 560, 612; chronology (1756–1885), 601; company men (EIC) in, 567, 599, 600, 606–608 and map; cotton production and, 608, 612, 677; durbar ceremonials in, 609–610, 611(illus.); immigrant labor from, 566, 617 and illus., 618, 665, 670, 672; industrialization in, 550, 566, 567, 612; tea production in, 608, 612, 671, 677, 735; nationalism in (1828–1900), 612–613, 672; opium trade and, 580, 586, 608; political reform in, 611–612; traditions in, 608; railroads in, 567, 612, 613(illus.), 627, 677; raj and rebellion in (1818–1857), 607–608, 610; trade in, 508, 512; independence movement in (1905–1945), 735–742, 757; World War I and, 687; Depression of 1930s and, 714; famine in, 735, 741, 759–760; influenza epidemic in (1918–1919), 738; irrigation in, 612, 678; women in, 612, 656
Indian Civil Service (ICS), 611–612, 736
Indian National Congress, 613, 736, 739; Nehru and, 740, 741
Indian Ocean (Indian Ocean trade). See also East Indies; and specific states; chronology (1405–1539), 387; exploration and settlement of, 388–390 and map; Islam and, 389; Portuguese explorers in, 395, 396; Portuguese monopoly of, 401–403, 407, 475, 492(illus.); European colonies in, 490(map); Dutch and, 461
Indigo plantations, 453, 630
Individual rights: See also Human rights; Rights; Voting rights; Enlightenment view of, 526; Declaration of Independence (US) and, 529; in Napoleonic France, 535
Indochina, 658. See also Burma; Cambodia; Laos; Southeast Asia; Thailand; Vietnam; Communist party in, 774, 776; French in, 669(map), 670, 722, 743–744
Indonesia (Indonesians). See also Dutch East Indies; Java; New Imperialism in, 670, 672; deforestation in, 671; independence of, 774, 775(map); relocation program in, 811; East Timor independence from, 825; Muslim terrorism in, 830
Indulgences, sale of, 416
Indus River Valley, cotton in, 637
Industrialization. See also Industrial nations; Industrial Revolution; in Europe, 558; in Egypt, 566; laissez faire economics and, 563–564; electricity and, 630; nonindustrial world and, 566–568, 619; environmental effects of, 550, 560; in Russia, 581; in Japan, 627, 643, 648, 694–695; New Imperialism and, 657; socialism and, 636, 638; technological change and, 627; working women and, 636; in British India, 612; in Soviet Union, 709,

711, 712; World War II, 718; environmental effects of, 709–710; import-substitution, 754, 757, 790; in Brazil and Argentina, 753, 754, 756, 790; Asian governments and, 797; Western culture and, 839
Industrial nations (developed world). See also Industrialization; Industrial Revolution; overseas trade of, 615; population and migrations, 631, 633; urban environments, 633–634; socialism and labor movement, 636, 638–639; social transformations in (1850–1900), 631–639; women's changing roles in, 634–636; technology in (1850–1900), 627–631; Latin American dependence on, 673; New Imperialism and, 674; revolution in sciences, 702–703; class and gender in, 701–702; modern technology and, 703–704; technology and environment, 704–705; Depression (1930s) in, 713–714; less-developed countries and, 734; social problems in, 789; Asian economies, 789, 798, 809; lower fertility in, 804–805; population growth in, 805–807; growing wealth of, 809; technology and economic growth in, 811–812; immigration to, 811; environmental concerns in, 813, 815; fast food in, 840; Kyoto Protocol and, 832
Industrial Revolution (1760–1851), 549–568. See also Great Britain, Industrial Revolution in; United States, Industrial Revolution in; agriculture and, 552; causes of, 550–553; changes in society, 563; chronology, 551; cities, 555(illus.), 559–560, 562; division of labor in, 553; emigration in, 565–566; gas lighting, 562; impact of, 559–563; iron industry, 555–556; laissez faire and, 563–564; limits of, outside the West, 566–568; mass production in, 553–554 and illus.; cotton industry in, 554–555; new economic and political ideas, 563–566; population in, 551–552, 559, 804; positivism and socialism, 564; preconditions for, 551–552; protests and reforms in, 564–565; railroads and, 558; rural areas and, 560; steam engines, 556–558, 557(illus.); telegraph and, 558; women and, 560, 563, 565; work conditions in, 560–561
Industries. See also Industrialization; Iron industry; Manufacturing; Textile industry; chemical, 554, 555(illus.), 630, 686, 687, 728; gender divisions in, 636; wool, 467, 554; robots for, 808, 812
Inequality: See also Equality; in Haiti, 537; industrialization and, 550; in Mexico, 748, 778; global poverty and, 788, 809–810
Infantry. See also Armed forces; Chinese, 389, 518 (See also Bannermen); in World War I, 685, 686(illus.)

Inflation: See also Prices; in Safavid Iran, 485; in Ottoman Empire, 477; in Spain, 436; in China, 501, 721, 728; German crisis (1923), 693, 715
Influenza epidemic (1918–1919), 690, 691, 701, 738
Inoculation (variolation), 509
Inquisition, 422, 430, 436
The Institutes of Religion (Calvin), 417–418
Institutional Revolutionary Party (PRI), 778
Insurance companies, 425, 552, 579
Intellectual life (intellectuals): Scientific Revolution, 420–422; Enlightenment, 525–526, 545; Russian, 582, 584, 647; Indian nationalism and, 613, 739; socialism and, 636, 638; in China, 799
Interchangeable-parts manufacturing, 556
Interest: 428; Japanese prices and, 498, 500
International Center for the Improvement of Maize and Wheat, 768
International Criminal Court, 832
International Monetary Fund (IMF), 769, 798, 824
International Rice Research Institute, 768
International Statistical Congress (1860), 622
International Style in architecture, 704
International Working Man's Association, 638
Internet, 836
Inventions. See Technology; specific inventions
Investment. See Foreign investment
Iran (Iranians): See also Safavid Empire (Iran); Armenian merchants in, 425; silk industry in, 478, 479; Shi'ite Islam in, 474(map), 481, 482, 796, 828; tobacco in, 480; Mughal India and, 487; Russia and, 582, 583; cotton in, 637; women's rights in, 832; oil wealth of, 783, 784(map), 822; Islamic Revolution in, 789, 796, 797, 822, 829; war with Iraq, 822; Ahmedinjad regime in, 822, 826, 827(illus.)
Iraq (Iraqis), 782; independence of, 700; after World War I, 697(map), 700; oil wealth of, 700, 783, 784(map); terrorism in, 830; war with Iran, 822; Persian Gulf War (1990–1991) and, 803–804; invasion and regime change in, 825, 826, 827–828
Ireland (Irish), 464, 769; Great Britain and, 433, 436, 646, 674; potatoes in, 427, 552; emigration from, 561, 565(illus.), 632; Catholicism in, 639; famine in (1847–1848), 565, 631
Irigoyen, Hipólito, 753, 754, 756
Iron curtain, 764, 765, 773, 785. See also Cold War; Warsaw Pact
Iron industry. See also under Steel; deforestation and, 427, 555; English, 427, 436; Industrial Revolution and, 555–556
Iroquois Confederacy, 454, 455
Irrigation: in British India, 612, 678, 735; in Egypt, 662, 678, 780
Isabella (Castile), 396

604; explosives, 590(illus.), 630; New Imperialism and, 657, 659(illus.); poison gas, 686, 729; World War I, 685, 686 and illus.; World War II, 716, 721, 725 and illus., 730; Soviet, 711; American, in Iran, 796; Cold War rivalry and, 772–773, 799; Persian Gulf War, 803

Weapons of mass destruction, 826

Weaving: See also Spinning; Textile industry and trade; African, 465; Industrial Revolution and, 554, 563, 567; mechanization of, 577

Webb, James L. A., Jr., 521

Weber, Max, 685

Wedgwood, Josiah, 553–554 and illus., 562

Wehrmacht (Nazi German army), 716(illus.), 718, 721, 722, 726, 730; Enigma machine and, 723 and illus.

Weizmann, Chaim, 688, 691

Welfare. See Social welfare

West Africa. See also specific countries; Gold Coast, 392(map), 395, 399; Portuguese in, 392(map), 395, 399–400; British trade with, 461, 615; slave trade in, 464; Islamic reform in, 600, 603; mission schools in, 605; new states in, 600, 602(map), 603; malaria in, 658; palm oil trade in, 604–605, 615; New Imperialism and, 658, 662, 663–664, 666; foreign traders in, 745; independence movement in, 747, 777; urban growth in, 810; trade agreement (ECOWAS), 822, 823(map)

West Bank, 828, 829

Western Europe: See also Europe; and specific countries or people; industrialization in, 550, 553, 560; telegraph in, 558; Ottoman reform and, 576; Russia and, 582, 583, 584; economies of, 631; Marshall Plan for, 769; NATO and, 765; low fertility rates in, 806; aging population in, 808; air quality in, 813

Western front (World War I), 684(map), 685–686 and illus., 690

Western Hemisphere. See Americas, the (New World; Western Hemisphere)

Westernization (Western culture). See also Industrialization; Modernization; in Egypt, 515–516, 517, 581; in West Africa, 605, 746; of Japan, 627–628, 637(illus.), 643 and illus.; New Imperialism and, 656; in British India, 735; eastern Europe and, 800; cultural imperialism and, 834–835; industrialization and, 839

Western Sudan, 662. See also Mali; Sudan

West Germany, 769, 770. See also Germany; reunification and, 801 and map

West India Company, Dutch, 425, 461

West India Company, French, 461

West Indies. See Caribbean Sea and region

Whaling, 491, 616

Wheat, 558, 566, 646; in Argentina, 674, 752; famine and, 759, 760; Green Revolution and, 768

Wheatstone, Charles, 558

Whistler, James McNeill, 581

White Lotus Rebellion (1794–1804), 585

Whitney, Eli, 555

Wichelle, Treaty of (1889), 666

Widow burning (sati), 612, 656, 736

Wilhelm I (Germany), 640, 646

Wilhelm II (Germany), 646, 690

Williams, Eric, 457–458

Willis, John, 671

Wilson, Woodrow, 675, 690, 749; Fourteen Points of, 698–699; League of Nations and, 691, 696

Winds: Atlantic, 393, 397; Roaring Forties, 493

Wine, 427

Winsor, Frederick Albert, 562

Witch-hunts, 418, 420 and illus.

Wojtyla, Carol (John Paul II), 800

Women. See also Family; Feminism; Fertility rates; Gender differences; Marriage; Women's rights; as nuns, 428; witch-hunts and, 418, 420 and illus.; carpet making and, 485; slave, 484; Ottoman, 471–472, 483 and illus., 577–578; as prostitutes, 428, 429, 531, 589, 612, 667; seclusion of, 483; in Yangzhou Massacre, 504–505; American Revolution and, 530; French Revolution and, 532, 535; Haitian independence and, 538; African, in markets, 457(illus.), 745; as domestic servants, 561, 635, 695; cult of domesticity and, 563; as abolitionists, 543; as teachers, 544, 635; education of, 429, 544, 595, 634–635, 806; in colonial New Zealand, 616; in textile industry, 427, 544, 561, 565 and illus., 635, 645(illus.), 695; Islam and, 483–484 and illus.; foot binding in China and, 589, 591, 719; rulers, in Acheh Sultanate, 489; widow burning, in India, 612, 656, 736; clothing manufacture by, 637; Japanese, 635, 645(illus.); Victorian separate sphere of, 634, 635–636; working-class, 544, 635–636, 637 and illus.; as missionaries, 656; colonial expansion and, 660; in World War I, 687; in colonial Africa, 660, 667; reform movements and, 696, 701–702; Nazi Germany and, 716–717, 730–731; cult of cleanliness and, 704; Soviet Union, 701, 712; Chinese Communism and, 719, 720; in World War II, 730–731

Women's Christian Temperance Movement, 701

Women's rights, 546, 831, 834; in Americas, 543–544; feminists and, 701, 794–795, 832, 839; to property, 578; in Soviet Union, 701, 712; voting rights (suffrage), 543, 544 and illus., 635, 696, 701, 781, 828; neo-liberalism and, 794–795

Women's rights conferences: New York state (1848), 543, 544(illus.); Beijing (1995), 832; Nairobi (1985), 832

Woodblock printing, 500(illus.)

Wool industry: See also Sheep raising; Navajo, 467; British, 554

Woren, 594–595

Workers (working class). See also Labor; Labor unions; Wages; French Revolution and, 532–533; housing for, 549–550; Industrial Revolution and, 560–561; Revolutions of 1848 and, 537; Russian urban, 647; strikes by, 502, 561, 564, 638; women, 544, 635–636, 637 and illus.; consumer goods for, 703; industrialized world, 701; Soviet Russia, 690, 781; Great Depression and, 713, 714; Mexican Revolution and, 751; in Argentina and Brazil, 753, 755, 756

World Bank, 768, 769, 810, 824

World economy. See Global economy

World Trade Center, attack on, 818–819, 820(illus.), 830

World Trade Organization (WTO), 822, 824

World War I (1914–1918), 681–692; alliances and military strategy in, 682–685, 684(map); origins of the crisis, 682–685; stalemate (1914–1917), 685–687; nationalism in, 682; in Europe, 684(map); Africans in, 687; casualties, 686, 687, 688; homefront and economy, 687; trench warfare in, 686 and illus.; impact of, 691; Indian soldiers in, 738; Japan in, 694–695; Ottoman Empire and, 684(map), 687–688; Russian Revolutions and, 688–690; end of, in Western Europe, 690; peace treaties, 691–692; recovery after, 693; reparations for, 692, 713; pursuit of normalcy following, 708–709

World War II (1939–1945), 721–731; Africa and, 731, 747; aircraft in, 725(illus.), 728–729; in Asia and the Pacific, 722, 725, 726(map), 727; bombing raids in, 727 and illus., 729; Brazil in, 756; casualties of, 728, 729–730 and illus.; character of warfare in, 728–731; chronology (1939–1945), 711; code-breaking in, 722, 723 and illus.; environment in, 731; in Europe and North Africa, 721–722, 724(map); Germany in, 721–722, 723 and illus., 724(map), 725(illus.), 726–727; Holocaust of, 729–730 and illus.; home front in, 730–731; India and, 740–741; Japan in, 727 and illus.; nationalism in, 721; science and technology of, 728–729; Sino-Japanese War and, 720–721; United States in, 725–726 and map, 727, 728; as war of movement, 721; end of, 725–727

World Wide Web, 836

Wright, Frank Lloyd, 704

Wright, Orville and Wilbur, 703

Writing (written language): See also Literacy; Script; Chinese, 518

WTO (World Trade Organization), 822, 824

Wu Sangui, 496